SKI AM BRYAN COLLEGE

Introduction to

marketing

Introduction to
marketing

theory and practice

Second edition
Adrian Palmer

OXFORD
UNIVERSITY PRESS

OXFORD
UNIVERSITY PRESS

Great Clarendon Street, Oxford OX2 6DP

Oxford University Press is a department of the University of Oxford.
It furthers the University's objective of excellence in research,
scholarship, and education by publishing worldwide in
Oxford New York

Auckland Cape Town Dar es Salaam Hong Kong Karachi
Kuala Lumpur Madrid Melbourne Mexico City Nairobi
New Delhi Shanghai Taipei Toronto

With offices in
Argentina Austria Brazil Chile Czech Republic France Greece
Guatemala Hungary Italy Japan Poland Portugal Singapore
South Korea Switzerland Thailand Turkey Ukraine Vietnam

Oxford is a registered trade mark of Oxford University Press in the UK
and in certain other countries

Published in the United States
by Oxford University Press Inc., New York

First published 2004
Second edition 2009

British Library Cataloguing in Publication Data
Data available

Library of Congress Cataloging in Publication Data
Data available

Typeset by Macmillan Publishing Solutions
Printed in Italy
on acid-free paper by
Lego S.p.A.
ISBN 978–0–19–955744–8

3 5 7 9 10 8 6 4 2

Preface

Marketing is an exciting subject to study. Markets are the basis for the wealth of western economies, and marketers help make markets become more efficient and effective. It is marketers who have been a driving force in making an ever-wider range of goods and services available to buyers, seeking a better understanding of buyers' needs, and trying to deliver better products at lower prices than competitors.

This book provides an introduction to the principles of marketing, beginning from the underlying theoretical bases which are often borrowed from the disciplines of economics, sociology, and psychology. Practical application of theory is provided through case studies and vignettes, and it is often noted that the theories of marketing are not always easy to implement in practice. This book tries not to present prescriptive solutions to marketing problems, but encourages discussion about causes and effects. Underlying much of the discussion in this book is the interplay between marketing as a rigorous science and as a creative art.

The book is arranged in four thematic parts. The first part begins by identifying the fundamental building blocks of marketing. Chapter 1 explores definitions of marketing and its essential characteristics. Marketing takes place within a complex environment of social, economic, political, and technological forces and the following chapter examines the continual interplay between marketing managers and their business environment. Chapter 3 is new to this edition, and takes a critical look at the social responsibilities of marketers in the context of increasing concern about environmental sustainability.

The second thematic part of the book focuses on consumers, and on understanding the complex factors that lead to buying decisions. An understanding of buying processes (explored in Chapter 4) calls for appropriate information gathering, analysis, and dissemination (Chapter 5). Knowledge of buyer behaviour, backed by good quality research, leads to the concept of segmentation and targeting (Chapter 6).

The third thematic part of the book focuses on how companies use knowledge about their consumers and the broader marketing environment to develop a sustainable competitive advantage. Chapter 7 introduces basic principles of competitive positioning. Subsequent chapters analyse how the elements of the 'marketing mix'—product, price, place, and promotion—are used to create a competitive advantage (Chapters 8, 9, 10, and 11).

The final thematic part of the book seeks to integrate the previous chapters and provides an overview of the marketing management process (Chapter 12) and the challenges presented by global marketing (Chapter 13).

The book has been divided into a number of chapters in order to provide some form of structure. In the real world, marketing cannot be neatly compartmentalized in this way. With a holistic vision, it will be seen that any change in one aspect of marketing is likely to have consequences in other aspects. In an attempt to emphasize these linkages, each chapter closes with a summary of how that chapter relates to other chapters. Vignettes and case studies provide integrative perspectives.

Current developments in technology affecting marketing (e.g. mobile broadband and RFID) are reflected in vignettes and case studies throughout the book. The growing recognition of the social and ecological responsibilities of marketing is stressed throughout the book and in the new Chapter 3. This book is published at a time of great debate about the nature of marketing knowledge and theory. New ideas and even claims of shifts in marketing paradigms appear regularly. This book seeks to develop a well-founded and balanced view of marketing and makes no apology for raising as many questions as it answers. Marketing is more about a way of thinking than a series of prescriptive rules.

This book is supported by an Online Resource Centre: http://www.oxfordtextbooks. co.uk/orc/palmer2e/. Here, you will find supplementary reading lists and web links relevant to each chapter which can be clicked through. For each chapter, additional case studies and questions are provided. Your knowledge can be tested with a series of multiple-choice questions. For tutors, PowerPoint slides and lecture plans are linked to each chapter. An additional multiple-choice test bank of questions is provided.

Adrian Palmer
January 2009
mail@apalmer.com

Acknowledgments

Countless colleagues, reviewers, and organizations, too numerous to mention here, helped to bring this book to fruition and their assistance is greatly acknowledged. Many authors and organizations kindly granted permission to reproduce copyright material and this is specifically acknowledged throughout the book.

Every effort has been made to trace and contact copyright holders but this has not been possible in every case. If notified, the publisher will undertake to rectify any errors or omissions at the earliest opportunity.

The author: Adrian Palmer is Professor of Marketing at the University of Wales, Swansea, UK.

Walk-through preface

CHAPTER OBJECTIVES

Faced with competing products, it is important for companies to understand how buyers go about choosing between the alternatives. A thorough understanding of buyer behaviour should be reflected in product design, pricing, promotion, and distribution, all of which satisfy the needs of individuals' buying processes. This chapter explores basic theories of behaviour. Distinctions between personal and organizational buyer behaviour are noted, especially in the composition of the decision-making unit. Companies generally seek to influence buyer behaviour so that the company becomes customers' first choice of supp This chapter reviews methods by which companies seek to turn one-off casual buying

Chapter objectives

Identify the abilities and skills you should demonstrate after reading the chapter.

MARKETING in ACTION

From word of mouth to word of mouse

Word-of-mouth recommendation can be an important way of influencing buyers' ch but it has traditionally been a fairly slow means of spreading recommendation about product. Now, the Internet has allowed the whole process to be speeded up and has its impact. From word of mouth, companies now talk about 'word of mouse', leading marketing', in which a purchase recommendation can spread very quickly as one per passes on a message to half a dozen friends, each of whom in turn passes on the m

Marketing in Action boxes

Examples of how marketing is used in a real-life context.

Chapter summary and key linkages to other chap

The management of channel intermediaries plays a key part in a company's at ensure that its goods or services are made available to the desired market s Making goods available where and when buyers need them is an importa adding activity which contributes towards a company's competitive advan rival producers (Chapter 7). Availability of a company's products must be c with its promotional messages (Chapter 11) and its price position (Chapte design of a marketing channel requires careful analysis and planning. For

Chapter summary and key linkages to other chapters

A summary of the key points covered in the chapter, useful for revision purposes, as well as cross-referencing to topics featured in other chapters for reference purpose.

KEY PRINCIPLES OF MARKETING

- An overriding aim of marketing is to develop a sustainable competitive advantage f organization.
- Competitors for a firm's products can be direct or indirect. Indirect forms of competi more difficult to identify.
- A brand is a means of identifying one company and its products from otherwise simi products supplied by other companies.
- The functional role of a brand should be distinguished from its emotional role.
- Brands are created through the management of the marketing mix. The marketing

Key principles of marketing

Key points highlighting the main principles of marketing covered in the chapter to aid clarification.

CASE STUDY

Small new phones, big investment risk?

The mobile phone industry is no stranger to product innovation. In fact, it is hard to belie sector barely existed just 20 years ago; now, most people in western developed count mobile phone. In fact, according to the telecoms regulator Ofcom, there are now m phones in use in Britain than there are people. Although we are all now familiar with mob we probably wouldn't recognize a mobile phone of 20 years ago—much heavier and

Case study

Each chapter ends with a case study that covers the themes that have been raised in the chapter and helps you to analyse and reflect upon them.

Case study review questions

1. Critically evaluate methods that mobile phone companies could use to assess buye response to new features, such as video on demand.
2. In terms of a new product development process, how could the development and Telepoint services have been improved in order to avoid the problems that were experienced? What lessons can be learnt for the development of 3G (or 4G service
3. Consider how the launch of 3G services in a less developed country with a less sophis telecommunications infrastructure may differ from a launch in a western developed

Case study review questions

These are designed to help you apply your understanding of the concepts and develop your knowledge further.

CHAPTER REVIEW QUESTIONS

1. What is the relationship between selling and marketing?
2. Critically evaluate the steps that companies can take to ensure that their direct ma become 'junk' mail.
3. What do you understand by the term 'promotional campaign', and how can a firm whether its campaign has been successful?

Chapter review questions

The questions can be used for assessing your understanding or for discussing in small groups.

Activities

Suggested activities for you to take part in either individually or with others to enable you to discuss what you have learned from the chapter.

ACTIVITIES

1. Choose two or three international service providers from the following sectors: hot airlines, fast food, car rental, accountancy services. Go to their websites and click th a selection of their national sites in countries with a different socio-economic profi own. Analyse what is common between the service offer and the promotional mess between the different countries in which the company operates. Then try and iden in which the service offer has been adapted to meet local conditions.
2. Go to the website of an international hotel chain such as Hilton or Holiday Inn. Che the price of a standard room on a particular date, for a selection of the company's different capital cities. What dispersion of prices for a basically similar room do y

References

A list of sources used throughout the chapter to help you find out extra information on the subject.

REFERENCES

Bateson, J. E. G. (1989), *Managing Services Marketing: text and readings*, 2nd edn. For USA: Dryden Press.
British Industrial Society (2001), 'Managing Best Practice'. *Occupational Stress*, London, Industrial Society, (83): 4-23.
Direct Marketing Association (2007), *Census of the UK Direct Marketing Industry*. Lon Marketing Association.
Financial Times (2007), 'MI5 Warns Banks of Chinese Hackers'. *Financial Times*, London, December.

Suggested further reading

Useful sources of further information to extend your learning.

SUGGESTED FURTHER READING

There are many texts on the subject of marketing management which focus on how a tion can implement measures to respond to a changing external environment. The fol useful:
Baker, M. J. (2007), *Marketing Strategy and Management*, 4th edn. Basingstoke: Palgra Macmillan.
Doyle, P. and Stern, Phil (2006), *Marketing Management and Strategy*, 4th edn. Londo Prentice Hall.
Kotler, P. and Keller, K. L. (2008), *Marketing Management: analysis, planning, implem*

Useful web links

A link to the Online Resource Centre accompanying the text-book which directs you to further resources that support and enhance your learning experience.

USEFUL WEB LINKS

Visit the companion website to this book, with lots of interesting additional material a for each chapter:
   www.oxfordtextbooks.co.uk/orc/palmer2e/

Key terms

A list of key terms used in the chapter to enable you to familiarize yourself with the main marketing concepts related to the chapter.

KEY TERMS

- Brand extension
- Brand family
- Brand personality
- Brands
- Co-branding
- Commodity
- Counterfeiting
- Differentiation

Online Resource Centre

The book is supported by an Online Resource Centre. Here students will find a host of additional resources including suggested additional reading, web links to relevant websites, additional case studies, and self-test multiple-choice questions. Lecturers will find a suite of resources to assist them with their teaching, including lecture notes and PowerPoint slides for each chapter, and suggested discussion points. Lecturers will also have access to a test bank of 400 multiple-choice questions.

 www.oxfordtextbooks.co.uk/orc/palmer2e/

Brief contents

Preface   v
Acknowledgments   vii
Guided tour of the textbook features   viii

PART 1   Marketing: the fundamentals

1   What is marketing?   3
2   The marketing environment   40
3   Socially responsible marketing   76

PART 2   Understanding customers

4   Buyer behaviour and relationship development 111
5   Marketing research   148
6   Segmentation, positioning, and targeting   180

PART 3   Developing the marketing mix

7   Competitor analysis and brand development   223
8   Developing the product   260
9   Pricing   302
10   Channel intermediaries   349
11   Marketing communications   394

PART 4   Bringing it together

12   Managing the marketing effort   465
13   Global marketing   499

Glossary of marketing terms   535
Subject index   543
Index of authors   548
Index of companies and brands   550

Detailed contents

Preface   v
Acknowledgments   vii
Guided tour of the textbook features   viii

PART 1 **Marketing: the fundamentals**

1 **What is marketing?**   3

Chapter objectives   3
Introduction   3
Marketing as a philosophy and as a set of techniques   5
   Foundations for success in business   8
   Production orientation   11
   Selling orientation   12
What organizations undertake marketing?   14
Key marketing concepts   15
   Customers   15
   Needs   16
   Value   17
   Exchange   19
   Markets   20
   The marketing mix   21
   Products   22
   Pricing   23
   Place   23
   Promotion   23
   People   24
   Process   24
   Physical evidence   24
   Interdependency of the marketing mix   24
Marketing management   25
   The marketing management process   25
   Marketing management structures   26
   Outcomes of the marketing management process 27
Marketing and its relationship to other business functions   27
Marketing and social responsibility   28
Is marketing a science or an art?   29
Marketing as an academic discipline   31

What makes a good marketer?   32
Chapter summary and linkages to other chapters   33
Key principles of marketing   33
Case study: The Body Shop—good luck or good marketing?   33
Chapter review questions   36
Activities   37
References   37
Suggested further reading   37
Useful web links   38
Key terms   38

2   **The marketing environment**   **40**

Chapter objectives   **40**
Introduction   **40**
The micro-environment   **42**
    Customers   42
    Competitors   43
    Intermediaries   43
    Suppliers   44
    Government   45
    The financial community   45
    Local communities   46
    Pressure groups   46
    Value chains   47
    Relationships between members of an organization's
        micro-environment   48
    Communication within the micro-environment   50
The macro-environment   **51**
    The macro-economic environment   51
    The political environment   55
    The social and cultural environment   56
    The demographic environment   59
    The technological environment   61
    The ecological environment   61
The internal environment   **63**
    The flexible organization   65
Monitoring and responding to environmental change   **66**
    SWOT analysis   67
Chapter summary and linkages to other chapters   **69**
Key principles of marketing   **70**
Case study: Ready meal manufacturers ready to respond
    to a changing marketing environment   70
Chapter review questions   72

Activities 72
References 73
Suggested further reading 73
Useful web links 74
Key terms 74

3　Socially responsible marketing　76

Chapter objectives 76
Introduction 76
Philosophical principles underlying responsible marketing 78
Ecologically sustainable marketing 82
Ethical responsibility 85
Marketing's responsibility for customers' privacy and security 89
Marketing's responsibilities to vulnerable people 92
Marketing's responsibility to employees 93
Marketing's responsibility for preserving
the competitiveness of markets 95
Responsible communication 97
Chapter summary and links to other chapters 102
Key principles of marketing 102
Case study: Problems in the air for low-cost flights? 103
Chapter review questions 105
Activities 105
References 106
Suggested further reading 106
Useful web links 107
Key terms 107

PART 2　Understanding customers

4　Buyer behaviour and relationship development　111

Chapter objectives 111
Introduction 111
　Buying situations 112
The buying process 113
　Needs as buying process initiators 114
　Information search 120
　Evaluation 122
　Decision 124
　Post-purchase evaluation 125

The decision-making unit (DMU) 127
    Influencers 127
    Gatekeepers 128
    Buyers 128
    Users 129
    Decision-maker 130

Models of buyer decision-making 130

Personal and organizational buyer behaviour compared 133

Developing ongoing relationships with buyers 134
    Reasons for the development of ongoing customer relationships 135
    Methods used to develop ongoing relationships with customers 138
    Problems of creating ongoing relationships with buyers 141

Chapter summary and linkages to other chapters 142

Key principles of marketing 142

Case study: How do you really understand young people's
    buying behaviour? 143

Chapter review questions 145
Activities 145
References 145
Suggested further reading 146
Useful web links 146
Key terms 146

5   **Marketing research** 148

Chapter objectives 148

Introduction 148

Market research *v.* marketing research 149

Major uses of marketing research 150

The marketing research process 152

Primary *v.* secondary research 154

Secondary research information sources 156

Primary research methods 157
    Sampling procedures 157
    Data collection methods 158

Quantitative *v.* qualitative research 162
    Quantitative research 162
    Qualitative research 166

Who carries out marketing research? 168

Marketing intelligence 169

Knowledge management 169

Demand forecasting 172

Chapter summary and key linkages to other chapters 174

Key principles of marketing   175
Case study: Drowning in data, searching for insight?   175
Chapter review questions   177
Activities   177
References   178
Suggested further reading   178
Useful web links   179
Key terms   179

6   Segmentation, positioning, and targeting   180

Chapter objectives   180
Why segment markets?   180
Criteria for effective segmentation   183
Is the basis of market segmentation useful to the company?   183
Are the segments of an economic size?   184
Can the market segments be measured?   185
Are the segments accessible to the company?   186
Bases for market segmentation   187
Demographic bases for segmentation   187
Socio-economic bases for segmentation   194
Psychographic bases for segmentation   196
Geodemographic bases for segmentation   198
Situational bases for segmentation   199
Comprehensive approaches to segmentation   202
Bases for segmenting business markets   203
Size of firm   203
Formality of buying processes   203
Industry sector   203
Evaluating market segments   204
Size of segment   204
Growth prospects   204
Profitability   204
Competition for the segment   205
Fit with company objectives   205
Selection of target markets   207
Undifferentiated mass marketing   208
Single-segment specialization ('niche' marketing)   209
Multiple-segment specialization   211
Segment development plans   211
Developing a position within the target market   212
Chapter summary and linkages to other chapters   214
Key principles of marketing   214
Case study: A bar for all tastes   215

Chapter review questions   217
Activities   218
References   218
Suggested further reading   218
Useful web links   218
Key terms   219

PART 3 Developing the marketing mix

7   Competitor analysis and brand development   223

Chapter objectives   223

Introduction   223

Who are a company's competitors?   224

Branding   228

The history of branding   229

Key characteristics of a brand   231
    Consistency   231
    Risk reduction   233
    Functional and emotional attributes   233

Creating a distinctive brand   235
    Choice of name   235
    Distinctive product features   237
    Creation of a distinctive brand personality   238
    Distinctive visual identity   238

Branding strategy   239
    Development of a single strong brand   240
    Differentiated brands   242
    Brand families   242
    Brand extension   242
    Co-branding   243
    Protecting a brand   243
    The organization as a brand   244
    The development of global brands   245

The changing role of branding   246

Positioning the brand   249
    Repositioning   252

The marketing mix   253

Chapter summary and key linkages to other chapters   254

Key principles of marketing   254

Case study: Fairy's brand bubble never seems to burst   254

Chapter review questions   256
Activities   257

References		257
Suggested further reading		258
Useful web links		258
Key terms		259

8	**Developing the product**		**260**
	Chapter objectives		260
	What do we mean by a product?		260
		Material goods	262
		Intangible services	264
		Ideas	265
		Locations and people	266
	Analysis of the product offer		266
	The product mix		267
	Quality		268
		Technical quality and functional quality	269
	Distinctive design		270
	Packaging		271
	'Greening' the product range		272
	The product life cycle		272
		The product life cycle and consumer adoption processes	273
		Limitations of product life-cycle theory	276
	Innovation and new product development		276
		What is innovation?	277
		What are new products?	277
	The new product development process		281
		Idea generation	281
		Idea screening	282
		Concept development and testing	283
		Business analysis	284
		Product development and testing	285
		Market testing	285
		Product launch	286
		Integrating the new product development process	288
	Strategic issues in expanding the product range		288
	Planning for growth		290
	Deleting products		292
	Chapter summary and linkages to other chapters		295
	Key principles of marketing		296
	Case study: Small new phones, big investment risk?		296
		Chapter review questions	299
		Activities	299

References   299
Suggested further reading   300
Useful web links   301
Key terms   301

9   Pricing   302

Chapter objectives   302
Introduction   302
Effects of market structure on pricing   303
The theory of supply and demand   305
  Demand   306
  Supply   309
  Price determination   311
  Imperfections to competition   312
  Elasticity of demand   314
  Oligopoly   317
  Monopolistic markets   318
Regulatory influences on pricing   319
  Direct government controls to regulate monopoly power   319
  Government controls on price representations   320
Pricing objectives of companies   321
  Profit maximization   321
  Sales growth   322
  Survival   322
  Social considerations   323
  Pricing strategy   324
  Pricing and the product life cycle   324
Price-skimming strategy   325
Penetration pricing strategy   327
  Customer lifetime pricing   329
Pricing methods   329
  Cost-based pricing   329
  Marginal cost pricing   331
  Competitors and pricing   332
  Demand-based pricing   333
Pricing a product range   339
  Price bundling   340
  Pricing models   341
The pricing of public services   341
Chapter summary and linkages to other chapters   343
Key principles of marketing   343
Case study: A fair price for 'free' hospital treatment?   344
Chapter review questions   346

Activities	346
References	346
Suggested further reading	347
Useful web links	347
Key terms	347

10	**Channel intermediaries**	**349**
	Chapter objectives	349
	Introduction	349
	What is a marketing channel?	350
	The role of intermediaries in a value chain	351
	Functions of intermediaries	352
	Types of intermediary	354
	Classification of retailers	354
	Designing a channel of distribution	356
	Influences on channel selection	357
	Channel alternatives	359
	Multiple channels	360
	Selecting specific intermediaries	360
	Power and conflict within distribution channels	361
	Integrated distribution channels	363
	Franchising systems	364
	Global channels of distribution	366
	The Internet and channel design	366
	Physical distribution management	369
	Physical distribution objectives	370
	Customer service objectives in logistics	371
	Identification of segments by service requirements	372
	Cost/service trade-offs	373
	Inventory management	375
	Just-in-time systems	376
	Information processing	378
	Order processing	379
	Materials and production planning	379
	Delivery planning	379
	Production and warehouse location	380
	Transport	382
	Trends in logistics management	382
	Rising expectations of end consumers	382
	From functions to processes	384

Competition between supply networks	384
Closer working relationships	384
Fewer channel members	385
Virtual organizations	385
Increasingly complex consumer needs	385
The Internet	386
Increasing public concern over the environment	386
Chapter summary and key linkages to other chapters	**387**
Key principles of marketing	**387**
Case study: Tesco tries to cut food miles from its supply chain	**388**
Chapter review questions	390
Activities	391
References	391
Suggested further reading	392
Useful web links	392
Key terms	393

11	**Marketing communications**	**394**
	Chapter objectives	**394**
	Introduction	**394**
	Marketing and promotional objectives	**395**
	The communication process	**397**
	The message source	**399**
	The message	**400**
	Encoding, decoding, and noise	401
	Perception and retention of the message	403
	The target audience	**405**
	Buyer readiness state	407
	Push v. pull messages	408
	Other important audiences for communication	410
	The channel	**410**
	Response: marketing communications models	**411**
	'Hierarchy of effects' models	412
	Integrated models	413
	Stages of the promotion planning process	**414**
	The promotion campaign	415
	The role of promotion agencies	416
	Setting budgets for promotional activity	**417**
	Monitoring and evaluating the promotional effort	**419**
	Introducing the promotion mix	**420**
	Advertising	**424**
	The role of advertising in the promotion mix	424
	How does advertising work?	424

Advertising media   425

Media selection and evaluation   430
Constraints on advertising   430
Personal selling   432
Types of selling   432
Tasks of a salesperson   433

Sales promotion   434
Sales promotion tools   435
Evaluation of sales promotion   437

Public relations   437
Public relations and corporate reputation   438
The characteristics of public relations   439
The tools of public relations   440
Evaluating public relations activity   442
Sponsorship   442

Direct marketing   443
The development of customer databases   444
Profiling and targeting   446
Direct marketing media   448

Online marketing   449
Choice of online channels   451
Integrating online with other media   452

Chapter summary and links to other chapters   454

Key principles of marketing   454

Case study: Online advertising goes mobile   455

Chapter review questions   458
Activities   458
References   458
Suggested further reading   459
Useful web links   460
Key terms   460

PART 4   Bringing it together

12   Managing the marketing effort   465

Chapter objectives   465
Introduction   465
The marketing management process   466
Strategic, tactical, and contingency planning   470
The dynamic marketing environment   471
Marketing planning and corporate planning   471
Planning as an inter-functional integrator   472

The mission statement   473

Organizing the marketing management function   474
    Management by functional responsibility   476
    Management by geographical responsibility   476
    Management by product type   476
    Management by market segment   477

Integrating marketing management with other
management functions   479

Marketing management and smaller businesses   482
    Internal marketplaces   485

Leadership   485

Managing information   487
    Using information for control   490

Improving organizational effectiveness for marketing   492

Chapter summary and key linkages to other chapters   494

Case study: Viva España! Marketing Spain as
    a tourism destination   494

Chapter review questions   497
Activities   497
References   497
Suggested further reading   498
Useful web links   498
Key terms   498

13   Global marketing   499

Chapter objectives   499

Introduction   499

Why export?   501
    National reasons for trade occurring   501
    Firms' reasons for developing foreign trade   502

A note on 'exporting' of services   503

Analysing foreign marketing opportunities   503
    Political factors   504
    Economic factors   506
    Social factors   507
    Technological factors   508
    A more detailed analysis of potential markets   510

Adapting the product offer to foreign markets   512
    Pricing in foreign markets   516
    Distributing goods and services in foreign markets   517
    People decisions   518

Market entry strategies 519
Timescale for foreign market development 519
Who should be involved in foreign market development? 521

Global e-commerce 524
Future trends in global marketing 526

Chapter summary and key linkages to other chapters 527

Key principles of marketing 528

Case study: Can Interbrew sell more beer to
the heavy drinking Czechs? 529
Chapter review questions 532
Activities 533
References 533
Suggested further reading 533
Useful web links 534
Key terms 534

Glossary of marketing terms 535
Subject index 543
Index of authors 548
Index of companies and brands 550

PART 1

Marketing: the fundamentals

What is marketing?

CHAPTER OBJECTIVES

There is much misunderstanding about what marketing is. Many people equate it with promotion, or 'trying to sell things that people don't really want'. With higher levels of business education, that misperception is changing. This chapter sets out the foundations of marketing and distinguishes between marketing as a fundamental philosophy and marketing as a set of techniques. While the techniques have now been widely adopted, many organizations still have a long way to go in developing a true customer focus, which is at the heart of the marketing philosophy. This chapter discusses the relationship of marketing to other organization functions and reviews current debate about the nature of marketing. It is essentially a foundation chapter, and many themes discussed will be returned to in more detail in later chapters.

Introduction

Next time you are in a grocery store, stop and think about why there is such a wide choice of goods competing for your custom. You might be quite a selective shopper, with a strong preference for one brand of cola over another. Or you may be very price-sensitive, and choose the one that appears to give you the best **value**. You might be so accustomed to being able to purchase your favourite drink each time you go into a shop, and very surprised if one day it is not there waiting for you on the shelves. Then think about the shop itself. You might take it for granted that the shop is open late into the evening, at times which may be convenient for you. You might have noticed that the shop has innovated with new services over recent years—so you can now top up your phone, or buy freshly made coffee, for example. So much in our patterns of consumption that we take for granted can be attributed to marketing. When you called in to buy a can of your favourite drink, you probably did not have on your mind questions such as 'why does the shop stock this brand but not another one?'; 'how did they decide which sizes of packaging to sell the drink in?'; 'how did they decide on the range of flavours?'; 'how were selling prices worked out?'; 'who decided on the current special **promotion** offer of "buy one get one free"?'; 'who evaluated whether this offer was successful?'. Some of these involve key strategic decisions; others are day-to-day matters, but they are all central to what marketing is about. To get a simple bottle of cola on to the shelf in your local store will have involved hundreds, possibly thousands of strategic and operational decisions by marketing people. When these decisions are the right ones, you are happy with a **product** that you enjoy, and the manufacturer and retailer are happy because they earn profits from you. If the wrong decisions are made, you will not like the product, so you will not buy it, at least not repeatedly, and the company selling it will not get your money. If it makes a series of wrong decisions, it may eventually go out of business.

Think also of higher-value new products that you see in the shops—new versions of iPods, this season's new fashion clothing, or a new microwaveable ready-prepared meal, for example. The companies behind these new products would most likely have invested a great deal of time and money researching these new products and their targeted buyers, so that when they are launched, they are snapped up by buyers, rather than having to be sold at a discounted 'clearance' price. Marketers have to be aware of your changing **needs** and expectations, because if another company offers a shiny new product, possibly at a lower price, you will probably be tempted by it, wouldn't you?

Contrast the situation described above—which we take for granted in western countries—with the situation in a centrally planned economy. There, the goods offered for sale are more probably the result of an internal production decision, without much regard to the needs of consumers. Without a competitive market-based economy to spur a company into action, there is less need for marketing managers. Companies may just carry on making the things that they like making, rather than what buyers actually want. At best, they may have a poor understanding of the complex needs that buyers seek to satisfy, and may have little idea about how these may change over time. Indeed, change may be seen as a threat rather than an opportunity, so companies would just carry on doing what they always did. This was clearly seen in the design of cars and household goods in eastern Europe during the period of communism, when many people claimed that design and innovation lagged a long way behind what was happening in western, market-based economies. Today, as **markets** become increasingly competitive, so too does the need for marketing. Rather than trying to justify the existence of marketing, just think what your next visit to the shops would be like if marketing did not exist.

There are many definitions of marketing which generally revolve around the primacy of **customers** as part of an exchange process. Customers' needs are the starting point for marketing activity. Marketing managers try to identify these needs and develop products that will satisfy customers' needs through an **exchange** process. Definitions of marketing have subtly changed over time, and in 2008 the American Marketing Association updated its definition, stating that:

Marketing is the activity, set of institutions, and processes for creating, communicating, delivering, and exchanging offerings that have value for customers, clients, partners, and society at large.

In the UK, the Chartered Institute of Marketing (CIM) has proposed a new definition of marketing, describing it as:

The strategic business function that creates value by stimulating, facilitating and fulfilling customer demand—it does this by building brands, nurturing innovation, developing relationships, creating good customer service and communicating benefits.

While customers may drive the activities of a marketing-oriented organization, the organization will be able to continue serving its customers only if it meets its own objectives. Most private sector organizations operate with some kind of profit-related objectives, and if an adequate level of profits cannot be earned from a particular group of customers, a firm will not normally wish to meet the needs of that group. Where an organization is able to meet its customers' needs effectively and efficiently, its ability to gain an advantage over its competitors will be increased (for example, by allowing it to sell a higher volume and/or at a higher price than its competitors). It is consequently also more likely to be able to meet its profit objectives.

Even in fully marketing-oriented organizations, it is not just customers who are crucial to the continuing success of the firm. The availability of finance and labour inputs may be quite critical, and in times of shortage of either one of these an organization must adapt its production processes if it is to continue meeting customers' needs. In addition, a whole range of internal and external pressures (such as government legislation and the emergence of new technologies) can affect its ability to profitably meet customers' needs. Organizations must adapt to a changing marketing environment if they are to survive and prosper. In Chapter 2 we will look more closely at these pressures on businesses.

Marketing as a philosophy and as a set of techniques

Marketing can be seen at two levels—as a fundamental, underlying philosophy, and as a set of applied techniques. As a *business philosophy*, marketing puts customers at the centre of an organization's considerations. This is reflected in basic values, such as the requirement to understand and respond to customers' needs and the necessity to search constantly for new market opportunities. In a truly marketing-oriented organization, these values are instilled in all employees and should influence their behaviour without any need for prompting. For a fast food restaurant, for example, the training of serving staff would emphasize those items—such as the speed of service and friendliness of staff—that research has found to be most valued by existing and potential customers. The human resources manager would have a selection policy that recruited staff who could fulfil the needs of customers rather than simply minimizing the wage bill. The accountant would investigate the effects on customers before deciding to save money by cutting stockholding levels. It is not sufficient for an organization simply to appoint a marketing manager or set up a marketing department—viewed as a philosophy, marketing is an attitude that applies to *everybody* who works for the organization.

To many people, marketing is simply associated with a set of *techniques*. For example, market research is seen as a technique for finding out about customers' needs, and advertising is thought to be a technique for communicating the benefits of a product

MARKETING in ACTION

Are they really marketing oriented?

Companies that have wholly embraced the marketing philosophy put customers at the centre of everything they do, so that being 'marketing oriented' becomes a state of mind for *all of their employees*. They should all be aware that if they don't put customers first, somebody else probably will and will win their profitable business. Here are some tell-tale signs of a company that may claim to be marketing oriented but where, in fact, not all of its employees have taken on board a genuine marketing orientation.

- In the car park, the prime parking spots are reserved for directors and senior staff rather than customers.
- Opening hours are geared towards meeting the social needs of staff rather than the purchasing preferences of customers.
- Management's attitudes towards lax staff are conditioned more by the need to keep internal peace than by the need to provide a high standard of service to customers.
- When confronted with a problem from a customer, an employee will refer the customer on to another employee without trying to resolve the matter him/herself ('it's not my job').
- The company listens to customers' comments and complaints, but has poorly defined procedures for acting on them.
- Advertising is based on what senior staff want to say, rather than a sound analysis of what prospective customers want to hear.
- Goods and services are distributed through channels that are easy for the company to set up, rather than on the basis of what customers prefer.

Can you think of any more tell-tale signs? Can you identify companies that exhibit the characteristics described above? Why do you think the company can behave in such a way? Are there insufficient competitive pressures facing the company to warrant change? What, if anything, would you do to bring about change in the company?

offer to potential customers. However, these techniques can be of little value if they are undertaken by an organization that has not fully taken on board the *philosophy* of marketing. The techniques of marketing also include **pricing**, the design of channels of distribution, and new product development. Although many of the chapters of this book are arranged around specific techniques, it must never be forgotten that all of these techniques are interrelated and can be effective only if they are unified by a shared focus on customers.

Of course, the principles of marketing are not new. Some of the elements of **marketing orientation** can be traced as far back as ancient Greece, the Phoenicians, and the Venetian traders. The bartering that still takes place in many eastern Kasbahs is a form of marketing. In modern times, marketing orientation developed in the more affluent countries, especially for products where supply was outstripping **demand** and suppliers therefore faced high levels of competition for custom. Marketing first became an important discipline in the United States in the 1930s and has since become dominant around the world. In a competitive business environment, an organization will survive in the long term only if it focuses on the needs of clearly defined groups in society and produces goods and services that satisfy their requirements efficiently and effectively. The emphasis is on the customer wanting to buy, rather than on the producer needing to sell.

There have been many attempts to define just what is meant by marketing orientation. (A good review has been provided by Lafferty and Hult, 2001.) Among empirical attempts to measure marketing orientation, a study by Narver and Slater (1990) identified three important components (Figure 1.1):

- **Customer orientation**: An organization must have a thorough understanding of its target buyers, so that it can create a product of superior value for them. Remember that value can be defined only by customers themselves, and can be created by increasing the benefits to the buyer in relation to the buyer's costs or by decreasing the buyer's costs in relation to the buyer's benefits. A customer orientation requires that a company understand not only the present value to the customer, but also how this is likely to evolve over time.

- **Competitor orientation**: As well as focusing on its customers, a firm should look at how well its competitors are able to satisfy buyers' needs. It should understand the short-term strengths and weaknesses and long-term capabilities and strategies of current and potential competitors.

- **Inter-functional coordination**: It is futile for marketing managers to develop marketing plans that are not acted upon by people who are capable of delivering promises made to customers. Many individuals within an organization have a responsibility for creating value—not just marketing staff—and a marketing orientation requires that the organization draw upon and integrate its human and physical resources effectively and adapt them to meet customers' needs.

Figure 1.1 Elements of a firm's marketing orientation

Source: based on J. C. Narver and S. F. Slater, 'The Effect of a Market Orientation on Business Profitability'.
Journal of Marketing, October 1990, pp. 20–35.

Foundations for success in business

So far, marketing has been presented as an indispensable approach to doing business.
In fact, marketing is not appropriate to all firms at all times and in all **places**. Essentially,
marketing is most important where the main factor constraining a firm's survival and
growth is the shortage of customers for its products. If a firm can be assured of selling
all that it produces, it may consider marketing to be the least of its worries. There are
other factors that may be critical for success to some companies:

- Where the raw materials and components that a company requires are scarce but
demand for its finished products is very strong, a company may consider that
obtaining inputs to its production processes is its top priority. During the late 1990s,
the shortage of organic vegetables, rather than a shortage of customers, posed the
biggest challenge to companies seeking to develop the market for organic products
(see 'Marketing in Action' later in this chapter).

- For firms requiring high levels of skill among their employees, being able to recruit
and retain the right personnel can be critical to business success. Firms in sectors as
diverse as computer programming, direct marketing, specialist craft industries, and
electrical engineering have had market-led growth held back by difficulties in filling
key positions.

- Where a company is given a licence by government agencies to provide a monopoly service, its actions may be motivated more by the desire to keep the regulatory agency satisfied than to keep its customers happy.

Modern marketing emerged in the 1930s at a time when the volume of goods supplied to markets was increasing faster than consumers' demand for them. Instead of taking markets as a given element of their business plans, firms had to actively address the needs of their markets—if they did not, the market would slip into their competitors' hands.

It is common to talk about the production-oriented firm, where production and not marketing is the focal point for business planning. However, when markets became more competitive, the first reaction of many companies was to take on board not the full philosophy of marketing, but only the selling function. Eventually, firms have come to realize that, instead of trying to sell products that buyers do not really want, it would be better to take on board the full philosophy of marketing, which puts customers' needs at the centre of all business planning.

Figure 1.2 In 2006, Smartphones which combined a phone, Internet browser, camera, music player, and personal digital assistant became a hot new product which helped to reinvigorate the mobile phone market. The market for mobile phones had become saturated and the basic mobile phone had become a commodity-type product. The new-type phones allowed companies to add features that consumers valued. But how long would it be before *these* phones became standard and customers were no longer willing to pay a premium price for them? What would be the next features and benefits that customers will value as the technology of mobile phones develops?

A production or a sales orientation may be appropriate to firms at certain stages in the evolution of markets. Where the dominant business environment is based on the need for good production planning above all else, the company that does this best will achieve the greatest overall business success. Likewise, in markets where customers face a lot of choice, the company that achieves the greatest business success is likely to be one that has the most effective marketing.

Because they are business environments that still occur in some markets in some places, production and selling orientations are described below. There has, however,

Figure 1.3 The fast-moving consumer goods (FMCG) sectors were the first to adopt modern marketing. The soap powder, toothpaste, and shampoo markets have become fiercely competitive and great efforts have been made by the manufacturers to develop differentiated versions of a fairly standard product in order to meet the needs of small groups of consumers more effectively than their competitors. Next time you are in a shop choosing toothpaste, look at all of the different product formulations, packaging design, and price offers that companies have deployed to try to get you to buy their product rather than the competitors'. It is often said that experience in the tough world of an FMCG company's marketing department is the best apprenticeship that a new marketer can serve. While FMCG sectors were early adopters of marketing, many more sectors have followed their example. (Photograph: Angela Parks)

Figure 1.4 The development of the dominant business environment

been an almost inevitable tendency for such business environments to progress to a full marketing orientation. Firms that have identified such trends and adapted have tended to survive, while those set in their traditional ways of doing business have fallen behind.

Production orientation

Marketing as a business discipline has much less significance where goods or services are scarce and considerable unsatisfied demand exists. If an organization is operating in a stable environment in which it can sell all that it can produce, why bother spending time and money trying to understand precisely what benefit a customer seeks from buying the product? If the market is stable, why take time trying to anticipate future requirements? Furthermore, if a company has significant monopoly power, it may have little interest in being more efficient in meeting customer requirements. The former state monopolies of eastern Europe are frequently cited as examples of organizations that produced what they imagined consumers wanted, rather than what they actually wanted. Planning for full utilization of capital equipment was often seen as more important than ensuring that the equipment was used to provide goods and services that people actually wanted. Production-oriented firms generally aim for efficiency in production rather than effectiveness in meeting customers' needs.

In the developed countries of America and Europe, production orientation was quite pervasive until the 1930s; up until then, a general shortage of goods relative to the demand for them, and a lack of competition, resulted in a sellers' market. In many goods markets, however, the world depression of the 1920s and 1930s had the effect of tilting the balance of supply and demand more in favour of buyers, resulting in sellers having to address more seriously the needs of increasingly selective customers. In most countries markets for services have tended to retain a production orientation longer than most goods markets, reflecting the fact that many key services, such as postal services, telecommunications, electricity, gas, and water supply, have been dominated by state or private monopolies which gave consumers very little choice of supplier—if consumers did not like the service they received from their water supplier, they could not switch their business to another water company. Management in such circumstances had greater freedom to satisfy its own interests than those of the consumer, and could increase profits more effectively by keeping production costs down rather than applying effort and possibly taking greater risk through developing new services based on consumers' needs.

During periods of shortages, production orientation sometimes returns to an industry sector. The shortage might come about through supply limitations caused by strikes or bad weather, or it could be the result of a sudden increase in demand relative to supply. For example, during a bus or train drivers' strike, taxi operators may realize that there is a temporary massive excess of demand relative to supply and so may be tempted to lower their standards of service to casual customers (for example, by responding to requests much more slowly and doing so in a less friendly manner than regular customers would have come to expect). During the boom in property prices that occurred in the UK during the mid 2000s, the services of builders were in short supply, especially in south-east England. Stories abounded of builders 'selecting' customers and delaying the completion of jobs because they knew that customers had very little choice.

Selling orientation

Faced with an increasingly competitive market, the natural reaction of many organizations has been to shout louder in order to attract customers to buy its products. Product policy was driven by the desire to make those products that the company thought it was good at producing, rather than seriously asking what benefits customers sought from buying its products. In order to increase sales, the focal point of the business moved away from the production manager to the sales manager, who set about increasing effective demand by the use of various sales techniques. Advertising, sales promotion, and personal selling were used to emphasize product differentiation and branding.

MARKETING in ACTION

Demand boomed for organics, but where were the vegetables?

Supermarkets today sell a wide range of 'organic' fruit and vegetables, with rival supermarket chains competing against each other on the price and quality of their produce. Some have gone further, and added ethical sourcing as a point of differentiation, for example through compliance with Fairtrade standards. But in the early days of the boom in organic vegetables, competition was not so keen, and those early days illustrate the point that when a company faces acute problems of supply, it may simply not be realistic for it to be customer-led, at least in the short term. In the UK during the late 1990s a combination of rising incomes, greater awareness of health issues, and a stream of food safety scares led to a rapid growth in demand for organic produce (see Chomka, 2002). But how could farmers grow organically on land that had been saturated by decades of artificial fertilizers? The Soil Association, which operates an accreditation scheme for organic produce, required that farmland should be free of artificial fertilizer for at least five years before any crops grown on it could be described as organic. So, despite the rapid growth in demand and the price premiums that customers were prepared to pay, retailers found it difficult to satisfy demand. Furthermore, with a difficult and intermittent supply, could retailers risk their brand names by being seen as unreliable suppliers of second-rate produce? Marks & Spencer launched a range of organic vegetables in 1997, only to temporarily withdraw them soon afterwards, blaming the difficulty in obtaining regular and reliable supplies. In the short term, it was suppliers and not customers who guided the retailer's policy on organic produce. However, by 2002 previous initiatives to grow more organic food were finally coming on stream, resulting in a glut of produce which depressed the prices that farmers received. It was now a buyers' market.

MARKETING in ACTION

New marketing, or old ideas?

Among the favourite words of marketers are 'new', 'improved', and 'innovative'. Each year brings its crop of new ideas about the philosophy and practices of marketing, some of them being dressed up in pseudo-scientific terminology by consultants and academics, eager to use their knowledge base to sell a new idea to people who fear being left behind. In fact, basic principles of marketing have been quite enduring, and claims for completely new approaches to marketing should be treated cautiously. For the experienced marketer, most new ideas are based on age-old underlying theory, and there is usually some form of precedent for new ideas.

The Internet was hailed as a completely new approach to marketing, and at the height of 'dot.com' mania around 2000, some advocates had a vision of the Internet allowing almost infinite and cheap communication possibilities, breaking down monopolies, international trade and cultural barriers in the process. The world of marketing would never be the same again.

The Internet has certainly changed the way that many companies practise marketing, but underlying principles have often won out over the hype. 'Disintermediation' was held out as a great opportunity by which the Internet would cut out intermediaries, as people buy airline tickets, books, and financial services directly from the producer, rather than using an agent, retailer, or broker as an intermediary; but basic theories of marketing suggest that people like to be presented with a manageable choice in one location. It should therefore have been no surprise that instead of 'disintermediation', many new information intermediaries such as Expedia.com, Amazon.com, and moneysupermarket.com emerged to fulfil this role. Internet auction sites such as eBay have been proclaimed as a new way of marketing to customers on a one-to-one basis, but the basic principles underlying them can be traced back to marketing practices found in ancient Kasbahs. Many of the big Internet service providers realize that successful Internet marketing requires a sound understanding of basic human behaviour, and many have appointed teams of anthropologists to try to understand users' deep-seated motivations, and how these relate to modern technology. Among current burning questions are whether 'Web 2.0' and social networking sites, such as Facebook and Bebo, really represent a new marketing approach, as buyers seek out information from their peers rather than through conventional advertising. Again, theories based in social sciences may suggest that although the technology is new, the nature of people's need to belong and their methods of developing trust are longstanding.

Practitioners of marketing make excessive use of the word 'new', to describe anything from a 'new and improved' breakfast cereal to a new way of looking at the world. However, we should never forget that many of the underlying principles of marketing are quite timeless. We really need to distinguish between genuinely new marketing ideas—which are quite rare—and old ideas that have been applied to a new marketing environment.

A **sales orientation** was a move away from a strict **product orientation**, but it still did not focus on satisfying customer needs. Little effort was made to research customers' needs or to devise new product offerings that were customer-led rather than production-led.

A sales orientation has been characteristic of a number of business sectors. UK package holiday companies have often grown through heavy advertising of their competitive price advantage, supported by aggressive sales promotion techniques, such as free child places. There are signs that this sales-led approach is now being replaced by a greater analysis of the diverse needs that customers seek to satisfy when buying a package holiday, such as reliable aircraft departures, and assurance about the standards of the booked hotel.

If a company were accurately identifying consumer needs and offering a product that satisfied these needs, then consumers would want to buy the product, and the company would not have to rely on intensive sales techniques. In the words of Peter Drucker (1973),

The aim of marketing is to make selling superfluous. The aim of marketing is to know and understand the customer so well that the product or service fits him and sells itself. Ideally, marketing should result in a customer who is ready to buy. All that should be needed is to make the product or service available . . .

The discussion about the relationship between selling and marketing has been brought up to date in a recent *Harvard Business Review* article by Kotler, Rackham, and Krishnaswamy (2006).

■ What organizations undertake marketing?

Marketing developed in competitive fast-moving goods (FMCG) sectors, with private sector services following in their footsteps. More recently, marketing has been adopted by various public sector and **not-for-profit organizations**, reflecting the increasingly competitive environments in which these now operate. Operationalizing marketing within these organizations poses a number of challenges (see Sargeant, 2004). If an organization has a market that it needs to win over, then marketing has a role; but without markets, can marketing ever be a reality? Many organizations claim to have introduced marketing when in fact their customers are captive, with no marketplace within which they can choose competing goods or services. What passes for marketing may be little more than a laudable attempt to bring best practice to their operations in selected areas, for example in providing customer care programmes for front-line staff; but if customers have to come to the company anyway (as they do in the case of many local authority services), is this really marketing?

Within the public/not-for-profit sectors, financial objectives are often qualified by non-financial social objectives. An organization's desire to meet individual customer's needs must be further constrained by its requirement to meet these wider social objectives. In this way, a leisure centre may set an objective of providing a range of keep-fit programmes for disadvantaged members of the local community, knowing that it could have earned more money by opening its facilities to the larger group of full fee-paying visitors. Nevertheless, marketing can be employed to achieve a high take-up rate among this latter group, persuading them to spend their time and money at the leisure centre rather than on other leisure activities. It can also be used to appeal to disadvantaged groups by encouraging them to take part in keep-fit activities rather than other forms of activity.

In recent years, the principles of marketing have been applied to organizations that essentially promote ideas, for example charities, political parties, and religious groups. Some of the principles of marketing may be evident in the way that the UK Labour Party 'rebranded' itself as New Labour after careful research of its audiences. This was backed up with a very effective advertising campaign, based on many of the principles of segmentation and targeting, which helped it to win the subsequent general elections. However, some purists would argue that, in its application to social and political causes, marketing is inappropriate because of the absence of markets and exchanges as conventionally understood by marketers.

Key marketing concepts

In this section, the philosophy of marketing will be developed a little further by defining a number of key concepts which go to the heart of the philosophy. The concepts of customers, needs, value, exchange, and markets will be briefly introduced, but returned to in following chapters.

Customers

Customers provide payment to an organization in return for the delivery of goods and services and therefore form a focal point for an organization's marketing activity. Customers can be described by many terms, including client, passenger, subscriber, reader, guest, and student. The terminology can imply something about the relationship between a company and its customers, so the term 'patient' implies a caring relationship, 'passenger' implies an ongoing responsibility for the safety of the customer, and 'client' implies that the relationship is governed by a code of ethics (formal or informal).

The customer is generally understood to be the person who makes the decision to purchase a product, and/or who pays for it. In fact, products are often bought by one person for consumption by another, therefore the customer and consumer need not be the same person. For example, colleges must market themselves not only to prospective students, but also to their parents, careers counsellors, local employers, and government funding agencies. In these circumstances it can be difficult to identify on whom an organization's marketing effort should be focused. The role of influencers in the decision process is discussed further in Chapter 4.

For many public services, it is society as a whole, and not just the immediate customer, that benefits from an individual's consumption. In the case of health services,

When does a student become a customer?

As a hospital *patient*, would you cringe at being referred to as a 'customer'? Or what about the transformation of rail users from 'passengers' to 'customers'? Some universities now refer to their paying students as 'customers'. The use of the word 'customer' may sharpen minds within an organization, making everybody aware that they cannot take users for granted. 'Passenger', 'patient', and 'student' are relatively passive terms, but 'customer' provides a reminder that custom can be quite transient. Do terms used by professionals, such as 'patient' and 'student', imply a professional code of ethics which puts some groups of consumers in a very special, trusting relationship with their supplier? Is it realistic to describe as 'customers' the users of some public services (such as the police and fire services) when there is no alternative supplier they could customize? Does the use of the generic title of 'customer' undermine this special relationship? Could the use of the term 'customer' even be a double-edged sword, by raising consumers' expectations about standards of service to levels that may be undeliverable? Can being a patient in an NHS hospital ever be likened to being a customer of Sainsbury's supermarket?

society can benefit from having a fit and healthy population in which the risk of contracting a contagious disease is minimized.

Different customers within a market have different needs which they seek to satisfy. To be fully marketing oriented, a company would have to adapt its offering to meet the needs of each individual. In fact, very few firms can justify aiming to meet the needs of each specific individual; instead, they target their product at a clearly defined group in society and position their product so that it meets the needs of that group. These sub-groups are often referred to as 'segments' and are explored in Chapter 3.

Needs

Consumers are motivated by their desire to satisfy complex needs, and these should be the starting point for all marketing activity. We no longer live in a society in which the main motivation of individuals is to satisfy the basic needs for food and drink. Maslow (1943) recognized that, once individuals have satisfied basic physiological needs, they may be motivated by higher-order social and self-fulfilment needs. Needs as motivators are explored further in Chapter 4.

'Need' refers to something that is deep-rooted in an individual's personality. How individuals go about satisfying that need will be conditioned by the cultural values of the society to which they belong. In some cultures the need for self-fulfilment may be satisfied by a religious penance, while other societies may seek it through a development of their creative talents.

Nature of need	Likely sources of need satisfaction in primitive societies	Likely sources of need satisfaction in western Europe
Status	Ownership of animals Multiple wives	Make and model of car Type and location of house
Excitement	Hunting Inter-tribe rivalry	Fast car Adventure holiday
Identification with group	Body painting Adopting rituals of the group	Wearing branded clothing Patronizing 'cool' nightclubs and bars

Figure 1.5 Some basic human needs and how people in different societies may go about satisfying them

It is useful to make a distinction between needs and **wants**. Wants are culturally conditioned by the society in which an individual lives. Wants subsequently become effective demand for a product where there is both a willingness and an ability to pay for the product. Marketers are continually seeking to learn more about underlying needs which may eventually manifest themselves as demand in the form of people actually being willing to pay money for its products.

It must not be forgotten that commercial buyers of goods and services also have complex needs which they seek to satisfy when buying on behalf of their organizations. Greater complexity occurs where the economic needs of the organization may not be entirely the same as the personal needs of individuals within the organization.

Value

For customers, value is represented by the ratio of perceived benefits to price paid. Customers will evaluate benefits according to the extent to which a product allows their needs to be satisfied. Customers also evaluate how well a product's benefits add to their own well-being as compared with the benefits provided by competitors' offerings:

$$\text{Customer perceived value} = \frac{\text{Benefits deriving from a product}}{\text{Cost of acquiring the product}}$$

Consumers often place a value on a product offer that is quite different from the value presumed by the supplier. Business organizations succeed by adding value at a faster rate than they add to their own production costs. Value can be added by better specifying a product offer in accordance with customers' expectations, for example by providing the reassurance of effective after-sales service.

Estimating customers' assessment of value is not easy for marketers. Chapter 9 deals with theoretical and practical approaches to pricing which aim to set prices at a level that meets the needs of buyer and seller. Segmentation is crucial to this exercise, as some groups of buyers are likely to place significantly higher values on the firm's goods

Figure 1.6 Traditional street markets and farmers markets have been experiencing a revival in the UK. Although market traders may not use many of the terms used in books on marketing theory, they are nevertheless very adept marketers. Traders learn very quickly which product lines are selling well and the effects of price changes on sales levels, among other things. They must adapt quickly, or risk business going to another trader in the same market who is more in tune with customers' needs, or to another trader outside the market. Market traders do not have layers of bureaucratic control that may slow up a decision and individual traders cannot easily shelter in a bureaucratic structure where blame can be passed around without the fundamental issue of responding to customers' needs being addressed. It is not surprising that market traders who have survived and prospered in this environment have gone on to establish and run successful enterprises. Many marketers from large organizations could benefit by taking a walk through their local market and reconnecting with the fundamental principles of marketing. (Reproduced with permission of National Market Traders Federation)

Figure 1.7 Value can be a very personal issue, and one person's highly prized object may be regarded by somebody else as their rubbish. Furniture and clothing have often been artificially aged to give a used appearance. The denim jeans shown in this illustration have been cut and made to look worn at the knees before being sold to customers. Many buyers have been prepared to pay a premium price for a pair of jeans that look as if they had been previously worn. To others, however, the idea of prematurely ageing clothes may sound like a sacrilege—for them, prematurely aged jeans should have a lower rather than a higher value. Value is essentially about personal judgements. (*Source:* © Photodisc)

than others (Chapter 6). If the price of a good is set too high, no sale may take place, or at least only a one-off sale which may be regarded by the buyer as a 'rip-off'. If the price is set too low, the supplier may achieve high levels of sales, but fail to make any profit because the price is too low to cover its costs. Firms need to understand not just what constitutes value today, but how customers' perceptions of value will change over time.

Exchange

Societies have different ways in which they arrange for goods and services to be acquired. In some less developed societies, hunting for food, or begging, may be a norm. In centrally planned economies goods and services may be allocated to individuals and firms by central government planners. In modern market-based economies, goods and services are acquired on the basis of exchange. Exchange implies that one party makes some sacrifice to another party in return for receiving something it values; the other

Figure 1.8 Needs, wants, demand, and exchange

party similarly makes a sacrifice and receives something that *it* values. Of course, the sacrifices and valuations of goods received and given up are essentially based on personal opinion and preferences, so there is no objective way of defining what is a 'fair' exchange, other than observing that both parties are happy with the outcomes. In market-based economies there is a presumption that each party can decide whether or not to enter into an exchange with the other. Each party is also free to choose between a number of alternative potential partners. Exchange usually takes the form of a product being exchanged for money, although the bartering of goods and services is still common in some trading systems.

Can the concept of exchange be generalized to cover the provision of public services? Some have argued that the payment of taxes to the government in return for the provision of public services is a form of social marketing exchange. Within marketing frameworks, the problem with this approach to exchange is that it can be difficult to identify what sovereignty consumers of government services have in determining which exchanges they should engage in.

A single exchange should not be seen in isolation from the preceding and expected subsequent exchanges between parties. Marketers are increasingly focusing on analysing ongoing exchange relationships, rather than one-off and isolated exchanges. (We will come back to this in Chapter 4.)

Markets

The term 'market' has traditionally been used to describe a place where buyers and sellers gather to exchange goods and services (for example, a fruit and vegetable market or a stock market). Economists define a market in terms of a more abstract concept of interaction between buyers and sellers, so that the 'UK cheese market' is defined in terms of all buyers and sellers of cheese in the UK. Markets are defined with reference to space and time, so marketers may talk about sales of a particular type of cheese in the north-west region for a specified period of time. Various measures of the market are commonly used, including sales volumes, sales values, growth rate, and level of competitiveness.

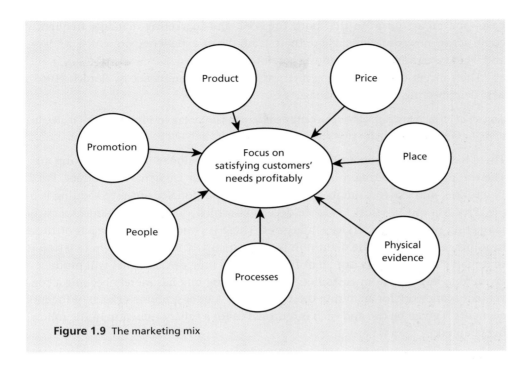

Figure 1.9 The marketing mix

The marketing mix

Central to **marketing management** is the concept of the **marketing mix** (Figure 1.9). In this section the elements of the marketing mix are briefly introduced, but they are returned to in greater detail in following chapters. The marketing mix is not a theory of management that has been derived from scientific analysis, but a conceptual framework which highlights the principal decisions that marketing managers make in configuring their offerings to suit customers' needs. The tools can be used to develop both long-term strategies and short-term tactical programmes.

A marketing manager can be seen as somebody who mixes a set of ingredients to achieve a desired outcome in much the same way as a cook mixes ingredients for a cake. At the end of the day, two cooks can meet a common objective of baking an edible cake, but using different blends of ingredients to achieve their objective. Marketing managers are essentially mixers of ingredients, and, as with the cooks, two marketers may each use broadly similar ingredients, but fashion them in different ways to end up with quite distinctive product offers. The nation's changing tastes result in bakers producing new types of cake, and so too the changing marketing environment results in marketing managers producing new goods and services to offer to their markets. The mixing of ingredients in both cases is a combination of a science—learning by a logical process from what has proved to be effective in the past—and an art form, in that both the cook and marketing manager frequently come across new situations where there is no direct experience on which to draw, and where a creative decision must therefore be made.

The concept of the marketing mix was first given prominence by Borden (1965), who described the marketing manager as,

a mixer of ingredients, one who is constantly engaged in fashioning creatively a mix of marketing procedures and policies in his efforts to produce a profitable enterprise.

There has been debate about which tools should be included in the marketing mix. The traditional marketing mix has comprised the four elements of Product, Price, Promotion, and Place. A number of people have additionally suggested adding People, Process, and Physical Evidence decisions, which can be important aspects of marketing planning in services industries. There is overlap between each of these headings, and their precise definition is not particularly important. What matters is that marketing managers can identify the actions they can take that will produce a favourable response from customers. The marketing mix has merely become a convenient framework for analysing these decisions. A brief synopsis of each of the mix elements is given below, and each is returned to for a fuller discussion in the following chapters.

Products

Products are the means by which organizations satisfy consumers' needs. A product in this sense is anything that an organization offers to potential customers which might satisfy a need, whether tangible or intangible. After initial hesitation, most marketing managers are now happy to talk about an intangible service as a product.

The elements of the product mix that the marketer can control include quality levels, styling, special design features, durability, packaging, range of sizes or options, warranties, after-sales service, and the brand image. Trade-offs are involved between these elements. For example, one firm may invest in quality control and high-grade materials to provide a durable, top-quality product requiring a low level of after-sales service, while another company might offer lower quality but would ensure that a much more effective after-sales service did not make their customers any worse off than if they had bought the higher-quality product. Brands are used by companies to help them differentiate their product from those of their competitors. A brand is a name, term, symbol, or combination of these intended to differentiate the goods of one seller from all other sellers (see Chapter 7).

The range of products offered by firms needs to adapt to changes in the marketing environment. As an example, cosmetics companies have responded to changes in male attitudes by launching new ranges of cosmetics targeted at men. (New product development is discussed in Chapter 8.)

Pricing

Pricing is a critical element of most companies' marketing mix, as it determines the revenue that will be generated. By contrast, the other mix elements are concerned essentially with items of expenditure. If the selling price of a product is set too high, a company may not achieve its sales volume targets. If it is set too low, volume targets may be achieved, but no profit earned. Setting prices is a difficult part of the marketing mix. In theory, prices are determined by the interaction of market forces, and the bases of such price determination is explored further in Chapter 9. In practice, marketers set prices for individual products on the basis of what they cost to produce, what the competition is charging, and what customers are prepared to pay. Marketing managers in many public utilities must additionally contend with interventions by government regulatory agencies.

Price decisions also involve deciding on the relationship between prices charged for different products within a firm's range (e.g. should the core product be sold at a low price in order to encourage sales of highly profitable optional extras?) and deciding a pricing strategy over time (should a new product be launched as a prestige product, and its price gradually lowered as it becomes more commonplace?).

Place

Decisions concerning place really comprise two related areas of decisions. Companies usually make their goods and services in places that are convenient for production, but customers prefer to buy them where the purchase process and/or consumption is easiest; so place decisions involve determining how easy a company wants to make it for customers to gain access to its goods and services. In the first place, this involves deciding which intermediaries to use in the process of transferring the product from the manufacturer to final consumer (usually referred to as designing a 'channel of distribution'). Second, it involves deciding how physically to move and handle the product as it is transported from manufacturer to final consumer (often referred to as 'logistics' or 'physical distribution management'). Place decisions are considered in more detail in Chapter 10.

Promotion

Promotion is used by companies in order to communicate the benefits of their products to their target markets. Promotional tools include advertising, personal selling, public relations, sales promotion, sponsorship, and—increasingly—direct marketing methods. Just as product ranges need to be kept up to date to reflect changing customer needs, so too promotional methods need to be responsive to changes in a firm's operating environment. Promotion decisions to be taken include: what message to use? which media? what timing for an advertising campaign? how much to spend? how to evaluate this expenditure? Promotional decisions are considered in more detail in Chapter 11.

People

People decisions are particularly important to the marketing of services. In the services sector, in particular, people planning can be very important where staff have a high level of contact with customers. Marketing effectiveness is likely to be critically affected by the actions of front-line employees who interact with customers. While a car manufacturer's employees may be unseen by its customers, a restaurant's waiters can make or break the benefits that visitors to the restaurant perceive. People decisions call for close involvement between marketing and human resource management functions to answer such questions as: what are the prerequisite skills for front-line employees? How should staff be rewarded and motivated?

Process

Process decisions are again of most importance to marketers in the services sector. The process of production may be of little concern to the consumer of manufactured goods, but it is often of critical concern to the consumer of 'high contact' services. A customer of a restaurant is deeply affected by the manner in which staff members serve them. For busy customers, the speed and friendliness with which a restaurant processes its customers may be just as important as the meal itself. Marketers must work closely with operations managers to design customer handling processes that are both cost-efficient and effective in satisfying customers' needs.

Physical evidence

Physical evidence is important in guiding buyers of intangible services through the choices available to them. This evidence can take a number of forms. At its simplest, a brochure can describe and give pictures of important elements of the service product—a holiday brochure gives pictorial evidence of hotels and resorts for this purpose. The appearance of staff can give evidence about the nature of a service—a tidily dressed ticket clerk for an airline gives some evidence that the airline operation as a whole is run with care and attention. A clean, bright environment used in a service outlet can help reassure potential customers at the point where they make a service purchase decision.

Interdependency of the marketing mix

The definition of the elements of the marketing mix is largely intuitive and semantic. The list of mix elements has much everyday practical value, because it provides headings around which management thoughts and actions can be focused. However, dividing management responses into apparently disconnected areas of activity may lead to the interaction between elements being overlooked. Promotion mix decisions, for example, cannot be considered in isolation from decisions about product characteristics or pricing. Within conventional definitions of the marketing mix, important customer-focused issues such as quality of service can become lost. A growing body of opinion is therefore suggesting that a more holistic approach should be taken by marketing managers in responding to their customers' needs. This view sees the marketing mix as a production-led approach to marketing in which the agenda for action is set by the seller and not by the customer. An alternative relationship marketing approach starts by asking what customers seek from a company and then proceeds to develop a response that integrates all the functions of a business in a manner that evolves in response to customers' changing needs. Although the chapters of this book roughly follow the elements of the marketing mix, the interlinkages between the mix elements must never be forgotten.

Marketing management

Successful marketing does not generally come about by accident: it needs to be managed effectively (although there are nevertheless many cases of successful marketing that occurred more by good luck than by judgement!). Three fundamental aspects of marketing management can be identified: processes, structures, and outcomes.

The marketing management process

Some companies, as they emerge from a production orientation, may think that they need only 'do some marketing' when trading conditions get tough. In fact, for well-managed businesses, marketing is an ongoing process that has no beginning or end (Figure 1.10). It is usual to identify four principal stages of the marketing management process, which involves asking the following questions:

- **Analysis:** Where are we now? How does the company's market share compare with that of its competitors? What are the strengths and weaknesses of the company and its products? What opportunities and threats does it face in its marketing environment?

- **Planning:** Where do we want to be? What is the mission of the business? What objectives should be set for the next year? What strategy will be adopted in order to achieve those objectives (e.g. should the company go for a high price/low volume strategy, or a low price/high volume one)?

- **Implementation:** How are we going to put into effect the strategy that will lead us to our objectives?

- **Evaluation and control:** Did we achieve our objectives? If not, why not? How can deficiencies be rectified? (In other words, go back to the beginning of the process and conduct further analysis.)

Marketing management structures

Internally, the structure and politics of an organization affect the manner in which it can respond to changing customer needs. An organization that gives all marketing responsibilities to just a narrow group of people may in fact create tensions within the organization that make it less effective at responding to change, compared with an organization where the philosophy and practice of marketing are shared more widely. Marketing plans cannot be developed and implemented without a sound understanding of marketing managers' relationship to other members of their organization. There has been extensive research into the internal barriers that prevent companies developing a marketing orientation (e.g. Harris, 2002; Morgan, 2002).

There are two aspects of management structure that particularly affect the role of marketers: the internal structure and processes of the marketing department itself (where one actually exists), and the relationship of the marketing functions to other business functions, which affects the marketing effectiveness of an organization. Issues of marketing management structures and processes are explored in Chapter 12.

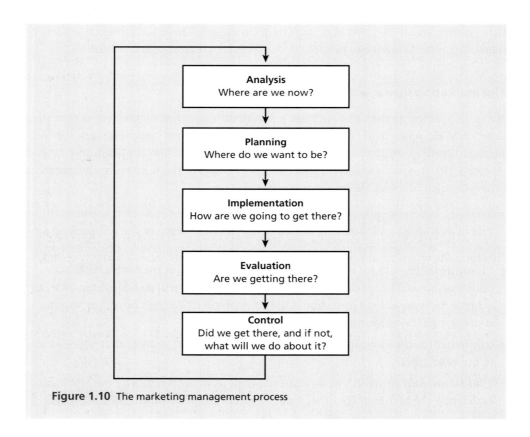

Figure 1.10 The marketing management process

Outcomes of the marketing management process

Ultimately, the aim of good marketing management is to allow a company to survive and produce an acceptable level of profits. Leading up to this, a tangible outcome of the management process is the marketing plan. A plan should be distinguished from the process of planning: a plan is a statement fixed at one point in time, while planning refers to an ongoing process, of which the plan is just one outcome.

Companies typically produce a strategic marketing plan for a five-year period. Over this time period, projections can be subject to a great deal of speculative estimation. Nevertheless, a five-year strategic plan can be vital to give a sense of direction to a company's marketing effort. Over the shorter term, companies usually produce an annual plan which gives more details of how the strategy will be implemented over the forthcoming 12-month period. Sometimes, where a marketing plan is based on a set of assumptions that are highly speculative, a company may choose to develop an additional contingency plan to use, should the assumptions on which the original plan was based turn out to be invalid.

There is continuing debate about the extent to which marketing plans should be flexible. If they are too flexible, they lose value in being able to act as a blueprint for all individuals in an organization to plan by. If the marketing department changes its sales targets halfway through the plan period, this might cause havoc in the production department, which had geared up to meet the original budgeted level of sales. On the other hand, fixed plans may become an irrelevance when the company's marketing environment has changed significantly.

Marketing and its relationship to other business functions

Companies have learned that their marketing departments cannot exist in isolation from the other functional departments of their organization. The importance attached to an organization's marketing activities is influenced by the nature of the environment in which the organization operates. In a production-oriented firm, a marketing department has little role to play, other than merely processing orders.

In a truly marketing-oriented company, marketing responsibilities cannot be confined to something called a marketing department. In the words of Drucker (1973),

Marketing is so basic that it cannot be considered to be a separate function. It is the whole business seen from the point of view of its final result, that is, from the customer's point of view.

In marketing-oriented organizations, the customer should be the concern not just of the marketing department, but also all of the production and administrative personnel whose actions may directly or indirectly create value in the mind of customers. In a typical company, the activities of a number of functional departments can affect customer value:

- The selection, training, motivation, and control of staff by human resources managers cannot be considered in isolation from marketing objectives and strategies. Possible conflict between the human resources and marketing functions may arise where, for example, marketing demands highly trained and motivated front-line staff, but the human resources function pursues a policy that places cost reduction and uniform pay rates above all else.

- A marketing manager may seek to respond as closely as possible to customers' needs, only to find opposition from production managers who argue that a product of the required standard cannot be achieved. Production managers tend to prefer long production runs of standardized products, but marketers increasingly try to satisfy market niches with specially adapted products.

- At a strategic and operational level, finance managers' actions in respect of the level of credit offered to customers, or towards stockholdings, can significantly affect the quality of service and the volume of customers with which the marketing department is able to do business.

Marketing orientation requires all of these departments to 'think customer' and to work together to satisfy customer needs and expectations. In practice, this can be very difficult to achieve, as witnessed by the many instances where it may appear that 'the left hand of the organization doesn't know what the right hand is doing'. A number of initiatives have sought to organize the activities of a company around processes that create value as perceived by customers (see Chapter 12). However, there is a danger that, as groups work more collectively, individual responsibilities and accountabilities can diminish.

🔵 Marketing and social responsibility

Traditional definitions of marketing have stressed the supremacy of customers, but this is increasingly being challenged by the requirement to satisfy the needs of a wider range of stakeholders in society. There have been many recent cases where companies have neglected the interests of this wider group with disastrous consequences, and we will look at some of these in Chapter 3. Scenes of protesters outside a company's premises and newspaper coverage of anti-social behaviour by firms can take away from the company something that its marketing department had spent years developing—its image. The opposite can be true where companies go out of their way to be good citizens.

There are segments within most markets that place high priority on ensuring that the companies they buy from are 'good citizens'. Examples can be found among consumers who prefer to pay a few pennies extra for products that have a low 'carbon footprint', or have been supplied by 'Fairtrade' companies.

Wider issues are raised about the effects of marketing practices on the values of a society. It has been argued by some that, by promoting greater consumption, marketing is responsible for creating a greater feeling of isolation among those members of society who cannot afford to join the consumer society where an individual's status is judged by what they own, rather than by their contribution to family and community life. Much advertising has been criticized as being socially harmful, for example for high-fat 'junk' food and alcohol, which may appeal against an individual's better judgement, bring bad health to millions, and raise the costs of health care for sufferers.

Determining the **social responsibilities** of organizations is a controversial subject and is discussed further in Chapter 3.

Is marketing a science or an art?

Is marketing based on a **scientific method** of inquiry, or is it essentially about an artistic process of creativity?

Studies of marketing using the scientific frameworks of the natural sciences have found favour with followers of the **positivist** approach. This holds that, from observations of the real world, it is possible to deduce models that are of general applicability. On this basis, models have been developed to predict consumer behaviour, the profitability of retail locations, and price–volume relationships, among many other phenomena.

The great merit of the scientific approach is its claim to great objectivity, in that patterns and trends can be identified with greater confidence than if they were based on casual observation. Many marketers have appreciated the value of this scientific approach. Most major retailers rely heavily on models of retail location before deciding where to locate their next outlet. Armed with trading statistics from their existing network of stores and background information about their locations (e.g. the number of people living within 20 minutes' driving time, passing vehicle traffic per day, proximity to competitors, etc.), a regression model can be developed which shows the significance of each specified factor in explaining sales success.

To many people, marketing has no credibility if it does not adopt a rigorous, scientific method of inquiry. This method of inquiry implies that research should be carried out in a systematic manner and results should be replicable: a model of buyer behaviour should be able repeatedly to predict consumers' actions correctly, based on a sound collection of data and analysis. In the scientific approach, data are assessed using tests of significance and models are accepted or rejected accordingly. In the UK the Chartered Institute of Marketing has launched an initiative to improve the standards of 'marketing metrics'.

To counter this view, it has been argued that marketing cannot possibly copy the natural sciences in its methodologies. Positivist approaches have been accused of seeking meaning from quantitative data in a very subjective manner which is at variance with scientific principles (Brown, 1995). Experimental research in the natural sciences generally involves closed systems in which the researcher can hold all extraneous variables constant, thereby isolating the effects of changes in a variable that is of interest. For social sciences, experimental frameworks generally consist of complex social systems over which the researcher has no control: a researcher investigating the effects of a price change in a product on demand from customers cannot realistically hold constant all factors other than price. Indeed, it may be difficult to identify just what the 'other factors' are that should be controlled for in an experiment, but they may typically include the price of competitors' products, consumer confidence levels, the effects of media reports about that product category, and changes in consumer fashions and tastes, to name some of the more obvious. Contrast this with a physicist's laboratory experiment, where heat, light, humidity, pressure, and most other extraneous variables can be controlled, and the limitations of the scientific methodology in the social sciences become apparent. Marketers are essentially dealing with 'open' systems, in contrast to the 'closed' systems that are more typical of the natural sciences.

Post-positivists place greater emphasis on exploring in depth the meaning of individual case studies than on seeking objectivity and replicability through large sample sizes. Many would argue that such *inductive* approaches are much more customer-focused, in that they allow marketers to see the world from consumers' overall perspective, rather than through the mediating device of a series of isolated indicators. Post-positivist approaches to marketing hold that the 'real' truth will never emerge in a research framework that is constrained by the need to operationalize variables in a watertight manner. In real-life marketing, the world cannot be divided into clearly defined variables that are capable of objective measurement. Constructs such as consumers' attitudes and motivation may be very difficult to measure and model objectively. Furthermore, it is often the interaction between various phenomena that is of interest to researchers, and it can be very difficult to develop models that correspond to respondents' holistic perceptions of the world.

There is another argument against the scientific approach to marketing, which sees the process as essentially backward-looking. The scientific approach is relatively good at making sense of historic trends, but less good at predicting what will happen following periods of turbulent change.

Creativity combined with a scientific approach can be essential for innovation. The scientific approach to marketing planning has a tendency to minimize risks, yet many major business successes have been based on entrepreneurs using their own judgement, in preference to that of their professional advisers. Consider the following cases.

- In the run-up to London's Millennium celebrations, the Millennium Dome (now called the O_2 Arena) was the outcome of a fairly bureaucratic process of planning. The forecasts turned out to be far too optimistic. By contrast, the London Eye was a great success, despite relying on largely intuitive estimates of likely demand.

- Demand for SMS text messaging services was greatly underestimated, partly reflecting a technological basis for forecasting, rather than a deeper understanding of individuals' lifestyles.

- A scientific analysis of the transatlantic airline market in the 1980s would have concluded that the market was saturated and there was no opportunity for a new British operator. This did not stop the entrepreneur Richard Branson from launching his own airline and, by using his own creative style, developing a distinctive and profitable service within the crowded market.

Marketing has to be seen as a combination of art and science. Treating it excessively as an art can lead to decisions that are not sufficiently rigorous. Emphasizing the scientific approach can lead a company to lose sight of the holistic perceptions of its customers. Successful firms seek to use scientific and creative approaches in a complementary manner.

Marketing as an academic discipline

It is only since the 1970s that marketing has featured significantly on university syllabuses. To some of the more traditional academic institutions, marketing has been seen as essentially a topic of application rather than a discipline in its own right.

Marketing has borrowed heavily from other discipline areas. Its roots can be traced back to industrial economics, but in the process of growth it has drawn on the following discipline areas.

- Psychology has been central to many studies of buyer behaviour. Psychological theory in the fields of human motivation and perception has found ready application by marketers.

- Because of the importance of peer group pressures on many consumer and commercial purchases, a body of knowledge developed by sociologists has been used by marketers. As an example, social psychologists have contributed an understanding of the processes by which interpersonal trust develops, which has been applied to the study of long-term buyer–seller relationships (e.g. Dwyer, Schurr, and Oh, 1987).

- In its claim to be a science, marketers are constantly borrowing statistical techniques. Large-scale empirical research into buyer behaviour, product design preferences, and pricing effectiveness draws heavily upon previously developed statistical techniques which have conceptual and empirical validity.

- The law represents an embodiment of a society's values, and legal frameworks are becoming increasingly important to the study of marketing.

- Finally, economics remains an important discipline area on which marketing draws. As an example, marketers' pricing strategy has to be based on an understanding of the underlying theory of price determination in different market conditions.

As marketing has developed, the flow of theory has become more two-way. As well as borrowing from other discipline areas, marketers have developed theory and techniques that have been adopted by other discipline areas. (For example, marketers contributed significantly to the development of conjoint analysis in the study of consumer preferences, and this statistical methodology has now found widespread application elsewhere.) In universities the subject has benefited from multi-disciplinary teams being brought together to develop new techniques that are appropriate to marketing. Unfortunately, the structure of many universities still has a tendency to inhibit research between discipline areas that are based in different faculties.

What makes a good marketer?

Finally, what characteristics make for a good marketer? Are good marketers born or bred? To answer this question, it is necessary to have a clear understanding of just what marketing is about. The ability to identify, anticipate, and respond to customer needs puts a lot of onus on skills of observation and analysis. Outdated ideas that marketing is all about selling harder by shouting more loudly were probably never appropriate to even the most aggressive sales personnel, for whom listening to customers' needs has always been crucial to developing a winning sales pitch. The great emphasis on listening skills is one explanation of the growing number of females who have made successful careers in marketing. Numerous studies have found that women have much stronger traits of empathy and listening ability than males.

Of course, marketing as a business function is very broad, and particular branches demand quite specific skills. Within the advertising sector, creativity is essential for successful copywriters, whereas a market analyst would be better equipped with patience and a rigorous methodical approach.

Can marketers be trained? There is a feeling among some employers that a little marketing knowledge by incoming employees may be quite dangerous. This idea holds that it may be better to take on staff who have an ability to think critically, communicate effectively, and show creativity. These abilities may have been developed in non-marketing environments, but the skills are easily transferable. Many engineers and biologists, to name but two science-based disciplines, have gone on to become very successful marketers, because of their ability to approach any new problem with clear, critical thinking combined with creativity.

This book seeks to cut through much of the jargon and mystique that has grown up around marketing and points out that many models are essentially based on straightforward critical analysis. By this argument, segmentation can be seen either as a specialist marketing technique or, more generally, as a logical process of breaking down a large problem (how to serve a market) into a series of smaller problems (how to serve different parts of that market). This book aims to develop a critical awareness of marketing theories and concepts, and to illustrate these with contemporary examples.

🔵 Chapter summary and linkages to other chapters

This chapter has introduced the basic principles of marketing that act as building blocks for more detailed discussion in the following chapters. Having read this chapter, you should be aware of the wide definition of marketing as a philosophy and a set of practices. Although subsequent chapters analyse marketing practices under a number of headings, it should never be forgotten that all elements of the marketing mix should support each other. Customers take a holistic view of a company and its product. Product decisions (Chapter 8), price decisions (Chapter 9), place decisions (Chapter 10), and promotions decisions (Chapter 11) must focus on meeting targeted customer segments (Chapter 6) effectively and efficiently in the face of competitors' products (Chapter 7).

☐ KEY PRINCIPLES OF MARKETING

- Marketing is essentially about organizations meeting customers' needs as a means of achieving the organizations' own objectives.
- Marketing is both a philosophy and a set of techniques. Marketing techniques have less value if an organization has not embraced the philosophy of marketing.
- The principles of marketing are not new, but a continually changing marketing environment demands new ways of applying the basic principles.
- Marketing can be adopted by both profit-seeking and not-for-profit organizations.
- Marketing operates in an environment in which stakeholders have rising expectations for the ethical standards of marketers.

CASE STUDY

The Body Shop—good luck or good marketing?

The Body Shop may have grown rapidly during the 1970s and 1980s, but its founder, the late Dame Anita Roddick publicly dismissed the role of marketing. Roddick ridiculed marketers for putting the interests of shareholders before the needs of society. She had a similarly low opinion of the financial community, which she referred to as 'merchant wankers'. While things were going well, nobody seemed to mind. Maybe Roddick had found a new way of doing business, and if she had the results to prove it, who needed marketers? But how could even such an icon as Anita Roddick manage indefinitely without consulting the fundamental principles of marketing? By embracing ethical issues, was she way ahead of her rivals in understanding the public mood, long before the major retailers piled into Fairtrade and 'green' products? Or did the troubles that the Body Shop suffer in the late 1990s indicate that a company may publicly dismiss the value of marketing while the going is good, but sooner or later it will have to come back to earth with good old-fashioned marketing plans?

Roddick had been the dynamo behind the Body Shop. From her first shop, which opened in Brighton in 1976, she inspired the growth of the chain of familiar green-fronted shops, which in 2006 comprised 2,100 stores in 55 countries around the world. She was the first to introduce socially and environmentally responsible business onto the High Street and was talking about fair trade long before it became a popular corporate buzz-word. Her pioneering products included naturally based skin and hair care preparations, such as Fuzzy Peach Bath and Shower Gel and Brazil Nut Conditioner. Her timing was impeccable, coming just at a time when increasingly afflu-ent consumers were becoming concerned about animal testing and the use of chemicals in cos-metics. She had not gone down the classic marketing route of understanding consumer trends and then developing the appropriate products with the right positioning. She simply had a passion for humanely produced cosmetics and was just lucky with her timing—more consumers were coming round to her view just as she was launching her business. As for planning a promotion campaign, she did not really need to do very much at all. With her boundless energy, outspoken views, and unorthodox dress sense, she was continually being talked about in the media. Her flair for publicity won free editorial space for the Body Shop worth millions of pounds.

Much of the company's success has been tied up with its campaigning approach to the pursuit of social and environmental issues; but while Roddick campaigned for everything from battered wives and Siberian tigers to the poverty-stricken mining communities of southern Appalachia, the company was facing major problems in its key markets. Yet until the late 1990s, she boasted that the Body Shop had never used, or needed, marketing.

By the late 1990s the Body Shop seemed to be running out of steam, with sales plateauing and the company's share price falling—from 370p in 1992 to just 65p in 2003. What was previously unique about the Body Shop was now being copied by others, for example, the Boots company matched one of the Body Shop's earliest claims that it did not test its products on animals. Even the very feel of a Body Shop store—including its decor, staff, and product displays—had been copied by competitors. How could the company stay ahead in terms of maintaining its distinctive positioning? Its causes seemed to become increasingly remote from the real concerns of shoppers. While most UK shoppers may have been swayed by a company's unique claim to protect animals, how many would be moved by its support for Appalachian miners? If there was a Boots or a Superdrug store next door, why should a buyer pay a premium price to buy from the Body Shop? The Body Shop may have pioneered a very clever retailing formula over 20 years earlier, but, just as the product range had been successfully copied by others, other companies had made enor-mous strides in terms of their social and environmental awareness. Part of the problem of the Body Shop was its failure fully to understand the dynamics of its marketplace. Positioning on the basis of good causes may have been enough to launch the company into the public's mind in the 1970s, but how could this position be sustained?

Many commentators blamed the Body Shop's problems on the inability of Roddick to delegate. She is reported to have spent much of her time globe-trotting in support of her good causes, but had a problem in delegating marketing strategy and implementation. Numerous strong managers who had been brought in to try to implement professional management practices apparently gave up in bewilderment at the lack of discretion that they had been given, and then left.

The Body Shop's experience in America had typified Roddick's pioneering style which frequently ignored sound marketing analysis. She sought a new way of doing business in America, but in doing so dismissed the experience of older and more sophisticated retailers—such as Marks & Spencer and the Sock Shop, which came unstuck in what is a very difficult market. The Body Shop decided to enter the US markets not through a safe option such as a joint venture or a franchising agreement, but instead by setting up its own operation from scratch—fine, according to Roddick's principles of changing the rulebook and cutting out the greedy American business community, but dangerously risky. Her store format was based on the British town-centre model, despite the fact that Americans spend most of their money in out-of-town malls. In 1996 the US operations lost £3.4 million.

Roddick's critics claimed that she had a naive view of herself, her company, and business generally. She had consistently argued that profits and principles do not mix, despite the fact that many of her financially successfull competitors have been involved in major social initiatives.

Critics claimed that, had Roddick not dismissed the need for marketing for so long, the Body Shop could have avoided future problems; but by the early 2000s it was paying the price for not having devoted sufficient resources to new product development, to innovation, to refreshing its ranges, and to moving the business forward in a competitive market and fast-changing business environment. It seemed that heroes can change the rulebook when the tide is flowing with them; but adopting the disciplines of marketing allows companies to anticipate and react when the tide begins to turn against them.

The year 2006 turned out to be a turning point for the Body Shop. In that year, the cosmetics giant L'Oréal acquired the company for £652 million. L'Oréal was part-owned by Nestlé, and both companies had suffered long disputes with ethical campaigners. L'Oréal had been the subject of boycotts because of its involvement in animal testing, and Nestlé had been criticized for its treatment of third-world producers. *Ethical Consumer* magazine, which rates companies' ethics on its 'Ethiscore', immediately down-rated the Body Shop from a rating of 11 to 2.5 out of 20, following the takeover by L'Oréal. A contributor to the magazine commented about the Body Shop:

I for one will certainly not be shopping there again and I urge other consumers concerned about ethical issues to follow my example. There are plenty of other higher scoring ethical companies out there.

Not to be outdone, Roddick dismissed claims that she was 'selling out to the devil' by arguing that she would be able to use her influence to change L'Oréal from inside the company. Suppliers who had formerly worked with the Body Shop would in future have contracts with L'Oréal, and through an agreement to work with the company for 25 days a year, Roddick would be able to have an input into its ethical sourcing decisions.

It seemed that the Body Shop was destined to become a safe, predictable company, carrying out marketing in more of the textbook fashion that had allowed its new owners to grow steadily but surely over the years. Maybe the missionary zeal had long ago gone out of the Body Shop, so perhaps having new owners who placed less emphasis on ethics would not be too great a price to pay in return for bringing the huge wealth of marketing experience of L'Oréal to the Body Shop. Part of the marketing experience of L'Oréal led it to treat the Body Shop as an independent brand and to respect its trusted heritage. It was aware that ecological concerns were rapidly rising up mainstream consumers' concerns, and having Roddick on board would not only be good for PR, it could also help change mindsets within L'Oréal more generally.

Roddick died soon after selling out to L'Oréal and her obituaries agreed that she had made a difference to the world. She certainly had put enormous energy into her mission and had been lucky with her timing. However, critics were more divided on whether she was a good marketer for the long haul; after all, it is relatively easy to make money when the tide is going with you and your luck is in, but much more difficult to manage a changing and increasingly saturated marketing environment. Like many entrepreneurs who have been good at creating things, but not so good at maintaining them, was it simply time for Roddick to hand over to classically trained marketers who could rise to this challenge?

Case study review questions

1. Critically assess the extent to which you consider the Body Shop to be a truly marketing-oriented organization throughout its 30+ years' history.

2. To what extent are the pursuits of profit and meeting the needs of wider groups of stakeholders incompatible? What companies, if any, have managed sustainably to reconcile these two aims?

3. What are the basic lessons in marketing that the Body Shop might have taken on board in its early years in order to improve its chances of long-term success?

☐ CHAPTER REVIEW QUESTIONS

1. Discuss how a car-wash business might operate if management embraced a production orientation? A sales orientation? A marketing orientation? A societal marketing orientation?

2. Analyse the nature of the needs which may be satisfied by a household mortgage.

3. What is the difference between selling and marketing?

⬚ ACTIVITIES

1. Go back to the 'Marketing in Action' vignette on page 6 which describes some tell-tale signs about whether a company is truly marketing oriented. Now apply these tests, and any additional tests you can think of, to an organization with which you are familiar. If you are studying at a college or university, how marketing oriented is it?

2. Use the extended '7p' marketing mix to produce a checklist of the headings for a marketing plan for a fashion retailer. Are there any additional headings that you consider would be important to develop a sustainable competitive advantage?

3. Review literature produced by a selection of public or quasi-public sector service providers, such as a doctor's surgery, housing association, or state-owned school. Assess the extent to which the organization balances its statutory duties with a marketing orientation.

⬚ REFERENCES

Borden, N. H. (1965), 'The Concept of the Marketing Mix'. In G. Schwartz (ed.), *Science in Marketing*. New York: John Wiley, pp. 386–97.

Brown, S. (1995), *Postmodern Marketing*. Routledge: London.

Chomka, S. (2002), 'Organic Market Figures Could Help Processors'. *Food Manufacture*, 77(9): 7–9.

Drucker, P. F. (1973), *Management: tasks, responsibilities and practices*. New York: Harper & Row.

Dwyer, F. R., Schurr, P. H., and Oh, S. (1987), 'Developing Buyer and Seller Relationships'. *Journal of Marketing*, 51 (April): 11–27.

Harris, L. C. (2002), 'Developing Market Orientation: an exploration of differences in management approaches'. *Journal of Marketing Management*, 18: 603–32.

Kotler, P., Rackham, N., and Krishnaswamy, S. (2006), 'Ending the war between sales and marketing'. *Harvard Business Review* (July).

Lafferty, B. A. and Hult, G. T. M. (2001), 'A Synthesis of Contemporary Market Orientation Perspectives'. *European Journal of Marketing*, 35: 92–109.

Maslow, A. (1943), 'A Theory of Human Motivation'. *Psychological Review*, 50 (July): 370–96.

Morgan, N. A. (2002), 'Antecedents and Consequences of Market Orientation in Chartered Surveying Firms'. *Construction Management & Economics*, 20: 331–41.

Narver, J. C. and Slater, S. F. (1990), 'The Effect of a Market Orientation on Business Profitability'. *Journal of Marketing*, (October): 20–35.

Sargeant, A. (2004), *Marketing Management for Not-for-profit Organisations*. Oxford: Oxford University Press.

⬚ SUGGESTED FURTHER READING

This chapter has taken a very broad overview of marketing and sets the scene for the subsequent chapters. Further reading that relates to issues raised in this introductory chapter will be listed in chapters where introductory topics are returned to for a fuller discussion.

To review the debate about the nature of marketing, the following are significant contributors to the debate:

Silk, A. J. (2007), What is Marketing?. Harvard Business School Press.

Lafferty, B. A. and Hult, G. T. M. (2001), 'A Synthesis of Contemporary Market Orientation Perspectives'. *European Journal of Marketing*, 35: 92–109.

Vargo, S. L. and Lusch, R. F. (2004), 'Evolving to a New Dominant Logic for Marketing'. *Journal of Marketing*, 68(1): 1–17.

Gronroos, C. (1989), 'Defining Marketing: a market-oriented approach'. *European Journal of Marketing*, 23(1): 52–60.

Gummesson, E. (2008), *Total Relationship Marketing: Marketing Management, Relationship Strategy and CRM Approaches for the Network Economy*. London: Butterworth-Heinemann.

Schultz, D. and Dev, C. (2005), 'In the Mix: A customer-focused approach can bring the current marketing mix into the 21st century'. *Marketing Management*, 14 (1).

Sargeant, A. (2004), *Marketing Management for Not-for-Profit Organisations*. Oxford: Oxford University Press.

⬜ USEFUL WEB LINKS

Visit the Online Resource Centre for resources that are relevant to this chapter, including web links, multiple choice questions, and additional case studies:
   www.oxfordtextbooks.co.uk/orc/palmer2e/

⬜ KEY TERMS

- **Competitor orientation**
- **Customer orientation**
- **Customers**
- **Demand**
- **Exchange**
- **Inter-functional coordination**
- **Marketing management**
- **Marketing mix**
- **Marketing orientation**
- **Markets**
- **Needs**
- **Not-for-profit organization**
- **Place**
- **Positivism**
- **Pricing**
- **Production orientation**
- **Products**

- Promotion
- Scientific method
- Selling orientation
- Social responsibility
- Value
- Wants

The marketing environment

CHAPTER OBJECTIVES

In the previous chapter we established that marketing is essentially about firms identifying customers' needs and responding to those changing needs with appropriate product offers. In this chapter we will explore how customers' needs are derived from the nature of an organization's marketing environment. The marketing environment can be defined as everything that surrounds an organization's marketing function and can impinge on it. Macro-environmental factors, such as a change in the birth rate, may seem inconsequential now, but could quickly have a direct effect on a firm's micro-environment, expressed through demand for its products. This chapter explores the relationships between the different elements of a firm's environment and how the firm can respond effectively to environmental change.

Introduction

In the previous chapter, marketing orientation was defined in terms of a firm's need to begin its business planning by looking outwardly at what its customers require, rather than inwardly at what it would prefer to produce. The firm must be aware of what is going on in its broader marketing environment and appreciate how change in this environment can lead to changing patterns of demand for its products.

An environment can be defined as everything that surrounds and impinges on a **system**. Systems of many kinds have environments with which they interact. A central heating system operates in an environment where a key environmental factor will be the outside temperature. A good system will react to environmental change, for example, by using a thermostat to increase the output of the system in response to a fall in the temperature of the external environment. The human body comprises numerous systems which constantly react to changes in the body's environment; for example, the body perspires in response to an increase in external temperature.

Marketing can be seen as a system that must respond to environmental change. Just as the human body may die if it fails to adjust to environmental change (for example, by not compensating for very low temperatures), businesses may fail if they do not adapt to external changes such as new sources of competition or changes in **stakeholders'** expectations of companies.

An organization's marketing environment is defined here as

the individuals, organizations, and forces external to the marketing management function of an organization that impinge on the marketing management's ability to develop and maintain successful exchanges with its customers.

Naturally, some elements in a firm's marketing environment are more direct and immediate in their effects than others. Sometimes parts of the marketing environment may seem quite nebulous and difficult to assess in terms of their likely impact on a company. It is therefore usual to talk about a number of different levels of the marketing environment.

- The **micro-environment** describes those elements that impinge directly on a company. The micro-environment of an organization includes customers, suppliers, and distributors. The company may deal directly with some of these, such as current customers. However, the micro-environment also includes companies and individuals with whom there is currently no direct contact, but their existence could nevertheless influence its policies (e.g. product policy could be affected by the changing attitudes of individuals whom a company may target in the future). Similarly, an organization's **competitors** could have a direct effect on its market position and form part of its micro-environment.

- The **macro-environment** describes things that are beyond the immediate environment but can nevertheless affect an organization. A business may have no direct relationships with legislators as it does with suppliers, yet legislators' actions in passing new laws may have profound effects on the markets it seeks to serve, as well as affecting its production costs. The macro-environmental factors cover a wide range of nebulous phenomena—they represent general forces and pressures rather than institutions, to which the organization relates directly.

- As well as looking to the outside world, marketing managers must also take account of factors within other functions of their own firm. This is often referred to as an organization's **internal environment**.

The elements within each of these parts of an organization's environment are described in more detail below and illustrated schematically in Figure 2.1.

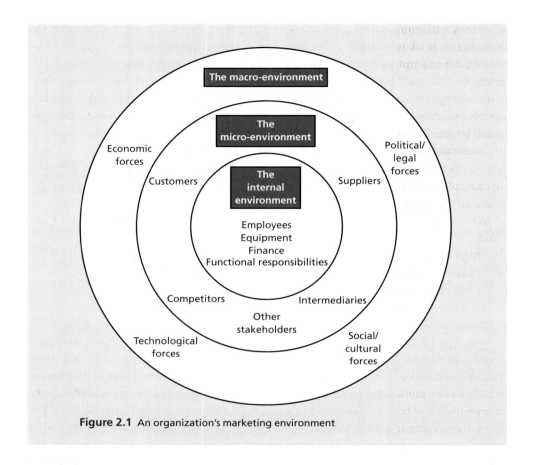

Figure 2.1 An organization's marketing environment

The micro-environment

The micro-environment comprises all those other organizations and individuals that, directly or indirectly, affect the activities of the organization. The following key groups can be identified.

Customers

These are a crucial part of an organization's micro-environment. For a commercial organization, no customers means no business. An organization should be concerned about the changing requirements of its customers and should keep in touch with these changing needs by using an appropriate information gathering system. Chapter 5 will return to the subject of collecting, analysing, and disseminating information. In an ideal world, an organization should know its customers so well that it is able to predict what they will require next, rather than wait until it is possibly too late and then follow. Most of this book is devoted to studying the interface between a company and its customers, for example, in terms of customers' responses to promotional messages and prices.

Increasingly, companies are being expected to take into account not just what a customer says they want, but also what is good for them—the two may be quite different, as can be seen in the case of 'junk food' companies who may promote good-tasting, but high-fat food to people to whom it is harmful to their health. Sometimes, firms' marketing efforts may wrongly suggest that their product would satisfy a customer's needs. As an example, in 2007 the website MoneySavingExpert.com launched a campaign against financial services companies which had sold payment protection insurance policies to individuals who could not possibly benefit from the insurance, because of terms and conditions that were not fully explained to them. Salespeople may have been tempted by a high level of commission to sell a policy that the customer did not understand and was clearly not in their best interest (*Financial Times*, 2008).

We will return to the issue of companies' broader responsibilities towards customers in the following chapter.

Competitors

You will recall from Chapter 1 that a competitor orientation is one of the defining characteristics of a marketing orientation. In highly competitive markets, keeping an eye on competitors and trying to understand their likely next moves can be crucial. Think of the manoeuvring and out-manoeuvring that appears to take place between competitors in such highly competitive sectors as soft drinks, budget airlines, and mobile phones. But who are a company's competitors? *Direct* competitors are generally similar in form and satisfy customers' needs in a similar way. *Indirect* competitors may appear different in form, but satisfy a fundamentally similar need. It is the indirect competitors that are most difficult to identify and to understand. What is a competitor for a cinema? Is it another cinema? A home rental movie? Or some completely different form of leisure activity which satisfies a similar underlying need for entertainment?

Because of the importance of competitors to a firm's marketing environment, in Chapter 7 we will have a more detailed analysis of competitors and how a company can position itself against these in order to gain a sustainable competitive advantage.

Intermediaries

Companies must not ignore the wholesalers, retailers, and agents who may be crucial interfaces between themselves and their final consumers. Large-scale manufacturing firms usually find it difficult to deal with each one of their final consumers individually, so they choose instead to sell their products through **intermediaries**. In some business sectors, access to effective intermediaries can be crucial for marketing success. For example, food manufacturers who do not get shelf space in the major supermarkets may find it difficult to achieve large-volume sales.

Channels of distribution comprise all those people and organizations involved in the process of transferring title to a product from the producer to the consumer. Sometimes products will be transferred directly from producer to final consumer—a factory selling specialized kitchen units directly to the public would fit into this category. Alternatively, the producer may sell its output through retailers; or, if these are considered too numerous for the manufacturer to handle, it could deal with a wholesaler who in turn would sell to the retailer. More than one wholesaler could be involved in the process.

Because of the importance of intermediaries in making a firm's goods and services accessible to its buyers, Chapter 10 is devoted to understanding how they are selected, motivated, rewarded, and controlled. In addition, the chapter reviews physical distribution management and the decisions that firms make in physically moving goods from where they are produced to where customers wish to buy them.

Intermediaries may need reassurance about the company's capabilities as a supplier that is capable of working with them to supply goods and services in a reliable and ethical manner. Many companies have suffered because they have failed to take adequate account of the needs of their intermediaries. (For example, Body Shop and McDonald's have faced protests from their franchisees, which felt threatened by a marketing strategy that was perceived as being against their own interests.)

Suppliers

These provide an organization with goods and services that are transformed by the organization into value-added products for customers. For companies operating in highly competitive markets where differentiation between products is minimal, obtaining supplies at the best possible price may be vital in order to be able to pass on cost savings in the form of lower prices charged to customers. Where reliability of delivery to customers is crucial, unreliable suppliers may thwart a manufacturer's marketing efforts.

In business-to-business marketing, it is important to understand how suppliers, manufacturers, and intermediaries work together to create value. The idea of a value chain is introduced later in this chapter. Buyers and sellers are increasingly cooperating in their dealings with each other, rather than bargaining each transaction in a confrontational manner. (Buyer–seller relationships are discussed further in Chapter 4.)

There is an argument that companies should behave in a socially responsible way to their suppliers. Does a company favour local companies rather than possibly lower priced overseas producers? For example, many supermarkets proudly promote locally produced ranges of food. Does it divide its orders between a large number of small suppliers, or place the bulk of its custom with a small handful of preferred suppliers? Does it favour new businesses, or businesses representing minority interests, when it places its orders? We will return to the subject of responsible marketing in the next chapter.

Government

The demands of government agencies often take precedence over the needs of a company's customers. Government has a number of roles to play in a commercial organization's marketing environment:

- Government agencies, such as the Health and Safety Executive, regulate many activities that have a direct or indirect impact on what products a company can offer to its customers, for example, UK legislation requiring employers to pay a minimum wage has added to the costs of companies, leading to price rises for many labour-intensive service industries such as restaurants, and movement of capacity to low-wage countries for many manufacturing companies.

- Governments—national, regional, and local—levy taxes that will most probably be incorporated into a firm's selling prices, thereby affecting the size of demand for its products. Some retailers in central London reported a fall in their number of customers, following the imposition of a congestion charge on motorists.

- Government is increasingly expecting business organizations to take over many responsibilities from the public sector, for example with regard to the payment of sickness and maternity benefits to employees.

- It is through business organizations that governments achieve many of their economic and social objectives, for example with respect to regional economic development and skills training.

As a regulator that impacts on many aspects of business activity, companies often go to great lengths in seeking favourable responses from such agencies. In the case of many private-sector utility providers, promotional effort is often aimed more at regulatory bodies than at final consumers. For UK water suppliers, promoting greater use of water to final consumers is unlikely to have a significant impact on a water utility company, but influencing the disposition of the Office of Water Regulation, which sets price limits and service standards, can have a major impact.

The financial community

This includes financial institutions that have supported, are currently supporting, or may support the organization in the future. **Shareholders**, both private and institutional, form an important element of this community and must be reassured that the organization is going to achieve its stated objectives. Many market expansion plans have failed because the company did not adequately consider the needs and expectations of potential investors.

Local communities

Market-led companies often try to be seen as a 'good neighbours' in their local communities. Such companies can enhance their image through charitable contributions, sponsorship of local events, and support of the local environment. This may be interpreted either as part of a firm's genuine concern for its local community, or as a more cynical and pragmatic attempt to buy favour where its own interests are at stake. If a fast-food restaurant installs improved filters on its extractor fans, is it doing this genuinely to improve the lives of local residents, or merely to forestall prohibitive action taken by the local authority? We will return to these issues in the following chapter.

Pressure groups

Members of **pressure groups** may have never been customers of a certain company and may never likely be. Yet a pressure group can detract seriously from the image of a company that its marketing department has worked hard to develop.

Pressure groups can be divided into those that are permanently fighting for a general cause, and those that are set up to achieve a specific objective and are dissolved when this objective is met. Pressure groups can also be classified according to their functions; for example, sectional groups exist to promote the common interests of their members over a wide range of issues (e.g. trades unions and employers associations), while promotional groups fight for specific causes (e.g. the Countryside Alliance campaigns for a range of countryside issues).

Pressure groups can influence the activities of businesses in a number of ways:

- Propaganda is used to create awareness of the group and its cause (e.g. through press releases to the media). Many pressure groups have effectively used social networking websites rapidly to mobilize opposition to companies that they see as operating in an anti-social way.

- The pressure group can seek to represent the views of the group directly to businesses on a one-to-one basis. (Many environmental pressure groups seek to advance their cause by 'educating' companies that may be ignorant of the pressure group's concerns.)

- Increasingly, pressure groups have resorted to direct action against companies, which can range from boycotts to physical attacks on a company's property. Organizations targeted in this way may initially put on a brave face when confronted with such activities by dismissing them as inconsequential, but often the result is to change the organization's behaviour, especially where the prospect of large profits is uncertain. Action by animal rights protestors contributed to the near collapse of Huntingdon Life Sciences (an animal-testing laboratory), and many farmers have been discouraged from taking part in GM crops trials by the prospects of direct action against their farms.

It should not be forgotten that businesses themselves are often active members of pressure groups, which they may join as a means of influencing government legislation that will affect their industry sector. The British Road Federation and the Tobacco Advisory Council are two examples of high-profile industry-led pressure groups.

Pressure groups themselves are increasingly crossing national boundaries to reflect the influence of international governmental institutions such as the EU and the increasing influence of multinational business organizations. Friends of the Earth and Greenpeace are examples of multinational pressure groups.

Value chains

The concept of a **value chain** will be explored more fully in Chapter 10 in the context of channels of distribution. Here it is introduced to help understand the complex marketing relationships that can exist between a company and its customers, suppliers, and intermediaries.

Most products bought by private consumers represent the culmination of a long process of value creation. The company selling the finished product probably bought many of its components from an outside supplier, which in turn bought raw materials from another outside supplier. This is the basis of a value chain in which basic raw materials

Value chain member	Functions performed
Grower	produces a basic commodity product—coffee beans
Merchant	adds value to the coffee beans by checking, grading, and making beans available to coffee manufacturers
Coffee manufacturer	by processing the coffee beans, adding other ingredients and packaging, turns beans into jars of instant coffee; through promotion, creates a brand image
Wholesaler	buys bulk stocks of jars of coffee and stores in warehouses close to customers
Retailer	provides a facility for customers to buy coffee at a place and a time that is convenient to them, rather than from the manufacturer
Coffee shop	adds further value by providing a ready-made cup of coffee in pleasant surroundings

Figure 2.2 A value chain for coffee

progressively have value added to them by members of the value chain. Value adding can come in the form of adding further components, changing the form of a product, or adding ancillary services to the product offer.

Consider the example shown in Figure 2.2 of a value chain for instant coffee. The value of the raw beans contained in a jar of instant coffee may be no more than a few pence, but the final product may be sold for over £2. Customers are happy to pay this amount because a basic product that they place little value on has been transformed into something that they perceive as highly valuable. Some consumers would be happy to pay an even higher price to buy their coffee ready prepared for consumption in a coffee shop rather than make it themselves at home. In the case of some trendy coffee shops such as Starbucks, customers may be prepared to pay quite a hefty premium for the at-mosphere in which the coffee is served—over £4 for a smartly presented cappuccino or a 'skinny latte' is not uncommon, even though the cost of the beans used in the coffee may be no more than a few pence. Value can be defined only in terms of customers' perceptions, so much of the transformation process described above may be considered by some people to have no value. Some coffee drinkers may consider that processing the coffee to make it into instant granules destroys value by spoiling the full taste that can be obtained from raw beans. For such people, the most important point in the value-creating process probably derives from the growing and selection of the coffee beans. For others, paying £4 for a skinny latte in Starbucks may be considered good value, because they particularly like the atmosphere in which the coffee is served.

Who should be in the value chain? The coffee manufacturer might decide that it can add value at the preceding and subsequent stages better than other people are capable of doing. It may, for example, decide to operate its own farms to produce beans under its own control, or sell its coffee direct to customers. The crucial question to be asked is whether the company can add value better than other suppliers and intermediaries could. In a value chain, it is only value in the eyes of customers that matters. If high value is attached to having coffee easily available, then distributing it through a limited number of company-owned shops would not add much value to the product.

The **Internet** has led to the development of a modified form of 'virtual value chain' to try and explain how information-based industries operate a value chain that is distinct from traditional models based on raw materials, production, and distribution (Rayport and Sviokla, 1995). Intermediaries such as Expedia.com (travel) and confused.com (insurance) create value by making available to consumers in one website a range of travel and insur-ance products, saving the effort of buyers in having to shop around. These intermediaries are also likely to add value by providing after-sales service.

Relationships between members of an organization's micro-environment

The discussion of value chains emphasizes the point that marketing effectiveness for a firm can be highly dependent upon its relationships with other members of its micro-environment. Very few organizations are able to produce and distribute every-thing they sell to customers entirely within their own resources. Instead, they will most probably outsource production, or use intermediaries to sell its products, for example. It follows that relationships between a company and these external organizations can be critical for delivering value to customers. The individuals and organizations that make up a firm's micro-environment are often described as its *environmental set*. An ex-ample of an environmental set for a computer manufacturer is shown in Figure 2.3.

An organization needs to be constantly alert to changes in the relationships between members of its environmental set. Consider the following recent changes in firms' environmental sets:

- There have been changes in the balance of power between set members (for exam-ple, between retailers, wholesalers, and manufacturers).

- New groups of potential customers may emerge (for example, elderly people have emerged as new groups of customers for fast-food restaurants), while other groups decline.

- New pressure groups are formed in response to emerging issues of widespread social concern.

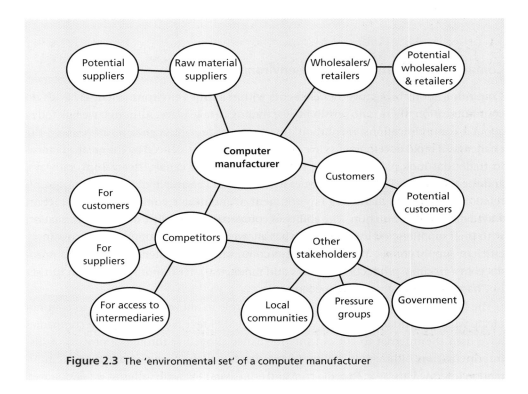

Figure 2.3 The 'environmental set' of a computer manufacturer

• The role of government in many sectors has increased with the introduction of new health and safety legislation (although in other sectors, deregulation and privatization have diminished the role of government).

In the UK in recent years there has been some significant redistribution in the power of manufacturers relative to retailers. The growing strength of retailers in many sectors has given them significantly increased bargaining power in their dealings with manufacturers whose goods they sell. By building up their own strong brands, large retailers are increasingly able to exert pressure on manufacturers in terms of product specification, price, and the level of promotional support to be given to the retailer. According to market research group TNS Worldpanel, the UK's big four grocery retailers—Tesco, Asda, Sainsbury's, and Morrisons—now account for more than three-quarters (76.2%) of the grocery market. However, while many manufacturers' may be dependent on the big four for further sales, this dependency is not reciprocated, with very few retailers relying on one single supplier for more than 1% of their supplies.

Increasingly, firms are changing the way they do business, away from one-off transactions that are individually negotiated, towards ongoing cooperative relationships. The process of turning casual, one-off transactions between buyers and sellers has often been described as **relationship marketing**. Chapter 4 provides further discussion of reasons for firms to seek closer relationships with their customers, and the methods adopted to achieve this.

Communication within the micro-environment

Communications bring together elements within a firm's environmental set. With no communication, there is no possibility for trading to take place. Although we talk today about a communications 'revolution', marketers of previous centuries have faced the challenge of rapid developments in communication, as evidenced by the great advances in trade that took place following the developments of canals, steamships, railways, and the telephone. Today, the Internet has become a versatile tool in an organization's relationship with its marketing environment, combining a communication function with a distribution function. The ability of companies to rapidly exchange information with their suppliers and intermediaries has allowed for the development of increasingly efficient supply chains. Without efficient communication systems, attempts to introduce 'just-in-time' production systems and rapid customer response (discussed further in Chapter 9) are likely to be impeded.

The Internet plays an increasingly significant role in allowing companies to communicate with their final consumers via e-mail and SMS text messaging. Some companies have used the Internet to cut out intermediaries altogether through a process of **disintermediation**, although in reality the Internet has allowed a new generation of 'information intermediary' (e.g. Expedia.com and esure.com) to create value, as we saw above.

The macro-environment

While the micro-environment comprises identifiable individuals and organizations with whom a company interacts (directly and indirectly), the macro-environment is more nebulous. It comprises general trends and forces which may not immediately affect the relationships that a company has with its customers, suppliers, and intermediaries, but sooner or later, as this environment changes, these trends and forces will alter the nature of such micro-level relationships. As an example, change in the population structure of a country does not immediately affect the way in which a company does business with its customers, but over time it may affect the numbers of young or elderly people with whom it is possible to do business.

Most analyses of the macro-environment divide the environment into a number of subject areas. The subject headings that are most commonly used are described below. It must, however, be remembered that the division of the macro-environment into subject areas does not result in watertight compartments. The macro-environment is complex and interdependent.

The macro-economic environment

An analysis of many companies' financial results will often indicate that business people attribute their current financial success or failure to the state of the economy. For example, in early 2008, the retailer Debenhams reported falling sales and profits as consumers cut their discretionary expenditure following sharp increases in food, fuel, and housing costs. Ten years earlier, a strong economy and rising house prices had led to a high level of consumer confidence, and booming sales for department stores such as Debenhams. But what do we mean by the macro-economic environment? The following headings are useful analytic headings.

Economic growth and the distribution of income

Few business people can afford to ignore the state of the economy, because it affects the willingness and ability of customers to buy their products. Marketers therefore keep their eyes on numerous aggregate indicators of the economy, such as **Gross Domestic Product (GDP)**, inflation rates, and savings ratios. However, while aggregate changes in spending power may indicate a likely increase for goods and services in general, the actual distribution of spending power among the population will influence the pattern of demand for specific products. In addition to measurable economic prosperity, the level of perceived wealth and confidence in the future can be an important determinant of demand for some high-value services. If consumers' confidence is low, a high proportion of income tends to be saved. If confidence is high, consumers are more likely to borrow, so that their expenditure is greater than their income (Figure 2.4).

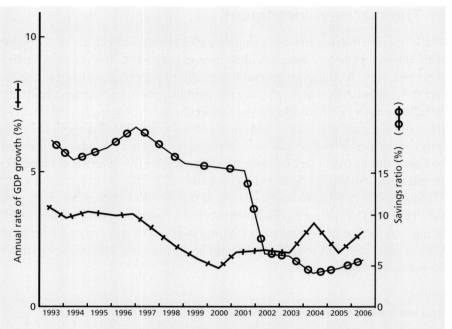

Figure 2.4 Two key macro-economic indicators that marketers pay attention to are the annual rate of growth in GDP and the savings ratio. The first shows how rapidly the national economy is expanding, and therefore the capacity of the economy to purchase more products. However, what is just as important to marketers is whether this economic wealth is saved or spent. If consumers' confidence is low, a high proportion of income tends to be saved. If confidence is high, consumers are more likely to borrow, so that their expenditure is greater than their income. The high levels of consumer confidence in the UK during 2002 saw record levels of mortgage borrowing, resulting in a house price boom and strong demand for many house-related items such as conservatories and furnishings. By 2008, GDP was falling while the savings ratios rose, as consumers became more cautious in their spending, and banks became more cautious in their lending.

Source: based on Annual Abstract of Statistics

The effects of government policy objectives on the distribution of income can have profound implications for marketers. During most of the post-war years, the tendency has been for income to be redistributed from richer to less well-off groups. In the UK, higher-rate taxation and the payment of welfare benefits have been instrumental in achieving this. During the late 1980s, this trend was reversed by a number of measures introduced by the Conservative government. Even under the subsequent Labour government, there is some evidence that the richest groups in the UK have grown richer, while the poor have grown poorer (*Financial Times*, 2007a).

Multiplier and accelerator effects

Through models of national economies, firms try to understand how increases in expenditure (whether by government, households, or firms) will affect their specific sector. The **multiplier effect** of increases in government spending (or cuts in taxation) can be compared to the effects of throwing a stone into a pond of water. The initial spending boost will have an initial impact on households and businesses directly affected by the additional spending, but through a ripple effect will also be indirectly felt by households and firms throughout the economy.

A small increase in consumer demand can lead, through an **accelerator effect**, to a sudden large increase in demand for plant and machinery as manufacturers seek to increase their capacity with which to meet this demand. Demand for industrial capital goods therefore tends to be more cyclical than for consumer goods, so when consumer demand falls by a small amount, demand for plant and machinery falls by a correspondingly larger amount, and vice versa.

Business cycles

Companies are particularly interested in understanding **business cycles** and in predicting the cycle as it affects their sector. If the economy is at the bottom of an economic recession, this may be the ideal time for firms to begin investing in new production capacity, ahead of the eventual upturn in demand. Adding new production capacity during a period of recession is also likely to be much cheaper than waiting until an upturn in the economy puts upward pressure on its input prices. During periods of economic boom, firms should look ahead to the inevitable downturn that follows. A problem of excess capacity and stocks can result when a firm fails to spot the downturn at the top of the business cycle. Analysing turning points in the business cycle has therefore become crucial to marketers. To miss an upturn at the bottom of the recession can lead to missed opportunities when the recovery comes to fruition. On the other hand, reacting to a false signal can leave a firm with expensive excess stocks and capacity on its hands.

It is extremely difficult to identify a turning point at the time when it is happening. In early 2006, the UK economy appeared to be going into recession, and many companies scaled back their investment in stocks and capacity. However, the economy soon bounced back after just a short blip, and the predicted recession did not set in until 2008.

Marketers try to react to turning points as closely as possible. Many subscribe to the services of firms that use complex models of the economy to make predictions about the future performance of their sector. Companies can be guided by key lead indicators which have historically been a precursor of change in activity levels for their business sector. For a company manufacturing process-plant equipment, the level of attendance at major trade exhibitions could indicate the number of buyers that are at the initial stages in the

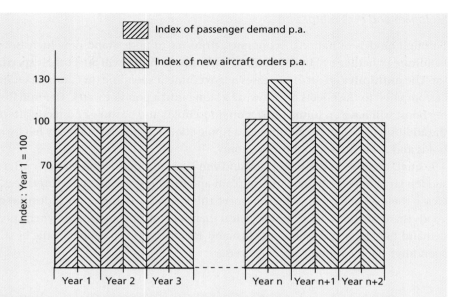

Figure 2.5 The accelerator effect can lead to volatility in demand for companies supplying capital equipment, as customers will rapidly change their orders for equipment in response to just a small change in final consumer demand. This can be illustrated by reference to the demand for new aircraft following a change in demand from passengers. In this simplified example, an airline operates a fleet of 100 aircraft and during periods of stable passenger demand buys ten new aircraft each year and retires ten older aircraft, retaining a stable fleet size of 100 aircraft. Then, some extraneous factor (e.g. a decline in the world economy) may cause the airline's passenger demand to fall by 3% per year. The airline responds to this by reducing its capacity by 3% to 97 aircraft (assuming that it can reschedule its aircraft so that it is able to accommodate all of its remaining passengers). The easiest way to achieve this is by reducing its annual order for aircraft from ten to seven. If it continued to retire its ten oldest aircraft, this would have the effect of reducing its fleet size to 97, in line with the new level of customer demand. What is of importance here is that, while consumer demand has gone down by just 3%, the demand facing the aircraft manufacturer has gone down by 30% (from ten aircraft a year to seven). If passenger demand settles down at its new level, the airline will have no need to cut its fleet any further, so will revert to buying ten new aircraft a year and selling ten old ones. If passenger demand picks up once more, the airline may seek to increase its capacity by ordering not ten aircraft but, say, 13.

buying process for new equipment. An alternative to trying to predict the economic performance of their sector a long way ahead is to manage operations so that a firm can respond almost immediately to changes in its macro-economic environment. The use of short-term contracts of employment and outsourcing of component manufacture can help a company to downsize rapidly at minimum cost when it enters a recession, and to expand production when a recovery occurs. This approach is particularly important when an organization needs to respond to an unforeseen shock to the macro-economic environment, as occurred following the terrorist attacks of 11 September 2001.

Market competitiveness

An analysis of the macro-economic environment will also indicate the current and expected future level of competitor activity. An oversupply of products in a market sector (whether actual or predicted) results in a downward pressure on prices and profitability. Markets are dynamic, and what may appear an attractive market today may soon deteriorate as the market matures. Market dynamics are discussed further in Chapter 7.

The political environment

The political environment in its broadest sense comprises governments, politicians, and the pressure groups that bring pressure to bear on politicians and government. The political environment can be one of the less predictable elements in an organization's marketing environment. Marketers need to monitor the changing political environment because political change can profoundly affect a firm's marketing. Consider the following effects of change in the political environment on marketing.

- While the countries of western Europe are generally politically stable, the instability of many governments in less developed countries has led a number of companies to question the wisdom of marketing in those countries.

- In countries with well-developed political systems, firms should understand the consequences for their business of a change in government. For example, how would a manufacturer of luxury cars react if a left-wing socialist government, pledged to impose higher taxes on expensive cars, was elected to replace a more right-wing government? Firms should not just wait for the election results, but should try and predict the likely results.

- Governments are responsible for protecting the public interest at large, imposing further constraints on the activities of firms (for example, controls on pollution, which may make a manufacturing firm uncompetitive in international markets on account of its increased costs).

- The macro-economic environment is very much influenced by the actions of politicians. Government is responsible for formulating policies that can influence the rate of growth in the economy and hence the total amount of spending power. It is also a political decision as to how this spending power should be distributed between different groups of consumers and between the public and private sectors.

- Government policies can influence the dominant social and cultural values of a country, although there can be argument about which is the cause and which is the effect. (For example, did the UK government's drive for economic expansion and individual responsibility during the late 1980s change public attitudes away from good citizenship and towards those of 'greed is good'?)

- Increasingly, the political environment affecting marketers includes supranational organizations, which can directly or indirectly affect companies. These include trading blocs (e.g. the EU, ASEAN, and NAFTA) and the influence of worldwide intergovernmental organizations whose members seek to implement agreed policy (e.g. the World Trade Organization).

The social and cultural environment

It is crucial for marketers to appreciate fully the cultural values of a society, especially where an organization is seeking to do business in a country that is quite different to its own. Attitudes to specific products change through time and at any one time can differ between groups in society.

Even in home markets, business organizations should understand the processes of gradual cultural change and be prepared to satisfy the changing needs of consumers. Consider the following examples of contemporary cultural change in western Europe and the possible responses of marketers.

- Leisure is becoming a bigger part of many people's lives, and marketers have responded with a wide range of leisure-related goods and services.

MARKETING in ACTION

EU legislators influence the UK, so UK marketers must try and influence the EU

The EU is playing an increasingly important role in firms' marketing environments. Protests at new legislation which would previously have been aimed at national legislators now often need to be aimed at the EU, because national legislators are simply implementing EU directives. The role of the EU in marketers' political environments was demonstrated when two EU directives came into force in 2005, placing all herbal medicines and vitamin and mineral supplements on the same regulatory basis as medicines. More than 300 widely used 'natural remedies' were banned altogether, and the cost of licensing each product—estimated at up to £2,000 per product—would be beyond the means of many of the small producers who dominated the market for natural remedies. The big pharmaceutical companies had been lobbying the EU to effect such a change, citing 'adverse reactions' from many herbal remedies and vitamin supplements such as vitamin B6. Of course, they knew that driving thousands of small herbal producers out of business would draw customers to the pharmaceutical companies' mass-produced products. The natural remedies producers were much more fragmented than the large pharmaceutical companies and were slow to get their lobbying together. In 2002, the sector presented to the UK government a petition protesting about the proposed changes. It contained over one million signatures, including those of Sir Paul McCartney and Sir Elton John, but it was too late, because the directives had already been passed by the EU and hence there was little discretion left for the UK government. The lobbyists of the pharmaceutical industry seemed to have outsmarted the lobbyists of the natural remedies firms and understood where and when to apply pressure.

- Many western European countries are becoming ethnically and culturally much more diverse. In the UK, the large number of Polish people who entered the country from 2004 has led to the development of many retail and financial services aimed specifically at this group (*Financial Times*, 2007b).

Figure 2.6 Busy lifestyles have opened new opportunities for marketers. The increasing number of money-rich, time-poor households has been targeted by suppliers of services ranging from home shopping to domestic cleaning personal coaching. Busy lifestyles have contributed to an increase in the number of parents seeking kindergartens for their young children. A desire for mothers to return to their career as soon as possible after the birth of their child and a decline in the geographically close extended family have led to an increase in private childcare services. (Reproduced with permission of Bushbabies Kindergarten)

- The role of women in society is changing as men and women increasingly share expectations in terms of employment and household responsibilities. According to the Office for National Statistics, women in 2006 represented 53% of graduates in the UK and 45% of the workforce (compared with 37% in 1971). Furthermore, a report by the Future Foundation predicted that women would be the major bread-winners in a quarter of families by 2030 (Doughty, 2007). Examples of business responses include variants of cars designed to appeal to career women and ready-prepared meals which save time for busy working women who need to juggle work, family, and social roles.

- Greater life expectancy is leading to an ageing of the population and a shift to an increasingly 'elderly' culture. This is reflected in product design which is increasingly emphasizing durability rather than fashionability.

- The growing concern, among many groups in society, with the **ecological environment** is reflected in a variety of 'green' consumer products.

Some indication of the minutiae of changing lifestyles and their implications for marketing was revealed in a report, *Complicated Lives II: The Price of Complexity* (The Future Foundation, 2002), commissioned by Abbey National from the Future Foundation. The report brought together quantitative and qualitative research with extensive analysis of a range of trends affecting families and their finances. The findings show that, between 1961 and 2001,

- the average time women spent in a week doing cleaning and laundry fell from 12 hours and 40 minutes to 6 hours and 18 minutes;

- the average time that parents spent helping their children with homework had increased from 1 minute a day to 15 minutes a day;

- time spent caring for children increased from 30 minutes a day to 75 minutes a day;

- the average amount of time spent entertaining went up from 25 minutes to 55 minutes;

- time spent cooking has decreased for women, down from more than 1 hour and 40 minutes to just over an hour (73 minutes) per day. At the same time, men marginally increased their time in the kitchen, from 26 to 27 minutes per day.

There has been much discussion recently about the concept of **cultural convergence**, referring to an apparent decline in differences between cultures. It has been argued that basic human needs are universal in nature and, in principle, capable of satisfaction with universally similar solutions. Many companies have sought to develop one core product for a global market, and there is some evidence of firms achieving this (for example, Coca Cola, McDonald's). The desire of a subculture in one country to imitate the values of those in another culture has also contributed to cultural convergence.

Critics of the trend towards cultural convergence point to a growing need for cultural identity which has been expressed, for example, in the rejection by some Muslim fundamentalist groups of the values of western society. This poses new challenges for western companies that seek overseas expansion. How can Coca Cola be sure that its brand name and product offer will be the object of aspiration for the dominant groups in a country, rather than a hated symbol of an alien system of capitalism?

The demographic environment

Demography is the study of populations in terms of their size and characteristics. Among the topics of interest to demographers are the age structure of a country, the geographic distribution of its population, the balance between males and females, and the likely future size of the population and its characteristics. Changes in the size and age structure of the population are critical to many firms' marketing. Although the total population of most western countries is stable, their composition is changing. Most countries are experiencing an increase in the proportion of elderly people, and companies who have monitored this trend have responded with the development of residential homes, cruise holidays, and financial portfolio management services aimed at meeting this group's needs. At the other end of the age spectrum, the **birth rate** of most countries is cyclical, resulting in a cyclical pattern of demand for age-related products such as baby products, fashion clothing, and family cars (Figure 2.7).

Consider the following changes in the structure of the UK population and their effects on marketers.

1. There has been a trend for women to have fewer children. (The average number of children for each woman born in 1930 was 2.35, it was 2.2 for those born in 1945 and it is projected to be 1.74 for those born in 1970.) There has also been a tendency for women to have children later in life. (The mean age at which women in the UK have their first birth has increased from 25.2 years in 1986 to 27.4 in 2006 (Office for National Statistics, 2008b).)

   In addition, there has been an increase in the number of women having no children. (According to the Office for National Statistics, this has risen from 10% of women born in 1950 to a projected 20% of women born in the early 1960s.) Fewer children has resulted in parents spending more per child (more designer clothes for children rather than budget clothes) and has allowed women to stay at work longer (increasing household incomes and encouraging the purchase of labour-saving products).

2. Alongside a declining number of children has been a decline in the average household size (from an average of 3.1 people in 1961 to 2.4 in 2007). There has been a particular fall in the number of large households with six or more people (down from 6% of all households in 1971 to 2% in 2007) and a significant increase in the number of one-person households (up from 18% to 29% over the same period) (Office for National Statistics, 2008a). According to Euromonitor, only 32.7% of all

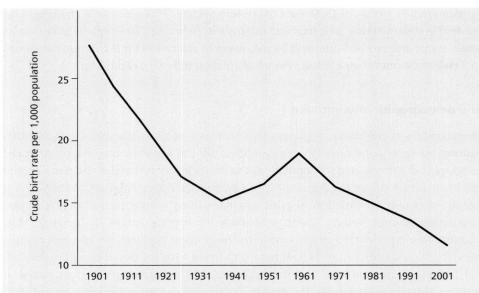

Figure 2.7 The UK birth rate fluctuated greatly during the past century. As one 'baby boom' generation grew up, they had children who contributed to a further baby boom. This figure shows how the number of births per 1,000 has fluctuated over time. For some companies, these changes can have a major effect on consumer demand. Inevitably, it is the specialist children's shops such as Mothercare that are first to feel the effects of a rise or fall in birth numbers, but eventually all companies who target specific age groups will experience a change in the number of buyers available to purchase their goods and services.

households in western Europe were comprised of couples with children in 2006, compared to 51.0% in Asia Pacific and 54.3% in Africa and the Middle East (Euromonitor, 2007).

The growth in small or one-person households has had numerous marketing implications, ranging from an increased demand for smaller units of housing to the types and size of groceries purchased. A single person buying for him or herself is likely to use different types of retail outlet compared with the household buying as a unit.

3. The ethnic composition of the UK population has become increasingly diverse. The Office for National Statistics has estimated that almost 60% of the 4.3 million population increase expected to occur between 2000 and 2025 will be accounted for by inward migration. Ethnic diversity has created new opportunities to cater for ethnic preferences in fields as diverse as food, travel, and music.

4. Marketers also need to monitor the changing geographical distribution of the population (between different regions of the country and between urban and rural areas). The current drift towards rural and suburban areas has resulted in higher car-ownership levels and a preference for using out-of-town shopping centres.

MARKETING in ACTION

McDonald's recognizes new family values

Statistics have continued to chart the decline of the stereotypical nuclear family of two parents and 2.4 children. However, advertisers have often continued to portray this ideal-type family in their advertising, despite the fact that fewer people can relate directly to it. The fast-food restaurant, McDonald's, recognized this trend with an advertising campaign that portrayed a boy arranging for a meeting between his separated parents in a branch of McDonald's. Behind the departure from the happy-families norm in fast-food marketing is the realization that the number of families in the UK with single parents has risen from 8% in 1971 to nearly one quarter in 2002. McDonald's claimed that it could not credibly position itself as a family restaurant and show only pictures of mum and dad and two kids without the risk of alienating parents and children from different households. But could McDonald's incur the wrath of critics who might accuse the company of actually contributing to family breakdown? With an eye on such worries, McDonald's advertisements left the impression that the couple were going to get together again.

The technological environment

The pace of technological change is becoming increasingly rapid, and marketers need to understand how technological developments might affect them in four related business areas:

- New technologies can allow new goods and services to be offered to consumers—mobile Internet, and new anti-cancer drugs, for example.

- New technology can allow existing products to be made more cheaply, thereby widening the market for such goods by enabling prices to be lowered. In this way, more efficient aircraft have allowed new markets for air travel to develop.

- New opportunities for companies to communicate with their target customers have emerged, with many companies using computer databases to target potential customers and to maintain a dialogue with established customers. The development of mobile Internet services offers new possibilities for targeting buyers at times and places of high readiness to buy.

- Technological developments have allowed new methods of distributing goods and services. (For example, amazon.com used the Internet to offer book buyers a new way of browsing and buying books.)

The ecological environment

Issues affecting our natural ecology have captured the public imagination in recent years. The destruction of tropical rain forests and the depletion of the ozone layer

MARKETING in ACTION

The Internet and the law of unintended consequences

The development of the Internet has had profound impacts on the marketing activities of some business sectors. As an example, the budget airline sector has capitalized on the ability of the Internet to cut out intermediaries and reduce the airlines' costs. The low-cost carrier easyJet now claims that over 95% of its bookings are made online.

However, while many observers correctly predicted that travel and financial services would rapidly embrace the Internet, some other predictions have proved wide of the mark, suggesting that there is a very complex interaction between the technological, social, and economic environments. Consider the following predictions, which were made in 2000 when 'dot.com' mania was at its height.

1. Predictions were made that commuting would lessen as more people would work from home, using the Internet to communicate with their work colleagues. Traffic congestion would disappear and commuter rail services would lose customers. In fact, 24/7 access to their work e-mail has allowed many people to choose a pleasant residential environment and to live much further away from their work, because access to the Internet now allows them to work from home for two or three days a week. Overall, the travelling distances of many people in this situation have actually increased, resulting in more rather than less total commuting.

2. Conferences were predicted to disappear in favour of video conferencing. Why bother travelling to a meeting or conference when you could meet 'virtually' from the comfort of your desk, and at lower cost? However, face-to-face conferences have continued to prosper. The technology that enables many people to work in isolation may have indirectly contributed to a desire to counter this with more face-to-face meetings with a greater social content.

3. High Street shops were being written off in 2000, when quite extraordinarily the pure Internet company lastminute.com had a market capitalization value far in excess of the 110-outlet Debenhams store. But the convenience of shopping in the High Street or at out-of-town shopping centres and the problems of arranging home delivery of Internet suppliers were underestimated by advocates of Internet-based shopping.

We seem to have an inherent tendency to overstate the short-term effects of technological change, but to understate the long-term effects on our behaviour. With the development of new technologies enabling high-speed mobile Internet services, further predictions were being made in 2008. Would we really want to download full-length feature films to watch on our mobile phones? Would large numbers of people really want to surf the net on a small screen while travelling on a train? Would there be unforeseen 'killer applications' such as SMS text messaging which was almost left out of the specification of first-generation mobile phones, because no useful role for it was foreseen? Perhaps the long-term effects of the Internet may be more subtle, by contributing to individuals' sense of connectedness with narrowly selected commercial and social groups, no matter where they may be located, while reducing the sense of community which has traditionally been associated with diverse groups of people living together in close proximity.

The unforeseen consequences of the Internet emphasize how difficult it can be to understand the consequences for the marketer of a changing marketing environment. These examples demonstrate the importance of understanding the linkages between different elements of the marketing environment, so developments in the technological environment can be sensibly understood only in conjunction with changes in the social environment.

leading to global warming have serious implications for our quality of life—not necessarily today, but for future generations. Marketing is often seen as being in conflict with the need to protect the natural ecology. It is very easy for critics of marketing to point to cases where greed and mismanagement have created long-lasting or permanent ecological damage. Have rain forests been destroyed partly by our greed for more hardwood furniture? More locally, is our impatience for reading our destination quickly the reason why many natural habitats have been lost to new road developments?

A market-led company cannot ignore threats to the natural ecology, for two principal reasons:

1. There has been growing pressure on natural resources, including those that, directly or indirectly, are used in firms' production processes. This is evidenced by the extinction of species of animals and the depletion of hardwood timber resources. As a result of overuse of natural resources, many industry sectors, such as North Sea fishing, have faced severe constraints on their production possibilities.

2. The general public has become increasingly aware of ecological issues and, more importantly, some segments have shown a greater willingness and ability to spend money to alleviate the problems associated with ecologically harmful practices (see Laroche, Bergeron, and Barbaro-Forleo, 2001).

Because of the growing importance of ecological considerations to the marketer, there is further discussion of the topic in Chapter 3.

The internal environment

Marketers do not operate in a vacuum within their organizations. Internally, the structure and politics of an organization affect the manner in which it responds to environmental change. We are all familiar with lumbering giants of companies who, like a super-tanker, have ploughed ahead on a seemingly predetermined course, and found it difficult to change direction. During the late 1990s such well-respected companies as Sainsbury's and Marks & Spencer were accused of having internal structures and processes that were too rigid to cope with a changing external environment. Simply having a strong marketing department does not guarantee that a firm will be best able to adapt to change. The existence of a central marketing department may in fact create internal tensions, which make them less effective at responding to changing consumer needs than where marketing responsibilities in their widest sense are spread throughout the organization.

Two aspects to a marketing manager's internal environment are of importance here: the internal structure and processes of the marketing department itself (where one actually exists), and the relationship of the marketing function to other business functions.

Marketing departments allocate responsibilities to individual managers on a number of bases, the most common being functions performed, products managed, customer

Figure 2.8 Labour-intensive service industries have long realized that recruiting, training, and motivating the right staff is an important basis for delivering value to customers. In conditions of full employment, companies must sell themselves as a good employer so that they can recruit the people who will ultimately deliver marketers' promises to customers. The *Sunday Times* conducts an annual survey of Britain's best companies to work for, and the shoe-repair and key-cutting chain Timpson has scored highly for a number of years. Employee benefits include maternity allowances above the statutory minimum, and cash payments to employees when they get married. One sign of the company's success is a low level of staff turnover—at least 40% of its staff have worked at the company for more than five years. Managers are given considerable discretion in how they run their branch, for example the prices that they charge. Customers have come to trust the chain and reward it with sustainable long-term profits. (Reproduced with permission of Timpsons)

segments, and geographical areas; but in practice, most marketing departments show more than one approach to structure. Chapter 12 will review some of the advantages and disadvantages of each of these approaches.

In a genuinely marketing-oriented organization, marketing activities cannot be confined to something called a marketing department. As Drucker (1973) noted, marketing is so basic that it cannot be considered a separate function: it has to be the whole business seen from the customer's point of view. In marketing-oriented organizations, customers should be the concern not simply of the marketing department, but also of all those operational and administrative personnel whose actions may directly or indirectly affect customers' perceptions of quality and value. Some of the most successful companies are those that have successfully integrated marketing into all functional areas of the organization.

An important element of an organization's internal environment is its dominant 'culture'. Culture in this sense refers to a set of values that are shared by all members of the organization. Some organizations, for example, have a culture that stresses that 'the customer is always right', while others have a bureaucratic culture that stresses the need to conduct business in an administratively 'correct' way. Numerous comparative studies into the performance of European, American, and Japanese-managed organizations have identified the concept of culture as a possible explanation for differences in competitive effectiveness.

It can be very difficult to change cultural attitudes within an organization, and the process of change can be painful for many. Some organizations appear to have successfully managed the transition from a production-oriented culture to one focused on customers (for example, many former state-owned bus companies). In many cases, however, this change has been slow, leading to competitive disadvantage where culture does not keep up with changes in the external environment. As an example, some people have claimed that UK clearing banks have continued to be dominated by a culture based on prudence and caution whereas in some product areas such as home insurance a more aggressive approach to marketing management is called for.

For some firms, the availability of an adequate number of trained staff may by critical for satisfying customer needs. A marketing manager for a change of fine dining restaurants may put together several promotional programmes to entice diners, but if the chain cannot find sufficient chefs to operate in its kitchens, it will not be able to meet its customers' needs and expectations. In order to encourage staff retention, in particular of women returning after having had children, companies have offered attractive packages of benefits, such as working hours that fit around school holidays, and have sponsored various events in order to promote a caring image.

Can going beyond the legal requirement for employees ever be considered altruistic rather than just good business practice? Quaker companies such as Cadburys have a historic tradition of paternalism towards their staff; but might such altruism result in a payback in terms of better motivated staff?

The flexible organization

Organizations differ in the speed with which they are able to exploit new opportunities as they appear in their environment, partly reflecting the flexibility of their employment practices. Being the fastest company in a market to adapt can pay good dividends, so recent years have seen attempts by firms to increase their **flexibility**. This can be seen in the way that companies have moved personnel from areas in decline to those for which there is a prospect of future growth. For example, the major UK banks have moved staff away from basic banking activities—which face mature markets and challenges from new technology—towards broader financial services, which have been seen as more promising growth areas.

The management of change is becoming increasingly important to organizations, driven by the increasing speed with which the external environment is changing. Where the external environment is changing fast, employees of the organization may feel threatened, and it is important that management understands their fears and encourages them to take on board change. Sometimes, change needs to be considered at a strategic level, for example the role of post office employees is having to change in response to the threats posed by the Internet, and the declining volume of letter business. At other times, flexibility needs to be considered on a more short-term, operational basis, for example a restaurant may need the flexibility to take on or lay off staff at very short notice, depending on the weather.

Flexibility within an organization's workforce can be achieved by segmenting it into *core* and *peripheral* components. Many organizations have given their core workers greater job security, with defined career opportunities. In return for this relative job security, core workers may have to accept what Atkinson (1984) termed 'functional flexibility' by becoming responsible for a variety of jobs, as and when required. During their career with a company, such employees may undertake a variety of roles. In contrast to this group, peripheral employees have less job security and relatively limited career opportunities. They are 'numerically flexible', and often are employed on short-term contracts or treated as self-employed sub-contractors. It is not just operational staff whose jobs have been casualized in this way. Increasingly, many management jobs are being 'outsourced', and undertaken by consultants who are taken on, as and when required. There is, however, debate about whether excessive use of short-term, flexible labour increases the effectiveness of an organization. Many have pointed to a possible downside in the form of reduced commitment of employees to the firm, which can ultimately damage the company's dealings with its customers.

Monitoring and responding to environmental change

There are many examples of firms that have failed to read their marketing environment and have eventually withered and died. To avoid this fate, a firm must:

- understand what is going on in its business environment, and
- respond and adapt to environmental change.

As organizations become larger and national economies more complex, the task of understanding the marketing environment becomes more formidable. Information about a firm's environment becomes crucial to environmental analysis and response.

Information about the current state of the environment is used as a starting point for planning future marketing strategy, based on assumptions about how the environment will change. Information is also vital to monitor the implementation of an organization's marketing plans and to note the cause of any deviation from plan. Information therefore has both a planning function and a control function.

Information collection, processing, transmission, and storage technologies are continually improving, as witnessed by the development of Electronic Point of Sale (EPOS) systems. These have enabled organizations greatly to enhance the quality of the information they have about their operating environment. However, information is becoming more accessible not just to one particular organization, but also to its competitors. Attention is therefore moving away from how information is collected, to who is best able to make use of the information.

Large organizations operating in complex and turbulent environments often use information to build models of their environment, or at least sub-components of it. Some of these can be quite general, as in the case of the models of the national economy which many large companies have developed. From a general model of the economy, a firm can predict how a specific item of government policy (for example, increasing the rate of value added tax on luxury goods) will impact directly and indirectly on sales of its own products.

The crucial role of information in marketing analysis and planning will be returned to in Chapter 5.

SWOT analysis

SWOT is an acronym for Strengths, Weaknesses, Opportunities, and Threats. SWOT analysis is a useful framework for assessing an organization and its marketing environment, summarizing the main environmental issues in the form of opportunities and threats facing an organization. These external factors are listed alongside the organization's internal strengths and weaknesses. An opportunity in an organization's external environment can be exploited only if it has the internal strengths to do so. If, on the other hand, the organization is not capable of exploiting these because of internal weaknesses, then they should perhaps be left alone. For this reason, the terms 'opportunities' and 'threats' should not be viewed as 'absolutes', but assessed in the context of an organization's resources and the feasibility of exploiting them.

The principles of a SWOT analysis are illustrated in Figure 2.9 by examining how an established manufacturer of ready prepared chicken products might view its strengths and weaknesses in terms of the opportunities and threats that it faces in its environment.

Marketing opportunities can come in many forms, and each should be assessed for its attractiveness and success probability. Attractiveness can be assessed in terms of potential market size, growth rates, profit margins, competitiveness, and distribution channels. Other factors may be technological requirements, the extent of government restrictions, availability of government grants, ecological concerns, and energy requirements. Measures of attractiveness must be qualified by the probability of success, which depends on the company's strengths and competitive advantage. Probability of success is likely to be influenced by, among other things, the firm's access to cash, lines of credit or capital to finance new developments, technological and production expertise, marketing skills, distribution channels, and managerial competence. A simple matrix can be constructed to show the relationship between attractiveness and success probability. We will return to this in Chapter 7.

Strengths	Weaknesses
Established and widely recognized brand name	Only has a narrow product range
Good distribution network	Shortage of production staff
Strong financial base	
Opportunities	**Threats**
Growing demand for chicken products	Possibility of health scares
Rising income will result in increased demand for ready prepared meals	Intense competition from supermarkets' own label products
	Tighter safety standards may increase costs

Figure 2.9 SWOT analysis for a hypothetical established UK manufacturer of ready prepared chicken meals

An environmental threat is a challenge posed by an unfavourable trend or development in a company's environment that would lead, in the absence of action by the company, to the erosion of the company's market position. In this case the threats should be assessed according to their seriousness and the probability of occurrence. A threat matrix can then be constructed.

In order for an environmental analysis to have a useful input to the marketing planning process, a wide range of information and opinions needs to be summarized in a meaningful way. The information collated from a detailed environmental analysis can be simplified in the form of an Environmental Threat and Opportunity Profile (ETOP). This provides a summary of the environmental factors that are most critical to the organization (Figure 2.10) and can be useful in stimulating debate among senior management about the future of the business. Some analysts suggest trying to weight these factors according to their importance, and then rating them for their impact on the organization.

Factor	Major opportunity	Minor opportunity	Neutral	Minor threat	Major threat	Probability of occurrence
Political						
New transport policy sees introduction of tax on use of cars in town centres					✓	0.1
Economic						
Tax on petrol increases by 5p				✓		0.4
Household spending falls for two quarters in succession					✓	0.2
VAT on new cars reduced	✓					0.1
Market						
Overseas competitors enter market more aggressively				✓		0.3

Figure 2.10 An Environmental Threat and Opportunity Profile, applied to a car manufacturer

Chapter summary and linkages to other chapters

The marketing environment comprises the individuals, organizations, and forces that impinge on the activities of marketers. Some of the effects are direct and relatively immediate (the micro-environment), while others are essentially forces for change in the future (the macro-environment). Marketers must also understand the internal structures and processes of their organization, as these can affect the development and implementation of marketing plans (the internal environment).

Marketers have developed methodologies for capturing information about the marketing environment and these will be developed in Chapter 5. Following analysis of their environment, marketers seek to develop a competitive position within that environment (Chapter 7). Increasingly, marketers are seeing the marketing environment in terms of not just the local market, but also the international environment (Chapter 13).

This chapter has stressed that marketers should understand the needs not just of their customers, but of a much broader range of stakeholders. Although social responsibility by firms can achieve long-term paybacks, there can still be doubt about what is the most responsible course of action. The issue of marketing's social responsibility is the focus for the next chapter.

▢ KEY PRINCIPLES OF MARKETING

- Marketing takes place within a broad system of economic, social, political, and technological relationships.
- Value is created through interaction with other individuals and organizations that make up the marketing environment.
- The marketing environment cannot be neatly divided into distinct areas. A good marketer seeks to understand the complex linkages between different parts of the marketing environment.
- Micro-environment influences may demand urgent attention, but macro-environment influences can have a more profound long-term effect on an organization's marketing.

CASE STUDY

Ready meal manufacturers ready to respond to a changing marketing environment

It is often said that 'we are what we eat', but it can also be said that what is on our dinner plates reflects the broader marketing environment. One big change in recent years has been the growing demand for ready prepared meals bought from a supermarket. Previously dismissed as unpalatable and a poor substitute for 'real' cooking, their sales have grown rapidly in recent years in many western developed countries. An analysis of the reasons for the growth in the ready prepared meals markets indicates the effects of broader factors in the marketing environment on the size of a particular market.

The research company Mintel reported in 2007 that the market for ready meals in the five largest European countries increased by 5% between 2006 and 2007 alone to reach €8.4 billion. Moreover, it predicted a further 18% growth to reach the €10 billion mark by 2011. In the UK, the market was worth a total of €2 billion, with a much higher level of sales per head of population than in France or Germany. Intel predicted that between 2006 and 2011, UK ready meals sales would reach €3.7 billion, with about a quarter of all Brits likely to eat a ready meal at least once a week. It seemed that the appetite for ready meals would grow more slowly in other European countries, for example Mintel predicted that by 2011, only 9% of Germans would eat a ready meal each week.

What has driven the growth in the ready meals market in recent years, and why should there be differences in market potential between countries?

Technology has played a big role in the growing take-up of ready meals. A report by the research body Leatherhead Food International described how new techniques have allowed companies to develop ready meals which preserve taste and texture, while still making them easy to use by the consumer. Furthermore, great advances in distribution management, in particular the use of information technology to control inventories, has allowed fresh, chilled ready meals to be quickly, effectively and efficiently distributed without the need for freezing or added preservatives.

The structure and values of society have contributed to the growth of the UK ready meal market, and may explain why growth here is greater than in France or Germany. Ready meals particularly appeal to single households, and those 'cellular' families in which individual family members tend to eat at different times. Mintel reported that the tradition of family meals together remains stronger in many continental European countries than in the UK, which may help to explain the greater popularity of individual ready meals in the UK. Some social commentators have reported that young people have lost the ability to cook creatively, as cookery has been reduced in importance in the school curriculum. Furthermore, many UK consumers no longer feel a social stigma attached to eating a ready meal, something which would be anathema to many people in France, a country which takes great pride in its national cuisine. Any remaining stigma has been reduced by the number of 'celebrity chefs' who have endorsed ready meals with their own brand image.

The impact of the economic environment on sales of ready meals is slightly more ambiguous. As individuals grow richer, they can afford to buy ready prepared foods, rather than spend time and effort preparing it themselves. With a tempting range of ready meals now available, from duck à l'orange to beef bourguignon, the consumer with money in his or her pocket will be tempted to splash out on a ready meal, rather than persevere at home with a 'quick' jacket potato or pizza. Although rising incomes have been associated with rising consumption of ready meals, increased sales have also been attributed to a deteriorating economic environment. As recession bit the UK in 2008, the manufacturer Northern Foods—a major supplier of ready prepared meals to Marks & Spencer—reported resilient sales. It seemed that consumers were trading down from expensive restaurant meals to the alternative of relatively cheap, gourmet ready prepared meals.

Of course, marketers should be more interested in predicting future effects of environmental change on consumption, rather than merely charting historical trends. So what do current trends hold for future sales of ready meals? The growing pressure on individuals' available time, matched with long-term rising disposable incomes, will doubtless continue to fuel the growth in UK ready meals sales.

In a market that is in its maturity stage, more attention will need to be paid to competitive differentiation, and understanding the way in which customers attribute value to a product. Many consumers have become increasingly concerned about the health implications of the food they eat, and ready meal manufacturers will need to continue responding to such concerns. For example, they have responded with a range of low calorie meals, and addressed specific, sometimes transient, health fads, for example with respect to trans-fatty acids and Omega 3 supplements. Many consumers have also become concerned about the ecological environment, and some suppliers, such as Marks & Spencer, have incorporated sustainability agendas into their ready meals, for example by reducing packaging and sourcing supplies from sustainable sources.

As other countries develop cellular household structures, with more professional, single people living alone, export opportunities may grow, and many companies in the sector have their eyes set on the Chinese and Indian markets, among others.

Sources: based on Mintel Oxygen Reports— 'Eating Habits: Improving the Appeal of Convenience Options'— August 2007; *Financial Times*, 'Quality ready meals hit the spot', 21 July 2006; Leatherhead Food International, European Ready Meals Market, 2001

- -

Case study review questions

1. Using an appropriate framework of analysis, briefly summarize the effects of change in the marketing environment on sales of ready meals.

2. Critically discuss the link between the economic environment and sales of ready meals.

3. Discuss the factors that might affect sales of ready meals in your country over the next five years.

CHAPTER REVIEW QUESTIONS

1. Explain briefly what you understand by the 'marketing environment' of a business.

2. 'Suppliers and intermediaries are important stakeholders in the micro-environment of the business.' Explain the evolving role and functions of these stakeholders in today's marketing-orientated business.

3. Critically discuss the links between the internal environment of an organization and its external marketing environment.

ACTIVITIES

1. Develop a checklist of points that you consider to be important indicators of whether an organization is responsive to changes in its business environment. Why did you choose these indicators? Now apply your checklist to three selected organizations: one a traditional manufacturing industry, the second a service-based commercial organization, and the third a government organization that serves the public. What, if anything, should your chosen organizations do to become more responsive to changes in their business environment?

2. Using a company of your choice, produce and justify an environmental set.

3. Giving examples, explain what is meant by the term 'pressure groups'. Provide a résumé of the tactics you would advise a high-profile company to use in managing relations with these groups.

REFERENCES

Atkinson, J. (1984), 'Manpower Strategies for Flexible Organizations'. *Personnel Management*, August, pp. 77–93.

Doughty, S. (2007), 'Women to be the Major Breadwinners in a Quarter of Families by 2030'. *Daily Mail*, 3 August, p. 17.

Drucker, P. F. (1973), *Management: tasks, responsibilities and practices*. New York: Harper & Row.

Euromonitor (2007), *Countries and Consumers*. London: Euromonitor International.

Financial Times (2007a), 'Inequality: growing income gap gives blueprint for action', 17 October.

Financial Times (2007b), 'UK immigration May be Close to Peak', 24 July.

Financial Times (2008), Insurance Threat to Loans', 6 June, p. 5.

Laroche, M., Bergeron, J., and Barbaro-Forleo, G. (2001), 'Targeting Consumers Who are Willing to Pay More for Environmentally Friendly Products'. *Journal of Consumer Marketing*, 18: 503–20.

Office for National Statistics (2008a), Social Trends No. 38, London: Office for National Statistics (available online at www.statistics.gov.uk/downloads/theme_social/Social_Trends38/Social_Trends_38.pdf.

Office for National Statistics (2008b), Population Trends, Spring 2008, No. 131, Office for National Statistics (available online at www.statistics.gov.uk/downloads/theme_population/Population_Trends_131_web.pdf.

Rayport, J. F. and Sviokla, J. J. (1995), 'Exploiting the Virtual Value Chain'. *Harvard Business Review*, (November–December): 75–85.

The Future Foundation (2002), *Complicated Lives II: The Price of Complexity*. London: EU Office of Statistics, The Future Foundation.

SUGGESTED FURTHER READING

A wide-ranging review of organizations' environment is given in the following:

Palmer, A. and Hartley, B. (2008). *The Business Environment,* 6th edn. Maidenhead: McGraw-Hill.

The following references provide further discussion of marketing relationships between a company and its suppliers and customers:

Donaldson, B. and O'Toole, T. (2007), Strategic Market Relationships: from strategy to implementation. London: John Wiley.

Mattsson, L.-G. and Johanson, J. (2006), 'Discovering Market Networks'. *European Journal of Marketing*, 40(3/4): 259–74.

Prenkert, F. and Hallén, L. (2006), 'Conceptualising, Delineating and Analysing Business Networks'. *European Journal of Marketing*, 40(3/4): 384–407.

The difficulties of understanding and assessing the impacts of change in the economic environment on a firm's marketing activities are discussed in the following:

Blanchard, O. (2008), *Macroeconomics*. Harlow: Pearson Education.

Burda, M. and Wyplosz, C. (2005), *Macroeconomics: A European Text*, 3rd edn. Oxford: Oxford University Press.

Griffiths, A. and Wall, S. (eds) (2007), *Applied Economics: An Introductory Course*, 11th edn. London: Prentice Hall.

Organizational culture has been referred to in this chapter as having a major impact on an organization's marketing effectiveness, and the following references explore internal and external dimensions of culture:

Hofstede, G. and Hofstede, G. J. (2004), *Cultures and Organizations: software for the mind.* Maidenhead: McGraw-Hill.

Ahmed, P. K. and Rafiq, M. (2002), *Internal Marketing: tools and concepts for customer focused management.* Oxford: Butterworth Heinemann.

USEFUL WEB LINKS

Visit the Online Resource Centre for resources that are relevant to this chapter, including web links, multiple choice questions, and additional case studies:
   www.oxfordtextbooks.co.uk/orc/palmer2e/

KEY TERMS

- **Accelerator effect**
- **Birth rate**
- **Business cycle**
- **Competitors**
- **Cultural convergence**
- **Demography**
- **Disintermediation**
- **Ecological environment**
- **Economic growth**
- **Flexible organization**
- **Gross Domestic Product (GDP)**
- **Intermediaries**
- **Internal environment**
- **Internet**
- **Macro-environment**
- **Marketing environment**
- **Micro-environment**
- **Multiplier effect**
- **Pressure groups**

- **Relationship marketing**
- **Shareholders**
- **Stakeholders**
- **System**
- **SWOT analysis**
- **Value chain**

3

Socially responsible marketing

CHAPTER OBJECTIVES

Marketing is coming under increasing scrutiny by members of the public who have ever higher expectations about the behaviour of commercial organizations. In the previous two chapters, we have presented marketing in simplistic terms whereby firms continually seek to maximize their profits by adapting what they sell to the needs of customers. Unfortunately, this simple approach may lead firms to adopt policies which society at large may consider to be irresponsible. This chapter explores the concept of marketing responsibility from a number of angles. It begins by reviewing the underlying philosophy of socially responsible business. It then explores the currently topical issue of sustainability in a world where many people have accused marketing of being responsible for unnecessarily depleting natural resources and harming the natural environment. Following this, the chapter will review issues of ethical standards by which marketers interact with their customers, suppliers, competitors, and government agencies. Finally, the chapter will make some observations on the duties of companies to communicate responsibly with their customers, in an era where customers and regulatory agencies are more prepared than ever before to criticize or sue firms for irresponsible communication.

Introduction

In Chapter 1, it was noted that satisfying customer requirements was a key defining element of marketing. The term 'customer is king' or 'the customer is always right' is often heard as the essential motivator that leads companies to try to satisfy customers' needs profitably. Of course, what the customer wants may be impossible for a company to provide at a profit, so the simplistic idea of 'customer is king' may not be followed through. It may also be highly irresponsible for a company even to attempt to satisfy customers' needs. In this chapter, we are going to explore further the reasons why the customer may not always be king, and why marketers may need to put responsibility before the short-term pursuit of profits.

Consider the following reasons why it may be considered irresponsible for a company to provide customers with what they want:

1. A product may be harmful to customers, and although it may be seen by them as being beneficial in the short term, it may have long-term harmful effects, of which they are not aware at the time of purchase. Addictive drugs and high-fat burgers may be sought by customers today, but they may regret their purchase in the future, when they are addicted to drugs, or are obese from eating too much high-fat food.

2. Some customers may not have the mental capacity to understand what they want. Children may choose to consume sweets and fizzy drinks all day, and may not be able to evaluate the consequences of their purchases.

3. Marketers have a particular responsibility to vulnerable groups of customers. Young children may be vulnerable, because they have not developed the capacity critically to evaluate purchases. However, vulnerability can have much wider effects, and a customer who is not vulnerable at one moment, may be vulnerable at another. A house-owner who desperately needs repairs to be carried out on his house following extensive storm damage in the area may be vulnerable to 'cowboy' builders who realize that customers suddenly have little choice of builders, and therefore that they can charge exploitative prices.

4. The company may present a false or misleading picture of a product, so the customer cannot realistically make an informed choice about whether or not it will satisfy their needs. In evaluating complex price details for mobile phones or gas tariffs, many customers may not understand exactly what they are buying, and what they are committing themselves to.

5. A customer may want to buy a product which could be directly harmful to others—for example, a shotgun. Should a company be allowed to supply it to them?

6. Similarly, a customer may wish to buy something that could be harmful to society more generally, for example by undermining its core values. Should customers be able to buy things from shops all day on Sunday, rather than treating Sunday as a day of rest and family togetherness?

7. Should companies promote products in a way that creates envy of those who have bought the product, and results in social divisions between a group of 'haves' and another group of 'have nots' that feels socially excluded? Should a teenager feel socially excluded because s/he does not have the latest fashion in trainers?

8. Could a customer's purchase harm future generations by depleting natural resources, or emitting harmful gases to the atmosphere? Customers may be happy to buy

'gas-guzzling' cars, but should their choice be restricted in order to reduce the emission of 'greenhouse gases'?

9. Is the customer actually presented with all the choice that should be available to them? What if a cartel of producers got together to try to restrict choice of a particular category of products?

How should a profit-orientated company act in each of these situations? Does it have a moral responsibility to treat its customers as an individual would treat their trusted friends? Is business essentially about letting the buyer beware, and if the customer says that they want something, why should the seller question this? Can foregoing sales and acting responsibly actually bring in more money to a company, because its brand comes to be seen more favourably by buyers?

In this chapter, we will explore issues of socially responsible marketing. Marketers have come under increasing levels of scrutiny by customers and the media, with newspapers and television programmes ever eager to pick up stories of bad practice by commercial organizations. Fast-food companies promoting high-fat foods which lead to obesity; car manufacturers encouraging high-emission four-wheel-drive cars which are only going to be used around town; and insurance policies sold to customers who will never be able to make a claim on them, are typical of marketing irresponsibility that has been reported recently.

This chapter raises many more questions than it provides answers. Many of the issues discussed here involve value judgements, so one person's idea of responsibility may be viewed by another person as irresponsible. Even if the chapter provides no definitive answer on certain subjects, you should at least beome aware of the issues involved, and frameworks for reconciling the sometimes conflicting aims of businesses and their broader group of stakeholders.

We will first explore the philosophical underpinnings of socially responsible marketing, before moving on to look at specific issues which may require us to modify the simple statement that marketing is primarily about satisfying customers' needs profitably.

Philosophical principles underlying responsible marketing

It is difficult to define precisely what is meant by socially responsible marketing, because there are essentially two views about why companies should act in a socially responsible manner.

1. In models of 'good' societies, organizations have a duty to think about the interests of society, and not just their own narrow interests. Businesses should do their bit to contribute towards a just and fair society, alongside the contributions of other institutions such as the family and the Church.

2. An alternative view is that firms take an instrumental approach to responsibility. If acting responsibly improves their chances of survival and prosperity, they will act responsibly—if not, they would act opportunistically and in their own self-interest.

For the purpose of this book, we will define socially responsible marketing as:

Marketing activities which acknowledge corporate responsibilities to all stakeholders who may be affected by such activities. Socially responsible marketing need not be incompatible with a profit-maximizing objective.

The philosophical approach of the firm as a 'good citizen' has been criticized by followers of Milton Friedman, who have argued that firms should concentrate on doing what they are best at—making profits for their owners. Expecting social responsibility by firms would allow business organizations to become too dominant in society. By this argument, any attempt by firms to contribute to social causes is a form of taxation on the customers of their businesses. Buyers should be aware of what they are buying, and make their own decisions about what is socially responsible.

The more pragmatic view is that where companies go out of their way to be 'good citizens', the cause of this can often be traced to a calculative, instrumental judgement by the company rather than to philanthropy. There are a number of reasons for such instrumentality:

- In a market in which product offers are all broadly similar and with saturation advertising, support of socially valuable causes may allow a company to develop a unique identity for its products. Such support may be a cheap way of gaining attention and provide a unique selling proposition.

- Acting responsibly may actually reduce a company's costs, rather than increase them; therefore, being a good citizen comes with no additional cost implications for a company. As an example, a restaurant chain that sources a high proportion of its food locally may appear to be acting responsibly by reducing 'food miles', but may also actually reduce its total costs. Sometimes, the biggest barrier to a company acting responsibly is the mindset of staff that can be difficult to change.

- Some of the company's customers may prefer to buy from a responsible company rather than an irresponsible one. Where there is much broadly similar choice available in a market, the cost to a customer of buying the 'responsible' product rather than an irresponsible one may be quite low. By appearing to be responsible, a company may have added to its brand reputation in much the same way as it would by investing in advertising and quality control.

- Sometimes companies change their behaviour ahead of new legislation. By changing early, they can gain positive publicity, which would be lost if they were seen to be pushed into change by legislation. The company may also gain cost-saving and learning advantages ahead of its competitors, before they too are forced to change when new legislation is introduced.

This chapter is about responsible *marketing*. However, it can often be difficult to separate marketing responsibility from other aspects of corporate responsibility. This reflects the recognition from Chapter 1 that marketing in its broadest sense is not just the responsibility of the marketing department, but of all functions within an organization. Consider some of the following cross-functional issues that impinge on responsible marketing:

1. The marketing department of a food retailer is desperately trying to reduce its supply costs, so that it can sell a range of ready prepared foods below a critical price point. It has cut its overheads as far as it can, so the only realistic method of selling its food at the specified price point, while at the same time retaining its profit margin, is to cut its production and wastage costs. Should it use chlorine in its washing processes, which will reduce washing costs and keep the finished product looking fresh for longer, even though there is a suggestion that chlorine may increase cancer risks and lead to the pollution of watercourses? The production manager may be happy to extend the shelf life, but what view should the marketing manager take?

2. Many service industries require a high level of flexibility by staff, with some staff being held on standby, and only called in for work if there is expected to be a high level of customer demand. Is it responsible that marketing's need to flexibly accommodate as many customers as possible, should lead to uncertainty among workers, who may come from disadvantaged groups in society anyway?

3. The marketing department of a retailer may desperately want to expand its store network, but the finance director needs to obtain new sources of funds. Should the finance director overstate recent profits in order to make raising new finance—and hence opening more stores—easier?

In all of these cases, it should be apparent that making decisions about what is responsible may not be easy. It is too naive and simplistic to say that commercial organizations should always act in a completely responsible manner. Just as there are few human beings who know no sin, so too there are very few companies that are beyond reproach. Acting responsibly may be crucial for a large organization with a differentiation strategy based on trust in its brand. In these cases, the brand is probably based on being perceived as a reliable, responsible one with which customers can do business. Therefore, companies such as Boots, Marks & Spencer and Virgin have gone to great lengths to appear as responsible members of the community. The Virgin group has used its reputation for responsibility to move into completely new markets, from music to airlines, to trains and telephones. For such companies, share values have sometimes suddenly fallen when stories or rumours have circulated about them acting in an irresponsible way. However, many smaller challenging companies may have fewer concerns about being seen as a responsible organization. A clothing retailer which is seeking to expand fast and appeal to a price-sensitive market through discount outlets may be prepared to take more risks when it comes to acting irresponsibly. If their main point of difference with competitors is price, rather than brand reputation, it may be more willing to turn a blind eye to dubious suppliers, or suppliers to those suppliers, who may have used toxic chemicals in their production process, or used child labour. They may reason that their brand is not particularly powerful, so therefore they have less to lose than a trusted brand. On the other hand, they would have everything to gain by undercutting the competition with cheaply sourced products.

Responsible marketing, then, is not a simple question of being good to all people at all times. In real life, marketing managers have to make hard decisions if they are to survive and stay in business. A business which was run purely on philanthropic lines probably would not last very long. However, a business that has a shrewd understanding of its business environment, and understands the broader expectations of buyers and legislators, may consider that acting responsibly yields good long-term dividends. It may even find that acting responsibly is less costly than acting irresponsibly. Read the 'Marketing in Action' vignette (below) about the retailer B&Q's decision to stop selling patio heaters, and judge for yourself whether you think the company was being shrewd in its decision.

MARKETING in ACTION

No more patio heaters at B&Q—who wins?

Global warming has become the big ecological issue of the early twenty-first century with a combination of financial incentives, new product development, and feelings of guilt leading to many consumers' desire to cut the greenhouse gas emissions to which their consumption contributes. Firms have been keen to associate with the cause of reducing greenhouse gas emissions, but how far would they go in helping the environment, or are they invariably guided by traditional corporate profit objectives? The DIY chain B&Q's decision in 2008 to end the sale of patio heaters at its stores illustrates the sometimes complex interplay between responsibility and profitability.

Patio heaters became a 'must have' accessory for many people during the prosperous years of the 1990s. For homeowners obsessed with style and obtaining the maximum utilization of their house space, a patio heater allowed use of their garden on chilly evenings. British people who had enjoyed al fresco eating in Benidorm could now enjoy the same on chilly evenings in Birmingham. Patio heaters were also a big hit with pubs, especially following bans on smoking in many countries. Pubs could still keep the trade of smokers, who could sit and smoke outside under a warm patio heater. According to the UK's Energy Saving Trust, there were 1.2 million patio heaters in the UK in 2007, and it predicted that within three years, this figure would almost double to 2.3 million.

Against this background of growing popularity among consumers, it may seem surprising that B&Q announced in January 2008 that it would stop selling patio heaters. Was it simply seeking favourable publicity, especially at a time when gas-powered patio heaters were drawing the wrath of environmentalists, who pointed out that each patio heater could emit as much carbon dioxide in a year as 1.5 cars? Was it being altruistic in its concern for the environment? Or could there have been pragmatic business benefit in discontinuing patio heaters?

First, B&Q could have expected the profits of selling patio heaters to be gradually falling. They were no longer the new product that they were a decade earlier, and the company now faced competition for sales—and pressure on margins—from a wider range of retailers. Also, after a decade of falling energy prices, gas prices started to increase sharply from 2007—would patio heaters fall out of favour as they became more costly to operate?

More importantly, pressure was mounting in the EU for a ban on sales of patio heaters which were seen as socially irresponsible. Was B&Q simply getting out while the going was still good? Did it foresee further government restrictions on the sale and use of such heaters, so if it got out now, it could gain the kudos for leading, rather than being pushed if it waited until later? Some cynics argued that B&Q had built up large stocks of patio heaters, and only committed itself to stop selling them when stocks ran out. Could the publicity have actually helped B&Q sell even more patio heaters than it would otherwise have done?

Ecologically sustainable marketing

There is no doubt that issues of **ecological responsibility** have been rising rapidly up the agenda of marketing. Global warming, tsunamis, violent storms, and the depletion of natural resources have led even the most doubting member of the public to the view that 'something must be done'. As individual consumers, we can decide to do our bit for the ecological environment, for example by walking rather than using the car, or buying locally produced food which has incurred fewer 'food miles'; but what should we expect businesses to do? Marketing is often seen as being irresponsible in its attitude to the natural ecology. Many of the products that we see in the shops probably have a substitute that is less harmful to the environment. Why should bottled water companies such as Volvic and Evian spend a lot of money promoting their product, using environmentally harmful transport to move it over long distances, when there is plenty of evidence that locally available tap water is just as good? Indeed, marketing could be accused of encouraging a throwaway society, which is good for increasing sales, but less **sustainable** for the environment. Taken to its logical extreme, consumption of the vast majority of goods and services can result in some form of ecological harm. For example, the most ecologically responsible means of transport is to avoid the need for transport in the first place. The most ecologically responsible holiday is for an individual to stay at home. Individuals with a true concern for preserving their ecological environment would choose to reduce their consumption of goods and services in total. At the moment, such attitudes are held by only a small minority in western societies, but the development of a widespread anti-consumption mentality would have major implications for marketers.

There are two principal reasons why marketers should be concerned about ecological responsibility:

1. The general public has become increasingly aware of ecological issues and, more importantly, some segments have shown a greater willingness and ability to spend their money in a way which minimizes ecological harm (see Laroche, Bergeron, and Barbaro-Forleo, 2001). It has been suggested that concern for the ecological environment is a luxury that can be afforded by developed societies who have achieved their wealth. Some have questioned the morality of western developed nations seeking to restrict growth in the less developed countries by imposing on them western standards of ecological protection.

2. There has been growing pressure on natural resources, including those that directly or indirectly are used in firms' production processes. This is evidenced by the extinction of species of animals and depletion of hardwood timber resources. As a result of overuse of natural resources, many industry sectors, such as North Sea fishing, have faced severe constraints on their production possibilities. The move towards sustainable resources implies that as resources are used in the consumption, they are replaced by freshly generated resources. In this way, timber grown in properly managed forests may be said to be sustainable, because a new tree will soon grow where an old one was felled. The use of other resources, such as oil, may be said to be unsustainable—when it is gone, it's gone, and it will take millions of years to create new oil. Many would argue that it is irresponsible of marketers to use unsustainable resources, when there are sustainable alternatives.

Marketers can face problems in coming to a view about what is ecologically responsible. Consumers (and marketers) may be confounded by alternative arguments about the consequences of their purchase decisions, with goods that were once considered to be environmentally 'friendly' suddenly becoming seen as enemies of the environment as knowledge and prejudice change (see Marketing in Action vignette on bio diesel fuels). Read the case study at the end of this chapter, and you might be surprised to hear that the chief executive of the airline Ryanair claimed to be a saviour for the ecological environment by using more efficient aircraft than its competitors.

Most consumers are not experts on ecological issues, and may therefore be easily persuaded by the most compellingly promoted argument, regardless of the technical merit of the case. Very often, a firm may have a technically sound case, but fail to win the hearts and minds of consumers who seem intent on believing the opposite argument that is in accordance with their own prejudices. For example, the nuclear power industry may claim to have won technical arguments about the much lower level of CO_2 emissions compared to fossil fuel energy sources, but many people remain implacably opposed to the concept of nuclear power.

Another confusing issue is the presumed benefits for the ecological environment of marketing new, efficient, low-energy products. If we save ecological resources in one form of activity, will that simply leave us with spare money to use more resources in other forms of activity? Consider the example of cars. It is certainly true that for any class of car, the typical fuel consumption has dropped over the past decade or so. A family-sized car such as the Volkswagen Golf, which 20 years ago might have achieved 34 miles per gallon, today may achieve over 40. Unfortunately, the associated reduction in running costs of a car have meant that customers can now afford a bigger and better car, which will doubtless use more fuel; so over the past decade or so, the fastest growth in car sales to private consumers has been in larger sports utility vehicles and multi-people vehicles. It is as if individuals have a set proportion of their income that they allocate to transport. If the cost per mile of running their vehicle comes down, they may trade up to the larger 'luxury' vehicle. Therefore, although car manufacturers might have been acting responsibly by improving the efficiency of cars, this has sent an ambiguous signal to consumers, and the overall contribution to the ecological environment may be neutralized by consumers' changed patterns of expenditure. This apparently perverse effect has been seen in a number of other sectors. The ecological benefits of increasingly fuel-efficient aircraft have been partly offset by the resulting lower prices of air transport, leading to more people taking short-break holidays. The Boeing 737-800 series aircraft not only uses much less fuel than the original Boeing-737 of 20 years ago, but this has also allowed budget airlines to develop a whole new market of low-cost air travel. Friends of the Earth has estimated that half a billion tonnes of carbon dioxide was emitted by aircraft into the atmosphere in 2006, up on previous years, despite the development of more efficient aircraft engines. The advent of budget airlines may also have brought tourists flocking to previously underdeveloped areas, causing ecological damage in the process.

The **green consumer** movement can present businesses with opportunities as well as problems. Proactive companies have capitalized on ecological issues by reducing their costs and/or improving their organizational image, pursuing a green marketing strategy. Here are some examples of how firms have adapted to the green movement.

- Many markets are characterized by segments that are prepared to pay a premium price for a product that has been produced in an ecologically sound manner. Some companies, such as the Organic Paint Company, have developed valuable niches on this basis. What starts off as a 'deep green' niche soon expands into a larger 'pale green' segment of customers who prefer ecologically sound products but are unwilling to pay such a high price premium.

- Being 'green' may actually save a company money. Often, changing existing environmentally harmful practices primarily involves overcoming traditional mindsets about how things should be done. For example, using recyclable shipping materials may involve overcoming traditional one-way supply chain logistics (see Unruh, 2008).

- In western developed economies, legislation to enforce environmentally sensitive methods of production is increasing. A company which adopts environmentally

MARKETING in ACTION

Bio diesel—from clean and green to mean?

In 2006, 'bio diesel', derived from renewable agricultural crops, was hailed as a great way forward to reduce carbon emissions and avoid depletion of our finite resources of fossil fuels. In a world which would eventually run out of oil, the prospect of renewable energy source which could be grown in clean and pleasant fields seemed like an answer from heaven. Moreover, bio diesel would have lower CO_2 emissions compared with alternative fossil fuels. The Virgin group, ever eager to gain a publicity advantage, announced that it would be converting part of its fleet of trains to run on bio diesel. The public were doubtless impressed by the ecological credentials of the boss of Virgin, Sir Richard Branson. They might just have seen through the hypocrisy of his attempts to save the planet by turning to bio fuels, while at the same time causing what many would regard as unnecessary and reckless ecological damage through his planned Virgin Galactica space travel project.

However, just a couple of years after Virgin's announcement, bio diesel had fallen out of favour with many groups. To many people, the analysis of carbon emission reductions was oversimplified and understated, for example destroying rainforest to make land available for bio fuels could actually increase greenhouse gas emissions. More seriously, there was a growing feeling that using agricultural crops to provide fuel for vehicles in the rich western countries would push up the price of basic food materials for people in developing countries. Was this ethical? Within a few months of Virgin seeking favourable reactions for its move to bio fuels, its rival, National Express, announced that it would be scaling back its project to use bio fuels. Did it have a better understanding of the reality of bio fuels and their likely future cost and availability? Had it responded to the public's flip-flop attitude on ecological issues, and sensed that the public now saw bio fuels as a problem rather than a solution?

sensitive production methods ahead of compulsion can gain experience and hence competitive advantage ahead of other companies.

Ethical responsibility

We now turn our attention to the broader subject of **ethics**, and the responsibilities of marketers to act according to a set of shared values, rather than simply pursuing short-term profits. Ethics has its roots in the study of philosophy, and for our purposes will be defined here as:

a philosophical framework within which decisions are made as to what constitutes right and wrong behaviour.

However, it can be difficult to agree just what is right and wrong, because no two people have exactly the same opinions. It can also be difficult to distinguish between ethics and legality; for example, it may not be strictly illegal to exploit the gullibility of children in advertisements, but it may nevertheless be unethical. Furthermore, culture has a strong influence on what is considered to be ethical, and culture's attitudes have a tendency to change over time, so that what is considered ethical today, may be considered unethical a few years later.

In western societies, ethical considerations confront business organizations on many occasions, as the following examples show.

- A food company may advertise a product and provide information which is technically correct, but omit to provide vital information about side effects associated with consuming the food. Many would argue that the company should be required to spell out the possible problems of using its products, as well as the benefits.

- A dentist is short of money and diagnoses spurious problems which call for unnecessary medial treatment. How does he reconcile his need to maximize his earning potential with the need to provide what is best for his patient?

- In order to secure a major new construction contract, a salesperson must entertain the client's buying manager with a weekend all-expenses paid holiday. Should this be considered ethical business practice in Britain? Or in South America? Cultural definitions of ethical conduct can differ markedly between countries.

With expanding media availability and an increasingly media-literate audience, it is becoming easier to expose examples of unethical business practice. Moreover, our expectations of business organizations are continually increasing. Many television audiences appear to enjoy watching programmes that reveal alleged unethical practices of household-name companies.

Firms are responding to increasing levels of ethical awareness by trying to put their own house in order. The following are some examples of how firms have gone about the task.

- Many companies have identified segments of their market that are prepared to pay a premium price in order to buy a product that has been produced in an ethical manner, or from a company that has adopted ethical practices. In the food sector, many consumers would consider the treatment of cattle grown for meat to be inhuman and unethical and would be happy to buy from a supplier who they knew acted ethically as to the manner in which the cattle were raised and slaughtered.

- Greater attention to training can make clear to staff just what is expected of them; for example, that it is unethical (and in the long term, commercially damaging) for an insurance company's sales personnel to try and sell to a person a policy that does not really suit their needs. Training may emphasize the need to spend a lot of time finding out just what the true needs of the customer are.

- More effective control and reward systems can help to reduce unethical practices within an organization. For example, sales personnel employed by a financial services company on a commission-only basis are more likely to try to sell a policy to a customer, regardless of the customer's needs, than a salaried employee who can take a longer-term view of the relationship between the company and its clients.

There are many documented cases to show that acting ethically need not conflict with a company's profit objectives, and indeed can add to profitability (e.g. Porter and Kramer, 2006).

Some societies can effectively use social pressure to bring about compliance with ethical **codes of conduct**. For example, it has been noted that in many traditional Far Eastern cultures, the distinction between an individual's social role and their business role is less clearly defined than it would be in most western countries. Therefore, acting unethically in business may bring shame on an individual, which may be a powerful incentive to act ethically. In modern western societies, there tends to be a clearer distinction between an individual's work and social environments, therefore social pressures alone may be insufficient to bring about compliance.

Over time, the ethics of a society tend to be incorporated into its laws. Initially, a group of companies acting through a trade association may develop an industry sector code of conduct. Codes of conduct do not in themselves have the force of law, but they can be very important to businesses. In the first place, they can help to raise the standards of an industry by imposing a discipline on signatories to a code not to indulge in irresponsible marketing practices, which—although legal—act against the long-term interests of the industry and its customers. Second, business organizations are often happy to accept restrictions imposed by voluntary codes of practice as these are seen as preferable to restrictions imposed by laws. The tobacco industry in the UK for a long time avoided statutory controls on cigarette advertising because of the existence of its voluntary code, which imposed restrictions on tobacco advertising. Third, voluntary codes of conduct can offer a cheaper and quicker means of resolving disputes between a company and its customers, compared with more formal legal channels. For example, the UK mobile phone sector has agreed a code of conduct with the industry regulator Ofcom that allows resolution of complaints about alleged mis-selling of phone services.

One industry sector that has frequently been accused of unethical practice is the car repair business. As cars become increasingly sophisticated, the typical customer may have little knowledge about the precise nature of a problem with their car, and may have to trust the car repairer's diagnosis and their subsequent solution. It is not surprising, therefore, that there is often a knowledge imbalance, and some car repairers have been accused of acting unethically by talking customers into having repairs undertaken which are not really needed, and which the customer cannot realistically evaluate afterwards. Car repairers in the UK who subscribe to the voluntary code of the Vehicle Builders and Repairers Association agree, among other things to: give clear estimates of prices; inform customers as soon as possible if additional costs are likely to be incurred; and complete work in a timely manner. In the event of a dispute between a customer and a member of the Association, a conciliation service is available which reduces the need to resort to legal remedies. However, in April 2005, the UK National Consumer Council accused the motor industry of failing adequately to regulate itself, by providing 'shoddy services and rip-off charges'. The council pledged to submit a 'super complaint' to the

Figure 3.1 **In market sectors which are dominated by basically similar product offers, an ethical positioning may give a business a competitive advantage in the eyes of some customer segments.** Many people would regard the major coffee shop chains as being essentially similar in what they offer, and many customers may question the disparity between the seemingly high price charged to consumers for a cup of coffee and the low price that third-world producers receive for raw coffee beans. Starbucks has developed a loyal following of customers for whom the atmosphere of its stores warrants a premium price. However, the company is conscious of critics who point to low prices paid to producers, and addresses this by offering 'Fairtrade' certified coffee. Fairtrade seeks to improve the lives of coffee growers by ensuring that they receive a fair price for their harvest. For many western consumers, this ethical positioning is a basis for differentiating Starbucks from other coffee shops. (*Source:* courtesy of Starbucks Coffee Company)

Office of Fair Trading (OFT) that would force the OFT to investigate its allegations, unless the industry took prompt remedial action. This raised the possibility of a licensing system for car repairers, something the industry had resisted so far and realized would be more onerous than a voluntary code of conduct.

Marketing's responsibility for customers' privacy and security

In a technological environment in which information about customers can be very quickly collected and disseminated, concerns have been expressed about the **privacy** of consumers and the security of data that is held about them. Firms have a responsibility to respect customers' privacy and their personal data, and this moral responsibility is increasingly being enshrined in codes of conduct and legislation.

There is nothing new in consumers' expectations that companies will treat their personal data as confidential and ensure its safe storage. Stories of banks' unshredded confidential waste being left out in the street where criminals as well as refuse collectors can obtain it have raised alarm among consumers. Today, personal information is likely to be held on servers which are accessible remotely by a range of authorized employees and unauthorized hackers. Instead of having laboriously to break into several bank branches to obtain large volumes of customer data, there have been many reported cases (and probably many more unreported cases) of skilled hackers being able to access a bank's database and view the records of thousands or even millions of customers (*Financial Times*, 2007). Where customer information is held on transportable discs, huge amounts of data can accidentally or deliberately end up in the wrong hands. In November 2007, many people in the UK were concerned to hear that the government had 'lost' two CDs containing personal information of 25 million recipients of government benefits. There was concern that this information could be used by criminals to wrongly impersonate another person and obtain credit or benefits to which they were not entitled.

There is also concern by some consumers that their personal data may be used irresponsibly—if not in a criminal way, certainly in a way that they would consider unethical. Junk mail, spam e-mail, and uninvited telephone sales calls may be considered intrusive by many, and can result from a company using personal data for a purpose for which it was never originally intended or authorized. Of course, much 'junk mail' is welcomed, and a survey by the Direct Marketing Association even claimed that a majority of UK consumers actually liked receiving it (DMA, 2007). However, most consumers would expect that if they gave their personal information and contact details to a bank when they took out a new credit card, the bank would act responsibly and not then pass on this information to a double glazing company who would use the details to make sales calls to them.

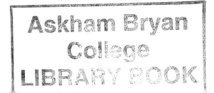

Intrusive advertising messages may be linked to **guerrilla marketing**. This has been defined as a way of getting a message through to the target audience when the audience would least be expecting a selling message (Levinson, 2007). Instead of perceptually filtering out what might be seen as a sales message, the target may be more amenable to persuasion. When guerrilla tactics are linked to the Internet, the results can be even more ethically questionable, as illustrated by the case of FriendGreetings.com. The company had built up a list of e-mail addresses and thousands of people followed its link to a greeting card which the company claimed was waiting for the recipient. Users were then invited to install an ActiveX control in order to view their e-card. Two lengthy end-user licence agreements were displayed stating that by running the application the user is giving permission for a similar e-mail to be sent to all addresses found in the user's Outlook address book. Of course, most users would not bother to read the licence agreement and therefore allowed numerous unwanted e-mails to be sent from their e-mail address. Such a 'worm', which creates a flood of unwanted e-mails, can be just as much a nuisance as a virus. Guerrilla tactics had achieved their aim of attracting attention. As the message took the form of an e-card sent by somebody that the user knew, they did not suspect that clicking onto the link would result in anything untoward occurring. Apart from being unethical in many people's minds, there is an argument that the approach adopted by FriendGreetings.com may be self-defeating. Even though the user had technically given their consent, unethical practices may tarnish the company's brand reputation and turn away many more potential customers.

The issue of privacy has also been raised by firms' attempts to collect information about them in a covert way. Marketers have used technology covertly to probe individuals' behaviour, but critics have argued that 'Big Brother' techniques may be exploiting consumers without their agreement. Many users of the Internet may be unaware that cookies lodged in their computer are 'spying' on them, trying to understand their buying behaviour. When an Internet service provider flashes a banner advert for car rental on a user's screen, it may not have appeared by chance, but an analysis of their previous search behaviour that led the system to deduce that the user was in the process of looking for a rental car. Similarly, Closed Circuit Television (CCTV) has been used by researchers to study how people move around a supermarket and the processes used in searching for products. Would you be happy in the knowledge that all of your indecisions, strained facial expressions, and bad tempers were being recorded, possibly to be replayed over and over again by researchers? In a nation which has been gripped by voyeuristic 'reality' television programmes such as 'Big Brother', it is not surprising that businesses should also try and gain a better insight into behaviour that might previously have been considered private. However, it can be very difficult to define at what point such practices become intrusive and irresponsible. Over time, there has been a tendency for the public to have higher expectations about how their privacy will be respected.

The response of marketers to issues of privacy and security has followed the familiar pattern of some firms developing best practice which has then been used as a basis for industry association codes of conduct, and where these have not worked, legislation has followed.

The first stage of this process, developing best practice, may be achieved by companies in a sector that have the profit margins (and the client base) to support their efforts at doing more than the minimum required by legislation. Within the banking sector, a bank such as Coutts, which has targeted high-wealth individuals with high expectations about privacy, could afford to implement more rigorous security and privacy procedures than a bank targeting mass-market customers with more basic banking services. Over time, the standards of the up-market banks would be expected to filter down to other banks, as customers' expectations rise. Widespread evidence of bad practice within a sector may lead the key players in the sector to cooperate in the development of a shared code of conduct that will avoid the whole sector being tarnished by the bad practice of a few firms. In the case of the banking sector, this has been achieved through the Banking Code, developed and monitored by the British Banking Association (www.bba.org.uk). This includes, among other things, a responsibility of member banks who subscribe to the code to treat customers' personal information as private and confidential, and operate secure and reliable banking and payment systems.

Voluntary codes of conduct have not managed to protect individuals' privacy in all sectors at all times, and one consequence of this failure has been legislation with which all designated companies must comply. Within the EU, the European Convention for Individuals with regard to Automatic Processing of Personal Data, implemented through Directive 95/46/EC, provides a framework for data privacy and security. This has been implemented in the UK in the 1988 **Data Protection** Act, and policed by the Data Protection Commissioner. The Act covers electronically stored data which can be used to identify a living person, including names, birthday and anniversary dates, addresses, telephone numbers, fax numbers, e-mail addresses, etc. A number of principles guide companies' use of data, and require, among other things, that personal data shall be processed fairly and lawfully, and shall not be used for any purpose that is not compatible with the original purpose. There is a requirement for companies to keep accurate records that are not unnecessarily excessive in detail, and shall not be kept for longer than is necessary for the purpose of collecting it. Appropriate technical and organizational measures must be taken against unauthorized or unlawful processing of personal data and against its accidental loss or destruction.

Legislation and voluntary codes of conduct can provide a dilemma for marketing managers who must reconcile the need to protect individuals' privacy and security with the need to make goods and services easily available. The only really secure way of holding data is to create a barrier to the outside world that nobody can penetrate. The only really secure form of Internet banking is a system that is not accessible from outside a bank's offices. Of course, this would defeat the whole purpose of Internet banking, and firms will find themselves reducing the barriers to access from the outside world, thus improving accessibility for legitimate customers, but also facilitating unauthorized access. Some customers may be reassured by lengthy security procedures to gain access to their accounts. Others may simply give up and either not buy, or go elsewhere.

Marketing's responsibilities to vulnerable people

We have seen that the basic principles of marketing are based on an assumption that customers know what they want and are able to evaluate the extent to which a product will meet their needs. Unfortunately, many people may not be able or willing to make a proper evaluation of a product and its likely impact on their physical and mental well-being. Some people may find themselves excluded from being able to buy in a market, leading to undesirable social consequences. Marketing managers are frequently faced with issues about what responsibilities—if any—they should have towards people who may not be able to make a free and fully informed choice by themselves.

The term **vulnerable customer** can be loosely used to describe any individual over whom a company has a high level of power which leaves the individual unable effectively to apply his own judgement. When anybody is taken out of their comfort zone or their area of expertise or knowledge base, they can potentially become vulnerable. In the UK, a 2007 report of an All Party Parliamentary Inquiry on Corporate Responsibility identified a number of generic bases for defining categories of vulnerable customers:

- *Vulnerabilities of personality*—an inherent factor within someone that makes them vulnerable to falling into consumption patterns that do them harm, e.g. gamblers, alcoholics, people with eating disorders.

- *Vulnerabilities of experience/understanding*—where either lack of worldly experience or barriers to understanding leave people vulnerable to people or processes that may harm them, e.g. children, people without financial education or maturity, people without good language or literacy skills.

- *Vulnerabilities of physical disorders*—where physical reactions to normal circumstances may lead to harm, e.g. people with allergies, immunity deficiency, certain disabilities.

- *Vulnerabilities of access*—where lack of financial resources or other barriers to accessing key basic services exist, leading to harm that goes beyond mere inconvenience.

The parliamentary committee report suggested that commercial organizations owed responsibilities towards these vulnerable groups. It pointed to a number of examples of good business practice, including Barclays Bank, which had introduced a basic bank account for groups who would not normally be accepted for full banking services. The bank had consulted extensively to ensure that this basic bank account met the target users' needs. It also pointed favourably to the mobile phone company O$_2$'s policies towards children. Children were considered vulnerable, on account of the potential health risks, and children's uncritical acceptance of advertising claims. The company worked with the Home Office and children's charities to draw up a code of practice to regulate the provision of content on mobile phones, e.g. any commercial content rated '18' has to be behind content controls which can only be accessed by someone verified to be over 18. O_2 agreed to a policy of only advertising in magazines or between television programmes where more than 50% of the audience is over 16.

Companies may attempt to develop voluntary codes of practice towards vulnerable groups, but in fiercely competitive markets this may be difficult to achieve, in which case legislation may be imposed. As an example, gas, water, and electricity suppliers in the UK must comply with the government regulator Ofgem's guidelines before they can withhold supplies from certain designated vulnerable groups.

Marketing's responsibility to employees

We saw in Chapter 1 that for many firms, especially service-based firms, marketing cannot easily be separated from human resource management. Where customers mainly judge a company on the basis of its front-line personnel, the recruitment, training, monitoring, and rewarding of employees should be something over which the marketing department has a strong influence, even if the marketing manager does not have final authority. It should also follow that the marketing manager owes some responsibility for the welfare of employees. Again, a fine balance often has to be made between what customers want, and what a responsible employer should provide for its employees. There is a widely held view that if employees are not happy with their jobs, customers will never be uppermost in their minds. Nevertheless, many have recognized the three-way fight between the firm, the employees, and the customer. Delivering goods and services is thus a 'compromise between partially conflicting parties' (Bateson, 1989).

In less developed countries with abundant supplies of low-cost and replaceable labour, employees have been expected to carry out tasks for customers that would be considered irresponsible in western developed countries. Circus acts in India, for example, have involved employees being shot from canons and performing daredevil stunts on motorbikes without safety equipment. Customers may have loved the acts, the employee may have welcomed the money they earned, but is it responsible for marketing to promote something that involves high levels of risk to employees?

Two recent issues illustrate the influences of responsibilities towards employees on the marketing function. First, many service-based companies have been keen to allow smoking in their establishments, on the basis that this is what a significant number of their customers want. For those customers who prefer to be in a smoke-free environment, separate non-smoking areas can be offered. But what about the effects of smoke

Figure 3.2 **The subject of smoking has caused a lot of anguish for operators of pubs and restaurants.** With mounting evidence of the harmful effects of smoking, and passively breathing in other people's smoke, bars may have been accused of endangering the health of its employees, and of their non-smoking customers. But despite the risks of being sued by employees for the effects of working in a smoky environment, most bars continued to allow smoking. Many realized that the bar was a haven for many people to smoke, away from homes and offices where such behaviour may have been frowned upon. There was also a suggestion that heavy smokers were also heavy drinkers, adding to the profits of a bar. As for protecting the workforce from the effects of smoking, employees were themselves quite likely to be smokers. It seemed that despite widespread recognition that smoking was 'bad', and mounting social pressure to discourage smoking, allowing it in bars satisfied the needs of many bar-owners and customers. Some bars and restaurants had bravely taken the moral high ground by introducing smoking bans, or at least designated no-smoking areas. But it took legislation from 2007 to force bars and restaurants to ban smoking completely. Should it have taken legislation to bring about such socially responsible behaviour by bars? With beer sales in pubs falling in the UK during the following year by over 10%, were bars right to hang on to smoking, evidenced by the desertion of bars after the ban by people who no longer felt that a bar met their needs? (*Source*: © Photodisc)

on the health of employees who serve customers in a smoky environment? There is growing evidence of the effects of passive smoking on individuals who are in the vicinity of smokers, so is it responsible for a firm to expose employees to such risk? In 2007, a ban on smoking was introduced in public places in England, Scotland, and Wales. Some companies had already voluntarily introduced bans, but following the ban, some companies, such as Gala Bingo, reported sharp falls in revenue, as smokers stayed at home where they were free to smoke. Without a change in the law, would marketers have been happy to go on satisfying their smoking customers' needs, while putting the health of their employees at risk? A second example which is currently exercising the minds of many marketing managers is the issue of 24/7 access to goods and services. What happens when a company's customers want access to its goods and services 24 hours a day, and they want immediate access, not a promise of delivery tomorrow or some time in the future? One consequence is often stress at work for those who are charged with responding to a company's promises, which it must make if it is to stay alive in a competitive business environment. The 24/7 culture has had a big impact on employees' lifestyles, with many individuals having to adjust to varying and often un-social shift patterns. Research undertaken by the Future Foundation (2004) predicted that by 2020, over 13 million people in the UK will be operating in an out-of-hours economy (outside the traditional Monday–Friday hours of 9 a.m. to 6 p.m.), compared to the 7 million who did so in 2003. Another study, by the British Industrial Society, showed that juggling home and work demands was a major source of stress for 70% of respondents, while half cited unrealistic deadlines and constant time pressures as an additional factor (British Industrial Society, 2001). The Future Foundation research found that while relatively wealthy customers benefit from 24/7 service availability, the downside of a vibrant 24/7 economy is an army of low-paid staff, many working for little above minimum wage, often trying to juggle multiple part-time jobs with study or looking after children. Responsible employers have sought to alleviate stress, setting standards for others to follow. This has not been entirely altruistic, as companies have recognized hidden costs to their operations that can result from high levels of stress at work. However, in some fiercely competitive business sectors, a voluntary approach to stress management has been insufficient, so the law (in the UK, the Health and Safety at Work Regulations 1999, specifically regs 3, 4, 13, and 19) is now requiring them to take some responsibility for employees' stress at work.

▣ Marketing's responsibility for preserving the competitiveness of markets

Marketing is all about markets—the space where buyers and sellers come together and where market forces ensure that buyers have available to them a wide choice of products, and they choose the products of the seller who offers them the best value. Unfortunately, fiercely competitive markets can be bad news for sellers, who may have their work cut out raising their efficiency and lowering their costs so that they can offer better value to discerning buyers than is offered by their competitors. Most business people would publicly acknowledge that competitive markets are a good thing, but quietly, many would be only too happy to come to an agreement with their competitors to limit the amount of competition between them. For sellers, a cosy **cartel** between them will put less pressure on them to reduce their costs. For buyers, the consequence would most likely be less choice and/or higher prices. Is it responsible for marketers to seek to undermine the power of market forces?

Consider the case of fruit and vegetable markets, which in many towns would comprise several stallholders competing against each other on price and quality. Just imagine that the market was the only source of food for miles around, and all the traders in it got together to agree prices that they would charge. They may agree, for example, that instead of them all selling a wide range of fruit and vegetables, each trader would sell only two or three ranges, thereby reducing their operating costs and reducing the amount of competition for each product. When customers visit the market, they will initially find less choice, and also prices would most probably have risen, because of the reduced level of competition for each product. This simple example may sound like an unrealistic scenario, but such collusion between suppliers is the basis for many attempts by businesses to undermine the power of markets, and to leave consumers worse off than they otherwise might have been.

A fine balance often exists between cooperation among firms which leads to lower prices/better products for consumers, and irresponsible cooperation, which leads to collusion and a reduction in consumers' choice. Cooperation between companies may result in greater benefits for consumers; for example, life is made easier for bank customers who can use their ATM card at the ATMs of competing banks, and not just the bank which issued the card. However, government regulators at national (and EU) levels are increasingly taking action against irresponsible actions by businesses that have the effect of restricting competition in a market. Recent cases investigated have highlighted irresponsible and illegal behaviour by many well-known companies.

- In 2007, OFT fined British Airways £121.5 million for colluding with Virgin Atlantic over the imposition of fuel surcharges. BA and Virgin appeared to increase their charges in step from when they were first introduced in May 2004. BA introduced a £2.50 surcharge on 13 May and Virgin did the same thing six days later. By April 2006, both airlines were charging £35 extra on a long-haul flight. In addition to the fine, British Airways was faced with a potential compensation bill of £80 million from customers who had been overcharged. Virgin escaped a fine from the regulator, because it had 'blown the whistle' on the price-fixing arrangement and provided evidence for the OFT. The investigation revealed a number of bad practices within British Airways, and shortly after publication of the report, the commercial director and communications director of BA resigned.

- Also in 2007, the OFT fined a number of UK supermarkets and dairy companies a total of just over £116 million after finding evidence that the retail chains, processors, and dairy companies had colluded to fix prices among themselves. It estimated that as a result of price fixing, the average additional cost of milk to each household was £11.25 during the period 2002–2003. The actions of the retailers and dairy producers has resulted in consumers paying an extra 3p on a pint of milk, 15p on a quarter of a pound of butter, and 15p on a half pound of cheese.

These cases illustrate the growing expectations of regulators that marketers should act responsibly by putting consumers' interests above what may be a natural desire to control a market. Actually detecting **anti-competitive practices** by marketers in the first place can be quite difficult. If all airlines change their fuel surcharge at the same time, is this evidence of collusion, or are they all simply responding simultaneously to the same external price pressures? Often, collusion is only revealed when one party decides to inform the regulatory authorities about what is going on. In return for being a 'whistleblower', an organization may escape punishment, in the way that Virgin Atlantic did not face the fines imposed on British Airways. Virgin could also claim to be acting in the public interest by exposing irresponsible practices, even though it had initially been part of that practice.

Responsible communication

The final aspect of responsible marketing that we will consider is in respect of firms' communication. In an ideal world, a company would act responsibly, and communicate honestly with its customers and key stakeholders. Unfortunately, there are too many cases where a company acts in an irresponsible manner, and then uses communication dishonestly to try and portray itself as acting responsibly. Responsibility in communication can be analysed at two levels: at a strategic level, whereby the company communicates an overall image of responsibility; and at a more tactical level, which involves the company acting responsibly in the way it communicates specific product features to its customers. We will look at these in turn.

Companies often go to great lengths in their communication to associate their brand with responsibility. Some organizations, such as the Body Shop, Innocent Smoothies, and Starbucks have associated themselves with good causes, and appeal to segments of customers who are happy to pay a few pennies more for the peace of mind, or social recognition which may come from association with a socially responsible brand. Starbucks, for example, has gone out of its way to stress its social responsibility through the use of 'Fairtrade' coffee. It has been suggested that organizations may be quite keen to support good causes that are popular with the public in general, or the particular groups of customers that they target. Many consumer goods companies, for example, have supported child and animal welfare charities, knowing that this will be popular with their target audiences. However, there may be other groups, such as refugees or the mentally ill, that represent even more deserving cases for a company to be associated with, but in general these groups have been shunned by the corporate sector.

Of course, where a company communicates a message to support a good cause, but does not in fact deliver its promise, this can add to criticism of the company by pressure groups who can now accuse it not only of the original bad practice, but also hypocrisy and dishonesty. In the case of companies making unjustified claims about their ecological responsibility, these claims may be dismissed as 'green wash' or 'green tosh'.

Communicating a position of responsibility can be a very long-term process, and a company cannot expect instant results from attempts to promote an image of responsibility. The true level of perceived responsibility can be tested during a crisis, when investigative journalists may dig deep into a company's past in the hope of digging up bad practice, which may help create create a further news story to add to the crisis in which a company finds itself. A company that had a consistent policy of acting responsibly would have little to worry about, but a company with a record of bad practice cannot expect a short burst of Public Relations to overcome its problems. For example, the train crash that occurred in the UK at Hatfield, involving a London–Edinburgh train in 2000 came following a series of widely reported failures by the privatized Railtrack company, which was perceived as putting profits before safety. The crash, in which four people were killed, appeared to be an indication of everything that was wrong with Railtrack. Partly because of the public's general distrust of Britain's railway operators, the industry, through its regulatory agencies, was forced to respond with drastic and costly measures, including system-wide speed restrictions. The industry was under intense scrutiny by a media that sensed that more bad practice would be found if it looked hard enough. It took several years for the sector to recover its trust in the eyes of its users. Railtrack, which was seen as incompetent, while rewarding its directors and shareholders, was subsequently taken into state ownership. By contrast, the coach operator National Express had a long history of safe operation, with very few major causes for complaints by its customers. It had been a long while since the public had read stories of overcrowded coaches travelling at excessive speed, driven by poorly trained, overworked, and tired drivers. When one of the company's coaches crashed in January 2007, killing two passengers and injuring several others, the media was generally sympathetic to the company. Senior executives were made available to answer media questions, the company provided an efficient and effective helpline for customers and the relatives of those affected. Above all else, the company had invested in a good reputation and even the most adversarial investigative reporters could not find a history of irresponsible management to prolong the crisis and open a 'can of worms' that would come back to haunt the company.

On some occasions, industry groups have come together to communicate a message of responsibility for the sector as a whole. As an example, many pub operators and alcoholic drinks manufacturers in the UK are members of the Portman Group, which has used a levy on members to pay for an advertising campaign to promote responsible drinking. One reason why members of the group are keen to promote social responsibility in drinking is to deter potentially harmful new legislation, such as restricted opening hours of pubs, or higher taxes on beer, which could harm members' interests. Industry-wide communication of responsible behaviour may work where there is a consensus within the sector, but may be difficult to achieve where this consensus is lacking. For example, the British Retail Federation had difficulty in communicating its members' views on proposed food-labelling regulations, because its members were divided over

Figure 3.3 Like many bars, this one loudly promotes a 'happy-hour' period during which alcohol is sold at a reduced price. For pub operators, such promotions may be vital to boost turnover, especially if all bars in the area are offering equally low prices. Unfortunately, one consequence of cheap alcohol and 'buy one, get one free' offers is an increase in 'binge drinking', with many town centres becoming noisy and violent areas at night-time, fuelled by excessive drinking. For any individual pub, how does it balance the need for aggressive price promotion to customers with the need to appear socially responsible, for fear of further government regulation of the sector? Adverts for alcohol now routinely include warnings about the consequences for the customer of excessive drinking, but often in much smaller print than the main price information. Should a pub simply stop '2 for 1' offers and earn a higher margin on a smaller volume of sales? Although this may seem to be a responsible and profitable approach, it is unlikely to work if other pubs continue with their cheap beer promotions—determined drinkers will simply make their way to the cheapest pub, or pick up their beer at a nearby supermarket. To illustrate the complexity of the task facing the sector, bar owners in some towns have voluntarily got together to try and agree collectively to stop price promotions that many believe lead to binge drinking. Agreement of all bar owners would be crucial, because otherwise drinkers would simply find the cheapest outlet, and other bars would be forced to defensively cut their prices to retain business. But did government see this as an example of good, socially motivated cooperation? Not the Office of Fair Trading, which gave a veiled threat to a group of Essex bar-owners that they could be prosecuted for operating a cartel by agreeing to keep prices artificially high.

what would be the best policy to pursue. If a sector cooperates too closely to communicate its views, it may be accused of illegally operating a cartel that has the effect of restricting consumers' choice (see above).

Issues about responsibility in communications also affect organizations at a much more operational level. Indeed, it could be argued that the long-term image communicated by a company is largely determined by a series of possibly isolated tactical communications. The issue of responsibility in everyday advertising is of regular concern to companies and the general public at large. Three or four decades ago, UK companies might have been able to get away with advertising claims which, while not factually incorrect, were misleading because they may have missed out vital information. They may also have been able to get away with statements that are today considered socially unacceptable (for example, adverts that are demeaning to women or ethnic minorities may have been considered acceptable then, but are not now).

In the UK, there are a number of voluntary codes which set standards for responsible advertising. The two most important codes affecting advertisers are administered by the Advertising Standards Authority (ASA) through two Committees of Advertising Practice: CAP—Broadcast (responsible for the TV and radio advertising) and CAP—Non-broadcast (responsible for non-broadcast advertisements, sales promotions, and direct marketing). The ASA codes are subscribed to by most organizations involved in advertising, including the Advertising Association, the Institute of Practitioners in Advertising, and the associations representing publishers of newspapers and magazines, the outdoor advertising industry, and direct marketing.

The Code of Advertising Practice (Non-broadcast) requires that all advertisements appearing in members' publications should be legal, honest, decent, and truthful. A case considered by the ASA in 2008 illustrates how the ASA interprets this. An advert in the *Daily Mail* for Ryanair under the headline 'Hottest back to school fares . . . one way fares £10' featured a picture of a teenage girl or woman standing in a classroom and wearing a version of a school uniform consisting of a short tartan skirt, a cropped short sleeved shirt and tie, and long white socks. The ASA considered the model's clothing, together with the setting of the ad in a classroom strongly suggested that she was a schoolgirl and considered that her appearance and pose, in conjunction with the heading 'Hottest', appeared to link teenage girls with sexually provocative behaviour. It considered the advert was likely to cause serious or widespread offence, and was in breach of the Code's sections governing social responsibility and decency.

Numerous other forms of voluntary controls on advertising exist. Some professional trade associations have codes which impose restrictions on how they can advertise. Solicitors, for example, were previously not allowed to advertise at all, but now can do so within limits defined by the Law Society.

In general, the system of voluntary regulation of advertising has worked well in the UK. For advertisers, voluntary codes can allow more flexibility and opportunities to have an input to the code. However, the Control of Misleading Advertisements Regulations 1988 (as amended) provides the legislative back-up to the self-regulatory system in respect of advertisements which mislead. The Regulations require the OFT to investigate complaints, and empower the OFT to seek, if necessary, an injunction from the courts against publication of an advertisement. In the case of television advertising, the Office of Communications (Ofcom) is the statutory regulator for broadcast advertising in the UK and has delegated its powers to the ASA. In addition, there are a number of laws that influence the content of advertisements in Britain. For example, the Trade Descriptions Act makes false statements in an advertisement an offence, while the Consumer Credit Act lays down quite precise rules about the way in which credit can be advertised.

Irresponsible communication by companies is about more than just misleading advertising. Many companies have been criticized for using dubious, high-pressure sales techniques (see Marketing in Action case below). Again, such practices may

MARKETING in ACTION

Irresponsible selling of payment protection insurance

Companies can sometimes be too eager to promote products that are not at all suitable for customers. Many salespeople have responded to bonus incentives offered by their employers to vigorously achieve sales which looked good at the time, but later came back to haunt the company. One of the key characteristics of a good salesperson is an ability to listen and to gain a good understanding of a buyer's needs; but what happens when the product on sale is complex and the buyer does not have the willingness or ability to understand exactly what s/he is buying? Furthermore, what happens when you couple this with a salesperson who would rather earn his/her sales commission as easily as possible rather than probing the true needs of the customer? The result has been a series of mis-selling scandals that have tarnished the reputation of a number of business sectors, especially financial services.

In the early 2000s, Payment Protection Insurance (PPI) became the latest financial product to be associated with irresponsible selling. The purpose of PPI is to cover loan or credit card repayments in the event of a borrower suffering an accident, sickness, or unemployment. It was estimated in 2008 that there were around 20 million PPI policies in the UK, generating over £5 billion a year for the companies involved (www.moneysavingexpert.com, 2008). There is nothing wrong with the principle of PPI, which can give valuable peace of mind to individuals who suddenly find that they cannot afford to repay their loan when they become unemployed. Unfortunately, many PPI policies were sold by sales staff who did not undertake a rigorous analysis of whether the policy was right for a customer. In many cases, a buyer would pay for a policy, but hidden in the small print would be clauses that would effectively prevent them from ever being able to make a claim on the policy. For example, self-employed people would most probably not be covered against unemployment, and many salespeople might not have mentioned that the policy would not pay out for existing medical conditions. A seller should have enquired about a customer's medical history, but many skipped over this, eager to earn their commission.

The term *caveat emptor* ('let the buyer be aware') has been used to excuse the situation where a salesperson sold an individual an item that was not at all suited to their needs. It was assumed to be the buyer's fault for buying wrongly, rather than the seller's fault for selling wrongly. The balance is now tilting in the consumer's favour as society's expectations of sellers rise. The Financial Services Authority (FSA) has a strict code of conduct that regulated sellers of financial services must follow. FSA guidelines require that a seller must establish the needs of a seller before completing a sale. Clearly, in the case of many PPI policies, these guidelines had not been complied with. The over-enthusiastic selling of PPI policies resulted in big fines being imposed by the FSA, and thousands of compensation claims from customers who claimed that they had been mis-sold a policy that was worthless to them. Companies were forced to rethink the way they managed their sales personnel, but this really just involved going back to traditional best practice for the sales force—listening to the customer and understanding what they really need; training the sales force with greater product knowledge; and structuring their rewards to recognize a balance between the need for short-term incentives and long-term relationships.

not be strictly illegal, but society has increasingly high expectations about the behaviour of salespeople. In previous times, a buyer who had made a bad purchase may have blamed themselves, but today, they may argue that the salesperson was irresponsible in selling them something which the salesperson knew was not suitable for the customer. Irresponsible selling may eventually cost the company money in terms of the poor reputation it gains, and possible fines from regulatory bodies.

◼ Chapter summary and links to other chapters

The aim of this chapter has been to provide a counterbalance to the first two chapters of this book which have portrayed marketing managers as single mindedly seeking to satisfy customers' needs as a means of meeting their organizations' objectives. This chapter has shown how listening to customers and supplying them with what they say they want might actually be considered irresponsible and this chapter has reviewed reasons why this might be so. Marketers are increasingly being expected to act responsibly with a high standard of ethics. It usually makes sound business sense for a marketer to act responsibly rather than irresponsibly. Where there is a tendency for marketers to act irresponsibly, voluntary industry sector codes of conduct may help to raise standards throughout the sector. If this is insufficient incentive to change firms' behaviour, the law may subsequently force companies to change.

Just as Chapters 1 and 2 were integrative chapters in defining the tasks and processes of marketing, this chapter is also integrative. Responsibility permeates all aspects of marketing, so we will return to the subject when we look at responsibility in promotion (Chapter 11); responsible pricing (Chapter 9), problems of abuse of power within a distribution channel (Chapter 10); and product design (Chapter 8). As we saw in this chapter, undertaking market research can raise ethical issues and these will be further explored in Chapter 5.

▢ KEY PRINCIPLES OF MARKETING

- Marketing responsibility does not necessarily imply any conflict between a company's profit objectives and its social responsibilities.
- Ethics is a moral code which defines what is right and what is wrong.
- Voluntary codes of conduct are generally preferred to legislation as means of bringing about social responsibility by firms.
- The customer is not always 'king'—they may not know what is really good for them, or what patterns of consumption are acceptable to society.
- Marketers have a responsibility to preserve freedom and choice in a marketplace.

CASE STUDY

Problems in the air for low-cost flights?

Global warming has emerged as a major concern to consumers throughout the world. Initially, awareness of the causes and consequences of global warming was confined to a small part of the population, but linkages with the destructive Tsunami of December 2004, and Hurricane Katrina of 2005 brought home to many people the possible long-term harmful consequences of excessive emissions of CO_2 to the atmosphere. Global warming was no longer a humorous subject where people in the developed countries of northern Europe and the United States focused on the benign consequences of mild winters and exotic new plants that they would be able to grow. Destructive winds, rising sea levels, and devastation of low-lying areas were increasingly coming to be seen as a consequence of our prodigious use of fossil fuels.

The reduction of CO_2 emissions had already been taken on board by many manufacturing companies, the largest of whom had seen reductions through a system of carbon trading initiated by the Kyoto treaty; but one business sector—civil aviation—had been quite notable for its apparent irresponsibility in not embracing the principles of reducing carbon emissions. Critics of the sector pointed out that as a result of worldwide agreements, aviation fuel was not taxed, in contrast with the steep taxation on most other forms of fuel. Although aircraft had become more efficient in their use of fuel during the 1990s, this was more than offset by booming demand for flights with no frills airlines such as easyJet and Ryanair. It seemed that the budget airline companies were very effective in communicating their low-price message to customers who filled their planes, often with more thought about a cheap weekend break by the Mediterranean, rather than the unknown and remote possibilities of global warming. Indeed, the general public seemed to be somewhat hypocritical about the effects of global warming. Some still thought that the problem would go away, and may have recalled previous 'scares' such as the imminent depletion of fossil fuels and the effects of 'acid rain', neither of which had really affected most peoples' lives, and had subsequently slipped down the news agenda. Even in respect of 'greenhouse gas' emissions, people may profess to being sympathetic to green causes, but then buy something which is anything but green. As an example, one survey of holidaymakers conducted in 2007 suggested that consideration of greenhouse gas emissions came way behind other evaluation criteria when choosing a holiday, including the ease of obtaining a sun lounger, proximity to the beach, and the range of nightlife available.

How should airlines respond to the apparent threat to their business model that had been thrown up by the issue of global warming? Should they put their head in the sand and hope that the problem would go away? Should they concentrate on giving customers what they have repeatedly said they wanted—cheap flights—and hope that human hedonism would win out over feelings of social responsibility? Or should airlines be on their guard against possible government intervention which could undermine their business model. How could they prevent new legislation? If it was introduced, how could they respond to it?

Politicians were becoming increasingly frustrated by the airlines' seeming lack of willingness to address issues of climate change. Already, the Bishop of London had described air travel as 'immoral', for the way that wealthy western travellers could inflict harm on people in the developed world through climate change. Could a significant number of airline passengers really begin to feel guilty about flying away for a cheap weekend break, and cut back their travelling by air?

In January 2007, the communications battle was stepped up when a UK government minister described Ryanair as 'the irresponsible face of capitalism'. He had argued that while other industries and consumers were cutting down their emissions, Ryanair had expanded at a phenomenal rate, churning out more CO_2 into the atmosphere. Friends of the Earth, in a report 'Aviation and global climate change', noted that commercial jets were adding 600 million tonnes of CO_2 a year to global warming, almost as much as for the whole of Africa. With such negative communication, would Ryanair suffer as people felt guilty about flying, and governments increasingly moved to regulate civil aviation and make it more expensive, especially for the price-sensitive segments that the no-frills airlines had been targeting?

Rarely known to be quiet, the chief executive of Ryanair, Michael O'Leary went on a communications offensive. Dismissing the minister as 'knowing nothing', he presented Ryanair as a friend rather than an enemy of global warming. He argued that travellers should feel reassured that Ryanair used one of the world's most modern and fuel-efficient fleets of aircraft. Moreover, Ryanair's business model of filling seats at the lowest price really meant that the carbon emissions per passenger were much lower than traditional full-service airlines, who often flew half-empty planes; and the fact that budget airlines operated an extensive point-to-point network avoided the costly and environmentally harmful effects of taking two indirect flights via a central hub airport.

The war of words that has ensued over airlines' contribution to global warming demonstrates the difficulty that many ordinary consumers have in evaluating rival environmental claims. Many may have taken to heart governments' and Church leaders' claims that made them feel guilty about flying; but even if hypocritical consumers were happy to carry on flying and were not backing their expressed concerns for climate change with changes in their behaviour, there was certainly a possibility that governments would intervene. Both the UK government and EU Commission had floated the idea of taxing aviation fuel and bringing aircraft emissions within the scope of the EU Emissions Trading Scheme. Some airlines, such as Ryanair, continued to sound off against the government, positioning them as the consumer's champion; but others, including easyJet, sensed the change in mood of the public and government bodies and openly supported the idea of bringing aircraft emissions into the carbon-trading regime. Was easyJet being philanthropic? Was it simply putting out a message that it thought its customers would want to hear, helping them salve their consciences and avoid feelings of guilt? Or was there a shrewd underlying commercial advantage, in which the modern, efficient easyJet fleet may use less than its allotted share of carbon emissions, which it could then sell on to less efficient 'legacy' carriers? Should the company begin planning for higher taxes on flying, and be prepared to reduce its growth plans if some marginal customers decided that a weekend break by the Mediterranean was no longer a luxury that they could afford?

Source: based on the Intergovernmental Panel on Climate Change's (IPCC's) *Special Report on Aviation and the Global Atmosphere*, published 1999. Available at www.unep.ch/ipcc/press/pr6-99.html; *Financial Times*, 'UK minister slapped down for attack on airlines', 5 January 2007; Ryanair corporate website (www.ryanair.com)

Case study review questions

1. If you were the marketing manager of an airline such as Ryanair, how would you address the ecological concerns raised in this article?

2. The case study refers to the apparent hypocrisy of consumers who may claim to be concerned about the environment, but nevertheless continue to fly. What might bring about a narrowing of this gap between what consumers think and what they actually do? How could a company such as easyJet measure and monitor consumers' attitudes?

3. What might be the consequences for the marketing of a budget airline of government policy measures which have the effect of doubling air fares in real terms? Critically discuss how the marketing manager of a budget airline might respond.

CHAPTER REVIEW QUESTIONS

1. Critically discuss the view that there is no such thing as altruism in marketing, but all apparently altruistic acts by marketers are in fact calculated attempts directly or indirectly to improve profitability.

2. What do you understand by the term ethics? Discuss the benefits to a marketing manager of having a thorough understanding of ethics.

3. What should be the response of businesses to pressure groups' claims that their activities are causing ecological damage?

ACTIVITIES

1. You are employed by a phone company as a commission-based sales assistant. The more people you persuade to sign up and switch from other phone companies, the more commission you will be paid. However, you know in your heart that most of the people you are selling to could gain a much better deal with another company. Moreover, you realize that hidden in the small print of the contract are clauses which will result in additional charges to the customer that are not mentioned in the glossy, colourful brochure that you send out.

   As a salesperson, would you consider yourself to be acting ethically by selling something when you know that buyers could find better elsewhere? Is it ethical not to alert buyers to the potentially disadvantageous terms contained in the small print, and just lure them to sign on the dotted line with the bait of free gifts and a glossy brochure?

   What would you do?

2. Select two or three campaigns by environmental pressure groups with which you are familiar, for example Greenpeace, Friends of the Earth, or the Countryside Alliance. Review their websites and recent press releases to assess the effects that their campaigning is likely to have on a manufacturer of consumer goods. How widely do you consider the opinions expressed by these groups represent the population as a whole? If you were a manufacturer, how would you address the issues raised?

3. Select a company with which you are familiar as a customer. Using some the headings in this chapter, undertake an audit to assess how responsible you consider the organization to be in its marketing.

REFERENCES

Bateson, J. E. G. (1989), *Managing Services Marketing: text and readings*, 2nd edn. Fort Worth, TX: Dryden Press.

British Industrial Society (2001), 'Managing Best Practice'. *Occupational Stress*, London: British Industrial Society, (83): 4-23.

Direct Marketing Association (2007), *Census of the UK Direct Marketing Industry*. London: Direct Marketing Association.

Financial Times (2007), 'MI5 Warns Banks of Chinese Hackers', 1 December.

Future Foundation (2004), 'Life in the 24/7? The Shape of Things to Come'. London: Future Foundation.

Laroche, M., Bergeron, J., and Barbaro-Forleo, G. (2001), 'Targeting Consumers who are Willing to Pay More for Environmentally Friendly Products'. *Journal of Consumer Marketing*, 18(6): 503–20.

Levinson, J. C. (2007), 'Guerrilla Marketing', 4th revd edn. London: Piatkus Books.

Porter, M. E. and Kramer, M. R. (2006), 'Strategy and Society: the link between competitive advantage and corporate social responsibility'. *Harvard Business Review*, 84(12) (December): 78–92.

Unruh, G. C. (2008), 'The Biosphere Rules'. *Harvard Business Review*, 86(2) (February): 111–17, 138.

SUGGESTED FURTHER READING

For a general review of ecological issues and their impacts on marketing, the following provide a useful overview of the issues involved:

Hitchcock, D. and Willard, M. (2006), *The Business Guide to Sustainability: practical strategies and tools for organizations*. London: Earthscan.

Rivera-Camino, J. (2007), Re-evaluating Green Marketing Strategy: a stakeholder perspective. *European Journal of Marketing*, 41(11/12): 1328–58.

Freeman, R. E., Pierce, J., and Dodd, R. (2005), *Environmentalism and the New Logic of Business*. Oxford: Oxford University Press.

For a discussion of business ethics the following texts are useful:

Crane, A. and Matten, D. (2006), *Business Ethics,* 2nd edn. Oxford: Oxford University Press.

Stanwick P. and Stanwick S. (2008), *Understanding Business Ethics*. New Jersey: Prentice Hall.

Harrison, R., Newholm, T., and Shaw, D. (2005), *The Ethical Consumer*. London: Sage Publications.

⬚ USEFUL WEB LINKS

Visit the Online Resource Centre for resources that are relevant to this chapter, including web links, multiple choice questions, and additional case studies:

   www.oxfordtextbooks.co.uk/orc/palmer2e/

⬚ KEY TERMS

- **Anti-competitive practices**
- **Cartel**
- **Codes of conduct**
- **Data protection**
- **Ecological responsibility**
- **Ethics**
- **Green consumers**
- **Guerrilla marketing**
- **Privacy**
- **Sustainability**
- **Vulnerable customers**

PART 2

Understanding customers

Buyer behaviour and relationship development

CHAPTER OBJECTIVES

Faced with competing products, it is important for companies to understand how buyers go about choosing between the alternatives. A thorough understanding of buyer behaviour should be reflected in product design, pricing, promotion, and distribution, all of which should satisfy the needs of individuals' buying processes. This chapter explores basic theories of buyer behaviour. Distinctions between personal and organizational buyer behaviour are noted, especially in the composition of the decision-making unit. Companies generally seek to influence buyer behaviour so that the company becomes customers' first choice of supplier. This chapter reviews methods by which companies seek to turn one-off casual buying behaviour into ongoing buyer–seller relationships.

Introduction

A company may think that it has developed the perfect product, one that customers will be queuing up to buy. But despite putting possibly years into new product development, it could find its efforts wasted as buyers reject its product in the few minutes, or sometimes even seconds, that it might take them to choose between competing products. The company may have failed to understand the complex processes by which buyers make purchasing decisions. It may, for example, have underestimated the role played by key **influencers** in the decision process and aimed its marketing effort at those individuals who really do not count for much in the final decision. It may have spent the bulk of its promotional effort at a time when buyers were not at a receptive stage in the buying process.

Companies undertake marketing activities in order to elicit some kind of response from buyers. The ultimate aim of that activity is to persuade customers to buy their products, and to come back again. Most of this book breaks down marketing activities into distinct areas of decisions that have to be made by marketing managers, for example pricing decisions and promotion decisions. However, while companies may break down their planning into small manageable chunks, customers make an assessment based on a holistic view of the total product offer. How customers perceive the whole offer and react to it may be quite different from what the company had expected when it was developing its marketing plan. In the case of sales to commercial buyers, the task of understanding who is involved in the buying process and what procedures are adopted becomes even more complex. Faced with a sometimes bewildering array of choices, buyers seek to simplify the choice process, for example by sticking with brand names with which they are familiar.

In short, buying processes can be complex, involving many people over a sometimes lengthy period of time. Making false assumptions about these processes can result in an otherwise good product not being bought.

This chapter will explore a number of dimensions in the complexity of buying behaviour:

- What factors motivate an individual to seek out a purchase in the first place?
- What sources of information are used in evaluating competing products?
- What is the relative importance attached by decision makers to each of the elements of the product offer?
- What is the set of competing products from which consumers make their final choice?
- Who is involved in making the purchase decision?
- How long does the process of making a decision take?
- How can a seller affect buyers' subsequent behaviour so that it becomes the preferred supplier, tied by a formal or informal relationship?

Buying situations

Of course, **buying processes** vary between products and between individuals. For the purpose of studying buying behaviour, a number of categories of buying situations can be identified.

- **Routine rebuy:** The buyer makes a purchase decision in these situations almost instinctively, without giving the process any thought. It is like routinely buying the same daily newspaper.
- **Modified rebuy:** The buyer may be familiar with a class of product, but this time wants something a little different. For example, she may often buy a tin of paint,

but on this occasion she needs paint specifically for a job in hand which may be novel to her (such as covering external masonry), so she is likely to engage in limited search processes to identify and evaluate alternatives.

- **Completely novel:** The buyer has no previous experience of buying this type of product, so the search process is likely to be longer, with a greater range of information sources being consulted.

In addition, the sophistication of the buying process is influenced by the level of involvement that a buyer has in the product being purchased.

- With high-involvement products, buyers have a close relationship with the product. The manner in which the product is used has the capacity to deeply affect their happiness and they cannot easily ignore the product. Items of clothing and many personal medical services fall into this category.

- Low-involvement products have less consequence for individuals' psychological well-being. If a mistake is made in choosing an unsuitable product, they will not worry about it unduly. They can normally live with the consequences of making a mistake in their washing powder purchase, but a mistake in their choice of outer clothing may affect their self-image.

Involvement is closely associated with risk. High-involvement purchase decisions are seen as being more risky in terms of their outcomes, so buyers are likely to spend more time and effort in trying to avoid a bad purchase for such products.

Further variety in the buying process is evident from the major differences that can occur between private individuals and organizations in the way they make purchase decisions. These differences are considered later in this chapter.

The buying process

The basic processes involved in purchase decisions are illustrated in Figure 4.1. Simple models of buyer behaviour usually see an underlying need triggering a search for need-satisfying solutions. When possible solutions have been identified, these are evaluated according to some criteria. The final purchase decision is often a result of the interaction between the final decision maker and a range of influencers. Eventually, after purchase and consumption, the consumer will develop feelings about the purchase that will influence future purchase decisions. In reality, however, purchase decision processes can be complex iterative processes involving large numbers of influencers and a variety of decision criteria. It is often unrealistic to see the stages of the buying process as being completely separate; for example, evaluation often takes place while the search for information is still ongoing.

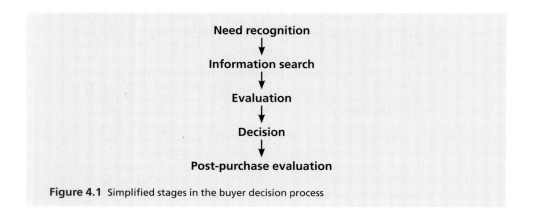

Figure 4.1 Simplified stages in the buyer decision process

Needs as buying process initiators

A need for something triggers the buying process. Needs provide a motive for an individual's action and can be very complex. Because they are a deep-seated initiator of buying behaviour, marketers are very keen to understand how needs are formed and manifested.

A *need* can be defined as a perceived state of deprivation, which motivates an individual to take actions to eliminate that sense of deprivation. A need is deep-rooted in an individual's personality. How the individual seeks to satisfy a need will be conditioned by the society of which he is a member. As an example, the need for status may be fairly universal, but its expression differs between cultures. In many less developed economies the need for status may be acquired by owning large numbers of cattle. In western countries the need is more likely to be satisfied by ownership of a particular brand of car. These manifestations of needs are sometimes referred to as *wants*. Wants are the culturally influenced manifestation of a deep-seated need. Of course, we can all want many products, but not buy or be able to buy them. Marketers are ultimately interested in *demand*, which can be defined as a willingness and ability to buy a product that satisfies a need.

An individual's needs are influenced by a wide range of psychological and sociological factors. We can begin our understanding of needs by focusing on those psychological factors that are inherent to an individual.

Physiological and psychological bases of needs

Genetic make-up clearly has some effect on buying behaviour. For example, physiological factors can influence an individual's appetite for food. Some people are said to be more 'impulsive' shoppers than others, and researchers have attributed part of the explanation for this behaviour to genetics. Differences have also been noted in the needs of male and female buyers and the way they approach purchasing decisions. Of course,

Figure 4.2 The market for sun protection products has become increasingly complex, as consumers' needs have changed. Marketers have recognized that the cheap bottle of sun oil from a pharmacy or supermarket is not going to satisfy the needs of increasingly discerning buyers who seek a sun oil that is suitable for their particular skin type. In addition, the desire for a natural tan has been supplemented with a growing awareness of the need to avoid the dangers of skin cancer. The Calypso brand has been progressively extended and developed to cater for these increasingly complex needs. (Reproduced with permission of Linco CARE Limited)

there is continuing debate about whether, and to what extent, such behaviours are inherent in our nature, or are the result of nurture through a socialization process. Either way, it is important for marketers to recognize differences between individuals in what motivates them to buy.

It is wrong to equate needs solely with physiological drivers. We no longer live in a society in which the main motivation of individuals is to satisfy the basic needs for food and drink.

Maslow (1943) recognized that, once individuals have satisfied these basic physiological needs, they may seek to satisfy social needs—for example, the need to have meaningful interaction with peers (see Figure 4.3). More complex still, western cultures see increasing numbers of people seeking to satisfy essentially internal needs for self-satisfaction. Products therefore satisfy increasingly complex needs. Food is no longer seen as a basic necessity to be purchased and cooked for self-consumption. With growing prosperity, people have sought to satisfy social needs by eating out with friends or family. Satisfaction of such social needs may be supplemented with a higher-order need to experience different types of meals. The great growth in eating out that occurred during the 1970s and 1980s has been followed by a growing diversity of restaurants that cater for people's need for variety and curiosity—hence the emergence in most larger European towns of Balti, Creole, and Far Eastern restaurants.

Maslow's **hierarchy of needs** is no more than a conceptual model, and it is difficult actually to measure where an individual is positioned on the hierarchy of needs. Furthermore, it is essentially based on western values of motivation, and there is a great deal of evidence of cultural influences on needs (e.g. Jai-Ok *et al.*, 2002). How, for example, would you explain religious sacrifice and penance, which are important motivators for many non-western consumers?

Figure 4.3 Maslow's hierarchy of needs: an application to the market for meat products

MARKETING in ACTION

Is Freud fit for marketing?

Freudian analyses of human motivation based on repression have sometimes achieved notoriety for their explanations of human behaviour. Is smoking really a substitute for the repressed desire of a child to suck its thumb? Think about the two following cases of supposedly repressed feelings, their explanation, and possible opportunities for marketers:

1. Children inherently dislike order and prefer creative chaos: it is only adults that teach children to be tidy and to structure their lives. Possible marketing opportunity—toys and novelties for adults that recreate a sense of chaos, such as 'silly string', party poppers, and some modern art.

2. Children like to be cared for by a mother figure. As adults we take on board such responsibilities, but we would sometimes be happy to go back to a simple dependent child– mother relationship. Possible marketing opportunity—a wide range of personal services aimed to pamper adults as if they were children again, including hairdressing, beauty salons, and health farms. Who else can exploit this desire to be a pampered, dependent child? Restaurants? Airlines?

Is an analysis of repression of any use to marketers in trying to understand human motivation? Or is it a highly speculative approach that may be intuitively appealing, but is only one of a number of possible explanations of the observed behaviour?

Maslow has presented one model of motivation that marketers have adopted widely as a conceptual framework. There are other frameworks for understanding the psychological bases for human motivation.

- **Freudian analysis** sees human behaviour as directed by a repression of feelings from early childhood. What comes naturally to a young child is often considered socially unacceptable, so such behaviour is socialized out before the child reaches adulthood. Behaviour is the outcome of the interaction between the id (the primitive unconscious basis of the psyche dominated by primary urges) and the ego (conscious **perceptions** that act as an inhibiting agency).

- **Stimulus–response models** of motivation have been widely used by marketers to understand needs. Analogies have been drawn between Pavlov's dog (who came to associate the sound of a bell with food) and everyday marketing situations. The existence of cues in the environment, such as advertising, can help trigger the buying process, even though the initial cue has no direct connection with the need an individual is seeking to satisfy. In this way, the sight of a well-known celebrity endorser can trigger the process of seeking out a brand of food that she endorses.

Sociological influences on needs

You will recall that needs were defined earlier as being inherent in an individual. However, the manifestation of these needs is influenced by the society in which an individual lives, and there is a great deal of research evidence of how these social influences work (see, e.g., Butcher, Sparks, and O'Callaghan, 2002). A number of levels of influence can be identified:

- The family influences a child's perception of the world, and this influence lasts into adulthood. Examples of this effect on buying processes can be found in adults' selection of a particular brand of breakfast cereal because it is the one that they were brought up with.

- Individuals are surrounded by **peer groups** (or **reference groups**) that act as a guide for behaviour. Peer groups can be primary and direct in their influence (e.g. colleagues at work and school), or they can be secondary and indirect (e.g. the guidance to behaviour provided by pop stars or media figures).

- Individuals can identify with a social class, and the values of this class can influence behaviour. As an example, individuals who identify with the 'working class' may feel alienated by an up-market retail outlet such as Gap compared with the traditional values epitomized in Woolworths.

- Culture in its widest sense influences our buying behaviour. Concepts such as self-centredness, the desire for immediate results, and deference to suppliers can differ significantly between cultures (see Hofstede and Hofstede, 2004).

Situational factors influencing needs

Our needs are also influenced by the situation in which we currently find ourselves. The subjects of age and socio-economic status can have profound effects on buying behaviour, as we will see in Chapter 5 when we look at market segmentation. In addition, the stage that an individual has reached in the **family life cycle** has a significant influence on needs (see Tinson, Nancarrow, and Brace, 2008). There have been numerous descriptions of the typical family life cycle. One of the earliest—and still widely cited—classifications was developed by Wells and Gubar (1966), who identified a number of stages, each associated with distinctive sets of needs:

1. Bachelor stage: young, single people not living at home
2. Newly married couples: young, no children
3. Full nest 1: youngest child under 6
4. Full nest 2: youngest child over 6
5. Full nest 3: older married couples with dependent children
6. Empty nest 1: older married couples, no children living at home

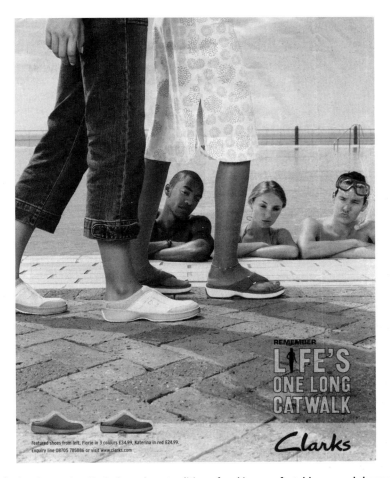

Figure 4.4 The shoemaker Clarks has a long tradition of making comfortable, rugged shoes which have created high levels of customer loyalty. However, among many younger people the company's shoes have been regarded as something their parents might wear, and not having the street credibility of shoes bearing the brand name of competitors such as Timberland. Clarks has set about the task of winning social approval for its shoes among younger segments' peer groups, something that is communicated in this advertisement. (Reproduced with permission of C. & J. Clark International Limited)

7.   Empty nest 2: older married couples, retired, no children living at home

8.   Solitary survivor: still working

9.   Solitary survivor 2: retired

More recent refinements of family life-cycle stages have sought to take account of their increasing complexity, brought about by the breakdown of the traditional nuclear family and the emergence of deviations from the norm such as single-parent families, extended cohabitation before marriage, and groups of young people sharing a house before they can afford their own. However, all family life-cycle models make the same important point: an individual's needs are likely to change as he or she goes through life. An individual moving from a bachelor stage to one with dependant children will face a reordering of priorities, reflecting a different set of needs. This will also most probably be matched by a reduction in discretionary expenditure.

Information search

Once a need has triggered a search for need-satisfying solutions, the search for information will begin; but where do buyers look for information when making purchases? In the case of the routine repurchase of a familiar product, probably very little information is sought about the product. Where there is a greater element of uncertainty, buyers will seek out information about the alternative ways in which they can satisfy their needs, especially where a high level of risk is involved. The following information sources are likely to be used.

- Personal experience will be a starting point, so, if a buyer has already used a company's products, the suitability of the proposed purchase may be assessed in the light of the previous purchases.

- **Word-of-mouth** recommendation from friends is important for many categories of goods and services where an individual may have had no previous need to make a purchase (Sweeney, Soutar, and Mazzarol, 2008). When looking for a plumber or a solicitor, for example, many people will seek the advice of friends. Increasingly, buyers are looking to the Internet to gather recommendations, through social networking sites, blogs, and discussion forums.

- Rather than referring to people we know, we may use various other reference groups to guide us. What type of sports shoes are our sports heroes wearing at the moment? What kind of drink is considered to be fashionable with our age group?

- Newspaper editorial content and trusted consumer review sources such as *Which?* magazine and www.moneysavingexpert.com may be consulted as a relatively objective source of information. Advertising and promotion in all of its forms is taken on board, sometimes being specifically sought and at other times just being casually noticed.

The greater the perceived risk of a purchase, the longer and more widespread is the search for information. Of course, individuals differ in the extent to which they are prepared to collect information methodically—some may make a purchase more impulsively than other, more calculating, individuals.

Perception

We may consciously seek out information, but may nevertheless fail to process the information that is presented to us. There are three key perceptual processes that can come in

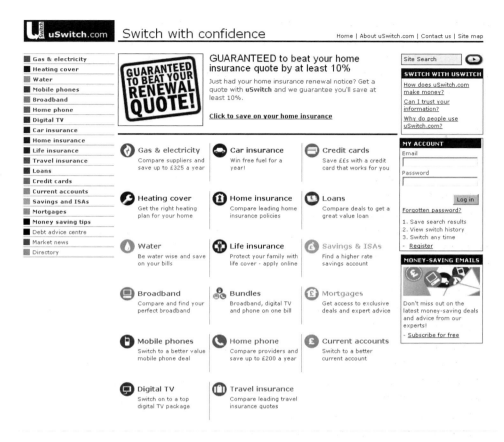

Figure 4.5 In the UK domestic gas and electricity supply market, consumers are faced with a sometimes bewildering and confusing choice of suppliers, all offering a basic commodity product, which by law cannot be differentiated. Evaluation is made more difficult because the different companies choose different bases for pricing, with many companies offering several different price plans. Some give introductory discounts, some give low-user discounts and most give discounts for payment by direct debit. The website www.uswitch.co.uk has become a popular choice for many consumers seeking comparative information on a novel purchase. This calculator for gas and electricity guides consumers through the choices available and identifies which supplier and price plan is best for them. It is claimed that an average family who switches suppliers on buy.co.uk or uswitch.com saves £140 on their annual energy bills. (Reproduced with permission of uswitch.co.uk)

the way between the presentation of information and the using of that information for evaluation:

1. We may fail to perceive the information because it fails to attract our attention (**selective attention**).

2. We may perceive the information, but then distort its content (**selective distortion**).

3. We may perceive the information, but then forget it very quickly (**selective retention**).

There is evidence that each sense receptor requires some minimum level of energy (or 'absolute threshold') to excite it before perception is organized. As well as the absolute threshold, there is a 'differential threshold', which is the smallest amount by which two stimuli must be different in order to be perceived as different. These thresholds are known to fluctuate, and differences between individuals' perceptions are influenced by their education, upbringing, experience, and many other factors.

We will return to the subject of perception in Chapter 10 when we look at communication processes within the context of the promotional mix.

Evaluation

In the process of gathering information, the total range of products available in the marketplace is gradually filtered down to a manageable number for evaluation (Figure 4.6). Choice is made from a select set of possibilities, and these choice sets can be classified according to their selectivity:

- The **total set** comprises all products that are capable of satisfying a given need.

- The **awareness set** comprises all of those products of which the consumer is aware. (The 'unaware set' is the opposite of the awareness set.)

- The **consideration set** includes those items within the awareness set that the consumer considers buying.

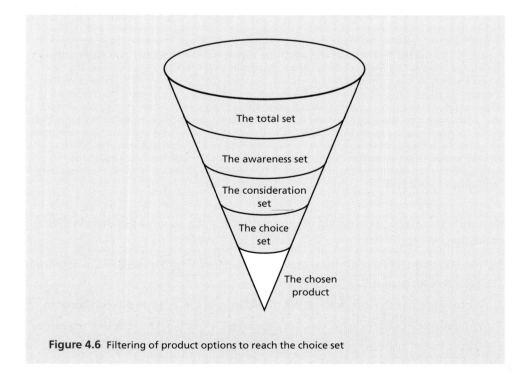

Figure 4.6 Filtering of product options to reach the choice set

- The **choice set** is the group of products from which a final decision is ultimately made.
- Along the way to defining the choice set, some products will have been rejected as they are perceived to be unavailable, unaffordable, unsuitable, etc. These comprise the **infeasible set**.

Research should seek to establish the choice set against which a company's product is being compared, and on this basis the marketing programme can be adapted in order to achieve competitive advantage against other members of the choice set.

A private buyer seeking to buy a low-value, low-involvement product such as an electric kettle may have narrowed down the choice set to four kettles. Analysts of buyer behaviour have developed a number of frameworks for trying to understand how a consumer chooses between these competing alternatives. In one such framework the consumer uses a sense of intuition as to which seems best. Such non-systematic methods of evaluation may be quite appropriate where the product in question involves low levels of cost, risk, and involvement.

Even apparently intuitive bases of evaluation can be reduced to a series of rules, implying some systematic foundation. One framework is a multiple-attribute choice matrix which holds that consumers refer to a number of component attributes of a product to evaluate its overall suitability. Figure 4.7 shows a typical matrix in which four competing MP3 players are compared in terms of five important attributes. In this matrix, the four short-listed MP3 players in the choice set are shown by the column headings A, B, C, and D. The left-hand column lists five attributes which research has suggested buyers use to make their purchase decision (reputation of the brand name, user-friendliness, memory size, price, battery life). The second column shows the importance the consumer attaches to each attribute of the service (with maximum importance being given a score of ten and a completely unimportant attribute a score of zero). The following four columns show how each MP3 player scores against each of the five evaluation attributes.

	Importance weights (out of 10)	Scores for each attribute for each MP3 player (0 = poor, 10 = excellent)			
		A	B	C	D
Brand reputation	10	10	7	8	10
User-friendliness	9	10	9	8	8
Memory size	8	10	10	9	9
Price	7	10	10	10	5
Battery life	6	4	10	10	4
Overall rating		44	46	45	36
Weighted rating		7.3	7.2	7.0	6.1

Overall rating = the sum total of scores for all attributes.
Weighted rating = the sum total of scores for all attributes, in which each attribute has been multiplied by its importance weight. (The importance weight is expressed as a percentage of the maximum score of 10 points.)

Figure 4.7 A hypothetical choice set for MP3 players: a multiple attribute matrix

If it is assumed that a consumer evaluates each product without weighting each attribute, MP3 player B will be preferred, as it has the highest overall rating. However, it is more realistic to expect that some attributes will be weighted as being more important than others; therefore the alternative *linear compensatory* approach is based on consumers creating weighted scores for each product. The importance of each attribute is multiplied by the score for each attribute, so in this case MP3 player A is preferred, as the attributes of A that consumers rank most highly are also those that are considered to be the most important.

A third approach to evaluation is sometimes described as a *lexicographic approach*. This involves the buyer in starting his evaluation by looking at the most important attribute and ruling out those products that do not meet a minimum standard; evaluation is then based on the second most important attribute, with products being eliminated that do not meet this standard. The process continues until only one option is left. In Figure 4.7 brand reputation is given as the most important attribute, so the initial evaluation may have reduced the choice set to A and D (which score highest on brand reputation). In the second round, user-friendliness becomes the most important decision criterion; only A and D remain in the choice set, and as A has the highest score for user-friendliness, it will be chosen in preference to A.

Decision

It is important to understand who is actually responsible for making a purchase decision. Both private and organizational purchases usually involve large numbers of people; for example, household purchases may involve joint decision-making between a husband and wife, with other family members acting as influencers. The subject of 'The Decision-Making Unit' is considered later in this chapter.

The outcome of the evaluation process may be a decision to do any of the following:

1. buy now;
2. do not buy at all;
3. defer the process;
4. start the process again.

Even when a positive decision to buy a product (e.g. the MP3 player used in the example above) is made, further decisions have to be taken to put the main decision into effect; for example:

- When will the product be bought?
- From which retailer?
- How many will be bought?
- Will any optional accessories be bought?
- How will the purchase be paid for (e.g. cash or credit card)?

Post-purchase evaluation

Wise marketers realize that purchasing activity does not end when a sale has been made. The buyer takes the product away and continues to develop feelings about it that will influence his decision next time he needs to make a purchase in that product category. The buyer will also be likely to tell his friends about the purchase, making either favourable or unfavourable comments. Many companies regard satisfied customers as their best form of promotion.

Cognitive dissonance

Buyers approach a purchase with a set of expectations about the performance of the product they are purchasing. A company's advertising and sales messages often serve to heighten expectations about the product's performance. Of course, these expectations are often not met. Maybe the product did not perform adequately, or the buyer's expectations were simply unrealistically high. In either case, the result is to create what is often referred to as **cognitive dissonance**, in which our expectations are out of line with the reality around us. We can handle dissonance in a number of ways.

- We can often simply return the goods and make a fresh purchase decision. The failed decision becomes part of a learning experience.

- Sometimes it is not possible to return the product. In the case of services that have already been consumed, this option is generally impossible. We may, alternatively, go about complaining and telling our friends about the bad product. Estimates vary,

> **Watsons**
>
> Thank you for shopping with us today.
>
> If you are happy with your purchase, tell us.
>
> If not, please tell us.

Figure 4.8 It is often said that a happy customer may tell a few friends about the company, but the dissatisfied customer will tell many more. This company encourages customers who have a complaint with its service to get in touch with it, so that the problem can be resolved before they tell others about it. Word-of-mouth recommendation is particularly important for high involvement goods and services where the buyer perceives a high level of risk.

but it is reckoned that on average a dissatisfied customer tells between five and ten people about his or her bad purchase.

- We can try and reduce dissonance by internal psychological processes. We may convince ourselves that we did not really make a bad decision, but our expectations were simply too high. We may clutch at minor features of the product that we like, to offset the major features that we dislike. We do not like to think that we made a mistake, so we may try to convince ourselves that we were right in our choice.

Companies often devote part of their promotional budget to reminding customers that they made the right choice in their purchase. Many companies write a short letter to recent customers, providing further reassurance to waverers that they have made the best choice. A convinced happy customer will be more likely to recommend a product to friends and to return to the same supplier next time.

In 2005, the computer manufacturer Dell was hit by influential blogger Jeff Jarvis complaining about poor customer service provided by Dell. Fellow consumers, no longer passive in their dissatisfaction, piled in with comments of their own, and stories of 'Dell Hell' rapidly became mainstream news. Companies cannot afford simply to watch these sites—to do so could result in a minor irritation spiralling into a serious problem. Traditional media have sometimes picked up dissent, but social networking sites allow such dissent to gain momentum much more quickly.

Increasingly, companies have been mingling in social networking sites, and have sometimes created their own sites as community forums. Dell, for example, established the Dell2Dell blog, in an attempt to gain some control over communication about it; but on other occasions, companies have sponsored blogs without declaring their hand. The retailer Wal-Mart covertly sponsored a blog that was supposedly operated by a couple camping in the store's car parks. It had hoped to manipulate content to put the company in a good light, but eventually the exercise turned into a PR disaster when news broke that the company had in fact been controlling the blog.

MARKETING in ACTION

From word of mouth to word of mouse

Word-of-mouth recommendation can be an important way of influencing buyers' choices, but it has traditionally been a fairly slow means of spreading recommendation about a product. Now, the Internet has allowed the whole process to be speeded up and has widened its impact. From word of mouth, companies now talk about 'word of mouse', leading to 'viral marketing', in which a purchase recommendation can spread very quickly as one person passes on a message to half a dozen friends, each of whom in turn passes on the message to another half a dozen friends. Chat rooms and websites devoted to customer complaints and comments (e.g. www.complaints.com; www.dooyou.com) allow happy or complaining customers to spread their message very quickly.

However, even though technology may have advanced, old questions remain, especially: why did a company allow itself to get into the position of exposing itself to criticism? Could this not have been foreseen? If there is little for people to spread bad stories about, the dissident websites would probably lose much of their support.

The decision-making unit (DMU)

In practice, few purchase decisions are made by an individual without reference to others. Usually, other people are involved in some sort of role and have a bearing on the final purchase decision. It is important to recognize who the key players in this process are, in order that a product can be configured to meet these people's needs, and that promotional messages can be adapted and directed to the key individuals involved in the purchase decision. A number of roles can be identified among people involved in the decision process (Figure 4.9).

Influencers

These are people or groups of people whom the decision-maker refers to in the process of making a decision. You will recall that reference groups can be primary in the form of friends, acquaintances, and work colleagues, or secondary in the form of remote personalities with whom there is no two-way interaction. Where research indicates that the primary reference group exerts a major influence on purchase decisions, this could

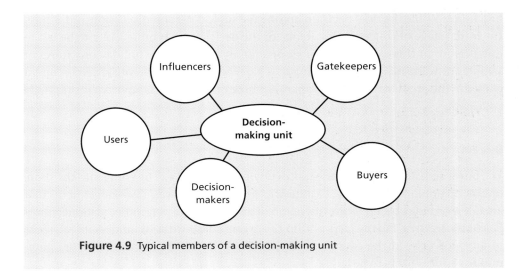

Figure 4.9 Typical members of a decision-making unit

indicate the need to take measures that will facilitate word-of-mouth communication—e.g. giving established customers rewards in return for the introduction of new customers. An analysis of secondary reference groups used by consumers in the decision process can help in a number of ways. It will indicate possible personalities to be approached who may be used to endorse a product in the company's advertising. It will also indicate which opinion leaders an organization should target as part of its communication programme in order to achieve the maximum 'trickle-down' effect. The media can be included within this secondary reference group—what a newspaper writes in its columns can have an important influence on purchase decisions.

Gatekeepers

These are most commonly found among commercial buyers. Their main effect is to act as a filter on the range of products that enter the decision choice set. **Gatekeepers** can take a number of forms—for example, a buying manager's personal assistant barring calls from sales representatives has the effect of screening out a number of possible choices. In many organizations it can be difficult to establish just who is acting as a gatekeeper; identifying a marketing strategy that gains acceptance by the gatekeeper, or bypasses him completely, is therefore made difficult. In larger organizations, and the public sector in particular, a select list of suppliers who are invited to submit tenders for work may exist—and if it is not on this list a supplier will be unable to enter the decision set.

Although gatekeepers are most commonly associated with purchases made by organizations, they can also be found in consumer purchase processes. In the case of many household goods and services, such as buying wallpaper or booking an overseas holiday, an early part of the decision process may be the collection of samples or brochures. While the final decision may be the subject of joint discussion and action, the initial stage of collecting the items for the decision set is more likely to be left to one person. In this way, one member of a family may pick up holiday brochures or samples of wallpaper, thereby acting as a gatekeeper and restricting the subsequent choice to the products of those companies whose brochures or samples were originally collected.

Buyers

The buyer actually undertakes the task of buying a product, e.g. by going into the shop, or ordering online. In the case of industrial goods and services, low-budget items that are not novel may be left to the discretion of a buyer. In this way, office stationery may be contracted by a buying clerk within the organization without immediate reference to anybody else. In the case of modified rebuys, or novel purchases, the **decision-making unit** is likely to be larger.

Users

The user of a product may not be the person responsible for making the actual purchase decision. This is typical of many items of clothing bought within household units. For example, it has been estimated that in the UK over half of all men's socks are bought by women. Parents buy products for their children, with varying levels of influence (or **pester power**) from the children who will be the actual users of the product. In the case of organizational purchases, there is often a separation between users

MARKETING in ACTION

Pester power pays

What role do children play in the purchase of the goods that they ultimately consume? There has been considerable debate about the extent of pester power, whereby parents give in to the demands of children. Increasingly, advertisers are aiming their promotional messages over the heads of adults and straight at children. The ethics of doing this have been questioned by many, and some countries, such as Sweden and Greece, have imposed restrictions on television advertising of children's products. A report published by the UK children's research company Childwise (ChildWise Monitor Trends Report, 2007) showed how children had become increasingly sophisticated shoppers. In a survey of 1,200 children, 78% of 10–12-year-olds said they enjoyed shopping. More than two-thirds liked collecting the latest things that their peers were collecting, and nearly half of 10–12-year-olds thought that brands are important when they buy. The average 10-year-old had internalized 300–400 brands, with a majority of even 5–6-year-olds able to name a brand of crisps or confectionery.

There was speculation about how children came to learn about these brands, with some pointing the finger at television advertising, especially during the breaks in children's programmes, while others who have studied children's behaviour claimed that children pick up 'cool' brands from their peer group. Despite a denial of its effects on children, many marketers of products consumed by children are quietly concerned by any moves towards EU integration of legislation on advertising to children. As a sign of regulators' increasing concern about the vulnerability of children to advertising, Ofcom, the UK broadcast regulator, issued new rules in 2007 banning television adverts for high-fat, salt, and sugar foods from programming likely to be popular with under 16s. While this may have seemed like good news to harassed parents, many felt that the restrictions did not go far enough, and called for a total ban on advertising such foods.

Even with advertising restrictions, companies have managed to get through to children in more subtle ways, for example by sponsoring educational materials used in schools and paying celebrities to endorse their products. When it comes to such items as confectionery and toys, just what influence do children exert on the purchase decision? And when football clubs deliberately change their strip every season, is it unethical for the clubs to expect fanatical children to pester their parents to buy a new one so that they can keep up with their peer group?

and buyers and research should be undertaken to reveal the extent to which users are important contributors to the decision process. In the case of the business air travel market, it is important to understand the degree of pressure that individual travellers can exert on their choice of airline, as opposed to the influence of a company buyer (who might have arranged a long-term contract with one particular airline), a gate-keeper (who may discard promotional material relating to new airline services), or other influencers within the organization (for example, cost centre managers might be more concerned with the cost of using a product, in contrast to the user's overriding concerning with its quality).

Decision-maker

This is the person (or group of individuals) who makes the final decision to purchase, whether he executes the purchase himself or instructs others to do so. With many family-based consumer products, it can be difficult to identify just who within the family carries most weight in making the final decision. Research into family purchases has suggested that, in the case of package holidays and furniture, women dominate in making the final decision, whereas in the case of financial services it is men who dominate. An analysis of how a decision is made can be achieved realistically only by means of qualitative in-depth research. In the case of decisions made by organizational buyers, the task of identifying the individuals responsible for making a final decision—and their level within the organizational hierarchy—becomes even more difficult.

■ Models of buyer decision-making

The buying process has now been portrayed as a highly complex one in which a variety of personal and environmental factors influence the decisions we make. We can process a great deal of information with outcomes that can sometimes be seen as quite irrational; so how can we attempt to model the buying process in order to establish some general rules that explain why a buyer decides to purchase one product rather than another?

A simple starting point is a **black box model** of consumer response (Figure 4.10). The inputs to the decision process are the range of psychological, sociological, economic, and situational factors. The outcome is the decision (e.g. whether or not to purchase; whether to purchase now or to defer; where to buy from; how many; etc.). In between is the black box, comprising our decision-making processes. The black box determines how we translate complex information into decisions. As individuals, we differ in the way that our processing occurs.

Of course, a black box is a simple representation of the input–decision–outcome process. In itself, it does not explain how a decision is actually made. For this, a number of

Figure 4.10 A simple black box model of consumer response

models of buyer behaviour have been developed. If a model is to have value to marketing managers, it should be capable of use as a predictive tool, given a set of conditions on which the model is based. Modelling buyer decision processes poses many problems. At one extreme, simple models may help in very general terms in developing marketing strategies, but are too general to be of use in any specific situation. At the other extreme, models of buyer behaviour based on narrowly defined sectors may lose much of their explanatory and predictive power if applied to another sector where assumptions on which the original model was based no longer apply. In any event, most models of buyer behaviour provide normative rather than strictly quantitative explanations of buyer behaviour, and there can be no guarantee that the assumptions on which the model was originally based continue to be valid.

One model that has been widely applied and subsequently developed is that developed by Howard and Sheth (1969). The principles of their model are shown in Figure 4.11.

The framework incorporates a number of elements:

- **Inputs:** This comprises information about the range of competing products that may satisfy a consumer's need. Information may be obtained from personal or published sources.

- **Behavioural determinants:** Individuals bring to the purchase decision a predisposition to act in a particular way. This predisposition is influenced by the culture in which they live and family and personality factors, among others.

- **Perceptual reaction:** Inputs are likely to be interpreted in different ways by different individuals, based on their unique personality make-up and conditioning that is a result of previous purchase experiences. While one person might readily accept the advertising messages of a bank, another might have been disappointed by that bank in the past, or by banks' advertising in general; she is therefore less likely to perceive such inputs as credible.

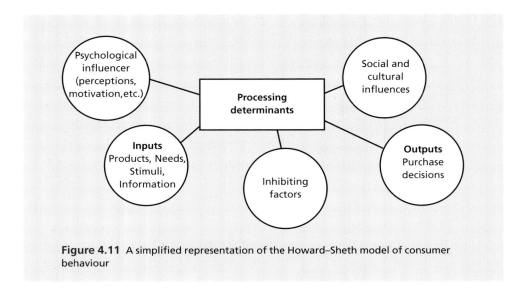

Figure 4.11 A simplified representation of the Howard–Sheth model of consumer behaviour

- **Processing determinants:** This part of the model focuses attention on the way in which a decision is made. Important determinants include the motivation of the individual to satisfy a particular need, the individual's attitude to a particular product or organization, and the weight attached to each of the factors used in the evaluation. For some consumers for some products, critical product requirements may exist which must be present if a product is to be included in the decision set. At other times, consumers attach weights to each of its attributes and select the product with the highest weighted 'score' (see Figure 4.7).

- **Inhibitors:** A number of factors might prevent an individual from making a decision to purchase a particular product, such as the ease of access to the product, its price, and the terms and conditions for delivery.

- **Outputs:** The outcome of the decision process may either be to go ahead and purchase, or alternatively, not to buy or to defer a decision until a later date.

More specific models of buyer behaviour have been developed as a result of research into specific sectors. Many of these have sought to rank in order of importance the factors that contribute towards the purchase decision, and to identify critical factors, the absence of which will exclude a possibility from a decision set. As an example, research into restaurant choice decisions by Auty (1992) identified five key factors, ranking food quality as the most important, then image and atmosphere. However, it was also noted that the importance attached to each of these factors differed according to the purpose of the visit to the restaurant; the factors influencing a choice of restaurant for a celebration were quite different from those used for a general social occasion.

Personal and organizational buyer behaviour compared

At the beginning of this chapter it was noted that buying processes are likely to differ for situations where it is an organization rather than an individual making a purchase. Instead of being seen as completely different processes, all personal and organizational buying processes can be placed along a continuum (Cova and Salle, 2008). However, there are a number of features which characterize organizational buying processes.

- Two sets of needs are being met when an organization buys a product: the formal needs of the organization, and the personal needs of the individuals who make up the organization. The former might be thought of as being the more 'rational'. However, individuals within the organization seek to satisfy needs that are influenced by their own perceptual and behavioural environment, very much in the same way as would be the case with private consumer purchases.

- More people are typically involved in organizational purchases. High-value purchases may require evaluation and approval at a number of levels of an organization's management hierarchy. Research might indicate, for particular organizations or types of organization, the level at which a final decision is normally made. The analysis of the decision-making unit might also reveal a wider range of influencers present in the decision-making process.

- Organizational purchases are more likely to be made according to formalized routines. At its simplest, this may involve delegating to a junior buyer the task of making repeat orders for goods and services that have previously been evaluated. At the other extreme, many high-value purchases may be made only after a formal process of bidding and evaluation has been undertaken.

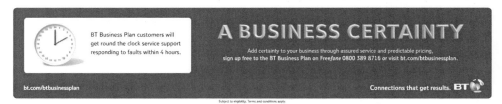

Figure 4.12 If a domestic telephone breaks down, it may cause no more than annoyance and inconvenience to the owner. However, for business users, the consequences of a failure can be much more serious, possibly leading to lost sales, delayed orders, and missed production. Few members of the organizational decision-making unit would want to carry the blame for selecting a phone provider which subsequently lets the company down. For business customers, telephone providers must appeal to all members of the decision-making unit by stressing that its services are reliable and have benefits in use which will be good value to the company. BT, the largest provider in the UK telecoms market, offers numerous packages for its domestic market. However, this advertisement aimed at the business sector stresses a particular concern of the business user—the need to get a faulty phone repaired quickly so that business is not interrupted. (Reproduced with permission of British Telecom PLC)

- The elements of the product offer that are considered critical in the evaluation process are likely to differ. For many products, the emphasis placed on price by many personal buyers is replaced by reliability and performance characteristics by the organizational buyer. In many cases, poor performance of a product can have direct financial consequences for an organization—a low-price but unreliable computer might merely cause annoyance and frustration to a private buyer, but might lead to lost production output or lost sales for an organizational buyer.

- The greater number of people involved in organizational buying also often results in the whole process taking longer. A desire to minimize risk is inherent in many formal organizational motives and informally present in the motives of individuals within organizations. This often results in lengthy feasibility studies being undertaken. In some new markets, especially overseas markets, trust in suppliers might be an important factor for purchasers when evaluating competing suppliers, and it may take time to build up a trusting relationship before any purchase commitment is secured.

Developing ongoing relationships with buyers

It was noted earlier that the buying process generally does not end when a purchase is completed. For many products, the purchase and subsequent use of the product provides input to the next purchase decision. Companies have recognized that it can be profitable to cultivate long-term customers; hence the emergence of 'relationship marketing' as an alternative to a one-off transaction-based approach to marketing. Marketing managers have seen the potential advantages of reducing levels of customer 'churn' by improving the retention rates of profitable customers (see Reichheld and Sasser, 1990).

Like all investments, some are worth more than others. How should a company decide which customers are worth investing in? And what level of investment can be justified in terms of the speculative future income that could result from the relationship?

MARKETING in ACTION

A £20 meal or a lifelong relationship?

What is the lifetime value of a restaurant customer? First-time customers may be spending only £20 on this occasion, but if they like what they get, how much are they likely to spend in the future? A typical diner eating out just once a month could be worth £2,000 in five years. If customers are happy, they are likely to tell their friends—if they're not, they are likely to tell even more of their friends. It follows that customers should be seen as investments, to be carefully nurtured over time. When things go wrong (for example, through overbooking) it would probably be to the restaurant's advantage to spend heavily on putting things right for the customer (e.g. by offering money off a future meal). Judged on the basis of the current transaction, the restaurant may make a loss, but it will have protected its investment in a future income stream.

Reasons for the development of ongoing customer relationships

Relational exchange is not a new concept; it has been observed, for example, in the pattern of exchanges between textile manufacturers and intermediaries in Victorian England. Also, while relationships may have been rediscovered in the west, they have remained a fundamental part of exchange in many eastern cultures (Lee, Pae, and Wong, 2001).

In recent times, organizations' growing interest in developing closer relationships with their private and corporate customers has come about for two principal reasons.

1. In increasingly competitive markets, good product quality alone may be insufficient for a company to gain competitive advantage. Superior ongoing relationships with customers supplement a firm's competitive advantage. This is evident in the car market, where the focal point of marketing has shifted from a preoccupation with better design, to better service and now to better relationships. Today, many private buyers of cars choose a car that comes with the best support package, keeping the car financed, maintained, insured, and replaced at the end of a specified period (Figure 4.13). For many, the three-yearly purchase of a car has been turned into an ongoing relationship with a car company to supply all the services that make a car available to the consumer.

2. The emergence of powerful, user-friendly databases has enabled large companies to know much more about their customers as individuals, recreating in a computer what the small business owner knew in his or her head. Many of the current developments in relationship marketing would have been unthinkable without modern information technology capabilities.

The main differences between traditional one-off transaction-based exchanges and relationship-based exchanges are summarized in Figure 4.14.

The extent to which the development of ongoing relationships with customers represents a desirable marketing strategy is dependent upon three main factors:

1. **The characteristics of the product:** Where products are complex and involve a high degree of uncertainty on the part of buyers, the likelihood of customers seeking a relationship is increased. Relationships are often a necessity where the stream of product benefits is produced and consumed over a period of time—a programme of medical treatment, for example. For some products, a relationship may allow preferential treatment or semi-automatic responses to requests for service, thereby reducing transaction costs associated with multiple service ordering. It has also been suggested that both suppliers and customers seek the security of relationships where the market environment is turbulent.

2. **The characteristics of customers:** Some customers may be happy to shop around each time they approach a purchase, while others may value the perceived security of an ongoing relationship with a supplier they have come to trust. Some buyers

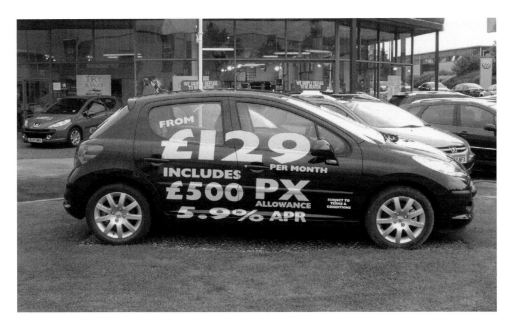

Figure 4.13 One of the great marketing successes of the car industry in recent years has been to transform the sale of a car into what is effectively an ongoing relationship with the car manufacturer. For many private buyers, the traditional way of buying a car has been to pay a sum of money for the car (either by cash or through a loan), keep the car for probably three or four years, then trade it in for a new one and make a fresh payment for the new car. Today, a wide variety of relationship-based service arrangements are available to private buyers that give them the use of a car for a defined period of time, and just as importantly, service benefits which allow them to make the greatest use of their car. A relationship-based approach to car sales typically includes a loan that is repaid over two or three years; an extended warranty; and a breakdown support service, some of which have been increasingly sophisticated in the benefits they offer car buyers to keep them mobile (for example, many support packages include the provision of a temporary replacement car, and overnight accommodation if necessary). Many agreements give the car buyer the option of returning their car at the end of a specified period and exchanging it for a newer model. Instead of spending £15,000 every three years for a tangible object, the car buyer now typically pays two or three hundred pounds a month for a service-based relationship with a car company and its dealers.

may value social aspects of an ongoing relationship and judge a transaction not just by its economic outcomes. Research has also suggested that the importance attributed to components of a relationship differ between groups, for example in the way that women place more emphasis on trust and commitment in their relationships than men (Shemwell, Cronin, and Bullard, 1994).

3. **The characteristics of suppliers:** By developing relationships with their customers, suppliers add to the differentiation of their products and give customers a reason to remain loyal. The extent to which organizations are relationship rather than product oriented can be related to their structure, processes, and core values. Organizations differ in the extent to which they are able, or willing, to calculate the lifetime value of a customer.

Traditional transaction-oriented marketing	Relationship marketing
Focus on a single sale	Focus on customer retention
Short-term orientation	Long-term orientation
Sales to anonymous buyers	Tracking of named buyers
Salesperson is the main interface between buyer and seller	Multiple levels of relationships between buyer and seller
Limited customer commitment	High customer commitment
Quality is the responsibility of production department	Quality is the responsibility of all

Figure 4.14 The components of transactional and relational exchange compared

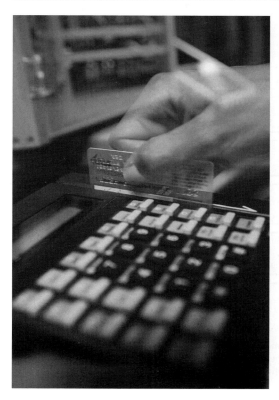

Figure 4.15 Boots is one of many retailers offering benefits to customers who sign up for their loyalty programmes. One of the challenges of Boots is to encourage the large number of people who visit its stores each day to spend more during their visit. Instead of just buying a bottle of shampoo, customers could be tempted to buy a sandwich, camera, or a new pair of glasses, rather than going to one of the company's competitors. A loyalty card offers an inducement to customers to place a larger part of their total expenditure with the company, especially where the rewards are seen as significant. However, the biggest benefit of a loyalty programme to a company is to gain a much deeper insight into the shopping behaviour of its customers. No longer does it have to base its marketing planning simply on till-receipt analysis; it can now understand individuals' patterns of buying over time. It can also link data collected at the point of sale with other demographic data provided by card-holders. Although some retailers have dismissed loyalty programmes as an expensive gimmick which adds to operating costs, many others have taken the view that the additional operating costs involved are a low price to pay for the rich data that is provided. (*Source:* @ Photodisc)

Methods used to develop ongoing relationships with customers

Companies seek to move buyers up what has often been described as a **ladder of loyalty** to the point where they become enthusiastic advocates for a firm's products (Figure 4.16). As customers move up this ladder, the relationship they have with a company changes from one based on convenience or necessity to one that is emotionally valued by the buyer.

However, considerable double-speak is often present in attempts by firms to develop customer relationships. In the service sector, many organizations are simplifying and 'industrializing' their processes, usually in an attempt to improve their operational efficiency and consistency of performance. Such companies may talk about relationship development with customers, based on dialogue that is driven by information technology; but such relationships can be qualitatively quite different from those based on social bonds founded on emotional commitment and trust. While UK clearing banks have become vigorous in their development of customer databases and named personal banking advisers, many customers may feel that the relationship with their bank today is qualitatively worse than when a branch manager was able to enter into a more holistic dialogue with them. Many unhappy customers do not switch banks, however, because the perceived financial and psychological costs are too great.

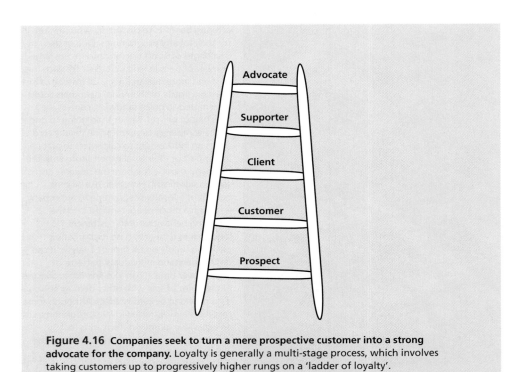

Figure 4.16 Companies seek to turn a mere prospective customer into a strong advocate for the company. Loyalty is generally a multi-stage process, which involves taking customers up to progressively higher rungs on a 'ladder of loyalty'.

Managers of firms seeking to develop relationships with their customers should avoid the arrogant belief that customers seek such relationships. Surveys have indicated that many categories of buyer are becoming increasingly confident in venturing outside a business relationship and increasingly reluctant to enter into an ongoing relationship. Relationship marketing strategies may fail where buyers' perceptions are of reduced choice and freedom to act opportunistically rather than the added value to be derived from a relationship. Added value must be defined by sellers in terms of buyers' needs, rather than focusing on customers as captives who can be cross-sold other products from a firm's portfolio.

Why, then should buyers wish to go back repeatedly to the same supplier? Below, we consider some of the methods used by companies to create ongoing relationships with customers.

Customer satisfaction

In a competitive marketplace, customer satisfaction can be the most important reason for customers deciding to make a repeat purchase, and telling their friends about their satisfaction. To achieve high levels of satisfaction requires the effort of all functions within an organization. Relationship development cannot simply be left to a relationship manager. There are many notable cases of companies that have not developed any explicit relationship marketing programme, but nevertheless achieve very high levels of recommendation by their customers. Consider, for example, the chocolate retailer Thorntons, which has developed strong loyalty from customers who return to its shops for indulgence and gift purchases of chocolate, despite having no formally stated relationship marketing programme.

Of course, many companies enjoy high levels of repeat business without providing high levels of customer satisfaction. Many train passengers may complain about the price and reliability of their train service, but they return because they have no realistic alternative.

Even companies that have an apparently poor standard of service can achieve high levels of repeat business in a competitive market by charging low prices. Retail chains such as Aldi and Lidl have developed strong loyalty from price-sensitive customers who consider that the total service offer (access to the store, range of products, cleanliness, friendliness, etc.) are acceptable in return for the price they have paid. The danger here is that competitors may enter the market with similarly low prices, but offering higher levels of service. Would customers still remain loyal?

Trust

The top of the loyalty ladder is more likely to be reached by a customer who trusts a company. Trust is a complex multi-faceted concept which has been extensively researched by marketers (e.g. Morgan and Hunt, 1994). Some retailers, such as Boots and John Lewis, consistently score highly in surveys of customers' trust in firms, and these companies generally tend to have high levels of customer loyalty. However, merely being trusted does not guarantee profitability for a firm—the rest of its operational and financial strategies must also be right.

Adding value to a relationship

A relationship, to be sustainable, must add value in the eyes of customers. This value can come about in a number of ways, including:

- making the reordering of goods and services easier (for example, many hotels record guests' details and preferences so that they do not have to be re-entered each time the guest checks in);

- offering privileges to customers who wish to enter into some type of formal relationship. As an example, many retailers hold special preview events for loyalty card holders, and send a free copy of the store's magazine. Loyalty cards allow companies to gather a great deal of valuable data about their customers' buying behaviour (see Meyer-Waarden, 2008). Customers will generally participate in a loyalty card programme only if they believe that they will gain something of value out of it. Many companies have been imaginative in creating value in the buyer's mind, beyond basic cash rebate schemes;

- developing an ability to jointly solve problems. For example, a car repair garage may endeavour to identify exactly what the problem is that a customer wants put right, rather than leaving it to the customer to specify the work that she wants carried out. Such joint problem solving requires a considerable level of trust to have been developed between the parties. In some cases, professional codes of conduct govern the delegation of problem-solving responsibilities.

Creating barriers to exit

Companies can bring about repeat buying by trying to make it difficult for customers to defect to a competitor. Customers can unwittingly walk into traps where they become dependent upon a supplier for continuing support. Suppliers of industrial machinery create ongoing relationships whereby they are the sole supplier of the spare parts or consumable items that the purchaser must buy in order to continue using their equipment. Many companies negotiate exclusive supply agreements with a supplier in return for a promise of preferential treatment. In both cases, the customer becomes dependent in the short term. However, such ties can usually be broken eventually (for example when the machinery is replaced, or when an exclusive supply contract comes up for renewal), and it is at that point that the true loyalty of a customer is put to the test. It has been pointed out that such ties may lead to customer *detention* rather than *retention*

(Dick and Basu, 1994) and that a company that has not achieved a more deep-seated emotional relationship with its customers may be unable to sustain those relationships if the legal or technological environment changes.

Problems of creating ongoing relationships with buyers

There are many situations in which buyers are not responsive to firms' efforts to create ongoing relationships. Many companies serve market segments where customers have no underlying need to make further purchases of a category of product that the company is able to supply. In the extreme case, a small-scale company may appeal to the curiosity of buyers, for whom a second-time purchase will have little of its original value—curiosity. This phenomenon is present in many tourism-related businesses in destinations of symbolic rather than aesthetic quality. (For example, many people make a religious pilgrimage once in their lifetime with little incentive to return again.) In the case of supplies to governmental organizations (and often to larger private-sector organizations), rules for tendering of new purchases may nullify sellers' attempts to develop continuing and uninterrupted relationships. Where relationships between commercial buyers and sellers are deemed to be against the public interest (for example, where they make it difficult for new entrants to enter a market), regulatory agencies may order them to be reduced in scope. (For example, soft drinks companies' exclusive supply agreements with retail customers have in some circumstances been held to be against the public interest.) Finally, attempts to create ongoing relationships by firms can be costly and may put a firm at a competitive disadvantage in markets where price is the most important decision factor.

MARKETING in ACTION

Spurious loyalty?

Just because customers repeatedly come back to a company does not necessarily mean that they have a loyal relationship to the company. This point was made, tongue-in-cheek, during a war of words between British Airways and Virgin Atlantic Airways. The latter had objected to BA's use of the advertising slogan 'The World's Favourite Airline'. Statistically, it was true at the time that more passengers travelled internationally with British Airways than with any other airline, but surveys of airline users had consistently put Virgin ahead of BA in terms of perceived quality of service. Virgin's Richard Branson claimed that on BA's logic the M25, London's notorious orbital motorway, could be described as the world's favourite motorway. Despite coming back to the motorway day after day, few motorists could claim to be loyal to it—they simply had no other choice.

The spat between BA and Virgin serves to underline the point that customer loyalty is about more than mere repetitive buying. True loyalty involves customers becoming enthusiastic advocates of a company.

🔳 Chapter summary and linkages to other chapters

A sound understanding of buying processes is essential for the development of an appropriate marketing mix. A purchase decision is influenced by a wide range of personal, social, economic, and situational factors, and varies between different types of product and different individuals. The outcome of the decision-making process may be to buy now, to not buy, or to defer a decision. Few buying decisions are made without reference to others, so it is important to identify the members of the decision-making unit. This is particularly true in the case of organizational purchases, where it is important to know what product features and promotional messages motivate different individuals.

Study of buyer behaviour is increasingly extending beyond the initial purchase by attempting to understand how buyers can be turned into loyal repeat customers. Relationship marketing is becoming an important part of many companies' marketing plans as they realize that it can be more profitable to take care to retain the customers they currently have, than to search expensively for new customers to replace lapsed ones.

In the first two chapters we noted in general terms that marketing is essentially about satisfying customers' needs profitably. This chapter has focused more specifically on buyers' evaluation of sellers' attempts to satisfy their needs. In subsequent chapters we will explore how companies undertake research into needs and buying processes (Chapter 5) and subsequently will group together buyers that have essentially similar needs (Chapter 6). Companies then develop a distinctive marketing mix which will give them a competitive advantage in satisfying the needs of the customers they are targeting (Chapters 7–11).

🔲 KEY PRINCIPLES OF MARKETING

- Buying is a process with a number of overlapping stages and a feedback loop from post-consumption to the start of the next buying cycle.
- The effort that buyers put into the buying process is influenced by their level of involvement with the product.
- We rarely make decisions entirely on our own. Marketers need to be aware of the broader decision-making unit of people who may knowingly or unknowingly influence a purchase decision.
- Models of buyer behaviour attempt to portray the buying process. Because of the situational nature of buying decisions, general models cannot hope to give any more than a general indication of these processes.
- It is generally more profitable for companies to retain existing customers than to replace lapsed customers with new ones.

CASE STUDY

How do you really understand young people's buying behaviour?

How can any marketer get inside *your* mind to understand how *you* actually make purchase decisions? Structured questionnaire surveys may have a role for collecting large-scale factual data, but they have major weaknesses when it comes to understanding individuals' attitudes. Complex sets of factors that influence our buying decisions can only rarely be captured by a questionnaire. Qualitative approaches such as those using focus groups can get closer to the truth, but participants often still find themselves inhibited from telling the full story. Many marketing managers, especially those without large research budgets, inevitably end up relying on their own personal experiences to understand how consumers behave. This may be easy for target markets that are in the 20–40 age range (the age of typical marketers), but how do you get inside the mind of teenagers, or elderly people?

Ethnographic approaches are becoming increasingly popular among marketers as a means of getting closer to the truth about consumer behaviour. Ethnographic research is nothing new, having been used by anthropologists in their study of the rituals of tribal people. Marketers have been relatively recent converts to the techniques of ethnography. One company that has applied ethnography to marketing is called Everyday Lives. Its clients have included Unilever, Proctor & Gamble, Pedigree, and GlaxoSmithKline. On behalf of its clients, it seeks to uncover hidden truths about the way people lead their lives, by paying volunteers to be followed for days on end, being filmed and having their every move recorded. According to the company, an observational survey would cost about £4,000–£6,000 per household, and a typical project for a client would involve a minimum of six households. For major international brands, many more than this number would be involved.

One essential feature of ethnographic research is that it must not have any predetermined agenda. There is little value in undertaking this type of research if the mindset of the researcher is expecting to see preconceived phenomena—it is the unexpected that is often of most interest, and that is so difficult to pick up through more structured forms of survey. Inevitably, participants in a survey may feel very self-conscious while they are being filmed, and the more interesting insights are likely to be observed when participants are feeling relaxed and off their guard. It is not just what people actually do that can be interesting, but what they almost do, and the body language used when members of the household are discussing an issue. It can take several hours of filming to yield just a few moments of true insights into participants' true attitudes and behaviour.

One example of the company's ethnographic research in action was provided by a project commissioned by the footwear brand Dr Martens. The company wanted to understand how young people used fashion brands in their everyday lives. Why, for example, did some brands, such as Nike trainers or baseball caps, become so iconic in youth culture? The researchers identified groups of young people around the world who corresponded to the Dr Martens target market. In return for a payment, volunteers were followed for several days and their daily routines filmed with a handheld digital camera. In total, 180 hours of captured film was edited to just one hour of highlights showing the key drivers of youth culture which are relevant to the Dr Martens brand.

It seemed that young people preferred fashions that allowed them to customize an item of clothing and in some way take 'ownership' of it. This was seen in the way that many young people wore a baseball cap the wrong way round, or pulled the tongue of a pair of trainers from behind the laces. The research drew the conclusion that iconic fashion items for young people had to have a distinctive label or style that made their wearers stand out as part of a tribe. The company's research brief did not go as far as designing shoes that might appeal to the target market—this is where the research had to be picked up by the brand owner and operationalized. Given the research evidence of young people's need to belong to a tribe, yet still be individual, how could Dr Martens develop its product? Could coloured shoelaces be one means of allowing young people to associate with a respected brand, yet at the same time show their individuality through different coloured laces?

What makes for good ethnographic research? EverdayLives has a number of tips for making the most of the technique. It suggests avoiding telling households what the research project is about, until it is over. That way, the chances of particpants deliberately playing to the camera can be reduced. Apart from that, involvement and total immersion of the researchers in the lives of the particpants is key to understanding their attitudes, beliefs, and lifestyles.

Ethnographic research has not been without its critics. Some have described it as 'psychobabble', arguing that it does not lead to original insights and explanation, but microscopic reflections of everyday events. At its worst, ethnographic research could be entertaining, easy, and quick, but superficial and the 'insights' of a poorly undertaken piece of research could be unduly influenced by the background and prejudices of the researchers. In short, hours of filming and 'analysis' could actually be a pointless cover for reinforcing established beliefs and prejudices. Some have questioned the ethics of ethnographic approaches, especially where participants are not fully informed about the purpose of the research. The participants themselves may not be representative of a product's target market, and insights may be biased towards outgoing, camera-seeking types, rather than quieter, more private types of people whose views will remain difficult to assess.

Sources: Daily Telegraph, 'Big brands turning to Big Brother', 29 March 2007, p. 17; Miles, L., 'Market Research: Living their Lives', *Marketing,* 11 December 2003, p. 15; EverydayLives website: www.everydaylives.com

----

Case study review questions

1. Critically assess the role of ethnographic research as a means of learning more about buyer behaviour.

2. Discuss the ethical issues that are raised by ethnographic research.

3. Discuss possible alternative approaches by which marketers may learn more about 'youth culture'.

CHAPTER REVIEW QUESTIONS

1. Is it realistic to represent the buying process as a simple linear process? What factors might complicate such apparently smooth progress?

2. Discuss the main ways in which buying processes for airline travel typically differ between private buyers and business buyers? How might airlines adapt their product offer to take account of these differences?

3. Critically assess methods used by banks to develop ongoing relationships with their personal customers.

ACTIVITIES

1. Reflect on the last time that you went for a night out with a group of friends to a bar/restaurant or nightclub. Analyse the decision processes, information sources, and evaluation criteria that you used in arriving at a decision as to where to go and what to order.

2. Refer to the buyer evaluation matrix shown in Figure 4.7. Now apply this to the decision-making process that you and your friends may go through if you were evaluating competing service offers from mobile phone service providers.

3. Review consumer magazines containing adverts for telecommunication services. Now review professional/trade magazines that also contain adverts for telecommunication services. Critically evaluate the ways in which the messages differ between the two types of magazine. What do the differences—if any—say about differences in the buying process between private buyers and business buyers?

REFERENCES

Auty, S. (1992), 'Consumer Choice and Segmentation in the Restaurant Industry'. *Services Industries Journal*, 12(3): 324–39.

Butcher, K., Sparks, B., and O'Callaghan, F. (2002), 'Effect of Social Influence on Repurchase Intentions'. *Journal of Services Marketing*, 16(6): 503–12.

Childwise Monitor Trends Report (2007), 'The Monitor Trends Report 2007'. Norwich: Childwise.

Cova, B. and Salle, R. (2008), 'The Industrial/Consumer Marketing Dichotomy Revisited: a case of outdated justification?'. *Journal of Business & Industrial Marketing*, 23(1): 3–11.

Dick, A. S. and Basu, K. (1994), 'Customer Loyalty: toward an integrated conceptual framework'. *JAMS*, 22(2): 99–113.

Hofstede, G. and Hofstede, G. J. (2004), *Cultures and Organizations: Software for the Mind*. Maidenhead: McGraw-Hill.

Howard, J. A. and Sheth, J. N. (1969), *The Theory of Buyer Behaviour*. New York: John Wiley.

Jai-Ok, K., Forsythe, S., Qingliang, G., and Sook, J. M. (2002), 'Cross-cultural Consumer Values, Needs and Purchase Behavior'. *Journal of Consumer Marketing*, 19(6): 481–502.

Lee, D.-J.; Pae, J. H., and Wong, Y. H. (2001), 'A Model of Close Business Relationships in China (guanxi)'. *European Journal of Marketing*, 35(1/2): 51–69.

Maslow, A. (1943), 'A Theory of Human Motivation'. *Psychological Review*, 50(4): 370–96.

Meyer-Waarden, L. (2008), 'The Influence of Loyalty Programme Membership on Customer Purchase Behaviour'. *European Journal of Marketing*, 42(1/2): 87–114.

Morgan, R. M. and Hunt, S. D. (1994), 'The Commitment–Trust Theory of Relationship Marketing'. *Journal of Marketing*, 58(3): 20–38.

Reichheld, F. F. and Sasser, W. E. (1990), 'Zero Defections'. *Harvard Business Review*, 68(5): 105–11.

Shemwell, D., Cronin, J., and Bullard, W. (1994), 'Relationship Exchanges in Services: an empirical investigation of ongoing customer service–provider relationships'. *International Journal of Service Industry Management*, 5(3): 57–68.

Sweeney, J. C., Soutar, G. N., and Mazzarol, T. (2008), 'Factors Influencing Word of Mouth Effectiveness: Receiver Perspectives'. *European Journal of Marketing*, 42(3/4): 344–64.

Tinson, J., Nancarrow, C., and Brace, I. (2008), 'Purchase decision making and the increasing significance of family types'. *Journal of Consumer Marketing*, 25(1): 45–56.

Wells, W. D. and Gubar, G. (1966), 'Life Cycle Concepts in Marketing Research'. *Journal of Marketing Research*, 3(4): 355–63.

◻ SUGGESTED FURTHER READING

There are numerous textbooks that provide a good overview of buyer behaviour, including the following:

Blackwell, R. D., Miniard, P. W., and Engel, J. F. (2005), *Consumer Behaviour*, 10th edn., London: Thomson Learning.

Evans, M., Jamal, A., and Foxal, G. (2006), *Consumer Behaviour*. Chichester: John Wiley.

Solomon, M., Bamossy, G., Askegaard, S., and Hogg, M. (2006), *Consumer Behaviour: a European perspective*, 2nd edn. London: FT Prentice Hall.

For an introduction to the general principles of relationship marketing and its role in turning buyers into regular customers, the following are useful:

Egan, J. (2008), 'Relationship Marketing: exploring relational strategies in marketing'. London: FT Prentice Hall.

Gummesson, E. (2008), Total Relationship Marketing: marketing management, relationship strategy and CRM approaches for the network economy. Oxford: Butterworth-Heinemann.

◻ USEFUL WEB LINKS

Visit the Online Resource Centre for resources that are relevant to this chapter, including web links, multiple choice questions, and additional case studies:

www.oxfordtextbooks.co.uk/orc/palmer2e/

◻ KEY TERMS

- **Black box model of buyer behaviour**
- **Buying process**
- **Cognitive dissonance**
- **Decision-making unit (DMU)**

- **Family life cycle**
- **Gatekeepers**
- **Hierarchy of needs**
- **Influencers**
- **Involvement**
- **Ladder of loyalty**
- **Models of buyer behaviour**
- **Need**
- **Peer groups**
- **Perception**
- **Pester power**
- **Reference groups**
- **Stimulus–response models**
- **Word-of-mouth**

5

Marketing research

CHAPTER OBJECTIVES

So far in this book, we have spoken in general terms of marketing being essentially about providing what the customer wants. But how do we know what the customer *actually* wants? How can we find out how buyers *actually* go about the buying process? How can we tell whether a company has succeeded in providing the goods and service that a buyer seeks? And how does a company gather, analyse, and disseminate information about its marketing environment, which we looked at in general terms in Chapter 2?

This chapter explores information as a valuable asset which can help marketers improve their knowledge of customers and their ability to meet customers' needs profitably. Marketing research is essentially about keeping in touch with a company's customers and its broader marketing environment, and this chapter reviews the main methodological approaches. Sources of data are discussed in terms of their timeliness and relevance. It is important that a company knows about its markets not just as they are now, but as they are likely to be in the future; therefore demand forecasting and knowledge management become crucial.

Introduction

Most definitions of marketing focus on a firm satisfying its customers' needs. But how does a firm know just what those needs are? And how can it try and predict what those needs will be in a year's time, or five years' time? A small business owner in a stable business environment may be able to manage by just listening to her customers and forming an intuitive opinion about customers' needs and how they are likely to slowly change in the future. But how can such an informal approach work in today's turbulent business environments, where the senior managers of very large businesses probably have very little contact with their customers?

Marketing research is essentially about the managers of a business *keeping in touch* with their markets. The small business owner may have been able to do marketing research quite intuitively and adapt her product offer accordingly. Larger organizations operating in competitive and changing environments need more formal methods of collecting, analysing, and disseminating information about their markets. It is frequently said that information is a source of a firm's competitive advantage, and there are many examples of firms that have used a detailed knowledge of their customers' needs to develop better product offers which have given the firm a competitive advantage. Interestingly, a recent trend has been for market researchers to rename themselves as 'Customer Insight Departments'. This is a recognition that marketers value insights above *everything* else—above being objective, above classic methodology, even above validity and reliability.

The range of techniques used by companies to collect information and turn it into actionable knowledge is increasing constantly. Indeed, companies often find themselves with more information than they can sensibly use. The great advances in Electronic Point of Sale (EPOS) technology, for example, have given retailers a wealth of new data of which not all companies have managed to make full use. As new techniques for data collection appear, it is important to maintain a balance between techniques so that a good overall picture is obtained. Reliance on just one technique may save costs in the short term, but only at the long-term cost of not having a good holistic view of market characteristics.

Market research *v.* marketing research

The terms 'market research' and 'marketing research' are often used interchangeably. This is incorrect, and the distinctive characteristics of each should be noted.

- **Market research** is about determining the characteristics of a *market*, for example in terms of its size, requirements, growth rate, market segments, and competitor positioning.
- **Marketing research** is broader and is about researching the whole of a company's marketing activities. In most organizations, such research would probably include monitoring the effectiveness of its advertising, intermediaries, and pricing position.

This chapter focuses on how a company goes about assessing its customers' needs. Of course, research into areas such as customers' perceptions of advertising messages is closely related to an understanding of their needs and expectations, so it is unwise to see the two aspects of research as completely separate.

Market research should be seen as just one component of a firm's information-gathering procedures. It is usual to talk about integrating market research within a company-wide marketing information system, which itself is part of a wider corporate management

Figure 5.1 The role of marketing research within a marketing information system

information system. From this, knowledge is created, and there is a lot of interest in how this knowledge can be shared to create a 'learning organization'.

In Figure 5.1, an attempt has been made to put market research in the context of a broader marketing information system.

◼ Major uses of marketing research

As markets become more competitive, marketing research is being called upon to perform an ever-increasing range of tasks. Some of the more important specific marketing research activities are listed below.

- **Research into customer needs and expectations:** Research is undertaken to learn what underlying needs individuals seek to satisfy when they buy goods and services. Identifying needs that are currently unmet by existing products spurs new product development. Needs should be distinguished from expectations, and a variety of qualitative techniques are used to study the often complex sets of expectations that customers have with respect to a purchase. For example, when buying a personal computer, what are customers' expectations with respect to reliability, after-sales support, design, etc.?

- **Customer satisfaction surveys:** Companies regularly try to find out from their customers how satisfied they are with the goods or services that they have bought. By identifying areas of dissatisfaction, a company can seek to improve its product offer in order to increase its sales. Customer surveys can have the dual function of providing a company with valuable information and providing a public relations tool, allowing customers to feel that they have made their feelings known to the company.

- **Communications effectiveness:** Companies may spend a lot of money on various forms of communication, such as advertising, sales promotion, and public relations, but may have little idea about how effectively its money was spent. Regular surveys may help a company to identify the communication channels which are most cost effective for producing sales leads.

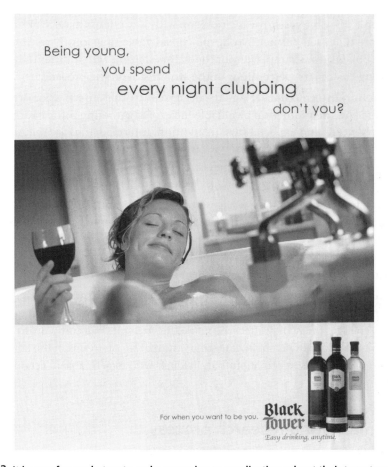

Figure 5.2 It is easy for marketers to make sweeping generalizations about their target market and detailed research is often required in order to understand the minutiae of buyers' lifestyles. Even the same person can take on quite a different lifestyle at different times of the day or week. Is the young male who drinks heavily with his mates on a Friday night likely to continue this drinking habit at home during the week? Is the goal-oriented career woman always driven by a desire to succeed in the fast lane? This ad for Black Tower reminds us of the need for marketers to get a complete insight into the lives of the target market and to identify apparent inconsistencies that can represent market opportunities. (Reproduced with permission of Reh Kendermann)

- **Similar industry studies:** By researching other companies, including competitors and companies in completely unrelated business sectors, marketing managers can learn a lot about how to improve their own marketing effectiveness. Through a process sometimes referred to as 'benchmarking', an organization can set itself targets based on best practice in its own, or a related, industry.

- **Key client studies:** Where a company derives the majority of its income from just a small number of customers, it may make special efforts to ensure that these customers are totally satisfied with its standards of service and prices. The loss of their business as a result of shortcomings of which it is unaware could otherwise be catastrophic. In some cases, the relationship with **key clients** may be of such mutual importance that each partner may spend considerable time jointly researching shared problems (for example, airport operators sharing with airlines the task of researching customers' perceptions of the airport's handling procedures).

- **Research into intermediaries:** Agents, dealers, and other intermediaries are close to consumers and therefore form a valuable means for gathering information about consumers' needs and expectations. In addition, intermediaries are themselves customers of manufacturers and service principals. It follows that the latter should be very interested in how they are perceived by their intermediaries, for example in relation to reliability, delivery times, and after-sales service.

- **Employee research:** For many services organizations, front-line employees are close to customers and are valuable sources of information about customers' needs. Research can also focus on employees as 'customers' of an organization, for example by measuring their attitudes towards the company. Employee suggestion schemes can form an important aspect of employee research.

- **Environmental scanning:** We saw in Chapter 2 that a company's marketing environment can be highly complex and that it is crucial to understand how even quite nebulous changes today may affect the marketing activities of a company in the future. Environmental scanning is about gathering information on trends in the environment and disseminating this information to individuals who may be able to act on it.

The marketing research process

The small business owner may have been able to get by with a fairly intuitive system of market research. Larger organizations operating in complex environments need to adopt a more structured approach to their market research activities. To be useful, keeping in touch with customers' needs should be carried out objectively, accurately, and should use a variety of methods. Casual, unstructured research may at best be wasteful, and at worst misleading. Data collected should be as up to date and relevant to a problem as time and cost constraints allow.

Figure 5.3 The marketing research process

The stages of the marketing research process can be described in a simple, linear format. A **model** of this process, which begins with the definition of the research problem and ends with the presentation of the findings, is shown in Figure 5.3. The process follows the basic pattern of scientific inquiry that is adopted for other forms of research.

The trigger for research can usually be related to a gap in the information that is currently available to a firm. For example, a company may have comprehensive information on the current market for its products, but lack information on new market opportunities for which its product range could be adapted.

Very often, marketing research activity fails because the 'problem' to be researched has been inadequately thought through and expressed as a research brief. For example, a company may be facing declining sales of a product and may then commission research to investigate customers' liking of the product's features relative to competitors' products. However, the real problem may be to understand the macro-economic environment, which may explain why sales of that category of product are declining.

The marketing research process operates at a number of levels.

- At the simplest level, a researcher may simply be required to provide a normative *description* of market characteristics (for example, defining the attributes that buyers evaluate when choosing between competing personal computer brands, or describing the buying behaviour of families buying a personal computer for the first time).

- The research task may additionally call for the *measurement* of market characteristics, for example by measuring the annual sales value of the UK personal computer market and the market shares of the main suppliers.

- A more thorough investigation would require an *analysis* of data, both quantitative and qualitative (e.g. an analysis of personal computer buying behaviour according to the age, income, or lifestyle of different segments of the population).

- With further analysis, a predictive *model* for targeting may be sought (e.g. a model to predict the level of computer sales based on individuals' occupation, family structure, and postcode).

Once the objectives of a research exercise have been defined, plans can be developed to collect relevant data. Data collection methods are considered below. A time plan is

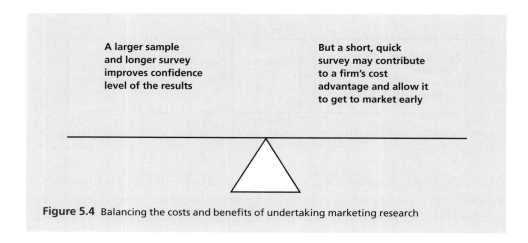

Figure 5.4 Balancing the costs and benefits of undertaking marketing research

essential to ensure that decision-makers can have the most up-to-date information on market characteristics as they are at present, rather than as they were some time ago. In rapidly changing markets, timeliness can be crucial. The outcome of market research should be actionable by those who receive it.

How extensive should a firm's marketing research processes be? The amount of time and expense incurred in undertaking research must be compared with the benefits that will result from it in terms of making a better informed decision. Very often, the issue is how harmful a badly informed decision could be to a firm. Where the capital costs involved in developing a new product are low, and the market is changing rapidly, it may make sense to do very little research and go straight to the market with a new product. This is true of many fashion designers, who can run up sample items and see how well they sell. If they sell well, follow-up production can be put in hand rapidly; if they fail to sell, they can be consigned to a bargain clearance store. Little will have been lost, whereas had the designer taken time to carry out lengthy market research, he could have got his designs to the market just as the current fashion was changing again, rendering his research historic and obsolete. Contrast this to the marketing research needed for a much more risky major infrastructure investment such as an airport, which will have a high capital cost and a long life-span. The research process here will typically last several years and take many forms (Figure 5.4).

Primary *v.* secondary research

A further question is whether to use primary data collection techniques, **secondary research**, or a combination of the two. Data sources are traditionally divided into two categories according to the methods by which they were collected. Secondary research is often referred to as desk research, while **primary research** is often called field research.

MARKETING in ACTION

A 'Wild West' for data?

The Internet has spawned a new generation of researchers who seem to have boundless amounts of web-generated data. But how valuable are these data?

One of the big advantages of doing business through the Internet is that all transactions are recorded in a form that is immediately available for analysis. No more transcribing the newspaper inquiry coupon into a database, or recording the essence of a customer's telephone call in a series of codes to be saved in a database. In both cases, creating a database can be time-consuming, costly, and subject to human transcription error—better to let the customer himself enter the data. Where a prospective customer approaches a company's website with an inquiry, the fact can automatically be recorded. Fairly simple software will allow a company to record how the visitor reached its site, how long she spent at each page, and the results of the visit (e.g. a request for further information, quotation request, purchase order). More sophisticated data are provided by companies, such as doubleclick.com, which inserts 'cookies'—often unknowingly—into users' PCs which are then used to send back to the company information about all of the sites that the user has visited. This can be very valuable information that third-party companies buy to improve their targeting. Of course, collecting information through use of such 'spyware' raises ethical questions.

Faced with such a huge amount of research data, just how valuable is it to marketers? Inevitably, there are some gems amidst a mass of debris. The ability to measure response rates to different page designs and/or different links to a company's site can sharpen marketers' analytic skills and improve their accountability for their actions. It is no longer good enough just to have a hunch that a website is effective when there is copious information to measure its performance.

How useful are the statistics that marketers routinely collect from the web? Simple records of visitors to a website are prone to many errors, including the problem of identifying 'unique' visitors from those who might repeatedly enter and leave a site in quick succession. Many apparent visits are actually hits recorded by 'spiders'—search engines that routinely seek out websites for indexing. A bigger problem of Internet data is the difficulty that often prevents Internet-based databases being integrated with existing records of consumers' behaviour, lifestyles, and attitudes. With concerns over Internet security remaining high, individuals may be reluctant to divulge personal information through the Internet that would allow a company to build up a full picture. Unfortunately, the people with the greatest concerns about privacy are often the people about whom companies are most interested in learning more (Ashworth and Free, 2006).

In its early days of development, the Internet was described as the new 'Wild West', where rules were few and far between and anything went. Unfortunately, this description can also be applied to many of the statistics circulating about website usage, with potential advertisers unsure about the true value of advertising on a particular site. Audit schemes (e.g. VeriSign) have helped to provide some reassurance to users about the validity of web statistics.

The development of the Internet as a marketing research tool has not always been helped by the sometimes confused communications between marketing and IT departments within a company. IT systems often fail to meet marketers' expectations, because needs have not been defined accurately. As in other aspects of marketing, getting the inter-functional dynamics of a company right can be crucial in the quest for competitive advantage, and may explain the success of, among others, Direct Line Insurance and First Direct.

Most organizations approach a research exercise by examining the available sources of secondary data. Secondary data refers to information which in some sense is second-hand to the current research project. Data can be second-hand because they have already been collected internally by the organization, although for a different primary purpose. Alternatively, the information may be acquired second-hand from external sources.

Secondary, or **desk research** can be a useful starting point for a research exercise. If somebody else has collected data or published a report in a closely related area, it is often much cheaper to buy that report than start to collect data afresh. Reports by organizations such as nVision and the Economist Intelligence Unit (EIU) may at first sight seem to be very expensive, but when set against the cost of undertaking the research from scratch the cost begins to look relatively good value.

Primary, or **field research** is concerned with generating new information direct from the target population. The phrase 'keeping in touch' was highlighted earlier, and marketing researchers spend most of their time designing and implementing such studies, either on a one-off or a continuous monitoring basis. Primary research tends to be much more expensive to conduct than secondary research, but the results are invariably more up to date and specific to a company's research objectives.

The range of primary research techniques is constantly increasing, and some of the important ones are discussed later in this chapter.

Secondary research information sources

A good starting point for secondary research is to examine what a company already has available in-house. Typically, a lot of information is generated internally within organizations; for example, sales invoices may form the basis of a market segmentation exercise. To make the task of desk research as easy as possible, routinely collected information should be analysed and stored in a way that facilitates future use. Of course, a balance needs to be struck between having data readily available, and spending money on the collection and storage of data that may subsequently (but not necessarily) be used.

The range of external sources of secondary data is constantly increasing, both in document and in electronic format. These sources include government statistics, trade associations, and specialist research reports. A good starting point for a review of these is still the business section of a good library. Some examples of secondary data sources are shown in Figure 5.5.

In many cases, other organizations, possibly even competitors, will have conducted similar studies to the one that is proposed. These may be available to purchase (or may be publicly available, as in the case of companies' annual reports, which often contain useful market information). There is also a dark world of espionage, where companies seek to gather information from competitors.

- Government departments and official publications—e.g. *General Household Survey, Social Trends, Transport Statistics*
- National media—e.g. *Financial Times* country surveys
- Professional and trade associations—e.g. Association of British Travel Agents, British Roads Federation
- Trade, technical, and professional media—e.g. *Travel Trade Gazette, Marketing Week*
- Local chambers of trade and commerce
- Yearbooks and directories, e.g. Dataquest
- Companies' Annual Reports and Accounts
- Subscription services, providing periodic sector reports on market intelligence and financial analyses, such as Keynote, Mintel, etc.
- Subscription electronic databases, e.g. Forrester Research, Gartner, Mintel Online

Figure 5.5 Examples of secondary data used in marketing research

Primary research methods

Primary, or field, research is becoming increasingly sophisticated, and this chapter can give only a brief overview of the range of techniques available. There are now many texts that go into market research methods in great detail (see the suggestions for further reading). We will begin by looking at methodological issues concerning primary research. Later, we will look at how data collected using these methods can be analysed to give a company new insights.

Sampling procedures

Primary research involves looking directly at the phenomena or individuals that are of interest, and recording the characteristics about them that are of particular interest. In most circumstances, it would be impractical to measure details of everybody who makes up the 'population'. (For example, if we were interested in the preferences of intensive mobile phone users in the UK, it would not be practical to talk to every single intensive user in the country.) As an alternative, primary research usually uses just a sample of the population that we are interested in. From this small sample, we can extrapolate to infer characteristics of the population as a whole. Any inference made about the population is limited by the extent to which the sample is truly representative of the population as a whole.

Sampling is essentially concerned with quantitative techniques, and there are a number of widely used techniques for sampling:

- A random sample implies that everyone within the target population has an equal chance of being selected for inclusion in the sample. For a completely random sample of all adult members of the population, the Electoral Register is frequently used and a proportion of names selected at random. (However, from 2002, UK residents have been able to 'opt out' of the part of the electoral register that is made available to commercial organizations.) A variant on this approach is stratified random sampling, in which the population is divided into a number of sub-groups and a random sample obtained from each sub-group. The proportion sampled from each sub-group can be varied according to the researcher's interest.

- Rather than picking specific individuals to be included in the sample, the researcher can specify the characteristics of each sub-group and the number required from each such group. The interviewer is then free to include in her *quota* sample individuals who meet the specification. This method of sampling is only as good as the specification of the quota's characteristics. If data collectors are given too much freedom to choose their sample, it can best be described as a *convenience* sample and is likely to be biased in terms of respondents' characteristics. (The researcher may consciously or unconsciously recruit respondents who are easiest to find, rather than those whom it is most valuable to learn about.) A biased sample may limit the generalizability of the research results to the population as a whole.

- Many survey techniques are effectively *self-selecting* in their sampling procedure. Where questionnaires are made widely available to the public, the researcher has little control over who will actually return a questionnaire. There is evidence that responses can be dominated by vociferous minorities of individuals who hold extreme views, which may not be typical of the views of the large group of 'average' customers. There is also evidence that retired people and housewives with more time to spare are more likely to volunteer to complete a survey, even though a research exercise may be more interested in the views of busy working people.

Data collection methods

The range of field research techniques is constantly increasing. Two main approaches to collecting primary data can be identified: by observation of the individuals in whom the researcher is interested, or by interaction with them through a survey.

Observation techniques

Observational techniques are limited to descriptions of behaviour, and cannot explore the reasons that might explain such behaviour. However, they do claim to be highly objective and free of bias from respondents.

The following are some examples of observation techniques.

- When a retailer is assessing the attractiveness of a proposed new store location, it may undertake observational research into pedestrian or vehicle flows past a proposed site.

- Many firms routinely monitor their competitors' marketing programmes, for example by collecting their brochures or by observing prices and products on offer in retail outlets and Internet sites.

- The use of **mystery shoppers** is becoming increasingly common among services companies who use them to check on standards of service delivery. Typical uses have been to assess the efficiency and friendliness of restaurant waiting staff, the attention received from staff in a car showroom, and whether a travel agent is recommending a sponsoring tour operator's products.

- Experimental laboratory research may observe how consumers interact with a product, for example by observing how, and in what order, an individual reads an advertisement.

- The Internet has created new opportunities for observing how individuals move around a company's website. Which hyperlinks were most productive in bringing visitors to the company's site? Which combination of pages did they visit? In what order were they visited? How long did they spend on each page? Companies often use alternative page designs which are randomly allocated to visitors, then the results (an order, further inquiry, etc.) compared.

- Developments in Radio Frequency Identity (RFId) technology is allowing tags to be attached to products, transmitting information to nearby receivers. This can potentially allow information about product usage to be transitted back to a base station. However, RFId tags are still too expensive for widespread application to low value, high-volume products. Their use has also raised many thical questions.

Observational techniques may be good at describing phenomena, but they do not in themselves provide explanations. For this, other techniques need to be used. Observational techniques can raise ethical questions, where those being observed are not aware that they are being studied. Many people may be unhappy at the thought that CCTV footage of them walking round a store is being used in a study of flow around the store. The use of unseen 'cookies' to observe Internet usage has been challenged by many on ethical and legal grounds.

Survey-based research methods

A survey questionnaire involves some form of interaction with the subject being studied and would normally seek some attitudinal, personal, or historical information about the respondent. Questions in a survey can be asked face-to-face, by telephone, or distributed for self-completion.

- *Face-to-face interviewing* is a traditional method of carrying out surveys. It can achieve high rates of response and can be free of the self-selection bias commonly associated with self-completion surveys. Bias can, however, occur where respondents give an answer that they believe the interviewer expects them to give, rather than one they truly believe. Face-to face interviewing, whether carried out house-to-house (which is the best approach for sampling purposes), in the street, or in hired locations, is labour-intensive. The cost and difficulty of obtaining good-quality, trained staff to undertake survey research, often at unsociable times of the day, has led researchers to search for lower-cost alternatives.

Figure 5.6 The UK supermarket operator Asda (part of Wal-Mart), appreciates the value of feedback from customers. Like many well-run companies, Asda provides comment cards and a freephone telephone number that customers can use to pass on their suggestions, complaints, and praise about the company's operations. Asda recognizes the value of this customer insight and goes one step further by making a donation to charity for each call that it receives on its freephone number. It also completes the process of information exchange by displaying in its stores a list of suggestions that customers have made, and actions that the company has taken in response to them. (*Source:* courtesy of Asda)

- An alternative to face-to-face interviewing is the *telephone survey*. While considerably cheaper than face-to-face interviews, the refusal rate for telephone surveys can be up to three times higher than for personal interviews, and response rates appear to be falling rapidly (Tuckel and O'Neill, 2002). The increased use of computer-assisted information collection for telephone (CATI) and personal interviews (CAPI) has speeded up the whole survey process dramatically, with responses being processed as they are received. Immediately prior to the 2005 UK general election, these systems were used in the next-day publication of survey results from total sample sizes extending into thousands.

- Online surveys have become increasingly popular, particularly among companies who target goods and services at young people who are likely to be heavy Internet users. There have been many reports of high response rates using this data collection method, although concerns have been expressed about the representativeness of samples obtained.

- In the case of *self-completion surveys*, respondents obviously self-select, so no matter how carefully the original sample to be contacted is chosen, the possibility of bias is highest. Furthermore, the response rate may be lower than 2%, particularly where a postal survey is used.

- In *qualitative research* (see below), the open-ended nature of the questions and the need to establish the confidence of respondents preclude the use of telephone and self-completion interviews. Face-to-face depth interviews are used, particularly in business-to-business research, where confidentiality is especially important and the scheduling difficulties and cost of getting a group of busy buyers together in one place can be a major problem; for this reason, it is usually most convenient for respondents to be interviewed at their place of work.

- In consumer markets, **focus group** discussions are frequently used. Groups normally consist of about eight people, plus a trained moderator who leads the discussion. Respondents are recruited by interviewers who use recruitment questionnaires to ensure that those invited to attend reflect the demography of the target market, and to filter out unsuitable respondents. Focus groups do not claim to be statistically representative of the population from which they come, but nevertheless there would be little value in recruiting a group that was not typical of the target population as a whole. In national markets, groups are arranged at central points throughout the country, the number of groups in each region reflecting the regional breakdown of the target population.

- There has been recent excitement among marketers that developments in medical technology will allow market researchers directly to study brain functions, so that instead of receiving a conditioned, verbal response to a question, the researcher can arive at something closer to the 'real' truth by studying brain pattern responses. However, such 'neuro marketing' research raises major issues about ethics and practicality (see Fugate, 2008).

Quantitative *v.* qualitative research

It was noted earlier that research techniques need to be varied and appropriate to the problem being studied. One important decision that needs to be made when developing a survey-based research plan is whether to conduct a qualitative or quantitative survey, or a combination of the two. Although quantitative and qualitative research are often seen as opposite ends of a research techniques spectrum, their methods overlap. Market researchers need to feel comfortable 'operating in all slices of the information map' (Smith and Dexter, 2001), incorporating harder, more scientific, objective data with softer, anecdotal, qualitative data.

Quantitative research

Quantitative research is used to measure consumers' attitudes and behaviour where the nature of the research has been defined. Quantitative research is designed to gather information from statistically representative samples of the target population. The sample size is related to the size of the total population being studied, the variability within it, and the degree of statistical reliability required, balanced against time and cost constraints. In order to achieve margins of error small enough to make the final measurements useful, however, quantitative research, as its name implies, is usually conducted among several hundreds, sometimes thousands, of respondents. For this reason, information is generally obtained using standardized structured questionnaires.

Unfortunately, many phenomena in which marketers are interested cannot easily be measured using single, simple indicators. In these cases, composite sets of scales are used and factor analysis is carried out to try and identify distinctive dimensions of a phenomenon. For example, marketers are often interested in whether customers trust a brand, but much research evidence has suggested that trust is a complex phenomenon; hence, it is not uncommon in quantitative studies to use 30 or more questions in a survey of trust. Perhaps the best-known multiple item measure used by marketers is the **SERVQUAL** methodology for measuring service quality. A company may wish to learn more about customers' perceptions of its service and to compare these with what they had expected. The methodology uses 22 questions to probe a respondent's attitudes about service quality. Previous research has shown that these 22 questions are reliable indicators of five distinct dimensions of service quality: reliability, attentiveness, tangibles, empathy, and responsiveness. The survey instrument has been widely used in the services sector to compare customers' perceptions of service quality between different branches, and to plot changes in performance over time.

The marketer has available a wide range of quantitative techniques with which to collect and analyse data. The following is a brief summary of the techniques most commonly used by marketers. Further details can be found in any good research methods book (see suggested further reading at the end of this chapter).

Correlation analysis

Marketers are often interested in the extent to which two phenomena are associated with each other, for example whether change in household income is associated with the amount that a household spends on eating out. A correlation coefficient of 1 would indicate perfect association between the two variables and 0 would indicate no association at all. A correlation does not imply causation, and, as with all quantitative techniques, care needs to be taken in interpreting a correlation coefficient. Researchers have, for example, found significant correlations between firms' advertising expenditure on a product and sales revenue for it. However, this correlation could imply either that advertising expenditure leads to increased sales, or that firms increase their advertising expenditure in response to increasing sales revenue, because advertising is now more affordable. Each of these hypotheses is plausible, and the observed correlation must be interpreted in the context of theoretical foundations and previous evidence. In the light of theory, it may be concluded that the most relevant correlation is between sales in one period and advertising revenue in the preceding period.

Regression analysis

Regression models are used to build a model of causes (independent variables) that lead to an effect (the dependent variable). Companies would use a historical database to test models that are assessed for the amount of variance in the dataset that they explain. A **regression analysis** would comprise one dependent variable, a constant, and any number of independent variables. The significance of each of these independent variables is calculated, allowing a company to understand which of them are having a significant effect on the dependent variable.

A typical application of regression modelling is retailers' use of it to predict sales at possible new sales locations. A regression model will be able to discover, on the basis of performance of the company's other sites, the relative contribution to sales that will be made by such factors as passing pedestrian traffic, passing vehicle traffic, proximity to a major attractor, and the number/proximity of competitors. Regression analysis is only as good as the data and context on which the initial model was calibrated. The model may not be relevant if it is applied outside the context of the original dataset (e.g. a UK-based model applied to US retailing), and environmental factors may change the validity of the model over time.

Analysis of variance

Analysis of variance, or 'ANOVA', is used to test hypotheses about differences between two or more means. It is widely used in experimental frameworks where the researcher wishes to examine the effects of two or more 'treatments' on customers. A store interested in the effects of background music on the daily value of sales may develop an experiment in which shoppers are treated to one of three types of background music: (1) slow, soft music; (2) strident, loud music; or (3) no music. Analysis of variance can be used to test whether there is any significant difference between sales values associated with different types of music.

ANOVA designs can be used to test for differences within subject variables and between subject variables.

Conjoint analysis

This is a versatile marketing research tool that can provide valuable information for market segmentation, new product development, forecasting, and pricing decisions. **Conjoint analysis** can analyse the real-life trade-offs that shoppers make when evaluating a range of features or attributes that are present in a range of products. Once data are collected about consumers' preferences for particular attributes and features, the researcher can conduct a number of 'choice simulations' to estimate market share for products with different attributes/features. This can improve the researcher's ability to predict which formulation of a product will be successful before a product is launched on the market. A limitation of this technique is that consumers' evaluation of individual attributes of a product may be quite meaningless on their own, and it is the creative combining of attributes that determines their final choice.

Cluster analysis

Segmentation exercises involve trying to allocate individuals within a sample/population into distinctive groups, so that differences *within* the groups are minimized relative to the differences *between* the groups. **Cluster analysis** is frequently used in segmentation studies, but does not provide the marketer with a unique solution, as the process of clustering involves subjective decisions about the grouping of data.

Neural network analysis

This technique splits a dataset into a training set and a testing set. It essentially combines the features of regression modelling with an ANOVA to give a 'best fit' model of dependent and independent variables.

Limitations to quantitative techniques

Quantitative surveys may give the appearance of a rigorous, scientific approach, and many marketers may delude themselves (and others) into thinking that you 'can't argue with the figures'. However, quantitative analysis techniques can suffer from a number of weaknesses.

Sampling error

Many quantitative studies fail because the sample is not truly representative of the population about which inferences are being made. A growing problem is non-response bias, which occurs when people who don't respond to a survey hold significantly different views from those who do respond, resulting in a biased estimate of population characteristics. A company will never know for sure what the views of non-respondents are, and how these differ from respondents, but there is some research evidence that, in the case of service quality surveys, responses are likely to be biased in favour of those who are either very happy or very unhappy with service levels, leaving the bulk of average customers under-represented. There are some methods to try and overcome this bias (e.g. comparing early respondents with late respondents), but the problem of non-response bias is a big one. (Typically, less than 5% of targeted individuals reply to a mail survey.) Concerns over data privacy, among other things, are exacerbating the problem.

Measurement error

This occurs where there is a difference between the true value of the information being sought and the information that is actually obtained by the measurement process. There are many sources of measurement error, the most common being using measurement variables that are inappropriate to the research problem; interviewer bias (which often occurs in face-to-face surveys where the respondent may give a 'polite' or 'expected' response, rather than the truth); problems with the research instrument (e.g. loaded questions used in a questionnaire); and processing errors (e.g. incorrect coding and data entry).

Significance level

Sample surveys can give only an estimate of population characteristics, and this estimate is subject to a margin of error. In general, as the size of the sample relative to the population increases, the confidence with which population parameters can be predicted increases. Also, greater confidence in predicting population parameters occurs where the amount of variability within the population is low. Before accepting an estimate of population characteristics, it is important to note the confidence interval of these predictions.

Inappropriate tests

Estimates of population may be invalidated because of the use of inappropriate statistical tests. Many of the tests described above are based on an assumption that data are normally distributed. If they are not, the test is invalidated.

Inappropriate interpretation

The interpretation of results can be highly subjective. This can derive from the validity of the measures being used—do they really measure the phenomena that they purport to (e.g. does SERVQUAL truly measure service quality as it applies in a specific industry sector)? Often a variety of significance tests are available to the researcher and a test may be chosen that is the most significant, but not the most valid. Finally, all inferences are subject to interpretation of meaning; for example, at what point does an observed fall in sales become a long-term trend rather than a temporary blip?

It should always be remembered that there are many 'noise' factors getting in the way of what is reported and the true state of the phenomenon that is being researched. Survey knowledge is a representation (researcher's interpretation) of a representation (data analysis) of a representation (survey instrument) of a representation (sample) of a representation (respondents' views of what really is going on) (Brown, 1998).

Qualitative research

Qualitative research techniques essentially seek to recreate the listening ear and interpretative mind that so many entrepreneurs use so well. In today's large corporation, key decision-makers are likely to be some way removed from everyday transactions with customers, so they employ qualitative researchers to be their listening ears for them.

Qualitative marketing research involves the exploration and interpretation of the perceptions and behaviour of small samples of individuals, and the study of the motivators behind observed actions. It can be highly focused, exploring in depth, for example, the attitudes that buyers have towards particular brand names. The techniques used to encourage respondents to speak and behave honestly and unselfconsciously are derived from the social sciences.

During the early stages of the research process, definitions and descriptions may be needed, and it is here that qualitative research is at its most useful. It can define the parameters for future studies, and identify key criteria among consumers that can subsequently be measured using quantitative research. For example, if a supermarket observed that its older customers were unwilling to register for its loyalty card programme, it might conduct some qualitative research among its older customers in order to develop greater understanding about why this particular group was reluctant to subscribe. (Perhaps it might uncover an underlying scepticism towards the idea of deferring rewards to the future; or there may be greater concerns over privacy; or perhaps a loyalty card may even subliminally bring back memories of wartime ration cards.)

Probably the most widely used qualitative approach in marketing research is the focus group. This entails inviting a group of individuals to discuss an issue about which a company is interested to learn more. Participants are invited to contribute to an understanding of an issue on the basis of their ability, rather than on the basis of being a statistically significant representation of the population being studied. A trained moderator will guide the discussion, but she needs to be careful not to put too many ideas into the minds of participants that might stifle their originality of thought. There are numerous approaches to managing a focus group that have the aim of reducing the bias caused by the intervention of the moderator and stimulating contribution from the invited members. Some researchers have had success by recording conversations between friends that tend to be relatively uninhibited. Although focus groups do not aim to be statistically representative of the population, some concerns have been expressed that they may become dominated by semi-professional participants, who make a living out of payments made to participants. Their views may be quite different from those of 'ordinary' consumers.

An alternative to the focus group is to use a one-to-one discussion format, which is especially useful for studying the behaviour and attitudes of employees of organizations, and also where confidentiality is an important concern of participants. Although one-to-one discussions may reduce problems of confidentiality, this approach does not allow the researcher to study peer-group interaction, which may be important when studying attitudes to items of ostentatious consumption.

In seeking to discover hidden meanings of phenomena, qualitative researchers use a number of techniques that are not available to the quantitative researcher. Projective techniques, including word association (often used in connection with research into proposed brand names), sentence completion, and interpreting a storyboard, are commonly used, but can demand skill in their interpretation.

It is very difficult to assess the validity of qualitative research techniques, and the tests for significance that are available for most quantitative techniques are largely lacking for qualitative techniques; so how can a client company that has commissioned qualitative research assess whether the findings are credible? Consider the following possibilities:

- Market research demands cooperation and trust between the client commissioning a study and the company carrying it out. The reputation that a market research agency has built for itself is particularly important where qualitative research is involved.

- Increasingly, qualitative research techniques are utilizing quasi-quantitative techniques in order to enhance their credibility (or at least the appearance of credibility). There are now a number of computer programs (e.g. NVivo) which essentially analyse the content of discussions and count key words, phrases, and contexts.

Qualitative research has been a major growth activity in marketing over the past couple of decades.

🔵 Who carries out marketing research?

Marketing researchers fall into two groups.

1. There are those employed by manufacturers and services companies (often referred to as 'client' companies) who collect internal data and commission research from outside organizations when needed.

2. A large industry of market research firms is available to carry out the research that client companies are unable or unwilling to carry out themselves. (Among the larger companies in this category are BMRB, Ispos MORI, and Taylor Nelson Sofres.) Staff employed by these companies can achieve a high level of expertise in particular research techniques or particular product areas. (For example, Verdict Research has achieved particular skills in the field of retailing.) Some of these companies undertake **omnibus surveys** on behalf of a number of clients simultaneously, thereby reducing the costs to each client.

The research process shown in Figure 5.3 allows for the expertise of both groups to be used at different stages. Client company researchers initially define a research problem, after internal discussion with marketing and other management. This is usually communicated to potential suppliers in the form of a research brief. The objectives of the study are determined by matching management information needs with what can realistically be obtained from the marketplace, particularly in the light of time and budgetary constraints, and these may well be defined after initial discussions with possible suppliers.

Specialist market research suppliers tend to dominate at the stage of data collection, for two main reasons. First, very few client companies, however large or diverse their product range, can generate sufficient research to warrant employing full-time specialist interviewers throughout the country. Much research is seasonal or one-off, and it would be more expensive for a company to retain research capacity that is required only intermittently, than to buy it in as and when required. The second reason is that respondents may be more likely to give honest answers to third parties than when replying directly to representatives of the organization being discussed. Data collectors are also less likely to be biased when they are working for a company that is independent of their own employer. However, commercial market research companies have sometimes been accused of focusing more on techniques than on identifying really useful information to a company (Savage, 2001).

Relationships between client companies and their suppliers can involve high levels of trust and cooperation, and many relationships between the two are very longstanding. Before deciding on the final plan, however, it is usual for client companies to approach several possible suppliers and ask for their suggestions in the form of a research proposal. The extent of involvement of the client company in the research process is largely dependent upon the size and expertise of its research department.

Marketing intelligence

Market research has so far been described in terms of establishing customers' characteristics and preferences in a structured manner. Another approach is to gather relatively unstructured information about the environment in a format that is often referred to as **marketing intelligence**. Business owners have developed over a long time the art of 'keeping their ear close to the ground' through informal networks of contacts. With the growing sophistication of the business environment, these informal methods of gathering intelligence often need to be supplemented. In contrast to market research, intelligence gathering concentrates on picking up relatively intangible ideas and trends, especially about competitors' developments.

Carson *et al.* (2001) described how marketing managers use networks, often haphazardly and informally, to gather information. They noted that for many small business owners, 'research' is inseparable from daily business. According to their study, research by networking is 'informal, often discreet, interactive, interchangeable, integrated, habitual, reactive, individualistic, and highly focused on the enterprise' (Carson *et al.*, 2001, p. 56).

Marketing managers can gather this intelligence from a number of sources, including the following.

- By regularly scanning newspapers, especially trade newspapers, a company can learn about competitors' planned new product launches.

- There are now many specialized media-cutting services that will regularly review published material and alert a company to items that fall within pre-determined criteria.

- Employees are a valuable source of marketing intelligence, especially in services organizations where they are in regular contact with customers. Sales personnel can act as the ears as well as the mouth for an organization. Staff suggestion schemes and quality circles are often used to gain market intelligence, in addition to informal methods of listening to front-line employees.

- Similarly, intermediaries are close to customers, and their observations are often encouraged through seminars, consultation meetings, and informal communication methods.

- When a firm feels that it does not have the resources to undertake any of the above, it may retain consultants to provide regular briefings.

Market intelligence is a valuable contributor to the development of corporate knowledge, which is considered next.

Knowledge management

Knowledge is one of the greatest assets of most commercial organizations, and its contribution to sustainable competitive advantage has been widely recognized (e.g. Pugh and Dixon, 2008). Information represents a bridge between the organization and its environment and is the means by which a picture of the changing environment is built up within the organization. Marketing management is responsible for turning information-based knowledge into specific marketing plans.

In 1991, Ikujiro Nonaka began an article in the *Harvard Business Review* with a simple statement: 'In an economy where the only certainty is uncertainty, the one sure source of lasting competitive advantage is knowledge' (Nonaka, 1991). A firm's knowledge base is likely to include, among other things, an understanding of the precise needs of customers; how those needs are likely to change over time; how those needs are satisfied in terms of efficient and effective production systems, and an understanding of competitors' activities. We are probably all familiar with companies in which knowledge seems to be very poor—the hotel reservation that is mixed up, the delivery that does not happen as specified, or junk mail which is of no interest at all. On the other hand, customers may revel in a company that delivers the right service at the right time and clearly demonstrates that it is knowledgeable about all aspects of the transaction. The small business owner may have been able to achieve all of this by himself, but in large organizations the task of managing knowledge becomes much more complex. Where it is done well, it can be a significant contributor to a firm's sustainable competitive advantage.

We need to distinguish between the terms 'knowledge' and 'information'. Even though in some senses they may be used interchangeably, many writers have suggested that the two concepts are quite distinct. Knowledge is a much more all-encompassing term, incorporating the concept of beliefs that are based on information. Knowledge also depends on the commitment and understanding of the individual holding these beliefs, which are affected by interaction and the development of judgement, behaviour, and attitude. Knowledge has meaning only in the context of a process or capacity to act. Drucker noted that 'There is no such thing as knowledge management, there are only knowledgeable people. Information only becomes knowledge in the hands of someone who knows what to do with it' (Drucker, 1999). Knowledge, then, is evidenced by its association with actions, and its source can be found in a combination of information, social interaction, and contextual situations which affect the knowledge accumulation process at an individual level. One outcome of a knowledge-based organization has often been referred to as the 'learning organization', in which the challenge is to learn at the corporate level from what is known by individuals who make up the organization.

Two different types of knowledge can be identified.

1. Knowledge that is easily definable and is accessible is often referred to as **explicit knowledge**. This type of knowledge can be readily quantified and passed between individuals in the form of words and numbers. Because it is easily communicated, it is relatively easy to manage. Knowledge management is concerned with ensuring that the explicit knowledge of individuals becomes a part of the organizational knowledge base and that it is used efficiently and contributes where necessary to changes in work practices, processes, and products.

2. The second type of knowledge comprises the accumulated knowledge of individuals, which is not explicit, but can still be important to the successful operation of an organization. This type of knowledge, often referred to as **tacit knowledge**, is not easy to see or express; it is highly personal and is rooted in an individual's experiences, attitudes, values, and behaviour patterns. Tacit knowledge can be much more difficult to formalize and disseminate within an organization. If tacit knowledge can be captured, mobilized, and turned into explicit knowledge, it will then be accessible to others in the organization and will enable the organization to progress, rather than require individuals within it continually to have to relearn from the same point. The owner of a small business could have all of this information readily available to him in his head. The challenge taken on by many large corporations is to emulate the knowledge management of the small business owner.

MARKETING in ACTION

Management by Walking About

Information is often described as management's window on the world. But what happens if management works in a large corporate head office, far removed from customers and day-to-day operations? It is sadly all too familiar for senior management to become cut off from the operations that they manage. In a BBC television series, 'Back to the Floor', chief executives were invited to spend a few days changing their role to that of a front-line employee. For some of the participants this was unfamiliar territory, which hadn't been witnessed at first hand for some time (if ever). The gulf between what these key decision-makers thought was happening and what was actually happening was sometimes quite marked. In one case, the then chief executive of the grocery retailer Sainsbury's seemed to be oblivious of customers' annoyance with shopping trolley design and availability, and in another the chief executive of Pickford's Removals couldn't understand why the company was so inflexible when minor changes in customers' requirements occurred. The managers of small businesses do not generally have such problems, as they are in regular contact with their customers and do not need structured information management systems to give them a window on the world. Their success in keeping in touch with customers has led many larger businesses to emulate some of their practices. **Management by Walking About** A has become a popular way in which senior executives try to gain knowledge about their marketing environment that is not immediately apparent from structured reporting systems. Archie Norman, when head of the retailer Asda, is reported to have introduced a number of innovations learned during his regular visits to the company's shop-floors. Some companies have adopted a formal system of role exchanges where senior executives spend a period at the sharp end of their business.

If you are studying at a university, do you believe that the vice chancellor really has a good understanding of the day-to-day issues that are of greatest concern to students? Some vice chancellors have taken the bold step of trying to live student life for a day or a week. What benefits can you see in this approach? Are there any possible problems in this approach?

The transition from individuals' information to corporate knowledge requires a sharing of knowledge by all concerned. This raises problems in which employees perceive that knowledge is a powerful asset which they can use in their negotiations with senior management or other functional departments. A knowledge management programme is needed to break down a laissez-faire attitude, and typically would include the following elements:

- a strong knowledge-sharing culture, which can emerge only over time with the development of trust;

- measures to monitor that sharing, which may be reflected in individuals' performance reviews;

- technology to facilitate knowledge transfer, which should be as user-friendly as possible;

- established practices for the capture and sharing of knowledge—without clearly defined procedures, the technology is of only limited value;

- leadership and senior management commitment to sharing information—if senior management does not share information, why should anybody else bother?

It must be remembered that marketing information cannot in itself produce decisions: it merely provides data which must be interpreted by marketing managers. Also, as information collection, processing, transmission, and storage technologies improve, information is becoming more accessible not just to one particular organization, but also to its competitors. Competitive advantage is more likely to go to those companies that are best able to make use of the available information.

Demand forecasting

It should never be forgotten that a key task of marketing management in general, and of marketing research in particular, is to gather a better picture of the future so that a company can be prepared for it more efficiently and effectively than its competitors. Demand forecasting can involve predicting general changes in the marketing environment that were discussed in Chapter 2. This in itself can be very difficult; for example, economists frequently disagree in their forecasts of economic growth during the year ahead. When it comes to predicting macro-environmental change, larger companies often retain expert consultants, such as the Future Foundation (www.futurefoundation.net), who employ economists, sociologists, and psychologists, among others, to try to build a picture of the world as it will evolve. Such macro-level forecasts can inform more detailed forecasts about market size, growth rates, market share, etc.

There have been many cases of spectacular failures to forecast demand accurately, of which the following are a few examples:

- When Carphone Warehouse launched its new 'free' broadband service in 2006, it experienced an unexpectedly high level of take-up, resulting in delays and frustration for potential customers.

- Many people in the industry expected the launch of 'Freeview' digital television services in 2002 to be a flop, following the previous low levels of take-up of ITV digital services. In fact, Freeview quickly became very popular, with reports of shortages of set-top adapter boxes.

- Each Christmas seems to witness another new toy which has become an unexpected success with children, leading to shortages, while other new toys fail to sell and end up being discounted in the January sales.

Figure 5.7 London's Millennium Dome (now known as the O$_2$ Arena), was open to the public for just one year in 2000, and proved to be a disappointment in terms of visitor numbers. Against forecasts of 12 million paying visitors, only about half this figure actually visited. Forecasts were made difficult because of the absence of comparable previous projects which might have given some idea of the likely take-up. Many uncertainties remained during the forecasting process, including the effects of competing millennium attractions, the impact of press reviews, the state of the national economy, and the capacity of the local transport infrastructure. Also, low initial numbers appeared to develop a momentum of its own, as the media talked down the success of the project, leading to many more people deciding to give the event a miss.

A forecast of likely demand is a crucial input to a firm's strategic and operational planning processes. In the case of Carphone Warehouse's broadband offer, the forecast of new customer applications was used as an input to the firm's human resource plan, so when the marketing demand forecast proved to be wrong, the human resource plan—which had recruited to cater for a lower level of forecast demand—also proved wrong.

The amount of effort that a firm puts into refining its demand forecasting techniques calls for a balancing of the cost of undertaking a detailed study against the cost of making an inaccurate forecast. Where capital costs are low, it may make sense to go straight to the market with a product to see what happens. It was noted earlier that this is common in the fashion clothing industry. At other times, a more analytic approach to demand forecasting is required (refer back to Figure 5.3).

Demand forecasting uses many of the analytic techniques—quantitative and qualitative—described earlier in this chapter. A starting point for demand forecasting is an examination of historical trends. At its simplest, a firm identifies a historic and consistent long-term change in demand for a product over time and seeks to explain this in terms of change in some underlying variables, such as household income levels or price levels. Correlation and regression techniques can be used to assess the significance of historical relationships between variables. However, a simple extrapolation of past trends has a number of weaknesses. One variable, or even a small number of variables, is seldom adequate to predict future demand for a product, yet it can be difficult to identify the full set of variables that have an influence. New variables may emerge over time. There can be no certainty that the trends identified from historic data are likely to continue in the future, and the data are of diminishing value as the length of time that they are used to forecast increases.

Models have become increasingly sophisticated in their ability to forecast consumer demand. This can be explained partly by a growing amount of readily available data (and staff who can use it), which can be used to build and validate a model. Reliability is improved by increasing the volume of data on which a model is based and the number of variables that are used for prediction.

Inevitably, models, no matter how sophisticated, need interpretation. This is where the creative side of marketing management is called for, especially in combining market intelligence with harder economic approaches. In interpreting quantitative demand forecasts, management must use its judgement, based on a holistic overview of the market situation.

Chapter summary and key linkages to other chapters

Understanding customers is critical to business success, and this chapter has discussed some of the approaches to market research. Marketing management is a combination of a science and an art, and this is reflected in approaches to gathering and analysing marketing information. The chapter has built on our review of the marketing environment (Chapter 2) and buyer behaviour (Chapter 4), which marketers must try to understand and predict into the future. Appropriate research methods are necessary for conducting segmentation exercises, to be discussed in Chapter 6. In the following chapters we will look at how research is used to inform decisions about a company's product development, pricing, distribution, and promotion activities.

▢ KEY PRINCIPLES OF MARKETING

- The ultimate aim of much of a company's research activity is essentially to gain a better understanding of its likely future marketing environment.
- Information is a source of a company's competitive advantage.
- Information on its own does not make decisions—management must use its judgement to interpret information.
- Learning organizations develop knowledge at a corporate level in order to provide a more efficient and effective response to environmental change.
- Research techniques need to be appropriate to the task in hand.
- Qualitative techniques provide for depth of understanding, while quantitative techniques provide for broad representation. The two techniques overlap.

CASE STUDY

Drowning in data, searching for insight?

Companies are able to capture ever-increasing amounts of information through electronically stored till receipts, order forms, registration cards, etc., from which almost endless correlation coefficients may be calculated. In recent times, researchers' analyses have shown correlations between an individual's height and his annual expenditure on clothing; shoe size and usage of gyms; and purchases of milk and purchases of paint. Some of these might at first sound quite spurious, and the researcher's task is to probe more deeply to establish whether there really is any direct causative relationship between the two variables, or whether there is some other intervening factor that may explain the observed correlation. Of course, sometimes the correlation is of little more than amusement value, and often it is used by research sponsors for its PR value. Would gym operators ever really want to target customers with large or small feet?

   The retailer Tesco is one of many companies that routinely gathers large volumes of data about its customers. Each year, it accumulates literally billions of pieces of information from its retail operations—sales of individual product lines, how these products are combined in customers' shopping baskets, data relating to the time of purchase and place of purchase, etc. For customers who registered with the company's 'Clubcard' loyalty programme, the quantity and quality of information is even greater. The card allows the company to track an individual's purchases over time, allowing it an opportunity to try to understand long-term trends at both the individual customer level, and possibly trends which are general between customers. The company also buys in information about customers, for example Clubcard holders give their address, and the postcode is used to match their expenditure with a particular 'ACORN' customer profile. From this information, the company can begin to build up a picture of spending habits related to postcode types.

Tesco's club card has both operational and planning functions. As an operational tool, it has been invaluable for targeting individual customers with offers that are of particular value to them as an individual. As an example, the company operates a mother and baby club which targets new mothers, and mothers-to-be with product offers to which they are likely to be particularly receptive. As a planning tool, the Clubcard allows the company to look for patterns in consumer spending. This can be useful, for example, for planning the location of new stores, allowing the company to have a better idea of likely sales and the best product mix, depending upon the previous spending pattern of local postcode types.

Using research data, the company frequently conducts experiments and monitors the results. A promotional offer can be mailed to a sample of people on its database and the results studied before the promotional offer is refined and targeted at a larger segment of its database. Experiments can be conducted with store layouts, opening hours, and product ranges and the results assessed before being rolled out nationally.

Although Tesco is sitting on a mountain of data, this alone is not always sufficient to give real insight into consumer behaviour. The story has frequently been told of an exercise undertaken by the company using data-mining techniques that apparently discovered a correlation between sales of beer and sales of babies' nappies. The two products were not in any way complementary to each other, so why should their sales appear to be associated? Was this just another spurious correlation, to be binned along with other gems of information such as a previously reported correlation between an individual's shoe size and their propensity to use a gym? The company didn't give up, and refined its analysis to study the correlation for different categories of store and by different times of day. Where it also had details of customers' demographic characteristics (gathered through its Clubcard programme) it was able to probe for further insights. The company was edging towards a better understanding of why the sales of these two products should be closely correlated. However, the data alone could not provide a complete answer, and to achieve this, the company had to resort to more traditional qualitative research techniques. Having identified individuals where this correlation was evident, the company is reported to have undertaken qualitative research to probe why these consumers were buying the two products in combination. From this, it appeared that men were offering to run a household errand to the shops in order to buy babies' nappies. This was an excuse to leave the family home in order to buy more beer for their own consumption. The company is claimed to have learned from this exercise and subsequently positioned the two products closer together in selected stores.

The story of Tesco's analysis of beer and nappy sales may have become distorted with telling, and may even come close to being an urban myth; but should it take a huge database and data-mining techniques to reveal these insights to buyers' behaviour? The landlord of the traditional

Irish bar spotted a very similar pattern of buyer motivation long ago, with bars doubling up as the local post office, bookseller, or grocer, giving the Irish drinker plenty of good excuses for visiting the pub. The Irish bar owner would have had none of the technology available to today's businesses, just a good set of ears and eyes.

It is sometimes said that today's marketers are drowning in data, but are often short of common sense. Do we sometimes look for complex technological solutions to understand customers, when the answer might be much easier to find using more traditional judgements?

Source: based on Clive Humby, Terry Hunt, and Tim Phillips (2003), *Scoring Points: How Tesco is Winning Customer Loyalty,* London: Kogan Page; Tesco corporate website (www.tesco.com)

Case study review questions

1. Critically evaluate the relative merits of quantitative and qualitative approaches to data collection for a large retailer.

2. Discuss the limitations of statistically based consumer databases of the type discussed here. Do qualitative approaches based on small groups offer any advantages?

3. What effects do you expect the development of interactive electronic media to have on retailers' collection of marketing research information from consumers?

CHAPTER REVIEW QUESTIONS

1. In what ways does information contribute to a firm's competitive advantage? Can a company ever have too much information?

2. What factors should influence the amount of time and money that a firm commits to the collection, analysis, and dissemination of marketing information?

3. The view is often expressed that quantitative survey techniques fail to tell the whole truth about customers' perceptions of a company's products. To what extent is this true, and how can companies address this issue?

ACTIVITIES

1. If you are studying at a university or college, identify a list of likely key marketing research objectives for the university.

2. Gather a selection of printed customer surveys from restaurants, hotels, etc. Critically discuss the insights that you think the surveys' sponsors will be able to gain from the survey form.

3. If you were considering opening a new Sushi bar in your local town, how would you go about researching likely demand? How would you try to identify the best location for your restaurant?

⬚ REFERENCES

Ashworth, L. and Free, C. (2006), 'Marketing Dataveillance and Digital Privacy: using theories of justice to understand consumers' online privacy concerns'. *Journal of Business Ethics*, 67(2): 107–23.

Brown, S. (1998), *Postmodern Marketing* 2: telling tales. London: Thomson International Business Press.

Carson, D., Gilmore, A., Perry, C., and Gronhaug, K. (2001), *Qualitative Marketing Research*. London: Sage.

Drucker, P. (1999), *The Frontier of Management: where tomorrow's decisions are being shaped today*. New York: Truman Talley.

Fugate, D. L. (2008), 'Marketing Services More Effectively with Neuromarketing Research: a look into the future'. *Journal of Services Marketing*, 22(3): 70–3.

Humby, C., Hunt, T., and Phillips, T. (2003), Scoring Points: how Tesco is winning customer loyalty. London: Kogan Page.

Nonaka, I. (1991), 'The Knowledge Creating Company'. *Harvard Business Review*, 69(6): 96–104.

Pugh, K. and Dixon N. M. (2008), 'Don't Just Capture Knowledge—Put It to Work'. *Harvard Business Review*, 86(5) (May).

Savage, M. (2001), 'A View from the Board Room'. *Research*, August: 16–18.

Smith, D. and Dexter, A. (2001), 'Whenever I Hear the Word Paradigm I Reach for my Gun: how to stop talking and start walking'. *International Journal of Market Research*, 43(3): 321–40.

Tuckel, P. and O'Neill, H. (2002), 'The Vanishing Respondent in Telephone Surveys'. *Journal of Advertising Research*, 42(5): 26–48.

⬚ SUGGESTED FURTHER READING

The market research process in general is described in more detail in a number of books. The following texts provide useful coverage of the principles introduced in this chapter:

Hague, P. and Hague, N. (2004), *Market Research in Practice: a guide to the basics*. London: Kogan Page.

Proctor, T. (2005), *Essentials of Marketing Research*, 4th edn. London: FT Prentice Hall.

Wilson, A. (2006), *Marketing Research: an integrated approach,* 2nd edn. London: FT Prentice Hall.

The following regularly updated UK government statistics are frequently used as a basis for marketing research:

Basic Statistics of the European Community.

Economic Trends: a monthly compendium of economic data which gives convenient access from one source to a range of economic indicators.

Family Expenditure Survey: a sample survey of consumer spending habits, providing a snapshot of household spending; published annually.

Population Trends: statistics on population, including population change, births and deaths, life expectancy, and migration.

Regional Trends: a comprehensive source of statistics about the regions of the UK allowing regional comparisons.

Social Trends: statistics combined with text, tables, and charts which present a narrative of life and lifestyles in the UK; published annually.

UK National Accounts (the Blue Book): the principal annual publication for National Account statistics, covering value added by industry, the personal sector, companies, public corporations, central and local government; published annually.

The subject of turning research information into corporate knowledge is addressed in the following:

Ichijo, K. and Nonaka, I. (2006), *Knowledge creation and management: new challenges for managers.* USA: Oxford University Press.

Hislop, D. (2004), Knowledge Management in Organizations: a critical introduction. Oxford: Oxford University Press.

▢ USEFUL WEB LINKS

Visit the Online Resource Centre for resources that are relevant to this chapter, including web links, multiple choice questions, and additional case studies:

www.oxfordtextbooks.co.uk/orc/palmer2e/

▢ KEY TERMS

- **Cluster analysis**
- **Conjoint analysis**
- **Correlation analysis**
- **Desk research**
- **Environmental scanning**
- **Explicit knowledge**
- **Field research**
- **Focus group**
- **Key clients**
- **Knowledge**
- **Management by Walking About**
- **Market research**
- **Marketing intelligence**
- **Marketing research**
- **Models**
- **Mystery shoppers**
- **Omnibus surveys**
- **Primary research**
- **Qualitative research**
- **Quantitative research**
- **Regression analysis**
- **Sampling**
- **Secondary research**
- **SERVQUAL**
- **Tacit knowledge**

6

Segmentation, positioning, and targeting

CHAPTER OBJECTIVES

Customers are becoming increasingly diverse in their needs and aspirations, and less inclined to accept an 'average' product. The purpose of segmentation is to identify groups of buyers who respond in a similar way to any given marketing stimuli. This chapter explores the bases for market segmentation and how these are used by companies to target selected groups. Some of the bases for identifying different types of customer are familiar and readily observable, such as age, gender, and geographical location. Others, such as attitudes and lifestyle, may be more difficult to identify, but can be crucial for understanding consumers' buying processes. To be effective, a company's products must be positioned relative to competitors' products in such a way that targeted segments find them the most attractive for satisfying their needs.

Why segment markets?

From Chapter 1 you will recall that a focus on meeting customers' needs is a defining characteristic of marketing. Organizations that make presumptions about customers' needs, or produce goods and services that are chosen for their convenience in production, are probably not truly marketing orientated. A true marketing orientation requires companies to focus on meeting the needs of individual customers. In a simple world where consumers all have broadly similar needs and expectations, a company could probably justify developing a marketing programme that meets the needs of the 'average' customer. In the early days of motoring, Henry Ford successfully sold as many standard, black Model T Fords as he was able to produce. In the modern world of marketing, few companies can have the luxury of producing just one product to satisfy a very large market. Some still can—for example, water supply utility companies generally produce a single standard of water for all of their customers—but this is the exception rather than the rule. Most companies face markets that are becoming increasingly fragmented in terms of the needs customers seek to satisfy. So, while Henry Ford's customers may have been quite happy to have a plain black car, today's car buyers seek out differentiated products in order to satisfy a much wider range of needs. The 'average' customer to whom Henry Ford appealed is increasingly becoming a myth.

Segmentation, then, is essentially about identifying groups of buyers within a marketplace who have needs that are distinctive in the way they deviate from the 'average' consumer (Figure 6.1). Some consumers may treat satisfaction of one particular need as a high priority, whereas others may regard this need as quite trivial. We saw in Chapter 4 how an understanding of needs is crucial to the study of buyer behaviour. We will pick up the question of needs again by considering the buying behaviour for cars. Buyers no longer select a car solely on the basis of a car's ability to satisfy a need to take them from A to B: in addition, they may seek to satisfy any of the following needs from a car purchase:

- to give them status in the eyes of their peer group;
- to provide safety and security for themselves and their families;
- to project a particular image of themselves;

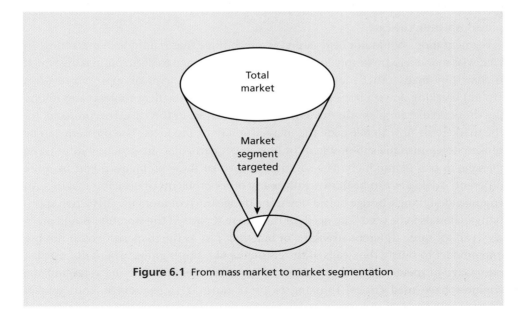

Figure 6.1 From mass market to market segmentation

- to provide a cost-effective means of transport;
- to be seen making a gesture towards the environment by buying a 'green' car;
- if it is a company car, to save company car tax.

There are many more possible factors that might influence an individual's choice of car. The important point here is that the market is composed of buyers who approach their decisions to buy a car in very different ways. Therefore, the features that each looks for in the product offer may differ quite markedly from the market average. It follows that, with a wide dispersion of market needs, a marketing plan based on satisfying the needs of the average buyer will be unlikely to succeed in a competitive marketplace. If another company can better satisfy the needs of small specialist groups, then the company that seeks to serve them with just an 'average' product offer will lose business from this group.

We will define the process of market segmentation as,

the identification of sub-sets of buyers within a market who share similar needs and who have similar buying processes.

In an ideal world, firms would tailor their product offering to the needs of each individual customer. In the case of some expensive items of capital equipment bought by firms, this indeed does happen. (For example, there are very few buyers of large power stations in the UK, so firms can justifiably treat each customer as a segment of one.) In the case of products that are relatively low in value and high in sales volume, it would be practically impossible for firms to cater to each individual's needs, although developments in technology are allowing for a much greater degree of customization than has previously been the case.

Segmentation should not be regarded as a technique that is unique to marketing. In fact, wise marketers are simply following a critical approach to decicion-making which is shared by many other professions and disciplines. The critical approach revolves around breaking down a large problem into a number of smaller problems and resolving those smaller problems in the most appropriate way. In this case, the 'problem' for the marketer is how to persuade the market to buy its products. The problem can be broken down into the sub-problems of how to get particular sub-groups within those markets to buy its products. The solution to each of these problems might be quite different. Analogies can be drawn with many other problems of decicion-making. An engineer designing a bridge breaks down the bridge into component parts when specifying materials to be used. The needs of the different parts of the structure would probably call for quite different strengths of material. Just as the marketer would not use one product to satisfy the needs of the entire market, the engineer would not use just one gauge of metal to build the entire bridge structure. Both the marketer and the engineer have used critical thinking to break down a large problem into smaller problems (Figure 6.2).

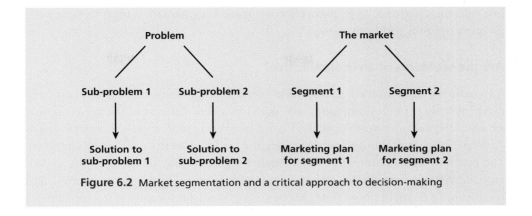

Figure 6.2 Market segmentation and a critical approach to decision-making

Criteria for effective segmentation

Market segmentation should be regarded as the product of critical thinking rather than as some predetermined set of procedures. There is no underlying theory to the process of market segmentation. It follows that what is an appropriate basis for segmenting one market may not be appropriate to all markets.

Before we begin to look at the bases on which marketers can segment any given market, we need to be aware of the criteria by which the effectiveness of any segmentation basis can be assessed. We will consider here four important criteria: usefulness to a company's marketing planning; size of the resulting segments; their measurability; and their accessibility.

Is the basis of market segmentation useful to the company?

It is easy to develop bases for market segmentation while losing sight of the purpose of the exercise. Essentially, the exercise is worthwhile only if it allows a company profitably to penetrate a greater proportion of its market than would have been the case if the exercise had not been undertaken. Groups identified as homogeneous market segments must be just that: similar in terms of the needs and buying behaviour of the individuals they contain. Many companies fail in their segmentation exercises because their assumptions about homogeneity within a segment overlook some critical differences within the segment that leads to varied responses to a product offer that has been specifically **targeted** at the segment. For example, a segment for overseas package holidays defined as 'affluent, married, working women' may overlook the fact that women within this segment have very divergent views on the features they seek from a holiday, depending on the age and structure of their families. The buying behaviour of those affluent, married, working women who seek to take their children away with them is quite likely to be significantly different from those who seek to travel by themselves or just with their partners. To be more effective, market segmentation must recognize the diversity of needs within this group.

Are the segments of an economic size?

Any basis for segmentation should yield segments that are of a size that a company can profitably exploit. Companies face a dilemma here, because as segments become smaller, they become closer to achieving the marketing philosophy of satisfying each customer's needs as though each one were the centre of all the company's attention. The problem for the company is that smaller segments may be uneconomic to provide for. What is a reasonable size of segment varies from one market to another, and is constantly changing over time. In the financial services industry, it is possible to develop quite specific products to target very small segments of a market. For example, it would involve relatively little effort by an insurance company to develop motor insurance policies that specifically meet the needs of people driving 'classic' vintage cars, further sub-divided into those who live in the north of England, and further sub-divided into those aged over 50 years. In principle, there are few operational reasons why an insurance broker should not focus on a segment that small. At the other extreme, a company manufacturing paint for the private household market might find it difficult to offer a range as customer-focused as this. For example, a paint manufacturer might wish to produce variants of paints for the following identified segments:

- users who are averse to painting (for this group, the manufacturer might develop a product that is non-spill and delicately perfumed);
- the 'professional' home decorator segment who seeks perfection through multi-coat application;
- the time-constrained perfectionist who seeks a one-coat paint with durable finish;
- the adventurous, who seek special-effect patterns from their paint (e.g. mottled effects).

To produce each new variant of paint, the manufacturer would probably have to stop its production lines to prepare for the next specialized product. Worse still, it would have to persuade its wholesalers and retailers to stock each such variant. When each colour variant is multiplied by the number of segment-specific formulations, it is clear that the stockholding problems for retailers and wholesalers could be immense.

Manufacturers are becoming increasingly able to offer specialized goods to meet the needs of small market segments. Service industries have had this flexibility for some time, and are now exploiting it to the full with the use of information technology. Within the manufacturing sector, flexible manufacturing systems are allowing smaller production runs to be achieved economically. For Henry Ford, producing even a slight variant of his original car would have meant stopping the production line and re-tooling

Figure 6.3 The marketing environment has tended to allow firms to target increasingly small market segments. Flexible manufacturing systems, interactive communication via the Internet and more flexible stock-handling methods have contributed to this. In the consumer market for paint, which is dominated in the UK by two large manufacturers and a handful of major retail outlets, a market exists for specialist organic paints. Ecos Organic Paints offers a range of environmentally friendly paints targeted at niche markets of paint buyers who may be concerned about allergies or environmental damage. Using flexible manufacturing and stock-handling systems, the company is able to offer next-day delivery of a wide range of paints. (Reproduced with permission of Ecos Organic Paints)

for a new model. Today, car assembly lines employ computerized design and manufacturing systems, which, combined with interchangeability of components, allow many different models to come off the same production line.

Can the market segments be measured?

Ideally, companies should be able to know the precise size of all market segments that it has identified. This is important in order that segments can be compared and their profit potentials assessed. Unfortunately, data are often not available to quantify market segments. Marketers therefore face a further dilemma in defining market segments. Should they go for segments that they believe exist but cannot measure, or should they define segments only on the basis of what can accurately be measured, but which may have little bearing on the homogeneity of consumers' needs and buying processes? As an example, the UK Population Census gives a wealth of valuable information that is frequently used as a basis for identifying market segments (for example, the age profile of an area, number of people per household, etc.). However, marketers are often interested in a more subjective assessment of individuals, such as their **attitudes** and **lifestyles**. Unfortunately, there is very little published information on these more subjective aspects of market segments. While we can know quite accurately the size of the segment of people aged over 60 and living alone in a particular area, there is very little readily available information about how many people living in that area can be described as 'environmentally aware' or 'liberal in attitudes' or any other measure of attitudes or lifestyle. Inevitably, marketing managers must make a trade-off between the need for information that is objective and reliable on the one hand and subjective and creative on the other.

Fortunately for marketers, the sources of information available that can be used to segment markets are constantly increasing. In addition to traditional government statistical sources, many private-sector organizations (for example, Mintel, Keynote, and nVision) frequently commission and publish research that is based on surveys of samples of the population.

Are the segments accessible to the company?

There is little point in going to a great deal of effort in defining segments of a market when those segments are not accessible to the company, or ever likely to be. Inaccessibility can come about for a number of reasons.

- The company may be prohibited by law from entering certain markets. (For example, many overseas governments restrict the rights of foreign companies to serve their domestic market.)

- Some buyers in a market may be tied to suppliers by long-term supply contracts. In the case of subsidiaries of large corporations, the holding company may require its subsidiaries to obtain its purchases from within the group.

- Although it may be possible, the cost of gaining access to a market segment may be prohibitive. A manufacturer of building materials in the UK may in theory be able to supply a segment of small building contractors in southern Italy, but the cost of transporting its bulky goods over the distances involved may make the segment effectively inaccessible.

Although a segment may be inaccessible to a company now, this may not always continue to be the case. Changes in legislation may make possible something that was previously illegal for a company. Policies of large companies towards the contracting out of supplies may present new opportunities. Even segments that seemed inaccessible because of high transport costs may become accessible through the development of a joint venture company.

Bases for market segmentation

A basis for segmenting a market should satisfy the criteria described above. It was noted that companies often need to make trade-offs in arriving at a basis for market segmentation that meets these criteria. It follows, therefore, that firms seldom use one basis for market segmentation alone. In Figure 6.4 a number of segmentation bases are plotted in terms of their measurability and usefulness to a typical manufacturer of ready-prepared meals. (Segmentation here is defined in terms of final consumers, although, as Chapter 10 will discuss, segmentation can also be applied to different types of intermediary who will handle the product.)

Markets can be segmented using a variety of philosophical approaches. In terms of operationalizing these approaches, demographic approaches, **socio-economic** approaches, and psychographic approaches are commonly used. Overlap often occurs between these approaches to segmentation.

Demographic bases for segmentation

Demography is the study of population characteristics, and demographers have used a number of key indicators in their studies of populations. Most methods of segmenting consumer markets make some use of demographic characteristics. In this section we

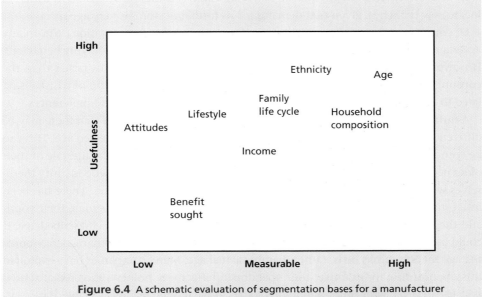

Figure 6.4 A schematic evaluation of segmentation bases for a manufacturer of ready-prepared meals, based on their usefulness and measurability

will consider a number of demographic-related bases for segmenting markets: age, the stage in the **family life cycle**, gender, and household composition.

Age

Age is probably one of the most widely used bases for market segmentation. It satisfies many of the criteria for effective segmentation discussed above. It is useful to companies because demand for many products appears to be age related. There are many obvious examples; for example, music buying peaks among the 18–25-year age group, and the purchase of cruise holidays increases after the age of 50. There are also more subtle age-related patterns of demand within particular categories of product. Within the UK retail sector, for example, many chains are associated with particular age groups. While the Arcadia clothing chain's Top Shop brand targets a mainly young 18–30-year age segment, its Principles brand is more attractive to the 21–40-year segment, and the BHS brand to 30+ shoppers. The usefulness of age can be explained partly by the observation that people's tastes change as they grow older. Some of this may be related to their stage in the family life cycle, which is age related, as well as to changes in disposable income (see below).

Age segmentation meets another important criterion in that it is generally easy to measure the size of segments. Population censuses record respondents' ages, while many privately collected sources of information (such as company-sponsored questionnaires) frequently ask for such information. A company can therefore be reasonably confident about how many people belong to a particular age segment within a specific area. This information might be vital to a retail chain seeking the best areas in which to locate new branches, given that demand for its format of stores is very age specific.

Of course, age alone is not usually a good basis for market segmentation. Within any age segment, individuals can be observed who exhibit quite different buying behaviour. However, differences often relate to the preference for specific brands rather than the consumption of a particular product. For example, while consumption of whisky is related to age, considerable diversity exists within age segments in brand preferences.

A further reservation on the use of age as a segmentation variable is that there may be differences between an individual's actual biological age and his perceived age. This can be seen at one extreme in 'wannabe' teenagers who seek to act out the lifestyle of their older peers, and at the other extreme by the elderly 'young at heart' who identify themselves with an age ten or twenty years younger than they actually are. There has been interesting research into the increasing desire of older people to perpetuate their youth and the effects on marketing of differences between actual age and self-ascribed age. It could be argued that the most important determinant of a person's buying behaviour is the age that he thinks he is, rather than his actual age. Many companies have exploited this opportunity; for example, tour operators offer activity holidays targeted at retired people. However, while information on biological age is often readily available, data relating to perceived age can generally be established only by sample survey approaches.

Family life cycle

Individuals typically go through a number of family roles, beginning with that of a dependent child and proceeding through a young single adult, a married adult with dependent children, a married adult with independent children, and finally a sole survivor. At each stage of development, an individual's buying preferences are likely to change—and, just as importantly, their ability to pay for those purchases will change too. There are many obvious marketing opportunities associated with specific stages in the life cycle. For example, a young adult with no financial responsibilities is a prime target for many leisure-related items such as music, while an individual with a young dependent family is an important target for firms selling childcare products. Figure 6.5 illustrates some of the changes in food-buying habits that may arise as an individual progresses through the family life cycle.

Marketers are often particularly interested in **trigger points** in people's lives. These are events that suddenly change a person's behaviour, and they are frequently family related. Setting up home together, the birth of a first child, and the death of a partner are examples of events that can profoundly affect what an individual buys and how she buys it.

Of course, the family life cycle shown in Figure 6.5 is an ideal type, and most western countries are seeing increasing deviation from it. Later marriage, adult children living with parents because they cannot afford to buy their own home, a rising divorce rate, and more single-parent families have created family units that do not fit into this ideal.

Stage in family life cycle	Possible main emphasis of food buying
Dependent child	Main food purchased is for snacks. Attracted by the novelty and packaging of food.
Young independent adult	Eating out, possibly at fast food outlets. Minimum effort put into preparing food at home—home-consumed food is often from simple ready-made meals.
Adult, married, no children	Quite likely to eat out at restaurants. Willing to experiment in home cooking, although may still buy ready-made meals for home consumption.
Adult, married, dependent children	Eating out is reduced and cooking at home concentrates on meeting the needs of the whole family. Budgeting becomes tighter and economy replaces variety as a driving force behind food purchases.
Adult, married, independent children	Greater time and money now available for eating out and being adventurous with home-prepared food. Can afford ready-made meals, but prefers to prepare own food.
Sole survivor	Average size of food purchase declines. Emphasis on food items that are easy to prepare.

Figure 6.5 Effects of stage in family life cycle on an individual's food-buying behaviour

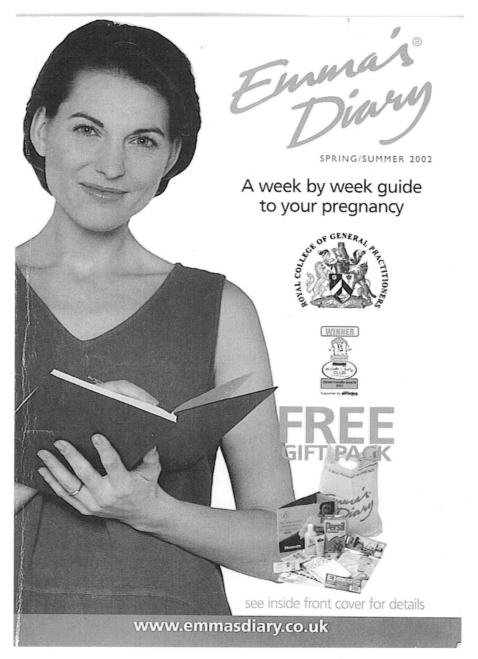

Figure 6.6 Market segments are often defined in terms of individuals who are at transition points in their lives. Life-cycle Marketing Limited publishes the pregnancy guide 'Emma's Diary' and an interactive website (www.emmasdiary.co.uk) that guide parents-to-be through the various stages of pregnancy and childbirth. By registering with the company, individuals receive further information and offers appropriate to their needs at the different stages of their pregnancy. The company has built up a valuable database of customers who have come to trust the advice given by Emma's Diary. Advertisers in its book and website realize that the birth of a child, especially the first one, is a significant trigger to new patterns of expenditure. Targeted individuals are likely to be highly receptive to the firms' messages. (Reproduced with permission of Life-cycle Marketing Ltd)

Marketers have responded to such change, for example by offering domestic support services aimed at busy, affluent, single-parent families.

Gender

It is quite evident that gender differences account for many variations in consumer buying behaviour. At first sight it might seem obvious that companies providing a wide range of goods and services will have developed product offers that are particularly targeted at males or females; so there are men's clothes and women's clothes; magazines aimed at women and those aimed at men; and cosmetics emphasizing their appeal to one gender or the other. Gender is a very commonly used basis for segmenting markets. Not only does it often correspond to crucial differences in buying behaviour, but it is also an easy one to measure. Firms can have a reasonably good idea of the gender-specific market in any given area.

We do, however, need to be careful how we use gender as a basis for market segmentation. In the first place, it has to be remembered that one of the criteria for effective segmentation is that it should identify homogeneity in *buying* behaviour. There is much evidence that for many products a person of one gender may buy a product that is intended for use by someone of the other gender. It has been estimated, for example, that in the UK over half of all men's underwear is purchased by women, with men playing a relatively minor part in the buying process. A segment of men's underwear buyers that should be of interest to manufacturers is therefore women. The way women buy underwear, the retailers from whom they buy, and the features for which they look are likely to be quite different from these processes of men.

A further reservation to the use of gender as a segmentation basis is its frequent confusion with a classification based on sex. Sex is essentially a biological description, which in itself explains many of the observed differences in products sought by men and women (e.g. the use of bras and tampons). Gender is essentially a social construct and is influenced by social conditioning. Western societies have seen a convergence in many male and female **values**, although there remains argument about just how far this has gone. Concepts such as aggressiveness, competitiveness, and sensation seeking, which have traditionally been associated with male values, are increasingly being seen in females (e.g. heavy drinking 'ladettes'). Similarly, some observers have suggested that 'new men' are taking on traditional female traits of caring, nurturing, and reconciling. Many marketers have therefore moved on from segmentation based on a dichotomous male/female sex classification to a segmentation basis which recognizes a wide range of gender orientations. For example, the lifestyle and buying behaviour of career women is likely to be quite different from that of housewives, and may be more similar to career-oriented men.

A further issue in gender-based segmentation is the emergence of segments of gay or lesbian people, whose buying behaviour may not fit neatly within dichotomous segments of male/female. Many companies have developed marketing programmes that are aimed at these groups, often seeking through promotional messages to promote accommodating and positive images of them. Manipulating gender images to accommodate different groups can create its own problems if not done carefully. If a company seeks to associate a product targeted at men with the values held by gay groups, it may alienate men with more traditional male values.

Ethnic group

The UK, like many other western countries, has become much more diverse in the ethnic backgrounds of its population. Despite years of integration, there is evidence that many ethnic groups retain distinctive preferences in their purchases that distinguishse them from the native community (Interfocus, 2001). For example, many Chinese migrants who have settled in the UK continue to buy authentic eastern-style food, providing a marketing opportunity for many small retailers that has arguably not been fully exploited by the larger supermarkets. Ethnic groups remain important segments for travel related services—for visiting friends and relatives, and for pilgrimages.

As in the case of gender, segmentation purely on the basis of biological origins may not be as useful as an individual's self-ascribed ethnic background. While some members of an ethnic group may wish to associate themselves primarily with the values and lifestyle of their host community, others may be proud of their background and make purchases that reinforce their ethnicity. This may lead, among other things, to such groups being accessible to a consumer goods manufacturer only if that firm distributes through the ethnically owned businesses to which this group may be loyal.

Household composition

A wide range of goods and services are bought by households as an economic unit. The weekly household shopping, the annual holiday, and the family car are typically purchased to meet the needs of the economic unit as a whole rather than of individuals within it. Households differ in their size and composition, and these differences are associated with diverse buying behaviour. Segmenting markets on the basis of the size of the household buying unit, therefore, makes a lot of sense for many products. Furthermore, there is a great deal of readily available information about **household structure** from the national census and other sources.

One indicator of household structure is the number of people that the household comprises. In the UK, as in most western countries, the average size of household units has declined as extended families have given way to nuclear families. More recently, there has been growth in the number of single-person households, which now account for over 10% of all households. The buying needs of a single-person household can differ quite markedly from those of a family unit; for example, it is more likely to seek smaller pack sizes and products which satisfy the needs of the individual buyer rather than the whole household. As with all bases of segmentation, it is important to avoid over-generalization, as the single-person household comprising a retired state pensioner is likely to behave very differently from that of a young, professional, single person.

MARKETING in ACTION

Segmentation or discrimination?

Segmentation and targeting are central to the marketers' task of meeting consumers' needs at a profit to their organization. But to other social commentators, the practices of segmentation and targeting may appear to be more like discrimination, with all the connotations of social divisiveness that have been associated with various forms of social discrimination. Admittedly, marketers seldom find themselves practising the kind of discrimination that typified South Africa during its years of apartheid, but there can be a thin line between the desirable aims of segmentation and the undesirable consequences of discrimination.

Legislation in most western countries is gradually squeezing out the opportunities for marketers blatantly to sell their goods and services to one group but not to another. The days when the owner of a bar could admit customers on the basis of their colour are now long gone. Nightclubs in the UK that once advertised different prices for men and women would now most likely find themselves breaking the Sex Discrimination Act. However, marketers have found more subtle ways of pursuing their segmentation and targeting strategies. A bar may subtly make its atmosphere more conducive to one ethnic group and less attractive to others; nightclubs have learned that discriminating on the basis of gender may be illegal, but a differential pricing policy based on whether a customer is wearing trousers or a skirt may come close to achieving the nightclub's objectives legally.

Despite a growing volume of legislation in developed countries to protect clearly identifiable groups based on sex, race, disability and, increasingly, on age, many people remain concerned that the processes of segmentation and targeting are leaving pockets of individuals who are denied access to many basic services. This is seen in the way that mainstream banks in most western countries have targeted relatively affluent individuals with a steady source of income. In the UK, a sizeable group of people find it difficult to borrow money from these banks, or even to open a basic bank account. Without a bank account, many life opportunities are closed to individuals, for example, without a credit or debit card, it can be difficult to buy goods and services online. In the United States, banks have been suspected of 'redlining' certain areas of towns, from which the banks will not take new customers. Many states have responded with legislation making illegal such geographically generalized bases for selection. In the UK, geodemographics remains an important basis for banks' segmentation and targeting, but although there is no legislation to prevent geodemographic targeting, the government has shown its impatience with banks' reluctance to target poorer groups, even with basic bank accounts. One initiative in response to this apparent problem was the creation of a 'Basic Bank Account' based on collaboration between the main banks and local post offices, making banking facilities available to poorer people with a bad credit history. In many service sectors providing essential public services, such as electricity, water, and telephones, regulatory agencies ensure that private sector companies do not unduly disadvantage poorer groups in their pursuit of profits.

When does segmentation become discrimination? To what extent should commercial organizations be expected to do business with individuals who, on a narrow commercial basis, are unlikely to be profitable? How far will companies' shrewd analysis of their social and political environment—and a visible response to problems of emerging discrimination—allow these issues to be resolved? Or will it take further government legislation to protect the interests of disadvantaged groups who may be further marginalized in society by commercial firms' segmentation and targeting policies?

A second indicator of household structure is the composition of individuals' roles within it. This is much more difficult to measure than size alone, but can be very useful because it is associated with quite distinctive buying patterns. In recent years, most western countries have seen a growth in the number of households that are composed of something other than the ideal-type family of husband, wife, and two children. A rising divorce rate has meant that there is a growing segment of consumers who live in single-parent households, and who are often (but not always) poorer than a two-parent family in terms of money and time. Some travel companies have specifically targeted this segment to fill capacity at quiet times of the year.

Other types of household that may present opportunities to particular companies include those comprising groups of friends sharing, an elderly parent living with grown-up children, and people living in institutionalized homes.

Socio-economic bases for segmentation

It has been traditional to talk about class differences as a factor that affects the way goods and services are purchased. We saw in Chapter 4 that an individual's perception of her class may be an important influence on her buying behaviour. However, marketers find the concept of **social class** too value-laden and imprecise to be of much practical use. Instead, more measurable indicators of social class are generally used; in particular, occupation and income.

Occupation

Since 1921, government statisticians in the UK have divided the population into six classes, based simply on occupation. This has resulted in the following familiar classification system:

Class category	Occupation
A	Higher managerial, administrative, or professional
B	Intermediate managerial, administrative, or professional
C1	Supervisory or clerical, and junior managerial, administrative, or professional
C2	Skilled manual
D	Semi-skilled and unskilled manual
E	State pensioners or widows (no other earners), casual or lower grade workers, or long-term unemployed

These segment labels have been widely used. For example, some newspapers have traditionally stressed the number of A/B readers they have. However, it became increasingly clear that six classifications could not fully explain the impact of class on buying behaviour. The government recognized that the uncertainty of work and the demise of a job for life had undermined the old classification system. From 2001 it implemented a new system, intended to take account of such things as the size of individuals' employing firms and their pension rights, effectively reflecting an individual's status in the purchasing marketplace.

Despite the improvements noted above, segmentation based on occupation remains fairly crude compared with the advances achieved using **geodemographic** methods (discussed below). Perhaps surprisingly, many marketers still refer to the old A/B/C1/C2/D/E basis of classification, perhaps because of its simplicity and a shared general understanding about the type of person contained in each of these groups.

Income

Many studies have shown that, as individuals' incomes increase, their expenditure on certain categories of product increases. For example, Mintel, in a study of the leisure industry, found a strong correlation between income and expenditure on a range of leisure activities.

There are three commonly used approaches to measuring income:

1. *Total income before taxation*: This is gross income, which is widely quoted and understood by most people.

2. **Disposable income**: This refers to the income that individuals have available to spend after taxation. It follows that, as taxes rise, disposable income falls.

3. **Discretionary income**: This is a measure of disposable income less expenditure on the necessities of life, such as mortgage payments. Discretionary income can be significantly affected by sudden changes in the cost of mortgages and other essential items of expenditure, such as heating and travel-to-work costs, which form a large component of household budgets.

All of these can be measured at the unit of the individual, or of the whole household.

Marketers are most often interested in consumers' discretionary incomes. A casual analysis of advertisements on television will show that most are aiming to gain an increased share of discretionary income—on an overseas holiday, a new mobile phone, or a takeaway meal, for example.

Despite its apparent correlation with buying behaviour, the use of income as a segmentation variable has some limitations. Obtaining data on individuals' incomes can be much more difficult than for occupation, and people are often reluctant to give this information when asked. Surveys that attempt to gather this information can be subject to misreporting by individuals. Even within segments of similar discretionary income, differences in actual spending levels arise, accounted for by differences in spending/saving ratios.

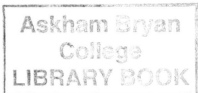

Psychographic bases for segmentation

So far, most of the bases for segmentation have been reasonably measurable. However, they are often criticized for missing the unique personality factors that distinguish one person from another, and many studies have suggested that **psychographic segmentation** has better predictive power than demographic bases (e.g. Lin, 2002). Under the heading of psychographic factors, we will consider the effects of lifestyle, attitudes, values, benefits sought, and loyalty.

Lifestyles

People of a similar age and socio-economic status can nevertheless lead quite different lifestyles, and firms have been quick to adapt their products to meet the needs of these lifestyles. Many companies in the tourism sector, for example, have been observed to base their segmentation and targeting on lifestyle factors (e.g. Gross *et al.*, 2008). It is very difficult to describe accurately a lifestyle and even more difficult to have any realistic measure of the size of segments of different lifestyle groups. Nevertheless, as societies fragment into ever smaller groups of shared interests and activities, companies have recognized the need to develop ideal types of lifestyle segment. The depth of research that underlies these approaches to segmentation can be questionable, with many segments being held up as ideal-type segments on only a weak empirically derived basis. Thus, segments described by terms such as 'Yuppies' and 'Dinkies' have come to acquire a meaning among marketers, if only as unquantified ideal-types of the segment being targeted. Many lifestyle segmentation methods have been developed for specific sectors. In one study of grocery retailing in the UK, the Henley Centre for Forecasting identified segments of shoppers using a multi-variable approach which took account of demographic factors such as age, sex, and income as well as lifestyle, personality, and finally attitude to the shopping experience. As with so many of these studies, the resultant new breeds of shopper were given glib titles:

- The Harried Hurrier was typically burdened with squabbling children and crippled by a severe lack of time. Hurriers were averse to anything that eats into their precious minutes such as having too much choice, which makes them impatient.

- Young-at-Hearts spent less money than the Harried Hurriers; they tended to be middle-aged, but, in contrast to the first group, had time on their hands and liked to try new products.

- An important and growing species of grocery shopper was identified as the Young, Affluent, and Busy (or 'YABs'); for these, money is not a major constraint in their quest for convenience and more interesting products, but they do have a low boredom threshold.

- The Fastidious were attracted by in-store hygiene and tidiness; these are expected to grow in importance.

- Begrudgers were mainly male and tended to shop only out of obligation to others.

- The Perfect Wife and Mother was concerned with the balanced diet; these appeared to be in numerical decline.

- To compensate for the decline in the Perfect Wife and Mother, the number of Obsessive Fad-Followers has been increasing; this group's choice of food tended to be dominated by brand image and current trends.

There have been many similar approaches to lifestyle segmentation. For example, Sony's Consumer Segment Marketing Division has a mission to 'develop an intimate understanding of Sony's end consumers . . . from cradle to grave', and divided its consumers into the following segments: Affluent; CE Alphas (early adopters); Zoomers (55+); SoHo (small office/home office); Young Professionals/DINKs (double income no kids, aged 25–34); Families (35–54); and Gen Y (under 25) (Elkin, 2002). While such approaches may be very useful for defining possible target markets, they are difficult to measure because of the absence of data beyond small sample surveys.

Attitudes

Lifestyles are observable, even if it can be difficult to do so, and to estimate how many of each lifestyle group exist in a particular population. Attitudes are much more difficult to identify and to measure, and may be revealed only in subtle ways. More importantly for marketers, what is a hidden attitude for an individual today may tomorrow become a behaviour that is manifested in purchase decisions to support a chosen lifestyle. Many people may possess an attitude towards an item but are afraid of being an early adopter of behaviour associated with that attitude. Among males, there may be a significant

MARKETING in ACTION

What your sandwich says about you

What does an individual's choice of sandwich say about him? The retailer Tesco has undertaken research that has revealed how complex the market for ready-made sandwiches has become, with clear segments emerging of people who look for quite different types of sandwich. In an attempt to define and target its lunch customers more precisely, the company found that well-paid executives invariably insisted on 'designer' sandwiches made from ciabatta and focaccia with sun-dried tomatoes and costing about £2.50. Salespeople and middle-ranking executives were more inclined to opt for meaty triple-deckers. Upwardly mobile women aged 25–40 chose low-calorie sandwiches costing around £1.49. Busy manual workers tended to grab a sandwich that looked affordable, simple, and quick to eat, such as the ploughman's sandwich that Tesco sold for £1.15. Tesco's research claimed that sandwiches have become an important statement made by individuals and need to be targeted appropriately. What do your snack meals say about you?

segment of the population that possesses an attitude that it should be acceptable for men to use cosmetics traditionally associated with women. They may, however, be reluctant to buy and use male cosmetics until they consider that it has become socially acceptable to do so. For this segment, the marketing programme should emphasize the need to gain gradual acceptability of the product among this group, for example by appealing to wives/girlfriends as key influencers on the decision to purchase.

Values

Sociologists have distinguished a deeper level of individual distinctiveness in the form of values. Values are standards, rules, norms, goals, ideals, or underlying evaluative criteria which we use when making judgements. They are deep-seated and tend to be fairly enduring within an individual. Attitudes and lifestyles are built on this substructure of values. Individuals have been attributed with having a number of underlying values; for example, values of self-centredness or of communality and sharing. Values can be even more difficult to measure than attitudes, and apparent inconsistencies may question the existence of a deep-seated value system. An individual may appear to have a value system based on caution when driving a car, but may nevertheless be quite reckless when investing in financial services.

Benefits sought

The same product may provide a variety of benefits to different people. A watch, for example, can be purchased by one segment primarily as an accurate timepiece, by another as a fashion item above all else, and by still others as items of ostentatious consumption. There will also be segments who buy a watch as a gift for someone. Each segment is likely to respond in different ways to variations in product design, packaging, pricing, and promotion. Inevitably, overlap between benefit categories exists and it is really possible to determine the size of each segment only on the basis of sample surveys.

Loyalty

In many markets, a segment can be found that shows considerable loyalty to one brand, while other segments will be prepared to switch between brands in response to products offering more benefits and/or lower prices. This may reflect differences in individuals' willingness to take on the risk of switching to a new supplier. For some people, loyalty may occur through inertia and a reluctance to take the perceived risk of changing supplier.

Geodemographic bases for segmentation

Marketers have traditionally used geographical areas as a basis for market segmentation. Very often, there have been very good geographical reasons why product preferences should vary between regions. The long, dark, cold winter nights of northern England and Scotland have led the inhabitants of these regions to take proportionately more winter sun holidays than their counterparts in the south of England, despite their having lower average levels of disposable income. Many companies have managed to adapt their product offer to meet the needs of different regional segments. National newspapers, for example, produce regional editions to satisfy readers' needs for local news coverage and advertisers' needs for a regional advertising facility.

More recently, geographical segmentation has been undertaken at a much more localized level, and linked to other differences in social, economic, and demographic characteristics. The resulting basis for segmentation is often referred to as *geodemographic*. The premise of geodemographic analysis is that where a person lives is closely associated with a number of indicators of his socio-economic status and lifestyle. This association has been derived from detailed investigations of multiple sources of information about people living in a particular neighbourhood. A very widely used system of geodemographic analysis is MOSAIC, provided by Experian Ltd (Figure 6.7). In the UK, ACORN codes seek to classify postcodes on the basis of their similarity of consumption patterns. Descriptions of each category can be seen by visiting the website www.upmystreet.com and entering any postcode.

Situational bases for segmentation

A further group of segmentation variables can be described as situational, because an individual may find herself grouped differently from one occasion to the next.

Stage in buying process

For some high-value goods, it may take a considerable time for an individual to arrive at a purchase decision. It has been estimated that the average time private buyers take in deciding on a replacement for their current car is about one year. At each stage of the process, their needs will be quite different. A price incentive aimed at a buyer in the early stages of the search process may achieve no success, while for a buyer who has gone through the search and evaluation processes and is now ready to commit himself to a particular product, it may prove successful.

Occasion of use

We often buy a product at different times for quite different reasons. A meal in a restaurant taken during the lunch hour will probably have to satisfy quite different needs compared with a meal taken during the evening. At lunchtime the most important selection criteria may be speed and value for money, whereas in the evening they may be good service and a relaxing atmosphere.

Group	Group Description	% Households	Type	Type Description	% Households
A	Symbols of Success	9.62	A01	Global Connections	0.72
			A02	Cultural Leadership	0.92
			A03	Corporate Chieftains	1.12
			A04	Golden Empty Nesters	1.33
			A05	Provincial Privilege	1.66
			A06	High Technologists	1.82
			A07	Semi-Rural Seclusion	2.04
B	Happy Families	10.76	B08	Just Moving In	0.91
			B09	Fledgling Nurseries	1.18
			B10	Upscale New Owners	1.35
			B11	Families Making Good	2.32
			B12	Middle Rung Families	2.86
			B13	Burdened Optimists	1.96
			B14	In Military Quarters	0.17
C	Suburban Comfort	15.10	C15	Close to Retirement	2.81
			C16	Conservative Values	2.84
			C17	Small Time Business	2.93
			C18	Sprawling Subtopia	3.08
			C19	Original Suburbs	2.41
			C20	Asian Enterprise	1.02
D	Ties of Community	16.04	D21	Respectable Rows	2.65
			D22	Affluent Blue Collar	3.12
			D23	Industrial Grit	3.82
			D24	Coronation Street	2.81
			D25	Town Centre Refuge	1.13
			D26	South Asian Industry	0.88
			D27	Settled Minorities	1.62
E	Urban Intelligence	7.19	E28	Counter Cultural Mix	1.36
			E29	City Adventurers	1.27
			E30	New Urban Colonists	1.36
			E31	Caring Professionals	1.08
			E32	Dinky Developments	1.10
			E33	Town Gown Transition	0.76
			E34	University Challenge	0.26
F	Welfare Borderline	6.43	F35	Bedsit Beneficiaries	0.71
			F36	Metro Multiculture	1.67
			F37	Upper Floor Families	1.72
			F38	Tower Block Living	0.49
			F39	Dignified Dependency	1.34
			F40	Sharing a Staircase	0.50
G	Municipal Dependency	6.71	G41	Families on Benefits	1.21
			G42	Low Horizons	2.64
			G43	Ex-industrial Legacy	2.86
H	Blue Collar Enterprise	11.01	H44	Rustbelt Resilience	3.00
			H45	Older Right to Buy	2.67
			H46	White Van Culture	3.17
			H47	New Town Materialism	2.17
I	Twilight Subsistence	3.88	I48	Old People in Flats	0.83
			I49	Low Income Elderly	1.63
			I50	Cared for Pensioners	1.43
J	Grey Perspectives	7.88	J51	Sepia Memories	0.75
			J52	Childfree Serenity	1.34
			J53	High Spending Elders	1.53
			J54	Bungalow Retirement	1.26
			J55	Small Town Seniors	2.71
			J56	Tourist Attendants	0.30
K	Rural Isolation	5.39	K57	Summer Playgrounds	0.29
			K58	Greenbelt Guardians	1.74
			K59	Parochial Villagers	1.64
			K60	Pastoral Symphony	1.31
			K61	Upland Hill Farmers	0.41

Figure 6.7 MOSAIC, a widely used method of geodemographic segmentation. Many companies provide data to help firms' segmentation, targeting, and positioning strategies. One of the most widely used is Experian, whose Mosaic™ consumer classification system gathers information under a number of headings shown in the diagram to build up a picture of every household in the UK. From this information, each household has been assigned to one of 61 household types (aggregated into 11 groups), some of which, with their descriptive titles, are shown in the table. For a company planning a mailshot, or deciding on the best location for a new retail outlet, such information about consumer behaviour at the household level can avoid wasted effort by targeting the company's efforts on those groups who are most likely to respond to a proposition. (*Source:* © Experian Ltd. Reproduced with permission)

Frequency of purchase

Infrequent buyers of a product may approach their purchase decision with caution and seek reassurance throughout the process. Their knowledge of prices and competing facilities available in the market may be low. At the other end of this segmentation spectrum, frequent buyers may have become much more price-sensitive, or more demanding in the features they expect from a category of product. A promotional programme that guides buyers through the stages of purchase will be less appropriate for this group.

Comprehensive approaches to segmentation

The preceding discussion has presented a seemingly bewildering array of segmentation variables, each of which has its strengths and weaknesses. In practice, a company uses a number of key variables which are most relevant to its product/market, and companies commonly segment consumers on the basis of multiple-category purchase data. Geodemographic segmentation has become particularly popular because of the close correlation between where an individual lives and other indicators of income, occupation, and lifestyle.

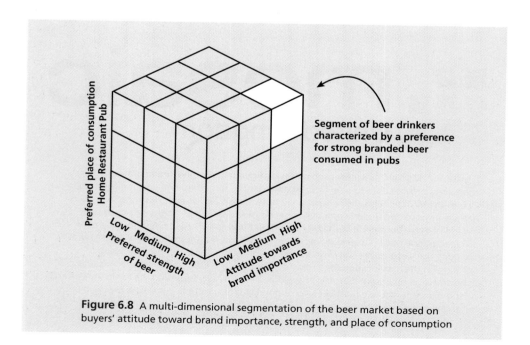

Figure 6.8 A multi-dimensional segmentation of the beer market based on buyers' attitude toward brand importance, strength, and place of consumption

Bases for segmenting business markets

The process of defining market segments for business buyers is similar in principle to that applied to consumer markets. Many of the bases described above, such as frequency of purchase and benefits sought, apply equally to private consumer purchases and business purchases. However, others, such as demographic and lifestyle bases, have little role to play, especially in segmenting very large corporate buyers. The following are additional bases for segmentation that are commonly used in business markets.

Size of firm

Within any industry sector, variations in corporate size are likely to be reflected in individual order sizes and the manner in which those orders are placed. In the printing industry, for example, very large printers obtain their inks direct from manufacturers, while smaller printers tend to rely on wholesale merchants. For a small intermediary, small printers may represent an important and accessible segment, whereas large printing companies may be considered inaccessible.

Formality of buying processes

As organizations grow, they have a tendency to formalize their buying processes. Nevertheless, within any size category of firm, variation can be observed in the formality of buying process, in terms of the number of people involved in making a decision and the level of the management hierarchy at which approval is required. Large state-owned organizations have sometimes been noted for having slow and complicated ordering procedures. It was noted in Chapter 4 that, in general, the more complex a firm's buying process, the greater the complexity of a seller's marketing that is called for. Instead of having to appeal to one individual with one set of needs, it must appeal to multiple influencers, who may each seek different benefits from a purchase.

Industry sector

An industry sector may be a large user of certain types of product but have little use for others. Within particular product categories, niche segments may appear in industries with quite specific needs. Many suppliers of industrial goods and services therefore target particular industry sectors or sub-sectors. In the case of information technology (IT) equipment, Fujitsu ICL successfully targeted the special computing needs of the retail segment, while NCR targeted the special needs of the banking segment.

Evaluating market segments

Defining market segments is a relatively passive task of analysis. While sound analysis is always important, the next stages involve critically evaluating the identified market segments and selecting one or more for targeting. In this section we consider the questions that a company should ask in deciding whether a segment is worth going after. In fact, a company is likely to avoid a dichotomous classification of 'develop/ignore' and prefer instead a ranking of segments ranging from 'very attractive opportunity' to 'let's ignore this one'.

Size of segment

In our criteria for effective segmentation, it was stated that to be useful a segment must be of a sufficient size that the company can serve it economically. What is an economic size varies between companies. A package holiday company selling low-cost holidays to popular destination may be able to operate economically only with segments of several hundreds of thousands of customers. On the other hand, a small specialist holiday company with lower overhead costs may be able to justify serving much smaller segments of, say, a few thousand people who have distinctive needs. It was noted earlier that the size of market segments that can be economically served has tended to come down with the development of flexible production systems.

Growth prospects

Our definition of marketing (Chapter 1) spoke not only about identifying current customer demands, but also of anticipating what these will be in the future. Markets are seldom static, and what is an attractive segment today may not be so in the future. Many banks competed with each other in the buoyant buy-to-let mortgage segment in the early 2000s, but from 2007, a 'credit crunch' among banks and falling property prices made the buy-to-let segment relatively unattractive. On the other hand, some segments that were once small have gone on to be very large before fragmenting into smaller sub-segments. In the UK the segment of adult ice cream consumers who sought sensual pleasures from consuming ice cream was small in the early 1980s, but grew significantly during the following decades. Suppliers of 'luxury' ice cream that had targeted this group saw their sales grow significantly faster than the ice cream industry average.

Profitability

The fact that a market segment is large does not necessarily mean that the segment can be served profitably. Many markets are characterized by a large segment which seeks low prices, and in which companies can make good profits only by stringent control of their costs, while a smaller segment is prepared to pay a premium for a product for which the additional cost of differentiation is less than the price premium charged.

Competition for the segment

Of course, the profitability of a segment is significantly affected by the level of competition for it. When a company is identifying potentially profitable segments to develop, the chances are that its competitors are doing exactly the same thing. The result is that an attractive segment soon becomes unattractive when large numbers of new entrants, all following the same logic, create intense competitive pressure. In evaluating a market segment, a company should consider not only how well *it* could develop the segment, but also how well its competitors could develop it. If its competitors in fact have more strengths with regard to this segment, the segment is likely to be less attractive to the company. Too many marketing plans fail because they make assumptions about a static market, when in fact markets are dynamic, with a changing composition of segments and of firms seeking to supply those segments.

Fit with company objectives

Many segments may appear large and profitable, but are then rejected because they would not sit easily within a company's broader marketing objectives and strategies. The following are some examples of market segments that might not 'fit' a company well.

- A manufacturer of high-value cars might be reluctant to serve a market segment that seeks more basic, low-value vehicles. What would happen to the image of BMW if it decided to develop the market segment for low-priced family hatchbacks using the BMW brand name?

- Will the image of a company be harmed by appearing to be too closely associated with a segment that is perceived by the public to be 'bad'? Many companies give priority to the preservation of their reputation, and being seen to supply products to a repressive government, for example, could cause unquantifiable damage to its long-term reputation.

- Has the company a core competence in serving this segment? Would its funds and management effort be better applied to a project that better fits its competencies, leaving this segment to a competitor that may have a stronger base for developing it?

MARKETING in ACTION

Targeting or spamming?

In the early days of the Internet, the ability of firms to target millions of customers cheaply and quickly through e-mail appeared to open up new opportunities. Schedules of press and TV advertising, optimized to minimize the cost per target audience, would be a thing of the past when the whole world could be targeted with a cheap e-mail message. In reality, e-mail may be an efficient way of targeting a lot of potential buyers, but is it effective?

Many online sites grew rapidly by building databases through sometimes dubious means. Some websites, such as 4anything.com, used the lure of a free sweepstake to build up a database of names which was subsequently used for sending promotional messages on behalf of other companies. Of course, to be effective, targeting requires a much more thorough understanding of potential customers than is possible using crude database building techniques. As with junk mail, 'spam' quickly finds its way to the bin. Many computer owners have installed anti-spam software to try and reduce the extent of the nuisance caused by junk e-mail. In response, some companies have developed ingenious methods of getting round such anti-spam filters. They might just be lucky in achieving a sale that would not have been possible had their e-mail been blocked, but their approach still appears very crude, and similar to targeting in the early days of modern marketing.

How can the Internet help segmentation and targeting for a company in a long-term and sustainable way? There are no surprises about the answer that traditional techniques work best. Targets are more likely to be responsive to a message where the message addresses a real need. Companies should amass information from multiple sources in order to build a profile of each potential target. The use of cookies allows Internet-based companies to understand quite a lot about a target from the websites the target has visited, but this seldom gives much insight into an individual's attitudes and lifestyle. Integrating online information with traditional data sources can greatly improve the effectiveness of targeting.

In an age of mass Information, consumers' concerns over their privacy have become increasingly important. This is reflected in the ideas of **permission marketing**. In his book of that title, Seth Godin, asserted that much of today's marketing is ineffective, as an overload of promotional messages is robbing people of one of their most precious assets—time. A target is more likely to be responsive to an e-mail message if it has previously given a sender permission to target him. Data protection legislation is also increasingly requiring permission to be given before an individual can be targeted with messages.

For the future, mobile Internet is offering new opportunities for targeting, offering the possibility of targeting individuals just at the time and in the place when they will be most receptive to a message (a special offer from a nearby restaurant in the early evening?). The possibility of walking down the High Street and being bombarded with SMS messages from nearby shops may fill many people with horror. How can companies avoid the mistakes of spam e-mail? If permission marketing is the way forward, how can that permission be obtained?

Figure 6.9 Mercedes-Benz identified a segment of car buyers who were seeking the benefits of a small city car that made a lifestyle statement about the individual. The company realized that targeting this segment with a small car might be inconsistent with the brand image that the company had built up in the market for larger luxury cars. It therefore decided to join a consortium to target this segment with the 'smart' car. (*Source:* © Daimler AG. Reproduced with permission)

Selection of target markets

The time has now come for a company to select one or more market segments for further development. At this point, marketing becomes a blend of scientific analysis and creative thinking. The segmental analysis that we have just discussed cannot in itself produce answers: it can only guide decicion-making, which is influenced by a range of company and environment-specific factors, many of which cannot be easily quantified.

True entrepreneurs are able to understand their marketing environment and to use their knowledge of a market to identify target markets which will grow and give them a period of profitable sales before the market becomes saturated with competitors. The following are some examples of successful targeting by entrepreneurs:

- Alan Sugar, founder of Amstrad, who had experience of launching low-cost versions of household electrical items and who correctly forecast the demand for a low-cost desktop computer for use by private households and small businesses;

- Stelios Haji-Ioannou, founder of easyJet, who understood the American airline market and sought to bring the benefits of low-cost domestic and European flights to the UK, where he had reasoned that there was a high level of suppressed demand from segments who were highly price-sensitive;

- Charles Dunstone, founder of the Carphone Warehouse, who foresaw the growth of privately owned mobile phones in the UK and of a segment that sought an impartial and independent retailer to guide them through the maze of competing networks and tariffs.

In each of these cases, success was a combination of good luck, good judgement, and good timing. Had there been a sudden rise in oil prices, or had its competitors responded more rapidly and vigorously, easyJet might have been sunk at an early stage. If mobile phones had failed to become popular consumer items (perhaps because of high taxes, network charges, or concerns over health), the ambitious plans of Carphone Warehouse might have come to nothing. The history books are littered with entrepreneurs (and large corporations) who have failed to understand and predict the dynamics of market segments, resulting in a failure to sell a product to a selected target market. The small C5 electric car is often cited as an example of an innovative product that just might have become a runaway success as a handy runabout or even a cult vehicle. It failed miserably, possibly because the entrepreneur behind the venture—Clive Sinclair—did not have sufficient understanding of the market segment he was targeting. (Possibly its failure could also be put to bad luck, as initial press coverage portrayed the car as ridiculous and dangerous rather than as a smart cult icon.)

A fundamental issue for a company is how many segments to exploit and how to enter those segments. A number of targeting strategies can be identified—for example, undifferentiated **mass marketing**, single-segment specialization, and multiple-segment specialization (Figure 6.10). While these are three ideal-type targeting strategies, companies frequently combine elements of all these approaches. The characteristics of each approach are described below.

Undifferentiated mass marketing

This does not really involve segmentation and targeting at all, as here a company seeks to satisfy the entire market with a single formulation of its product. It worked well for Henry Ford, and cases can still be seen where companies serve the entire market with one product (for example, electricity and water supply companies, which have traditionally offered one standard of service delivery to all of their domestic customers). Over time, however, consumers' needs tend to fragment into segments of different needs. Where markets are competitive, a company may no longer be able to ignore the special needs of small groups of its customers, because if it does its competitors may exploit the opportunities available. Very often, these groups with special needs represent the most profitable segments to serve. In the UK even the market for electricity has fragmented, spurred on by increasing competition which raises the expectations of consumers that their distinctive needs are capable of being met. Customers now have the choice of different pricing plans, bundling of electricity with other energy supplies, and a range of electrical appliance maintenance services to supplement the basic electricity supply.

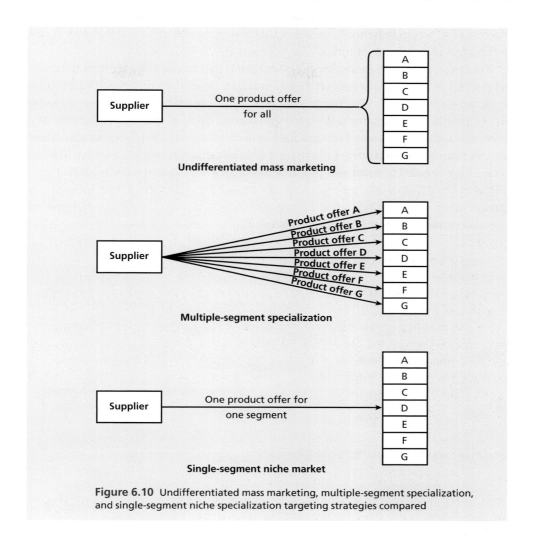

Figure 6.10 Undifferentiated mass marketing, multiple-segment specialization, and single-segment niche specialization targeting strategies compared

Single-segment specialization ('niche' marketing)

Many companies succeed by producing a specialized product aimed at a very focused segment of the market (**niche marketing**). The Freeminer Brewery in Gloucestershire targets the small proportion of beer drinkers who can be described as real ale enthusiasts. By this strategy, the company gets to know the needs of its target segment extremely well and puts all of its efforts into satisfying their needs. This can give it strength over competitors whose efforts are spread more diffusely among a number of segments. It also avoids the problem of tarnishing a brand by associations with 'inferior' segments (Freeminer Brewery does not carry any of the bland, mass-produced associations of the larger brewers). By specializing in one particular segment and achieving a high level of success in it, a company might be able to achieve economies of scale that give it cost advantages over its competitors.

The danger of targeting a single market segment is that a company's fortunes rise or fall with those of its chosen target. UK hotels that had targeted premium-rate US business customers suffered badly after the terrorist attacks of 11 September 2001, when the number of business people travelling across the Atlantic declined sharply. The ability of a company to adapt its product to small market niches is not a guarantee of success. Many Internet companies that offered a high level of personalization on their sites, e.g. Garden .com, have closed. The niche was probably too small to be satisfied economically.

MARKETING in ACTION

Cars in any colour except black

Henry Ford would have been amazed at the lengths to which the car company he founded now goes in order to satisfy the needs of specific market segments. Car manufacturers have for some time recognized the differing needs of differing groups of buyers, for example:

- 'Boy racers' typically want plenty of features and external manifestations of the power and status of their car (e.g. 'GTI' badges and spoilers).
- Affluent elderly males put the emphasis on refinement of the interior, comfort, and reliability, but seek no vulgar manifestation of status.
- The family buying a 'runabout' car seeks low initial cost and subsequent low running costs; they are not too worried about comforts, but the car needs to be hard-wearing to stand up to rough treatment by dogs, children, etc.
- The professional career woman, although a difficult market to typify, often seeks a light and airy colour, reliability, and easy maintenance.
- Company car buyers look for an economical and reliable car which will have a high residual value after three years and will satisfy the status needs of employees.

A look through the brochure for a Ford model such as the 'Focus' indicates how far the company has been able to adapt its cars to meet the needs of each of these segments: the 'ST' has been aimed at the boy racers, the 'Titanium' at the affluent young professional; the 'Econetic' includes many features designed to appeal to ecologically conscious buyers. The 'Studio' is a basic version aimed for use as a low-cost family runabout; in the past, Ford has produced a co-branded 'Elle' version of the car specifically targeted at professional career women.

The logistical problems of satisfying so many segments have been significant, with one basic car available in three basic body forms, with five different engines, 12 colour options, and the choice of automatic or manual transmission. After allowing for permutations that are not available, Ford promotes 72 versions of the Focus. Making these available on demand at each of its dealers has called for flexible manufacturing systems and a centralized stock-management system. Can the company be accused of offering too much choice? Can too much choice actually confuse customers, leading to them making no purchase decision at all? Or is the key to good market segmentation giving each targeted segment a small choice of, say, four or five options which buyers in the segment think have been selected specially for them?

Multiple-segment specialization

A third ideal-type strategy is for a company to seek to serve multiple markets, but to differentiate its products in a way that meets the needs of each of the segments it seeks to serve. The aim here is to develop slightly differentiated products that add to customer value faster than they add to production costs. Car manufacturers have become quite skilful at adapting a basic car to meet the needs of different groups (see vignette above). Many retailers have developed different brand formats to target different groups (for example, the Arcadia group with its Top Shop, Principles, and Dorothy Perkins chains, among others).

Segment development plans

Most companies entering a new market realize that it would be unrealistic to use their limited financial and management resources to satisfy all possible segments from the outset. They therefore develop a strategy to 'roll out' their marketing plan from an initial segment through further segments. The roll-out plan can be defined geographically. (McDonald's restaurants did this in the UK, working out from the London-based market to provincial markets.) Very often, companies initially target high-value segments. Such segments may be prepared to pay a premium for the benefits of novelty, but soon the premium attached to this novelty wears off. The company meanwhile has established an 'upmarket' image for itself from which to appeal to aspiring segments of potential buyers. In the UK, mobile telephone companies have moved from segments of business users who are prepared to pay a premium for a mobile phone that will give them a competitive advantage, to more price-sensitive segments for whom a mobile telephone is a useful but not essential accessory.

Market attractiveness analysis

Of all the market segments that a company has identified, which ones should it target? A conceptually useful analytic tool is a grid comprising two dimensions: market attractiveness and competitive position (Figure 6.11). Market attractiveness includes such factors as the size of a market, its projected growth rate, and its earnings performance. Competitive position refers to a company's brand strength, its experience in a market, and the availability of financial, technical, and human resources to serve that market. In developing an index, weights must be attached to each of these components and a sometimes subjective assessment made of each component. Ownership of a strong brand may be an essential element of competitive advantage for a soft drinks firm and would therefore be given a relatively high weighting, although the task of assessing how strong a brand is remains very subjective.

For the purpose of analysis, each of the scales in Figure 6.11 is divided into two classifications, resulting in a matrix of four cells.

Figure 6.11 Market attractiveness–competitive position portfolio classification and strategies

- **Box 1:** A market may appear attractive, but if a company has only a weak competitive position, it should think carefully before investing large amounts of cash. The market will appear attractive also to other companies, which may have a stronger competitive position.

- **Box 2:** A highly attractive market in which a company has a strong competitive position is the best position in the matrix, and in such a market the company should invest and build for future growth.

- **Box 3:** Unattractive markets for which a company does not have a strong competitive position should be avoided. However, a company may find that it has products in this box that were previously high performers, but whose market characteristics have changed. The best thing a company can do with the remaining products in this box is to refrain from new investment and to manage the products for the cash they generate.

- **Box 4:** Market attractiveness is low, but the company's competitive position is strong. The company should exploit its strengths by selectively investing in this market and building for future market growth.

As a basis for targeting, the grid focuses attention on finding strategies that match an organization's internal strengths and weaknesses with the opportunities and threats presented by its operating environment. The key to making this model useful in formulating marketing strategy is to measure the two dimensions of the grid not only as they are at the present time, but as they are likely to become in the future.

Developing a position within the target market

Having chosen a segment to target, a company must decide how to position itself in relation to the competitors for that segment. **Positioning** could be on the basis of the product's unique selling proposition, its price, design characteristics, method of distribution, or any other combination of factors that allow for differentiation. Within any market, **position maps** can be drawn to show the relative positions adopted by the principal competing products in respect of key customer evaluation criteria. In Figure 6.12, a position map has been drawn relating two important criteria used by customers in selecting a restaurant: speed of service, and the range of services provided by staff (e.g. whether the restaurant is self-service or waiter service). Position maps can use any criteria that are of relevance in influencing consumers' choices, and in reality they may be multi-dimensional rather than just two-dimensional, as in this example. Here, a number of UK restaurants have been plotted on this map in terms of two out of many possible relevant criteria.

The fact that a position on a map is unoccupied does not necessarily mean that it is an unexplored opportunity waiting to be targeted. There is always the possibility that a product offering in that position will not satisfy the needs of a sufficiently large market segment. However, many gaps on product position maps have been identified and exploited successfully. In the UK there was for a long time a gap between low-price fast food restaurants offering little choice and higher priced gourmet restaurants offering a wide range of menu options. Restaurant chains such as Brewers Fayre and Harvester have since successfully exploited this mid-market position.

It must be emphasized that a product position map is essentially product-focused rather than customer-focused. By itself, it does not address the underlying needs of

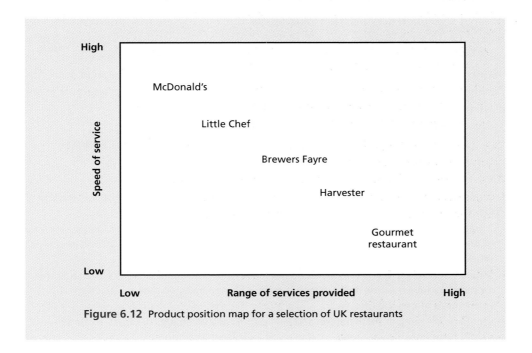

Figure 6.12 Product position map for a selection of UK restaurants

customers that a company seeks to satisfy. The process of adopting a product position is essentially about selecting specific target markets. In a market-oriented company, product features are developed only in response to the needs of clearly identifiable segments of consumers. We will return to the subject of competitive positioning and discuss it in more depth in Chapter 7.

Chapter summary and linkages to other chapters

This chapter has emphasized the need for market-oriented companies to break markets down into segments comprising groups of people with similar needs and buying processes. Numerous bases for segmenting markets have been identified, but there is no unique 'right' way of segmenting a market. The best way is the one that allows a company most profitably to exploit the greatest possible share of a market. Segmentation alone does not produce a marketing plan. To this end, a company must evaluate the segment opportunities open to it and assess how well it will be able to exploit each of them. There are a number of approaches for entering a market, and companies often seek to exploit one segment at a time with products that are uniquely adapted to that segment.

The crucial importance of segmentation to the philosophy of marketing is reflected in the extensive linkages between this chapter and others. In Chapter 4 we saw how buying behaviour differs among individuals, and these differences form an important basis for segmentation. In Chapter 5 we explored methods by which companies can research the differences between individuals and thereby identify and evaluate segments. In the next chapter, we will pick up issues of competitive positioning which were introduced towards the end of this chapter. We will see how the development of brands facilitates the task of targeting and positioning. Subsequent chapters deal with the elements of the marketing mix that allow a company to develop products that are particularly suited to the needs of targeted segments.

⬭ KEY PRINCIPLES OF MARKETING

- Segmentation is fundamental to marketing because of its emphasis on meeting the needs of identified groups of consumers.
- A trade-off must be made between the desire of individuals to be treated as a unique segment of one, and companies' desire to achieve segments that are large enough to achieve economic efficiencies.
- Segmentation exercises by themselves do not make decisions for management. Management must use creative thinking and a scientific analysis of segmentation data to decide which segments to target.
- Segments are rarely static in nature, and in deciding which segments to target, a company should focus on what each segment is likely to look like in the future.

CASE STUDY

A bar for all tastes

A few decades ago, the centre of most British towns would have had many small bars, all looking fairly similar to each other, with relatively few points of differentiation. The market for drinking in pubs was fairly homogenous, comprising mostly males, who went to the pub mainly to drink, and only very rarely to eat. Today, the bar scene in any British town centre is much more complex, and the key to understanding this complexity is the pub chain's increasingly sophisticated segmentation techniques, which seek to address a market which is much more heterogeneous than a few decades ago.

Going to pubs, clubs, and bars continues to be a popular leisure activity in the UK with over 72% of adults visiting at least once a month. In 2006, the annual sales of the UK pubs were estimated to be about £25 billion. The pub market has benefited from a growth in eating-out, which has increased faster than growth in GDP. This growth has been achieved despite numerous challenges facing pub operators, including higher taxes on alcohol, growing competition from supermarkets for 'off sales', a smoking ban introduced in most parts of the UK from 2007, and generally rising operating costs.

To achieve the greatest return from their investment, pub operators have had to focus the design of bars on meeting the needs of smaller and smaller market segments. No longer is the pub market dominated by males going out to drink—professional women and families are among many segments who may never have thought about going into the traditional bar, but may be tempted with a format which appeals to them. No loud music or big screen television? Good quality coffee served as well as beer? Bright, airy decor? Drinks served to the table, rather than queuing at the bar? These may have been design features that were unsought or unwanted by the traditional male heavy drinker, may strongly appeal to other market segments.

Punch Taverns owns one of the largest pub portfolios in the UK and its portfolio is constantly developing through acquisition, investment, and the changing trends of the pub sector. It has identified 11 types of pub which meet the needs of clearly defined market segments:

Basic Local	These are community pubs, mostly located in high-density residential areas. Trade is focused on regular drinkers and tends to be wet-led with little food. Beer, cider, and spirits are the big sellers. Most show televized sport. Customers are predominantly male with the proportion of female customers relatively low.
Mid-market Local	The 'traditional British pub' as depicted in television soaps. Again, they are situated in residential areas and most offer some sort of food. There may also be themed evenings, quizzes, darts, or pool. Customers tend to use the pub to meet friends and relax.

Upmarket Local	While still community pubs, upmarket locals are generally found in low-density housing areas. They are likely to offer high-quality food, representing a significant part of the trade. For this reason the proportion of women using these pubs is higher than most of the locals.
Young Local	Younger customers aged 18–30 are the focus here. Pubs draw custom from the surrounding area—they are still 'locals' rather than on the drinking circuit. The pubs tend to have a modern, trendy feel. Amusements including pool tables and machines will feature and chart music and video screens will be prevalent. Draught lagers are the most popular drink.
City Local	As the name suggests, these are found in city or town centres but away from the young people's circuit. Trading is highly competitive and the offer will include basic pub food and snacks. Local workers and shoppers provide passing trade in the daytime—residents will normally use the pub in the evening.
City Dry-led	Centrally located but offering high levels of food, city dry-led pubs target the same customers as city locals. These pubs tend to be larger and they may have function rooms and restaurant areas.
Chameleon	Also centrally located but the pub's character changes from day to night to attract different types of customer. The venue may be a subdued coffee bar in the day serving office workers and shoppers, but a vibrant young people's bar with loud music by night.
Circuit	These pubs will be on or near the young people's circuit. Expect loud music, possibly a dress code, and door staff. Food is less important while lager and spirits generate strong sales.
Premium Dining	These are destination food-led pubs in more upmarket areas. Restaurant-quality food served with flair will account for more than 50% of sales. These pubs are a refuge for adults away from children.
Value Dining	Again focusing on food, these pubs offer good value for money, so often attract families. They are welcoming to families particularly during the weekend and early evening.
Venue	Distinctive, wet-led pubs that draw clientele from a wide catchment area because they offer something special. This may be live music or entertainers. The pub could also be a meeting point for a specific customer group; for example, bikers.

The company, like most of its competitors, has developed a computerized-mapping program that helps it to identify the best location for any given format of pub. Postcode data using ACORN analysis gives an indication of how many typical consumers for each pub format would live within range of any location. However, segmentation cannot be based simply on where people live, and must recognize their mobility and movement patterns. Therefore, for some sites located in town centres or on busy roads, an understanding of people's work patterns and commuting habits can be crucial. Being near a main train station may be crucial for attracting a target market of urban professionals who want somewhere to stop off to meet friends before catching a train home.

Pub operators such as Punch make extensive use of consultants and geodemographic mapping systems to show the cultural, social, and economic make-up of an area; but data analysis on its own will not always provide a complete answer when choosing between locations or formats. Simply being on the wrong side of the road may be the difference between success and failure—will people be prepared to cross a busy road in order to go from the housing area to a pub? Data may drive the segmentation process, but simply getting out and having a feel for an area can provide a lot of detail not present in computerized systems.

What does the future hold for the pub industry in Britain? Operators face increasingly challenging times, and the campaign group CAMRA estimated that in 2006, 816 pubs closed throughout the UK, i.e. 68 per month or 15.7 per week. Many younger drinkers who might previously have gone to the pub now sought out coffee bars, which had been equally active in identifying different market segments and providing formats and drinks that appealed to different groups. In an increasingly competitive environment, in which pubs compete with other leisure outlets, identifying and comprehensively satisfying the needs of distinct market segments will become increasingly crucial for success.

Source: based on Office for National Statistics, Social Trends; Mintel Oxygen Report—Lager, August 2007; Punch Taverns website (www.PunchTaverns.com); Campaign for Real Ale website (www.camra.org.uk)

- -

Case study review questions

1. Critically evaluate the bases that bars may use to segment their markets.

2. In the context of bars, discuss the relative merits of quantitative and qualitative approaches to market segmentation.

3. Examine the bars in your area and try to identify the segments—using those described above—to which the bars are appealing.

▢ CHAPTER REVIEW QUESTIONS

1. 'Too much segmentation can be costly and can result in a paralysis by analysis.' Discuss the view that for many markets Henry Ford's approach of producing a limited range of products for the 'average' customer may be the most profitable option for a company.

2. Critically evaluate the likely future trend in segmentation techniques. Illustrate your answer with reference to a specific market sector.

3. Given the increasing fragmentation of society, and an apparent desire for greater individuality among consumers, are current scientific methods of analysis and segmentation a short-sighted oversimplification?

☐ ACTIVITIES

1. If you are familiar with the UK, visit the website www.upmystreet.com and enter postcodes of yourself and your friends and family. You will see an ACORN description of each postcode and associated spending patterns. How well do you think this classification system describes the spending pattern of individuals living in these areas? What are the limitations of such geodemographc methods of market segmentation?

2. Gather together a sample of national newspapers. Discuss the typical readership of these papers, and the extent to which this is reflected in who advertisers in the papers are targeting.

3. For a market sector of your choice, analyse the positions adopted by companies in the market. Use the framework in Figure 6.12 as a basis for your analysis.

☐ REFERENCES

Elkin, T. (2002), 'Sony Marketing Aims at Lifestyle Segments'. *Advertising Age*, 73 (11): 3–4.

Gross, M. J., Brien, C., and Brown, G. (2008), 'Examining the Dimensions of a Lifestyle Tourism Destination'. *International Journal of Culture, Tourism and Hospitality Research,* 2(1): 44–66.

Interfocus (2001), *Marketing to Ethnic Minorities*. London: Interfocus.

Lin, C.-F. (2002), 'Segmenting Customer Brand Preference: demographic or psychographic'. *Journal of Product & Brand Management*, 11(4): 249–68.

☐ SUGGESTED FURTHER READING

Segmentation, and targeting are discussed in more detail in the following:

Yankelovich, D. and Meer, D. (2006), Rediscovering Market Segmentation. *Harvard Business Review*, February.

Dibb, S. and Simpkin, L. (2007), *Market Segmentation Success: making it happen!* New York: Haworth Press.

Cahill, D. J. (2006), *Lifestyle Market Segmentation*. New York: Haworth Press.

Positioning is discussed in the following:

Ries, A. and Trout, J. (2001), *Positioning: the battle for your mind: how to be seen and heard in the overcrowded marketplace*. New York: McGraw-Hill.

D'Aveni, R. A. (2007), 'Mapping Your Competitive Position'. *Harvard Business Review*, November.

☐ USEFUL WEB LINKS

Visit the Online Resource Centre for resources that are relevant to this chapter, including web links, multiple choice questions, and additional case studies:

www.oxfordtextbooks.co.uk/orc/palmer2e/

⬜ KEY TERMS

- **Attitudes**
- **Differentiation**
- **Discretionary income**
- **Disposable income**
- **Family life cycle**
- **Geodemographics**
- **Household structure**
- **Lifestyle**
- **Mass market**
- **Niche marketing**
- **Permission marketing**
- **Positioning**
- **Position map**
- **Psychographic segmentation**
- **Segmentation**
- **Social class**
- **Socio-economic classification**
- **Targeting**
- **Trigger points**
- **Values**

PART 3

Developing the marketing mix

7

Competitor analysis and brand development

CHAPTER OBJECTIVES

This chapter marks a transition point in the book. In previous chapters we have been focusing on how companies can gain a better understanding of the external environment from which they earn their sales revenue. In the following chapters we will consider how companies try to develop the right products, and sell them through the right channels at the right price and with the right promotional messages. In this chapter we introduce concepts associated with competitive markets. We will explore what is meant by a competitor and how a company can develop a sustainable competitive advantage over its competitors. A large part of this chapter is given to the development of brands. These form the focal point of a firm's product, pricing, promotion, and distribution plans and aim to create a distinctive position for a product. Branding lies at the heart of marketing strategy and seeks to remove a company from the harsh competition of commodity-type markets. By differentiating its product and giving it unique values, a company simplifies consumers' choices in markets that are crowded with otherwise similar products.

Introduction

Marketing is a dynamic process of ensuring a close fit between the capabilities of an organization and the demands placed upon it by its external environment. It follows that what a company offers to a market will need to evolve continually over time in order to meet changes in the company's internal objectives and in its external business environment. It is not good enough for a company to develop a marketing plan that works for a short period, but then fails to make good long-term profits for the company because the plan is not sufficiently responsive to changes in its marketing environment.

History is full of marketing plans that looked too good to be true. A company may have found a very high level of sales in the short term, but failed to earn sufficient profits over the longer term. It may be that such a company has underpriced its products, leaving it an insufficient margin to cover its fixed costs. Or it may have invested heavily in product design and promotion but failed to generate a sufficient level of sales to pay for such investment. It is not difficult to develop short-term marketing strategies that at first appear highly successful when judged by sales levels. It is much more difficult to develop a marketing strategy that is sustainable over the longer term by producing adequate levels of continuing profits. Central to this long-term strategy is the development of strong **brands** which can allow a company to charge premium prices for products that consistently deliver a high level of customer-defined value.

Many companies that have been hailed as successful market-led businesses have not managed to achieve a sustainable long-term success. In the UK companies such as Next, Amstrad, and Laura Ashley have risen rapidly and gained many 'Business of the Year'-type awards on the way. But each of these ended up in serious financial difficulties just a short while later. It has been noted that very few of the so-called 'excellent' companies identified by Peters and Waterman (1982) in their book *In Search of Excellence* were considered to be excellent 15 years later. The marketing strategy that had led to short-term success was not sustained.

Who are a company's competitors?

Any plan to develop a competitive advantage must be based on a sound analysis of just who a company's competitors are. At first sight, it may seem obvious who the competitors are, but, as Theodore Levitt (1960) pointed out, a myopic view may focus on the immediate and direct competitors while overlooking the more serious threat posed by indirect and less obvious sources of competition. When railway companies in the 1930s saw their main competitors as other railway companies, they overlooked the fact that the most serious competition would come from road-based transport. More recently, banks have been made to realize that their competitors are not just other banks, or even other financial services organizations, but any organization that has a strong brand reputation and customer base. Through these, supermarkets, airlines, and car companies have all developed various forms of banking services which now compete with mainstream banks.

It is usually possible to identify direct and indirect competitors. **Direct competitors** are generally similar in form and satisfy customers' needs in a similar way. **Indirect competitors** may appear different in form, but satisfy a fundamentally similar need.

Product	Typical underlying need	Direct competitors	Examples of indirect competitors
Overseas holiday	Relaxation	Rival tour operators	Garden conservatories
Restaurant meal	Social gathering	Other restaurants	Ready-prepared gourmet meals for home consumption
Television programme	Entertainment	Other television programmes	Internet service providers
Rolex watch	Social status	Other watches	Armani suit; Gucci handbag

Figure 7.1 Underlying needs, direct and indirect competitors for selected products

Consider the examples of products and underlying needs shown in Figure 7.1. The table shows, for each product, possible direct and indirect competitors.

A sound analysis of the direct and indirect competitors of a firm is crucial in defining the business mission of an organization. (This is discussed further in Chapter 12.)

A useful framework for analysing the competition facing a company in a market has been provided by Michael Porter (1980). His model illustrates the relationship between existing competitors and potential competitors in a market and identifies **five forces** requiring evaluation:

1. the threat of new entrants;
2. the threat of substitute products;
3. the intensity of rivalry between competing firms;
4. the power of suppliers;
5. the power of buyers.

Figure 7.2 What business is the Parker Pen company in? At first sight, the company may appear to be in the pen business, or possibly the 'writing implement' or maybe even the 'communication' business. In fact, the company understands that the majority of its sales are made for gift giving. Gifts can be personal (e.g. to mark a relative's personal achievement or anniversary) or corporate (as when companies give away free pens as a sales incentive to reward a new order). The company is essentially in the 'gift' business, so its competitors are not just other pens, but any gift. Within this broad definition, MP3 players, alarm clocks, and overnight bags could all be regarded as competitors.

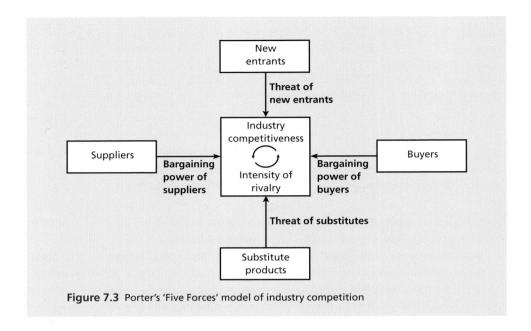

Figure 7.3 Porter's 'Five Forces' model of industry competition

Understanding the structure of competition within a market is a vital prerequisite for developing a strategy to develop a sustainable competitive advantage. The model is shown in Figure 7.3 and the nature of these five forces is discussed below.

The threat of new entrants

The threat of new entrants is greatest where there are low barriers to entry. New entrants may already be active in a similar market sector, but in another geographic market. The threat becomes reality when a company that is strong in one geographical market decides to exploit other geographical markets. As an example, the full service airlines have been challenged on many routes by newer low-cost 'budget' airlines. Having established a base, these airlines have often gone on to further challenge the established airlines by creating new operating bases. (For example, the budget airline Ryanair posed a new threat to Belgian and German carriers after expanding to those countries from its UK and Irish bases.)

Alternatively, new entrants may arrive from outside the industry. Bic, whose technology base was plastic moulding, was well established in the disposable ballpoint pen market. They were able to diversify successfully into the wet shave razor market with plastic disposable razors, thereby challenging established market leaders such as Gillette and Wilkinson in their core business.

The threat of substitute products

Substitute products are likely to emerge from alternative technologies, particularly as the economics of production change. Initially, the new technology may have high costs associated with it and serve only small niche markets. As the technology and experience develop, the level of investment rises and production volumes increase, resulting in economies of scale that are associated with falling production costs. Many products have been consigned to obscurity by the development of new technologies; for example, the market for typewriters has been almost eliminated by the development of personal computers, and the market for sugar has been reduced by the development of artificial sweeteners. These substitutes may change the whole economics of an industry and threaten the survival of manufacturers of the traditional product.

Intensity of rivalry between competing firms

The intensity of rivalry may be high if two or more firms are fighting for dominance in a fast-growing market. For example, this occurred in the UK's personal phone market during the mid-1990s. There may also be a fight to establish the dominant technology in a sector, something that occurred in the mid-2000s in the fight to establish a common standard for high-definition DVD players. The Sony-supported Blu-ray system was pitched against Toshiba's rival HD-DVD system. By 2008, Blu-ray seemed to be winning the battle, with sales outnumbering those of HD-DVD, and more importantly, it had the support of Walt Disney, 20th Century Fox, and Metro Goldwyn Mayer who had chosen Blu-ray for their new releases. The need was for a format to become established as the dominant technology or brand before the industry matures. Companies are likely to engage heavily in promotional activity involving advertising and promotional incentives to buy. In a mature industry, particularly if it is characterized by high fixed costs and excess capacity, the intensity of competitive rivalry may be very high. This is because manufacturers or service providers need to operate at near maximum capacity to cover overhead costs. As the industry matures or at times of cyclical down-turn, or when a number of companies have invested in new capacity, firms fight to maintain their maximum level of sales.

The power of suppliers

The power of suppliers is likely to be high if the number of suppliers is small and/or the materials, components, and services they offer are in short supply. The suppliers of silicone chips and patented medicines have at times held a powerful market position as a result of their dominance of technology and the high demand for their products.

The power of buyers

Buyers' power is likely to be high if there are relatively few buyers, if there are many alternative sources of supply, and if buyers incur only low costs in switching between suppliers. During the past couple of decades, Britain's grocery retailing sector has become increasingly dominated by a small number of very large organizations. According to a Competition Commission report, Asda, Co-operative Stores, Iceland, Morrisons, Sainsbury's, Somerfield, and Tesco held over three-quarters of UK grocery market share by turnover in 2007 (Competition Commission, 2008). Power in the marketplace has shifted away from the manufacturers of grocery products to the retailers, seven of whom may buy around three-quarters of many manufacturers' total output.

Branding

Fierce competition may at first sight appear very attractive for the welfare of society as a whole, but it can pose problems for sellers. In a fiercely competitive market, an individual firm is subject to considerable direct competition from other firms and must take its selling price from the market. An implication of fierce competition is that firms will be unable to make a level of profits that is above the norm for their market. If they did achieve higher-than-normal profits, this would act as an invitation to new market entrants, whose presence would eventually increase the level of competition in the market and drive down profits to the minimum level that makes it attractive for firms to continue in the market.

To try to avoid head-on competition with large numbers of other suppliers in a market, companies seek to **differentiate** their product in some way. In doing so, they create an element of monopoly power for themselves, in that no other company in the market is selling a product identical to theirs. To some people, the point of difference may be of great importance in influencing their purchase decision, and they may be prepared to pay a price premium for the differentiated product. Nevertheless, such buyers remain aware of close substitutes that are available, and may be prepared to switch to these substitutes if the price premium is considered to be too high in relation to the additional benefits received. The co-existence of a limited monopoly power with the presence of many near substitutes is often referred to as **imperfect competition**. (We will come back to this again in Chapter 8.)

For a marketing manager, product differentiation becomes a key to gaining a degree of monopoly power in a market. It must be remembered, however, that product differentiation alone will not prove to be commercially successful unless the differentiation is based on satisfying clearly identified consumers' needs. A differentiated product may have significant monopoly power in that it is unique, but if it fails to satisfy consumers' needs, its uniqueness has no commercial value.

Figure 7.4 Perfect competition, imperfect competition, and the role of brands

Out of the need for product differentiation comes the concept of branding. A company must ensure that customers can immediately recognize its distinctive products in the marketplace. Instead of asking for a generic version of the product, customers should be able to ask for the distinctive product that they have come to prefer. A brand is essentially a way of giving a product a unique identity which differentiates it from its near competitors. The means by which this unique identity is created are discussed in this chapter.

Through adding values that will attract customers, a company can provide a firm base for expansion and product development and protect itself against the strength of intermediaries and competitors. There has been much evidence linking high levels of advertising expenditure to support strong brands with high returns on capital and high market share (see de Chernatony, 2006).

Branding through product differentiation may not be possible in all markets. Where products involve consumers in low levels of risk and there are few opportunities for developing a distinctive product, competitive advantage may be based on cost leadership rather than brand development. Examples of **commodity** strategies are evident in many low-value consumer and industrial markets where a significant segment of customers seek a product with a basic and substitutable set of characteristics. Milk and cheese are everyday items of consumer purchase where manufacturers' brands have had relatively little impact and most consumers are happy to buy the generic milk or cheese offered by a retailer.

The history of branding

The term 'branding' pre-dates modern marketing and is generally believed to have originated in agricultural practices of the Middle Ages. Farmers who allowed their cattle to graze on open common land needed some means of distinguishing their cattle from

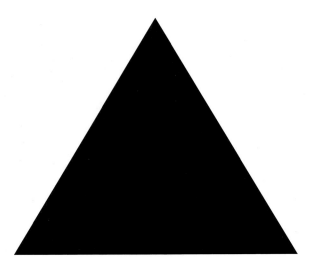

Figure 7.5 In early nineteenth-century England, consumers of beer may have had little knowledge about the quality of beer from the expanding industrialized breweries. Many brewers were reputed to add salt to their beer, in order to make the drinker thirstier, so that he would buy more beer—by which time he probably wouldn't notice any impurities. One of the emerging brewers of the time, Bass, developed what is acknowledged to be one of the earliest brand logos in order to provide reassurance of quality to a segment of the market that was more discerning. By drinking Bass beer, the buyer could, over time, come to be reassured that it was worth specifically selecting that brand of beer, because it could be confident that no salt had been added. The logo was simply a plain triangle, and essentially the same logo is still in use today.

those that were owned by other farmers sharing common grazing rights. They therefore 'branded' their animals with a branding iron, leaving an indelible mark which would clearly identify the owner of a particular animal. The role of a brand in identifying products with a particular source is shared by the medieval farmer and the modern corporation.

Economies in an early stage of development are characterized by small-scale production processes and relatively local markets. Where there are few opportunities for economies of scale in production, brands had only a limited role to play. With poor transport facilities and few opportunities to profitably expand business beyond the immediate area of production, consumers could readily identify the source of goods. In early nineteenth-century Britain, most communities had their own baker, brewer, and carpenter. None had developed the ability to achieve competitive advantage through economies of scale, while poor road and rail transport would have prevented their goods being exported to neighbouring communities. People in local communities knew where their goods had come from and were not confused by competing products from distant towns. Buyers were able to learn through personal experience of the abilities, consistency, and reliability of a supplier, while suppliers were able to adapt simple production methods to the needs of individual customers who were known personally.

Through personal knowledge and trust, a supplier was likely to be able to judge the creditworthiness of each customer.

In the UK, the industrialization that occurred in the nineteenth century meant that many goods could now be produced efficiently in centralized factories rather than in small cottage industries. An efficient centralized factory could produce more output than could be consumed by the local community. Furthermore, improvements in transport infrastructure allowed the surplus production to be shipped to markets around the country. What one company could do efficiently in one factory, another company could probably do equally as well in another factory elsewhere. Therefore, firms became involved in competition in distant markets. This, however, led to a problem for buyers, whose buying process was now made more complicated. Instead of having just the local brewer's products available, they now had a range of beers from which to choose. Buyers probably had little knowledge of the distant firms who were now supplying their market, or of the quality and consistency of their products. Branding emerged essentially to simplify the purchase processes of buyers who faced competing sources of supply.

Key characteristics of a brand

A brand, then, is essentially a way of distinguishing the products of one company from those of its competitors. To have value, a brand must have consistency, reduce buyers' level of perceived risk, and offer a range of functional and emotional attributes that are of value to buyers.

Consistency

Consistency is at the heart of branding strategy. To have value in simplifying buyers' purchasing processes, consumers must come to learn that a brand stands for the same set of attributes on one purchase occasion as on all subsequent and previous occasions. Consider a brewery offering draft bitter to the market. The distinctive characteristics of the beer that contribute towards its brand values may be described as:

• taste: light hop flavour;

• strength: above-average gravity;

• appearance: clear light colour.

Consumers come to prefer the particular taste/strength/appearance of beer that is described in shorthand by a brand name. If the taste of a brand varies between one pint and the next, the ability of the brand name to act as a shorthand description of a whole bundle of attributes is significantly weakened. Next time the buyer may not bother sticking with the brand, which it does not now trust, if it has just as much chance of achieving the desired bundle of attributes from another product.

Figure 7.6 Many of our most familiar fast-moving consumer goods brands have a long history.
Typhoo Tea, which can trace its origins back to 1820, is typical of a brand that has been associated
with consistency in its appeal. Despite numerous changes in ownership of the brand and many new
product formulations (such as different shapes of tea bag), many consumers remain loyal to the
Typhoo brand, and this loyalty is often passed down through generations of families.

The ability of a company to secure consistency of product delivery is crucial to the
development of branding. This helps to explain why branding was fastest to develop for
those products that were produced using factory techniques in which quality control
procedures could be used to ensure consistent standards every time. Soap powders,
cigarettes, and soft drinks were all examples of products for which manufacturers developed an ability to control production standards and were early adopters of brands.

Brands have been relatively slow to develop in the services sector, partly because of
the difficulty of maintaining consistent standards. Some service sectors have successfully taken on board the 'industrialization' of their production processes to ensure that

a service delivered on one occasion is very similar to that delivered on all previous and subsequent occasions. Fast-food restaurants have been notable in this field, and have been associated with the development of many strong international brands. On the other hand, many one-to-one services such as those provided by hairdressers, solicitors, and dentists have difficulty in 'industrializing' their service offer, and consequently corporate brands have had much more limited impact; the brand identity is essentially limited to the individual performing the service.

The term 'consistency' was noted above as an important attribute of a brand. As well as referring to specific product attributes (as in the case of the beer described earlier), consistency can refer to more general values about a producer or its range of products. As an example, the Co-operative brand name has been associated with ethical values, and these values have been applied consistently across the UK organization's activities, including retailing, banking, and travel services.

Risk reduction

In simple economies where buyers personally knew the producers of the goods and services they bought, the personal relationship helped to manage the buyer's exposure to risk. In the absence of that relationship, a brand acts as a substitute in managing buyers' exposure to risk. Branding simplifies the decision-making process by providing a sense of security and consistency for buyers that may be absent outside a relationship with a supplier.

A brand addresses a number of dimensions of purchase risk that have been identified as:

- physical (will the product cause me harm?);
- psychological (will this product satisfy my need for peace of mind?);
- performance (does the product work in accordance with my requirements?);
- financial (will this product provide adequate performance within my budget?).

Risk levels are perceived as being higher for products that fulfil important needs and for which there is a high level of involvement by the consumer.

Functional and emotional attributes

There have been many conceptualizations of the unique qualities of brands (see de Chernatony and McDonald, 2003). These usually distinguish between dimensions that can be objectively measured (such as taste, shape, reliability) and the subjective values that can be defined only in the minds of consumers (such as the perceived **personality of a brand**). In an early study, Gardner and Levy (1955) distinguished between the 'functional' dimensions of a brand and its 'personality'. Similar attempts to distinguish

MARKETING in ACTION

Can a university be branded?

Are universities unique places of learning, or brands to be marketed just like any other product? The language of brand management has been entering the vocabulary of university vice chancellors throughout the UK. 'Good' universities have known for some time that they have their reputation to preserve, but more recently many universities have begun talking about 'managing brand values'. Research among applicants to UK universities has consistently shown that prospective students have very poor knowledge about the actual facilities on offer, such as the standards of teaching, accommodation, and library facilities. However, some universities have come to be rated more highly than others, often on the basis of non-academic information, such as the triumphs of the university's sports teams or the nightlife in town.

Many of the UK's 'new' (post-1992) universities have made a priority of developing a strong brand image with which to challenge the established universities. Even students feel that it is important to have a degree from a university that has a 'good' name, in the same way as people have always wanted to belong to 'good' clubs. The view has spread that a university's 'good' name needs to be nurtured and maintained in just the same way as any fast-moving consumer product. Simply having technical excellence is not good enough.

De Montfort University has been one of the pioneers in university brand-building, supporting its efforts with television advertising. It undertook research among current students which showed, perhaps surprisingly, that many preferred limited university funds to be spent on a brand-building advertising campaign than on improvements in academic facilities, such as additional books for the library. Graduating from a known rather than an unknown university was seen as being important to many students.

Cynics have been quick to criticize efforts to market universities as brands. How can any brand be sustained over the long term if the infrastructure and facilities of a university are under pressure from ever-diminishing resources?

the dimensions of brands have been made by others—e.g. utilitarianism versus value expressive (Munson and Spivey, 1981), and functional versus representational (de Chernatony and McWilliam, 1990). It has been suggested that brands need to be positioned somewhere in a 'brand space', defined by the degree of abstraction (whether the brand has become independent from its associated product) and the degree of enactment (whether the brand focuses more on the meaning of a product or its functionality) (Berthon, Holbrook, and Hulbert, 2003). With increasing affluence, the emotional or non-functional expectations of brands have become more important.

A number of dimensions of a brand's emotional appeal have been identified, including trust, liking, and sophistication, and it has been shown that products with a high level of subjective emotional appeal are associated with a greater level of customer involvement than a product that provides essentially objective benefits. This has been demonstrated in the preference shown for branded beer as opposed to a functionally identical generic beer (Allison and Uhl, 1964), and in the way that the emotional appeal of brands of analgesics contributed significantly in relieving headaches (Branthwaite and Cooper, 1981). As consumers buy products, they learn to appreciate their added value and begin to form a relationship with them. For example, there are many coffee shops competing for customers, but individual chains such as Starbucks and Costa Coffee have each tried to develop their own personality, expressed through the ambience of their stores, the personality of their staff, and their linking to good social causes.

There is an extensive literature on the emotional relationship consumers develop between a brand and their own perceived or sought personality. Brands are chosen when the image they create matches the needs, values, and lifestyles of customers. Through socialization processes, individuals form perceptions of their self, which they attempt to reinforce or alter by relating with specific groups, products, and brands. There is evidence that branding plays a particularly important role in purchase decisions where the product is conspicuous in its use and in situations where group social acceptance is a strong motivator.

Creating a distinctive brand

Branding creates a product with unique physical, functional, and psychological values and can help to transform commodities into unique products. To be successful, a brand must have a competitive advantage in at least one aspect of marketing, such that it meets the complex needs of consumers better than competitors. This section discusses the strategic issues involved in creating a strong and distinctive brand.

Choice of name

A brand is much more just than a name. Nevertheless, a name is usually vital to the identity of a brand and can be the most difficult to change. Many products have been redesigned and relaunched as they have gone through their life cycle, yet their brand name has remained unchanged. In the car market, Volkswagen introduced its first Golf model in 1974. Since then, the car has gone through four completely new body designs, three new series of engines, and countless minor modifications to styling, features, engine ranges, and colours. The Golf of 2008 is larger and much better equipped than its predecessor of a quarter of a century ago; yet the brand name remains the same. Instead of symbolizing a set of narrowly defined product characteristics, the name 'Golf' has come to stand for reliable, mid-size, safe, value-for-money motoring. These values have been essentially unchanged for over 30 years. The public has come to learn what is associated with the name 'Golf', and therefore new model launches do not have to start from scratch in explaining what the car stands for.

Companies frequently engage specialist firms to develop brand names for their new products. This is often a wise investment, in view of the possible downside costs of getting a name wrong and the difficulties of subsequently changing it. A brand naming team may be made up of linguists, psychologists, sociologists, and media analysts, among others. The following are some of the factors that previous experience shows should lead to a brand name being successful.

- The name should have positive associations with the benefits and features of the product (e.g. 'Bostik' suggests adhesive qualities; 'Flash' sounds like it will clean thoroughly and quickly).

- There should be no negative associations with words that sound similar. (For example, Volkswagen had to think long and hard about the wisdom of using the

---

MARKETING in ACTION

A Bum name or a Sic brand?

Getting a brand name wrong can cost a company dearly. For a major brand, re-tooling to change product formulations can be a relatively minor matter compared with the costs of changing a brand name. Sometimes brands fail because the underlying product has failed to meet customers' expectations. At other times a brand fails because its name was chosen with insufficient care. Occasionally, the world outside a brand name changes in a way that destroys the appeal of a once well-liked name; for example, the slimmers' biscuits called Aids had to be renamed in the light of HIV scares.

With increasing globalization of markets, firms have to be careful that a brand name is capable of translation into overseas languages without causing offence or ridicule. The following brand names may have been well thought out in their own home market, but they failed to take account of local interpretations in potential overseas markets:

- General Motors may have wondered why its Nova car wasn't selling well in Spain, then realized that in the local language the brand name suggests that the car 'doesn't work'.

- British visitors to Spain are often amused to find 'Bum' crisps on sale—they probably wouldn't go down too well in an English-speaking market.

- Similarly, the French drink 'Sic' wouldn't be easy to export to Britain.

Care must also be taken in choosing a corporate brand name. Corporate mergers and restructuring during the 1990s spawned numerous abstract names, many of which promptly had to be changed following public ridicule. Royal Mail should have had one of the most sought-after corporate brand names in the world, but nevertheless it decided to change the company's name to 'Consignia'. Public ridicule led it to abandon this name in 2002 and revert to its original name. There was incredulity in 2002 when the accounting firm Price Waterhouse Cooper proposed changing its name to 'Monday'. One financial analyst calculated that, during the period 1997–2000, just under half of all FTSE 100 companies that had taken on a new abstract corporate name were ejected from the FTSE 100 list within two years.

name 'Sharan' in the UK for a new model. Although the name worked well in other countries, it sounded too similar to Sharon, a girl's name which at the time had been much maligned in the media.)

- The name should be memorable and easy to pronounce. (There is research evidence to suggest that names including the letter 'x' are particularly memorable, such as Andrex, Durex, Radox, etc.)

- The name must be in a tone of language that is understood and appreciated by the product's target market.

- The name must be checked my legal experts to ensure that it does not infringe on another company's brand name.

- A company must ensure that the product's name is available as an Internet domain name. Ideally, it should also be able to register all similar sounding domain names in order to prevent unauthorized sites appearing.

Despite these guidelines, brand names exist which appear to break all the rules and would almost certainly not have been chosen today. In a world that is sceptical of offal from animals, who would have named a range of meat products 'Brains'?

Distinctive product features

Sometimes the distinctive features of a product do not really require a brand name to prompt immediate recognition. Distinctiveness can be based on the physical design of a product (e.g. the distinctive shape of Toblerone chocolate); distinctive packaging (e.g. the lemon-shaped container used to package Jif lemon juice), or distinctive service

Figure 7.7 The packaging of some products is so distinctive that a brand is recognizable even without a name or logo. The chocolate bar Toblerone has a distinctive shape which differentiates it from competitors and which the company guards against imitators. The brand owner has gone to great lengths to legally protect its distinctive design from competitors who have imitated the triangular shape.

processes (e.g. the manner in which waiting staff in a TGI Fridays restaurant serve customers). Companies make great efforts through the use of **patents** to protect the distinctive characteristics of their products from competition, although this can be much
more difficult in the case of intangible service processes.

Creation of a distinctive brand personality

It will be recalled that a brand possesses functional and emotional attributes. The emotional attributes are of particular importance in contributing to a brand's personality.
This can best be described as the psychological disposition that buyers have towards a
particular brand. Brands have been variously described as having personalities that are
'fun', 'reliable', 'traditional', and 'adventurous'. The Virgin group has evolved a personality for its brand which can be described as reliable, slightly offbeat, and value for
money. This personality has been developed consistently across the group's product
ranges, from air travel to banking and investment services.

There has been some debate about whether the emotional aspects of a brand are
becoming more or less important in consumers' overall evaluation of a product. One
argument is that consumers are becoming more 'marketing literate' and increasingly
sceptical of firms' attempts to create abstract images that are not underpinned by reality. On the other hand, there is no doubt that, as consumers become more affluent, they
buy products to satisfy a much wider and more complex range of needs, which they
seek to satisfy with distinctive brands. (Refer back to the discussion of needs in Chapter 4.) A brand personality can help an individual reinforce her own self-identity, for
example, in the way that clothes are worn bearing brand names that have a personality
of their own. An individual who wears a Gap sweatshirt is probably identifying herself
with the personality that Gap has created for its brand.

Distinctive visual identity

Companies often go to great lengths to invest their brands with a distinctive **visual
identity**. Sometimes this can be achieved simply on the basis of a colour. The Easy
group of companies has come to be associated with the colour bright orange, which it
has applied to a wide range of products, from airline services, to hotels, car rental, and
cinemas. Many people would associate the distinctive colour with the company, without needing any reference to the brand name. The importance of colour was demonstrated in 1996 when Pepsi Cola sought to adopt the colour blue in the UK cola market
to distinguish itself from its predominantly red competitors. The fact that the change
appeared to result in no short-term increase in sales provides a reminder that buyers
may not be influenced simply by a superficial change which does not increase the product's perceived value. This may be especially true for low-involvement products such as
soft drinks. One of Pepsi's arch rivals, Virgin, exploited the opportunity by stating in

advertisements that it pays more attention to the *contents* of the can than to its colour.

The extent to which a company can legitimately 'own' an identifying colour is questionable. Many suppliers of generic products have copied the colours used by their branded competitors; for example, many supermarkets' own brands of coffee have shared a very similar colour scheme to that of the market leader, Nescafé. This has frequently led to allegations that they are 'passing off' their goods as if they were the manufacturer's branded product, especially where the packaging and typography are also used to imitate the brand leader. The owner of easyJet successfully challenged the owner of easyRealestate.co.uk which had used easyJet's colour, orange. A court held that, by using a similar name and colour, the company had sought to wrongly imply an association with easyJet.

Colours have often come to be associated with certain product features. Bright reds and yellows are often used to signify speed (e.g. fast food, one-hour film developing), and white is often associated with purity (low-fat, additive-free foods). However, the meaning of colours has to be seen in their cultural context—although white may be associated with purity in most western countries, in some other countries it is associated with bereavement.

To achieve maximum effect, corporate visual identity should be applied consistently. For a typical service-based company, this would mean applying a design and colour scheme to the company's advertising, buildings, staff uniforms, and vehicles.

Logos are an important part of corporate visual identity. The aim of a logo is to encapsulate the values of a brand and to provide an immediate reminder of the brand each time it is seen by customers and potential customers. A good logo should:

- give some indication of the business which a company is in, or the product category to which its output belongs (e.g. the logo for many water utility companies includes stylized waves of water);

- stress particular advantages of a product or organization (e.g. the most advanced, the fastest, most caring, longest established);

- not be over-complicated. The simplest logos tend to stand the test of time best;

- be updated to keep it in tune with styles and fashions of the time (for example, the Shell oil company's logo has gone through numerous minor styling changes during its 70-year history that have retained the central theme of a shell, but adapted the shape and the emphasis on particular details.

Branding strategy

Once a firm has decided on a distinctive brand identity for a product, the next issue is to have a strategy for developing the brand. In this section, a number of alternative strategic routes are explored which each lead to a company differentiating its products from

Figure 7.8 These logos are so powerful that most people could readily identify with the 'true' owner, despite the use of a false name

those of its competitors. One strategy is to develop a single strong brand. As an alternative, differentiated brands or brand families may be developed (Figure 7.9). Finally, once a strong brand has been developed, companies are often keen to extend its use.

Development of a single strong brand

One approach to branding is to apply the same brand name to everything that a company produces. The big advantage of this approach is the economies of scale in promotion that this can bring about. Instead of promoting many minor brands through small campaigns, a company can concentrate all of its resources on one campaign for one brand. This approach has been used successfully by many large multinational companies, such as IBM, Kodak, and Cadbury, who, with a few exceptions, put their single brand name on everything they sell.

The main disadvantage of this approach is that it can pose significant risks of confusing the values of a brand. If a company positioned its product range as premium priced, top quality, confusion may arise in consumers' minds if it applied the same brand name to a budget version of its product—does the brand still stand for top quality?

Worse still for a company, a poorly performing product carrying its brand can tarnish all products carrying that name. This is a particular problem for new product launches which are of unproven reliability. (For example, the Virgin group's reputation for dependable, no-nonsense service undoubtedly suffered when it applied its brand name to train services with a very poor reliability record.)

A final problem of the strong single corporate brand is that it can make it more difficult for a company to dispose of the manufacture and marketing of products that no longer fit in its corporate plan. Very often, the main value of the products to a corporate buyer is their brand name, so the company may be forced into a

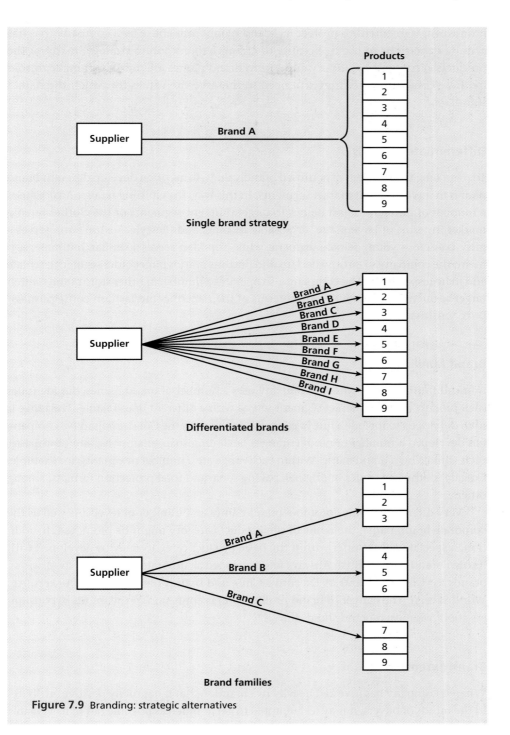

Figure 7.9 Branding: strategic alternatives

monitoring agreement to protect its brand name from abuse by a company that has acquired the right to use it. Because of changes in corporate strategy, many of the products carrying the Cadbury and Virgin brand names are not in fact made or sold by these companies, yet they still need to preserve the values for which the names stand.

Differentiated brands

To overcome the problem of confused brand values, firms often develop different brand names to serve different market segments. In this way, the clothing retailer Arcadia uses a number of different brand names to target different segments of the clothes buying market in terms of buyers' age, disposable income, and lifestyle. So Top Shop serves a price-conscious young female segment, while Top Man serves a similar, but male, segment; the company's Dorothy Perkins and Burtons brands target older segments, female and male respectively. The company also operates a number of other store brands which target segments that are different in terms of their age/income/fashion consciousness/price sensitivity.

Brand families

A **brand family** occurs where a company uses a number of brand names, but identifies each product range or market segment served with a different brand name. The range is then developed to include a line of products. In this way, the Colgate Palmolive company has developed a number of product ranges, including soap, shampoos, and toothpaste, each with its own brand name. Within each range are a number of variants; for example, Colgate toothpaste comes in original, baking soda, and total protection formats, among others.

Very often, companies promote brand names at a number of levels. As well as the corporate brand name, the name of the product category might be promoted. In addition, a special package offer within the basic product category may be developed with its own brand name. British Airways has developed a corporate brand (British Airways), brands for Club Class and its Executive Club, and brands for special offer tickets (e.g. World Savers). The danger of brand proliferation is confusion in the minds of consumers about what each brand stands for.

Brand extension

Where a company has invested heavily in a brand so that it has many positive attributes in the minds of buyers, it may feel tempted to get as much as possible out of its valuable asset. Given the increasing costs of developing strong brands, many companies have attempted to extend their brand to new product ranges. The attraction is quite clear. Rather than having to start from scratch with a new product and a new name, the company can at least start with a name with whose values buyers are familiar; so if a manufacturer of chocolate has developed a brand that stands for good taste and consistency, those values will be immediately transferred to a new range of ice cream products that the company may consider adding to its range.

Of course, extending a brand to new products poses dangers as well as opportunities. If the extension goes too far into unrelated product areas, the core values of the brand may be undermined. Consider the case of BP oil, which introduced a line of dishwashing detergent to the private consumer market. How could consumers avoid the feeling that the detergent was oily? The line was subsequently withdrawn. Considerable research has been undertaken to assess the effects of **brand extensions** on consumers' perceptions of a brand (e.g. Grime, Diamantopoulos, and Smith, 2002).

Co-branding

Opportunities often arise for the owners of two quite different brands to work together jointly to develop a new product that carries the brand name of both partners, resulting in an otherwise unattainable gain to both. **Co-branding** is increasingly common in the food sector, where, for example, a branded manufacturer of meat products may develop a 'beef and ale pie' in which it co-brands the product with its own brand name and that of the beer brand that makes up one of the ingredients. The owner of the beer brand gets exposure and distribution through a new channel, while the pie-brand owner adds to the distinctiveness and perceived value of its pies. As with any brand extension (see above), co-branding presents dangers where expectations of each brand are not met. A previously loyal customer of the beer brand used in the pie may have his faith in the brand reduced if the process of incorporating it into the beer leaves a nasty taste.

Protecting a brand

Once they have been created, brands can become very valuable assets to the companies that own them. Attempts to value brands usually try to estimate the price premium they command in their market, multiplied by estimated sales. A discounted cash flow calculation takes into account the value of earnings in future years. The enormous value of brands such as Coca Cola is a reflection of the significant price premium they can command and their enormous annual sales worldwide.

Like any asset of value, criminals will be tempted to appropriate the asset for themselves. If somebody else has developed a strong brand name, why not 'borrow' it to promote your own goods? The result is counterfeit goods, which carry all the superficial manifestations of brand identity, but may fail to deliver the performance that has come to be expected with the brand. **Counterfeiting** of goods with false brand names has been found in products as diverse as beverages, perfumes, watches, computer chips, and aircraft engine components. Sometimes consumers may be quite happy buying a low-priced branded product knowing that it is a counterfeit copy—this is especially true of goods bought for conspicuous consumption, such as the fake Rolex watches that many tourists bring back from the Far East for just a few pounds. Research undertaken by CDR International, a brand protection consultant, suggested that the most desirable consumer demands for counterfeiting were Nike, Calvin Klein, Rolex, Adidas, and Levi Strauss. At other times buyers may be defrauded into thinking that they have bought the genuine brand, often with dangerous consequences where the integrity of the product has safety implications. There have been many cases of counterfeit drugs being sold cheaply, but having harmful effects on the consumer.

For the owner of a brand, counterfeit copies hit it in two ways. First, it loses sales to counterfeiters that it would probably have made itself. Second, and more importantly, buyers may come to mistrust the brand. How can they be sure that they are buying the genuine article? Firms often go to great lengths to stay one step ahead of counterfeiters, for example by regularly introducing new designs which are hard to copy.

Brand owners resort to the law to protect their assets. In the UK, the common law provides a general remedy against companies seeking to 'pass off' counterfeit products as though they were the real thing. Passing off can include attempts to copy any of the distinctive brand characteristics discussed above. As an example, a bus operator was accused of passing off by painting its buses a similar colour to those of its main competitor and running on a similar route. It had been relying on public confusion to pass off its service as the one people had been expecting. Further protection is provided by legislation. The Trade Marks Act 1994 (which implements the EU Trade Marks Harmonization Directive no. 89/104/EEC), provides protection for **trademarks**, which are defined as any sign that can be represented graphically which is capable of distinguishing goods or services of one undertaking from those of other undertakings (Trade Marks Act 1994, s. 1(1)). Where a company has a patent for a product, the Patents Act 1977 provides protection against unauthorized copying of the product specification during the currency of the patent.

The organization as a brand

The traditional role of a brand has been to differentiate a product from competing products and to create a liking of it by target customers. The process of branding has been increasingly applied to organizational image, too. This has been particularly important for services, where the intangibility of the product causes the credentials of the provider to be an important component of consumers' choices. The notion of an emotional relationship to a product has been extended to develop an emotional relationship between an organization and its customers.

Many service organizations have found the development of brands to be attractive where their service offer is highly complex and consumers find the offer mentally as well as physically intangible. In the UK the pensions industry has found it difficult to explain its products to an audience that is not receptive to technical details of a product, but nevertheless may consider a pension to be a vital provision for old age. Furthermore, the Financial Services Act 1986 limits the ability of companies to promote their pensions in creative ways. (For example, companies may quote only standard industry-wide expected rates of return.) This has led many companies to embark on comprehensive brand building programmes which say very little about the details of the products on offer, but a lot about the nature of the company offering them. The Prudential Assurance Company has built its brand image on the superior lifestyle that can result from dealing with the company, while Legal and General used the brand image of an umbrella as the symbol of a protective company.

Many companies have used their corporate image successfully to extend the range of products that they offer. Retailers such as Tesco and Sainsbury's have developed strong, trusted brands, associated with reliable products sold at good value prices, with a high standard of customer services. They have used this trusted brand reputation to extend their activities to banking services, insurance, and telephone services, among others. Customers may not be knowledgeable on these additional services, but by inference, if they trust Sainsbury's with their weekly shopping, they will trust it with their banking services.

The development of global brands

With the volume of international trade growing at around four times the rate of world Gross Domestic Product, companies are increasingly having to include exports as part of their marketing plan. It follows, therefore, that the process of branding should be considered in global terms. The world's top 20 **global brands** are shown in Figure 7.10. Economies of scale can be achieved by developing a global brand; for example, visitors from overseas can automatically recognize a McDonald's restaurant, giving it an advantage over a local branded restaurant which starts with no overseas name recognition. There are many pitfalls in the development of brands that work in overseas markets as well as the domestic one. There is an argument that individuals' need for cultural identity is making it more difficult to justify the cost of developing a global brand (Williams, 2002). This chapter has highlighted some of the problems that occur with an inappropriate choice of name. We will return to the subject of global brands in Chapter 13.

1	Coca Cola
2	Microsoft
3	IBM
4	General Electric
5	Intel
6	Nokia
7	Disney
8	McDonald's
9	Toyota
10	Marlboro
11	Mercedes-Benz
12	Citigroup
13	Hewlett-Packard
14	American Express
15	Gillette
16	BMW
17	Cisco
18	LVMH Moët Hennessy Louis Vuitton
19	Honda
20	Samsung

Figure 7.10 The world's top 20 global brands

Source: based on *Business Week*/Interbrand Top 100 Global Brands Scoreboard, 2005

Note: The table was based on the asset value of global brands, defined as those that derived 20% or more of sales from outside their home country. Brands were only included if there was publicly available marketing and financial data on which to base a brand valuation.

The changing role of branding

The philosophy and practices of branding have seen a number of developments in recent years. There is debate about whether these represent shifts in the underlying principles of branding, or merely a change in application.

As societies become more affluent, the emotional aspects of branding have tended to become more important than the functional elements. Characteristics such as purity, reliability, and durability may have traditionally added value to a brand, but these are increasingly enshrined in legislation and therefore are less capable of being used to differentiate one product from another. An example of the effects of legislation on brand loyalty can be observed in the taxi market by contrasting buyer behaviour in areas with strict licensing (e.g. London) with areas where a relatively unregulated market exists. In London, legislation has reduced the product to a commodity meeting strictly specified standards, whereas in the other towns, customers are more likely to seek the reassurance of a branded operator. In western countries, consumers choice of beer brand is no longer dominated by questions about its purity (this is ensured by a great deal of food safety legislation, and government inspectors to enforce it), but by the emotional messages that the brand develops, and with which the buyer associates. A casual observation of nearly all advertising for beer will show very little mention of the beer itself, but much that is related to abstract lifestyle associations with its consumption.

Another issue affecting branding is the claim that consumers are becoming increasingly critical of the abstract messages for brands developed by big, faceless corporate organizations. In her book *No Logo*, Naomi Klein (2001) painted a bleak picture of a 'brandscape' in which public space is dominated by such unaccountable multinational organizations. To her, brands such as Nike, Shell, Wal-Mart, Microsoft, and McDonald's had become metaphors for a global economic system gone awry and she made a call to arms to fight the dominance and abuses of multinationals. It has also been noted that individuals who are disillusioned with a brand are increasingly likely to use web-based social networking sites to challenge the authority of the brand (Hollenbeck and Zinkhan, 2006).

Against this, proponents of branding have argued that the idea of a confident, educated consumer who despises big brands does not reflect reality. Some, such as Cova (1997) have argued that in an increasingly fragmented society, individuals need to belong to groups through which they acquire identity. Where once church and family provided an individual with their identity, today this role is more likely to be fulfilled by their attachments to brands. Some have spoken of **tribal marketing**, by which brands only acquire value if they have collective meaning to groups of people who adopt them, and of a 'Brandscape' as an increasingly important type of community. In such communities, consumers feel emotionally linked to one another, either formally or informally, through the brands that they consume (Ouwersloot and Odekerken-Schröder, 2008). Members of a gym or up-market fashion retailer may feel this sense of linking, and increasingly, the Internet has been used to develop online branded communities such as YouTube and Bebo.com.

A significant development in most countries in recent years has been the emergence of strong retailers' brands, which have come to challenge manufacturers' brands. When Tesco sales large volumes of its own branded lager, some would say that this represents the declining importance of brands—the customer is simply buying the cheapest alternative that is available in the supermarket. This essentially treats the product as a commodity evaluated solely on the basis of price and availability. An alternative view is that retailers have been very active in developing their own brands, which consumers have come to trust. The consumer may select the Tesco lager rather than the Carlsberg branded lager because they have come to trust Tesco for all the other products that it buys. The buyer may also come to have a favourable emotional attitude towards Tesco

MARKETING in ACTION

Can brands be socially divisive?

Some of the healthiest food products we could buy are inexpensive but are shunned because they are not supported by brand-building activities, in contrast to possibly more harmful and expensive alternatives which have the power of branding behind them. Consider the following examples.

- The market for bottled water in the UK has increased markedly during the past couple of decades, helped by the development of strong brands including Perrier, Highland Spring, and Volvic. This is despite repeated analyses suggesting that filtered domestic tap water is purer and more beneficial than most bottled water, yet is a fraction of the cost. The water supply utility companies have not marketed the benefits of their water, partly held back by a regulatory system that prevents them raising prices for the water they supply. Meanwhile, bottled water suppliers have promoted their product, increasingly relying on 'lifestyle' associations to command ever-higher prices.

- Children are exposed to a vast amount of advertising for snack foods, and peer-group pressure leads them to demand 'cool' brands of drinks and snacks. Meanwhile, fresh fruit—which is considered by nutritionists to be much more beneficial to children—is overlooked as it lacks strong brand-building support. A fragmented industry made up of countless growers and importers and a generic range of products that cannot generally be protected by patent have resulted in very little investment being made available for brand-building. Support is generally limited to national growers' associations promoting a national product, with little effort to develop lifestyle brands. Would children eat more apples and fewer crisps if apples were supported by a multi-million pound advertising campaign to portray them as a 'cool' brand?

- A comparison by *Which?* magazine suggested that retailers' own-brand training shoes costing around £10 are just as hard wearing and beneficial to children's feet as top brand shoes advertised using sports heroes, but costing over £60. Critics have accused branded sports shoes companies of exploiting the children's susceptibility to peer-group pressure and their consequent desire to be seen in only the coolest brand of sports shoes.

Are brands a form of exploitation which creates social divisiveness? Critics of branding in particular, and the capitalist system in general, have argued that brands contribute towards a division in society between the 'haves' and 'have nots', with ostentatious displays of brands creating a feeling of grievance among those who aspire for brands but cannot afford them. Brands may particularly appeal to less secure individuals as a means of establishing an identity for themselves, yet these are often the people who can least afford to pay for premium brands.

Would life be better without brands? Buying would certainly be a lot more difficult without the shorthand code of a brand which comes to stand for a whole bundle of functional and emotional benefits, and simplifying our choice processes. As far as the emotional aspects of lifestyle brands are concerned, have not all societies had some means of differentiating individuals within the society? Maybe we do not have the tribal dresses that have been used in the past by individuals to give them identity, so are modern-day marketers spot on when they talk about 'tribal marketing' by appealing to individuals' inherent desire to identify with a group?

that may be greater than the emotional attitude towards Carlsberg. Many retailers such as Tesco have also gone on to create distinctive sub-brands with their own product positioning (Tesco has developed a 'value' brand for the price-conscious, and a 'Tesco finest' brand for more quality-oriented buyers).

Finally, brands are not only aimed at customers, but also increasingly at employees. The brand values that appeal to customers should be the same as those with which employees identify, and there has been a lot of talk among labour-intensive service organizations about delivering their 'brand promise' through employees (Knox and Freeman, 2006). If employees do not believe in their employer's brand, why should customers?

Positioning the brand

Positioning strategy for a brand is a crucial part of developing a sustainable competitive advantage for the brand. Positioning puts a firm in a sub-segment of its chosen market, and so a firm that adopts a product positioning based on 'high reliability/high cost' will appeal to a sub-segment that has a desire for reliability and a willingness to pay for it.

For some marketers, positioning has been seen as essentially a communications issue, where the nature of the product is given and the objective is to manipulate consumers' perceptions of it. However, others have pointed out that positioning is more than merely advertising and promotion, involving the management of the whole marketing mix. Essentially, the mix must be managed in a way that is internally coherent and sustainable over the long term. A marketing mix positioning of high quality and low price may attract business from competitors in the short term, but the low prices may be insufficient to cover costs of delivering high quality, and therefore profits may be unsustainable over the long term.

A company must examine the strengths and weaknesses of its brands within their marketplace and the opportunities and threats that they face. From this, its brands take a position within their marketplace. A position can be defined by reference to a number of scales, such as price, quality, availability, durability, etc. Level of comfort and price are two dimensions of positioning that are relevant to cars. It is possible to draw a *position map* in which the positions of key players in a market are plotted in relation to these criteria. A position map plotting the positions of selected cars in respect of their price and level of comfort is shown in Figure 7.11. Both scales run from high to low, with price being a general indication of price levels charged relative to competitors and level of comfort being a subjective evaluation of features provided with the car. The position map shows that most cars lie on a diagonal line between the high-comfort/high-price position adopted by Mercedes-Benz and Lexus and the low-price/low-comfort position adopted by Proton and Kia. Points along this diagonal represent feasible positioning strategies for car manufacturers. A strategy in the upper-left quadrant (high price/low quality) can be described as a 'cowboy' strategy and generally

Figure 7.11 A simplified product-positioning map for selected cars

is not sustainable. A position in the lower-right area of the map (high quality/low price) may indicate that an organization is 'overdelivering' by failing to achieve a sufficiently high price to match the level of quality that it is providing. Of course, this two-dimensional analysis of the car market is very simplistic, and buyers make judgements based on a variety of criteria. Low levels of comfort may be tolerated at a high price, for example, if a car carries a strong, aspirational brand name.

The example of cars used two very simplistic positioning criteria. Wind (1982, pp. 79–81) has suggested six generic scales along which all products can be positioned. These are examined below by reference to the positioning opportunities of a leisure centre.

- **Positioning by benefits or needs satisfied:** The leisure centre could position itself somewhere between meeting pure physical recreation needs and meeting pure social needs. In practice, positioning may accommodate the two sets of needs.

- **Positioning by specific product features:** The leisure centre could promote the fact that it has the largest swimming pool in the area, or the most advanced solarium.

- **Positioning by usage occasions:** The centre could be positioned primarily for the occasional visitor, or the service offer could be adapted to aim at the more serious user who wishes to enter a long-term programme of leisure activities.

- **Positioning by user categories:** Should the leisure centre be aimed primarily at individual users, or institutional users such as sports clubs and schools?

- **Positioning against another product:** The leisure centre could promote the fact that it has more facilities than its neighbouring competition.

- **Positioning by product class:** Management could position the centre as an educational facility rather than a centre of leisure, thereby positioning it in a different product class.

Of all the position possibilities open to a company, which position should it adopt? Selecting a product position involves three basic steps (illustrated in Figure 7.12).

1. **Undertake a marketing audit to analyse the position opportunities relative to the company's strengths.** A SWOT analysis should be undertaken to assess the opportunities and threats in a marketplace and the strengths and weaknesses of the company in meeting opportunities as they arise. An important consideration is often the position that customers currently perceive a company as occupying. If a company is perceived as being 'down-market', this may pose a major weakness in exploiting opportunities arising for more 'up-market' products. An organization that is already established in a particular product position will normally have the advantage of customer familiarity to support any new product launch. A car manufacturer such as Mercedes-Benz, which has positioned itself as a high-quality/high-price producer, can use this as a strength to persuade customers to pay relatively high prices for a new product range, in this case a small compact car. Sometimes a weakness can be turned into a strength for positioning purposes; for example, the Avis car rental chain has stressed that, by being the number two operator, it has to try harder.

   It often happens that opportunities are greatest in budget range, low-quality, low-price positions. If a company has established a position as a premium position

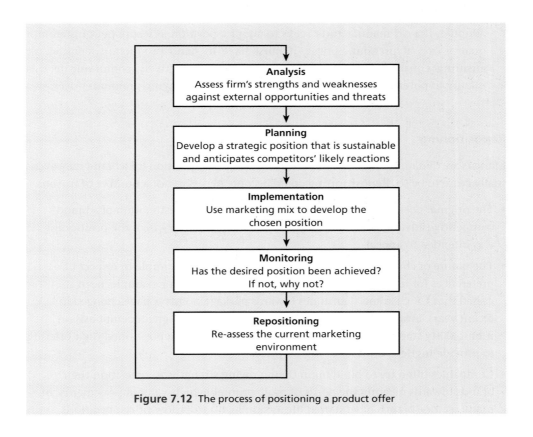

Figure 7.12 The process of positioning a product offer

supplier, should it seek to exploit a lower market position when the opportunity arises? It must avoid tarnishing its established brand values by association with a lower quality product. One solution is to adopt a separate identity for a new product which assumes a different position. In this way, the Volkswagen car group offers different price/quality positions with its Volkswagen, Audi, and Skoda brands.

2. **Evaluate the position possibilities and select the most appropriate.** In undertaking a SWOT analysis, a number of potential positions may have been identified, but many may have to be discarded if they result in uneconomically small market segments, or are too costly to develop. Other positions may be rejected as being inconsistent with an organization's image. Selection from the remaining possibilities should be on the basis of the organization's greatest differential advantage in areas that are most valued by target customers. When it entered the Indonesian market, the UK retailer Marks & Spencer realized that its UK brand positioning of everyday clothes at good value prices would be unsustainable against low-cost local competition. It therefore adopted a much more exclusive position, with smaller shops, limited product ranges, and relatively high prices.

3. **Use the marketing mix to develop and communicate a position.** Organizations must develop programmes to implement and promote the position they have adopted. If a car manufacturer seeks to adopt a position as a supplier of premium quality cars at premium prices, it must have in hand production facilities for ensuring consistently high quality. It must also effectively communicate this quality to potential customers in order to justify their paying premium prices.

Repositioning

Markets are dynamic, and what was once an appropriate position for a brand may eventually cease to be so. **Repositioning** could become necessary for a number of reasons.

- The original positioning may have been based on an overestimation of a brand's competitive advantage or of the size of the sub-segment to which the positioning was intended to appeal.

- The nature of customer demand may have changed, for example in respect of preferences for high quality rather than low price. It has, for example, been suggested that UK customers' attitudes towards package holidays have changed in recent years, away from an emphasis on low price towards greater emphasis on high-quality standards. Many tour operators accordingly repositioned their offering to provide higher standards at higher prices.

- Companies often try to build upon their growing strengths to reposition their brands towards meeting the needs of more profitable high-value sub-segments. In many sectors, brands have started life as simple, no-frills, low-price operations, subsequently gaining a favourable image which they use to 'trade up' to relatively high-quality/high-price positions. This phenomenon is well established in the field of retailing and has become known as the 'Wheel of Retailing'. This contends that retail businesses start life as cut-price, low-cost, narrow-margin operations which subsequently trade up with improvements in display, more prestigious premises, increased advertising, delivery, and the provision of many other customer services which serve to drive up expenses, prices, and margins. Eventually retailers mature as high-cost, conservative, and 'top-heavy' institutions with a sales policy based on quality goods and services rather than price appeal. This in turn opens the way for the next generation of low-cost innovatory retailers to find a position vacated by maturing firms.

The marketing mix

The marketing mix has already been mentioned a number of times in this book. In the following chapters we will look in detail at how companies go about using the marketing mix in order to build brands that satisfy consumers' needs and at the same time allow the company to make a sustainable level of profits.

So what exactly is the marketing mix? You may recall from Chapter 1 that the marketing mix is not a scientific theory, but merely a conceptual framework that identifies the principal decisions marketing managers make in configuring their offerings to suit customers' needs. The tools play a pivotal role in developing the sustainable competitive advantage which has been discussed in this chapter. The tools of the marketing mix can be used both to develop long-term strategies and short-term tactical programmes.

There has been a lot of debate in identifying the list of marketing mix elements. The traditional marketing mix has comprised the four elements of product, price, promotion, and place. A number of people have additionally suggested adding people, process, and physical evidence decisions, which are very important for services businesses. There is overlap between each of these headings, and their precise definition is not particularly important. What matters is that marketing managers can identify the actions they can take that will produce a favourable response from customers. The marketing mix has merely become a convenient framework for analysing these decisions. Some would go further and argue that the concept of a marketing mix is harmful because it encourages managers to take a narrow and compartmentalized approach to each of the mix elements. By this argument, customers buy the whole product offer and are not concerned about how decisions relating to individual components are arrived at—just so long as the total product offer is coherent and creates value in their eyes. Many critics of the marketing mix see the move towards relationship marketing (Chapter 4) as a move towards a focus on customers' holistic values and away from a narrower obsession with management of a producer-defined marketing mix.

The following chapters have been arranged in accordance with traditional definitions of the marketing mix elements, but it must never be forgotten that each element is closely related to all other elements.

Chapter summary and key linkages to other chapters

Developing a sustainable competitive advantage involves a sound understanding of a firm's strengths and weaknesses relative to the opportunities and threats in its marketing environment. Research into buyer behaviour and appropriate targeting, issues discussed in Chapters 4, 5, and 6, provides input to the development of a distinctive marketing mix, discussed in the following chapters. A crucial link between the needs of customers and the capabilities of a firm is the development of a brand. The process of branding allows a company to develop a distinctive identity and position for itself and its products, so as to differentiate its products from those of competitors. By doing this, a company can avoid the worst excesses of price competition. We will look in more detail at how a company uses the marketing mix to develop a distinctive brand in the following chapters.

KEY PRINCIPLES OF MARKETING

- An overriding aim of marketing is to develop a sustainable competitive advantage for an organization.
- Competitors for a firm's products can be direct or indirect. Indirect forms of competition are more difficult to identify.
- A brand is a means of identifying one company and its products from otherwise similar products supplied by other companies.
- The functional role of a brand should be distinguished from its emotional role.
- Brands are created through the management of the marketing mix. The marketing mix is merely a convenient listing of interrelated decisions to be taken by managers.

CASE STUDY

Fairy's brand bubble never seems to burst

It is often said that somebody who has been trained in marketing at Procter & Gamble can go on to successfully market anything. The markets in which Procter & Gamble operates—mainly low-value consumer goods, such as household detergents—are among the most fiercely competitive, and building successful brands is key to long-term profitability. Differentiating one product from another in the minds of consumers can be extremely difficult, with one packet of detergent looking very much like another, and in many cases also performing similarly. An analysis of one of the company's flagship brands—Fairy Liquid—illustrates how the company has carefully nurtured the brand, adapting it to changes in consumers' preferences, and maintaining consistent standards while exploiting new market opportunities.

Fairy was rated as Britain's number one cleaning brand by *The Times* in February 2007 and has been a regular household feature since the name first appeared in 1898 on a bar of soap. Procter & Gamble first launched Fairy Liquid in the UK market in 1960. At that time, the market for washing-up products was still in its infancy, with most consumers using solid soaps, and only 17% of households using liquid soap. As market leader, Procter & Gamble stood to gain most from a change in consumers' habits. Its first task was therefore to educate the public on the benefits of using washing-up liquid. The launch of Fairy involved distributing 15 million trial bottles to about 85% of households in the UK.

Creating early awareness and trial of the product led to Fairy gaining a market share of 27% by 1969. Strong promotional support was, and remains, a key to the brand's success. Since its launch, promotional messages have focused consistently on the mildness of the product, its long-lasting suds, and a proud positioning as a slightly more expensive product which is better value and worth paying the extra for. Mother and child images have been used extensively in advertising. This helps to create brand values of a soft, caring, homely image. A discussion thread on the Bebo website featured many reminiscences from adults who associated the brand with happy days of their childhood. Fairy has a trusted heritage which has been passed down from generation to generation. However, messages have been adapted around the core theme in response to changing attitudes; for example, a commercial in 1994 for the first time used a father instead of a mother at the kitchen sink. Various celebrities have been used to endorse the brand's values, including a lengthy spell of endorsement by the actress Nanette Newman. The consistency of the brand's message has been reinforced with a promotional jingle that has been modified only slightly since it was first introduced in 1960.

During the first 20 years of the brand's life, product innovation had been relatively modest. However, since then an increasingly competitive market and more discerning customers have forced the company to innovate in order to maintain and strengthen its market share. With the emergence of many 'me too' competitors from supermarkets, Fairy needed to offer additional unique advantages to supplement its long-lasting suds.

In 1984/5 the company introduced a lemon variant of Fairy and its total market share increased to 32%. By 1987 the market share had increased to 34% with the newly introduced lemon variant accounting for one-third of sales. In 1988 a new formulation was launched, offering '15% extra mileage', as well as more effective grease eradication.

In 1992 the original Fairy Liquid was replaced with Fairy Excel, which claimed to be '50% better at dealing with grease'. This helped to increase the market share to 50%. In the following year a concentrated version of Fairy Excel Plus was launched, with the slogan 'The power of four for the price of one'. The company launched this low-bulk, high-concentration product with one eye to retailers, who were tiring of filling their valuable shelf space with more and more variants of basically low-value products. Excel Plus offered supermarkets more cost-effective and profitable use of their shelf space.

Increased ownership of domestic dishwashing machines posed a threat and also an opportunity to Fairy. The threat came from a relative decline in sales of liquids used for handwashing of dishes. The opportunity arose from increased demand for dishwasher cleaning fluid and the Fairy brand was extended to dishwashing detergents. In 2006 Procter & Gamble introduced Fairy Active Bursts for dishwashers.

During the lifetime of Fairy, the market for detergents in different European countries has gradually converged. As a result, Excel Plus was launched simultaneously in the UK, Belgium, Denmark, Finland, Germany, Holland, Ireland, and Sweden.

Innovation and reliability have been at the heart of Fairy's branding strategy, in a market which has been fiercely contested by other manufacturers' brands, and increasingly by supermarkets' own-label brands. In what other ways could Fairy evolve to retain its brand leadership? Preferences for new scents of detergent are continually emerging and provide an opportunity for innovation. Following a series of food safety scares, some observers of the market have pointed to a potential market for anti-bacterial food washes that would satisfy consumers' increasing concern over residues on the surface of fruit and vegetables.

Source: based on Procter & Gamble website (www.pg.com), accessed 25 April 2008; British Brands Group, case study—Fairy Liquid (www.britishbrandsgroup.org.uk/brands/case-studies/brands); Talking Retail, 'Fairy adds two new dishwashing products', (www.talkingretail.com/products/9181/Fairy-adds-two-new-dishwash-pr.ehtml), accessed 25 April 2008.

Case study review questions

1. How would you explain the success of the Fairy brand?

2. How do you think Procter & Gamble has been able to increase its market share at a time when competition from supermarkets' own-label brands has intensified?

3. To what extent can the principles and practices of brand management used for Fairy Liquid be applied to other goods and services, such as televisions and package holidays?

CHAPTER REVIEW QUESTIONS

1. In the context of a sustainable competitive advantage, what is meant by customer value? How can a company ensure that it continues to deliver value?

2. With increasing levels of consumer protection legislation designed to protect buyers from faulty products and misleading advertising claims, do we still need brands? How can brands adapt to increasing levels of legislation?

3. Using examples, discuss the problems that are likely to result from a firm seeking to reposition its product offer.

ACTIVITIES

1. Consider the case of a restaurant in your local town. Identify the restaurant's direct and indirect competitors. Think far and wide about what may constitute an indirect competitor and justify your reasoning.

2. Look through a Sunday newspaper magazine supplement and examine a selection of adverts. What brand message is communicated by these adverts? Identify the functional and emotional elements of the firms' branding strategy.

3. Examine the branding strategy used by banks or financial services organizations with which you are familiar. Critically examine the message that is communicated by the brand. Which market segments is a brand particularly addressing? Are there any important segments that may be alienated by the brand message? To what extent has the service provider used brands and sub-brands to segment its market?

REFERENCES

Allison, R. and Uhl, K. (1964), 'Influence of Beer Brand Identification on Taste Perception'. *Journal of Marketing Research*, 1(3): 36–9.

Berthon, P., Holbrook, M. B., and Hulbert, J. M. (2003), 'Understanding and Managing the Brand Space'. *MIT Sloan Management Review*, 44(2): 49–55.

Branthwaite, A. and Cooper, P. (1981), 'Analgesic Effects of Branding in Treatment of Headaches'. *British Medical Journal*, 282(6276): 1576–8 (16 May).

Competition Commission (2008), *The Supply of Groceries in the UK Market Investigation*, 30 April. Available at: www.competition-commission.org.uk/rep_pub/reports/2008/538grocery.htm.

Cova, B. (1997), 'Community and Consumption—Towards a Definition of the "Linking Value" of Product or Services'. *European Journal of Marketing*, 31(3/4): 297–316.

De Chernatony, L. (2006), *From Brand Vision to Brand Evaluation*. Oxford: Butterworth-Heinemann.

De Chernatony, L. and McDonald, M. (2003), *Creating Powerful Brands*, 3rd edn. Oxford: Butterworth-Heinemann.

De Chernatony, L. and McWilliam, G. (1990), 'Appreciating Brands as Assets through Using a Two-Dimensional Model'. *International Journal of Advertising*, 9(2): 111–19.

Gardner, B. and Levy, S. (1955), 'The Product and the Brand'. *Harvard Business Review*, 33(2) (March/April): 33–9.

Grime, I., Diamantopoulos, A., and Smith, G. (2002), 'Consumer Evaluations of Extensions and their Effects on the Core Brand: key issues and research propositions'. *European Journal of Marketing*, 36(11/12): 1415–38.

Hollenbeck, C. R. and Zinkhan, G. M. (2006), Consumer Activism on the Internet: the role of anti-brand communities. *Advances in Consumer Research*, 33: 470–85.

Klein, N. (2001), *No Logo*. London: Flamingo.

Knox, S. and Freeman, C. (2006), 'Measuring and Managing Employer Brand Image in the Service Industry'. *Journal of Marketing Management,* 22(7): 695–716.

Levitt, T. (1960), '*Marketing Myopia*'. *Harvard Business Review*, 38(4): 45–56.

Munson, J. M. and Spivey, W. A. (1981), 'Products and Brand Users: stereotypes among social classes'. In K. Munroe (ed.), *Advances in Consumer Research*. Ann Arbor, MI: CAR.

Ouwersloot, H. and Odekerken-Schröder, G. (2008), 'Who's Who in Brand Communities—and Why?'. *European Journal of Marketing, 42*(5/6): 571–85.

Peters, T. J. and Waterman, R. H. (1982), *In Search of Excellence: lessons from America's best run companies*. New York: Harper & Row.

Porter, M. E. (1980), *Competitive Strategy: techniques for analysing industries and competitors*. New York: Free Press.

Williams, L. (2002), 'Pursuit of Holy Grail Comes with Global Warning: the jury is out on whether the cost of creating a world brand is worth it'. *Daily Telegraph*, 14(6) (November).

Wind, Y. J. (1982), *Product Policy: concepts, methods and strategy*. Reading: Addison-Wesley.

◉ SUGGESTED FURTHER READING

The following provide insights into competitor analysis:

Hooley, G, Saunders, J., and Piercy, N. (2007), *Marketing Strategy and Competitive Positioning*, 4th edn. Hemel Hempstead: Prentice-Hall.

D'Aveni, R. A. (2007), 'Mapping Your Competitive Position'. *Harvard Business Review*, November.

The following book provides a general and authoritative introduction to the principles of branding:

De Chernatony, L. and McDonald, M. (2003), *Creating Powerful Brands*, 3rd edn. Oxford: Butterworth-Heinemann.

The following provides a more critical perspective on the role of branding:

Klein, N. (2001), *No Logo*, London: Flamingo.

For further discussion of the application of general branding principles to not-for-profit organizations, refer to the following:

Stride, H. and Lee, S. (2007), 'No Logo? No way: branding in the not-for-profit sector'. *Journal of Marketing Management*, 23(1/2): 107–22.

◉ USEFUL WEB LINKS

Visit the Online Resource Centre for resources that are relevant to this chapter, including web links, multiple choice questions, and additional case studies:

www.oxfordtextbooks.co.uk/orc/palmer2e/

☐ KEY TERMS

- Brand extension
- Brand family
- Brand personality
- Brands
- Co-branding
- Commodity
- Counterfeiting
- Differentiation
- Direct competitors
- Five Forces model
- Global brands
- Imperfect competition
- Indirect competitors
- Patent
- Positioning
- Repositioning
- Trademark
- Tribal marketing
- Visual identity

8

Developing the product

CHAPTER OBJECTIVES

The product is at the heart of a company's marketing mix planning. Customers buy a firm's products in order to satisfy their needs as cost-effectively as possible. This chapter begins by discussing the nature of the product offer. Products comprise complex bundles of attributes which must be translated into valuble benefits for customers. Companies typically offer a range of products, each of which can be expected to go through some form of life cycle.

Product mix planning is discussed in the context of the product life cycle. This chapter explores the methods used by companies to keep their product ranges up to date. Innovation is an important differentiating factor for many firms, and this chapter explores methods by which innovative products can be developed, tested, and brought to market. When products approach the end of their life cycle, it is important that they are deleted in a rational and cost-effective manner.

What do we mean by a product?

Products are the focal point through which companies seek to satisfy customers' needs. It must be remembered that people do not buy products as an end in themselves. Products are only bought for the benefits they provide. In other words, a product is of value to someone only as long as it is perceived as satisfying some need.

Most people, when they consider the marketing of products, tend to think of fast-moving consumer goods such as soap powder or chocolate bars. In fact, the term 'product' can mean many things. In this chapter a 'product' is any tangible or intangible item that satisfies a need. A product can be any of the following:

- a material good;
- an intangible service;

- a combination of the above;
- a location;
- a person;
- an idea.

Most products that we buy are actually a combination of two or more of the above.

It is useful to begin this chapter by trying to classify products in a way which reflects differences in the way they are marketed. Within the different categories of product that are described below, some broad similarities in marketing requirements can be identified. Figure 8.1 attempts to classify products according to two important dimensions:

1. the level of involvement required on the part of the purchaser (e.g. the purchase of sugar calls for only very low levels of emotional involvement by the buyer, whereas in the case of fashion clothing, involvement may be very high);

2. the level of availability that is typically required by purchasers (e.g. a buyer will expect a can of soft drink to be available immediately and without having to travel to get it, whereas she would be prepared to travel further, and possibly wait, to purchase some specialist hi-fi equipment).

These are just two dimensions that contribute towards the design of an appropriate marketing mix. Others could include buyers' price sensitivity, brand loyalty, frequency of purchase, etc. The idea of placing products somewhere on a position map is introduced at this stage to emphasize an important reason for categorizing products in the first place: to explore whether marketers of one product can learn from the marketing of another product which may at first appear to be quite different, but is really quite similar in terms of the needs that it satisfies.

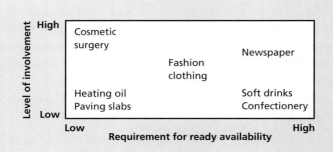

Figure 8.1 A schematic classification of products based on buyers' levels of involvement and desired levels of access to the product, showing examples of product positions

Material goods

Material goods can be classified under two major headings: consumer goods and **business-to-business goods**. (The latter are also often referred to as industrial goods.)

Consumer goods

Consumer goods are those that are purchased to satisfy individual or household needs. They can be classified as follows:

- **Convenience goods:** These items tend to be relatively cheap and are purchased on a regular basis—tea, coffee, toothpaste, etc. They are often referred to as **fast-moving consumer goods (FMCGs)**. The purchase of this type of product is likely to involve very little decision-making effort on the part of the buyer, and in many cases an individual will tend to purchase a particular brand on a regular basis.

  Within the broad category of convenience goods, products as diverse as ice cream and toothpaste may at first appear to have very little in common; but in fact the marketing of them can be quite similar. Convenience goods are generally sold through many retail outlets so that buyers have easy access to the product. There is therefore a tendency to spend large amounts on advertising and on sales promotions. The packaging aspect of the marketing mix is also likely to be important, with the package acting as promotional tool in its own right. A company must invest in an extensive network of distributors, so that its product is easily available to large numbers of people. These items tend to be cheaply priced with the aim of selling high volumes at low margins.

- **Shopping goods:** Consumers generally put much more effort into choosing 'shopping' goods. Their bases for evaluation may be much wider than those used for FMCGs, and may typically include price, credit facilities, guarantees, after-sales service, etc. Examples of shopping goods include dishwashers and freezers (which are examples of what are known as 'white goods'), mobile phones, and cameras.

  These products are distributed through fewer retail outlets and therefore there is likely to be a higher margin for the retailer. Customers are usually more willing to travel to an outlet to find a product, rather than expecting it to be available on their doorstep. Large amounts of money may be spent on advertising these goods and developing strong brands, and the amount of effort put into personal selling tends to be greater than for FMCGs.

- **Speciality goods:** For these products, consumers may spend a great deal of effort in the decision-making process. Speciality goods have one or more unique characteristics and are sold in relatively few outlets. A quality image is usually communicated as a result. Designer clothing would be an example of a speciality good. Such goods are bought infrequently, and tend to be expensive. Buyers may go to considerable effort to find the product of their choice.

- **Unsought goods:** Some goods initially may be considered by an individual not to be necessary, but they are nevertheless sold aggressively on the market. Many home owners may not be aware of, or concerned about limescale damage to their dishwasher, and may therefore not seek out products which may reduce such damage. Consumers may only purchase these products if they are aggressively sold.

Business-to-business goods

These are purchased for use in a firm's production processes or to make other goods. They are often bought by a large decision-making unit in which organizational as well as individuals' needs have to be satisfied (see Chapter 4).

Business-to-business goods can be divided into the following types:

- **Raw materials:** These are basic materials that are needed as inputs to the early stages of production of a product or its components, e.g. iron ore, chemicals, etc. They are often purchased in bulk and sold as a commodity, with little attempt at product differentiation which would justify a price premium.

- **Major equipment:** This category includes large machines and tools used in production processes. They tend to be expensive and are expected to last a number of years. The decision to purchase this type of equipment tends to be made at a high level in an organization, and the purchase process can take a long time and involve a number of people. There is a need to build important relationships between buyers and sellers in this process, as it is likely to involve not only the agreement to purchase the equipment but also agreement on financing, maintenance contracts, guarantees, future purchases, etc.

- **Support equipment:** This includes goods that are used in the production process or allied activities but are separate from the final 'product' itself. Examples of support equipment include computer software, tools, etc. These goods are generally cheaper than major equipment and the purchase process is less involved.

- **Component parts:** When put together, component parts produce a finished good. Buyers purchase such items according to their own requirements for quality and delivery time so that they can ensure that their own end product can be produced effectively and efficiently. Just-in-time delivery of component parts has become an important element of the total product offer.

- **Consumable supplies:** These goods help in the production process and do not become part of the product; for example, lubricating oil is vital to many production processes but does not become incorporated into the product. These items are typically purchased routinely by organizations with very little search effort.

Intangible services

Services can be described as 'products', although some people still find it amusing that bank accounts, package holidays, and even pop stars can be described as products. Although the term 'product' is traditionally associated with tangible goods, it can be more correctly defined as anything of value that a company offers to its customers. This value can take tangible or intangible forms.

There has been a big increase in recent years in service industries, which do not offer physical goods for sale but instead offer intangible benefits to buyers. A car mechanic offers expertise in maintaining vehicles; a decorator or plumber sells his service. It is essentially their skills in performing a service process that are being offered for sale, rather than any physical good. At other times, the service is essentially about paying for use of an asset, such as a rental car or car-parking space. In most western economies, services now account for around three-quarters of Gross Domestic Product.

The marketing of services can be quite different from the marketing of goods, although in practice most products are a combination of a good and a service. (For example, a meal in a restaurant combines the tangible elements of the food with the intangible service that is provided.) The distinguishing characteristics of services are described below:

- **Intangibility:** Services cannot be seen, tasted, or touched. This means that it is very difficult for a customer to examine a service in advance. In fact, most material goods have some intangible service aspects to them, and likewise most services have at least some physical elements. Indeed, it is likely to be a question of degree of intangibility that will help in the identification of whether a product is a service.

- **Inseparability:** The provision of a service normally requires the involvement of both customer and service provider simultaneously. Production and consumption cannot be separated in the way that manufacturing companies are able to mass-produce their goods in a central factory and transport them to customers for consumption.

- **Variability:** As a result of inseparability, each service tends to be unique, and the standard of service delivery can vary from one occasion to the next. A consequence of this is that service quality is difficult to standardize and to guarantee. The best that can be achieved are minimum standards (e.g. answering the telephone after a stated number of rings) or standards relating to the physical aspects of the service (such as the percentage of time that a bank ATM machine is available for use).

- **Perishability:** Services cannot be inventoried like material goods. If a service is not sold at the time it is produced, e.g. an empty airline seat after a plane has departed, then the service offer disappears forever. This has important implications for service providers as they cannot store up services when demand is low in order to satisfy demand when it increases.

In much the same way as for goods, services can be further broken down into categories, although there tend to be fewer commonly used shorthand classification titles, such as 'FMCGs' and 'white goods'. However, some important bases for classifying services are:

- **Consumer services:** These are used up by the final consumer and no further economic benefit arises (e.g. a meal in a restaurant, a visit to the cinema).

- **Business-to-business services:** These are bought by businesses in order to add value to their own production processes (e.g. the services of a commercial bank or courier delivery service).

- **People-based v. equipment-based services:** The nature of interaction between a company and its customers tends to be different depending on whether the service is primarily provided by machines (e.g. a telephone service) or people (e.g. many personal health services).

- **Knowledge-based services:** Some services essentially comprise the exchange of specialized knowledge, rather than the exchange of goods or undertaking of a service process (e.g. consultants may be engaged primarily for their knowledge).

The debate about the factors that distinguish or unite goods and services was crystallized recently in an article by Vargo and Lusch that talked about a new 'service dominant logic' of marketing (Vargo and Lusch, 2004). They argued that marketing was originally built on a goods-centred, manufacturing-based model of economic exchange developed during the Industrial Revolution. Services were then added to these frameworks, but in seeking to broaden its scope to include services, marketing was constrained by the language and models of manufactured goods. Vargo and Lusch have turned this argument around, by arguing that everything we buy is essentially service-based, and goods play a secondary, facilitating role in any product offer. Services provide *value in use* for a tangible product which might otherwise be of little value to the consumer. Think of a bottle of beverage that you have bought and all of the services that were essential to create value in use at a time and place where you need it. Without the services of intermediaries and transport companies, the beverage would still be in the manufacturer's factory and of no value to you.

Ideas

Ideas can also be considered as products. Political parties have developed marketing strategies to promote their own particular policies to the electorate, as have groups that are attempting to market particular issues, such as the environment, equal opportunities, etc. The key feature of these types of product is that they are intangible and have many similar characteristics to services. However, where an idea is the focus of marketing, it can be unclear just who the 'customer' is, and it can be difficult to conceptualize the exchange that takes place between the 'buyer' and the 'seller' of the idea.

Locations and people

The term 'product' can also be used to denote places (e.g. holiday resorts) and people (e.g. footballers, rock stars). These involve both tangible and intangible elements, and therefore the marketing mix should be configured accordingly.

Analysis of the product offer

Products can be complex entities, and it is useful to identify a number of levels of the product offer. Three levels will be identified here (see Figure 8.2):

1. **The core level:** The best way to think of this is to consider an item and identify the key benefit from its ownership. For example, the core benefit of buying food is to overcome hunger, and the core benefit of undertaking a marketing course is personal development. Every product has a core element, and it is the secondary and augmented elements that put 'flesh on the bones' and give a product an individual identity.

2. **The secondary level:** The secondary level of a product includes those physical features that the product actually possesses. Such elements include colour, design,

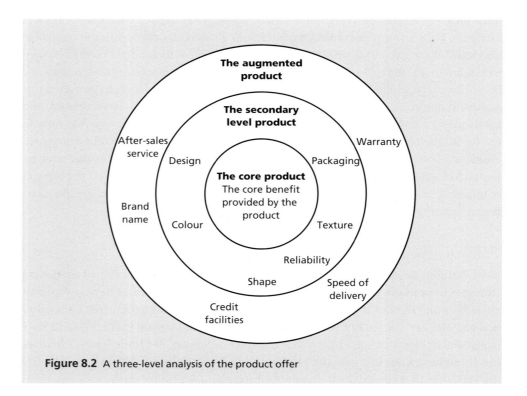

Figure 8.2 A three-level analysis of the product offer

shape, packaging, size, etc. A television, for example, may have entertainment as a core benefit but the secondary elements would include such features as the shape of the box, the type of screen, the size of screen, the quality of sound, the colour of the unit, whether there is a stand, etc.

3. **The augmented level:** It is this that differentiates a particular product from its competitors. The augmented level of a product tends to include intangible features such as pre-sales and after-sales service, guarantees, credit facilities, brand name, etc.

This is a fairly traditional three-level analysis, which may be appropriate to tangible goods, but it has less value in the analysis of intangible services. For services, the augmented level may be the key distinguishing feature of the service. It is more appropriate, therefore, to talk about two levels of the product offer, with a core level representing the primary benefit and a secondary level representing the distinguishing characteristics of the service. Remember also the argument of Vargo and Lusch, who see services as the focal point of all marketing activity. By their argument, it is goods which become the differentiator to a service, rather than services being one of the elements of the secondary offer which differentiates one good from another.

The product mix

The product mix comprises the complete range of products that a company offers to the market. A number of elements of a typical product portfolio can be identified and the following terms are commonly used (see Figure 8.3).

- **Product item:** This is the individual product, with its core, secondary, and augmented elements (for example, a Fuji A340 camera).

- **Product line:** This is a collection of product items that are related by the type of raw materials used, similar technology used, or merely as a commonsense grouping (e.g. a line in digital cameras). A truly effective product line should be customer-focused and therefore should link to the range of needs of the particular segment/s targeted by the firm (e.g. the need for recording memories).

- **Product mix:** This is the total range of products that the company has on offer to customers and within this product mix there is what is known as the depth and the width of the product. The **depth** of the product mix refers to the number of products offered within a product line. The more products within a line, the greater the depth of the product mix. For example, the electrical retailer Currys has many different types of camera within its line of cameras. The **width** of the product mix refers to the number of product lines a company has, and the more lines, the greater the product mix width. Currys, for example, would have other lines as well as cameras, including televisions, audio equipment, computers, etc.

Figure 8.3 Elements of the product mix

Quality

Quality is an important feature of a product, and buyers make choices among competing products on the basis of the ratio of quality to price. Most people would accept that a Sony DVD recorder is of higher quality than one marketed by Alba and would be prepared to pay a higher price for it. Many will nevertheless be quite happy with the quality of the Alba machine, preferring its lower price.

But what do we mean by product quality? Quality is an extremely difficult concept to define in a few words. At its most basic, quality has been defined as 'conforming to requirements' (Crosby, 1984). This implies that organizations must establish customers' requirements and specifications. Once established, the quality goal of the various functions of an organization is to comply strictly with these specifications. However, the questions remain: whose requirements, and whose specifications? A second series of definitions therefore state that quality is all about fitness for use (Juran, 1982), a definition based primarily on satisfying customers' needs. These two definitions can be brought together in the concept of customer-perceived quality. Quality can be defined only by customers, and exists when an organization supplies goods or services to a specification that satisfies their needs and expectations.

The problem remains of identifying precisely what consumers' needs and expectations are. A company may think that it has the best-quality product based on its own criteria, but customers may have completely different criteria for judging quality. Sometimes there are benchmarks for measuring quality that can be readily agreed upon, for example that an 18-carat gold ring is better quality than one that is only 9 carats. At other times, the quality of a tangible good can only be defined in the mind of the buyer, for example some people might rate fast food as being higher quality than a gourmet meal in a fine restaurant. In the case of intangible services, it can be much more difficult to agree the criteria for assessing quality, because few tangible manifestations exist. This has led many people to draw a distinction between the technical and functional dimensions of quality.

Technical quality and functional quality

Technical quality refers to the relatively quantifiable aspects of a product that can easily be measured by both customer and supplier. Examples of technical quality include the waiting time at a supermarket checkout and the reliability of a new car. However, consumers are also influenced by *how* the technical quality is delivered to them. This is what Gronroos (1984) has described as *functional quality*, and it cannot be measured as objectively as the elements of technical quality. In the case of the queue at a supermarket checkout, functional quality is influenced by such factors as the environment in which queuing takes place and consumers' perceptions of the manner in which queues are handled by the supermarket's staff.

A great deal of research has gone into trying to understand the processes by which buyers form expectations about the quality of a product. It is widely accepted that a

Figure 8.4 Meat has traditionally been sold as a commodity-type product, with the main branding being confined to that of retailers who sell meat. Retailers have earned the trust of customers for supplying good quality meat, but this trust has been increasingly challenged by food scares and reports of alleged inhumane treatment of animals. To provide further reassurance to meat buyers, industry bodies have developed a number of certification or accreditation schemes. Many buyers will specifically seek out meat which carries a mark such as the tractor logo in the knowledge that they are buying a product which is of greater value to them than an unmarked commodity-type product. (*Source:* © Assured Food Standard. Reproduced with kind permission)

product could be deemed to be of poor quality simply because it did not meet the buyer's expectations. A company's promotional material may have built up unsustainable expectations, resulting in perceptions of poor quality, even though an objective outside observer may have considered the technical quality to be high.

To try to provide reassurance to buyers, many companies incorporate some sort of guarantee of quality into their product offer. These can take a number of forms, including:

- The manufacturer may specify the standards in the product descriptions (e.g. bread made without preservatives; light bulbs tested for a life of 10,000 hours; clothing manufactured to be water-resistant).

- Often, product quality statements are backed up by specific guarantees of performance (e.g. the paintwork on a new car may be guaranteed to remain intact for six years).

- 'Customer charters' are often used to state the standards of service that a customer can expect. (Train-operating companies have customer charters which, among other things, can provide compensation for late-running trains.)

Distinctive design

It has been noted many times in this book that the development of a distinctive product is the basis for strong brand development. However, distinctiveness in itself is irrelevant if buyers do not value the distinction. Marmite-flavoured ice cream may be distinctive, but would you buy it (Ofek and Srinivasan, 2002)?

A product's distinctiveness can be protected by a **patent**. This is a right given to an inventor that allows her exclusively to reap the benefits from the invention over a specified period. To qualify for a patent, a product must satisfy certain criteria: it must be novel, and it must include an inventive step. In the cases of services, for which patent protection is difficult to obtain, the registration of a **trademark** can protect a company's distinctive identity. If a patent or trademark is infringed, the patent holder will be entitled to an injunction and to damages. A company can also challenge a 'copycat' product under the common law doctrine of 'passing off'. It can be difficult to define the point where a competitors' copycat product infringes on the original company's legal protection. There have been many examples of alleged infringement. The crisp maker Walkers challenged Tesco over what it believed to be an amazing similarity in packaging between its premium Sensations range and Tesco's Temptations crisps. Coincidentally, one of Walkers' more unusual flavours, Sea Salt and Cracked Black Pepper, also appeared in the Tesco range.

Ownership of patents can make enormous differences to the profitability of a product range, especially within the pharmaceutical sector. The shares of the pharmaceutical company Merck fell sharply in April 2008 after regulatory authorities refused a licence for its new anti-cholestorol pill, wiping out most of the value of its patent on the drug (*Financial Times*, 2008a). However, the ownership of patents alone may not be sufficient for market success. It has been noted that the cosmetics company L'Oréal owns over 28,000 patents for components of its cosmetics, but the main reason behind its market success is the image that it has successfully created for its products (Mills, 2003).

Packaging

The **packaging** of goods performs four major functions: handling, transport, storage, and the communication of product information.

Packaging is needed to ensure that goods are delivered to customers in a sound condition. The packaging should enable distributors and end users to handle and transport the product from one place to another. In addition, packaging should allow the product to be stored, and therefore the shape should be conducive to it being stocked on shelves and, where appropriate, in the home, office, or business. Packaging should protect the product from deterioration and from breakage.

Where goods are sold to customers using self-service methods, packaging can perform an important information and promotional role. The package can inform the customer of what is inside and can communicate the brand name, both directly through name association and indirectly by associating the brand with a distinctive type of packaging. (For example, most people would recognize a bar of Toblerone chocolate by the shape of its packaging alone.)

The results of redesigning packaging without changing the contents can sometimes be quite dramatic—see the 'Marketing in Action' vignette on how long-life milk sales were boosted by changing its packaging.

MARKETING in ACTION

A pint of powder pulls a punch

The British have a long tradition of buying fresh bottles of milk delivered daily to the front door. Although today most milk is bought in plastic or cardboard containers, buying milk in a bottle still seems appealing to most people. Powdered milk had been around for a long time and, despite being nutritious, has been looked down upon by most people as an inferior product. Yet a market existed for dried milk as a 'reserve supply' of milk for those times when fresh milk was temporarily not available. But the product still had an image problem, not helped by many people's wartime memories of rations of dried milk being provided in tins and boxes. One solution identified by St Ivel was to put its dried milk in familiar shaped milk bottles. It could then sit in the fridge next to the fresh milk. The image of the product improved and sales soared.

'Greening' the product range

We saw in Chapter 3 that many consumers and governments are showing increasing concern for the ecological impacts of the products that they consume. The idea of individuals reducing their 'carbon footprint' has become a topical subject for discussion, even if, as we saw in Chapter 3, most consumers probably do not have a thorough understanding of the complexities of ecological impacts.

Ecologically concerned consumers can present marketers with product development opportunities, as well as problems. Pro-active companies have capitalized on ecological issues by reducing their costs and/or improving their organizational image. Go back to Chapter 3 to review some examples of firms' responses to the need to make their product ranges more ecologically responsible.

The product life cycle

There is a general acceptance that most products go through a number of stages in their existence, just as humans and most living organisms go through a number of life-cycle stages. When a new product comes onto the market, there will probably be a lot of promotional effort by a company to secure sales. It is likely that the company will have incurred high costs in the development of such a product, costs that in the early stages may not be covered by revenue. Potential customers for a new product may be few and far between and therefore sales in the early stages may be quite slow. This stage is known as the **introduction stage**.

If the new product proves popular, more people will show an interest and start purchasing it. As more people buy, the firm will discover a number of cost savings in producing larger quantities. Raw materials can be purchased in bulk and therefore at a cheaper cost per unit. Machinery and employees will become more efficient at producing larger quantities, resulting in economies of scale. Any initial teething problems with the product will start to be ironed out and more people will purchase the product on the basis of word of mouth rather than merely the firm's formal promotion campaign. Falling costs and rising revenues will improve profitability in what is usually referred to as the **growth stage**.

As sales of the product increase, other competitors are likely to be attracted to the market and as a result, there will be increasingly fierce competition and a tendency for downward pressure on prices. Promotion on the part of all competitors will tend to increase, and yet the number of customers for the product will have ceased to grow. Over a period of time, the increase in sales starts to slow down and this is known as the **maturity stage**.

As time goes by, sales start to stabilize, marking the **saturation stage**. At this point most demand is replacement demand rather than new demand, and total sales start to

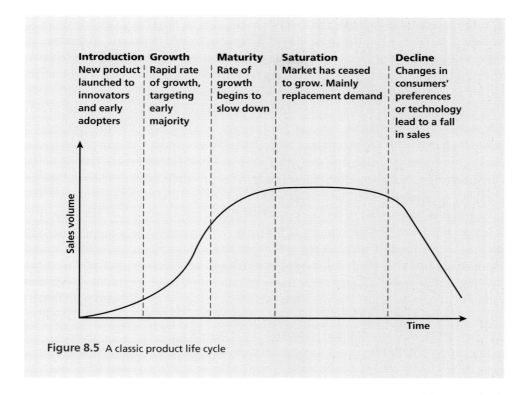

Figure 8.5 A classic product life cycle

fall. The mobile phone market in the UK reached this point in 2002 when total sales fell for the first time (*The Times*, 2002). Falling sales eventually lead to the **decline stage**. Figure 8.5 displays this classical **product life cycle**.

The product life cycle fits well with the explanation put forward of how new products are adopted (Rogers, 2003). Different types of customer are identified according to the speed at which a new product is adopted, and we will turn to this now.

The product life cycle and consumer adoption processes

When an innovative product is introduced onto the market, only a small number of people will be interested in purchasing it as it is an untested item and usually quite expensive. Such people are categorized as **innovators**, and they tend to buy new products because they like to be seen owning something that is new and generally untried. People in this category are likely to have been among the first to buy mobile phones, digital cameras, and widescreen televisions when they were launched. Despite the existence of innovators, new product launches may nevertheless be unsuccessful, as witnessed by the launch of WAP mobile phone services and the Sinclair C5 vehicle.

As the successful product begins to move to the growth stage, more people show an interest in it. The price of the product by this time has started to fall and, as innovators inform other people of the benefits of the product, more people begin to purchase it. The next wave of people to buy the product are known as **early adopters**. A key characteristic of early adopters is that they can be very influential in the groups with whom they interact, so they can be considered as opinion leaders. These individuals are generally looked on as experts in a particular field among the group, and therefore if they feel generally happy with the purchase of this relatively new product, they are likely to influence others to purchase it as well. This next group of customers are known as the **early majority**, and the product is now firmly in the growth stage of its life cycle. As the competition starts to enter the market and prices begin to fall ever more quickly, the next group of people start to consider purchase. These are known as the **late majority**. It is after this point that the number of potential new customers for a product starts to decline, as the product starts to move through to its maturity and saturation stages. Products are sold at lower prices as companies try and sell excess stock. The market has by now almost ceased to grow, with most demand now being replacement demand rather than new demand. There is a relatively small group of people who tend to purchase products at the end of their life cycles, and such people are known as **laggards**. The pattern of product adoption is illustrated in Figure 8.6.

The concept of the life cycle is useful in that any marketing activity applied to a product can be closely related to the stage in the life cycle that the product has reached. Promotional planning, for example, can be closely related to the life cycle. In the introductory phase emphasis will be typically placed on creating awareness through public relations activity, building on this through the growth phase with advertising. Sales promotion activity will typically be used as the market reaches maturity and becomes

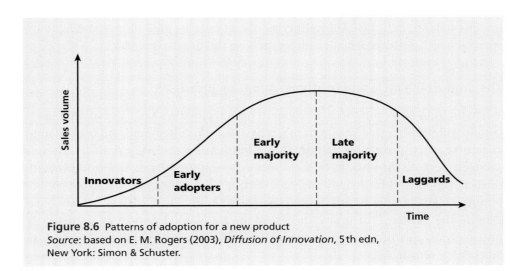

Figure 8.6 Patterns of adoption for a new product
Source: based on E. M. Rogers (2003), *Diffusion of Innovation*, 5th edn, New York: Simon & Schuster.

more competitive. Finally, all promotional activity may be dropped in the decline stage as the product is allowed to die naturally.

All aspects of the marketing mix can be altered to fit the various life-cycle stages. For example, for an innovatory product, a high price may be achievable in the introductory stage, eventually falling as the competition gets stronger and costs fall. Different distribution policies can be applied to the different stages.

Is there one particular pattern of product life cycle that is applicable to all products? In fact, different products move through the stages at different speeds, and not all products follow the 'classic' shaped cycle. Some have an introduction stage but fail to go any further. Others reach the growth stage and then for some reason sales fall very rapidly. Still other products go through the introduction, growth, and maturity stages but then stay at the maturity stage for a seemingly indefinite period. In reality, a number of different types of life cycle can exist, and some of these can be seen in Figure 8.7.

In the first example, the product has a high level of sales at an early stage but then there seems to be no change in sales. In the second example, there is a constant increase in sales volume in each subsequent time period. The third example displays the complete opposite: here, each subsequent period of time brings with it a fall in sales volume after a period of initially strong sales. This could be a result of the entry of strong and

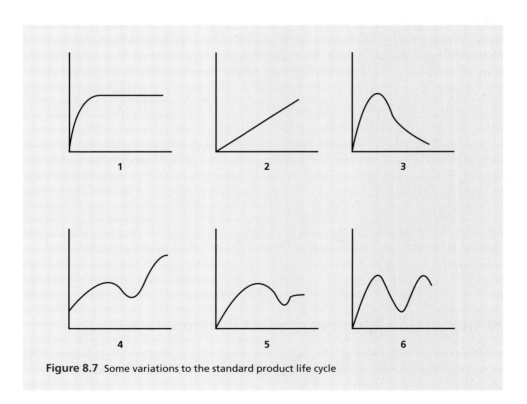

Figure 8.7 Some variations to the standard product life cycle

powerful competition. The fourth type of life cycle displays the situation where a firm actually influences the degree to which a product follows the life cycle. In this situation the product has been saved from decline, either through intense sales promotion activity or possibly through some form of product modification; alternatively, external factors such as a change in customer tastes, etc., may have led to the improvement in sales. Whatever the cause, the product here displays further growth before moving once again through to a decline phase, although sales are still higher now than they were at the original decline phase. The fifth example once again shows that the product has been saved from decline, but in this case the new cycle is at a lower stage than existed at first. The final example displays a typical life-cycle pattern for a fashion item where there is a steep drop in sales once the product is considered unfashionable, but it may subsequently become popular again.

Limitations of product life-cycle theory

Life-cycle theory may look intuitively appealing when viewed with hindsight, but can be difficult to apply for short-term forecasting purposes. More fundamentally, it is difficult for marketers to identify where a product currently lies on its life cycle. For example, if sales are stabilizing, it is difficult to ascertain whether the product has reached its peak in terms of growth and is about to decline, or whether there is just a temporary stabilization owing to external influences and that, if left alone, sales may start to increase once again in the near future. Indeed, the shape of the life cycle can be influenced by the actions of the marketer, and as a result there could be a self-fulfilling prophecy. For example, if there is a belief that the product is about to reach the decline phase, marketers may consciously reduce the marketing effort in response to this belief; as a result of this action, sales may fall and the product may indeed move into the decline phase.

Another observation is that the shape and duration of a life cycle is dependent upon whether it is the product class, the product form, or a specific brand that is being considered. For example, the life cycle of men's trousers is quite flat, taken over a long period of time, compared with specific types of trouser (e.g. jeans, chinos), which come into and go out of fashion. Within each type of trouser, brand names will go through a life cycle of popularity. (For example, Levis rose in the 1980s but lost ground by the end of the 1990s to newer brands such as Diesel and DKNY.) These differing life cycles are illustrated in Figure 8.8.

◉ Innovation and new product development

We have seen how products go through a life cycle, and that therefore most products can expect eventually to go into decline. It is therefore important for a company to develop new products to replace those that have reached the end of their life. Marketing managers

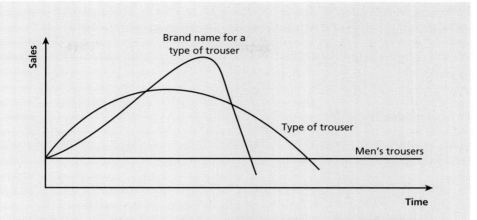

Figure 8.8 A comparison of life cycles for different levels of product specification. When defined very broadly, a product life cycle may appear quite flat, but individual variants and brands can have much more pronounced life cycles.

must recognize the need to develop new products in response to shortening life cycles, which in turn result from rapidly changing technology and competitive pressures.

What is innovation?

For many marketing managers, **innovation** means new or better products, and innovation has often been identified as a source of a company's long-term competitive advantage. Indeed, some nations as a whole can be described as more innovative than others, and there appears to be a link between a country's spending on **research and development** and its economic performance.

It should be remembered that innovation is not confined to a company's product offer, but applies to all marketing functions, including distribution and promotion. Innovation must be linked to a firm's objectives, and of course must relate to creating value in the eyes of customers.

What are new products?

It may not be that easy actually to define what is meant by a 'new product'. Companies' routine efforts at continuous quality improvement are often closely linked to innovation, and it can be difficult to distinguish between the two. New products could in fact comprise any of the following:

- improvements/revisions to existing products;
- additions to existing lines;

- 'new to the world' products;
- repositioning (existing products in new segments/markets).

We will consider below the distinction between product modifications and innovative products.

Product modifications

Many so-called new products are in fact modifications of existing products. Changes tend to be incremental and may include the following:

1. Minor changes can be made to how the product actually performs: this could involve the addition of new features and/or changing the packaging.
2. The quality of the basic product can be improved.
3. The style of the product can be modified, without changing its basic function. (For example, cars tend to undergo styling changes to keep in line with current design preferences.) In style-conscious industries such as fashion clothing, regularly updating a product's style can be crucial to continuing success. A Mintel report noted that soft drinks manufacturers have responded to consumers' desire for novelty and variety with a raft of new flavours and bottle designs (Mintel, 2002).
4. Non-product attributes can be altered to produce a change of image. A change in advertising message can be used to alter the image of a product. This occurred, for example, with the change in image of Guinness from a working man's stout to a trendy social drink, and the repositioning of After Eight mints as an all-time chocolate for all ages (Mills, 2002).

Innovative products

Truly new products are comparatively rare compared with product modifications, but they can be very important in certain circumstances.

- If consumer tastes are changing radically, existing products may no longer satisfy their needs. (This is often the case in many parts of the fashion clothing industry.)
- Technological change may make existing products obsolete. (For example, dot matrix printers were made obsolete by the development of ink jet and laser printers.) However, it has been noted that new technologies need not necessarily have a better performance than those they replace (Adner, 2002). For example, many professional photographers still prefer to use traditional 35 mm cameras than the newer digital cameras.
- New products may be required as a result of changes in internal processes such as accounting, office management, or labour relations. If a product becomes

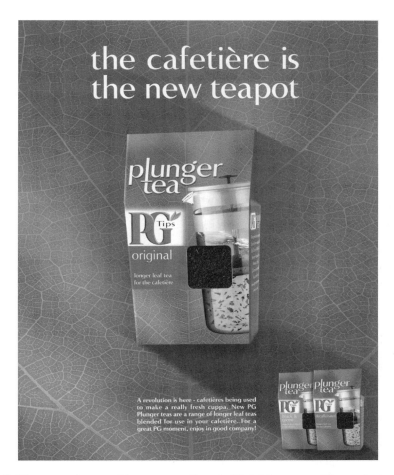

Figure 8.9 Many people regard tea as an easily substitutable commodity product, so it can be a tough market for a company to gain a competitive advantage in. Innovation has been a key to successful marketing of this age-old product. Some niche players have innovated with herbal teas, but not all innovation has been successful (for example, 'instant' powdered tea never became as popular as instant coffee). PG Tips has used innovation to gain a competitive advantage in the UK tea market. It has successfully launched new formats of tea bags that improve the taste of the tea and that are easier for consumers to use. More recently, it has capitalized on consumers' growing familiarity with cafetieres by launching 'Plunger Tea' specifically for cafetieres.
(Reproduced with permission of Unilever Bestfoods UK Ltd)

dangerous or illegal to produce (as has happened in the UK with many derivatives of beef products), a motivation is provided to develop a new replacement product.

- New products may be required to meet the need of intermediaries. (For example, concentrated forms of soap powder were introduced partly to satisfy retailers' demand that they take up less shelf space.)

- The social and economic environment may have changed, creating new needs in the market. For example, a growing number of Muslims in the UK population led many UK banks to develop bank accounts based on the principles of Sharia law to target this group (*Financial Times*, 2008b).

- If competitors are actively developing new products, a company must do likewise if it is not to lose market share.

- New products may be developed to fill under-utilized capacity. (For example, many business hotels have filled their empty rooms at the weekend by offering innovatory weekend leisure activity breaks, such as a course in aromatherapy.)

Critical to the development of many new products has been a 'product champion' within an organization. A champion can continually press the case for a new product to be developed and provide the impetus for development which may be lost if responsibility is dispersed too widely. Without such people, it is likely that many innovations that we take for granted today would not have been seen through to development and launch.

MARKETING in ACTION

Here's the product, now where's the market?

Marketers might like the idea that they carefully study consumers' needs and then develop the products which satisfy their needs. You may recall from Chapter 1 that this is essentially what distinguishes marketing orientation from production orientation. But the world is full of products which appeared almost by accident out of research laboratories, with no prior analysis of what customer needs were being targeted by new product development. Consider these examples:

1. 'Post it' notes were a by-product of 3M researchers looking for new forms of permanent adhesive. A partially sticky material was found, and a use subsequently found for it.

2. The drugs manufacturer Pfizer was researching an anti-angina drug, when it noticed side effects in trials with patients. It capitalized on this and eventually launched Viagra.

3. Even champagne, which we now take for granted, was developed by the accidental discoveries of a seventeenth-century Benedictine monk, Dom Pierre Perignon, who had been trying to eradicate bubbles from white wine.

When researchers make a discovery, it can be difficult to tell whether it will satisfy a need. If consumers have no experience of the product, it may be difficult for them to articulate their thoughts, which may be dominated by familiarity with what is currently available. After all, it took Dom Perignon some time to convince the seventeenth-century aristocracy that white wine with bubbles was not a sign of a dud vintage, but a refreshing drink in its own right. But he persevered, and the rest, as they say, is history.

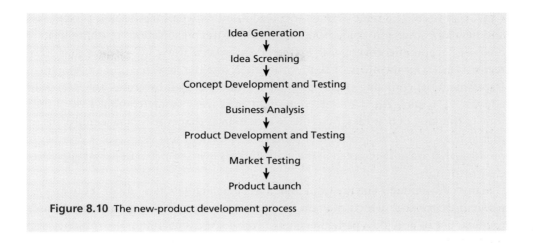

Figure 8.10 The new-product development process

The new product development process

Having a formal **new product development** process in place is generally more likely to be effective than adopting a haphazard approach to developing a product. Indeed, where costs and risks are high (as they are in many major infrastructure developments), a system needs to be in place to help keep such risks to a minimum.

It is usual to talk about a new product development process comprising a number of stages which span from having an initial idea through to the launch of the new product. We will look at each of these stages in turn, although it must be recognized that the stages often overlap each other (Figure 8.10).

Idea generation

New products come from a variety of sources rather than merely being initiated by the firm through the use of market research and the identification of untapped needs.

An important source of new product ideas is the customer. For products bought by businesses, new uses for an existing product or new ideas for a new one tend to be communicated to the sales force. For services, the important characteristic of inseparability means that there are plenty of opportunities for customers to inform service providers of new ideas or possible improvements to service processes.

Another source of new product ideas is a firm's competitors. Creative imitation does not carry the same risks as developing something totally new. A consideration of the flaws that exist in a competitor's product can also produce useful ideas for new products.

Some organizations see the importance of developing new products as part of their long-term competitive strategy and try to instill an internal organizational culture that positively thrives on new ideas. For example, Sony, the electronics company, encourages employees to move around and get involved in other departments. New perspectives and new ideas therefore come from every level of the organization, resulting in hundreds of new products every year. Similarly, 3M expects to receive new product ideas regularly from all members of staff, rather than just the Research and Development Department. Its corporate ethos has for some time included two rules: the '15% rule' and the '25% rule'. The '15% rule' states that employees should commit 15% of their time to thinking of new ideas, and the 25% rule states that every manager must ensure that at least 25% of his portfolio of products is less than five years old. A number of products that are now accepted in the marketplace have originated from this approach, e.g. Post-It notes.

Many new products emerge from 'blue skies' research laboratories, or more applied research exercises in which the aim is not to develop a particular customer-focused product, but to develop a particular area of technology. Sometimes, new products can emerge quite by accident without any planning or prior analysis of buyers' needs (see 'Marketing in Action: Here's the product, now where's the market?').

Idea screening

Whether a firm responds positively to ideas for new products very much depends on its internal resources. As well as considering whether there are the financial resources to develop a new product (in particular, the availability of cash flow in the short term), a firm needs to consider other internal issues. For example, is there enough production capacity to cope with likely demand? Are there suitably trained personnel? Will new staff have to be recruited or present staff retrained? In addition, the firm needs to consider the availability of the raw materials or components required to produce the new product.

Another consideration is time. New product development can take a long time from inception to final production and launch. Some developments can take as little as a few months whereas others can take years to come to fruition, especially where safety testing is protracted, as in the case of new drugs. The pressures of competition today mean that speed is becoming increasingly important.

Another important aspect that needs to be considered is the possibility that a new product could take sales from a product that is already in the firm's portfolio, through a process of 'cannibalization', resulting in only a small increase in total company sales. Alternatively, adding a new product may help to improve the sales of existing products as the product line becomes more comprehensive. This may be particularly important to companies that seek to expand their relationships with key customers and obtain a greater share of their total expenditure.

Screening should ensure that the new product fits within the firm's overall image. With current concern among many consumers about ecological issues, how well does a new product contribute to a company's image as an ecologically responsible organization.

Figure 8.11 Every now and again, a new product gets launched which goes on to become a high-profile 'flop'. When Clive Sinclair launched his C5 vehicle, it could have become a cult car and might have found many valuable off-road uses. But it was launched at the wrong time of year, and journalists soon got to work ridiculing the vehicle. The car was never a commercial success. But at the idea-screening stage, how could its developer have assessed whether the car would have become a premium-priced cult car, or the non-selling joke that it became?

At this stage, many new product ideas will be dropped because they do not fit with overall marketing strategy. If the proposal passes this filter, the company can proceed to the next stage. Although the filtering stage has been portrayed here as a rational process, there is evidence that the final selection of ideas for further development is typically affected by intuitive and political factors (Forlani, Mullins, and Walker, 2002; Bolton, 2003).

Concept development and testing

It has often been claimed that around three-quarters of all new products fail. One way of reducing the failure rate is to ensure more rigorous screening so that 'no hope' ideas do not get through to the next stage; but even this can be easier said than done, because by this approach, Sony would have rejected its Walkman concept, and IBM the idea of developing a photocopier. At the time, both were dismissed as concepts with no potential.

A new product concept can be tested using a number of methods, and such testing should take place before any significant amount of further investment is made in product development. Initial market research should aim to discover potential customer attitudes to the concept and, more particularly, whether they would be interested in purchasing the product if it came on to the market. This may be quite a difficult task if the new product is a major innovation and customers have no experience of such an idea (see 'Marketing in Action: The unimaginable may be indescribable?').

Business analysis

A financial analysis needs to take place in order to assess whether the product concept can be made into a profitable proposition. An income and expenditure statement, together with the associated balance sheet and cash flow analysis, therefore need to be prepared. The key to this financial analysis is that the product should at least break even over a period of time. However, any financial forecasts may be based on very crude assumptions about the likely volume of sales, the selling price, distribution costs,

MARKETING in ACTION

The unimaginable may be indescribable?

When it comes to forecasting take-up for completely new products, simply asking potential buyers whether they would buy it can be fraught with difficulties. In the case of intangible services, it can be difficult to present potential customers with a mock-up of the product in a way that manufacturing companies often do to test likely reaction to a new product. Around the year 2000, for example, there was much discussion about just what features and benefits customers would use when high-speed mobile Internet services become widely available and affordable. Simply asking somebody what they would use such a service for is likely to be limited to the scope of respondents' imagination. In the context of developing a low-cost car, Henry Ford is famously reported as saying that if he had asked people what they wanted, they would have simply replied 'faster horses', rather than being able to imagine ever owning a car. For intangible services, the problem of consumers' limited vision can be even greater, requiring more sophisticated research methods that seek to understand deep-seated needs and motivators. Where possible, companies have sought to experiment with new goods and services targeted at trial groups, before committing themselves to large-scale provision. This may be a valid approach where capital commitments are high and the market is relatively stable, but in fast-moving markets, too much time spent understanding consumer behaviour may lead competitors to gain a lead in an emerging new service sector. In the early days of the Internet, many new online services were developed with very little research; indeed, in those days, the problem of Henry Ford's horses was even more present, with most consumers having little idea of how they might use the Internet. So, in order to be first to market and have a 'first mover' advantage, the process of concept testing was often based more on intuition and judgement than rigorous analysis.

and the cost of producing the item. Cost and revenue estimates can be closely linked with each other, so that high-volume sales results in lower unit production costs, which in turn improves profitability. This can be a very difficult and speculative part of the process. According to one estimate, 30,000 new products annually vie for the 25,000 total spots in the average supermarket. Will a new consumer product even get supermarket shelf space? Of all new package-goods products, 52% fail before their second year (Dipasquale, 2002).

Because there are many unknowns in the financial analysis, a sensitivity analysis is often carried out to assess the impact on overall profitability of changes in the underlying assumptions. Would the concept still be profitable if selling prices were only half those that had been predicted?

Product development and testing

This is the translation of the idea into an actual product that can be delivered to customers. It is at this point that the decision is made to physically develop the product, and large amounts of money can be poured in at this stage. The various elements of the product have to be designed and tested. However, this testing should be more rigorous than at the concept-testing stage. In the case of tangible goods, customers can now see the product as it might actually look, and the company can identify possible problems that need to be resolved.

There is a need to consider the requirements for repeat purchase in addition to the single one-off purchase decision, and therefore the factors that influence trial, first purchase, adoption, and purchase frequency need to be identified. In addition, customer response to promotional material needs to be assessed.

Even given the increased rigour in this testing process, there are still difficulties. Testing consumers' responses to intangible elements of a new product can be more difficult.

Market testing

A market test aims to replicate everything that is likely to exist in the entire market but on a smaller scale. A company is testing not only the product itself, but the way in which it is promoted, priced, and distributed. Test marketing can take place in a television viewing area, a test city, particular geographical regions, or, in the business-to-business context, on a sample of key customers.

Designing a market testing exercise involves making a number of decisions. Where should the test market be? What is to be tested? How long should the test last? What criteria should be used to determine success or otherwise?

Although market testing should reduce the potential risks before launch, it is important to realize that there are still potential problems. Market testing is not cheap, and in some cases can be nearly as expensive as a full-scale launch. Even a large test market is unlikely to be totally representative of the market, because in reality small test markets may lead to distortions that wouldn't be present in a national launch. Market testing is also likely to warn competitors of what is to come, and as a result the competition may act more quickly in response or may interfere with the test itself. Competitors may study the test very carefully through retail audits and their own qualitative research and may learn a lot which will allow them to launch a competitive product, but without having incurred much of the development and testing costs so far.

Product launch

Actually launching the product (assuming that it has survived this far) involves a number of issues. Replacing an existing product with a new one tends to be a popular approach. There is likely to be an existing customer base for the new product and therefore the risks are lower, although even here mistakes can be made. When Coca Cola sought to replace its existing cola with a new formulation, it became apparent that it had misinterpreted its market research and had to reinstate the old product as 'Classic' Coke. A company may choose to sell both the old and new products simultaneously for a period of time, although this might meet with reluctance from retailers who will be required to commit twice as much shelf space to the products.

Time is a key issue. The longer a new product goes through the various developmental stages, the greater the chance that competitors will enter the market before launch. The firm can be a pioneer and enter the market first or be a follower and reduce its risks considerably. In the UK there was a race in 2003 to launch the first 'third generation' mobile phone network. The new operator 3 created some publicity as the first to launch a network (on 3 March 2003), despite the fact that no handsets were available until some time afterwards (Fagan, 2003). There is also the issue of stock levels—a company would normally avoid launching a new product when it had large unsold stocks of an older model that would become more difficult to dispose of after the launch of the new one.

For companies operating globally, timing of the launch in different national markets can be critical, as markets are likely to be at different stages of development and a global rollout may be inefficient for a company to manage (Wong, 2002). A staggered rollout allows a company to exploit profits from one market before moving on to progressively less attractive markets, thereby maintaining a portfolio of products at different stages of market development. However, in the case of some easily transported products such as computer software, it may not be realistic to have a staged rollout, as sales would soon occur through a 'grey' market. Most launches of new products by Microsoft have involved almost simultaneous launch, demanding a high level of global commitment by the company.

MARKETING and the INTERNET

How long will the queue be at the e-bank?

The online bank Egg has now established itself as one of Europe's leading online financial services providers, with over 3 million customers by the end of 2007. By 2002, Egg had attained brand awareness with 88% of adults in the UK, which is impressive for such a young company, and managed to acquire 600,000 new customers in 2001 alone—100,000 more than the total number of customers for its nearest UK Internet rival (*ABA Banking Journal*, 2002). But despite careful planning, the launch of Egg got off to a bumpy start.

When ATM machines first appeared a couple of decades earlier, many people thought they would never work because people liked to go into a branch and deal with a human being. Would people have the same fears about Internet banking? In 1998 the Internet was only beginning to catch the public's imagination, and there were still major concerns about privacy, security, download speed, and access to the Internet. Would Internet banking be a runaway success, or just another over-hyped new service development, of which there were many at the height of the dot.com boom?

Egg targeted busy people with neither the time nor inclination to shop around for financial services. But how many customers should the company have geared itself up to handle when it launched its new product? Launching a new product often involves a lot of guesswork. If the number is underestimated and the company does not have the capacity to cope with large numbers, frustration and harm to the brand reputation can soon build up.

Egg's then-parent company—Prudential—undertook the testing of its new banking service among a small group of customers. This allowed it to understand more about demand when it eventually went for a full public launch, backed by heavy online and offline advertising. Despite this, it soon became apparent that its servers could not cope, as potential customers complained of spending hours trying to log on to the bank's website. Egg's call centre was similarly overwhelmed, despite being available 24 hours a day, seven days a week. It seemed that the bank had inadequately understood the peaked nature of demand, which meant that call-centre operators might be rushed during the early evening, but idle during much of the night and early morning.

Taking a longer-term perspective, the launch of Egg was a success. It managed to gain a 'first mover' advantage in the emerging market for online banking service, something that might have been lost had it spent more time researching its market. Since launch, it has learned a lot more about its customers and has embraced emerging technology to launch Egg TV in April 2000, which was the first interactive digital TV service from a financial services provider in Britain.

Integrating the new product development process

So far, the stages of new product development have been presented as if they are steps that necessarily have to be tackled in a sequential order. In fact, the time taken to go through this process can be considerable, allowing competitors to gain a lead. There have therefore been many attempts to carry out some of the steps simultaneously. Virtual reality systems, for example, are allowing customers to get a feel of the final product at a very early stage, allowing this to take place at the same time as concept testing and avoiding the need to wait until all steps of the process are progressed (Dahan and Hauser, 2002).

The new product development process can be extremely complex, with many examples of cost overruns and delayed results (Kim and Wilemon, 2003). A key to more effective new product development activity is close working relationships between marketing and manufacturing functions (Rodríguez *et al.*, 2007). In one study of 467 completed product innovation projects, increased marketing–manufacturing joint involvement was associated with better project performance (Song and Swink, 2002). Even simple administrative matters such as rapid communication following the results of one stage can help to speed up the new product development process.

As can be seen, the new product development process can be time-consuming and complex. This has led many companies to outsource the whole process to specialist companies who have developed an expertise in product development and market testing (Howley, 2002).

Our discussion of new product development processes has focused on how large companies might typically go about the process in a logical and structured manner. There is a lot of research evidence that in smaller companies the process is much more intuitive (e.g. Enright, 2001). In one study of SMEs it was found that marketing-related activities were undertaken less frequently and were less well executed than technical activities in developing new products, and the existence of a new product strategy seemed to have a significant positive impact on marketing activities (Huang, Soutar, and Brown, 2002).

Strategic issues in expanding the product range

Earlier in this chapter we introduced the idea of a product mix, which comprises the range of products offered by a company. Product life-cycle theory reminds us that a product mix cannot remain static, as some products will eventually cease to be profitable elements of that mix. But which direction should the new product mix take?

Product management involves ensuring that there is a succession of products available that are at different stages of their life cycles. The planning process should involve the firm's business being managed in the same way as an investment portfolio, with attention paid to developing, maintaining, phasing out, and deleting specific elements.

MARKETING in ACTION

From dairymen to hypermarket operator

Should a company 'stick to its knitting' and do what it is good at, or should it search continually for new products and new markets? Countless companies have reported disastrous results after going into areas about which they knew very little. The rapid growth of Next from its core of fashion retailing into newsagents, travel, and home furnishings contributed to its near collapse in the late 1980s. *WHSmith* went through bad years in the mid-1990s when the newsagent's diversification into DIY retailing and television failed to work. Abbey National expanded in the late 1990s from its core of domestic mortgage lending into merchant banking and train and aircraft leasing, only to have to write off millions of pounds of losses and withdraw from these sectors in 2003.

But isn't change essential for companies, especially those facing static or declining markets for its core products? One of the UK's leading grocery retailers, Asda (now a subsidiary of Wal-Mart), would not be where it is today had not the Associated Dairy Company taken a risk and set up a retailing operation. Milk was a facing a mature market, but new opportunities for product development were available further down its distribution chain as more people sought the benefits of shopping in large supermarkets. The company therefore created its Asda superstores. The security services company Securicor knew that it was taking a risk when it invested in a joint venture with British Telecom to create the Cellnet (now O_2) mobile phone network. And a small company manufacturing shopping baskets called WPP (standing for Wire Plastic Products) took huge risks in diversifying its product range on its way to becoming owners of some of the world's leading advertising agencies.

It is fine, with hindsight, to criticize a firm's decisions about which direction its product portfolio should take; but in an uncertain world, risks have to be taken. A sound analysis of a company's strengths and weaknesses and of its external environment certainly helps, but success also depends upon an element of luck.

This process can lead management to identify where there may be market potential and therefore where investment can be most profitably made.

For a company to put all of its efforts into supplying a very limited range of products to a narrow market segment is potentially dangerous. Risk-spreading is therefore often an important element of **portfolio planning** that goes beyond marketing planning. Some companies deliberately provide a range of products that—quite apart from their potential for cross-selling—act in contrasting manners during the business cycle. There is a long tradition to this practice; for example, the ice cream manufacturer Walls became more sustainable as a business unit by adding sausages to its product portfolio. Sausages tended to have their highest demand in winter, counterbalancing the sharp peak in summer for ice cream. Similarly, accountancy firms have become potentially more stable units as they have amalgamated, by allowing pro-cyclical activities such as management buy-out expertise and venture capital investment to be counter-balanced by contra-cyclical activities such as insolvency work. Sometimes statutory requirements may require a balanced portfolio of products. The Bank of England's regulation of the UK banking system, for example, imposes constraints on banks' freedom to be market-led in the pattern of their lending decisions. Also, with the development of relationship marketing strategies, firms are increasingly keen to develop opportunities for offering customers a broad range of products which attract a higher share of their total expenditure. For all of these reasons, organizations seek to manage their growth in a manner that maintains a desired portfolio of products.

Planning for growth

Most private-sector organizations pursue growth in one form or another, whether this is an explicit aim or merely an implicit aim of its managers. Growth is often associated with increasing returns to shareholders and greater career opportunities for managers. Growth may be vital in order to reach a critical size at which economies of scale in production, distribution, and promotion can be achieved, thereby contributing to a company's sustainable competitive advantage. But where should the growth be focused?

The development of new products or new markets are more risky options than simply selling more of its existing product to existing customers. More risky still is **diversification** into new markets and new products. The dimensions of product development and market development form the basis of the Product/Market Expansion Grid proposed by Ansoff (1957). Products and markets are each analysed in terms of their degree of novelty to an organization, and growth strategies are identified in terms of these two dimensions. In this way, four possible growth strategies can be identified. An illustration of the framework, with reference to the specific options open to a company that is currently marketing a range of organic fruit and vegetables, is shown in Figure 8.12.

The four growth options are associated with differing sets of problems and opportunities for a company. These relate to the resources required for implementation, and the level of risk associated with each. It follows, therefore, that what might be a feasible growth strategy for one organization may not be for another. The characteristics of the four strategies are described below.

1. **Market penetration strategies:** This type of strategy focuses growth on the existing product range by encouraging higher levels of sales to current target customers. In this way, a food manufacturer serving the growing market for organic produce could grow—all other things being equal—simply by maintaining its current marketing strategy. If it wanted to accelerate this growth, it could do this first by seeking to sell more products to its existing customers and second by attracting customers from its

Figure 8.12 An application of Ansoff's Product/Market Growth Matrix to a company that is currently marketing a range of organic fruit and vegetables

competitors. If the market was in fact in decline, the company could grow only by attracting customers from its competitors through more aggressive marketing policies and/or cost reduction programmes. This strategy offers the least level of risk to an organization—it is familiar with both its products and its customers.

2. **Market development strategies:** This type of strategy builds upon the existing product range that an organization has established, but seeks to find new groups of customers for them. In this way the organic foods manufacturer that had saturated its current market might seek to expand its sales to new geographical regions or overseas markets. It could also aim its marketing effort at attracting custom from groups beyond its current age/income groups—for example, by targeting children with organically produced snacks. While the company may be familiar with the production side of its growth plans, it faces risks because it may have poor knowledge of different buyer behaviour patterns in the markets it is attempting to enter. For an organic food company that has built its business in the UK, it may have little knowledge about consumer buying behaviour in continental European countries, for example. It may face even greater risk in developing a marketing strategy aimed at children, whose needs it has little previous experience of satisfying.

3. **Product development strategy:** As an alternative to selling existing products in new markets, a company may choose to develop new products for its existing markets. The organic food company may add new ranges of ready meals or drinks, for example. While the company minimizes the risk associated with the uncertainty of

new markets, it faces risk resulting from lack of knowledge about its new product area. Often, a feature of this growth strategy is collaboration with a product specialist who helps the organization produce the new product, leaving it free to market it effectively to its customers. Rather than setting up its own facility to produce ready-prepared meals, the organic foods company may leave the specialized task of doing this and undertaking quality controls to a more experienced food manufacturer.

4. **Diversification strategy:** Here, a company expands by developing new products for new markets. Diversification can take a number of forms. The company could stay within the same general product/market area, but diversify into a new point in the distribution chain. For example, the organic food producer may move into retailing its products, rather than just selling them exclusively to wholesalers and retailers. Alternatively, it might diversify into completely unrelated areas aimed at quite different market segments, for example by offering residential cookery courses. Because the company is moving into both unknown markets and unknown product areas, this form of growth carries the greatest level of risk from a marketing management perspective. Diversification may, however, help to manage the long-term risk of the organization by reducing dependency on a narrow product/market area.

In practice, most growth that occurs is a combination of product development and market development. In very competitive markets, a company would most likely have to adapt its product slightly in order to become attractive to a new market segment.

Deleting products

Good product management demands not only that new products are developed, but also that failing ones are deleted. Deciding when a product has reached the decline stage of its life cycle can be quite difficult, because a down-turn could simply be a temporary blip. If a down-turn seems to have set in, it can sometimes be difficult to decide whether it is worth trying to revive the product, or to just let it die. Even the manner of a product's deletion requires careful thought—should it be allowed to die gradually, or suddenly killed off?

In general, there is a tendency to 'add on' rather than subtract, and therefore many products do not die but merely fade away, consuming resources of an organization which could be better used elsewhere. 'Old' products may not even cover overheads. In addition, there are a number of hidden costs of supporting dying products that need to be taken into consideration; for example:

- a disproportionate amount of management time can be spent on them: this can delay the search for new products;

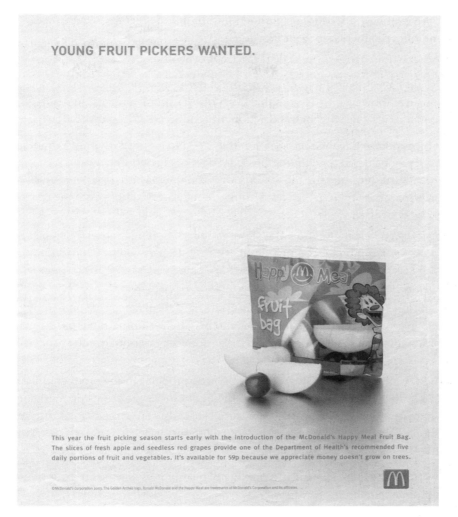

Figure 8.13 Fast food was a great marketing success story of the 1980s and 1990s. Chains developed in response to changes in the pattern of family meal eating, growing levels of disposable income (especially among younger adults), a growing desire for variety seeking, and increasing concern with value for money. McDonald's has a long record of innovation with the development of new menus and new formats in new countries. However, by the end of the 1990s, there was growing concern in many western countries about problems of obesity caused by eating too much high-fat food. McDonald's has continued its pattern of innovation with products which address the changed needs of the early twenty-first century, including McCafes and here, a fruit bag which is aimed at making fresh fruit more appealing to children (and their parents). (Reproduced with permission of McDonald's Corporation)

- short and relatively uneconomic production runs may be required where the demand for a product is small and irregular;
- they often require frequent price and stock adjustments.

Firms should have a logical planning system for deciding which products to delete. It would be naive, however, to assume that deletion is a simple process. In reality, there are a number of reasons why logical deletion procedures are not readily followed:

- Often firms do not have the information they need to identify whether a product needs to be considered for elimination. Even if an organization is aware of a potential deletion candidate, the reasons for its failure may not be known and therefore management may just leave things as they are and hope that the problem will go away by itself.
- Managers often become sentimental about products, hoping that sales will pick up when the market improves. Sometimes marketing strategy will be blamed for the lack of success, and there may be a belief that a change in advertising or pricing, for example, will improve the situation.
- Political issues within organizations may create barriers to deletion. Some individuals will have vested interests in a product and may fight elimination efforts. In fact, some individuals may hide the true facts of a product's performance to ensure that deletion is not considered at all.
- Finally, a company may fear that the sale of other products in the product range will fall if a product is deleted. With the growing importance of relationship marketing, many firms are keen to ensure that they are able to satisfy all of their target customers' needs for a particular category of product. If a product is deleted, the whole relationship may be lost.

Where weak products are identified, a number of possibilities may be open for trying to revive a product, including:

- modifying the product so that it meets changed market requirements;
- decreasing promotional expenditure, in order to minimize costs: this may be a sensible idea if there is a small loyal market;
- increasing promotional expenditure, assuming that sales are sufficiently responsive to this increased promotion;
- decreasing the price, if demand is elastic and an increase in sales revenue is likely to result;
- increasing the price, if there remains a core market that is strongly loyal to the product: by doing this, total revenue may be increased, even if sales volumes decline;
- changing the distribution system, in order to cut costs, and/or open up sales opportunities in new market segments.

If none of these options is considered feasible, the company must decide how best to delete the product. This is not always a simple task, and a number of options can be identified.

1. Ruthlessly eliminate 'overnight'. This may seem the simplest solution, but will customers take their business to competitors? Will they take their business for other products in the company's mix with them? There may also be the problem of what to do with existing stocks of finished goods and work in progress. Sometimes a company may be contractually obliged to continue supplying a product for many years into the future, especially in the financial services sector, where products such as mortgages and pensions cannot be completely deleted until all customers' policies have reached the end of their contracted term. A sudden withdrawal of a product without notice may create bad publicity for a company, especially if customers have come to depend upon it.

2. Increase the price and let demand fade away. This may sound to many loyal customers like exploitation, but it could mean that the firm makes good profits on the product while demand lasts.

3. Reduce promotion or even stop it altogether. Again, this could increase profitability while demand lasts.

Chapter summary and linkages to other chapters

Products are the means by which a company satisfies its customers' needs. However, it must be remembered that customers seek the benefits of the product rather than the product itself. Products can be grouped according to the similarity of their marketing requirements, and a number of bases for classifying products have been suggested. Services can be described as products, but the characteristics of 'pure' services can be quite distinct from those of 'pure' goods. For all products, quality is an important defining characteristic. Change in the marketing environment (Chapter 2) causes most products to go through some form of life cycle which affects the way they are marketed.

Because most products eventually go into decline, it is important that a portfolio of established and new products is maintained in order to develop a sustainable competitive advantage (Chapter 7). This chapter has emphasized new product development as a process. The length of this process will depend upon product and market characteristics. Shortening the new product development process can give a firm a competitive advantage, but can also increase the risk of a failed launch.

The opposite of new product development is deletion, and a rational approach to deletion can prevent a firm becoming weighed down with a large number of minor products which consume a lot of management time but return very little, if any, profit.

Product decisions are just one element of the marketing mix, and the following chapters will discuss how price, distribution, and promotion are used to develop a distinctive and profitable market position for a product.

⬡ KEY PRINCIPLES OF MARKETING

- A customer's definition of a product focuses on the benefits provided and how the product will satisfy a need.
- A product can comprise anything that can be offered to a market. Marketers classify types of product according to the similarity of their marketing needs.
- In a dynamic marketing environment, products can expect to go through a life cycle of development, launch, growth, saturation, and decline.
- Product life-cycle theory implies that new products will be required to replace products that go into decline and are eventually deleted from a product portfolio.

CASE STUDY

Small new phones, big investment risk?

The mobile phone industry is no stranger to product innovation. In fact, it is hard to believe that the sector barely existed just 20 years ago; now, most people in western developed countries own a mobile phone. In fact, according to the telecoms regulator Ofcom, there are now more mobile phones in use in Britain than there are people. Although we are all now familiar with mobile phones, we probably would not recognize a mobile phone of 20 years ago—much heavier and without the cameras, MP3 players, and web-browsing gizmos that we associate with today's mobile phones.

The life cycle of mobile phones as a broad product category is now at the mature stage—some would say saturated. But when individual product formats are examined, a pattern of continual development, launch, growth, and eventual decline is evident. First-generation phones based on analogue technology were soon replaced by digital technology. From 2003, it seemed that the 'new' digital technology would be replaced by a third generation of mobile phones (3G). By 2008, work was well underway with the development of the next generation (fourth generation) of mobile phones.

The pace of growth has posed enormous risks for the companies involved, especially where new technologies displace the technology that went before them, calling for ever-increasing capital investment, and no chance of a return from customers until long after the initial investment has been made in new capacity. Each time, the stakes involved in new product development seemed to get bigger, with uncertainty about just what take-up there would be for the new technology. Companies had in the past been wrong in their predictions of mobile phone usage. WAP (wireless access protocol) phones capable of surfing the Internet turned out to be a flop. On the other hand, SMS text messaging, which was originally considered not worth including in the specification for GSM phones, went on to be a runaway hit.

Many commentators saw 3G technology as the key to a whole new world of mobile telephony in which the mobile phone would be positioned not just as a device for voice communication, but as a vital business, leisure, and information tool. In 2000, the UK government held an auction for five new 3G mobile phone licences, and the mobile phone companies paid a total of £22 billion for licences. Would they get back their huge investment, not only in licence fees paid, but also the infrastructure that was needed to support the new 3G networks?

During 2003, the Hong Kong-based Hutchison Whampoa became the first company to launch a 3G service in the UK, with its '3' network. The launch was accompanied by endless hype about the wireless Internet and video capabilities. The world was going to be transformed by streaming of video and football matches live to customers' mobile phones, and a whole new world of mobile advertising media would open up. Location-Based Services (LBS) had been a small but growing sector of the mobile phone industry. A report by Concise Insight (2004) noted that Vodafone UK's mobile content reached 1.9% of total revenue for March 2004, almost double the 1.0% a year before. It seemed that location technology was underpinning value-added data services. Even the emergency services stood to benefit from 3G's ability to pinpoint precisely a caller's location. By 2004, 60% of calls to the UK emergency services were made from mobiles, but in many instances callers did not know exactly where they were, and ambulances and fire brigades only had very approximate locations.

But after long delays in rolling out the new phones and networks, followed by sluggish uptake of the early services, 3 found itself in 2004 focusing on more mundane marketing issues, such as the cost of old-fashioned voice calls. The costs of recruiting new customers were high, with Mark James, telecoms analyst at Japanese investment bank Nomura, estimating that 3's customer acquisition costs in its first year were £600 per customer—around four times the European average. Analysts estimated that Hutchison, which had placed a $US22 billion bet on the fledgling technology, was seeing a worldwide 3G cash-burn of about HK$100 million ($12.8 million) per day. Rival operators that were preparing their own 3G launches would aim to start by pricing the technology at a premium. But their problem was that 3 was already pricing its phones and services—which offered ITN news and premiership football clips among other features—at cut-throat prices. Their best hope was that 3's model would prove unsustainable. After all, anyone can get customers if they effectively give their product away.

Hutchison is not new to taking big risks in the mobile phone market. It was behind the 'Rabbit' network of semi-mobile Telepoint phones launched in the UK in the 1980s. These allowed callers to use a compact handset to make outgoing calls only, when they were within 150 metres of a base station, these being located in public places such as railway stations, shops, petrol stations, etc. As in the case of many new markets that suddenly emerge, operators saw advantages of having an early market share lead. Customers who perceived that one network was more readily available than any other would—all other things being equal—be more likely to subscribe to that network. Operators saw that a bandwagon effect could be set up—to gain entry to the market at a later stage could become a much more expensive market challenger exercise.

Such was the speed of development that the Telepoint concept was not rigorously test-marketed. To many, the development was too much product-led, with insufficient understanding of buyer behaviour and competitive pressures. Each of the four companies forced through their own technologies, with little inclination or time available to discuss industry standard handsets which could eventually have caused the market to grow at a faster rate and allowed the operators to cut their costs. The final straw for the Rabbit network came with the announcement by the UK government of its proposal to issue licences for a new generation of Personal Communications Networks—these would have the additional benefit of allowing both incoming and outgoing calls, and would not be tied to a limited base station range. While this in itself might not have put people off buying new Rabbit handsets, it did have the effect of bringing new investment in the network to a halt, leaving the existing networks in a state of limbo.

Could the point about leapfrogging technology—which had wiped out Hutchison's Rabbit network—happen again with 3G technology? By 2006, the next generation of mobile phone services was under development, with Japanese trials of '4G'—faster than 3G. 3G phones were also challenged by the development of alternative wireless access services, notably WiFi. Many companies, such as T-Mobile, had begun offering mobile WiFi services, which allow users to log on to a local access point and gain access to their e-mail and browse the Internet. Subscribers to 'VOIP' telephony services could also effectively make free phone calls from a WiFi access point. For many business travellers, using their laptop, WiFi access seemed a more attractive and less expensive option than using a 3G phone connection to check for e-mail. It was likely to become even more attractive, with development of longer range WiMax services that extended beyond the very limited 50 metre or so range of WiFi. The pressure on 3G services was intensified when the UK government announced in 2006 that it would license the development of a national WiFi network.

Could 3G become old hat before it had even reached a profit table stage in its life cycle? Would the history of the short-lived Rabbit network be repeated? Had the owners of the 3 network, Hutchison, failed to learn from the Rabbit failure? Or should Hutchison point to its record with another of its previous new product launches—the launch of the UK Orange network in the early 1990s, which critics initially dismissed as a costly failure, but which went on to become one of the UK's strongest mobile phone brands?

Source: based on *Financial Times*, '3UK seeks to project a new image', 18 October 2005, p. 25; *Financial Times*, 'Hutchison 3G unit hits profitability target', 27 May 2008, p. 31; Concise Insight Europe, European Location-Based Services, 2004.

Case study review questions

1. Critically evaluate methods that mobile phone companies could use to assess buyer's likely response to new features, such as video on demand.

2. In terms of a new product development process, how could the development and launch of Telepoint services have been improved in order to avoid the problems that were experienced? What lessons can be learned for the development of 3G (or 4G services)?

3. Consider how the launch of 3G services in a less developed country with a less sophisticated telecommunications infrastructure may differ from a launch in a western developed country.

⬡ CHAPTER REVIEW QUESTIONS

1. Critically discuss the usefulness of the product life-cycle concept to marketing managers.

2. To what extent can the various stages in the new product development process be distinguished? How could they be integrated more fully?

3. With reference to specific examples, examine the practical problems of deleting products from a company's product range.

⬡ ACTIVITIES

1. Take a look inside your local post office. Post offices have been undergoing a transformation in many countries, as governments deregulate mail services, and many of the functions traditionally undertaken by post offices have migrated to online. Identify ideas for possible new product development by the post office, and critically evaluate their likelihood of success.

2. Consider a poorly performing service with which you are familiar, such as a bus service which seems to run empty, or a university course that has a falling number of students. Consider the merit of deleting the selected service. If you consider that the service justifies deletion, identify the most cost-effective strategy for deleting it, so that the reputation of the service provider is maintained and as many customers as possible are maintained.

3. If you are following a course of study at a college or university, list your ideas for new services, or service improvements offered by the college or university. Explore how your ideas could be most effectively communicated to senior decision-makers, and identify possible barriers to actually implementing your ideas.

⬡ REFERENCES

ABA Banking Journal (2002), 'What's Egg?'. *ABA Banking Journal*, 94(9): 60–1.

Adner, R. (2002), 'When Are Technologies Disruptive? A demand-based view of the emergence of competition'. *Strategic Management Journal*, 23(8): 667–88.

Ansoff, I. H. (1957), 'Strategies for Diversification'. *Harvard Business Review,* 35(5): 113–24.

Bolton, L. E. (2003), 'Stickier Priors: the effects of nonanalytic versus analytic thinking in new product forecasting'. *Journal of Marketing Research*, 40(1): 65–80.

Concise Insight (2004), *European Location-Based Services 2004: Market Opinions.* London: Concise Insight.

Crosby, P. B. (1984), *Quality without Tears*. New York: New American Library.

Dahan, E. and Hauser, J. R. (2002), 'The Virtual Customer'. *Journal of Product Innovation Management,* 19(5): 332–51.

Dipasquale, C. B. (2002), 'Catalina Service to Track New Products'. *Advertising Age*, 73(38): 59.

Enright, M. (2001), 'Approaches to Market Orientation and New Product Development in Smaller Enterprises: a proposal for a context-rich interpretative framework'. *Journal of Strategic Marketing*, 9(4): 301–13.

Fagan, M. (2003), 'Three Launches 3G Services—but without Handsets'. *Sunday Telegraph*, 2 March.

Financial Times (2008a), 'Commodities Sell-off Drags Materials Lower', 30 April, p. 36.

Financial Times (2008b), 'UK Leads in Sowing Seeds for a Sector', 17 June.

Forlani, D., Mullins, J. W., and Walker, O. C. Jr (2002), 'New Product Decision Making: how chance and size of loss influence what marketing managers see and do'. *Psychology & Marketing*, 19(11): 957–81.

Gronroos, C. (1984), 'A Service Quality Model and its Marketing Implications'. *European Journal of Marketing*, 18(4): 36–43.

Howley, M. (2002), 'The Role of Consultancies in New Product Development'. *Journal of Product & Brand Management*, 11(7): 447–58.

Huang, X., Soutar, G. N., and Brown, A. (2002), 'New Product Development Processes in Small and Medium-Sized Enterprises: some Australian evidence'. *Journal of Small Business Management*, 40(1): 27–42.

Juran, J. M. (1982), *Upper Management and Quality*. New York: Juran Institute.

Kim, J. and Wilemon, D. (2003), 'Sources and Assessment of Complexity in NPD Projects'. *R & D Management*, 33(1): 16–30.

Mills, D. (2002), 'Ad of the Week'. *Daily Telegraph*, 5 November.

Mills, D. (2003), 'L'Oreal Patents: are they worth it?'. *Daily Telegraph*, 18 February.

Mintel (2002), *The Sports Drinks Market*. London: Mintel.

Ofek, E. and Srinivasan, V. (2002), 'How Much Does the Market Value an Improvement in a Product Attribute?'. *Marketing Science*, 21(4): 398.

Rodríguez, N. G. M., Sanzo, P. J., and Trespalacios Gutiérrez, J. A. (2007), 'Interfunctional Trust as a Determining Factor of a New Product Performance'. *European Journal of Marketing,* 41(5/6): 678–702.

Rogers, E. M. (2003), *Diffusion of Innovation,* 5th edn. New York: Simon & Schuster.

Song, M. and Swink, M. (2002), 'Marketing—Manufacturing Joint Involvement across Stages of New Product Development: effects on the success of radical *v.* incremental innovations'. *Academy of Management Proceedings*, B1–B6.

The Times (2002), 'Mobile Phone Sales Fall', 12 March, p. 25.

Vargo, S. L. and Lusch, R. F. (2004), 'Evolving to a New Dominant Logic for Marketing'. *Journal of Marketing,* 68(1): 1–17.

Wong, V. (2002), 'Antecedents of International New Product Rollout Timeliness'. *International Marketing Review*, 19(2/3): 120–32.

◌ SUGGESTED FURTHER READING

The following provide contemporary insights into the role of innovation in organizations and the relationship between marketing and R&D:

Trott, P. (2008), *Innovation Management and New Product Development*, 4th edn. London: FT Prentice Hall.

Dodgson, M., Gann, D., and Salter, A. (2008), *Management of Technological Innovation: strategy and practice.* Oxford: Oxford University Press.

Christensen, C. M., Anthony, S. D., and Roth, E. A. (2004), *Seeing What's Next: using the theories of innovation to predict industry change.* Harvard Business School Press.

New product development processes in the context of service industries are discussed in the following:

Stevens, E. and Dimitriadis, S. (2005), 'Managing the New Service Development Process: toward a systematic model'. *European Journal of Marketing,* 39(1/2): 175–98.

Smith, A. M. and Fischbacher, M. (2005), 'New Service Development: a stakeholder perspective'. *European Journal of Marketing*, 39(9/10): 1025–48.

The methods used by organizations to search for new ideas are discussed in the following:

Matthing, J., Sandén, B., and Edvardsson, B. (2004), 'New Service Development: learning from and with customers'. *International Journal of Service Industry Management*, 15(5): 479–98.

Olsen, N. V. and Sallis, J. (2006), 'Market Scanning for New Service Development'. *European Journal of Marketing*, 40(5/6): 466–84.

USEFUL WEB LINKS

Visit the Online Resource Centre for resources that are relevant to this chapter, including web links, multiple choice questions, and additional case studies:

www.oxfordtextbooks.co.uk/orc/palmer2e/

KEY TERMS

- **Business-to-business goods**
- **Consumer goods**
- **Convenience goods**
- **Diversification**
- **Fast-moving consumer goods (FMCGs)**
- **Innovation**
- **New product development**
- **Packaging**
- **Patent**
- **Portfolio planning**
- **Product life cycle**
- **Product line**
- **Product mix**
- **Quality**
- **Research and Development**
- **Shopping goods**
- **Speciality goods**
- **Trademark**

9

Pricing

CHAPTER OBJECTIVES

Pricing can be a very difficult part of the marketing mix to get right, but getting it right can have a big impact on sales volumes and profitability. In the first part of this chapter we will look at the economic theory underlying price decisions. Perfectly competitive markets are introduced as one extreme in which the marketer must take prices as given from the market. From this, various other market structures are discussed and their impact on pricing decisions assessed. The second part of the chapter focuses on situations where a firm has developed some degree of uniqueness for its product, such as a brand, which sets it aside from perfectly competitive markets. Here firms have more discretion over pricing, and this chapter explores firms' objectives, strategies, and tactics in setting their prices.

Introduction

Most of the decisions made by marketing managers involve spending their company's money—on advertising, paying sales personnel, setting up distributor networks, new product development, and so on. Price is the one element of the marketing mix that directly affects the income that a company receives. In businesses with high turnover and low profit margins, a miscalculation of selling prices can have a big effect on a firm's annual profits. If the company charges too little for its products, it may find that, although it has achieved a very respectable level of sales, the low price charged is insufficient to give it any profit. Too high a price, and it may be unable to sell sufficient output to cover its fixed overhead costs. It may also end up with unsold stocks of obsolete products.

For most firms, setting prices is a difficult task which involves both scientific analysis and intuitive trial and error. This is especially true of new product launches, where a company has no historical precedent on which to base its expectations of how much customers will be prepared to pay.

In the first part of this chapter, we will look at some of the basic theory underlying firms' pricing decisions. Taking a broad perspective, firms cannot ignore market forces, so it is important to understand the relationship between market structure and the way in which prices are determined. The approach to pricing of a firm operating in a fiercely competitive market will differ quite markedly from the approach of a firm in a market where there are very few competitors.

The second part of this chapter considers more applied issues of pricing, which are applicable to companies that have some discretion in the prices they charge (that is, they are not operating in a perfectly competitive market where prices are determined solely by the market). Firms develop strategies in order to respond to the competitive nature of their environment; for example, they may aim to be a price leader across their range of products. For individual new product launches, a company may pursue a strategy of starting with a high price, and gradually lowering it over time. In terms of setting prices for individual products, firms pursue a variety of approaches, including basing their selling price on their production costs, on the prices that competitors are currently charging, and on customers' ability and willingness to pay.

Governments often seek to control the prices of key goods and services, such as electricity and telephones, so it is important to understand how firms can reconcile the sometimes conflicting approaches of market forces and regulation.

Of course, pricing should never be seen as an isolated element of a firm's marketing decision-making. What the company is able to charge is closely related to, among other things, the quality of its products, the advertising images that it has created, and the effectiveness of its distribution strategy.

Effects of market structure on pricing

The market conditions facing suppliers of goods and services vary considerably. Customers of water supply companies may feel that they are being exploited by high prices and poor service levels provided by companies that know that their customers have little choice of supplier. On the other hand, customers are constantly being wooed by seemingly countless credit card companies, all trying to offer deals that buyers will consider to be better than those offered by competitors. The differences in the pricing behaviour of these two groups of organizations can be related to the structure of the markets in which they operate. The term **market structure** is used to describe:

- the number of buyers and sellers operating in a market;
- the barriers that exist to prevent new firms from entering the market (or prevent existing companies from leaving it);

Figure 9.1 A continuum of market structures from perfect competition to monopoly

- the extent to which the supply of goods and services is concentrated in the hands of a small number of buyers (or, less frequently, the extent to which purchases are concentrated in the hands of a few buyers);
- the degree of collusion that occurs between buyers and/or sellers in the market.

An understanding of market structure underpins all pricing decisions made by marketers. Market structure influences not only the pricing decisions made by marketers within a firm, but also the nature of the response from other firms operating in the market.

Economists have developed a number of labels to describe different types of market structure. At one theoretical extreme is the model of perfect competition and at the other is pure monopoly. In practice, examples of the extremes are very rare, and most markets are referred to as being in a state of *imperfect competition* (Figure 9.1).

We are first going to spend some time looking at perfectly competitive markets. These are characterized by the following conditions.

- There are many producers supplying to the market, each with similar cost structures and each producing an identical product. No single supplier on its own can influence the market price.
- There are also many buyers in the market, none of which can, on their own, influence the market price.
- Both buyers and sellers are free to enter or leave the market; that is, there are no barriers to entry or exit.

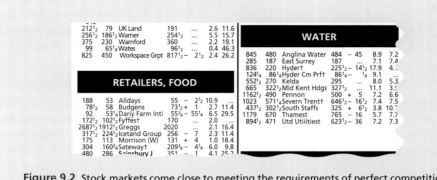

Figure 9.2 Stock markets come close to meeting the requirements of perfect competition, with large numbers of buyers and sellers resulting in daily fluctuations in a company's share price

- There is a ready supply of information for buyers and sellers, for example about competing alternatives.

These may seem quite unrealistic conditions for many markets, although a few markets do come close to meeting them (for example, the 'spot' market for oil products, and stock markets where shares are bought and sold). However, the real value of studying competitive markets is that it teaches us the basic rules of supply, demand, and **price determination** (Figure 9.2).

The theory of supply and demand

In perfectly competitive markets, firms are **price-*takers***, and their ability to set prices is limited by the level of demand and supply within the market they serve. If total demand goes up, all other things being equal, the going rate of prices in the market for their product will rise. Likewise, if there is a drop in total supply for whatever reason (for example because of bad weather), there will be further pressure for prices in the market to rise. The final price paid in the market will reflect the balance between supply-side and demand-side factors.

A market as defined here need not be a physical location where exchange takes place (as happens in retail and wholesale grocery markets). A market in the economist's sense refers to all individuals and firms who wish either to buy or to sell a specified product. A market is defined in terms of product and geographic descriptions, so the UK soft drinks market refers to all individuals in the UK who seek to buy soft drinks and the suppliers to that market.

Demand

Demand refers to how many people in a market are actually willing and able to buy a product at a given price and given a set of assumptions about the product and the environment in which it is being offered. Demand is also expressed in terms of a specified time period, for example thousands of litres of soft drinks per week. It is important to add the caveat that demand is about the quantity of a product that consumers are *willing* and *able* to buy at a specific price over a given period of time. It is important to distinguish these conditions from what people would merely *like* to buy—after all, most people would probably *like* to buy more expensive holidays and cars.

For most products, as their price falls, so the demand for them (as defined above) can be expected to rise. Likewise, as the price rises, demand could be expected to fall. This relationship can be plotted on a simple graph. In Figure 9.3, a *demand curve* for dessert strawberries is shown by the line D1. This relates—for any given price shown on the vertical axis—the price to the volume of demand, which is shown on the horizontal axis. So at a price of £8 per kg demand is 20,000 units per period within a given area, while at a price of £4 the demand rises to 30,000 units.

The demand curve shown in Figure 9.3 refers to *total* market demand from all consumers, and is not simply measuring demand for one strawberry grower's output. The importance of this distinction will become clear later, because in imperfect markets each producer seeks to develop a unique demand function for its own differentiated product.

In drawing the price–volume relationship D1, a number of assumptions were made. These include, for example, assumptions that the price of substitutes for strawberries will not change, and that consumers will not suddenly take a dislike to strawberries.

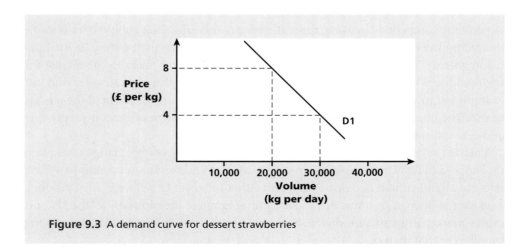

Figure 9.3 A demand curve for dessert strawberries

Figure 9.4 Alternative demand curves for strawberries, based on differing assumptions

Demand curve D1 measures the relationship between price and market demand for *one given set of assumptions*. When these assumptions change, a new demand curve is needed to explain the new relationship between price asked and quantity demanded.

In Figure 9.4, two sets of fresh assumptions have been made and new price–volume relationship curves D2 and D3 drawn, based on these new sets of assumptions. For new demand curve D2, more strawberries are demanded for any given price level. (Alternatively, this can be restated in terms of any given number of consumers demanding strawberries being prepared to pay a higher price.) A shift from D1 to D2 could come about for a number of reasons, including the following:

- Increased spending power available to consumers could lead to more of all goods, including strawberries, being bought.

- The demand for strawberries may be dependent upon demand for some complementary goods. For example, if demand for cream increases (perhaps because of some newly discovered health benefit), it is just possible that demand for strawberries will also rise.

- There could have been an increase in the price of substitutes for strawberries (such as peaches or raspberries), thereby increasing demand for strawberries.

- Heavy advertising of strawberries may increase demand for strawberries.

- Consumer preferences may change. This may occur, for example, if strawberries are found to have positive effects on health.

In the case of the movement in the price–volume relationship from D1 to D3, corresponding but opposite explanations can be put forward, including reduced spending power of consumers; a fall in demand for a complementary product; a fall in the price

Figure 9.5 £99.99 represents an important price point in many people's minds. Through a process of rationalization, customers of this shop may be able to justify to themselves spending £99.99 on a luxury, whereas £100.00 may be considered unacceptable. Where the market allows it, companies use various forms of psychological pricing to induce a response that would probably not be expected on the basis of assumptions about a linear demand curve. (Reproduced with permission of Carphone Warehouse)

of substitutes; reduced advertising; and new evidence linking strawberries with harmful effects on health.

Most price–volume relationships slope downwards, as in Figures 9.3 and 9.4, indicating that as price rises demand falls, and vice versa. While this is usually the case, there are exceptions. Sometimes, as the price of a product goes up, buyers are able and wiling to buy more of the product. This can occur where a product becomes increasingly desirable as more people consume it. Many Internet websites were of little value to advertisers when only small numbers of people used the site, but as more customers used it the price of advertising on the site increased.

Although the price–volume relationships shown in Figures 9.3 and 9.4 are straight, this is a simplification of reality. Demand curves are usually curved, indicating that the relationship between price and volume is not constant for all price points. There may, additionally, be discontinuities at certain price points where buyers in a market have psychological price barriers (see Jeffrey and Harris, 2006).

Drawing a conceptual diagram relating price to volume of demand is relatively easy compared with the problems of collecting data and actually measuring the relationship. The problems are both theoretical and practical.

Data can be obtained by one of two principal methods.

1. They could be collected at one point in time by comparing sales volumes in one area, at a given price, with sales volumes in another area, where a different price is charged. Retailers often experiment by charging different prices at different stores to

build up some kind of picture about the relationship between price and volume. This is referred to as *cross-sectional data*. To be sure that this is accurately measuring the price–volume relationships, there must be no extraneous differences between the points of observation (such as differences in household incomes) which could partly explain differences in price–volume relationships.

2. Alternatively, a firm can change the price of a product over time and see what happens to sales volumes. This is referred to as *longitudinal data*. Again, it can be difficult to keep assumptions constant throughout the duration of the data collection, so that rising incomes or changing consumer preferences could explain sales variations just as much as changes in a product's selling price.

Supply

Firms' willingness to supply products to a market will be influenced by the prevailing price in the market. If the price they receive for selling their goods is low, they will be less willing to supply to the market than if the selling price is high. As in the case of demand, a price–volume line can be drawn, relating the market price of strawberries to volumes supplied by all farmers to the market (Figure 9.6).

The supply curve in Figure 9.6 slopes upwards from left to right, indicating that, as the market price rises, more suppliers will be attracted to supply strawberries to the market. Conversely, as prices fall, marginal producers (such as those who operate relatively inefficiently) will drop out of the market, reducing the daily supply available.

Supply curve S1 is based on various assumptions about the relationship between price and volume supplied. If these no longer hold true, a new supply price–volume relationship needs to be drawn, based on the new set of assumptions. In Figure 9.7, two new

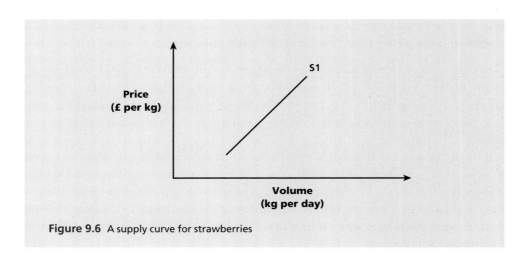

Figure 9.6 A supply curve for strawberries

Figure 9.7 Alternative supply curves for strawberries, based on differing assumptions

supply price–volume relationships, S2 and S3, are shown. S2 indicates a situation where, for any given price level, total supply to the market is increased. This could come about for a number of reasons, including the following:

• In the short term, extraneous factors (such as favourable weather conditions) could result in a glut of perishable strawberries which must be sold, and the market would therefore be flooded with additional supply.

• Improvements in production methods could result in suppliers being prepared to supply more strawberries at any given price (or, looked at another way, for any given volume supplied, suppliers are prepared to accept a lower price).

• Governments may give subsidies to strawberry growers, thereby increasing their willingness to supply to the market at any given price level.

New supply curve S3 indicates a situation where, for any given price level, total supply to the market is reduced. This could come about for a number of reasons, including adverse extraneous factors (e.g. bad weather for growers), increased production costs (e.g. rising wage costs), and reduction of government subsidies and/or imposition of taxes.

It should be noted that some changes in the actual volume of supply might take time to occur. So if strawberry prices went up today, it may not be until the next growing season that this results in increased planting of strawberry plants and hence a larger supply of strawberries to the market. Refer back to the discussion in Chapter 1 of the organic vegetable market and the time that it took firms to satisfy customers' demand for more organic produce.

Figure 9.8 Price determination: the interaction of supply and demand for strawberries

Price determination

In competitive markets, selling prices are determined by the interaction of demand and supply. This can be illustrated by superimposing the supply curve on the demand curve (Figure 9.8).

The supply curve indicates that at lower prices fewer strawberries will be supplied to the market. But at these lower prices, customers are willing and able to buy large volumes of strawberries—more than the suppliers collectively are willing or able to supply. The demand and supply curves intersect at precisely the point where the price–volume relationship is similar for both buyers and sellers. This is the point of equilibrium where demand and supply are precisely in balance. At any lower price, there will be more demand than suppliers are willing to cater for. At any higher price, excessive supply could result in the build-up of unsold stocks.

Changes in the equilibrium market price can come about for two principal reasons.

1. Assumptions about buyers' ability or willingness to buy may change, resulting in a shift to a new demand price–volume relationship.

2. Assumptions about suppliers' ability or willingness to supply may change, resulting in a shift to a new supply price–volume relationship.

The effects of shifts in supply are illustrated in Figure 9.9. From an equilibrium price of £7 and a volume of 15,000 kg, the supply curve has shifted to S2 (perhaps in response to higher wage costs). Assuming that demand conditions remain unchanged, the new point of intersection between the demand and supply lines occurs at a volume of 12,000 kg and a price of £6. This is the new **equilibrium price**. A similar analysis could be

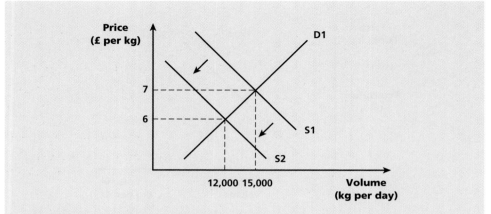

Figure 9.9 New equilibrium market price for strawberries, based on a shift in the supply price–volume relationship

undertaken with a shift in the demand curve and noting the new point of intersection between the demand and supply lines.

Markets vary in the speed with which new equilibrium prices are established in response to changes in demand and/or supply. In pure **commodity markets** where products are instantly perishable, rapid adjustments in price are possible. Where speculators are able to store goods, or large buyers and sellers are able unduly to influence a market, adjustment may be slower (see Bell, Iyer, and Padmanabhan, 2002). The extent of changes in price and volume traded is also dependent on the elasticity of demand and supply, which are considered later in this chapter.

Imperfections to competition

The model of **perfect competition** presented above is rarely seen in practice. The forces of competition may usually be ideal for consumers because of the tendency of market forces to minimize prices and/or maximize firms' outputs. But in such markets, suppliers are forced to be price-*takers* rather than price-*makers*. In a perfectly competitive market, firms are unable to use marketing strategies to affect the price at which they sell. At a higher price, buyers will immediately substitute identical products from other suppliers. Lower prices would be unsustainable in an industry where all firms had similar cost structures.

It is not surprising, therefore, that firms try to overcome the full effects of perfectly competitive markets. There are two principal methods by which a firm can seek to deviate from the workings of perfectly competitive markets to its own advantage: operating at lower costs than other firms in the market, and differentiating its products.

Operating at a lower cost

If a company operates at a lower cost than other firms, and is able to remain at a lower cost than other firms, it will be able to sustain lower prices than its competitors. In many industries **economies of scale** are available to firms, so that as they grow bigger their unit costs fall. This allows them to charge lower prices and still make an adequate profit. Lower prices result in a greater demand for a firm's products, which in turn can allow it to achieve even more economies of scale. This virtuous circle of lower costs leading to competitive advantage can result in a small number of firms gaining a dominant position in the marketplace, thereby violating an important assumption of perfect competition. This can lead to a situation of oligopoly or monopoly (see below), in which the dominant firms have significant power to dictate prices.

Of course, gaining a competitive advantage through economies of scale is not an option open to firms in all industries. Where production and distribution methods are simple, there may be no economies of scale available to exploit. As an example, many firms in service industries such as plumbing and decorating would find it difficult to gain a cost advantage over competitors by operating at a larger scale. Indeed, there may be diseconomies of scale associated with being too large.

Differentiating the product

We saw in Chapter 7 that an entrepreneur can try to avoid head-on competition by selling a product that is somehow differentiated from competitors' products. So in the market for strawberries, a strawberry grower may try to get away from the fiercely competitive conditions that occur in wholesale fruit and vegetable markets. In such markets, the price of products is determined by the market forces alone. Instead, the strawberry supplier could try a number of differentiating strategies, including:

- concentrating on selling specially selected strawberries, for example, ones that are of a particular size or ripeness;
- offering strawberries in distinctive protective packaging;
- offering a delivery service to local customers;
- offering a money-back guarantee of quality;
- offering strawberries in combination with other complementary elements of a fruit salad;
- processing the strawberries by tinning or freezing them;
- as a result of any of the above actions, it could develop a distinctive brand identity for its strawberries, so that buyers do not ask just for strawberries, but for 'Brand X' strawberries by name.

In this example, the supplier has taken steps to turn a basic commodity product into something that is quite distinctive, so it has immediately cut down the number of direct competitors it faces. In fact, if its product really was unique, it would have no direct competition. (In other words, it would be a monopoly supplier of a unique product.) For some differentiated products, this may seem very true in many customers' minds; for example, some people would see a Rolex watch as being quite different to any other watch. Part of the differentiation may be only in buyers' minds, resulting from brand images and lifestyle associations that have been built up over time.

It must not, however, be forgotten that, although the way a supplier has presented its product may be unique, the product is still broadly similar to many competing products in terms of the ability to met buyers' basic needs. The strawberry trader therefore will still face indirect competition from suppliers of other types of fruit.

If a supplier has successfully differentiated its product, it is no longer strictly a price-taker from the market. So the strawberry supplier that has specially selected or packaged its strawberries may be able to charge a few pence per kilogram more than the going rate for basic commodity strawberries. However, it will achieve this higher price only if customers consider that the higher price is worth paying for a better product. It will be able to experiment to assess how customers value a product, and to see just how much more buyers are prepared to pay for its differentiated product.

Elasticity of demand

Price **elasticity of demand** refers to the extent to which demand changes in relation to a change in price. It is a useful indicator for business organizations because it allows them to predict what will happen to volume sales in response to a change in price.

Price elasticity of demand can be expressed as a simple formula:

$$\text{Price elasticity of demand} = \frac{(\%) \text{ change in demand}}{(\%) \text{ change in price}}$$

Where demand is relatively unresponsive to price changes, it is said to be *inelastic* with respect to price. Where demand is highly responsive to even a small price change, it is described as being *elastic* with respect to price.

We have seen that firms face a downward-sloping demand curve for their products, indicating that as prices fall demand increases, and vice versa. By lowering its price, a firm may be able to increase its sales, but what is important to firms is that they increase their total revenue (and profits). Whether this happens depends upon the elasticity of demand for the product in question.

- If it is possible to substitute a product with another that is very similar, price elasticity is said to be high. What constitutes a similar and substitutable product can be defined only in the minds of customers. Two pairs of training shoes may seem technically similar, but their images may be so different that for many buyers they are not at all substitutable.

- The absolute value of a product and its importance to a buyer can influence its elasticity. As an example, most people would not bother shopping around for the best price on infrequently purchased boxes of matches. However, the same percentage difference in price between competing brands of television sets makes a sufficiently large difference to encourage buyers to shop around.

- It is important to understand how price cuts will be perceived by people who are the target of the cuts. A large price cut may lead some people to ask 'Why do they have to make such a cut—surely the product cannot be very good?'

Figure 9.10 Budget airlines discovered a highly elastic demand for air services and have grown rapidly as a result. The price of a return fare from London to Glasgow can now cost less than the price of a pair of jeans and low prices have tempted more people into the airline market. For some, low prices by air meant that they switched from competing rail and road services. For others, new possibilities for taking short holidays or visiting friends were opened up that had previously not been affordable. (Reproduced with permission of easyJet Airline Co. Ltd)

Figure 9.11 A comparison of elasticities of demand for beverages at different levels of product specificity, from a general product form to a specific brand

A number of demand curves describing a firm's market can be described, ranging from the general product form to the specific brand, each with differing elasticity. For example, in the market for beverages the demand curve for beverages in general may be fairly inelastic, on the basis that people will always want to buy drinks of some description (Figure 9.11). Demand for one particular type of beverage, such as cola, will be slightly more elastic, as people may be attracted to cola from other drinks such as carbonated fruit juices and soda water on the basis of their relative price. Price becomes more elastic still when a particular brand of cola is considered. To many people, Coca Cola can be easily substituted with other brands of cola, so if a price differential between brands developed, switching may occur.

In general, firms will find that their products are much more inelastic to changes in price over the short term, when possibilities for substitution may be few. But over the longer term, new possibilities for substitution may appear. (For example, petrol is very inelastic over the short term but much more elastic over the long term, when motorists have a chance to adapt to less fuel-intensive cars and alternative methods of transport.) In addition to *price* elasticity of demand, economists measure a number of other types of elasticity that are of relevance to marketers in determining selling prices. Probably the most important of these is *income* elasticity of demand, which measures the responsiveness of demand to changes in buyers' incomes and can be expressed in the following way:

$$\text{Income elasticity of demand} = \frac{(\%) \text{ change in demand}}{(\%) \text{ change in income}}$$

MARKETING in ACTION

A small penny—a big price difference?

Many business sectors have been accused of deliberately confusing customers in the way prices are presented, and the 'no frills' airline sector has attracted particular criticism from government agencies and consumer groups. Many of the 'tricks of the trade' used by the sector go back a long way, for example the use of '99' pricing rather than whole pound pricing to make a buyer feel that the price is below a psychologically important price barrier (Jeffrey and Harris, 2006). Airlines have been fined for advertising low 'lead in' prices in bold print, but when customers have tried to find such prices, they have not been available. Airlines may have had an excuse for non-availability when printed price lists became out of date, but how could they excuse misleading lead-in prices for web-based adverts which can be automatically updated in real-time from a database?

The practice of some airlines of showing a low basic price in large figures, while hiding compulsory additional costs in small print has been widely criticised. For many budget airline tickets, taxes and security charges may amount to more than the basic price of the ticket, but the total cost of the ticket might only be found at the point where a potential buyer is about to complete their purchase. One critic has likened airlines' practice of making separate charges for taxes and security charges as being similar to car manufacturers making an additional charge for the steering wheel.

There is some evidence that consumers may make irrational choices, based on apparently misleading price information. This may be evidenced by paying a higher price for a ticket with a low basic price, compared with a similar ticket for which total price is expressed upfront (Palmer and Boissy, 2009). Should governments intervene to stop such practices? Or should the old maxim apply that a buyer should beware, and study the small print before committing to a purchase? Do most buyers have the time or inclination to go through every company's small print with a fine toothcomb? One sign of governments' impatience with airlines' pricing practices was a statement in 2006 by the EU Transport Commissioner Mr Barrot, that the EU would press ahead with proposals to make fares easily comparable between airlines.

In general, as an individual's income rises, her demand for most products rises, giving rise to a positive income elasticity of demand. Where there is a particularly strong increase in demand in response to an increase in incomes, a product is said to have a high income elasticity of demand. This is true of luxuries such as long-haul package holidays and fitted kitchens, whose sales have increased during times of general economic prosperity but declined during recessionary periods. On the other hand, there are some goods and services for which demand goes down as income increases. These are referred to as inferior goods, and examples in most western countries include rural bus services and household coal.

Oligopoly

Imperfect competition can develop to a point where market structure can be described as oligopolistic. **Oligopoly** lies somewhere between the two extremes of perfect competition and pure monopoly. An oligopoly market is dominated by a small number of sellers that provide a large share of the total market output. The crucial point about oligopoly markets is that all suppliers in the market are interdependent. One company cannot take price or output decisions without considering the specific possible responses of the other companies.

Markets are most likely to be oligopolistic where economies of scale are significant; for example, oligopoly is typical of oil refining and distribution, pharmaceuticals, car manufacturing, and detergents. Customers of oligopoly organizations may not immediately appreciate that the products they are buying come from an oligopolist, as such firms frequently use a variety of brand names. (The detergent manufacturers Unilever and Proctor & Gamble between them have over 50 apparently competing detergent products on sale in the UK.)

Oligopolists pay particular attention to the activities of their fellow oligopolists, and there is often a reluctance to upset the established order. One firm is often acknowledged as the price leader, and the other firms await its actions before adjusting their prices. In the UK household mortgage market, for example, Halifax has often been the initiator of price changes which other banks and building societies then follow. It has been suggested that firms may not match upward price movements, in the hope of gaining extra sales, but would match downward price changes for fear of losing market share. Oligopolists have often been accused of collusion and of creating barriers to entry for newcomers (such as signing exclusive distribution rights with key retailers).

Price wars between oligopolists can be very expensive to participants, so there is a tendency to find alternative ways to compete for customers, such as free gifts, coupons, added value offers, and sponsorship activities. This occurred in the UK in 2007 as the main cable television networks—Sky and Virgin—challenged each other with price cuts and special bundles of additional services which were included free of charge.

Monopolistic markets

In its purest extreme, **monopoly** occurs where there is only one supplier to the market, perhaps because of regulatory, technical, or economic barriers to entry which potential competing suppliers would face. A pure monopoly means that one person or organization has complete control over supply to that market. A monopolist can determine the market price for its product and can be described as a 'price-maker' rather than a 'price-taker'. Where there are few substitutes for a product, and where demand is inelastic, a monopolist may be able to get away with continually increasing prices in order to increase its profits.

Sometimes monopoly control over supply comes about through a group of suppliers acting in collusion in a **cartel**. As with the pure monopoly, companies would join a cartel in order to try and protect themselves from the harmful consequences of competition. Cartels have been suspected in many industry sectors, for example, rings of cement suppliers in a region who covertly agree to share markets between themselves and not to undercut each other's prices.

A pure monopoly rarely occurs in practice. Even in the former centrally planned economies of eastern Europe, there were often active 'shadow' markets that existed alongside official monopoly suppliers. Most products have some form of substitute which reduces the monopolist's ability to set prices. Also, a firm that has significant monopoly pricing power at home may nevertheless face quite severe price competition in its overseas markets.

A company may have monopoly power over some of its users, but it may face competition if it wishes to attract new segments of users. It may therefore resort to differential pricing when targeting the two groups. As an example, many rail operators in the London area have considerable monopoly power over commuters, who need to use their train services to arrive at work by 9 a.m. on weekdays. For such commuters, the alternatives of travelling to work by bus or car are very unattractive. However, leisure travellers wishing to go shopping in London during off-peak periods may be much more price sensitive. For them, the car or bus provide realistic alternatives, and so train companies offer a range of price incentives aimed at the off-peak leisure market, while charging full fare for their peak period commuters.

In theory, a company with significant monopoly power could continually raise its prices in order to exploit its monopoly. However, marketing managers who think strategically may be reluctant to exploit their monopoly powerfully. By charging high prices in the short term, a monopolist could give signals to companies in related product fields to develop substitutes that would eventually provide effective competition. Blatant abuse of monopoly power could also result in a referral to the regulatory authorities (see below).

Regulatory influences on pricing

Because of the presumed superiority of competitive markets, prevailing laws in most developed countries have been used to try to remove market imperfections where these are deemed to be against the public interest. Private-sector companies must take account of various regulations in setting their prices. These can be classified as:

- direct government controls to regulate monopoly power;
- government controls on price representations.

Direct government controls to regulate monopoly power

Governments have a range of measures which can be used to prevent exploitative pricing by monopolists. At a European level, Articles 85 and 86 of the Treaty of Rome limit the ability of firms to collude with their fellow producers or distributors in fixing prices. In the UK, the Enterprise Act 2002 strengthened the previous Competition Act 1998 by making provision for criminal sanctions with fines and a maximum penalty of five years in prison for individuals that operate agreements to fix prices, share markets, limit production, and rig bids. The Director General of the Office of Fair Trading (OFT) has power to order an investigation by the Competition Commission of alleged anti-competitive practices that may have the effect of restricting choice or causing prices to be higher than they need be. In 2006, the OFT found that an agreement between 50 of the UK's fee-paying independent schools to exchange detailed fee information was in breach of the Competition Act, and imposed penalties totalling just under £500,000 on the schools. The schools concerned had exchanged confidential information relating to their intended fee levels for boarding and day pupils through a survey known as the 'Sevenoaks Survey'.

Utility companies with a monopoly position usually have their prices limited by the regulator for that industry. In the UK Ofgem, Ofwat, and Ofcom regulate certain prices of gas/electricity, water, and broadcasting/telephone service providers, respectively. Governments have deregulated some utility markets, in the hope that this results in lower prices through competitive pressure (for example, numerous companies have been licensed to compete with British Telecom in the UK). However, in many cases measures to increase competition have had only limited effect, as in the very limited competition faced by the privatized water supply companies; hence the continuing need for direct price controls. Even within the apparently more competitive tele-communications sector, the regulator has frequently intervened with instructions to operators to reduce specific categories of prices. In 2006, Ofcom—with the European Regulators Group (ERG), a body of EU telecoms regulators—investigated mobile phone roaming charges throughout Europe and was instrumental in the development of an EU directive to regulate these charges throughout Europe.

Government controls on price representations

In any marketplace, buyers and sellers need rules to govern their conduct and prevent abuses of their respective positions. So, as well as controlling or influencing the actual level of prices, government regulation can have the effect of specifying the manner in which price information is communicated to potential customers. At a general level, the Consumer Protection Act 1987 requires that all prices shown should conform to the Code of Practice on pricing—misleading price representations which relegate details of supplementary charges to the small print or give attractive low lead-in prices for ser-vices that are not in fact available are made illegal by this Act. Other regulations affect specific industries. The Consumer Credit Act 1974 requires that the charge made for credit must include a statement of the annual percentage rate (APR) of interest. Also within the financial services sector, the Financial Services Act 1986 has resulted in quite specific requirements regarding the manner in which charges for certain insurance-related services are presented to potential customers.

Pricing objectives of companies

We are now going to look at the decisions taken by firms that are able to act as price-*makers* rather than price-*takers*; in other words, those that have established some degree of differentiation from the rest of the market. Marketers must consider pricing not just at one point in time, but over the life of a product. So a price based on differential advantage over competitors may need to change over time as competitors gradually erode a company's differential advantage. Simplistic economic analyses of pricing tends to overlook the complex interdependencies that can exist between different products within a firm's product range, and we will explore the subject of product mix pricing.

First, we need to consider the objectives of an organization as an important influence on its pricing decisions. Simple models of perfect competition assume that firms are motivated primarily by the desire to maximize their short-term profits. In a commodity market, where prices are taken from the market, a company cannot be expected to have any other objectives, or it would soon go out of business. However, where a company has differentiated its products to give it a degree of monopoly power, it is able to pursue a more diverse range of possible objectives. Below, we consider the effects of diverse objectives on an organization's pricing policies.

Profit maximization

Economists' models of perfect competition assume that firms in a market act rationally in order to maximize their profits. In less competitive markets, the notion of **profit maximization** becomes much more complex to understand. The first complicating issue is the possible divergence between short-term and long-term profit objectives. A company that aims to maximize its profits over the short run may unwittingly reduce its ability to achieve long-term profit objectives. By charging high prices in a new market, it may make that market seem very attractive to new entrants. This could provide a major incentive for new competitors to appear, thereby increasing the level of competition in subsequent years, and therefore reducing long-term profitability. Drugs companies selling medicines that have just come out of their period of patent protection must decide whether to continue charging the high prices to which buyers have been accustomed, or to lower the price to a point where it deters new market entrants who can no longer be sure of making a quick short-term profit.

Organizations differ in the urgency with which they need to make profits from a new product. It is frequently suggested that the open shareholding structure of UK firms makes shareholders restless for short-term profits. Managers are therefore likely to set prices to achieve these short-term objectives, even if this is at the expense of longer-term profitability. By contrast, the relatively closed capital structure of many Japanese companies has allowed them to take a longer-term view on profitability, relatively free of short-term stock market pressures. A longer-term profit objective may allow an organization to tap relatively small but high-value segments of its markets in the first year and save the exploitation of lower-value segments until subsequent years.

Finally, while it is easy to talk about firms calculating the effects of their pricing on their profits, in reality many marketing managers have little understanding about the relationship between costs, sales volumes, and profitability. This can be especially true of new and emerging markets where there are few historical data on which to predict the outcome of price changes.

Sales growth

Management often does not directly receive any reward for increasing its organization's profits, so its main concern may be to achieve a *satisfactory* level of profits rather than the *maximum* possible. Managers often benefit personally where their company pursues a sales growth strategy, a point that has been made by many behavioral studies of how managers act (e.g. Cyert and March, 1963).

There are also some very good reasons why a company may benefit over the longer term by seeking to boost its short-term sales growth, even if this does mean charging very low prices and sacrificing short-term profits in order to do so. In many industries it is essential to achieve a critical size in order to achieve economies of scale in buying, production, promotion, and distribution. On the basis of these economies of scale, a firm may be able to achieve a competitive advantage. Companies in sectors as diverse as grocery retailing, civil aviation, and publishing have used low prices to achieve short-term sales growth in the hope that this will lead to long-term profit growth.

Finally, sales growth may be an important objective, influencing pricing, because managers may have practical difficulties in establishing relationships between marketing strategy decisions and the resulting change in profitability. Going for growth may be perceived by managers to be their safest option.

Survival

For many struggling companies, the objective of maximizing profits or sales volume is quite unrealistic when they are fighting desperately to avoid bankruptcy. In these circumstances, prices may be set at very low levels, simply to get enough cash into the organization to tide it over. Many retailers have found themselves in this situation when there has been a sudden down-turn in consumer demand and they are left with too much stock and expensive overheads to pay. Cash is now tied up unnecessarily in stock. In a bid to stay afloat, many desperate retailers have held stock liquidation sales,

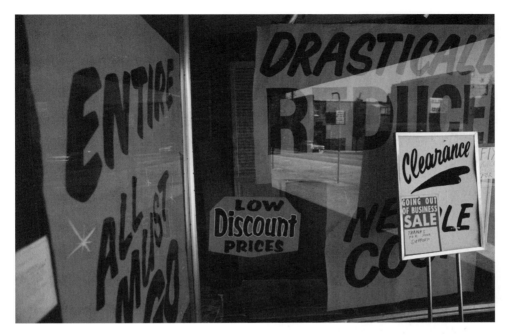

Figure 9.12 Sometimes the use of advertising statements such as 'Closing Down Sale', 'Everything Must Go', and 'Stock Liquidation Sale' may be just advertising spin. Often, however, these sales reflect the fact that the company is desperately short of cash and will sell its stock at very low prices, just so that it can raise enough cash quickly enough to satisfy its creditors. Low prices may be vital just for survival, but such prices will not sustain the business indefinitely. (*Source:* © Photodisc)

in which stocks have been sold at almost any price, just to keep cash flowing in (*Daily Telegraph*, 2007). Even if the prices charged did not cover the original cost of goods, such pricing could satisfy managers' short-term objective of survival.

Social considerations

Talk about maximizing sales or profits may have little meaning within the public and not-for-profit sectors, where there is more emphasis on maximizing social benefits (e.g. the number of operations performed by a hospital). The price of many public services represents a tax levied by government based not on market forces, but on an individual's ability to pay, with many services being provided at no charge. In the UK, many basic health services are provided without charge to patients, and where charges are made, these often reflect the ability of individuals to pay, rather than the need for the health authority to maximize its revenue (e.g. lower dental and prescription charges for disadvantaged groups).

Although social objectives are normally associated with public-sector services, they are sometimes adopted by private-sector organizations also. Many companies provide goods and services for their staff (such as canteens and sports facilities) at below their market price, with the aim of adding to staff's motivation and sense of loyalty to their organization.

Pricing strategy

Strategy is the means by which an organization seeks to achieve its objectives. Strategic decisions about pricing cannot be made in isolation from other strategic marketing decisions; so, for example, a strategy that seeks a premium price position must be matched by a product development strategy that creates a superior product and a promotional strategy that establishes in buyers' minds the value that the product offers.

The concept of positioning was discussed in Chapter 6, where it was noted that combinations anywhere along a line from high price/high quality to low price/low quality are sustainable strategic positions to adopt. A strategy that combines high price with low quality may be regarded by customers as poor value and they are likely to desert such companies where they have a choice of suppliers. For most companies such a strategy is not sustainable. A high quality/low price strategic position may appear very attractive to buyers, but it too may not be sustainable. Many companies in their public pronouncements claim this to be their strategic position, but it can pose problems for them, in the following ways.

- Are they selling themselves short and failing to recover their full costs in their bid to please customers? Unless they are operating more efficiently than other companies in their sector, there is the possibility that they will fail to make sufficient profits. In the mass market restaurant sector, for example, portion control can be quite critical to financial success. Customers may love the value offered by bigger servings, but many restaurants have gone out of business because they offered their customers too much value.

- If a company is genuinely able to offer lower prices for any given level of quality on the basis of greater efficiency, it must realize that its competitors may soon learn and copy its own levels of efficiency. Its prices will therefore no longer be the only sustainable low prices in the sector. In the European scheduled airline industry, many low-cost operators such as easyJet and Ryanair have undercut the established airlines' prices. However, their competitive advantage has often been eroded when the established operators have then implemented many of the cost-cutting measures pioneered by their new competitors.

Pricing and the product life cycle

In Chapter 8 the concept of the product life cycle was introduced, and you will recall that many aspects of a product's marketing strategy are closely related to the position

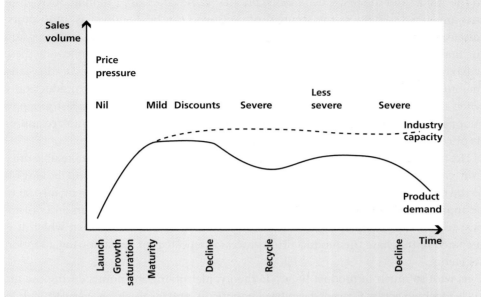

Figure 9.13 As a product passes through its life cycle, the pressures on pricing will change. This graph shows the likely pricing response for a typical innovatory high-tech product.

that it has reached in its life cycle. Pricing strategy is no exception. An effective marketing strategy must identify how the role of price is to function as a product goes through different stages in its life from the launch stage through growth to maturity.

Where a company is supplying a market in which product differentiation is possible, it is able to take a long-term view on its price position. However, pressure on the product's price, and hence on its profitability, will vary during the life of the product. Figure 9.13 illustrates the typical pressures on a product's price as it progresses through its life cycle.

Price-skimming strategy

One approach to product life-cycle pricing is for a firm to start by charging a high price for a newly launched product, on the basis of its uniqueness. As its uniqueness is copied by other firms, the price will then have to be reduced to match those of the competitors.

This strategy is suitable for products that are genuinely innovative—the first microwave cookers in the 1970s; the first portable phones in the 1980s; the first digital cameras in the 1990s, and the first video mobile phones in the 2000s, for example. Such products are aimed initially at the segment of users who can be described as 'innovators' (discussed in Chapter 8). These are typically consumers who have the resources and inclination to be the trendsetters in purchasing new goods and services. Following these will be a group of early adopters, followed by a larger group often described as the 'early majority'. The subsequent 'late majority' group may take up the new product only when the product market itself has reached maturity. 'Laggards' are the last group to adopt a new product and would do so only when it has become commonplace and/or its price has fallen sufficiently.

The basic principle of a **price-skimming strategy** is to gain the highest possible price from each market segment, beginning with the highest-value segments and moving on to the next lower-value one when the purchasing ability of the first segment appears to be approaching saturation level. At this point the price level is lowered in order to appeal to the 'early adopter' segment, which has a lower price threshold at which it is prepared to purchase the product. This process is repeated for the following adoption segments.

As with so much of product life-cycle theory, identifying the points during the life cycle at which action is needed can be very difficult, and it can also be very difficult to map out a price strategy with any degree of confidence. Consider the following problems, all of which make a price-skimming strategy difficult to formulate.

- What is the saturation level of individual market segments? At what point should the company decide to lower its prices to appeal to lower value segments?

- How long will the firm's product remain genuinely innovative in the eyes of consumers? To what extent will the appearance of competitors diminish its uniqueness and therefore the firm's ability to charge premium prices?

- How quickly are new competitors likely to appear?

- Should the firm avoid charging very high initial prices, as this may be a signal to competitors to enter the market? How strong are the barriers to entry for new competitors?

Price-skimming strategies work for consumer markets as well as business-to-business markets. Diffusion patterns for products sold mainly to business buyers can be different from those for consumer products. Business buyers generally have less of a desire to be a trendsetter for its own sake, and a different kind of rationality in purchase decisions. This limits the opportunities for price-skimming to situations where commercial buyers can use innovative products to give them a productivity advantage, which in turn will give them a competitive advantage in selling their own products to their customers at a lower price and/or a higher standard.

For many innovative products, falling prices may be further stimulated by falling production costs. Lower costs can occur because of economies of scale in production,

Figure 9.14 Skimming and penetration pricing strategies compared

promotion, and distribution. (For example, the cost of microwave cookers and mobile phones came down partly as a result of improved production efficiency, which itself was partly a refection of economies of scale.) Costs may also fall as a result of the **experience effect**. This refers to the process by which costs fall as experience in production is gained. By pursuing a strategy to gain experience faster than its competitors, an organization lowers its cost base and has a greater scope for adopting an aggressive pricing strategy.

Penetration pricing strategy

Genuinely innovative new product launches are few and far between. The vast majority of product launches are simply copies of products that consumers can already buy in substantially the same form. Consider the following product launches:

* a new television listings magazine;
* a new type of chocolate biscuit;
* a new coffee shop.

The principle of initially appealing to high-value segments and then dropping the price will be unlikely to work with any of these, as buyers in all segments have access to competitors' products which are essentially similar. Buyers must have a good reason for choosing to try the new product instead of sticking with the product they are currently purchasing. There are many ways in which a company can encourage trial of its product, including a product design that offers real benefits to buyers, heavy advertising, sales promotion, and sponsorship activity. One method used by many companies to encourage trial is to offer prices that are sufficiently low that a large number of buyers will switch from their existing suppliers. Sometimes the new product will even be given away, in order to get potential buyers to try it. (For example, cosmetics companies often give away free samples with magazines.)

Naturally, companies will not want to go on charging low prices for very long. Their hope is that, once buyers have tried and enjoyed their product, they will come back again. At this stage, the price can be raised to something that approaches competitors' price levels. The buyers no longer have to be tempted with a low price. Over time, they may even come to prefer the product over competitors', so the company may be able to charge a price premium.

Of course, **penetration pricing strategies** have their dangers. Companies often find it difficult to develop sufficient loyalty from customers that will allow them to raise prices. Customers who were attracted by low penetration prices may be just as easily lost when a competitor or another new market entrant tries offering low prices in its turn. This pricing strategy also presupposes that buyers have a high awareness of prices. Research has shown that in many markets buyers have a very poor knowledge of prices, so competing for market share on the basis of low price alone may not work (Shugan, 2006).

MARKETING in ACTION

One nibble and customers are nobbled

Companies use many pricing techniques to get people to try out a product and then seek to lock in the customer at ever-increasing price levels. Is this exploitation, or just good marketing? Knowing that customers who were attracted by a low price may just as easily be lost to a competitor who tries to tempt them back with low prices, companies try to lock customers in once they have tried a new product. Many new magazines launch with low prices and include series or articles which it is hoped readers will get attached to and so will carry on buying the magazine, even after the publisher has put the price up midway during the series. Many fast-moving consumer goods manufacturers include competitions or gift offers with their launch sales, for which tokens need to be collected. Where the collectible items include children's toys, 'pester power' may add to the motivation to carry on buying the product. Meanwhile, the company may have taken a strategic decision to increase the price of the product while customers are part-way through collecting the required number of tokens. Is this ethical?

In some cases a company can exploit the fact that customers have become physically hooked on their product. Tobacco companies have recognized the power of addiction for some time, even though they may have not publicly accepted that it happens. The effects can be seen in other products too. So with the biscuit 'Hob Nobs', a suspicion arose that individuals could become addicted to the biscuit after their initial trial, regardless of its price. Is this brilliant marketing, in that the manufacturer has perfected its product to such an extent that buyers are prepared to pay a premium price for it? Or is this an example of cynical manipulation of buyers to put them in a position of dependency?

Customer lifetime pricing

As well as the product life cycle, we can also consider the customer life cycle. You will recall from Chapter 4 that the development of ongoing buyer–seller relationships is becoming a much more important part of business strategy. Rather than bargaining over each transaction, companies are trying to view each transaction with a customer in the context of those that have gone before, and those that they hope will follow. The price offered to a prospective new client may start off relatively low and build up progressively as both buyer and seller come to recognize the value of their relationship. Think back to our example in Chapter 4 of a new customer going into a restaurant. Should the profit of that individual be measured just in terms of that one meal, or in terms of the lifetime of meals it is hoped that he may buy? Viewed in the latter context, there may be scope for offering a low-price incentive to encourage newcomers to give the restaurant a try.

🍩 Pricing methods

Strategies need to be translated into methodologies for actually setting prices. Faced with a new product, the task of determining a selling price can sometimes appear to be quite daunting. If it is a completely new product, there may be very little historical guidance for setting prices. Companies may resort to a hunch or guesswork. However, even guesswork can be reduced to a series of rule-based decisions. Essentially, there are three questions that need to be asked when setting the price for any product:

1. How much does it cost us to make the product?
2. How much are competitors charging for a similar product?
3. What price are customers prepared to pay?

An additional factor affects marketing managers in many public utility sectors:

4. How much will a government regulator allow us to charge customers?

The relationship between these bases for pricing is shown in Figure 9.15. Each will be considered in turn.

Cost-based pricing

The cost of producing a product sets the minimum price that a company would be prepared to charge its customers. If a commercial company is not covering its costs with its prices, it cannot continue in business indefinitely (unless, perhaps, the business has a wealthy owner and the business is kept going for reasons of prestige, as in the case of many national newspapers). The principle of a direct linkage between costs and prices

Figure 9.15 Bases for determining prices showing maximum and minimum constraints on a firm's pricing decisions

may be central to basic price theory, but marketing managers rarely find conditions to be so simple. Consider some of the problems in relating costs to prices:

- The cost of a particular product is often very difficult to calculate. This is especially true where production costs involve high levels of shared overhead costs which cannot easily be allocated to specific products.

- While it may be relatively easy to calculate historic costs, it is *future* costs that may be crucial in determining profitability. An office furniture manufacturer, for example, may find it difficult to set fixed prices for customers today for furniture that will be built and delivered at some time in the future. It may be difficult to predict inflation rates for labour and materials used.

- **Cost-based pricing** in itself does not take account of the competition that a particular product faces at any particular time, nor of the fact that some customers may value the same service more highly than others.

Despite these shortcomings, cost-based pricing is widely used in many sectors. In its most straightforward form, 'cost-plus' pricing works like this: a company calculates its total costs and divides these by the total volume of resources used, in order to determine the average cost of each unit of resource used; it then calculates a selling price by estimating the number of units of resources to be used, multiplying this by the unit cost and adding a profit margin. Cost-based pricing is widely used by solicitors, plumbers, and other labour-intensive service industries where the cost of labour is a major component of total costs. So a plumber may price a job on the basis of the total number of hours estimated to complete a job, multiplied by the historical cost per hour (including

Cost information for most recent trading year:

Total employees' wage cost	£1,000,000
Total hours worked	70,000
Cost per employee-hour	14.28
Total other overhead costs	£600,000
Overhead cost per employee hour worked	8.57
Total chargeable amount per hour	22.85
Required profit mark-up	40%

Price calculation for a job requiring 100 hours of labour and £500 materials:

100 hours @ £22.85 per hour	£2,285
Materials	500
Sub-total	2,785
Add 40% mark-up	1,114
Price	3,899

Figure 9.16 An example of a cost-based approach to pricing for a building contractor

overheads) of its employees, plus materials used, plus a profit margin. The principles are illustrated in Figure 9.16.

Marginal cost pricing

Another form of cost-based pricing that is widely used is referred to as **marginal cost pricing**. Here, a company calculates the *marginal* cost of producing one additional unit of a product (that is, the addition to the company's total costs of selling one extra item). In some industries with high levels of fixed costs, the marginal cost of producing one extra unit of output can be surprisingly small. The cost of carrying one extra passenger on an aeroplane that is about to depart with some empty seats can be little more than the cost of the airport handling charges, possibly a meal, and marginally additional fuel. This explains why many airlines and holiday companies are keen to offer last-minute standby airfares, as some revenue is better than having an unsold seat, just so long as the price charged more than covers the marginal costs.

Pricing based on marginal costs may work up to a point, but companies must realize that a sufficient number of customers must be willing to pay full costs in order for others to be charged a much lower price reflecting only marginal costs. Many airlines and holiday companies have gone bankrupt because too high a proportion of their customers have been sold tickets at the marginal cost, leaving the fixed overhead costs uncovered.

Calculating marginal costs can sometimes be quite difficult. In the long term, all of a company's costs are marginal in that there is always the option to close down entire business units or even the whole company. While the marginal cost of one seat on an

Product	Fixed costs	Marginal costs
Meal in a restaurant	Building maintenance Rent and rates Head chef	Food
Bank mortgage	Head office staff time Building maintenance Corporate advertising	Sales commission Paper and postage
Hairdresser	Building maintenance Rent and rates	Shampoos used

Figure 9.17 A classification of typical fixed and marginal costs for three service industries. Note that even fixed costs could in the long term become marginal costs if the whole business unit is being evaluated

Figure 9.18 Travel companies have for a long time used marginal cost pricing, mindful that some revenue is better than an empty plane seat or hotel room. They have realized that some people could be tempted by low-price offers to fill its spare capacity at very short notice. The online travel intermediary lastminute.com makes full use of marginal cost pricing by bringing together companies that have spare capacity with buyers who are looking for a bargain. (Reproduced with permission of lastminute.com)

aeroplane may be low, if the unit of analysis is the whole journey or even the whole route, the level of marginal costs becomes much higher (see Figure 9.17).

Competitors and pricing

Very often, a marketing manager may go about setting prices by examining what competitors are charging. But what is the competition against which prices are to be compared? From Chapter 7, you will recall that competitors can be defined at different levels:

• similar in terms of product characteristics;

or, more broadly,

• similar just in terms of the needs that a product satisfies.

As an example, a video rental shop can see its competition purely in terms of other video shops, or it could widen it to include cinemas and satellite television services, or widen it still further to include any form of entertainment.

Once it has established what market it is in and who its competitors are, a company can go about setting comparative prices. First it must establish what price position it seeks to adopt relative to its competitors. This position will reflect the wider marketing mix of the product, so if the product is perceived by buyers as being superior in quality to the competitors' products, it may justify a relatively higher price. Similarly, heavy investment in promotion or distribution channels may give it a competitive advantage that is reflected in buyers' willingness to pay relatively high prices.

In markets that show some signs of interdependency among suppliers, firms can often be described as price-makers, or price-followers. Price-makers tend to be those who, as a result of their size and power within a market, are able to determine the levels and patterns of prices, which other suppliers then follow. Smaller estate agents in a local area may find it convenient simply to respond to pricing policies adopted by the dominant firms—for them to take a proactive role themselves might bring about a reaction from the dominant firms that they would be unable to defend, because of their size and standing in the market.

Where it is difficult for a company to calculate its production costs (perhaps because of the high level of fixed costs), charging a 'going rate' can simplify the pricing process. As an example, it may be very difficult to calculate the cost of renting out a video film, as the figure will be very dependent upon assumptions made about the number of uses over which the initial purchase cost can be spread. It is much easier to take price decisions on the basis of the going rate charged by close competitors.

Many business-to-business goods and services are provided by means of a sealed-bid tendering process where interested parties are invited to submit a bid for supplying goods or services in accordance with specifications. In the case of many government contracts, the organization inviting tenders is often legally obliged to accept the lowest priced tender, unless exceptional circumstances can be proved. The first task of a bidding company is to establish a minimum bid price based on its costs and the required rate of return, below which it would not be prepared to bid. The more difficult task is to try and put a maximum figure on what it can bid. This will be based on expectations of what its competitors will bid, based on an analysis of their strengths and weaknesses.

Demand-based pricing

What customers are prepared to pay represents the upper limit to a company's pricing possibilities. In fact, different customers often put different ceilings on the price they are prepared to pay for a product. Successful demand-oriented pricing is therefore based on effective segmentation of markets and **price discrimination** that achieves the maximum price from each segment.

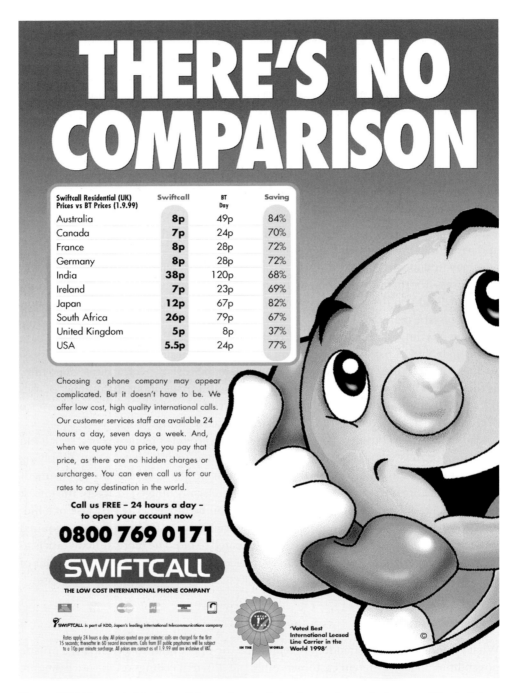

Figure 9.19 The market for long-distance phone calls has become increasingly competitive in the UK, and for many people price is the only means of differentiating between one supplier and another. Swiftcall is one of several companies to challenge the dominant provider, BT. Its advertising picks out a few key destinations and provides direct price comparisons with BT, providing an immediate comparison of price advantages. (Reproduced with permission of Swiftcall)

The bases for segmenting markets were discussed in Chapter 4 and are of direct relevance in determining discriminatory prices. It was noted that, in addition to socio-economic factors, geographical location of buyers, their reason for purchase, and the time of purchase are all important bases for segmentation. Their impact on price determination is considered below.

Price discrimination between different groups of buyers

Sometimes price discrimination can be achieved simply by offering the same product to each segment, but charging a different price. This is possible with some services that are not transferrable from one individual to another. So a hairdresser can offer students a haircut that is identical to the service offered to all other customer groups in all respects except price. The justification could be that this segment is more price-sensitive than other segments, and therefore additional profitable business can be gained only by sacrificing some element of margin. By selling more haircuts, even at a lower price, a hairdresser may end up deriving increased total revenue from this segment, while still preserving the higher prices charged to other segments.

On other occasions, however, where one segment was paying more than other segments for an identical product, price discrimination would not be sustainable. It would always be open for members of the segment being charged a higher price to try to buy the good in lower-price markets. Sometimes they will do this directly themselves, as seen by the number of British buyers who have taken advantage of lower cigarette and alcohol prices in continental Europe. Sometimes entrepreneurs will seek out goods in low-priced market segments and offer them for resale in the higher-price market (a practice that retailers such as Superdrug and Tesco have carried out in respect of branded perfumes, which are sold in many overseas markets at lower prices than in the UK).

To be sustainable, price discrimination is often associated with slight changes to the product offer. This can be seen in the market for air passenger services. Airlines offer a variety of fare and service combinations to suit the needs of a number of segments. One segment has to travel at short notice and is typically travelling on business. For the employer, the cost of not being able to travel at short notice may be high, so this group is prepared to pay a relatively high price in return for ready availability. A sub-segment of this market may seek extra comfort and space and is prepared to pay more for the differentiated Business Class accommodation. For non-business travellers, another segment may be happy to accept a lower price in return for committing themselves to a particular flight just two weeks before departure. Another segment with even less income to spend on travel may be prepared to take the risk of obtaining a last-minute standby flight in return for a still lower priced ticket.

Price discrimination by point of sale

Some companies charge different prices in different places. Hotels frequently charge much higher prices in some prime locations, despite there being little difference in facilities

MARKETING in ACTION

Entrepreneurial senior citizens seize price discounts

Many service-sector companies have offered reduced prices for segments of senior citizens, calculating that these segments are more price-sensitive than others and could usefully fill spare capacity at a profit, even at the lower prices charged. But can this apply to the sale of goods? With services, a supplier can insist that only senior citizens receive the benefit of the service they have paid for (for example, by insisting on seeing proof of age during a train journey). But goods can be bought by members of a low-price segment and sold on to those of a relatively high-price one. The pitfalls of this approach to market segmentation were learned by a German grocery retailer which offered 20% off the price of all purchases made by senior citizens. Entrepreneurial senior citizens were then seen lining up outside the supermarket offering to do other customers' shopping for them. The 20% price saving was split between the senior citizen and the person needing the goods, saving effort for the latter, providing additional income for the former—but making a mockery of the retailer's attempts at price discrimination.

offered between locations. The reason for this discrimination can be a combination of cost factors (e.g. land and staff costs for a hotel are higher in central London than in northern England) and demand factors. (To large segments of potential buyers, a hotel room in central London will be considered more valuable than one located in northern England.)

Price discrimination by location is much more effective for services than for goods. Services cannot generally be transferred from the point where they are produced to another area where a buyer most wants to consume them. (For example, a Sheffield hotel room can be consumed only in Sheffield and cannot be brought to London where it would be more valuable.) Airlines often charge more at one end of a route than the other, depending on strength of demand in different national markets, and one American Express study calculated that business travellers out of the UK were being charged up to 54% more for transatlantic flights than travellers from other European cities (*Daily Telegraph*, 2002). By contrast, differences between areas in the price of goods will soon be exploited by entrepreneurs who are able to buy in the lower-price market and sell on in the higher-price one (as has happened with cosmetics sourced from low-price Far Eastern markets and resold in the UK).

Price discrimination by type of use

A similar product can be bought by different people to satisfy quite different needs. A train journey may be perceived as an optional leisure purchase by one person, but as a means of getting work done on the way to an important business meeting by another. Train-operating companies have therefore developed different fares aimed at groups with different journey purposes (e.g. off-peak fares for price-sensitive leisure travellers and first-class facilities for business executives).

Figure 9.20 It is not just large companies that practise price discrimination. Many smaller businesses, such as this hairdressing salon, charge different prices for different groups, typically offering discounts for students and senior citizens. Price discrimination would work for a haircut (unlike most goods), because one person cannot buy a cheap haircut and sell it on to another person who is not eligible for the lower price. However, even small businesses must ensure that discriminatory pricing does not create feelings of resentment from those who pay a higher price for an essentially similar service.

Even the same person may buy a product repeatedly but seek to satisfy different needs on each occasion. There are many examples of this. Most people when eating out are more likely to be price-sensitive for a regular midday meal during their lunch hour than for a social meal with friends in the evening. Many restaurants have responded to this by offering special lunchtime menus which are very similar to meals offered in the evening, except that the price is lower.

Price discrimination by time of purchase

It is quite common for suppliers of services to charge different prices at different times of supply. Services often face an uneven demand which follows a daily, weekly, annual, seasonal, cyclical, or random pattern. At the height of each peak, pricing is usually a reflection of.

- the greater willingness of customers to pay higher prices when demand is strong, and
- the greater cost that often results from service operators trying to cater for short peaks in demand.

The greater strength of demand that occurs at some points in a daily cycle can be for a number of reasons. In the case of rail services into the major conurbations, workers generally must arrive at work at a specified time and may have few realistic alternative means of getting to work. A train operator can therefore sustain a higher level of fares during the daily commuter peak period. Similarly, the higher rate charged for telephone calls during the daytime is a reflection of the greater strength of demand from the business sector during the day. Price can also occur between different periods of the week (e.g. higher fares for using many train services on a Friday evening), or between different seasons of the year (e.g. holiday flights at busy holiday periods).

Price discrimination by time can be effective in inducing new business at what would otherwise be a quiet period. Hotels in holiday resorts frequently lower their prices in the off-peak season to try to tempt additional custom. Many utility companies lower their charges during off-peak periods in a bid to stimulate demand—for example, lower telephone charges at weekends.

Bartering and auctions

Bartering is one of the oldest forms of price determination. It is still normal practice in many Middle Eastern and Asian bazaars, where buyer and seller go through a process of determining each others' price limits before eventually converging on an agreed price. The seller will try to establish the maximum price that an individual is prepared to pay. To western tourists visiting these markets this may seem quite daunting, but the seller has doubtless worked out in his mind principles for negotiating. From previous experience, the seller may have come to recognize that such factors as the buyers' nationality, the size of their group, the length of time that they have been in the country, and their general appearance all give clues about the sales price that could be achieved. Although bartering is associated with many less-developed economies, it is typical of many high-value business-to-business sales elsewhere. There is also some evidence that it is making a resurgence in western consumer markets. It seems that individuals buying cars or hotel accommodation are increasingly prepared to haggle for a better price rather than accept the list price (*Daily Telegraph*, 2008).

Auctions are used where it is difficult for a seller to determine the maximum price that might be achieved for a product. Unlike bartering, which is carried out on a one-to-one basis, auctions involve many people bidding against each other for an item; the seller achieves the highest price based on what the highest bidder is prepared to pay. Although traditionally auctions have been associated with high-value, difficult-to-value items, such as art and unusual houses, the Internet has enabled a new generation of auctions selling relatively low-value items, such as the auction service provided by eBay (www.ebay.com). As well as consumer sales, Internet auctions have found a valuable role for business-to-business procurement. A company can put out a tender and invite suppliers to bid, following which it chooses the lowest price bidder.

Although bartering and auctions may seem an attractive method of extracting the maximum price from a seller, and therefore a good method of demand-based pricing, they do have problems. Price lists were developed in order to simplify the purchasing process, especially where high-volume, low-value goods are concerned. Going round Sainsbury's supermarket haggling over the price of every item of groceries would take up a lot of time and effort for buyer and seller alike. Anybody who has used an Internet auction site will appreciate the uncertainty created by the buying process, in which you may not know for some time whether you have got yourself a bargain or will have to start the purchase process all over again. For a seller, an auction may be good in the short term for clearing surplus stock, but in itself does nothing to develop strong brand values. In fact, auctions may treat a product like a commodity in which the only distinguishing feature is price.

Pricing a product range

Most organizations sell a range of products, and the price of each individual item should recognize the pricing strategy adopted for other products in the range. Some companies may have many thousands of individual items, for each of which a price must be set.

For any given product, a company can allocate the other items in its product range to one of three categories for the purposes of pricing.

1. **Optional additional items** are those that a buyer may or may not choose to add to the main product purchased, often at the time the main product is purchased. As a

matter of strategy, an organization could seek to charge a low lead-in price for the core product, but to recoup a higher margin from the additional optional items. Simply breaking a product into core and optional components may allow for the presentation of lower price indicators, which through a process of rationalization may be more acceptable to many customers. Research may show that the price of the core product is in fact the only factor that potential customers take into account when choosing between alternatives. In this way, mobile phone companies may cut the basic monthly charges for their calling plans, but make this up with higher prices for optional extras such as multi media message bundles, or insurance.

2. **Captive items** occur where the core product has been purchased and the provision of additional services can be provided only by the original provider of the core product. Where these are not specified at the outset of purchasing the core product, or are left up to the discretion of the supplier, the latter is in a strong position to charge a high price. Against this, the company must consider the effect that the perception of high exploitative prices charged for these captive items will have on customer loyalty when buyers are next considering the purchase of the core product. An example of captive product pricing is provided by many manufacturers of computer printers that sell their printers at a low initial price, but seek to make up for this through sales of ink cartridges. In 2002, the manufacturer Epson took this one stage further by fitting a chip to some of its printers that prevented users saving money by buying cheaper refill cartridges from other suppliers.

3. **Competing items** within the product range occur where a new product targets a segment of the population that overlaps the segments served by other products within the organization's mix. By a process of **cannibalization**, a company could find that it is competing with itself. In this way, a confectionery company with a large market share that launches a new organic chocolate bar may find that its new launch is taking sales away from its existing range of chocolate bars.

Price bundling

Price bundling is the practice of marketing two or more products in a single package for a single price. Bundling is particularly important for goods and services that have a high ratio of fixed to variable costs. Furthermore, where there is a high level of interdependency between different types of output from an organization, it may be difficult and meaningless to price each individual item. In this way, the provision of an ATM card and Internet banking become an interdependent part of the current bank account offering that most UK banks do not charge for separately.

Price bundling of diverse products from an organization's product mix is frequently used as a means of building relationships with customers. In this way a health insurance policy could be bundled with a travel insurance policy or a legal protection policy.

Where the bundle of service represents ease of administration to the consumer, the service organization may be able to achieve a price for the bundle that is greater than the combined price of the bundle's components.

Different groups of consumers have differing expectations about what they would expect to see in a price bundle. Car buyers in the UK, for example, expect a high level of equipment (radio, wheel trims, etc.) to be bundled in with the main price of a car, while many buyers in continental Europe would expect to pay for each item separately.

Pricing models

A pricing model reflects the fact that companies can generate revenue through a variety of combinations of the basic price and prices charged for optional additional items. Some price models may be sustainable by giving away a product at very low price initially, but then charge higher prices for essential items that are needed to make the product function (razor manufacturers may make only a small charge for the initial razor unit, but make more money out of selling the replacement blades, which are specific to that brand). Sometimes, the dominant pricing model in a market is challenged by a new entrant, with the result that consumers' expectations are changed. This was seen in the pricing models adopted for broadband services in the UK. Until 2006, the dominant model was for firms to charge a fixed monthly fee for broadband services, in addition to basic telephone line rental charges. But in that year, Carphone Warehouse introduced a new model with its 'Talk Talk' plan, in which broadband was given away for (almost) free, and the company made up for this with its pricing of line rental.

The pricing of public services

Many of the pricing principles discussed above, such as price discrimination and competitor-based pricing, may be quite alien to some public services. It may be difficult or undesirable to implement a straightforward price–value relationship with individual users of public services for a number of reasons.

- Pricing can be actively used as a means of social policy. Subsidized prices are often used to favour particular groups; for example, prescription charges favour the very ill and unemployed, among others. Sometimes the interests of marketing orientation and social policy can overlap. Charging lower prices for unemployed people to enter museums may provide social benefits for this group, while gaining additional revenue from a segment that might not otherwise have been able to afford a visit to the museum.

- Benefits to society at large may be as significant as the benefits received by the individual, so there may be a case for the government subsidizing low prices. Education and training courses may be provided at an uneconomic charge in order to add to the level of skills available within an economy generally.

Figure 9.21 Companies often bundle a number of products together and charge one inclusive price. Like many sellers of lunchtime snacks, the Co-op offers a discounted 'Meal Deal' to customers who buy a sandwich, a drink, and selected crisps/snack bars together. For many buyers, the 'Deal' price becomes the reference price which they use to compare prices between retailers. For the retailer, a bundled price offer encourages additional spending by the customer and the discounted price of the bundle is likely to be made up from the additional margin from selling three, rather than just one item. (Reproduced with permission of Oxford, Swindon, and Gloucester Co-op)

Figure 9.22 Road users within the UK have not generally been charged directly for the benefits they receive from the road system, largely because of the impracticality of road pricing and issues of equity between users. Instead, users have paid for the use of roads through direct and indirect taxation. However, with improved technology and growing realization of the social and economic costs of traffic congestion, there has been a move towards pricing the use of roads. The London Congestion Charge, introduced in 2003, provides evidence that pricing a public service can change consumers' behaviour, with traffic volumes falling by about 10% since the introduction of the charge.

Problems can occur in public services that have been given a largely financial, market-oriented brief, but in which social policy objectives are superimposed, possibly in conflict. Museums, leisure centres, and car park charges have frequently been at the centre of debate about the relative importance to be attached to economic and social objectives. Museums have sometimes overcome this dilemma by retaining free or nominally priced admission charges for the serious, scholarly elements of their exhibits, while offering special exhibitions which match the private sector in the standard of production and the prices charged.

Chapter summary and linkages to other chapters

This chapter began by discussing the underlying theory of price determination. Perfect competition is an idealized market structure which rarely occurs in its pure extreme, but the principles of such competition provide a relevant background to many of the pricing decisions made by marketers. Firms seek to create a distinctive product, which reduces the impact on them of intense price competition. Because imperfect markets are generally held to be against the public interest, various regulatory measures exist to improve the competitiveness of markets.

Where a company has developed a distinctive product, it becomes a price-maker rather than a price-taker. Its pricing behaviour will be influenced by its organizational objectives. Prices can be set in relation to production costs, the strength of demand, competitors' prices, or a combination of all three. Market segmentation (Chapter 6) is used to identify groups that may be able and willing to pay higher prices than average. Pricing strategy contributes towards a company's sustainable competitive advantage (Chapter 7). However, pricing must be closely related to a firm's product policy (Chapter 8), its distribution (Chapter 10), and its promotional strategies (Chapters 11) in order to create a coherent positioning for its products.

KEY PRINCIPLES OF MARKETING

- In competitive markets, prices are influenced by the interaction of supply and demand.
- Marketing seeks to develop a unique product which is subject to less direct competitive pressure and therefore allows marketers more discretion in setting prices.
- The maximum price that a company can charge is what customers are able and willing to pay (or what a government regulator will allow it to charge).
- Price should be distinguished from costs. Costs determine the minimum price that a company will charge.

A fair price for 'free' hospital treatment?

Organizations with a broad range of products often price different products within their portfolio in quite different ways. They may have developed a price 'model', which describes the way that it uses pricing of its product portfolio to maximize its overall revenue. So, one product may be charged at a very low price, on the assumption that this will bring in business which is then prepared to pay relatively high prices for related products. There are many examples of this practice in action, ranging from humble household goods, through to complex industrial equipment. A simple refillable air freshener unit may initially be sold at a very low price, but the refills sold at a much higher price. With a patent on the refills—preventing copycats undercutting its price—a manufacturer may benefit from several years of revenue from high-price refills, more than offsetting the low-priced base units which were sold as a 'loss leader'. In some sectors, a number of different pricing models co-exist. For example, in the emerging multi-channel television broadcasting market, some channels are provided free of charge to users, but make revenue from selling advertising space, while others charge a subscription to users, either on a monthly/annual basis, or a 'pay to view' basis. In the UK, the BBC provides a further model, where most services are provided without charge to users or advertising revenue. Instead, government provides funding.

The idea of a pricing model is familiar to private sector organizations, but do they have a role to play in the public sector? In the UK, pricing models are increasingly being discussed and developed for services which have previously been considered a vital service available freely to all. The National Health Service (NHS) has a long and proud tradition of providing health services to all, according to an individual's need, paid for out of general taxation, according to an individual's means. Pricing has historically had barely a role to play in the NHS. Both socialist and right-wing Conservative governments have encountered opposition when they suggested an American-style market-based approach to charging for health services. But from the 1990s, the need to increase revenue became a priority for cash-strapped NHS trusts, at a time when increasing demand for services was not fully matched by increased government funding. Could NHS Trusts copy some of the ideas of pricing models from the private sector?

Although the principle of a health service free at the point of use has been firmly enshrined in the minds of politicians and users, a number of charges have been introduced over the years, for example for prescriptions. However, these tended to be centrally determined with exemptions for those in greatest need. But from the mid-1990s, individual NHS trusts began exploiting charges for ancillary services as a means of boosting their revenue. One of the first targets for charging was users of hospitals' car parks. Trusts argued that providing car parks was not central to the mission of NHS Trusts, and conveniently, government was encouraging more people to use public transport and leave their cars at home. Critics argued that patients were essentially captive and public transport was not a realistic alternative for most people. What began for most hospitals as a small charge soon became a cash cow for hospital finance directors, mindful of the lack of alternatives available to patients. A House of Commons Health Select Committee investigation in 2006 found evidence that some patients did not go to hospital for treatment because of the cost of parking. It showed that at one hospital in London, a patient who attended A&E on the advice of her GP was charged £3.75 for the first two hours' use of the hospital car park and £7.50 thereafter. She was 10 minutes over the two-hour period and therefore had to pay the higher charge. She also questioned the fact that charges were reduced to £1 per hour after 6 p.m., when many hospital departments were closed. For private sector services, lower evening prices—when there is not much demand from customers, and plenty of spare capacity—is quite common. But is it right that a hospital should only charge lower prices at the very time when much of the hospital itself is closed? If lower prices are designed to stimulate additional demand, is this a realistic prospect when many hospital departments are only available between 9 a.m. and 5 p.m.?

Another source of revenue exploited by many hospital trusts comes from the use of bedside telephones by patients. Many trusts entered agreements with private telephone service providers that allowed incoming and outgoing patient calls only through the officially appointed system, which used a premium rate number. A proportion of the revenue was retained by the hospital. Conveniently, Hospital Trusts pointed to evidence that mobile phones could harm sensitive medical equipment, and therefore used this to eliminate competitive pressure from patients' mobile phones, forcing them to use the hospital's own telephone system. The ethics of hospital telephone pricing was challenged by the House of Commons Health Select Committee, which accused some trusts of using excessively long recorded messages at the beginning of each incoming and outgoing call, adding to patients' costs, and boosting hospitals revenues. It cited a hospital in Essex where people wishing to telephone patients were being charged 49p per minute at peak time and 39p off-peak. By comparison, a typical household rate for a long distance phone call was around 7p in the peak and 2p in the off-peak. One relative of a patient in a Gloucester hospital claimed to have run up a bill of nearly £1,200 for phoning a disabled patient in hospital. The select committee also expressed doubts about whether a ban on mobile phones in hospitals was actually a result of possible interference with medical equipment and recommended that visitors should be able to use mobile phones within certain areas of hospitals. By banning mobile phones, had hospitals been more concerned about creating a monopoly environment for pricing their telephone service, rather than any possible risk to their equipment?

Summing up, the Select Committee on Health described the system of NHS pricing as a mess, with Lord Lipsey of the Social Market Foundation describing it as 'a dog's dinner'. Successive governments had shied away from an overt market-based framework for pricing services provided by the NHS. However, it appeared that pricing was coming in through the back door, raising issues about the ethics of charging apparently exploitative prices that reflect patients' captivity. Or were managers of NHS Trusts simply being realistic and pragmatic, charging as much as they could for ancillary services so that they could invest more in what a hospital is essentially all about—providing better health treatments?

Source: based on *The Times,* 'Hospitals making £78m a year from car park charges', 18 July, 2006; House of Commons Health Select Committee, NHS Charges, 2006; NHS, 'Our NHS, our future', www.ournhs.nhs. uk/, accessed 20 June 2008.

Case study review questions

1. What do you understand by the concept of a 'pricing model'. Critically discuss their relevance to a public sector service such as the NHS.

2. What factors should influence the level of charges at an NHS car park?

3. If you are studying at a university or college, critically reflect on the pricing strategy that it has adopted for ancillary services.

CHAPTER REVIEW QUESTIONS

1. Critically assess methods used by companies to reduce the effects on them of intense price competition.

2. 'Elasticity of demand is a fine theoretical concept of economists, but difficult for marketers to use in practice.' Critically assess this statement.

3. What are the main challenges facing an oligopolist when determining prices? Is the task of an oligopolistic marketer more or less difficult than that of a marketing manager in a sector dominated by small businesses?

ACTIVITIES

1. Gather together price lists from a selection of any of the following services organizations in your area: sports centres; cinemas/theatres; restaurants. Analyse their pricing and the extent to which cost-based, customer-based, and competitor-based pricing is being applied.

2. Examine prices charged by a selection of public sector organizations with which you are familiar, for example, swimming pools, museums, and universities. Assess the extent to which prices are influenced by market forces as distinct from government social policy considerations.

3. Study the price list shown in Figure 9.20. What, if any, changes in pricing practice would you suggest, based on a similar service provider with which you are familiar?

REFERENCES

Bell, D. R., Iyer, G., and Padmanabhan, V. (2002), 'Price Competition under Stockpiling and Flexible Consumption'. *Journal of Marketing Research*, 39: 292–303.

Cyert, R. M. and March, J. G. (1963), *A Behavioural Theory of the Firm*. Cambridge, MA: Blackwell.

Daily Telegraph (2002), 'High-Price Airlines Fail to Get Message', 4 November, p. 36.

Daily Telegraph (2007), 'Wet Weather Compounds High Street Turmoil', 8 July.

Daily Telegraph, (2008), 'Ten simple tips to save money on your mobile', 16 June.

Jeffery, P. B. and Harris, C. (2006), 'The Effect of 9-Ending Prices on Retail Sales: a quantitative UK based field study'. *Journal of Marketing Management*, 22(5/6): 601–7.

Palmer, A. and Boissy, S. (2009), 'The effects of airline price presentations on buyers' choice'. *Journal of Vacation Marketing*, 15(1): 39–52.

Shugan, S. M. (2006), 'Are Consumers Rational? Experimental Evidence'. *Marketing Science*, 25(1) (January–February): 1–7.

▢ SUGGESTED FURTHER READING

This chapter has provided only a very brief overview of the principles of economics as they affect pricing. For a fuller discussion, the following texts provide more detailed frameworks:

Lipsey, R. G. and Chrystal, K. A. (2007), *Economics*, 11th edn. Oxford: Oxford University Press.

Begg, D. and Ward, D. (2006), *Economics for Business*. Maidenhead: McGraw-Hill.

Sloman, J. and Hinde, K. (2007), *Economics for Business*. London, FT Prentice Hall.

For an overview of pricing strategy as practised by marketers, the following provide useful insights:

Nagle, T. and Holden, R. (2001), *The Strategy and Tactics of Pricing*. Englewood Cliffs, NJ: Prentice-Hall.

Avlonitis, G. J. and Indounas, K. A. (2006), 'Pricing Practices of Service Organizations'. *Journal of Services Marketing*, 20(5): 346–56.

Trout, J. and Rivkin, S. (1998), 'Prices: simple guidelines to get them right'. *Journal of Business Strategy*, 19(6): 13–17.

▢ USEFUL WEB LINKS

Visit the Online Resource Centre for resources that are relevant to this chapter, including web links, multiple choice questions, and additional case studies:

www.oxfordtextbooks.co.uk/orc/palmer2e/

▢ KEY TERMS

- **Auctions**
- **Bartering**
- **Cannibalization**
- **Cartel**
- **Commodity market**
- **Cost-based pricing**
- **Customer lifetime pricing**

- Demand
- Economies of scale
- Elasticity of demand
- Equilibrium price
- Marginal cost pricing
- Market structure
- Monopoly
- Oligopoly
- Penetration pricing strategy
- Perfect competition
- Price bundling
- Price determination
- Price discrimination
- Price-maker
- Price-skimming strategy
- Price-taker
- Profit maximization

10

Channel intermediaries

CHAPTER OBJECTIVES

Most companies would encounter administrative and logistical problems if they tried to deliver their goods and services directly to each of their end consumers. Instead, companies more often than not use intermediaries to distribute their products. The first aim of this chapter is to develop an understanding of the 'place' element of the marketing mix and the role of intermediaries in making goods and services available to buyers, at a time and place that is convenient to them. Approaches to designing a channel of distribution and issues in the management and control of intermediaries are discussed.

The second part of the chapter considers *how* goods are physically moved between the producer and the end consumer. It seeks to develop an understanding of how efficient and effective distribution can add to a firm's competitive advantage. The chapter reviews the objectives of physical distribution management, strategic approaches to supply chain management, and the key elements of a physical distribution system. The influence of information technology (IT) on channels of distribution will become apparent as we proceed through the chapter.

Introduction

This chapter discusses issues concerning what is often called the 'place' (P) of the traditional marketing mix. Decisions about channel intermediaries (or 'middlemen', to use an outdated, yet user-friendly, term) and the management of physical distribution fall under this heading. 'Placing' products involves managing the processes supporting the flow of good or services from producers to consumers. The process has sometimes been described as developing the best 'routes to market' for a firm's products.

We shall examine the distribution of services later in this chapter, but most of our initial attention will focus on making goods available to buyers. Goods must be made available in the right quantity, in the right location, and at the times when customers wish to purchase them—all at an acceptable price (and cost to the producer and/or intermediary). Achieving these concurrent aims is not easy, but is essential for an organization wishing to gain a sustainable competitive advantage. There is evidence that the design of distribution channels can explain differences in marketing and sales performance (Löning and Besson, 2002).

Sometimes a manufacturer will decide to dispense with intermediaries altogether. The computer manufacturer Dell has pursued a distribution strategy which makes very little use of intermediaries, but instead relies on the company communicating directly with customers through advertising and direct mailshots (among others), and delivering computers directly from the company's factories to the buyer's home or office. But many companies have realized that not all buyers want to deal with the manufacturer, so they must develop multiple 'routes to market' involving intermediaries. Even Dell—which for a long time emphasized the benefits of dealing directly with the company—now sells its computers through a number of intermediaries. In the following pages we will explore the complex set of issues involved in managing distribution channels in today's fast-shifting economic environment.

What is a marketing channel?

A **marketing channel** has been defined by the American Marketing Association as:

a set of practices or activities necessary to transfer the ownership of goods, and to move goods, from the point of *production* to the point of *consumption* and, as such, which consists of all the *institutions* and all the *marketing* activities in the marketing process.

Channel **intermediaries** are those organizations that facilitate the distribution of goods to the ultimate customer. The roles of intermediaries, which are explored in the following section, may include taking physical ownership of products, collecting payment, and offering after-sales service. Since these activities can involve considerable risk and responsibility, it is clear that, in attempting to ensure the availability of their goods, producers must consider the needs of channel intermediaries as well as those of the end consumers. Marketing channel management refers to the choice and control of these intermediaries, although, as we shall see, the ability of manufacturers to exert influence over intermediaries such as retailers varies considerably, especially in channels for fast-moving consumer goods (FMCGs).

In addition to deciding who should be involved in a channel of distribution, it is important for marketing managers to understand the *overall* movement, storage, and availability of goods. Later in this chapter we will look at the physical distribution processes that allow goods to flow from materials suppliers to manufacturers and on to the end customer. In taking a wider perspective that extends beyond marketing channel considerations, it is common to visualize this entire **supply chain** as a *pipeline*.

The role of intermediaries in a value chain

The **value chain** was introduced in Chapter 2; it describes the activities involved in the manufacture, marketing, and delivery of a product or service by a firm (see Figure 10.1). You will recall that value can be added at all points in a value chain, from transformation of basic raw materials into components, and then into finished goods, and later through making those goods and services available at a time and place that is most highly valued by the buyer. Another way of looking at a value chain is as a supply chain. Although the two terms are not strictly synonymous, a value chain implies channels through which goods and services are supplied from the producer to the end consumer.

Marketing channels can perform an important role in the later stages of a value chain, in particular outbound logistics (e.g. order processing, storage, and transportation); marketing and sales (e.g. market research, personal selling, sales promotions), and after-sales service (e.g. repair, training, spare parts). It is rare for a producer to undertake all of these activities itself, and therefore the management of channel intermediaries, in terms of both minimizing costs and maximizing competitive advantage, plays a vital

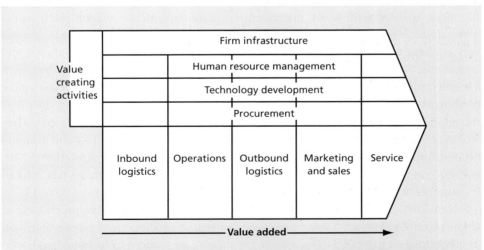

Figure 10.1 A value chain showing how value is progressively added to a product as different processes are preformed. Some of these processes may be performed more efficiently by intermediaries than by the manufacturing firm itself.

part in boosting the value added by any marketing channel. The concept of a value chain applies to services as well as goods, in fact many sources of added value are essentially service-based. Value chains can also exist in an Internet environment, even though no physical goods may be directly involved, as a service offer is jointly created by a number of different companies, for example an Internet travel agent can add value by providing choice to consumers (Porter, 2001).

In order to decide whether a firm should undertake its own distribution direct to consumers or whether it would be more efficient and effective to use intermediaries, it is necessary to understand the functions of intermediaries.

Functions of intermediaries

Perhaps the most significant role of channel intermediaries is to reconcile the differing needs of manufacturers and consumers. Essentially, producers like to produce their product in bulk in order to achieve economies of scale, whereas consumers may typically just want to buy one or two units. Furthermore, the producer would typically prefer to make the product in one central location where production economies can be maximized, whereas the buyer wants the product to be available close to them, where their own costs of obtaining the product are minimized.

Intermediaries' play a valuable role by reducing this *discrepancy of assortment* between what the producer wants to produce and what the buyer wants to buy. They do this by reducing dramatically the number of contacts required between suppliers and the end customers. If a manufacturer had to deal with each consumer individually, they would have to maintain thousands, possibly millions of individual distribution channels. Furthermore, if there were many manufacturers competing in the market, each would maintain large numbers of direct channels. For low-value, high-volume goods, it is not very efficient to have such a large number of lines of contact between producers and consumers. This pattern could be greatly simplified if the manufacturers only dealt with a smaller number of intermediaries, rather than the thousands or millions of individual consumers. There is a further benefit to consumers, because they could now go to any of the intermediaries and obtain a selection of products from a number of producers. They would not have to go to each producer separately. Take a look at Figure 10.2 and it should become apparent that the use of intermediaries greatly simplifies communication between a company and its customers, In this case, the use of intermediaries has reduced the number of potential channels between producers and consumers from 30 to 13.

Intermediaries can add value by breaking bulk. This might involve purchasing in large quantities from a manufacturer and then selling smaller, more manageable, volumes of stock on to retailers. *Discrepancies of quantity* are reduced by intermediaries who provide consumers with individual items that suit their needs.

In many cases, intermediaries can offer superior knowledge of a target market compared with manufacturers. Retailers can therefore add value to the producer's goods by

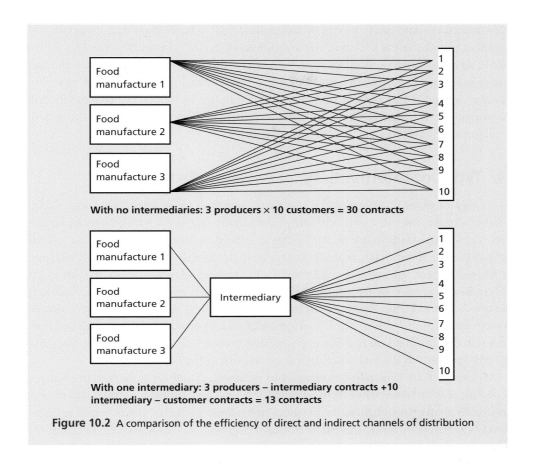

With no intermediaries: 3 producers × 10 customers = 30 contracts

With one intermediary: 3 producers – intermediary contracts +10 intermediary – customer contracts = 13 contracts

Figure 10.2 A comparison of the efficiency of direct and indirect channels of distribution

tailoring their offerings more closely to the specific requirements of consumers, for example by ensuring that goods are stocked that match the economic and lifestyle needs of shoppers who live in the area.

Intermediaries might also offer after-sales services in the form of guarantees and customer advice hotlines. If these services can be provided with a high level of expertise, then manufacturers may feel able to relinquish control of these parts of the value chain. Ahmad and Buttle (1998) described the relationship between a foreign-based manufacturer of office equipment (fax machines, photocopiers, printers, etc.) and its UK dealers. The manufacturer provided basic service training for the dealers' technical staff and allowed the dealers to sell consumables such as toners. More complex repair queries, however, were handled by a head office telephone helpline for both dealers and end users.

Probably the most important gaps between consumers and producers in channel management are those of location and time. A *location gap* occurs owing to the geographic separation of producers and the consumers of their goods and services. Goods manufacturers (and many service providers) generally want to produce their goods and services in one central location, but consumers typically want to buy them locally. A *time gap* arises when consumers want to purchase products at a time when a manufacturer may consider it inconvenient to make them available. Manufacturers may like producing goods and services from 9 a.m. to 5 p.m. on weekdays, but consumers may want to buy in the evenings or at weekends. Intermediaries can facilitate the task of making goods and services available at these times.

Types of intermediary

A variety of types of intermediary can participate in a value chain. For most FMCG manufacturers, the two most commonly used intermediaries are **wholesalers** and retailers. These organizations are normally described as **distributors** (or 'merchants'), since they take title to products, typically building up stocks and thereby assuming risk, and then resell them. Wholesalers sell to other wholesalers and retailers; retailers sell to the ultimate consumers. Other intermediaries, such as agents and brokers, do not take title to goods. Instead, they arrange exchanges between buyers and sellers and in return receive commissions or fees. The use of agents often involves less of a financial and contractual commitment by the manufacturer and is therefore less of a risk, but their lack of commitment to the manufacturer can sometimes be problematic.

Wholesalers are typically less obvious to us as individual consumers than retailers, but they play an important role in servicing retailers (in consumer markets) and organizational clients (in industrial or business-to-business markets). It can prove prohibitively expensive for a manufacturer of industrial goods, such as a simple bolt fastening, to maintain a large sales force. In this case, access to a wide range of industrial customers may be facilitated more efficiently via a few specialist wholesalers. Smaller retailers are often serviced by wholesalers specializing in sourcing and selecting stock for a particular product line. These wholesalers can offer detailed product knowledge and in-store merchandising services to retailers.

Classification of retailers

We now turn our attention to retailing, which represents a highly visible form of intermediary. A **retailer** is simply an organization that buys products for the purpose of reselling them to end consumers. Having said this, a number of different types of retailer may be identified.

- **Department stores**, e.g. Debenhams. Here, we find product lines laid out into separate departments, such as ladies' and men's clothing, home furnishings, cosmetics, etc. Companies may operate as 'shops-within-shops' and pay rent as a percentage of takings to the host store.

- **Supermarkets**, e.g. Sainsbury's. These are large, self-service stores carrying a very wide range of FMCGs. They are typically located in out-of-town retail parks, although many supermarket chains have recently opened smaller city-centre sites. The supermarket chains are often the first with new customer initiatives such as loyalty cards and in-store bakeries. Low prices based on large-scale efficiency are hard for smaller independent stores to match.

- **Discount sheds or 'category killers'**, e.g. Toys 'R' Us. These stores often stock bulky items such as furniture and electrical goods. The 'category killer' terminology results from the tendency of some very large specialist stores to put competing independent retailers out of business.

- **Speciality shops**, e.g. clothing (Next), music (HMV), mobile phones (Carphone Warehouse). These are typically found in central business districts of towns where prime sites are vitally important. As it is frequently only the large national chains that can afford the high rents of such sites, it might be said that many UK High Streets are now very similar in the choice they offer to the shopper.

- **Convenience stores**, e.g. Spar, 7-Eleven. Geographically, and also in terms of the range of products on offer, these stores fill the gap between edge-of-town supermarkets and the 'traditional' corner shops situated close to housing estates. While independently-owned convenience stores have tended to decline in number in recent years, the major UK supermarket operators have expanded into this area.

- **Cash-and-carry warehouses,** e.g. Costco. These usually offer cheaper groceries and durable goods to consumers or catering trades and small retailers.

- **Catalogue showrooms**, e.g. Argos. These stores lower their costs by maintaining only a limited display of goods, with consumers making their selection via a catalogue and collecting their purchase from a stockroom attached to the store.

- **Market traders**. These remain significant outlets for many low-value products. Although they have generally declined in importance in recent years, some types of market, e.g. farmers' markets, have expanded.

- **Online retailers**. Some online retailers, e.g. amazon.com, have no physical shops that interface with the public. However, most online retailing is in fact accounted for by 'bricks and mortar' retailers. (For example, it is reported that the supermarket operator Tesco was the biggest online retailer in the UK in 2006, measured by value of online sales (Deloitte, 2006).)

Within these differing types of store, we can find some interesting trends. One of the most significant changes in retailing structure has been the increased proportion of trade taken by large multiple store retail chains. In the grocery sector, multiples are usually defined as retailers with over ten outlets. This change has taken place largely at the expense of independent retailers, but has also eroded the market share of the cooperatives. It is notable that, collectively, the cooperative societies represent one of the largest

Figure 10.3 New forms of retailing are continually emerging. One recent innovation in the UK is the outlet mall, which sells a range of brand-name products at clearance prices. For shoppers, outlet malls, such as this one in Bicester, Oxfordshire, have been developed into day-out attractions in their own right, attracting visitors from a wide area. For retailers and manufacturers, they provide an opportunity to sell old-season stock which would otherwise clutter their High Street outlets.

retailers in the country. The problem for the Co-op is that it comprises a large number of mostly autonomous societies and does not pool its buying resources into a fully integrated retailing organization. Independent retail stores are typically run by a sole trader or as a family business. Changing social trends conspire against the independent convenience store, which is constantly having to look for ways to differentiate itself, usually through flexible opening hours and specialist **inventory**. One response of independent retailers has been to form voluntary or 'symbol' groups where buying and marketing is provided centrally in return for the retailers buying a proportion of their goods from particular wholesalers. Examples include Spar and Happy Shopper for groceries, and Euronics for electrical goods.

Designing a channel of distribution

Manufacturers need to take a holistic view of distribution, and to adopt a 'channel vision' to maximize their opportunities to reach customers. The starting point for designing a channel of distribution should be a producer's distribution objectives. These should be derived from the organization's positioning strategy and must be consistent with the remaining marketing mix tools used by the marketing manager to gain a sustainable competitive advantage (see Chapter 7). For example, a strategy to sell large volumes of a low-priced FMCG in a fiercely competitive market may be inconsistent with a distribution strategy which concentrates on just a small number of retailers.

We can identify three approaches to designating a channel of distribution:

1. **Intensive distribution**: This is generally used for FMCGs and other relatively low-priced or impulse purchases. Put very simply, the more outlets that are stocking your product, the greater the likelihood of its being bought. The convenience factor is often very important for these goods. An interesting development here is the increasing range of products available from petrol stations—everything from groceries to snacks and gifts. In terms of the discrepancies of assortment and location discussed earlier, a highly intensive distribution network with wide geographical cover can prove extremely efficient. Although not a conventional 'product', consider the huge number and variety of outlets where National Lottery tickets may be bought.

2. **Exclusive distribution**: Here, distribution may be limited to a small number of intermediaries that manage to gain better margins and exclusivity. In return, the manufacturer seeks more control over how the product is marketed, and there is likely to be dedicated merchandising and sales support from the retailer. The intermediary may also agree not to stock competing lines. This is often done for expensive products with an up-market brand image, such as Oakley sunglasses or designer label clothing. Manufacturers can become upset when retailers whom they see as not having the appropriate brand image attempt to stock their products or, worse, offer them at discounted prices. This can be seen in the reaction of the perfume industry to Superdrug's stocking of fine fragrances, or Calvin Klein's protests at Tesco selling its underwear range.

3. **Selective distribution**: This represents a compromise between intensive and exclusive distribution. The manufacturer is looking for adequate market coverage, but still hopes to select supportive dealers. This usually occurs for 'shopping' products such as audio and video hardware.

Influences on channel selection

There are a number of key influences on channel selection strategies.

1. First, the expectations of the **end customer** must be addressed. Do they expect to buy locally, or are they prepared to travel to a retailer that stocks a product? This might mean taking into consideration factors such as a geographical preference to buy locally, or a tendency to feel more comfortable visiting a particular type of store.

Do they expect the retailer to be capable of undertaking warranty repairs? Decisions must be made based on sound marketing research into buyer behaviour patterns (see Chapters 4 and 5). This is also true for business-to-business markets. For example, suppliers of electronic components need to determine whether business customers prefer to deal with the company's direct sales force (often the case for larger organizational clients with expert purchasing departments) or with a specialist distributor (typically used by smaller clients without this in-house expertise). In international markets, it may be essential to use an agent with an intimate knowledge of the cultural nuances of doing business in target countries (see Chapter 13).

2. **Producer-related factors** include a number of issues in addition to the distribution levels sought. An important constraint is the resources that are available to the manufacturer to bring the product to market. Some companies lack the finances to recruit and reward a sales force and so will use a wholesaler or agent instead. This is often the case for companies making a very narrow range of products. Also critical is what the manufacturer believes to be its core competence. If, for instance, this is the design and production of innovative goods, then the distribution of these goods may well be better left to a specialist channel intermediary. Another consideration is the desired level of channel control sought by the manufacturer.

3. **Product attributes** can be important. Fresh produce that is highly perishable requires fairly short channels. Northern Foods, a manufacturer of chilled meals for Marks & Spencer, claims that it takes just 24 hours from the time a fresh egg arrives at the factory to its appearance in a custard tart on the shelves of an M&S store anywhere in the country. Heavy or large goods are frequently not suited to inner-city retail locations where consumers cannot easily drive to pick up their purchases: instead, they may be more suitable to out-of-town retailers or sold to order via direct distribution. Some products may be so complex that personal contact between producer and buyer is essential. This can be the case for the installation of highly technical machinery.

4. Finally, the activities of the **competition** must be considered. If competitors have exclusive deals with intermediaries, the choices open to a new market entrant seeking to place its products may be limited. Beverage manufacturers seeking to build distribution have often encountered refrigerator exclusivity deals between small retailers and the major suppliers such as Coca Cola, preventing them getting immediate access to such stores. In fact, such agreements are increasingly being scrutinized by competition regulators, and outlawed where they are held to be an anti-competitive practice. Sometimes, a manufacturer's most significant competitor is the 'own label' product of the supermarket itself. When this happens, it can be very difficult to gain retailer support, as shown by the battles of Coca Cola to gain what it saw as adequate display space in Sainsbury's. A solution may be for the manufacturer to target convenience stores instead, or to set up alternative distribution channels such as company-owned chilled vending machines.

Figure 10.4 Alternative channel structures for consumer markets

Channel alternatives

Figure 10.4 shows some alternative *consumer* channels. Channel A represents a direct producer-to-consumer channel, using **direct marketing** techniques (e.g. Dell, Avon Cosmetics). Channel B represents the producer–retailer–consumer route. This is typically used by large retailers such as Sainsbury's, who have the buying power to order large quantities of goods direct from manufacturers with no need of a further middleman. The addition of the wholesaler in Channel C is more commonly used by smaller retailers with relatively small order quantities and, from the producer's perspective, by manufacturers of convenience goods, such as cigarettes, which need intensive distribution. The even longer structure of Channel D, with the inclusion of agents, is often used by producers entering foreign markets, where a local agent's expertise may be essential to overcome trade barriers (see Chapter 13).

Figure 10.5 shows alternative channels used in order to reach *industrial* (business-to-business) customers. In general, these channels are shorter than those for consumer goods.

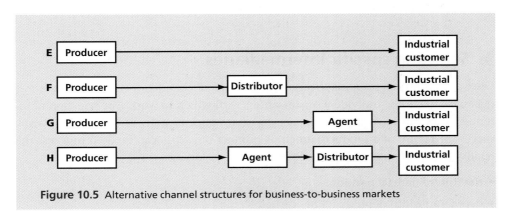

Figure 10.5 Alternative channel structures for business-to-business markets

The shortest structure, that of Channel E, represents the direct manufacturer-to-customer course. This is a viable alternative for many high-value industrial products, as customer numbers here are fewer and often less geographically widespread than for consumer markets. Channels for large, expensive, and highly technical products such as railway engines, the development of which may require the solving of considerable mechanical problems, frequently follow this pattern.

Channel F represents the manufacturer–industrial distributor–customer route. It is used for more frequently purchased, less expensive products that are required by a wider range of industrial customers, for example tools used by garage repair workshops. The use of an agent, as in Channel G, can occur when a manufacturer chooses not to set up its own dedicated sales force, and has therefore to 'outsource' the agent's marketing and selling services. This can be a relatively quick option, but, as we have noted previously, the support offered by agents may be less than that provided by a title-taking distributor. Finally, the lengthier structure of Channel H may arise when it is found that organizational buyers in a particular market prefer to use nearby distributors. This can happen when customers need to be resupplied frequently, for instance with paper used by office photocopiers.

◼ Multiple channels

In reality, many producers use a combination of channels to distribute their goods. Think of the many different places you can purchase a can of Coca Cola, for instance. Also, some manufacturers, such as those in the personal computer sector, sell to both consumers and organizations. There is rarely one simple solution to the decision concerning which channel type should be selected by a company. Indeed, bearing in mind the power of some retailers, the problem for producers often comes down to: which channel intermediary will select *us*? This complexity is explored further in the following section.

◼ Selecting specific intermediaries

Once a decision has been made regarding the type of channel or channels to use, it is necessary to choose individual organizations with which to work. The selection of intermediaries can have a major impact on what happens afterwards, for example the success or failure of a product launch. A number of *criteria* can be used to assess the relative merits of potential channel participants, including:

* the firm's financial position;
* depth and width of product lines carried;

- whether competitive lines are carried;
- evidence of marketing, sales, and promotional ability;
- approach to order processing and order fulfilment;
- evidence of investment in new technologies;
- reputation within industry;
- willingness to share data;
- local market knowledge.

Some of these selection criteria may be particularly important to the company, for example if it is entering a completely new market, and intermediaries' local knowledge may be critical.

The issue can arise of *reverse selection* in a channel of distribution, in which the intermediary effectively selects the producer, rather than the other way round. This is becoming increasingly common among large supermarket chains, who may design a new food product in their research laboratories, then approach different specialist meal manufacturers for their ability to mass-produce the products to the supermarket's specification. The flexibility of such manufacturers as S&A Foods in providing Asian-style chilled meals to order, as well as in developing their own recipes, has resulted in the growth of a number of large food manufacturers whose products are sold under supermarkets' own labels, with customers completely unfamiliar with the identity of the manufacturer (e.g. Northern Foods and Samworth Brothers).

Power and conflict within distribution channels

From the previous discussion, it is clear that some members of the distribution channel may have dominant power over the others. Sometimes, this may be a manufacturer who has a strong brand which retailers feel they must stock in order to satisfy the expectations of their customers. Increasingly though, it is the retailers themselves who are exercising power within the channel. If power is used in a manner believed to be unfair by one or more channel members, then conflict may arise. Conflict need not necessarily be destructive, since it can encourage managers to question the *status quo* and find ways of improving their distribution systems. Sometimes, however, strategies employed by firms can create unstable, adversarial relationships between producers and intermediaries. The following are examples of conflict which may arise in channels:

- **Bypassing channels**: a producer may seek to cut out intermediaries by dealing directly with the public. Retailers may feel aggrieved that they have opened up a market for the producer, but are now cut out of any resulting benefit.

- **Over-saturation**: a manufacturer may be accused of using too many distributors within a given geographical area, making it difficult for any individual distributor to achieve a satisfactory level of sales.

- **Too many links**: in the supply chain: an intermediary may be required to buy stocks from a larger dealer, who may be perceived as a competitor, rather than a co-operative channel member.

- **New channels**: these can have a similar effect to bypassing an intermediary, for example many manufacturers have opened up Internet sales channels, thereby taking sales away from established intermediaries.

- **Cost-cutting**: in order to increase volume sales, a manufacturer may seek to distribute through higher volume, low cost intermediaries, which may make it more difficult for a smaller, full service intermediary to sell that product.

- **Inconsistency**: appearing arbitrarily to treat some intermediaries more favourably than others, for example through incentives and rewards.

In recent years, power in UK distribution channels has tended to pass to a small number of dominant retailers and away from manufacturers. The growing strength of grocery retailers has put them at the focal point of a value chain. By building up their own strong brands, large retailers are increasingly able to exert pressure on manufacturers in terms of product specification, price, and the level of promotional support to be given to the retailer. According to market research group TNS Worldpanel, the UK's big four grocery retailers—Tesco, Asda, Sainsbury's, and Morrisons—now account for more than three-quarters (76.2%) of the grocery market. However, while many manufacturers may be dependent on the big four retailers for their sales, this dependency is not reciprocated, with very few retailers relying on one single supplier for more than 1% of their supplies. Most countries have legislation which prevents one company having dominant power in a market, unless there are public interest benefits.

Some evidence of the power of grocery retailers was provided in a 2008 report by the UK Competition Commission on supermarkets (Competition Commission, 2008). It found evidence of the large supermarkets using their dominant position retrospectively to demand discounts from suppliers, who felt obliged to pay, for fear of losing a large contract. It also highlighted how supermarkets had used their power to charge the cost of shoplifting to manufacturers, when the manufacturers' products were stolen while in the supermarket. The Competition Commission argued that the retailers were transferring excessive risk to suppliers, and proposed a new ombudsman, dubbed 'Offshop', to investigate grievances by suppliers at the hands of supermarkets. The new regulator would be able to hear and investigate complaints from farmers and any other traders in the grocery supply chain, including abattoirs, dairies, processors, the food service industry, wholesalers, and manufacturers.

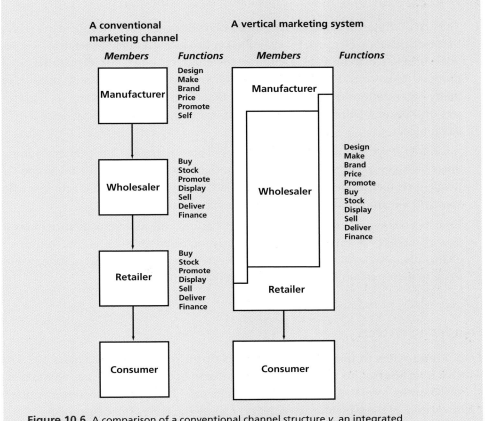

Figure 10.6 A comparison of a conventional channel structure *v.* an integrated distribution channel
Source: adapted from D. J. Kollat, R. D. Blackwell, and J. F. Robeson, *Strategic Marketing*, New York: Rinehart & Winston, 1972, p. 321.

🌰 Integrated distribution channels

It follows from the previous discussion of conflict, that channel participants may be keen to integrate their functions, in order to reduce conflict and improve efficiency and effectiveness. An integrated channel is seen as having a number of advantages over a channel where the individual components operate quite independently (see Figure 10.6):

- they reduce channel costs by eliminating duplication of functions;
- they minimize conflict among channel members;
- they maximize the experience and expertise of members.

There are three general types of integrated marketing channel:

1. The first of these, the *corporate* system, involves one company owning many stages in the distribution channel, for example a coffee producer may own farms, wholesalers or retailers to provide it with raw materials, or outlets for its manufactured product. This form of channel integration is becoming increasingly rare, since many organizations either cannot afford to, or do not wish to, invest in fixed assets or skills at a point in the value chain where they do not have a competitive advantage.

2. *Administered* systems arise when participants are financially independent but are effectively controlled by the most powerful channel member. In the UK, most independent retailers of new cars are very closely managed by car manufacturers, who specify the manner in which their cars are sold.

3. In *contractual* systems channel members' rights and obligations are defined by legal agreements. These can include collaborative agreements such as the voluntary chains discussed earlier in this chapter, where separate firms share resources and agree to joint purchasing initiatives and franchise arrangements.

Franchising systems

Franchising refers to trading relationships between companies (see Figure 10.7) in which a franchisor grants the right to a franchisee to operate a business using the franchisor's business format. The franchisor and franchisee have legally separate identities, but the nature of the franchise agreement can make them very interdependent.

Franchising is a rapidly growing type of business relationship. According to the annual Nat West/British Franchise Association annual survey, the total number of franchise systems in the UK in 2005 was 718. These were linked to a total of 31,300 franchisees, with an annual turnover of £9.1 billion and employed an estimated 327,000 people (British Franchise Association, 2006).

Franchising offers both manufacturer/retailers and entrepreneurial intermediaries the opportunity to undertake relatively rapid market development at relatively low risk. Consequently, for many companies operating internationally, franchising has become the cornerstone of their global expansion activity. Having said this, problems in controlling standards among individual franchisees can occur. This, for example, is claimed to have contributed to the failure of some of the Body Shop's outlets in France. When this takes place, the image of the franchisor can be seriously dented. From a different perspective, Benetton's franchisees in Germany were outraged at the company's controversial advertising campaigns, which they blamed for poor sales. Bitter disputes can develop where franchisor and franchisee differ in their assessment of the costs and benefits associated with their involvement in a franchise.

Figure 10.7 Domino's Pizza is now recognized as the world's leading pizza delivery company.
Founded in 1960, Domino's makes and delivers nearly 6 million pizzas a week in more than 60 countries
around the world. By 2006, it had 8,190 stores serving a total of over 1 million pizzas a week. From
humble beginnings in 1960, franchising has been a key element of the company's mission to bring
pizza to the world. By 2007, 85% of its outlets were owned by franchisees. The UK was an early target
for Domino's expansion, and it established a subsidiary company, Domino's Pizza Group Ltd, which
holds the exclusive master franchise to own, operate, and franchise Domino's Pizza stores in the UK
and Ireland. For Domino's, franchising allowed the company to expand quickly, by using the capital and
entrepreneurship of independent franchisees. And in 2004, Domino's reported that ten of its
100+ UK and Ireland franchisees owned businesses which were worth more than £1,000,000 each.
Domino's franchisees earned around £120,000 a year on average (although some considerably more)
which was more than three times the average income of a typical business manager (£38,107).
Although franchising is the dominant form of distribution for Domino's, the company retains a
proportion of directly managed outlets. As well as providing an internal benchmark against which
franchisees can be judged, these outlets are useful for developing new service ideas which may be too
risky for individual franchisees to undertake on their own. One outcome of this process has been the
development of a bluetooth and GPS-enabled system which can pinpoint a pizza delivery person's
exact location via satellite. Information can then be transmitted to the delivery person's bluetooth
headset, providing advice about the best route to take to their next customer. Would such
developments be possible without the support of a strong centrally managed franchise?
(*Source*: © Domino's Pizza Group Ltd. All rights reserved)

Global channels of distribution

Increasingly, channels of distribution are designed to cross national borders. There are a number of reasons for this. Retailers, who we have seen now have increasing power in a value chain, have sourced their goods from overseas countries where costs can be considerably lower than production at home. In recent years, retailers such as Tesco and Primark have been able to compete with extremely low prices, such as a pair of jeans for £5.00, or an expresso coffee machine for just £6.00, because they have sourced these from the cheapest manufacturers in the world. If the lowest price of a delivered pair of jeans involves manufacture in the Philippines, then the retailer's supply chain must be extended back to incorporate overseas manufacturers. We will consider logistics later in this chapter, when it will become evident that part of the retailer's competitive advantage lies not just in obtaining a cheaper pair of jeans at the factory gate, but also shipping it quickly and cheaply to its shelves.

The second reason for channels of distribution becoming increasingly international derives from retailers' desire to operate at an international, rather than purely national or regional scale. By operating internationally, retailers can achieve significant economies of scale through buying in bulk more cheaply; spreading the cost of product design over a greater range of output; and extending their management skills across a large network of outlets. Many west European retailers have moved into less developed markets, where their skills of inventory control, merchandising, and information technology can shake up the local market.

There are many examples of retailers who have sought to become truly global, including America's Wal-Mart, Britain's Tesco, and France's Carrefour. However, many retailers have encountered problems in overseas markets, where the business environment may be quite different to what they have been used to. Even Tesco, which has successfully developed stores in eastern Europe and the Far East, is reported to have faced problems when it sought to develop its 'Fresh and Easy' convenience stores in the United States (*Financial Times*, 2008a).

We will return to the subject of global marketing in Chapter 13.

The Internet and channel design

The trend towards direct delivery from producer to consumer has been speeded up by the growth of Internet access. Although 'bricks and mortar' companies may have been a little late into the fray, they are now doing well compared to some dot.com start-ups. According to websites listing the top UK retail sites traditional 'bricks and mortar' retailers are very well represented. Many high street names have transformed themselves into 'clicks and mortar' companies, including Argos (general household goods), Tesco (groceries), Comet (electrical appliances), PCWorld (computers), WHSmith (books and stationery). Many offer a variety of options including 'buy on line and pick up from store' which gives them an advantage. Although research estimates and sales forecasts vary widely, most agree that travel is the largest e-retailing sector by far.

Some retailers have closed a number of branches or reduced their sales force and instead offer customers access to their product range via a website. Several UK suppliers of books, music, computer games, and flowers have the logistical support to develop their business on the Internet. In the longer term, it is possible that FMCG suppliers may use the Internet to regain some of their lost power in channel relationships. Car manufacturers are recognizing the impact of the Internet on their traditional dealership-based channels of distribution, with evidence that the Internet is increasingly being used for selecting new cars.

However, while the Internet may facilitate direct communication between producers and end-consumers, the chances of dialogue actually taking place are lessened by the proliferation of content on the Internet, which presents a bewildering array of choice to consumers. The response has been the development of a new breed of information intermediary, or 'infomediary'. The new generation of infomediaries has effectively become a new form of value-adding member in a virtual value chain. Within the travel and financial services sectors, airlines' and insurance companies' attempts to create direct dialogue with customers have often been overshadowed by the development of powerful infomediaries such as lastminute.com, Expedia.com, and esure.com.

The advance of the Internet as a distribution channel has been affected by the speed with which consumer and commercial buyers have adopted the medium. There is considerable evidence that young people have been more ready to adopt the medium than older people. In a study using a technology acceptance model, it was found that consumers' perceived ease of use was affected by a range of factors, including opinion leadership, impulsiveness, shopping orientation, and perceived web security (O'Cass and Fenech, 2003).

Of course, it is not just in business-to-consumer markets that the Internet is reshaping distribution channels. In business-to-business channels, the Internet (and intranets and extranets) have replaced previous EDI systems for handling transactions between businesses. Government and not-for-profit organizations have also incorporated the Internet into their distribution channels, both for procuring purchases (Timmins, 2003) and for making services available to users. (For example, NHS Direct makes medical advice available to the public through call centres and the Internet.)

Despite the enormous potential of the Internet to simplify communication between a company and its customers without recourse to intermediaries, problems of final delivery remain where tangible goods are involved (see Yrjölä, 2001). There are also many high-involvement goods where buyers feel more comfortable being able to see and feel the goods before they commit to a purchase. The failed Internet clothes retailer boo.com encountered the reality that many people would probably find it much easier and reassuring

Figure 10.8 The Internet has opened up a powerful distribution channel by which a company can communicate directly with each of its customers, providing rapid, low-cost distribution which need not involve intermediaries. The budget airline easyJet has embraced the Internet and claims to be the 'Web's favourite airline', with over three-quarters of the airline's customers using the company's website for booking their tickets. The company boasts that it does not pay commission to intermediaries, and can pass on these savings in the form of lower ticket prices. (*Source:* Reproduced with permission of easyJet Airline Co. Ltd)

to try on clothes in a shop than rely on a computer image, thereby ensuring a continuing role for traditional High Street retailers (although 'bricks and clicks' retailers such as Next have quietly developed a substantial level of clothes sales via their website).

Physical distribution management

A channel of distribution must support the task of moving goods from the producer to the consumer so that the right goods are available to the right people in the right place at the right time. This must be done as cheaply as possible. In other words, the distribution must be both *efficient* and *effective*. Physical distribution also concerns most services organizations that have to move supporting goods (e.g. supplies of brochures for travel agents; supplies of burgers for a fast-food chain). In western countries we have often come to take for granted that our favourite products will be on the shelves in a shop when we visit. Business buyers have come to depend on the prompt delivery of inputs to their production process. But when physical distribution goes wrong, customers will soon notice, and the financial effects on a company whose distribution has failed can be harsh, even threatening the survival of the company. During 2001, the children's retailer Mothercare opened a new UK distribution centre at Daventry. The aim was to increase the efficiency and effectiveness of deliveries to the company's nationwide store network. In reality, poor IT systems caused stock to be lost within its system instead of getting 'hot' products to the shelves where customers were eager to buy them. By the time they had arrived, market preferences had changed and goods had to be sold at discounted 'clearance' prices. As a direct result of its distribution problems, the company was forced to issue a series of profit warnings and its share price slumped, threatening the continued independent existence of the company (Keers, 2002).

In the next few pages, as well as examining the movement of goods between producers and these downstream channel participants, we shall also be considering the flow of raw materials and components from suppliers that are *upstream* from the manufacturer. Furthermore, we shall explore the vital role played by the flow of information between supply chain members, as shown in Figure 10.9. In the figure, second-tier suppliers usually provide the raw materials (e.g. plastic resin) for first-tier suppliers to convert to component parts (e.g. steering wheels), which are then manufactured into the end product (e.g. cars) by the producer. Note that not all supply chains will contain both tiers of suppliers: we shall discuss more examples of supply chains later.

Let us begin with some definitions, and attempt to show how the terms 'physical distribution' and 'logistics' differ. **Physical distribution** refers to the movement of finished goods outward from the end of the manufacturer's assembly line to the customer, frequently via intermediaries. Functions under this heading can include warehousing, transport (often undertaken by third-party specialists), customer service, and administration. **Logistics** describes the entire process of materials and products moving into, through, and out of a firm. The US Council of Logistics Management (CLM) has defined

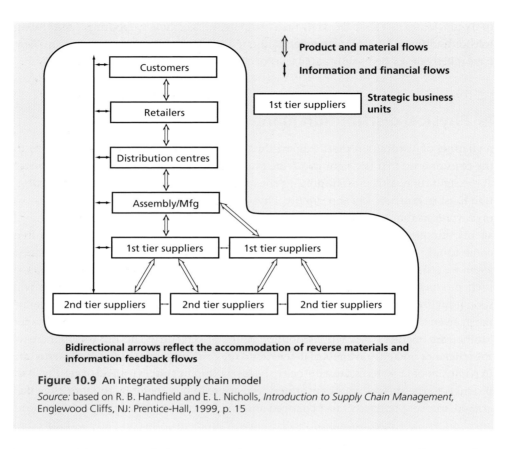

Figure 10.9 An integrated supply chain model

Source: based on R. B. Handfield and E. L. Nicholls, *Introduction to Supply Chain Management,* Englewood Cliffs, NJ: Prentice-Hall, 1999, p. 15

logistics as 'the process of planning, implementing and controlling the efficient, effective flow and storage of goods, services and related information from the point of origin to the point of consumption for the purposes of conforming to customer requirements'. Physical distribution may therefore be seen as 'outbound logistics', while 'inbound logistics' covers the movement of materials from suppliers and is closely linked to the manufacturer's purchasing or procurement function. 'Materials and inventory management' describes the movement and stockholding of goods within a firm.

It should also be remembered that distribution is often a two-way process. Most companies have to deal with customers' returns, and a facility to move these backwards through the distribution chain should be incorporated (Nairn, 2003). Increasingly, legislation is requiring companies to recycle used products, requiring collection and return services.

Physical distribution objectives

As with all elements of the marketing mix, the ultimate objective of a firm's physical distribution management is to develop a sustainable competitive advantage. However, this is becoming increasingly difficult as customers, instead of just seeking a better designed product, seek value in a much wider sense. A critical component of such customer value is *service*, and a key part of service value is *availability*. In other words, there is no value in a product until it is in the hands of the customer. Recall in Chapter 8 that it was noted that 'service dominant logic' holds that goods only have *value in use*, in other words they are of no value until they are actually made available to the end user (Vargo and Lusch, 2004).

Customers often only have a *preference* for a particular brand, rather than strong brand loyalty; so when their preferred brand is not available, many customers will quite readily choose an acceptable substitute. This is equally true in both business-to-business and consumer markets. The choice of suppliers by a just-in-time (JIT—see below) manufacturer will be greatly influenced by delivery reliability, and not just product quality.

Companies that are responsive to customers' needs must also focus on *time* as a source of competitive advantage. Essentially, the less time it takes for a company—or indeed an entire supply chain—to do things, the more flexible it can be in response to changes in the marketplace. The clothes retailer Primark, for instance, is able to respond to the popularity of certain colours in its ranges extremely quickly, thanks to its advanced logistics systems. Information from points of sale, flexible manufacturing, and global distribution all mean that Primark's *lead times* (i.e. the time taken from receipt of a customer's order to final delivery) are shorter than clothing industry averages.

In addition to lead times, manufacturers should consider the impact of shorter life cycles on new product development (see Chapter 8). If innovation is a company's key source of competitive advantage, then the time taken to get a new product on to the shelves will be crucial to prevent obsolescence.

Customer service objectives in logistics

From the manufacturer's perspective, customer service impacts not only on the end user but also on intermediate customers. Marketing has traditionally focused on the consumer by seeking to promote brand values and to generate a demand 'pull' within the market for a company's products. It is now recognized that this by itself is often not sufficient. Because of shifts in channel power towards the retailer, it has become vital to develop strong relations with such intermediaries. In other words, marketers must design their distribution systems around the needs of both *trade* and *consumer* buyers. The benefits of both of these groups can be enhanced or diminished by the efficiency of the supplier's logistics system. It is only when the three components are working optimally together that marketing effectiveness is maximized.

The primary objective of any logistics customer service strategy must be to reduce the customer's cost of ownership. Ownership in this context can include the cost of ordering, the holding stocks, and the consequences of running out of stock. As an example, a delivery twice a week instead of once reduces the customer's average inventory by half and therefore cuts the cost of carrying that inventory. Similarly, reliable on-time delivery means that a retailer can reduce the need to carry safety stock, again resulting in lower stockholding costs.

In a physical distribution context, customer service objectives can be described based on three sets of questions:

1. **Pre-transaction elements:** How quickly should we respond to requests for information from new potential customers? What level of flexibility should we offer individual customers?

2. **Transaction elements:** What should be the time taken from order to delivery? What is the target reliability of this lead time? What percentage of demand should be met from stock? What proportion of orders should be completely filled? How long should it take us to provide order status information?

3. **Post-transaction elements:** What level of availability of spare parts should we provide? What should be the target call-out time for our engineers? How quickly should we aim to deal with customers' complaints?

Precise questions will inevitably vary from one company to another. However, a key issue for marketers to grasp is that it is essential first to understand the differing requirements of different market segments (see Chapter 4), and then to tailor the company's service offering accordingly. For some customers, frequent deliveries of small quantities may be more important than occasional deliveries of large volumes. It has become fashionable to talk about 'marketing logistics', which starts by asking how customers want to receive the product (see Chapter 4 on buyer behaviour) and then works backwards to the retailing, warehousing, transport, inventory, and design of the goods in order to meet customers' expectations. The amount of information needed by managers to make appropriate marketing logistics decisions is clearly vast. Fortunately, it is becoming increasingly available, due to advances in technology, and we shall discuss some of these advances in more detail at the end of this chapter.

Identification of segments by service requirements

The marketing logistics manager first needs to determine the elements of service that customers most value, for example speed, reliability, or availability. Some form of marketing research is likely to be needed here. It is probable that the market will not be homogeneous: some market segments may be willing to pay high prices to obtain premium service, while others may attach greatest importance to low prices and be willing to accept minimum service levels. In attempting to meet buyers' requirements, managers must, of course, also consider cost/service trade-offs and the logistics standards set by the competition. Looking at the company's performance in relation to its main competitors is known as *benchmarking*, and allows it to identify areas for improvement. An example of a benchmarking study is shown in Figure 10.10. Which service elements do you think should be addressed by the company concerned?

Figure 10.10 Customer service benchmarking—a comparison of one company's performance against a benchmark competitor

Once target service levels have been identified (e.g. to deliver 95% of orders within two days; to ensure 98% availability in selected stockists of product X), the company must design a physical distribution system which can deliver them at minimum cost. The key issues for marketing logistics managers to consider include:

- How can we speed up communications and order processing?
- Where should we produce goods and store them?
- How much stock should be held?
- How can we best handle transport?

Cost/service trade-offs

We need to recognize that there are costs as well as benefits in providing high levels of customer service, and therefore the appropriate level of service will need to vary from customer to customer. While companies want to attract and retain customers by offering superior service to that provided by competitors, there comes a point when diminishing returns set in. For example, a chemicals supplier might continually have to keep very large stocks of a particular product because of the demands of a key customer—say, an oil company. Eventually the cost of holding that inventory (perhaps in terms of storage space, or insurance bills) may force the supplier to reconsider the service levels it offers to the customer. Figure 10.11 shows the typical nature of the cost–benefit trade-offs in service-level decisions.

Figure 10.11 indicates that the shape of the revenue curve is dictated by customers' response to the service level offered. The slope is initially fairly flat, since in many markets

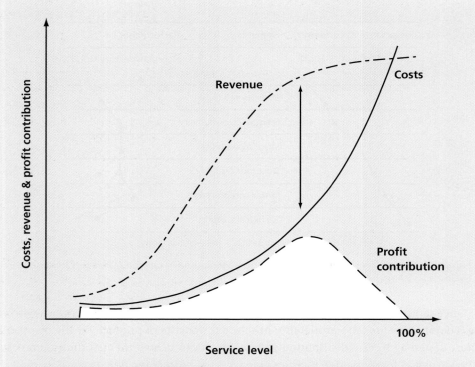

Figure 10.11 The trade-off between the level of service provided and costs/revenue/profits
Source: based on M. Christopher, *Logistics and Supply Chain Management,* London: Pitman, 1992, p. 42.

there will be a minimum threshold of acceptable service which most competitors will be providing, for example delivery within seven days. Once the threshold is passed, increasing returns to service improvements (say, getting delivery times down to five, then three, days and so on) should be achieved as customers place more orders with the company. At the top, the curve flattens out again when additional returns can only be achieved with greatly increased amounts of expenditure. At this point, there may be a case of 'service overkill'. The cost curve is usually a steeply rising curve, as shown, because of the need to keep high levels of inventory. By investing in IT to improve the flow of information about customer requirements, a company might, however, be able to push this curve to the right, thereby boosting overall profitability at all levels of service.

In setting physical distribution objectives, it is important for managers to understand the *total cost* of attempting to meet a specified service level. When assessing alternative approaches, the costs of some functions will increase, others will decrease, and still others may remain unchanged: the objective is to find the approach with the lowest overall cost. The concept of cost trade-offs recognizes these changing patterns, for example the 'trading' of additional information, via IT-based control systems, as an alternative to higher inventory levels; or perhaps the 'trading' of an extra regional warehouse as an alternative to a larger fleet of national delivery trucks.

Commercial organizations seek to maximize their ROI (return on investment) with a 'reduced asset base'. The need for marketing managers to work closely with other functional areas, such as finance, is vital. An understanding of accounting should tell you that, since ROI is a ratio of returns to investment, a company might attempt to improve this ratio by increasing sales revenue through improved service levels/volumes, and/or it might reduce the asset base on which the ratio is calculated. This can be achieved by a better management of inventory, thereby tying up less money in stocks. The use of 'just-in-time' (JIT) techniques to address this issue is discussed later in the chapter.

Inventory management

You should by now be aware of the strategic importance of inventory management. Ultimately, stockholding represents costs such as storage space, obsolescence, deterioration, and interest payments. Yet, ideally, a company should carry enough stock to meet customers' orders immediately. If the desired goods are not available, then a sale may be lost, and a customer may be lost to a competitor. If too much stock is held, the company may find itself with large quantities of goods which it is later forced to mark down. This is often the case in fashion retailing, as we saw with Mothercare. The objective of inventory management is therefore to find a balance between customer service and the cost of carrying stock.

A number of methods are used to achieve the desired balance in stockholding. Perhaps the most basic method is that of the *reorder point*. This approach recognizes that waiting to reorder stock until an extremely low level has been reached is risky, because it takes time to replenish stock. The reorder point system triggers reordering at a stock level a little higher than this 'danger' level, so that by the time new stock is received the danger level of the old stock has only just been reached. Stock is typically counted manually in small organizations, or via computerized sales systems such as 'electronic point of sale' (EPOS) (see below), which compare daily sales with starting stock levels. Safety stock levels are usually based on historical sales data, often seasonally adjusted. Another approach is to use the **economic order quantity** (EOQ) formula:

$$EOQ = \sqrt{2do/ic}$$

where d = annual demand in units; o = cost of placing an order; i = carrying costs as a percentage of cost of one unit; and c = the cost of each unit. The principle of the EOQ model is shown in Figure 10.12. This shows an idealized theoretical relationship between order-processing costs and inventory-carrying costs to give the order-quantity size that minimizes total costs.

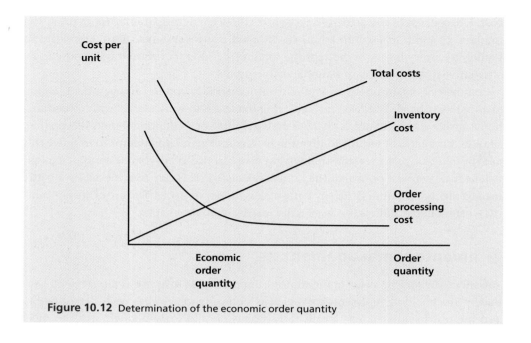

Figure 10.12 Determination of the economic order quantity

Unfortunately, as with many economic models, the EOQ model does not take into sufficient account variations in customer and supplier behaviour. Where demand is unpredictable, or when stocks cannot be replenished relatively quickly, the model may be inadequate. Also, the reorder quantity means that a company will be carrying more inventory than is actually required over practically the complete order cycle (the time between placing separate orders with the supplier); for example, if the EOQ is 100 units and daily usage is 10, then on the first day of the cycle the buyer would be overstocked by 90 units, on the second day by 80, and so on.

Just-in-time systems

The **JIT** philosophy is based on the view, commonly attributed to the Japanese, that inventory is waste and that large inventories merely hide problems such as inaccurate forecasts, unreliable suppliers, quality issues, and production bottlenecks. The JIT concept aims to eliminate any need for safety stock, with parts for manufacture (or goods for reselling) arriving just as they are needed. As a result, small shipments must be made more frequently. Order requirements can specify the exact unloading point and time of day, with suppliers having to respond accordingly. For example, Toyota schedules its car production to minimize sharp fluctuations in daily volume, and to turn out a predicted number of each model every day. Suppliers are automatically notified of orders and

	Traditional 'just-in-case' logistics	**With the development of a 'just-in-time' approach to logistics**
Inventory levels	Large inventories resulting from manufacturing economies of scale and safety stock provision	Low inventories resulting from reliable, 'continuous flow' delivery
Flexibility	Minimal flexibility with long lead times	Short lead times and customer service drive flexibility
Relationships between logistics channel members	Tough, adversarial negotiations	Joint venture partnerships
Number of logistics channel members	Many, to avoid sole dependency	Fewer, but in long-term relationships
Communications	Minimal and with many secrets	Open communication and sharing of information to enable joint problem-solving

Figure 10.13 The effects on organizational behaviour of the transition to a 'just-in-time' logistics system

given a stable production schedule so they will not deliver the wrong components on the date of final assembly. This level of planning also occurs, for instance, with retailers such as Marks & Spencer stipulating delivery 'windows' for its carriers. In the fast-changing world of personal computers, many companies have taken the lead of Dell, which builds computers to customers' specific requirements. This reduces the risk of obsolescence, but requires carefully planned logistics if promised delivery dates are to be met.

The increasing popularity of JIT delivery among business customers clearly means that, for suppliers, the logistics service elements of availability and reliability, plus, of course, uniformly excellent product quality become paramount. Successful implementation of JIT systems relies on high levels of cooperation between supplying and buying organizations, and on the development of long-term partnerships. These closer relations can exist both upstream and downstream from the producer/manufacturer. This can affect the whole culture of an organization and the way that it goes about business. Figure 10.13 summarizes the changes within an organization as it moves from a 'just-in-case' mentality to one of 'just-in-time'.

The JIT concept is not without its problems. The *Financial Times* (1994) reported that suppliers in the Japanese plastics industry have been in 'revolt' against JIT, claiming that it is too expensive. During the 1980s, suppliers tolerated the system because it strengthened the relationship between supplying firms and customers. Once manufacturers had become used to a steady flow of materials from one company, they were unlikely to go elsewhere. The cost to the suppliers of additional freight and stockholding was bearable because the Japanese plastics sector was highly profitable. However, when the demand for plastics fell, many suppliers felt that the costs of frequent small deliveries (up to three per day) had become insupportable. Eventually, *en masse*, the Japanese petrochemicals industry association decided to tell its customers that deliveries would be limited to once a day, with additional calls available, only if paid for by the customer. Buyers were also encouraged to take larger quantities in each order.

Information processing

It should be clear from the previous sections that an effective and efficient supply of information is crucial to logistics management. IT is facilitating the creation of *integrated logistics systems* that link the operations of a company, such as production and distribution, with suppliers' operations on the one hand and customers on the other. A model of information within the logistics function is shown in Figure 10.14. This shows how information about customers should drive strategic issues, such as the design of channels of distribution, through to implementation issues such as order processing and delivery. IT is providing more information to improve management decision-making. The support activities of the value chain have also benefited from developments such as computerized accounting and costing procedures, electronic mail, and online ordering procedures.

We will now look at some of the impacts of IT on logistics activity.

Channel member	Focus for information collection
Final customer	Preferences with respect to product configuration and delivery. Payment/order processing
Intermediaries	Availability of stocks Availability of warehouse capacity Order/delivery preferences Availability and location of transport
Manufacturer	Manufacturing schedule Raw material supplies Availability of stocks Availability of warehouse capacity Availability and location of transport

Figure 10.14 Levels of information within a logistics system

Source: based on M. Christopher, *Logistics and Supply Chain Management,* London: Pitman, 1992, p. 215.

Order processing

The physical distribution process starts when the company *receives an order*. This may be direct from the end consumer, as in the case of Dell's sales of its personal computers; it may involve a head office 'order-taker' noting a replenishment order from a major retailer; or it may be generated by an account manager visiting a major client and entering its order for some new equipment on to a lap-top. Copies of this order are then usually directed to relevant company departments, which may include those responsible for purchasing, credit control, manufacturing, dispatch, warehousing, and invoicing. As far as possible, the company should ensure that this communication takes place *concurrently*, rather than consecutively. This avoids an order being slowed down because it gets 'stuck' in one particular department before being passed to the next. Increasingly, integrated computer systems can automatically pick goods from warehouse shelves, produce shipping documentation, bill customers, update stock records, and confirm delivery arrangements to the customer. An integrated system can inform the production department of the potential need to make new stock, and the purchasing department of the need to order new supplies, as well as warning suppliers of the producing company's imminent requirements. A good IT system allows account managers to provide instant status reports on the progress of their customers' orders, to check inventory levels, and to make alternative recommendations for out-of-stock items.

Materials and production planning

Manufacturing resource planning (MRP) is a computer-assisted method of managing production inventory. It takes into account the producer's master production schedule (MPS), sales forecasts, existing orders, inventories, and a bill of materials (BOM) listing all the necessary inputs. It allows companies to control production inputs carefully, yet still be able to respond quickly to demand-driven production requirements.

Delivery planning

You will recall the earlier discussion of value in use—a product is of no value to a customer until it is delivered to them. IT can increase this value by improving the speed and reliability of the delivery process, and doing so at reduced cost. A good example of the impact of IT on physical distribution can be seen in the scheduling and routing of delivery vehicles. Manual methods for this process are slow and relatively inefficient, and are now being superceded with *computerized vehicle routing and scheduling* systems (CVRSs). These allocate vehicles to sets of delivery locations and build routes linking these destinations. More recently, CVRS systems have been linked to global positioning systems (GPSs), allowing a company to track delivery vehicles and to alert drivers to any

Figure 10.15 Some express parcel companies have extended their parcel-tracking facility to allow customers to log on to the Internet to find out for themselves where an expected delivery is. DHL is a leading express parcel and logistics company with worldwide operations, whose operations add value to supply chains by speeding up deliveries and improving the confidence of channel members that goods will actually arrive in the place where they are needed, and at the time that they are needed. DHL allows customers to track the status of their parcels at any time of the day, anywhere in the world. With increasing importance of Just-in-Time production methods, this valuable facility allows customers to manage their production and inventory levels more effectively. (Reproduced with permission of Deutsche Post AG)

need to reroute during their journey. The benefits to companies of CVRSs include: a significant overall reduction in transport costs, greater vehicle utilization, and a more responsive service to customers.

⬤ Production and warehouse location

In traditional models of distribution, the production facility was given, then it was the task of the manufacturer's marketing department to find customers for its output. We saw earlier that the more modern idea of marketing logistics works backwards from the customer, so using this logic, the location of factories becomes a marketing decision, and not just a production decision.

Regarding the logistic chain as a whole, it is important to ask how many manufacturing plants there should be, and where they should be located. Larger factories generally achieve lower levels of cost per unit of output, but this has to be set against the cost and time involved in getting finished goods to customers. The trend in most industries has been for small manufacturing plants to be replaced by larger factories, operating at a national, European, or even world level.

Companies in fiercely competitive markets often calculate that it is cheaper to manufacture a product in a low-cost country such as China and to ship the finished product to the country where there is demand for it. Most British clothes companies now manufacture the bulk of their clothing in less developed countries where wages paid to staff can be a fraction of what would be paid to UK staff. This can more than offset higher transport costs and allow the company to compete on price, especially where there are significant price points above which buyers will not buy an item. However, locating manufacturing facilities a long way from customers extends the time between identification of a market need and the delivery of goods to meet that need. While fashion for basic underwear and socks may not change much over time, outerwear tends to be much more volatile, with preferred styles and colours changing frequently. If it takes several weeks to get the latest 'hot' fashion from China to Chichester, it might arrive in the shops just as customers have moved on to a new 'hot' fashion. For this reason, manufacturers supplying goods to highly volatile markets are more likely to favour manufacturing facilities closer to home. There is also an issue of maintaining quality control in low-cost countries.

Locational advantages can change over time, and what was once a cost effective production location may cease to be so if local production costs or transport costs change. It has been noted, for example, that many German car-component manufacturers who relocated production to low-cost eastern European countries in the early 2000s found their cost advantage undermined by local increases in wage costs, and some subsequently relocated again to cheaper Far Eastern countries (Maskell *et al.*, 2007). The rapid increase in fuel costs which occurred from 2008 led many supply chains to reconsider the merits of manufacturing goods a long way from their markets. In 2008, the FMCG manufacturer Procter & Gamble claimed that it was spending more on transport and storage than on running its factories, causing a major rethink of its extensive supply network (*Financial Times*, 2008b).

Warehouse location decisions also have to be made to balance the often conflicting needs for low handling costs per unit, against the need for rapid delivery to customers. We may view decisions here in terms of the familiar 'trade-offs' concept: the greater the number of warehouses used, the greater the potential for rapid delivery. But more warehouses will increase costs and capital employed, thus reducing ROI. Warehouses may not necessarily be owned by manufacturers: many manufacturers and retailers use the warehouse facilities of specialist companies in order to achieve economies of scale, and to improve their operational flexibility.

Transport

The appropriate choice of transport mode is a key part of physical distribution management. This is especially important in markets where JIT delivery is the norm. A number of criteria should be used to select transport, including costs, transit time, reliability, capability (important if goods require special handling, such as chilled temperatures), security, and traceability.

For most goods, road transport continues to be the dominant mode, although increasing road congestion in many countries has had serious consequences for the reliability and efficiency of distribution channels. For companies seeking to operate with 'lean' production methods, paying a truck driver to sit in a traffic jam, and being unsure when the truck will arrive can greatly increase the cost of a distribution channel, because of the need to keep spare stocks 'just in case'. In 2003 the DIY chain B&Q claimed that congestion on southern England's roads had become so severe that it moved its main import centres from Felixstowe and Tilbury to Humberside. Congestion (or 'southern discomfort', as the company called it), was contributing to a reported 5% or 10% failure rate in getting goods delivered on time. The company even estimated that the cost of UK road haulage was accounting for about half the total cost of getting a product from a Far East factory into a B&Q store (*The Times*, 2003).

Trends in logistics management

In a landmark article in 1962, the management guru Peter Drucker claimed that physical distribution was the US economy's 'dark continent'. He said: 'We know little more about distribution today than Napoleon's contemporaries knew about the interior of Africa. We know it is there, and we know it is big; and that's about all' (Drucker, 1962). In the 40 years since Drucker made this claim, there have been massive advances in the efficiency and effectiveness of distribution systems. The impact of improved logistics on national economies should not be underestimated. The UK's Chartered Institute of Purchasing and Supply has claimed that a 1% improvement in the cost of managing the supply chain can boost the bottom line of a company by as much as 15%.

So far in this chapter we have identified a number of trends that have influenced the shape of logistic systems as they are today. Now we will summarize some of the key trends for the future.

Rising expectations of end consumers

Logistics for the most part is an invisible part of marketing—it is unseen by the final consumer, and we tend to appreciate its significance only when things go wrong, such as a supermarket running out of potatoes, or an expected home delivery not arriving. Logistics managers deliver what other people in the marketing function promise.

Figure 10.16 Suppliers of goods and services must consider the location where their products will have greatest value for end consumers. Many supermarket operators have identified groups of consumers who would prefer to have their groceries delivered to their home rather than having to visit a supermarket to collect them. The development of the Internet has resulted in home shopping for groceries being a growth area for many supermarket operators. Tesco has become one of Europe's largest online retailers, with a turnover of over £400 million for its Tesco.com division in 2002. The company's logistics task must incorporate an additional link to the final consumer. Tesco serves its home delivery customers from selected individual stores, where customers' orders are assembled manually. Some companies (e.g. Ocado) have chosen instead to develop strategically located automated distribution centres specifically to serve customers requiring home delivery. (Reproduced with permission of Tesco Stores PLC)

Consumers' expectations of availability and reliability of delivery have tended to in-crease over time. Whereas consumers might previously have readily accepted that an item they had ordered was not available when they expected it, today they may complain and take their business elsewhere. The rising expectations of consumers has sharpened minds throughout channels of distribution. In recognition of consumers' rising expectations, some companies have offered guarantees about delivery and/or availability, with compensation paid where they fail (Posselt *et al.*, 2008).

From functions to processes

Effective and efficient logistics focus on processes rather than functional responsibility. It is a challenge to overcome the problem of functional isolation where senior managers come to regard functional area as their 'territory' and who often jealously guard their own departmental budgets. A typical problem is a production manager wanting to min-imize costs by running large batch quantities, even though this may mean creating an inventory greater than what is needed.

The solution to these problems lies in recognizing that a customer order and its associated information flows should be at the heart of any business. This means moving from an *input-focused and budget-driven* organization to an *output-focused, market-driven* one, managing processes rather than functions; and ensuring the rapid sharing of accurate information. These are not solutions that are quick to implement, and furthermore, shared responsibility may sound fine in theory, but somebody should be accountable and responsible for achieving objectives.

Competition between supply networks

It is becoming too simplistic to see competition as existing between companies at just one level of the supply chain—rather, it takes place between integrated supply chains. A retailer may be the public face of competition to most consumers, but their source of competitive advantage increasingly lies in the networks of suppliers and distribution companies that provide the right goods at the right time for their stores, as cheaply as possible. Many commentators have pointed to weaknesses in its supply chain as a con-tributor to the difficulties that Marks & Spencer faced in the late 1990s, in contrast to the well-developed, flexible, responsive, and low-cost distribution network developed by upcoming competitors such as Primark and Zara.

Closer working relationships

We have seen how the need to share information has led to close working relationships becoming crucial to a successful distribution chain. In most channel relationships is-sues of power are never far from the surface, and they can destabilize the whole channel where one party seeks to exert power in the chain that others regard as unreasonable.

Power in distribution channels has tended to move towards retailers and away from producers of goods.

Fewer channel members

There has been a tendency for channels to be simplified by reducing the number of members involved at each level. A good example of this is provided by the major car manufacturers, which have progressively reduced their number of component suppliers while from their remaining suppliers demanding a commitment to quality, innovation, and cost reduction.

Virtual organizations

With the growth of outsourcing as a business philosophy, some commentators have suggested that formal company structures are giving way to informal networks, giving rise to a *virtual organization* (Holcomb and Hitt, 2007). In the case of logistics, key teams might be linked electronically to perform critical activities in an integrated fashion. Work teams could share common information regarding customer requirements and performance measures while retaining local control to achieve a high level of logistical core competency. This is essentially a form of 'electronic keiretsu'. ('Keiretsu' is a Japanese term for a loosely affiliated group of firms that share common practices and are committed to cooperation.) The fact that companies could join forces to achieve common goals and then disband presents significant challenges for the management of partnerships.

Increasingly complex consumer needs

Society is fragmenting into smaller and smaller groups with specialized interests, needs, and expectations. We saw in Chapter 8 how marketers have responded by trying to develop products that closely meet the needs of each group. This can itself create a logistical challenge, as the proliferation of variants of a basic product means higher stockholdings if buffer stocks of each product variant are to be kept. For a simple product such as Coca Cola, the product range has proliferated from one flavour, three packaging types, and three sizes in the 1970s to today's five flavours/formulations (e.g. Diet/Caffeine-free), five basic packaging types, and five sizes, plus special promotional packages. In order to satisfy the needs of each group that has been targeted with these differentiated products, stocks of all must be continually available.

With the development of a 24-hour society and increasingly busy lifestyles, logistics management has to face the challenge of delivering goods to individual consumers' front doors not just between 9 a.m. and 5 p.m., but at other times that are convenient to consumers.

The Internet

We have seen that information technology has drastically changed the nature of logistics management. It is increasingly changing the way that consumers buy goods, with Internet sales set to grow further. The Internet has enabled many retailers to service customers without having to maintain expensive High Street shops, but just a warehouse on a relatively low-cost industrial estate. However, the delivery of goods to the final consumer has not shown the productivity gains that Internet-based ordering has achieved. This is probably not surprising when it is remembered that home delivery remains a labour-intensive activity in which two of the main costs—labour and transport—are likely to continue to increase in real terms. We should not forget that in the UK the milkman has almost disappeared because efficiency of delivery cannot be improved relative to the cost of consumers collecting milk from large, efficient supermarkets. The logistics function must also face the challenge of being able to deliver goods when somebody is at home, or of providing alternative secure storage arrangements.

Increasing public concern over the environment

Ecological concerns have impacts on logistics in a number of ways. To a large extent, public concerns over ecologically harmful practices in logistics have not attracted the same level of attention as the goods themselves, possibly reflecting the fact the point noted earlier that logistics tends to be a relatively invisible process, which is only noticed when things go wrong. It is much easier to focus attention on a visibly harmful product such as 'gas guzzling' 4×4 vehicles, rather than the resources used up in transporting manufactured goods between warehouses. However, this situation is changing, for example the subject of 'food miles' is gaining more public attention. The case study (below) discusses impacts of distribution systems which some critics have argued causes goods to be transported unnecessarily long distances, with impacts on greenhouse gas emissions.

Governments seem increasingly likely to impose environmental constraints which directly impact on distribution systems. The transport of goods, for example, is affected by measures to restrict trucks from town centres. Proposals to impose taxes on air freight may change the rationale for very long distance supply chains (e.g. will it continue to be cost-effective to use air freight to move exotic fresh fruits from low-cost Far East countries to western markets?). Recycling will become an increasingly important environmental issue, and an EU directive has placed on certain manufacturers a responsibility to recycle discarded products after their use (e.g. car components that have reached the end of their life). This calls for reverse logistics. Many distribution channels already collect waste materials for recycling (e.g. cardboard packaging) and use empty vehicles to return such material to the distribution centre where it is consolidated and forwarded to a recycling plant. With higher recycling targets being set, getting waste products from consumers will need to be considered more carefully as part of the logistics plan.

Chapter summary and key linkages to other chapters

The management of channel intermediaries plays a key part in a company's attempts to ensure that its goods or services are made available to the desired market segments. Making goods available where and when buyers need them is an important value-adding activity which contributes towards a company's competitive advantage over rival producers (Chapter 7). Availability of a company's products must be consistent with its promotional messages (Chapter 11) and its price position (Chapter 9). The design of a marketing channel requires careful analysis and planning. For this to be done effectively, firms must be aware of the roles that intermediaries can perform and of their relative power bases.

Logistics is concerned with coordinating the flow of goods from suppliers to the manufacturer, through the production process, and on to the customer. The overall aim of marketing logistics management is to provide customer value through service, which for many customers (both consumers and commercial) comprises the key elements of availability and timeliness. There have been numerous developments in physical distribution and logistics in the past few decades, most of which has been facilitated by advances in IT.

KEY PRINCIPLES OF MARKETING

- Value chains are at the heart of marketing. Value is added to a product as it passes through a channel of distribution.
- There is not one channel design that is appropriate in all situations; the design of an optimal channel is influenced by a range of customer, product, supplier, and competitor characteristics.
- Physical distribution may be a largely unseen activity, but it is crucial for delivering promises communicated in a company's promotional messages.
- Distribution efficiency and effectiveness must be consistent with a company's product/price/ promotional positioning.
- Logistics involves a series of trade-offs in order to optimize a cost/service/profit level.

CASE STUDY

Tesco tries to cut food miles from its supply chain

For previous generations, the availability of fresh fruit and vegetables was governed by the time of year, and where you lived. If you lived in the heart of the countryside, you would probably be spoiled for choice of fruit and vegetables during summer and autumn. But the middle of the great conurbations in winter might have seen choice reduced to basic items such as potatoes, cabbage, and apples, supplemented by canned fruit and veg. Look in a Tesco supermarket today, and you may find it difficult to tell the season of the year or the distance from the countryside, simply based on the fruit and veg which are on display. With so many exotic fruits available, you might even wonder in which part of the world you are.

The UK supermarket sector is intensely competitive, and has seen continuous innovation in the way it seeks to satisfy customers' needs. As consumers have become wealthier, the supermarkets realized that buyers would no longer be content with the staple foods such as cabbage and potatoes in the depths of winter—significant numbers of them now wanted excitement on a plate, and all year round. Furthermore, if they were planning a menu, they wanted to be sure that when they went to their local supermarket, the Jerusalem artichoke or mangetout which their recipe demanded would be on the shelves, and not sold out.

By and large, supermarkets have been key drivers of the value chain for the groceries that they sell. They have been close to their customers and identified their changing needs. They have built trust with their customers, who can trust the freshness, and provenance of the food they sell, and the reliability of supply. It is therefore the supermarkets who have gone seeking sources of supply, rather than the growers seeking aggressively to sell the produce that they have available. Before the development of very large supermarket chains, retailers were more fragmented. They did not have the power or resources to innovate with new product lines which they could then commission a grower to produce. Today, supermarkets such as Tesco invest heavily in their food technology laboratories, and can then go to suppliers and place large orders with exacting standards with regard to price, quality, and delivery. Above all else, supermarkets have put themselves at the centre of a slick distribution system which connects an international network of growers through transport networks of trucks, ships, and planes to put fresh produce in their network of stores, every day, all year round. The efficiency of the logistics, and the bargaining power of the supermarkets has often led to the price being charged at a British supermarket being lower than the price charged in supermarkets thousands of miles away where the fruit and vegetables were grown. Tomatoes grown in Bulgaria and sold in Britain can be cheaper in Britain than in local Bulgarian shops.

The bizarre situation has occurred where the supermarkets import apples from France to be sold in Kent, the traditional home of British apple-growing; plums from Poland to be sold in the traditional plum-growing area of Worcestershire, and cauliflowers from Spain to replace the locally grown product in Lincolnshire. Supermarkets argue that sourcing from overseas is not just an issue of cost-saving: more importantly, the supermarkets seek a continuity of supplies from large growers who can guarantee to deliver a specified quantity at a specified time and place. The supermarkets have claimed that the fragmented nature of agricultural growers and distributors in Britain is not capable of achieving this. British supermarkets are among the most efficient in the world, and their desire to ensure that customers can always get what they want may explain the mass transport of food. Local farmers' markets may sound environmentally friendly, but they rarely guarantee a continuity of supplies.

As part of their drive for efficiency, supermarkets have a tendency to move food between large warehouses and processing centres. Friends of the Earth have noted the paradox of potatoes being transported several hundred miles between distribution centres before they end up on a supermarket shelf just a few miles from where they were grown. The environmental campaigning group Sustain has estimated that the average chicken travels 2,000 km between the farm where it was grown and the supermarket shelf (Sustain, 1999).

By the mid-2000s, the supermarkets' slick supply chains appeared to be coming under greater challenge. Global warming had become an important issue with many consumers, and there was growing concern that supermarkets' practice of transporting fresh produce long distances around the world was irresponsibly adding to greenhouse gas emissions. Conscientious consumers who did not want to be seen harming the ecological environment were apparently seeking out local produce, and often telling their friends about their moral stand. A survey for the Institute of Grocery Distribution in 2008 found that one in six (16%) of respondents claimed that distance travelled was one of their top five concerns about food production, up from 9% in 2003. The most contentious food miles are clocked up by fresh fruit and vegetables flown in by plane from overseas. Although air-freighted produce accounted for less than 1% of total UK food miles, it was the fastest-growing way of moving food around, according to figures published in 2007 by the Department for Environment, Food and Rural Affairs (Defra). Furthermore, air transport is responsible for around 11% of the total CO_2 emissions from UK food transport, because transport by plane generates 177 times more greenhouse gases than shipping per unit of food.

One response by Tesco was to introduce a greater proportion of local produce. To achieve this, it placed buyers and marketing teams in the regions in order to gain a clearer picture of local markets and to develop closer relationships with suppliers. By 2007, Tesco claimed to have 7,000 regional lines from throughout the UK that were promoted as local produce, supporting local growers and reducing greenhouse gas emissions. Later that year, the company announced that contracts for the supply of organic fruit and vegetables worth £12 million pounds had been reallocated from overseas suppliers to UK growers.

Throughout its history, Tesco has demonstrated its ability to listen to what customers want, and this has been true in respect of its distribution system. At a time when the media enjoyed bashing the big supermarkets, being seen to source products locally and being good to the environment helped to restore the standing of the company. However, critics were quick to point out some of the weaknesses and occasional hypocrisy in Tesco's approach. One observer from Friends of the Earth noted that 'local produce' sold at a branch of Tesco in Essex had in fact travelled several hundred miles as it was moved from the grower to a regional processing centre, then to a regional distribution centre, and finally back to the supermarket where it was sold. There has also been debate about whether sourcing fruit and vegetables locally actually reduces greenhouse gas emissions. There is an argument that it would be better for the environment to grow them in countries where they need less heating and artificial fertilizers than if they were grown in Britain. The greenhouse gas emissions resulting from growing them locally in Britain may be more than the emissions associated with transporting them from warmer countries.

Another distribution quandary facing Tesco and its customers occurred with respect to its home delivery service. With the launch of its Tesco online service, the company effectively extended the supply chain right through to customers' own homes, adding value to its product offer by avoiding the need for customers to even visit a supermarket. Was it good for the environment to have fleets of delivery vans scurrying around town and countryside? Simple evaluations were difficult to make, but again, Tesco was keen to be seen as a good citizen in this final leg of its value chain, for example by launching electric delivery vehicles which the company claimed had a low carbon footprint.

Source: based on Institute of Grocery Distribution, Shopper Trends—Five Years On, 2008; *The Times*, 'Buy British food? No thanks, we're from the Government', 13 November 2007, p. 13; Tesco PLC website (www.tesco.com)

- -

Case study review questions

1. Identify the elements of the value chain involved in the supply of fresh fruit and vegetables to Tesco stores.

2. Critically discuss the factors influencing Tesco's sourcing of fresh fruit and vegetables.

3. Assess the level of power that Tesco exercises in the supply chain for fruit and vegetables.

▢ CHAPTER REVIEW QUESTIONS

1. Why does conflict so often occur between manufacturers and intermediaries? How might this conflict be resolved?

2. Contrast JIT inventory management with conventional reorder methods. Do you think the adoption of JIT techniques is viable for every sector? Where might it not be so relevant?

3. Giving examples from both the manufacturing and retailing sectors, discuss the effects of the Internet on logistics and physical distribution management.

◻ ACTIVITIES

1. Compare the prices of a bottle of soft drink/jar of coffee/chocolate bar in different retail outlets in your area. What do the different prices for an identical product say about the nature of its value chain? Is there a consistent trend of retailers charging a price premium for providing availability of the item in prime locations and/or at anti-social hours?

2. Construct a diagram showing the channel alternatives for a manufacturer of coffee to get its products to the final consumer.

3. Undertake an audit of local fast-food restaurants in your area. Can you tell whether there are differences in the style and standard of service provided between franchised and company owned outlets? If you were a franchisor, how would you go about monitoring and maintaining the standards of service provided by the franchised outlets that you have observed?

◻ REFERENCES

Ahmad, R. and Buttle, F. (1998), 'Bridging the Gaps between Theory and Practice: a case of the retention of dealers of office equipment products'. In *Proceedings of Academy of Marketing Conference*. Sheffield: Sheffield Hallam University (8–10 July), pp. 16–21.

British Franchise Association (2006), The NatWest/British Franchising Association Annual Survey of Franchising. Henley-on-Thames: BFA.

Christopher, M. (1992), *Logistics and Supply Chain Management*. London: Pitman.

Competition Commission (2008), 'Grocery Markets Investigation'. London: Competition Commission.

Deloitte (2006), 'The Global Powers of Retailing 2006'. London: Deloitte.

Drucker, P. (1962), 'The Economy's Dark Continent'. *Fortune*, 103 (April).

Financial Times (1994), 'Just-in-time Now Just Too Much', 14 January, p. 20.

Financial Times (2008a), 'Tesco's Trolley may have Started to Wobble', 4 April.

Financial Times (2008b), 'Oil Costs Force P & G to Rethink its Supply Network', 27 June, p. 22.

Holcomb, T. R. and Hitt, M. A. (2007), 'Toward a Model of Strategic Outsourcing'. *Journal of Operations Management,* 25(2): 464–81.

Institute of Grocery Distribution (2008), *Shopper Trends: Five Years On.* London: Institute of Grocery Distribution.

Keers, H. (2002), 'Mothercare Slips into Red as Warehouse Woes Grow'. *Daily Telegraph,* 22 November.

Löning, H. and Besson, M. (2002), 'Can Distribution Channels Explain Differences in Marketing and Sales Performance Measurement Systems?'. *European Management Journal*, 20(6): 54–62.

Maskell, P., Pedersen, T., Petersen, B., and Dick-Nielsen, J. (2007), 'Learning Paths to Offshore Outsourcing: From Cost Reduction to Knowledge Seeking'. *Industry & Innovation,* 14(3): 239–57.

Nairn, G. (2003), 'Not Many Happy Returns: reverse logistics causes headaches and eats into already thin margins'. *Financial Times,* 5 February, p. 5.

O'Cass, A. and Fenech, T. (2003), 'Web Retailing Adoption: exploring the nature of internet users web retailing behaviour'. *Journal of Retailing & Consumer Services*, 10(2): 81–94.

Porter, M. E. (2001), 'Strategy and the Internet'. *Harvard Business Review* (March–April); 63–78.

Posselt , T., Gerstner, E., and Radic, D. (2008), 'Rating E-Tailers' Money-Back Guarantees'. *Journal of Service Research,* 10(3): 207–19.

Sustain (1999), *Food Miles: still on the road to ruin*. London: Sustain.

The Times (2003), 'B&Q Plans Freight Escape from Southern Route', 20 January, Business, p. 4.

The Times (2007), 'Buy British food? No thanks, we're from the Government', 13 November, p. 13.

Timmins, N. (2003), 'Online Auctions: e-commerce has arrived in the public sector as a way to reduce the civil procurement bill'. *Financial Times,* 29 January, p. 12.

Vargo, S. L. and Lusch, R. F. (2004), 'Evolving to a New Dominant Logic for Marketing'. *Journal of Marketing,* 68(1): 1–17.

Yrjölä, H. (2001), 'Physical Distribution Considerations for Electronic Grocery Shopping'. *International Journal of Physical Distribution & Logistics Management*, 31(10): 746–61.

SUGGESTED FURTHER READING

For a more detailed review of the channels of distribution literature, the following develop many of the issues raised in this chapter:

Coughlan, A., Anderson, E., Stern, L. W., and El-Ansary, A. (2007), *Marketing Channels*, 7th edn. London: FT Prentice Hall.

Fung, P. K.O., Chen, I. S. N., and Yip, L. S. C. (2007), 'Relationships and Performance of Trade Intermediaries: an exploratory study'. *European Journal of Marketing*, 41(1/2): 159–80.

Löning, H. and Besson, M. (2002), 'Can Distribution Channels Explain Differences in Marketing and Sales Performance Measurement Systems?'. *European Management Journal*, 20(6): 54–62.

For further discussion of logistics and supply chain management, consult the following:

Cousins, P., Lamming, R., Lawson, B., and Squire, B. (2007), *Strategic Supply Management: Principles, Theories and Practice*. London: FT Prentice Hall.

Bowersox, D., Closs, D., and Cooper, M. B. (2007), *Supply Chain Logistics Management*, 2nd edn. USA: McGraw-Hill.

Rushton, A., Croucher, P., and Baker, P. (2006), *The Handbook of Logistics and Distribution Management*. London: Kogan Page.

USEFUL WEB LINKS

Visit the Online Resource Centre for resources that are relevant to this chapter, including web links, multiple choice questions, and additional case studies:

www.oxfordtextbooks.co.uk/orc/palmer2e/

⬤ KEY TERMS

- ▪ **Direct marketing**
- ▪ **Distributors**
- ▪ **Economic order quantity**
- ▪ **Franchising**
- ▪ **Intermediary**
- ▪ **Inventory**
- ▪ **Just-in-time (JIT)**
- ▪ **Logistics**
- ▪ **Marketing channel**
- ▪ **Physical distribution management**
- ▪ **Retailers**
- ▪ **Supply chain**
- ▪ **Value chain**
- ▪ **Wholesalers**

Marketing communications

CHAPTER OBJECTIVES

It is sometimes said that a well-designed product, appropriately priced and distributed, should require little or no promotion. Instead, customers should be queuing to buy it. Some new products do find themselves in a seller's market, and their producers can sell all they can make without a need for promotion. But the reality of most markets is fierce competition between suppliers in which each supplier has to communicate to potential buyers the unique benefits of buying its products rather than the competitor's. This chapter aims to develop an understanding of promotion planning as an integral part of the marketing and business planning process. It then discusses the key stages of the promotion planning process, the range and variety of promotional techniques, basic models of communication, and how promotional activity can be monitored. The characteristics of the different media that make up the promotion mix will be explored.

Introduction

As consumers, we are surrounded and constantly bombarded by marketing communications stimuli. These stimuli derive from a range of promotional activity, such as television advertising, mailshots, e-mail messages, and face-to-face selling, delivered through a variety of different channels and media. Alongside such overt messages, the broader marketing mix is also communicating messages to us, more covertly (for example, the packaging of a product and its price send out messages about the nature of the product).

This chapter focuses on firms' efforts to communicate the features and benefits of their products in particular, and their corporate image in general. Communication in its broadest sense can incorporate firms' communication with key stakeholder groups, including shareholders, employees, and government agencies. This chapter will concentrate on communications which take the form of promotional activity aimed at customers. Although the words 'communications' and 'promotion' are sometimes used interchangeably, this chapter will focus on this narrower understanding of promotion.

A key theme of this chapter is the need for companies to integrate their communications, and this integration can take a number of forms. The message that is sent out by the firms' promotional material must be consistent with the product that it is selling, or the distribution channels that it is using. The promotional media themselves must be integrated, so that, for example, the message seen on a television advert is reinforced by Internet banner ads. 'Integrated Marketing Communications' has become an important concept, and although this chapter looks in detail at individual aspects of promotion, you should never forget the need to develop an integrated approach, which is what customers will see.

Managing an organization's communications involves a lot of detail. As an example of recent developments, many people are employed to optimize a company's search engine rankings, which can involve complex knowledge of algorithms. This introductory chapter cannot hope to go into great detail on operational issues, which are covered in more specialist books. This chapter will adopt a more strategic approach to managing communications. It may not give you the answers to the detailed questions that communications managers ask every day, but at least it will help you to identify the important questions that need to be asked within a strategic marketing management framework.

Marketing and promotional objectives

We will begin by exploring the link between promotional activity and other aspects of marketing activity. To understand fully the role of promotion planning, it is necessary to see it within the context of an organization's overall business and marketing plan, and in particular its objectives and strategy. Promotion activity should not be seen as a stand-alone series of activities which bear little relation to the organization's goals, purpose, and markets.

At its most basic, promotion planning can be visualized as a top-down process (Figure 11.1). It should be seen as one element of the business and marketing planning cycle, with the aim of ensuring that:

- the messages being communicated are consistent with an organization's corporate and marketing activity;
- promotion activity supports and adds synergy to the overall business and marketing strategy;
- consumers hear 'one voice' and not a range of disparate messages and behaviour.

The starting point of a company's promotional planning is a clear understanding and articulation of the promotional objectives, in order that appropriate messages are accurately targeted through the most appropriate channels in the most cost-effective manner possible. Typical communication objectives might be:

- to develop an awareness of an organization and its products;
- to communicate the benefits of purchasing a product;
- to build a positive image of the organization and its products;
- to influence eventual purchase of the product;
- to differentiate the company and its products from its competitors;
- to remind people of the existence of the organization and its products.

Ideally, promotional objectives should be quantified as far as possible. From the general objectives specified above, the following specific objectives are typical of those that might be set by a newly established budget airline.

- Of all A/B/C1 adults within the south-east region of England, 30% should be aware of the airline's brand name by the end of year 1, rising to 50% after year 2, and 70% after year 3.

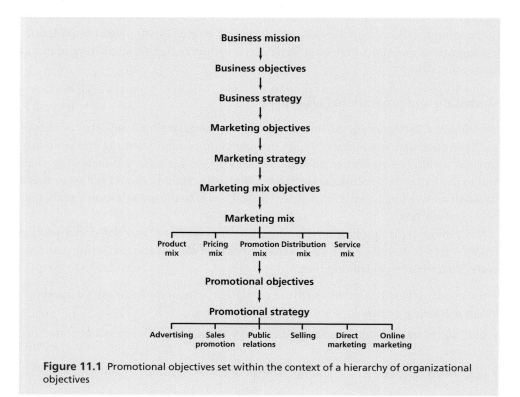

Figure 11.1 Promotional objectives set within the context of a hierarchy of organizational objectives

- Awareness levels among A/B/C1 adults who regularly fly from London area airports should be 60%, 80%, and 90% over the same time periods.

- The airline should receive 5 million hits on its website during year 1, rising to 10 million in year 3.

- By the end of year 3, the airline should be the first low-cost airline to be recalled by regular air travellers in the south-east in an unprompted survey of brand recognition.

- Ultimately, promotion effort should contribute to the sale of 1 million seats in year 1, rising to 3 million in year 3.

Promotional objectives are likely to change throughout the life cycle of a product, as the above example would suggest. We will see later in this chapter how firms' promotion planning responds to changing objectives.

The communication process

To understand the principles of promotion, we first need to understand what is happening when a company sends messages to potential customers telling them about the benefits of buying its product. Some people see promotion as essentially a proactive means of persuading people to do something that they would not otherwise have done. (For example, they would not have gone to a new nightclub if they had not known about it.) An alternative view is that promotion is essentially a communication process which aims to remove the barriers that prevent an individual doing something. Think further about why you might not have visited a new nightclub in town:

- You may not have been aware of its existence.

- If you had known about it, you might not have had sufficient information to allow you to take action. (Where is it? What times does it open?)

- You might have wondered what benefits it would offer over the nightclub that you regularly patronize—what motivation would there be for you to break away from your present club, with which you are perfectly happy?

- You may have regarded a visit to the new nightclub as risky. (Will there be a rough clientele? Will they rip me off for drinks prices?)

Promotional planning must address all of these issues, which are likely to vary in importance as the nightclub passes through its life cycle. It must not be assumed that the communication process is complete once a targeted individual has become a customer. A customer is likely to need the reassurance that her chosen nightclub is the best choice, and much promotional activity is directed at reducing the cognitive dissonance that a person may have if she believes that she has made a wrong purchase decision. Further-more, an individual may fear ridicule of her peer group if the nightclub is not continu-ally promoted as the coolest place in town. Other nightclubs, including new challengers, may step up their promotional efforts in a bid to attract defectors from established clubs. Communication can involve maintaining an ongoing dialogue with the cus-tomer, for example by informing established customers of new product offers, or giving rewards for loyalty. Communication is a key aspect of firms' efforts at developing rela-tionship marketing strategies.

Communication, then, is a continual process, and we need to identify a number of elements of this process:

- the message source;
- the audience to which the message is addressed;
- the message itself;
- the processes by which a message is encoded by the sender and decoded by the receiver, and the noise factors that may cause distortion of the message;
- the channels through which the message is communicated;
- the desired and actual response of the audience;
- a feedback loop by which future communication with the target audience may be reconfigured following evaluation of the current communication.

The development of electronic **channels of communication** is making this process increasingly interactive, so now, instead of waiting a long time for feedback following a communication, this can often come back instantly. The elements of the process are illustrated in Figure 11.2 and are described in more detail below.

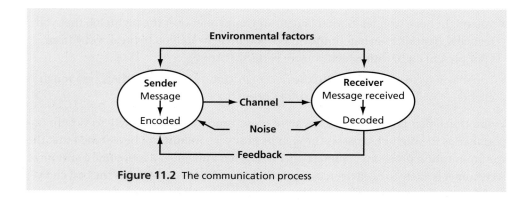

Figure 11.2 The communication process

The message source

The company seeking to promote a product is the ultimate source of a message. Sometimes the identity of the source may be quite clear, but very often a company will use distinctive individuals as the apparent source of its messages. The identity of the message source can be important, because the source of a message—as distinct from the message itself—can influence the effectiveness of any communication. The following factors affect the credibility of a message source:

1. If a source is perceived as having power, then the audience response is likely to be compliance.

2. If a source is liked, then identification by the audience is a likely response. Important factors here include past experience and the reputation of the organization, in addition to the personality of the actual source of the communication. A salesperson, any contact personnel, a TV/radio personality, etc., are all very important in creating *liking*.

3. If a source is perceived as credible, then the message is more likely to be internalized by the audience. Credibility can be developed by establishing a source as important, high in status, power, and prestige, or by emphasizing reliability and openness. Consider the following examples of messages in which companies have selected a message source to add to the credibility of its products:

   • Pharmaceutical companies frequently use doctors dressed in white coats to explain the benefits of an over-the-counter medication in their television adverts. Even if the role of doctor is played by an actor, the presence of the doctor's white coat is likely to increase the chances that we would trust the message. (Would we believe the message as much if it was communicated by a comedian?)

   • Many companies seeking to stress the robust design of their product have used Germans—popularly associated with engineering superiority—to endorse the product.

   • For many low-risk, low-involvement products, endorsement by an individual's peer group can be important. 'If people who are like me are happy with the product, then I will be happy with it as well' is a typical rationalization.

Celebrities are often used to endorse a product or an organization. We have a tendency to impute to the endorsed product the qualities that we have come to like about our favourite celebrity characters. There have been numerous studies of the effects of celebrity endorsement (e.g. Cummings, 2007; Chung-kue and McDonald, 2002). To be effective, the celebrity must be carefully chosen to match the aspirations of a product's target market. Consider the following examples of celebrity endorsement.

- Children develop a liking for television and film characters, whether they are real or inanimate. The popularity of Harry Potter books and films with children (and their parents) has led to manufacturers of products as diverse as breakfast cereals, confectionery, stationery, and computer hardware being endorsed with the character of Harry Potter (Lynch, 2001).

- The TV chef Jamie Oliver has developed a loyal following among aspirational cooks which has been exploited by the grocery retailer Sainsbury's, which employed the chef to front its advertising campaign demonstrating meals made with Sainsbury's groceries.

- Companies often pay to have their products 'placed' in films. When the James Bond movie *Casino Royale* was released in 2006, several companies, including Sony, Ford, Dell, and Federal Express, helped to pay for the film, in return for having their products included in the storylines.

Of course, a celebrity endorsement loses a lot of its value if the celebrity subsequently acquires a negative reputation. Naomi Campbell, for example, was notoriously dropped from her involvement in a charity campaign against wearing animal skins when she was photographed draped in fur on the catwalk. And in 2005 fashion brands Burberry and Hennes & Mauritz dropped Kate Moss from their advertising campaigns after she was seen taking illegal drugs.

The message

Central to an organization's communication effort is the message that it wants to communicate. The message must be derived from a sound analysis of an organization's product offer and the positioning of its brand. To be effective, a message must identify the target audience and communicate in a manner that addresses its needs and expectations. A message may be communicated for a number of reasons. Usually, the focus for a message is communication of specific product features and benefits. Often, however, a message will say very little about specific product details, but will instead focus on communicating core brand values that encourage customers and other stakeholders to trust the organization and its brands. Sometimes, messages have to be communicated following a crisis, for example in the aftermath of a food-poisoning incident.

A message must be able to move an individual along a path from awareness through to eventual purchase. In order for a message to be received and understood, it must gain attention, use a common language, arouse needs, and suggest how these needs might be met. All of this should take place within the acceptable standards of the target audience. However, the product itself, the channel, and the source of the communication also convey a message, and therefore it is important that these do not conflict.

Three aspects of a communication message can be identified: content, structure, and format. It is the content that is likely to attract attention, and change attitude and intention. The appeal or theme of the message is therefore important. The formulation of the message must include some kind of benefit, motivator, identification, or reason why the audience should think or do something. Appeals can be rational, emotional, or moral.

Messages can be classified into a number of types, according to the dominant theme of the message. The following are common focal points for messages:

- **The nature and characteristics of the organization and the product on offer:** For example, television advertisements for Volkswagen have traditionally stressed their robust build quality.

- **Advantages over the competition:** Promotion by the airline Ryanair has emphasized the low cost of its fares compared with its competitors.

- **Adaptability to buyers' needs:** Many insurance companies stress the extent to which their policies have been designed with the needs of particular age segments of the population in mind.

- **Experience of others:** Testimonials of previous satisfied customers are used to demonstrate the benefits resulting from use and the dependability of a company. (For example, Weight Watchers has used real customers to say how they successfully managed to lose weight using the company's products.)

Recipients of a message must see it as applying specifically to themselves, and they must see some reason for their being interested in it. The message must be structured according to the job it has to do. The points to be included in the message should be ordered (strongest arguments first or last) and consideration given to whether one-sided or two-sided messages should be used. Some messages use criticism of competitors' products, although there is some research evidence that negative advertising may be counter-productive (Richardson, 2001).

Encoding, decoding, and noise

The message that a company seeks to put across to its audience may be lengthy and involve a lot of technical description. However, the audience may have an attention span of only a few seconds; moreover, it is likely to be expensive to buy sufficient access to channels of communication to allow the company to put across its message in full. Furthermore, a company may define its products in terms of their features, but it is important to remember that the audience must be *rapidly* made aware of its *benefits* to them. The creator of a message must therefore encode it into some acceptable form for an audience, which will then decode it.

Unfortunately, there is likely to be interference between the stages of **encoding** and **decoding**, so the message that a company sends out may not be the one the audience

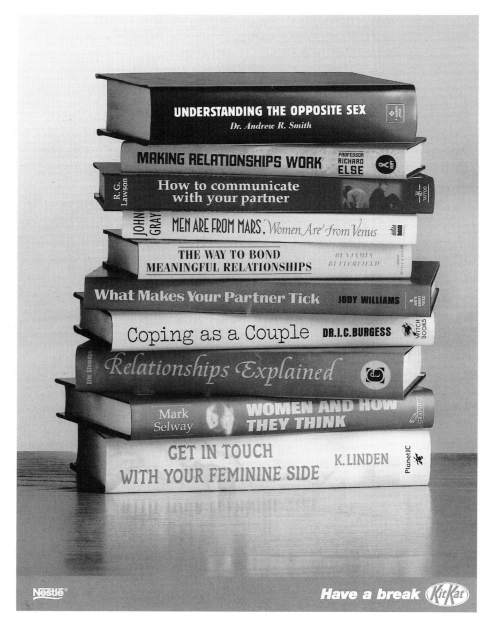

Figure 11.3 Advertisers must fight to gain the attention of an audience; simply stating the benefits of a product may be inadequate to gain attention or to create a distinctive identity. This advertisement does not say much about the product on offer and is not likely to achieve any sales in the short term, but it does raise awareness of the KitKat brand and it helps to give it a distinctive and humorous position in the competitive market for confectionery products.

picks up. **Noise** occurs between the encoding and decoding of a message. Although it is difficult to eliminate such interference in the communication process totally, an understanding of the various elements of this noise should help to minimize its effects.

Noise factors can be divided into two major types.

1. **Psychological factors:** No two individuals are the same in terms of their psychological make-up. Each person undergoes different experiences influencing their personality, perceptions of the world, motives for action, and attitudes towards people, situations, and objects. Therefore, it is not surprising to find that different people will interpret an advertisement differently.

   An individual's past experience of a product or supplier is an important influence on how messages about that company's products are interpreted. Both positive and negative experiences predispose an individual to decode messages in a particular way. For example, a person may have a negative attitude towards an insurance company as a result of having previously had an insurance claim turned down by that company. This negative attitude is likely to distort their interpretation of any marketing communication from the company. Also, an individual's current motives can influence how a message is decoded (an advert for food may be viewed differently when you are hungry, compared to when you have just eaten).

2. **Sociological factors:** In addition to the essentially personal characteristics that influence their behaviour, people are influenced by the presence of others around them. Individuals develop attitudes as a result of a conditioning process which is brought about by the culture in which they live and the specific actions of family, friends, and work associates. People develop attitudes from a number of sources. In addition to the family, there are many other social groupings that influence how consumers see the world and how they decide what to purchase. These include *reference groups* with which an individual closely identifies. Reference groups can be divided into those of which an individual is a member ('membership groups') and those to which membership is aspired ('aspirational groups'). Both types of reference group can affect how an individual makes decisions on goods and services purchases. (Think of how many people copy their best friend's or their favourite pop star's hairstyle or clothing.)

Perception and retention of the message

We are unlikely to remember, let alone notice, all of the messages that we come across. In a typical day, the average person in the UK may be exposed to hundreds of commercial messages, including television and newspaper adverts, messages given out by cereal packets at breakfast time, posters seen on the roadside on the way to work, and banner

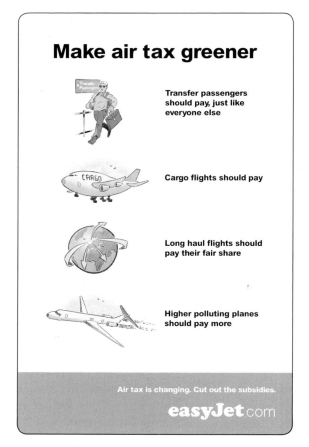

Figure 11.4 Addressing customers' concerns for the ecological environment has become an increasingly important basis for films' messages. During its first ten years of operation, the low-cost airline easyJet stressed low fares above all else. In early adverts, the company likened the price of an air ticket to a low-cost item of clothing. Over time, the airline placed a little more emphasis on the extensiveness of its route network, and for passengers travelling on business, it promoted ease of booking, and flexible tickets which would allow business people the possibility of changing their travel arrangements at short notice. But from 2007, a potentially serious threat faced easyJet, and other low-cost airlines, in the form of EU proposals to tax airlines more heavily. The public had become increasingly concerned about the harmful ecological effects of aviation. Some passengers may even have felt guilty about flying, and many more people thought that 'something must be done' to tackle the problem of greenhouse gas emissions caused by aircraft. But a new tax on airlines could have hit easyJet hard. Had the company ignored pressure for greater controls on civil aviation, and simply carried on advertising cheap flights, it might have alienated the public it sought to serve, and more importantly, the legislators who would decide its fate. An important message of easyJet, therefore, turned towards addressing the needs of these wider groups of stakeholders. In this advert, the company is accepting the need for some form of increased taxation on aviation. In doing so, it comes over as a more responsible airline, and may overcome some passengers' feelings of guilt about flying. Just as importantly, the company was keen to preserve its business model and sought to engage in debate about how new taxes should be implemented, so that low-cost airlines did not lose competitive advantage to airlines with different business models. The target of this advert was legislators, as much as passengers themselves. (Reproduced with permission of easyJet Airline Co. Ltd)

ads encountered while surfing the Internet. Past experience, personality, motivation, attitudes, and the influence of reference groups can all affect what we perceive and retain, leading to noise, which can distort an audience's perception and interpretation of a promotional message.

Individuals are likely to select only the stimuli perceived as being important to them.

- **Selective perception** occurs where communication is perceived in such a way that it merely reinforces existing attitudes and beliefs.

- **Selective reception** occurs where individuals make active decisions as to which stimuli they wish to expose themselves to. For example, a committed Conservative Party supporter may consciously avoid advertising by the Labour Party.

- **Selective retention** occurs when an individual remembers only those aspects of the message perceived as being necessary to him.

Even if an individual decides to give attention to a message, understands it, and remembers it, comprehension may still be different from what the communicator of the message expected. This perceptual distortion could be caused by those noise factors previously noted, poor encoding on the part of the communicator, or poor understanding by the audience itself. It is therefore important to pre-test all advertising before a full campaign is launched.

The target audience

A fundamental principle that underlies most promotional activity is that communication should be designed and placed to reach a specific type of audience. This audience represents a *market segment*. A market segment is any group of people who exhibit similar needs or demographic, social, psychological, or behavioural characteristics that will enable them to be targeted with a distinct marketing mix. Go back to Chapter 6 if you wish to review different bases for defining market segments.

The importance of rigorous market segmentation and targeting varies between products and some promotion succeeds with only very broad definitions of their target market. One example is the UK national lottery, which has gained wide market appeal aimed at a very wide target market. For the majority of products, however, such a homogeneous market and message is unlikely to be cost-effective.

Once potential market segments have been identified and **target audiences** selected, a company will need to determine the positioning of its product in the marketplace and in the minds of consumers. It is not feasible to develop promotional plans until a clear understanding of the product positioning has been determined. Positioning was discussed in Chapter 7.

The matching of media to target markets is increasingly being done using state-of-the-art technology to manipulate quantitative and qualitative data. The accuracy of such market information is critical for effective promotion management. The media industry has traditionally been provided with a wealth of market research data such as the Target Group Index, which mixes product usage data with demographic, socio-economic, and attitudinal data. The Broadcasters Audience Research Board (BARB) uses a panel of households to monitor television viewing data, and National Readership Surveys (NRS) provide data on newspaper and magazine readership. Internet-based advertisers have available to them a wealth of information measuring visitors' behaviour, for example the source of hits to a website, the length of time spent on specific pages, and the progression of visitors from one page to another. Embedded cookies can allow a company to analyse the websites that an individual had visited before coming to its own website. Alongside these data, advertising agencies and market research

MARKETING in ACTION

Magazines for men

Until a few years ago, the shelves of most newsagents would have been loaded with many general interest women's magazines (e.g. *Woman's Own*, *Women's Weekly*, *Cosmopolitan*), but very few general interest magazines aimed at men. Why? Some cynics might have argued that women were more likely to have spare time at home and could sit around reading, while 'busy' men were out at work, in the pub, or watching sport, and did not have time to read magazines. There may just have been a bit of truth in this, but the main reason has been that women's magazines have been popular with advertisers, who generally provide a high proportion of total income for a magazine publisher. In the traditional household, it has been women who have made decisions on a wide range of consumer goods purchases. Advertising the benefits of toothpaste, yogurt, or jam would have been lost on most men, who had little interest in which brand was put in front of them, and played little part in the buying process.

Take a look at the news-stand now and you will find that it carries a wide range of men's general interest magazines, such as *FHM, Loaded, Maxim,* and *Esquire*. Why have they suddenly mushroomed in number and in readership? Again, the answer lies in their attractiveness to advertisers. Talk of a male identity crisis may have spurred some sales, and it is evident that men are now involved in a much wider range of purchasing decisions than ever before. While some 'new men' may be taking a more active interest in the household shopping, many more are marrying later after having indulged themselves in personal luxuries, an option that is less readily available to their married counterparts. With support from advertisers, the leading men's magazine in the UK, *FHM*, had a circulation of 315,149 copies per issue in 2007 (Audit Bureau of Circulation). In the late 1990s, *FHM* had even overtaken the leading women's monthly magazine, *Cosmopolitan*, although competition from the Internet and a proliferation of men's titles, such as *Zoo* and *Nuts*, resulted in *Cosmopolitan* taking back the lead—in 2007, it had a circulation of 460,276. Advertising to men still looked very attractive.

organizations conduct their own detailed research to help match target markets with the media audiences.

Buyer readiness state

It is often important to define an audience in terms of the level of involvement of potential recipients of the communication. For example, a distinction can be made between those people who are merely aware of the existence of a product, those who are interested in possibly purchasing it, and those who definitely wish to purchase it. This is crucial, because it was noted above that the aim of communication is to move target customers through the stages from mere awareness, through liking, to eventual purchase. Segmentation of audiences does not end there, however: many communication messages are aimed at people who have already bought a product, with the aim of reducing any *cognitive dissonance* they may have, and encouraging them to recommend the product to their friends. A communication can sometimes succeed in targeting buyers at all stages the buying process, but generally it is more likely to be focused on buyers at just one or two stages of the process.

It is also important to note that people differ markedly in their readiness to try new products, and a number of attempts have been made to classify the population in terms of their level of risk aversity or risk-seeking inclination. For purchases that are perceived as being highly risky, customers are likely to use more credible sources of information (e.g. word-of-mouth recommendation) and to engage in a prolonged search through information sources. Rogers (2003) defined a person's 'innovativeness' as the 'degree to which an individual is relatively earlier in adopting new ideas than the other members of his social system'. In each product area, there are likely to be 'consumption pioneers' and early adopters, while other individuals adopt new products only much later.

A typical adoption pattern, applied to the market for mobile video-phones, is illustrated in Figure 11.5. 'Innovators' are willing to try new ideas at some risk. Some people will always want to have the latest gadgets, and the promotion of new video mobile phones to this group should stress not only the technical features of the product, but also the status benefits that an early adopter of the new technology will receive. 'Early adopters' are opinion leaders in their community, adopting new products early but carefully. The 'early majority' adopt new ideas before the average person, taking their lead from opinion leaders; for this group communication should be moving towards an emphasis on the practical benefits of video mobile phones, rather than concentrating on their status benefits. The 'late majority' are sceptical, tending to adopt an innovation only after the majority of people have tried it. Finally, 'laggards' are tradition-bound, being suspicious of changes. This group adopts a new product only when it has become sufficiently widespread that it has now taken on a measure of tradition in itself. Communication aimed at them would probably emphasize low price and easy availability.

Figure 11.5 A message has to reflect the position of a service in its life cycle and differences between buyers in their motivations to try new services. Rogers described a diffusion model in which a small group of 'innovators' are first to respond to a new service offer, and a message to them may emphasize the novelty of the purchase and the social benefits that may derive from being a consumption pioneer of an exclusive product. Over time, ownership will become diffused to progressively wider audiences, helped by falling costs and increasing competitive pressure. Instead of stressing exclusivity, the advertising message is likely to increasingly emphasize easy availability and an affordable price. A final group of 'laggards' may only become receptive to a message if it implies that what was once an exclusive product has now become a necessary item which even they can afford. Mobile phone services as a category have gone through this diffusion process, with previous 'snob appeal' messages about mobile phone messages giving way to more general price-based promotion. Nevertheless, mobile phone operators are continually developing new services, such as live sports events delivered to customers' phones, that has the effect of starting the process again with a new group of innovators, before this new product development itself becomes adopted by a mainstream audience.

Push *v.* pull messages

Should a company aim its message at the final consumer who will actually use its product? You should recall from Chapter 4 the existence of a decision-making unit (DMU) and noted that the person who actually consumes a product may not be the best person to target a message at. (For example, a high proportion of men have very little influence in the purchase process for the socks that they wear.) Just as importantly, we need to consider whether messages should be aimed at the end buyer/user, or at intermediaries who will influence the purchase decisions of the end buyer/user.

This distinction forms the basis for 'push' and 'pull' models of communication (Figure 11.6). In a traditional push model, a manufacturer promotes its products heavily to wholesalers, which in turn promote to retailers, which in turn use their sales skills to sell

Figure 11.6 'Push' and 'pull' channels of communication compared

to the final buyer/user. In many markets, the end consumer may have little awareness of brands and may rely totally on what is offered to them by an intermediary. How many people visiting their dentist would specify a type of filling material by brand name that they would like the dentist to use in their filling? How many people visiting an independent financial adviser (IFA) for advice on pensions would have a preference for one pension company rather than another? In these circumstances, a company is most likely to achieve higher levels of sales by targeting its promotional efforts at intermediaries rather than the end consumer.

The problems to a manufacturer of a 'push' approach should be apparent. In order for its message to reach the end buyer/user, it must be transmitted efficiently and effectively by each of the intermediaries who handle the message. There is a great danger that noise factors could drastically change the message from what is sent out by the manufacturer to what is received by the end buyer/user. Because the manufacturer has very little control over a message as it passes through a push channel, it may seek to go over the heads of intermediaries by developing a pull channel. Here, the message is aimed at the end buyer/user. If it has an effect in changing their behaviour, buyers will go into a retail outlet and demand the brand by name. The retailer will then demand a particular brand from the wholesaler, which in turn will demand the product from the manufacturer. In the field of financial services, the efforts of savings and pensions companies to develop strong brands have been designed to bring buyers to an intermediary with a prior preference for one brand over others. In computing, Intel broke with tradition by going over the heads of dealers and computer assemblers with the message to end users that they would benefit by choosing a computer with an Intel processor.

Other important audiences for communication

It should be remembered that promotion is not always aimed solely at buyers or their immediate decision-making units. Other key audiences, or 'stake-holders' can include the following:

- suppliers;
- distributors/agents;
- competitors;
- employees and trades unions;
- political bodies and regulatory agencies;
- financial institutions;
- pressure groups and local community groups;
- the media and opinion leaders.

Each of these stakeholder groups at varying times can have a significant influence upon the organization in terms of its overall effectiveness, efficiency, and image. Many privatized utility companies realize that the most important target for their communication is often not the consumers who buy or use their services, but the regulators who control the prices that can be charged, or politicians who can change the legislative framework within which the utilities do business. It is often necessary to strike a balance between the short-term goals of the organization and the longer-term interests of these key groups. Communication is a vital link between the organization and its key stakeholders and Public Relations (see below) is often the primary tool used for communicating with such stakeholders.

● The channel

A message must be communicated to the target audience by some means. In a very few cases, a company may be able to do the bulk of its communication face-to-face with its current and potential customers. A trader at a fruit and vegetable market probably has no advertising or paid promotional activity, but relies on attracting passing trade through a display of his products and face-to-face communication with each customer. Larger and more complex companies cannot rely on such simple methods. They must develop impersonal means of communication in place of face-to-face contact. We talk about communication being conducted through a *channel*, such as television, newspapers, or posters. Some of these channels may nevertheless still retain a high degree of personal contact, for example **personal selling**.

Channels have a tendency to distort the message that was sent. We saw earlier how messages are encoded by the sender and also by the receiver, and part of the noise that occurs between the two can be explained by the nature of the channel. Some channels are able to accommodate a lengthy message without distortion. Contrast this with a typical 30-second radio advert, where a complex message must be conveyed in a short time using only one of the senses—sound. While some channels have a facility for immediate feedback from the person receiving a message (online channels are good at this), immediate response is lacking from most channels; for example, a newspaper advert in itself does not allow a customer to speak back to a company that has transmitted a message through the pages of the newspaper.

Companies put a lot of effort into optimizing their use of channels so that they get the maximum number of messages through to the most number of people in their target market, at minimum cost. We will consider general approaches to evaluation later in this chapter.

The term **promotion mix** is often used to describe the range of channels, such as advertising, e-mail, and face-to-face selling, that are available to companies as methods by which they can get their messages to target customers. We will look in more detail at the elements of the promotion mix, and their relationship to each other, later in this chapter.

Response: marketing communications models

Having identified the target audience and its characteristics, the communicator must consider the type of response required from it. The required response will have an influence on the source, message, and channel of communication.

It was noted above that in most cases customers are seen as going through a series of stages before finally deciding to purchase a product. It is therefore critical to recognize these buyer-readiness stages and to assess where the target audience is at any given time. The communicator will be seeking any one or more of three audience responses to the communication:

1. **Cognitive responses**—the message should be considered and understood.

2. **Affective responses**—the message should lead to some change in attitude.

3. **Behavioural responses**—finally, the message should achieve some change in behaviour (e.g. a purchase decision).

Many models have been developed to show how marketing communication has the effect of 'pushing' recipients of messages through a number of sequential stages, finally resulting in a purchase decision. These models portray a simple and steady movement through the various stages, and the probabilities of success in each stage cumulatively decline because of noise, and therefore the probability of the final stage eventually achieving an actual purchase can be very low.

We will now look briefly at some widely used marketing communication models which seek to understand buyers' responses to communication stimuli.

'Hierarchy of effects' models

Hierarchy of effects models propose a sequence of responses that occurs as a result of a message being received by a target audience. The two most common such models are referred to as AIDA and DAGMAR (Figure 11.7).

The principle that underlies these models is that communication acts as a stimulus which gives rise to a 'conditioned' response. Communication can therefore be developed to achieve the objective of moving people through a sequence of responses:

- To gain initial awareness of a product, advertising may be the most effective method.

- To gain liking, comprehension, and desire, brochures may provide more detail that will be needed to make a subsequent purchase decision.

- To achieve an actual sale, personal selling and sales promotion activity may be best.

Hierarchy of effects models suggest how communications affect the mind and behaviour of the audience. The major benefit of such models is that they enable the purpose of a particular promotion to be defined and pre- and post-campaign surveys can be carried out to demonstrate the communication effect.

The models have many weaknesses, the most significant being their simplification of a complex psychological and behavioural process. The audience is seen as a passive recipient of messages as opposed to active seekers and participants in the **communication process**. Consumer research has shown that many consumers set predetermined parameters within which a purchase decision might be made, such as price range and style of a product. The buyer therefore selects those messages that support her in her purchase decision as opposed to being passively pulled through the sequence. These models also

Figure 11.7 AIDA and DAGMAR models of communication processes

ignore psychological factors, such as the influence of attitudes/beliefs, motivation, and perception on behaviour. Furthermore, they assume that the sequence of response is universal, when in fact instances occur where awareness of, and commitment to, a product can occur at the same time as the point of purchase but with limited understanding, as happens with impulse purchases. Finally, the assumption that specific promotional effects can be measured in isolation is a simplification of a complex communication environment. In reality, it is difficult to isolate one single cause as a communication effect. We are bombarded daily by many communication signals, each one playing its part in influencing behaviour.

Integrated models

A model that identifies and integrates psychological and behavioural elements was developed by Timothy Joyce and is shown in Figure 11.8. This model recognizes that to understand how promotions work we need to understand the nature of the promotion, people's purchase behaviour, their individual psychology, and how the relationships between these factors interrelate. The effect of communication is seen not as a passive relationship but more as a continuing relationship, with habit and consistency forming an integral part of an individual's behaviour. The inclusion of perception and the selective attention to

Figure 11.8 A model of communication, incorporating psychological and behavioural elements

Source: adapted from T. Joyce, 'What do we know about how advertising works?', ESOMAR, 1967

communication stimuli recognize that the consumer will not take in all of a communication message and that individuals make associations in their own minds as to the nature of the communication they have received. The model also recognizes that attitudes can be influenced by both pre- and post-purchase experience and that consumers may actively seek promotional material to reduce their feelings cognitive dissonance, which can occur where they believe that they may not have made the best purchase choice. Promotion can therefore have a role in reinforcing the correctness of the buyer's choice.

◉ Stages of the promotion planning process

Promotional activity is unlikely to be effective unless it forms part of a cohesive and integrated promotional plan. A useful framework within which to consider promotional planning is the SOST '4Ms' proposed by Smith and Taylor (2004), which sees the process beginning with a general review of a company's situation, and proceeds through objectives, strategy, and tactics.

1. **Situation**

   (a) Company—sales and market share trends, summary strengths and weaknesses

   (b) Product service range—features, benefits, and Unique Selling Proposition; product positioning

   (c) Market structure—growth, opportunities and hazards, target markets and competition

2. **Objectives:** short, medium, and long term

   (a) Marketing objectives

   (b) Communication objectives

3. **Strategy:** how the objectives will be achieved; this can be a summary of the promotional mix and can include the marketing mix (no tactical details here)

4. **Tactics:** the detailed activities to implement strategy; the detailed planning of how, when, and where various promotional activities (communication tools) occur

5. **4Ms**

   (a) *Men*: men (and women!)—Who is responsible for what? Are there enough suitably experienced men and women in-house to handle various projects? Have they got spare capacity to take on extra tasks? Are outside agencies needed, or should extra permanent staff be recruited?

   (b) *Money*: budget—what will it cost? Is it affordable? Is it good value for money? Should the money be spent elsewhere? Does the budget include research to measure the effectiveness of various other activities? Is there an allowance for contingencies?

(c) *Minutes*: time-scale and deadlines for each stage of each activity—proposals, concept development, concept testing, regional testing, national roll-out, European launch.

(d) *Measurement*: monitoring the results of all activities helps the marketing manager to understand what works well and what is not worth repeating in the next campaign. Clearly defined and specific objectives provide yardsticks for measurement. The monitored results also help the manager to make realistic forecasts and ultimately to build better marketing communication plans in the future.

The situation analysis should ideally be part of a comprehensive audit of an organization's competitive position. It should highlight market trends, market position, competitor activity, consumer perceptions, etc. From this analysis a clearer understanding of the situation can be obtained and appropriate objectives and strategies agreed. It is also important to conduct an internal audit of the organization to determine resource requirements and availability.

After analysing the situation, objectives are set. A mnemonic that provides a useful framework by which to formulate objectives is SMARTT. Objectives should be **S**pecific, **M**easurable, **A**chievable, **R**elevant, **T**imed, and **T**argeted.

The choice of promotional strategy will be determined by the objectives. A range of promotional options are likely to be available, for example whether to have a low-key launch of a new product, or to go for an aggressive promotional build-up prior to launch. Strategy is not about doing things, but about setting the direction, scope, and breadth by which things will be done, and allocating resources. The strategy should provide guidance on the future implementation of promotional activity and its evaluation.

The promotion campaign

A campaign brings together a wide range of media-related activities so that, instead of being a series of unrelated activities, they can act in a planned and coordinated way to achieve promotional objectives. The term 'Integrated Marketing Communications' is often used to describe the way in which one promotional medium works in conjunction with others, in order to convey a consistent message cost-effectively. The first stage of campaign planning is to have a clear understanding of promotional objectives (see above). Once these have been clarified, a message can be developed that is most likely to achieve the objectives. The next step is the production of the media plan. Having defined the target audience in terms of its size, location, and media characteristics, media must be selected that achieve the desired levels of exposure/repetition with the target audience. This should specify the timing of media activities (Figure 11.9). A media plan must be formulated which specifies:

• the allocation of expenditure between the different media;

Product X	Schedule of Promotional Activity									
	J	F	M	A	M	J	J	A	S	O
TV adverts	X	X				X	X			
Magazine adverts		X	X	X			X	X	X	
Press releases	X	X			X	X			X	X
Sales promotions			X	X	X				X	X
Trade promotions	X	X			X	X			X	X
Field sales	X	X			X	X			X	X
Telephone sales	X	X	X			X	X	X		
Sponsorship				X			X			
Exhibition				X						
Community event							X			

Figure 11.9 A schedule such as the one shown above is typically used to plan media-related activities over the coming 12-month period. While a plan such as this helps to control budgets and provides more certainty in interfunctional planning, the media schedule may need to be revised at short notice, for example if consumer spending falls unexpectedly, or a new competitor appears with a large media budget.

- the selection of specific media components—for example, in the case of print media, decisions need to be made regarding the type (tabloid *v.* broadsheet), size of advertisement, and whether there is to be national or local coverage;
- the frequency and timing of insertions;
- the cost of reaching a particular target group for each of the media vehicles specified in the plan;
- the inter-relationship between different media (e.g. how an Internet banner ad may reinforce a television advert).

The role of promotion agencies

Should a company undertake its own campaign management, or give the task to a specialist agency? There are many benefits in giving the task to an outside agency. The culture of a company, especially large ones operating in stable or regulated environments, may not be conducive to the creativity that promotion demands and therefore it may be better to leave promotional activity to an outside organization which has a more creative culture. It may be easier for an outsider to be more customer-focused and to see opportunities for promotion that are not immediately apparent to insiders who are too close to the product. A further major benefit of using an outside agency is its ability to use its expertise in developing and executing campaigns. Such agencies can usually purchase media on more favourable terms than a single company acting alone. External agencies have tended to become much broader in their abilities. While many still specialize in one type of promotion (e.g. advertising or direct mail), there has been a tendency for agencies to offer their clients a broad range of promotion management services. Clients' requirement for integrated marketing communications planning (sometimes referred to as 'media neutral planning') in an increasingly complex and fragmented media world has been one reason for the development of large multi-media promotion agencies. An integrated approach implies consistency in the structure of communications and the attitudes they develop (Fill, 2006).

Against these benefits, external agencies are sometimes accused of losing sight of the true nature of a product and its target customers. While an agency may be free to take risky innovations, these can sometimes prove disastrous and need to be disowned by the client company. The relationship between an advertising agency and its client company is critical. There are many examples of very long-lasting relationships which have been mutually beneficial and have given the agency considerable experience in understanding the client's needs. Dissatisfaction with the relationship may result in the client company's inviting rival agencies to 'pitch' for its account. Large organizations frequently use a number of agencies to cover different product and/or geographical areas. Where a company uses the specialized services of different media agencies, there is a danger that these could seek to use more of the client's money on the medium in which they specialize, rather than on the medium that is best suited to the client. A specialist advertising agency may see a direct marketing agency as a threat, rather than part of an integrated solution which would benefit the client.

Setting budgets for promotional activity

Promotional expenditure can become a drain on an organization's resources if no conscious attempt is made to determine an appropriate budget and to ensure that expenditure is kept within the budget. A number of methods are commonly used to determine the promotional budget.

- **What can be afforded:** This is largely a subjective assessment and regards promotion as a luxury which can be afforded in good times and cut back during lean times. In fact, expenditure may need to be increased rather than reduced in bad times. This approach is used by many smaller companies to whom advertising spending is seen as the first and easy short-term target for reducing expenditure in bad times.

- **Percentage of sales:** By this method, advertising expenditure rises or falls to reflect changes in sales. In fact, sales are likely to be influenced by advertising rather than vice versa, and this method is likely to accentuate any given situation. If sales are declining during a recession, *more* advertising may be required to induce sales, but this method of determining the budget implies imposing a cut in advertising expenditure.

- **Competitive parity:** Advertising expenditure is determined by the amount spent by competitors. Many market sectors see periodic outbursts of promotional expenditure, often accompanying a change in some other element of firms' marketing mix. As an example, operators of satellite and cable television services in the UK became involved in an escalating campaign during 2007, as the two main contenders—BSkyB and Virgin—launched a series of new services, backed by levels of promotion expenditure which were designed to outbid the other. However, merely increasing advertising expenditure may hide the fact that other elements of the marketing mix need adjusting in order to gain a competitive market position in relation to competitors.

- **Residual:** This is the least satisfactory approach, and merely assigns to the advertising budget what is left after all other costs have been covered. It may bear no relationship to promotional objectives, especially as a down-turn in the business cycle may call for greater expenditure rather than less.

- **Objective and task:** This approach starts by defining promotional objectives. Tasks are then set that relate to specific targets. In this way, advertising is seen as a necessary—even though risky—investment in a brand, ranking in importance with other more obvious costs such as production and salary costs. This is the most rational approach to setting a promotional budget.

It has been common to talk about 'above-the-line' and 'below-the-line' promotional budgets, referring respectively to advertising and other forms of promotion. In large organizations, having separately managed budgets for different elements of the promotion mix may have served the status needs of individual managers, but the result may have been a fragmented promotion plan. With increasing emphasis on integrated communications, this distinction has become increasingly irrelevant. Also, instead of the advertising manager engaging an advertising agency and the direct marketing manager recruiting a direct marketing agency, there has been a tendency for agencies to become multi-channel, operating 'through the line', thereby allowing a client company to hand its entire promotional planning activity over to one agency.

It was also noted above that many of a firm's activities that communicate messages about the firm and its products do not fit neatly under the heading of 'promotion', and therefore may not be included in the promotional budget. While there has been a tendency to bring under the budget heading some items that were previously considered outside of it (e.g. direct marketing activities), others are difficult to include. Should a company's website be included within the promotional budget, or should it be seen as part of a company's wider budget for supporting its distribution system? More seriously, how should temporary price discounts be handled? Should these be included as a promotional item of expenditure, perhaps on the basis that they are a temporary means of stimulating sales? Or should they be regarded not as a cost, but as a reduction in revenue budgets? There are also issues about the extent to which promotion managers should have budgetary responsibility for the customer-facing messages that are given out by a company's buildings and staff. Some would argue that the promotion budget for a fashion retailer should include provision for a designer-look store frontage that conveys a message about the clothes within the store.

Monitoring and evaluating the promotional effort

It is very important to monitor and evaluate the effectiveness of an organization's promotional activities, in order to better inform future campaign planning. However, it can be very difficult to assess effectiveness, and in respect of advertising, Lord Rothermere once famously said that half of all advertising was wasted, but the trouble was he could not tell which half. In one study of 135 campaigns by 40 advertising agencies, it was found that almost none of the agencies really knew, or ever could know, whether or not their campaigns were successful (Henderson, 2000). While much evaluation relies on instinct and gut feeling, methods of evaluation are becoming increasingly sophisticated. Databases are making it possible for direct marketing companies to measure the response to a message, allowing them to refine their efforts in future targeting. The development of the Internet has allowed previously unimaginable levels of information about an audience's behaviour with respect to a message. Cookies embedded in an individual's computer can enable a company to learn how the viewer arrived at a company's site, the range of sites that she had previously visited, her movements around the site, how long she spent on different pages, where she went to subsequently, and whether she made a purchase/inquiry for further information.

It should not be forgotten that evaluation of communication must be made against the objectives set for that communication. A message that had the objective of creating awareness of a brand should not be criticized if it failed to achieve a short-term increase in sales. Instead, evaluation should be based on changes in the level of awareness of the brand among the target market.

In combination, a number of techniques can be used to try to assess the effectiveness of an individual advert or an advertising campaign:

- Prior to launching a message, companies use focus groups to test its effectiveness. Researchers are particularly concerned to identify memorable parts of the message and how far an individual progressed before he skipped to the next subject. Prior evaluation of an advert can help companies to avoid running adverts that subsequently turn out to be offensive or misinterpreted.

- Routine monitoring of a sample panel's television viewing is undertaken by BARB. Similar monitoring of the press is undertaken by the National Readership Survey. While such monitoring can estimate how many people see an advertisement, they provide little evidence of whether the advert was recalled or acted upon.

- To overcome the above problem, a number of panels are retained by market research agencies and are consulted regularly to ascertain which recent advertisements or other promotional messages they can recall, either spontaneously or with prompting. One example is the NOP weekly telephone omnibus survey carried out among 1,000 adults on behalf of sponsoring companies.

Introducing the promotion mix

Communication is received by audiences from two principal sources: those within an organization, and those external to it. The latter includes **word-of-mouth**/word-of-mouse recommendation from friends, editorials in the press, etc., which may have high credibility in the product evaluation process. Sources originating within an organization can be divided into those originating from the traditional marketing function (which can be divided into personal two-way channels such as personal selling and impersonal one-way channels such as advertising), and those originating from front-line production resources. In the case of services that involve consumers in the production process, the promotion mix has to be considered more broadly than is the case with manufactured goods. Front-line operations staff and service outlets become a valuable channel of communication.

The promotion mix comprises those activities and channels that a company uses to promote its products and its corporate image to customers, potential customers, and the key stakeholder groups described above. These activities are conventionally identified by a number of headings, although they overlap. As with the marketing mix itself, definitions of the promotion mix elements are not in themselves particularly important—what is more important is to recognize the interdependencies between them. The most commonly used headings for promotion mix elements are advertising, sales promotion, selling, public relations, direct marketing, and online marketing. Within each of these categories a further range of options can be identified. (For example,

Figure 11.10 Key elements of the promotion mix

advertising involves mixing a variety of media, such as newspaper, television, and radio advertising.) Figure 11.10 outlines the key elements of the promotion mix.

The choice of a particular combination of communication channels will depend primarily on the characteristics of the target audience, especially its habits in terms of exposure to messages. Other important considerations include the present and potential market size for the product (advertising on television may not be appropriate for a product that has a local niche market, for example), the nature of the product itself (the more personal the product, the more effective the two-way communication channel), and of course the costs of the various channels.

An important trend affecting promotional planning is the increasing fragmentation of markets, resulting in smaller market segments, and hence smaller audiences for a highly specific message. Fortunately, this has occurred at a time of growing media availability and choice. Sophisticated database technology and the Internet have opened new possibilities for communicating messages to narrowly defined audiences, while the development of the mobile Internet through 3G mobile phones, WiFi, and global positioning systems allows targeting not only by individual, but also according to where and when a company believes that the individual will be most responsive to a message. Such fragmentation of both markets and media availability confirms the need for increased sophistication of market segmentation and targeting techniques within the promotion planning process. Another key trend is the emergence of peer-to-peer communication through the Internet. **Social networking sites** such as Facebook and You-Tube can provide user generated sources of messages which compete with the 'official' message from the company whose products are being talked about.

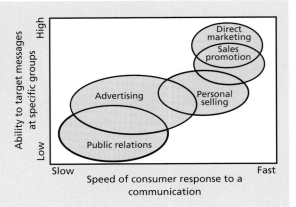

Figure 11.11 A schematic map showing the capabilities of the main promotional mix elements in terms of their ability to target specific audiences and to achieve short-term rather than long-term results

The elements of the promotion mix vary in the extent to which they can achieve the diverse communication objectives described earlier in this chapter. Advertising, for example, is generally fairly good at developing an image for a company, but is less capable of conveying complex factual information about a product. Direct marketing is much better at adapting a message to very small audiences, but is less useful for image building. Two important aspects of communication objectives are shown in Figure 11.11:

1. the extent to which a message can be adapted to the needs of a specific audience;

2. the extent to which a message can achieve a short-term or a long-term response from the audience.

In the figure a two-dimensional grid has been drawn, in which the main elements of the promotional mix have been located. The diagram shows that, while different mix elements may have distinctive functions, there is nevertheless some overlap. Some media, such as advertising, are capable of spanning a range of objectives.

Different elements of the promotion mix are brought together in a promotional campaign, and for any given product, the emphasis placed on different elements are likely to change as a product goes through its life cycle. Advertising and public relations are more likely to form important channels of communication during the introductory stage of the life cycle, where the major objective is often to increase overall audience awareness. Sales promotion can be used to stimulate trial, and in some instances personal selling can be used to acquire distribution coverage. During a product's growth stage the use of all communication channels can generally be reduced, as demand during this phase tends to produce its own momentum through word-of-mouth communications. However, as the product develops into its maturity stage, there may be a call for an increase in advertising and sales promotion activity. Finally, when the product is seen to be going into decline, advertising and public relations are often reduced, although sales promotion can still quite usefully be applied. Sometimes

Press (newspapers, magazines, and directories)	45.3%
Television	25.4%
Direct mail	12.5%
Outdoor and transport	5.5%
Internet	7.2%
Radio	3.1%
Cinema	1.0%.

Total advertising expenditure in 2006 was £19 billions

Figure 11.12 Estimate of UK display advertising by medium, 2007

Source: based on Advertising Association estimates

products in decline are allowed to die quietly with very little promotion. In the case of many long-life financial services, which a company would like to delete but cannot for contractual reasons, the service may be kept going with no promotional support at all. Figure 11.12 gives some indication of the relative importance of the different elements of the promotion mix, as measured by expenditure.

An organization's image can be projected through channels other than the formal promotional process. There is a lot of evidence, for example, that, when comparing professional and personal services providers, customers prefer to be guided by information from friends and other personal contacts rather than a company's formal promotion mix (e.g. Susskind, 2002; Walker, 2001). Of course, positive word-of-mouth recommendation is generally dependent on customers having good experiences with an organization. An important communication objective for firms is often therefore to leverage 'free' positive promotion through word-of-mouth recommendation, and to limit the damage caused by negative word-of-mouth. Word-of-mouth recommendation has been further facilitated by the Internet. As well as telling their friends, messages left with social network sites can spread a message very rapidly. Many companies have embraced the Internet to develop **viral marketing**, in which a message can be spread rapidly from one person to a handful of friends, who each in turn inform a handful of their friends (Ferguson, 2008). In one case, the online marketing firm NewGate distributed advance excerpts of a new children's book to online forum leaders. When the forum leaders read the pre-released chapters they quickly spread the excitement and anticipation for the book, which ended up being on the *New York Times* bestseller list. The company had used more than 400,000 discussion boards and message forums across the net, targeting about 11 million 'e-fluentials', who in turn reached 55 million consumers by spreading the word (Cardwell, 2002). However, Internet-based communication can also pose a threat to companies as social networking sites can rapidly spread the views of dissatisfied customers. As an example, the bank HSBC announced in 2007 that it intended to end interest-free overdrafts for students after they had graduated, but was subsequently forced to do a u-turn and restore the facility. Many commentators attributed this change of heart to the strength of feeling expressed through Facebook circles of friends.

We will now look in more detail at each of the main elements of the promotion mix. We can only cover broad strategic issues relating to each of these, and for more discussion of the practical problems and opportunities of implementation, refer to the suggestions for further reading at the end of this chapter. Remember also as you read through the list of promotion mix elements that the headings used can overlap, for example, Internet promotion may be seen as a form of advertising.

Advertising

The role of advertising in the promotion mix

Advertising is defined here as 'Any paid form of non-personal communication of ideas, goods, or services delivered through selected media channels'. This definition incorporates a wide range of activities, from a 30-second slot on prime-time television through to a postcard in a newsagent's window. Advertising 'media' simply refers to where the advert is placed. In addition to television and newspapers, a hot-air balloon with an advertising message and football hoardings seen at stadiums are all different forms of advertising media.

The selection of media is critical. In an ideal world, a specific advertisement would be seen and read by all of its intended target audience. In reality, such coverage is difficult to achieve. Different media are therefore selected to increase the probability of a member of the target audience seeing the advert at least once. The combination of types of media used for this purpose is often referred to as the *media mix*.

Advertising is defined as non-personal. Advertisements are targeted at a mass audience and not to a specific individual. One of the benefits of advertising is its ability to reach a large number of people at relatively low cost. That is not to say that advertising costs are low. If an advertiser wishes to reach a prime-time television audience or to place a full-page advert in a high-quality magazine or newspaper, then the costs will range from tens of thousands of pounds to hundreds of thousands of pounds just for one spot or insertion. When we consider the cost per 1,000 people, however, this can work out to be relatively low. With large audiences or readerships, the cost of an advertisement per 1,000 viewers or readers can often fall to just a few pence. Advertising, like the other mix elements, cannot be seen in isolation. Advertising is frequently used, for example, to support sales promotion and direct marketing activity.

How does advertising work?

Think back to the discussion earlier in this chapter about the objectives of communication. You will recall that a message may be required to do a number of things, from simply creating awareness of a product, through to achieving a final sale. Advertising can be used to achieve a wide range of objectives, but it is generally best suited to building a longer-term image for an organization and its products. Advertising is also best at targeting broadly defined target audiences where dialogue is not called for.

An advertising message must be able to move an individual along a path from awareness through to eventual purchase. In order for a message to be received and understood, it must gain attention, use a common language, arouse needs, and suggest how these needs may be met. The content, structure, and format of an advert must be developed in order to achieve promotional objectives. A complex message needs to be encoded before being transmitted, but the presence of noise may result in the receiver decoding a message quite differently to what had been intended.

The role of advertising often does not end when a sale has been achieved. Advertising is often aimed at customers after they have made a purchase, to encourage them to feel that they made the correct choice (thereby reducing 'cognitive dissonance') and to foster further purchases from the company. It was noted in Chapter 4 that organizations increasingly seek to build relationships with their customers, so the behavioural change (the sale) should be seen as the starting point for making customers aware of other goods and services available from the organization.

Advertising media

Effective advertising requires a good understanding of the media habits of the target audience. If a firm's target market is not in the habit of being exposed to a particular medium, much of the value of advertising through that medium will be wasted. Information about target audiences' media habits is obtained from a number of sources. Newspaper readership information is collated by the National Readership Survey. For each newspaper, this shows reading frequency and average readership per issue (as distinct from circulation) broken down into age, class, sex, ownership of consumer durables, etc. Television-viewing information is collected by BARB. This indicates the number of people watching particular channels at particular times by reference to two types of television rating (TVR): one for the number of *households* watching a programme/advertising slot, and one for the number of *people* watching.

Using such sources of information, the media characteristics of a particular target audience can be ascertained and a media plan produced which achieves maximum penetration of the target audience.

The choice of advertising media is influenced by the characteristics of each medium and its ability to achieve the specified promotional objectives. The following are some of the most common types of media and their characteristics.

Newspapers. Daily newspapers tend to have a high degree of reader loyalty, reflecting the fact that each national title is targeted at specific segments of the population. This loyalty means that the printed message can be perceived by readers as having a high level of credibility. Therefore, daily papers may be useful for prestige and reminder advertising. They can be used for creating general awareness of a product or a brand as well as providing detailed product information. In this way, banks use newspapers both for adverts designed to create a brand awareness and liking for the organization, and for adverts giving specific details of savings accounts. The latter may include an invitation to act in the form of a website address or freephone telephone number where a transaction can be completed.

Daily newspapers, however, are normally read hurriedly, and therefore lengthy copy is likely to be wasted. Sunday newspapers also appeal to highly segmented audiences but are generally read at a more leisurely pace than daily papers. They are also more likely to be read at home and shared by households, which may be important for appealing to family-based purchase decisions.

Local newspapers offer a much greater degree of geographical segmentation than is possible with national titles. Within their circulation areas, they can also achieve much higher levels of readership penetration. In the case of free newspapers that are given away free, high levels of circulation may be achieved, although actual readership levels are more open to question. While national advertising through local newspapers is expensive and inefficient, it is useful for purely local suppliers, as well as national organizations wishing to target specific areas with local messages, or to pre-test national advertising copy.

The distinction between national, regional, and local papers has become blurred as flexible printing systems allow local editions of national and international newspapers to be produced, appealing to advertisers seeking tightly specified audiences. Many commentators have forecast the demise of newspapers in the face of competition from electronic sources of news, but newspapers have fought back and adapted. There is, however, a trend towards lower newspaper readership by some groups, especially young people (Lauf, 2001). Local newspapers have suffered, as much of their traditional classified advertising—for jobs, cars, and houses—has transferred to the Internet, which provides a constantly updated and searchable source of information, accessible from anywhere.

Magazines/journals. Within the UK, and most western countries, there is an extensive selection of magazine and journal titles. While some high-circulation magazines appeal to broad groups of people (e.g. *Radio Times*), most titles are specialized in terms of their content and targeting. In this way, *What Car?* magazine may be a highly specific medium for car manufacturers, dealers, and loan companies to promote their goods and services to new car buyers. Specialist trade titles allow messages to be aimed at intermediaries; for example, manufacturers of catering equipment will gain access to an audience of key buyers through *The Caterer* magazine. The amount of advertising placed in magazines has been falling recently, as advertisers, especially specialist trade and classified advertisers, have moved to searchable online media. According to Outsell, a research firm which advises the information industry, trade publishers' revenues fell by more than 10% between 2005 and 2007, with a number of specialist titles, such as *Hospital Doctor* and *Independent Practitioner* closing.

MARKETING in ACTION

What does your newspaper say about you?

In most countries, advertisers are attracted to national newspapers by the highly segmented audience of each newspaper. Not only do we tend to be loyal to our preferred newspaper, but we may be inclined subconsciously to regard advertisements placed in it as being more believable. An individual's choice of national newspaper can say a lot about his or her values, attitudes, and lifestyle. Researchers have developed a number of detailed indicators of the profile of a newspaper's readership, but the following tongue-in-cheek analysis of UK newspaper readership may not be too far from the truth:

- *The Times* is read by the people who *run* the country.
- *The Financial Times* is read by the people who *own* the country.
- *The Telegraph* is read by people who think that the country should be run the way that it was *in the past*.
- *The Mail* is read by the *wives* of the people that run the country.
- *The Independent*'s readers keep an *open mind* about who should run the country.
- *Sun* readers do not care who runs the country, so long as she *looks good* on page 3.

What does your preferred newspaper say about you?

Although advertising in magazines may at first seem relatively expensive compared with newspapers, it represents good value to advertisers in terms of the high number of target readers per copy and the highly segmented nature of their audiences.

Television. This is an expensive, but very powerful, medium. Although it tends to be used mainly for the long-term task of creating brand awareness, it can also be used to create a rapid sales response. The very fact that a message has been seen on television can give credibility to the message source, and many companies add the phrase 'as seen on TV' to give additional credibility to their other media communications. The power of the television medium is enhanced by its ability to appeal to the senses of both sight and sound, and to use movement and colour to develop a sales message.

The major limitation of television advertising is its cost. For most small businesses, television advertising rates start at too high a level to be considered. The high starting price for television advertising reflects not only high production costs, but also the difficulty in segmenting television audiences, either socio-economically or in terms of narrowly defined geographical areas. Also, the question must be asked as to how many people within the target audience are actually receptive to a television advert. Is the target viewer actually in the room when an advertisement is being broadcast? If the viewer is present, is he receptive to the message? The use of video recorders and remote controls has important implications for the effectiveness of television advertising. Television advertisers must use their creative talents to ensure that a short 30-second slot creates sufficient impact that a viewer pays attention to the whole of the advertisement.

With the development of digital broadcasting and the proliferation of television channels, the ability of the medium to segment audiences is increasing. There are now numerous channels that have developed distinctive audiences, such as the Discovery Channel, MTV, and Sky Sports. With the development of interactive television, advertising can be used to elicit an immediate response. (For example, a pizza company can use an advert to create an awareness and liking of its brand, as well as offering immediate ordering and delivery of a pizza.)

Commercial radio. Radio advertising in the UK has seen considerable growth in recent years, recovering from its traditional perception as the poor relation of television advertising. The threshold cost of radio advertising is much lower than for television, reflecting much more local segmentation of radio audiences and the lower production costs of radio adverts. With radio, the audience can be involved in other activities—particularly driving—while being exposed to an advertisement. Inevitably, a radio message is less powerful than a television message, relying solely on the sense of hearing. Although there are often doubts about the extent to which an audience receives and understands a radio message, it does form a useful reminder medium when used in conjunction with other media.

Cinema. Because of the captive nature of cinema audiences, this medium has the potential to make a major impact. It is frequently used to promote local services such as food outlets, whose target market broadly corresponds to the audience of most cinemas. However, without repetition, cinema advertisements have little lasting effect, although they can be useful for supporting press and television advertising.

Outdoor advertising. This is useful for reminder copy and can support other media activities. The effect of an advertisement on television or in the national press can be prolonged if recipients are exposed to a reminder poster on their way to work the following day. Some poster sites can appeal to segmented audiences; for example, London Underground sites in the City of London are seen by large numbers of affluent business people. The sides of buses are often used to support new products available locally (e.g. new store openings) and have the ability to spread their message as the bus travels along local routes. Posters can generally be used only to convey a simple communication rather than complex details.

Online media. The Internet has opened up new opportunities for companies to communicate with their target markets. Much of the development in this area allows companies to enter into a one-to-one dialogue with customers that is not strictly a form of advertising as defined here. The use of the Internet for one-to-one communication and distribution is considered in more detail later in this chapter. In addition, most companies have their own websites which address mass audiences. Creating an awareness of these sites has become a major challenge for companies, with conventional media often being used to promote the website address. As a further method of attracting 'hits', companies frequently pay for hotlinks out of other companies' websites. 'Search' marketing has become very important for identifying web-based audiences who are actively seeking a particular category of product, and will be considered later (Jones, 2008).

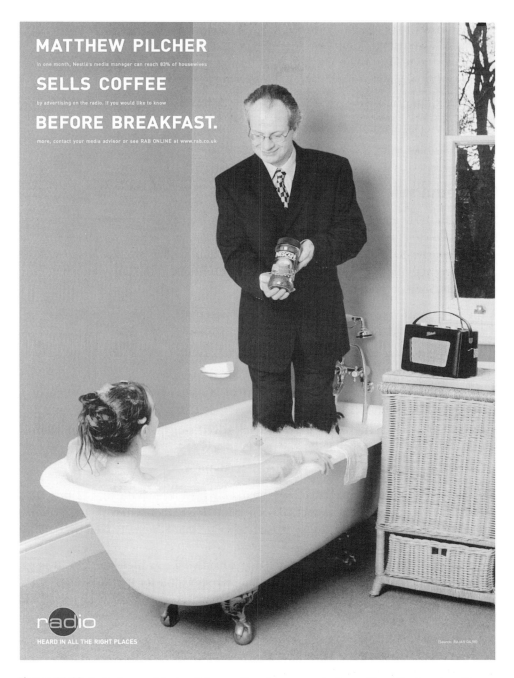

Figure 11.13 Radio is a useful advertising medium for communicating with audiences when they are captive and/or open to persuasion. This advertisement demonstrates the power of radio in communicating a message about a fast-moving consumer good, just at the moment when the audience may be most receptive to a message about the product. (Reproduced with permission of the Radio Advertising Bureau)

Other innovative media. Advertising media can become very cluttered by the sheer volume of advertising. Companies that spot new media may avoid some of this clutter by having the field to themselves, at least until it too becomes cluttered. Innovative media that have targeted specific groups in recent years include:

- adverts on milk bottles promoting breakfast cereals;
- adverts on petrol pumps promoting car insurance;
- adverts on the sides of cows promoting ice cream.

Media selection and evaluation

Faced with the availability of such a great variety of media, advertising managers need some criteria to assess the most effective mix of media to meet their objectives. Increasingly sophisticated computer programs are available which produce a schedule of advertising activities, based on their ability to get through to the target audience cost-effectively. Such programs take into account:

- the *cover* or reach of an advert, defined as the percentage of a particular target audience reached by a medium or a whole campaign;
- the *frequency*, or number of times a particular target audience has an 'opportunity to see/hear' an advertising message;
- the impact an advertisement will have on the target audience—how many people can remember seeing an advert?
- the extent to which the effects of a particular advertising message 'wear out' over time and require reinforcement;
- the cost of advertising through a particular medium.

The cost of using different media varies markedly, and a medium that at first sight appears to be expensive may in fact be good value in terms of achieving promotional objectives. A key measure is the cost of each message that is actually seen by, or acted upon, by the target audience.

Although it is commonplace to think that advertising can increase sales, it is extremely difficult to prove that advertising alone is responsible for a sales increase. Sales, after all, can be the result of many intervening variables, some of which are internal to the organization (e.g. public relations activity, pricing policy), while others are external (e.g. the state of the national economy).

Constraints on advertising

You will recall from Chapter 3 that firms are increasingly expected to act in a socially responsible manner, and this is particularly the case in respect of their advertising.

Figure 11.14 Trade journals are particularly valuable for targeting highly specific groups of business buyers. *Construction News* is the most widely circulated publication within the UK building and civil engineering sector with a total ABC average circulation figure of 21,203 (July 2006–June 2007). This makes it an ideal medium for promoting a range of construction-related products, such as plant and equipment. A fuller understanding of the publication's readers is provided by an in-depth readership survey which is conducted every two years. Among other things, the survey has established that on average, four people read each copy of *Construction News*, giving an industry-wide readership of about 85,000 per issue. (Reproduced with permission of *Construction News*)

Britain, like most developed countries, recognizes the possibly harmful effects that advertising can have on vulnerable buyers and the values of society. Advertisers therefore face a number of controls on the content and distribution of their adverts. The content of advertisements is influenced by both **voluntary codes** and legislation, although the effect of EU legislation has been to move more towards legislation; for example, from 2003 it has been illegal to advertise tobacco products. Refer back to Chapter 3 for more discussion of the voluntary and legislative constraints on advertisers.

Personal selling

Personal selling involves interpersonal dialogue between a prospective customer and a salesperson. Such dialogue may occur face-to-face or by other personal forms of communication. Personal selling is not simply about persuasion and persistence, although undoubtedly such skills and attributes do come in useful. Professional selling is also about gathering market and customer information; listening, interpreting, and understanding customer needs; managing the customer–supplier relationship interface; and communicating clearly to the customer the benefits of purchasing a particular product that meets their needs.

Selling as a profession is often devalued and misunderstood. Much of this misunderstanding comes from the activities of sectors of the profession itself, particularly the sleazy end represented by pressurized selling techniques, which traditionally were (and still commonly are) practised in several consumer service and goods industries such as double glazing, time-share property, and kitchens/bathrooms. In a business-to-business context, professional selling is more highly regarded.

The interrelationship between sales and marketing has been discussed at length. There is only limited evidence to support the view of Drucker (1973), who stated that if organizations got their marketing activity right they would not need a sales force, as customers would come beating a path to their door. Such a statement is naive and does not recognize the complex nature of many purchase decisions and the importance of human relationships and the sales function in business transactions. Steward (1993) suggested that to omit the importance of selling as an integral component of the marketing activities of an organization is akin to 'omitting a striker from a football team, a gun without a firing pin, and a chemical formula without a catalyst . . .'. Contemporary issues about the relationship between selling and marketing have been explored by Kotler, Rackham, and Krishnaswamy (2006).

Types of selling

Selling includes activities that range from a shop assistant selling a bar of chocolate for a few pence to teams negotiating a multi-million pound contract to supply aircraft. A salesperson's role can be described as any of the following, or combination of them:

- **Deliverer:** Although a person may have the title of 'salesperson', their job is mainly concerned with delivering the product, e.g. milk, beer, bread, and there are few selling responsibilities. Increases in sales are more likely to stem from a good service and a pleasant manner.

- **Order taker:** The salesperson is predominantly an order-taker but works in the field and is sometimes able to negotiate additional sales. Here, selling may be done at a central or regional office, and the salesperson simply records and processes the customers' orders. Sometimes, there is scope for making additional sales, for example a waiter in a restaurant may have a role to encourage customers to add additional items to their order. Good service and a pleasant personality may lead to more orders, but the salesperson has only limited opportunity for creative selling.

- **Missionary selling:** The salesperson does not actually take orders but rather, builds up goodwill, educates the actual or potential user, and undertakes various promotional activities, e.g. a salesperson for a pharmaceutical company who makes doctors and pharmacists aware of the benefits of prescribing a new drug.

- **Technical selling:** Many companies in business-to-business markets use sales engineers or salespeople with technical knowledge where product and application knowledge is a central part of the selling function.

- **Managing key accounts:** With the development of relationship marketing strategies, many companies have appointed people to manage the relationship that the company has with its most important customers. They are given responsibilities for selling the company's range of products, based on a thorough understanding of the client's specific and changing needs. They are also likely to have responsibility for ensuring the customer's satisfaction, although they are given little authority over operational people who are responsible for delivering the company's promises.

Tasks of a salesperson

A number of tasks undertaken by salespeople can be identified. The importance of each of these tasks depends on the type of selling situation in which a salesperson is employed: The most common tasks are

- **Prospecting:** A key function of many selling roles is to help in identifying and generating sales leads. Unsophisticated prospecting involves door-knocking; searching through telephone directories, trade directories, and other general listings of companies, etc. The probability is that only a small percentage of those contacted will be interested in what the organization has to offer. The generation of sales leads from referrals by customers, suppliers, or other business/social contacts will usually provide better prospects. Similarly, leads generated by exhibitions, conferences, seminars, and responses to advertisements will prove to be 'warmer' leads.

- **Targeting:** deciding how to allocate time among prospects and customers. Having established a customer prospect list, the salesperson should conduct some form of evaluation of each potential buyer in terms of their business, markets, products, and probability of purchase. Those prospects that appear to offer the most potential can then be shortlisted for contact.

- **Selling:** This is at the heart of many salespeoples' roles and involves clearly understanding the needs of a buyer; recognizing the barriers to them making a purchase (financial, psychological, administrative, etc.); communicating the benefits of the product as they affect the buyer; overcoming objections from the buyer; recognizing buying signals; and eventually closing the sale. A good salesperson will have the flexibility to adapt their communication to the emerging requirements of the buyer. This is almost likely to be important for complex, high-value sales, and less important for selling situations where the salesperson is essentially an order-taker.

- **Servicing:** Salespeople are often expected to check that an order has been successfully delivered. They may also have a role of routinely checking with the buyer about their future requirements. With the development of **key account management**, the servicing function has become an increasingly important task linked to selling.

- **Information gathering:** Salespeople need to gather information about a buyer so that they can adapt their sales pitch to their needs. In addition, sales personnel may be expected to conduct market research and intelligence work to inform a company's sales and marketing decisions.

- **Allocating:** Where goods or service capacity is in short supply relative to demand, sales personnel may become involved in deciding which customers will have priority for deliveries.

The range of these roles and responsibilities will vary between organizations and sectors, particularly in terms of the level of complexity. For a retail salesperson the primary role may be to meet customers who enter the shop and through dialogue to encourage purchase of a product. Such a salesperson may also be responsible for maintaining the appearance of the stock on the shelf and providing support and advice to customers. A telephone salesperson requires a different range of skills, often following a predetermined and well-tested script.

🎏 Sales promotion

Sales promotion involves those activities—other than advertising, personal selling, and public relations—that stimulate customer purchase and the effectiveness of intermediaries. The Institute of Sales Promotion defines sales promotions as:

a range of tactical marketing techniques designed within a strategic marketing framework, to add value to a product or service in order to achieve a specific sales and marketing objective.

Although sales promotion activity can be used to create awareness, it is usually used for the later stages of the buying process, that is to create interest and desire, and—in particular—to bring about action. Sales promotion can quite successfully complement other tools within the promotion mix, for example by reinforcing a particular image or identity developed through advertising. Traditionally, sales promotion has been used tactically to encourage brand switching, as a response to competitors' activity, or to create a short-term increase in the level and frequency of sales. Whereas advertising tends to encourage brand loyalty, sales promotion tries to undermine loyalty to competitors' brands with a short-term incentive to switch brands. Increasingly, sales promotions are being used more strategically and are being integrated into an overall communications strategy. Sales promotions can be targeted at consumers with the aim of pulling sales through a channel of distribution, or at intermediaries with the aim of pushing products through the channel, or at a combination of both.

Over the last few years there has been a rapid increase in the use of sales promotion. This can be attributed to the increasingly competitive nature of many markets, and new technology in targeting which has resulted in an increase in the efficiency and effectiveness of sales promotion.

Sales promotion tools

A wide and ever-increasing range of sales promotion tools are available to marketers. Some of the more commonly used tools aimed at the final consumer include the following.

- **Free samples/visits/consultations:** These encourage trial of a product and can be valuable where consumers are currently loyal to another supplier. They could, for example, be used by a breakfast cereal manufacturer to entice potential customers to try their brand. In the case of new products which are perceived as being expensive and of poor value to a consumer, they can encourage trial. Satellite television companies, for example, have often used this approach with free trial offers. However, for established products, the excessive offering of free samples can demean the value of the product on offer and buyers may become reluctant to pay for a product that they have seen being given away freely.

- **Money-off price incentives:** Price incentives can be used tactically to try to counteract temporary increases in competitor activity. They can also be used to stimulate sales of a new product shortly after launch or to stimulate demand during slack periods where price is considered to be a key element in a customer's purchase decision. Price incentives tend to be an expensive form of sales promotion, as the incentive is given to customers regardless of its motivational effect on them. A restaurant reducing its prices for all customers is unable to extract the full price from those customers who may have been willing to pay the full price. There is also a danger that price incentives can become built into consumers' expectations so that their removal will result in a fall in business.

- **Coupons/vouchers:** These allow holders to obtain a discount off a purchase and can be targeted at quite specific groups of users or potential users, often combined with the direct marketing techniques discussed later in this chapter. To encourage trial by potential new users, vouchers can be distributed to non-users who fit a specified profile. In this way, a manufacturer of cosmetics may provide a voucher with a women's magazine whose readership corresponds with the manufacturer's target market. To encourage repeat usage, vouchers can be given as a loyalty bonus. Voucher offers tend to be much more cost-effective than straight price incentives because of their ability to segment markets. As an example, a tourist attraction can recognize that visitors from overseas might see the full price as being only a small part of their total holiday cost and representing good value, while a local family might need an incentive to make more frequent visits to the attraction.

- **Gift offers:** Companies often provide the incentive of a gift to encourage short-term sales. Gifts can take many forms, such as a Marks & Spencer gift token or a T-shirt, and can encourage immediate and/or repeated purchase. The gift can satisfy a number of objectives. In order to promote initial inquiry, many firms offer a gift for merely inquiring about their products. This provides an opportunity to submit, with the gift, samples and brochures of the firm's products. A gift can also be used to bring about immediate action—for example, a free clock radio if a purchase is made within a specified period. For existing customers, gifts can be used to develop and reward loyalty. Sometimes, a company might charge a small amount for a 'gift'. If the gift is inscribed with the company's logo, the message will be seen by the user and others for some time to come. Some gifts are provided collaboratively between companies with quite different product ranges. For example, a grocery retailer may give rewards of money-off vouchers at a chain of restaurants, satisfying the promotional criteria of the retailer (rewarding loyalty) and the restaurant (encouraging trial).

- **Competitions:** The offer of a competition adds to the value of the total offer. Instead of simply buying an insurance policy, a customer buys the policy plus a dream of winning a prize to which she attaches significance. Competitions can be used both to create trial among non-users and to encourage loyalty among existing customers (e.g. a competition for which a number of proofs of purchase are necessary to enter).

The sales promotion tools described above are predominantly aimed at the final consumer of a product. In addition, a company may use sales promotions aimed at the intermediaries who sell its products. The following are commonly used:.

- **Short-term sales bonuses:** These can be used to stimulate sales during slack periods or to develop loyalty from intermediaries in the face of competitor activity.

- **Competitions and gifts:** These can be aimed at sales personnel working for intermediaries and can help increase awareness of a brand and, if entry to the competition is dependent upon sales , can encourage additional sales.

- **Point of purchase material:** To stimulate additional sales, a supplier can provide a range of incentives to help intermediaries. Many consumer goods suppliers offer retailers and field-sales staff a range of eye-catching displays to demonstrate the benefits of their product at the point of purchase.
- **Cooperative advertising:** Suppliers can agree to subscribe to local advertising by an intermediary, for instance when a car manufacturer promotes the location of its dealers as well as the core benefits of its cars. Cooperative advertising is often undertaken in conjunction with a significant event, such as the opening of a new outlet by the intermediary, or the launch of a new product.

Evaluation of sales promotion

The performance of the promotion needs to be assessed against the objectives set. If objectives are specific and quantifiable, measurement would seem to be easy. However, extraneous factors can account for the apparent success of many sales promotion activities; for example, competitive actions or seasonal variations may influence customers' decision-making. It can also be extremely difficult to separate the effects of sales promotion activity from other promotional activity—or indeed from other marketing mix changes, such as a lower price. A further problem is that sales promotion activity may simply bring demand forward, resulting in buyers building up stockpiles which depresses demand for the product in future periods. This is especially true of products that are of low value and have a long shelf-life. This effect is illustrated in Figure 11.15.

While some firms would use sales promotion tactically to boost sales at specific times and/or locations (e.g. during a quiet time of year, or to support a new store opening), others have a tendency to use a continuous series of sales promotions in a strategic way. A retailer may, for example, have a strategy of always offering a small number of lines at exceptionally low prices in order to attract people into its store, and hopefully buy other products as well as the promotional items. However, it should be remembered that sales promotion activities in themselves generally do not create long-term customer loyalty.

Public relations

Public relations (PR) is used to establish and enhance a positive image of an organization and its products among its various publics. It is defined by the Institute of Public Relations as:

the deliberate, planned and sustained effort to establish and maintain mutual understanding between an organization and its publics.

Figure 11.15 Sales promotion activity, such as a short-term 'Buy one, get one free' offer, can simply bring demand forward, resulting in stockpiles which depress demand after the promotion has ended. This graph illustrates the difficulties in trying to assess the effectiveness of sales promotion activities.

The words 'deliberate', 'planned', and 'sustained' are crucial here, as companies cannot simply 'do a bit of PR' in isolated bursts and hope for the type of result that comes from a more concerted effort. Public relations as a professional activity is treated with suspicion by many people, but this probably reflects a perception of a short-term opportunistic activity, rather than the long-term commitment advocated by public relations professionals. A good long-term PR strategy will make it much easier for a company to use PR tools when it has a real emergency and needs to communicate with its audience. As an example, a food manufacturer that has carefully used PR to develop a good mutual understanding between itself and its principal publics will be better placed to use PR to counter a food-safety incident than a manufacturer that uses PR tools only as and when needed.

Because public relations is involved with more than just customer relationships, it is often handled at a corporate level rather than at the functional level of marketing management, and covers communication with investor and community groups, among others.

Public relations and corporate reputation

Public relations is very important for maintaining a firm's reputation, especially where it is facing a crisis, for example following a food-poisoning scare. Public relations was called upon extensively by the chocolate manufacturer Cadburys following an outbreak of salmonella at one of its factories in 2007. The company had to carefully manage its reputation immediately following the outbreak by recalling all stocks swiftly, and also later on, when investigations suggested that poor working practices had led to contamination within its factory.

For highly variable goods and services (such as airline and train services), there is always the possibility that the media will pick up one bad incident and leave their audience thinking that this is the norm for a particular organization. Media editors have a tendency to write stories that they believe their audiences would like to hear, so if a bad news story about a train company can be assured of a sympathetic hearing it will most likely be run. It would take a lot of effort by train operators to prove to editors that they are out of touch with the reality facing their readers or viewers.

With the development of a 24/7 media environment and 'Web 2.0' social network sites, companies' reputations can be destroyed more quickly and easily than ever before. It took very little time for the accountancy firm Arthur Andersen to be brought down from having a multi-million-pound income with blue-chip clients and an international network, to being picked over by competitors and deserted by long-term clients. By all accounts, Andersen was still doing good work at its offices in Singapore and Auckland, but its involvement with just one client—Enron—had changed the public's perceptions of the company to the point where business leaders were going out of their way not to be associated with it. The pervasiveness of news media meant that what could have been a local difficulty had led to a multi-national organization being brought down (*The Times*, 2002).

The characteristics of public relations

Some of the more important characteristics of public relations are described below.

- **Relatively low cost:** PR tends to be much cheaper, in terms of cost per person reached, than any other type of promotion. Apart from nominal production costs, much PR activity can be carried out at almost no cost, in marked contrast to the high cost of buying space or time in the main media. To make the most use of this apparently free resource, many companies pay outside PR consultants.

- **Can be targeted:** Public relations activities can be targeted to a small specialized audience if the right media vehicle is used.

- **Credibility:** The results of PR activity often have a high degree of credibility, compared with other promotional sources such as advertising. Where information is presented as news, readers or viewers may be less critical of it than if it is presented as an advertisement, which they may presume to be biased.

- **Relatively uncontrollable:** A company can exercise little direct control over how its public relations activity is subsequently handled and interpreted. If successful, a press release may be printed in full, although there can be no control over where or when it is printed. At worst, a press release can be misinterpreted and the result can be unfavourable news coverage. This is in contrast to advertising, where an advertiser can exercise considerable control over the content, placing, and timing of an advert.

The tools of public relations

In general, the tools of public relations are best suited to creating awareness of an organization and its products, or a liking for them, and tend to be less effective in directly bringing about action in the form of purchase decisions. Some of the more important tools of public relations are described below.

- **Press releases:** This seeks to secure *editorial* space in the media, as distinct from paid-for advertising space. Because of the competition from other organizations for press coverage, there can be no guarantee that any particular item will actually be used. Indeed, it is often suggested that over 90% of press releases sent to media editors end up in the bin without being used.

- **Press conferences:** These are used where a major event is to be announced and an opportunity for a two-way dialogue between the organization and the media is considered desirable.

- **Lobbying:** Professional lobbyists are often employed by a company in an effort to inform and hence influence those key decision-makers who may be critical to its success. Lobbying can take place at a local level (e.g. a fast-food company seeking to convince members of a local authority about the benefits of allowing them to locate in a sensitive area); at a national level (e.g. lobbying by UK brewers to bring UK tax on beer down to the lower levels of many other European countries); and at a supranational level (e.g. the lobbying of the EU Commission by airlines campaigning against proposals in 2007 to introduce additional taxes on airlines).

- **Education and training:** In an effort to develop a better understanding—and hence liking—of an organization and its products, many firms aim education and training programmes at important target groups. In this way, food manufacturers frequently supply schools with educational material that will predispose recipients of the material to their brand. 'Open days' are another common method of educating the public by showing them the complex processes that occur 'behind the scenes' in order to ensure a high quality of output for customers.

- **Exhibitions and trade shows:** Most companies attend exhibitions not with the intention of making an immediate sale, but to create an awareness of their organization which will result in a sale over the longer term. Exhibitions are used to target both consumer and commercial audiences. Many trade shows are important events in their respective business sectors, where a high proportion of key decision-makers are likely to be present. The annual World Travel Market in London, for example, is an ideal opportunity for travel-related organizations to communicate with their key business customers.

- **In-house journals:** The number of in-house magazines produced by companies is now huge, with examples spanning sectors from airlines to banks and supermarkets.

By adopting a news-based magazine format, the message becomes more credible than if it were presented as a pure advertisement. Often, outside advertisers contribute revenue which can make such journals self-financing. Airlines often publish in-flight magazines that are read by a captive audience.

- **Sponsorship:** There is argument about whether this strictly forms part of the public relations portfolio of tools. It is, however, being increasingly used as an element of the promotion mix and is described in more detail later in this chapter.

- **Internet**: Companies now routinely use the Internet as one of their PR tools, often to support the activities described above. For example, press releases in practice are most likely to be circulated by e-mail. Companies have also become active in creating blogs, and some, such as that associated with Innocent Smoothies, have developed a loyal following. At other times, PR professionals 'lurk' in social network sites, in order to understand better what the public is saying about a client company. Smart PR professionals also prepare to address issues raised through such networks, although there is debate about whether they should do this covertly, passing off as an ordinary member of the community, rather than declaring their attachment to the company being discussed.

Resort Devastated
Extensive damage is reported in the coastal regions south of Catler Ridge where many seaside apartments have been washed into the sea. **A spokesman for the tour operator Thomson Holidays** confirmed that very few people were staying in this area, with most staying in Miami

Figure 11.16 Faced with a news story that the media wishes to cover, a newspaper or radio station may seek specialists within an industrial sector who are knowledgeable on the issues involved. A local tour operator may be asked by a local newspaper to comment upon the consequences of a natural disaster in an overseas resort. This helps both the reporter and the tour operator in question, whose representative is fielded as an expert.

Evaluating public relations activity

The need for evaluation of PR activity was dismissed by many on the grounds that it was very difficult to do, and the low cost of PR activity did not justify the effort. Today, there is greater awareness of the need for evaluation and an increasing range of tools to do so. Media content analysis and press cuttings are the most commonly used evaluation techniques, and companies typically measure, 'advertising value equivalents' and 'opportunities to see'. Innovations in computer software are providing new tools which can allow for rapid tracking of media coverage and a calculation of the likely audience.

Another important aspect of PR evaluation is the pre-testing of messages. Where time allows, this may identify any possibilities of misinterpretation that may subsequently arise.

Who should do the PR evaluation? Many PR consultancies provide an evaluation service to their clients using agreed criteria. Meanwhile, many specialist evaluation companies have emerged that may be contracted directly by the client, or sub-contracted by a consultant to provide detailed evaluation.

Sponsorship

Sponsorship does not fit neatly into a categorization of the main elements of the promotion mix. It uses a combination of advertising, public relations, sales promotion, and direct marketing to associate a company's product or corporate image that may be unknown or misunderstood with the image of something that is well understood. As the general clutter of media advertising has increased in recent years, sponsorship has come to play a more important role in the promotion mix. With consumers becoming increasingly critical of organizations' societal credentials, sponsorship has been seen by many organizations as a cost-effective means of enhancing their image.

Sponsorship involves a company's investment in events or causes in order to achieve objectives such as increased awareness levels, enhanced reputation, etc. Sponsorship activities include a brewer sponsoring tennis matches (e.g. the Stella Artois tournament) and an organization sponsoring specific television programmes (such as Cadbury's sponsorship of *Coronation Street*).

As with promotional planning in general, segmentation is crucial to successful sponsorship. A company must have a good definition of the audience to which it wishes to communicate its message, and must then seek sponsorship vehicles whose audiences match that target market. As an example, the tour operator Kuoni Travel's sponsorship of Classic FM programmes matches Kuoni's target market with Classic FM's audience. Sponsorship often takes place at a local level; for example, an estate agency moving into an area may seek to increase awareness of it by sponsoring a school fête or a local theatrical group.

It is difficult to evaluate sponsorship activities because of the problem of isolating the effects of sponsorship from other elements of the promotion mix. Direct measurement is likely to be possible only if sponsorship is the predominant tool. Sponsorship should therefore be seen as a tool that complements other elements of the promotion mix.

Figure 11.17 Sponsorship of sporting events allows a company's brand name to be seen by viewers of the event and to associate the brand with the values of the sport concerned. Cheltenham & Gloucester is the third largest provider of household mortgages in the UK, and has to compete with dozens of other banks and building societies for buyers' attention. By sponsoring a public activity, the brand name is exposed to potential buyers, especially, in this case, cricket fans, for whom C&G may be high on the list of brands which are spontaneously recalled. The company's financial services products are also likely to be attributed with some of the characteristics of cricket—traditional, very English, reliable, etc. (Reproduced with permission of Cheltenham & Gloucester)

Direct marketing

Direct marketing entails companies opening up a dialogue directly between themselves and the end consumers of their products, thereby avoiding the need to communicate through indirect media such as press and television advertising. It can also allow a firm to communicate directly with its customers without having to go through retail or wholesale intermediaries. However, direct marketing is also compatible with a company using intermediaries (for example, the manufacturer may use direct marketing to direct potential customers to its intermediaries). Direct marketing activities described in this section are often used to support other elements of the promotion mix and should not therefore be seen in isolation.

There is no universally agreed definition of what constitutes direct marketing, but we will begin with the definition used by the UK Direct Marketing Association. It defines direct marketing as:

Communications where data are used systematically to achieve quantifiable marketing objectives and where direct contact is invited or made between a company and its customers.

Direct marketing has been growing very rapidly. In 2006, organizations spent a total of £37 billion on direct marketing, of which over £14 billion can be attributed to media spend (Direct Marketing Association, 2007). As a further indicator of its significance to the marketing community, the Institute of Direct Marketing has estimated that 10% of all new graduates entering marketing careers begin in direct marketing.

An important advantage of direct marketing is that it can target segments as small as one. This is fine for companies that produce high-value goods and services that are tailored to the needs of specific customers. It helps to explain the popularity of direct marketing in such sectors as computer hardware and motor insurance. However, many goods and services are capable of appealing to large groups of customers in their 'standard' form without any attempt at differentiation. Where the value of the goods is low and volume sales are high, the cost of attempting to communicate directly with each individual customer may be prohibitive.

The development of customer databases

At the heart of companies' direct marketing efforts is a **database** identifying prospective customers, current customers, and lapsed customers. The effectiveness of direct marketing is critically dependent on the quality of customer details held on the database. To many people, direct marketing has become synonymous with 'junk mail'. But mail becomes junk in the hands of the recipient only if it has been poorly targeted so that it does not meet the needs of the person to whom it has been sent. Consider the following cases:

- A company selling bulbs and shrubs for domestic gardeners sent its catalogues to people living in upstairs flats in an inner-city area of London.
- A bank that had just refused a loan to an individual shortly afterwards sent out a mailing to that same customer enclosing details of its loans and an application form.
- A company manufacturing baby nappies sent promotional material and a trial offer for its products to a resident of a retirement home.

In each of these cases, it is just possible that the companies concerned had carefully studied their target market and made a decision that successfully hit their target market, even though it seemed intuitively ridiculous. (For example, the firm supplying bulbs and shrubs may have identified a group of flat dwellers who went away to their country cottages at the weekend.) However, the above examples serve only to show that the individual dialogue that is a defining characteristic of direct marketing cannot exist where a company is speaking to people who have no motivation whatsoever to enter into a dialogue.

So how does a company develop a database that at least allows it to enter into an appropriate dialogue with the right people? The most commonly used sources are:

- **Routine customer inquiries:** Increasingly, companies are taking an inquirer's postcode very seriously. By analysing postcodes using a geodemographic system such as MOSAIC, much can be learned about the background of an inquirer. At the very least, a careful analysis of postcodes tells the company something about the geographical spread of its inquiries, something that may be vital to planning future marketing communications. It should also be able subsequently to identify which postcode areas result in the highest 'conversion' rate (that is, in a sale). Companies often go beyond asking for an inquirer's name and address. Typical additional questions include: where did you see the advertisement? (helps monitor the effectiveness of the firm's advertising); when do you intend to buy? (helps the company follow up an inquiry at a later date if the purchase intention is not immediate); do you currently own a specified item? (can help to distinguish first-time purchasers from replacement purchasers who may approach the purchase decision in quite different ways); and basic demographic details, such as age group and marital status (helps to develop a profile of an inquirer's needs specifically, and a profile of inquirers generally). Of course, companies can go too far in the information they collect from a casual inquiry and risk alienating the inquirer. There is also a danger that a firm's intermediaries may be suspicious of its opening a dialogue directly with what they regard as their own customers.

- **Customer orders:** Once a prospect has become an actual customer, a company can track subsequent purchases, building up a more refined profile of the customer's needs. From this it should spot opportunities for opening a dialogue to sell related or replacement products. If a company has maintained its database effectively, it should instantly be able to build up a picture of each of its customers. So when a customer calls in with an enquiry, any individual within the company taking the call should have available full details of the enquirer's recent transactions, notes about his preferences, and any problems that he might have encountered in the past.

- **Buying in mailing lists:** Leasing **mailing lists** has become a major industry in its own right, with numerous specialists marketing services companies offering mailing lists tailored to the needs of individual client companies. These list brokers gather information from multiple sources, including the electoral register, credit rating reports, consumer survey data, and other geographic data accumulated by recording an individual's previous transactions with other companies. Lists can become out of date very rapidly, so some mailing lists may be of dubious reliability. People moving house, deaths, and companies going out of business are typical reasons for a name on a mailing list no longer being a prospect. The better suppliers of mailing lists use multiple sources of information to confirm the existence of an individual on the list and to delete any if they have not had a recent positive confirmation of their existence. Merging multiple lists can be a highly complex task, with electronically stored lists coming in a variety of formats.

The manner in which companies buy and sell information about individuals raises a number of ethical and legal issues. Should a customer of a company have a right to consider the dialogue she enters into with the company to be private between the two parties? Is it then unethical for the company to sell on information about its customers to third-party companies? In the UK, the Data Protection Act 1998 gives individuals a general right to prevent a company from passing on their details to organizations other than the one to which they initially gave the information. There are also voluntary codes of conduct which restrict the ability of firms to exchange customers' personal information, for example in the UK, the Mailing Preference Service allows individuals to opt out of receiving direct mail. The direct marketing industry has become concerned at the rising number of people who choose not to allow their details to be passed on to other organizations. While the volume of junk mail has been reduced by better targeting by companies, junk e-mail ('spam') is a growing problem.

There has been much talk of 'permission marketing', in which dialogue is based on buyers' giving permission for a company to communicate with them (Godin, 2007). This puts greater control of marketing communications in the hands of the buyer, and technology is increasingly facilitating buyers' ability to be selective in what communications they choose to receive

Profiling and targeting

With direct marketing, a company can use its database to develop a **profile** of who its best customers are. Consider the case of a direct response company advertising in the national press to promote a satellite navigation system, a product it has no previous experience in selling. It would probably have a reasonable idea of its target market from previous related selling experience, and may choose to advertise in national newspapers and magazines whose audience closely matches its own target market. Prospective customers would be invited to return a coupon or telephone for further information about the offer. The company would learn about the geodemographic profile of customers who responded, and through which medium they originally saw the promotional message. From its initial response, a company can get a reasonable idea of what type of person is showing most interest in its product. A further analysis is made to establish which types of respondent are the most successful prospects in terms of conversion to paying customers. Very often a company may find that a high level of initial inquiry among one segment is matched

GUARANTEE REGISTRATION CARD

Name   Mr/Miss/Mrs/Other _____ First Name _____ Surname _____

Address   _____

Postcode   _____

Model No. of product purchased   HN _____

Where did you buy this product? _____

Which of the following best describes your reason for purchase?

Gift _____
Replacement for existing equipment _____
Purchase of addition equipment _____
First time purchase of this type of product _____

What is your age group?   Under 18 ☐   18–25 ☐   25–35 ☐

                               36–45 ☐   46–55 ☐   56–65 ☐

                               65+ ☐

Male or female?   Male ☐   Female ☐

Your occupation _____

Please tell us whether you own, or are considering buying, the following:

	Already own	Considering buying
Mobile telephone	☐	☐
Widescreen television	☐	☐
Home computer	☐	☐

Tick this box if you would NOT like to be informed from time to time of new products and special offers. ☐

THANK YOU

Now return this card to the address shown overleaf.
You will also be entered in our monthly prize draw.

Figure 11.18 Guarantee registration cards can say a lot about an individual. Cards such as this one offer consumers who complete it a number of benefits, such as priority attention in the event of a safety recall of the product and entry into a prize draw. But the main beneficiary is the manufacturer, who gets to learn a lot about the profile of the buyer and his reasons for buying its products.

by a below-average level of conversions. Where this is the case, the company needs to examine the appeal of the offer to this segment. Was the product appropriately specified? Was it overpriced? Were the benefits of ownership stressed sufficiently?

For the initial inquirers who were converted into customers, the company can seek to obtain further information at the time of ordering (e.g. do they already own a navigation system, whether the purchase was for their personal use, business use, or a gift for someone else). If the company is offering credit facilities, this gives a further legitimate reason to collect more information to build up a profile of customers wishing to buy on credit.

Having started out with only a general idea about who constitutes its target market, the company now has a fairly detailed profile of who its customers are. If it is offering a range of accessory products, it would be able to identify who the most profitable customers will be in terms of the total value of their orders. The company can go on to track the purchases of those customers it had attracted with its initial offer. It may find that some converts went on to become regular customers not only of its navigation systems, but of its related product offers. These represent particularly attractive customers for the company, and it would seek to establish whether frequent buying is associated with any particular combination of an individual's demographic characteristics (e.g. aged under 30, living in a better residential area, and reading *FHM* magazine). The company may make particular efforts to obtain an initial purchase from this group, in the knowledge that there is a high probability of such buyers' going on to become regular, profitable customers.

Finally, a profile analysis of an organization's customers may suggest that some are not at all profitable and are unlikely to ever become profitable. Just as a company requires a means of adding new prospects to its database, it requires a means of 'exiting' those who have not responded profitably to its attempts to create a dialogue. Companies may adopt a graduated process of removing individuals from their active database. They may invite individuals to confirm that they want to continue mailings or reduce the frequency of mailings.

Companies are amassing increasing volumes of data with which to profile their customers and prospective customers. However, it is felt by many that the ability of companies to use such data effectively is lagging behind the growth in volume of data. Techniques such as Artificial Intelligence, Fuzzy Logic, and Neural Networks have been used to find patterns in large databases, and in particular to identify those variables that are most closely associated with sales and profitability (Ratner, 2001).

Direct marketing media

In 2006, organizations spent over £14 billion on media to support direct marketing (Direct Marketing Association, 2007). One of the problems in defining and quantifying direct marketing is that it uses a wide range of media; so advertising could be used as part of a traditional mass marketing strategy, or it could be used to try and initiate a direct dialogue between a company and its prospective customers. **Direct mail** (sending

MARKETING in ACTION

Telecoms companies are particularly bad at communicating, says report

The phenomenal development of telecommunications over the past couple of decades should have opened up tremendous new opportunities for two-way communication between a company and its customers—actual and potential; but there is still evidence that service companies can be slow to embrace the interactive communication abilities of the telephone and Internet. Research undertaken in 2006 by the e-services provider Transversal showed that the UK telecoms sector—which should have been at the forefront of the telecommunications revolution—was actually performing badly at communication. The report found phone companies to be among the slowest at answering their phones, with some, such as Carphone Warehouse, apparently being overwhelmed at their call centres. Answering a phone is generally more expensive than having customers communicating through a website, entering all data themselves and using their time rather than a call centre operator's time to search for results; but the phone companies did not seem to do well here either. The report found that only a third provided an online customer search function, down from 70% in 2005. Furthermore, the telephone companies' websites could answer an average of just two out of 11 most basic customer questions such as 'How do I upgrade my phone?'. Online users who sent an e-mail to the company to resolve a problem would typically wait 48 hours for a reply, and many e-mail requests for information simply did not get answered.

It is easy to say that telecommunications improve the ability of companies to communicate with their customers, but technology alone will not improve communication. Telecommunications companies should be at the leading edge when it comes to the enabling technology, but did they have the management abilities to put the technology to good use? Or were they simply victims of their own success, and as they grew, their capacity to handle calls continually lagged behind customer demand? Had the communications revolution led to higher expectations by customers, who may have been happy to wait several days for an answer, but now want an instant response, 24/7? And with communication costing money, could facilitating easier communication simply result in more calls from customers, adding to a company's costs and putting it at a disadvantage in a price-sensitive market?

printed materials to individual customers through the mail), and **telemarketing** (using the telephone inbound and outbound calls) are more likely to be used once a customer profile has been developed.

Online marketing

We have already mentioned some of the advantages of **online marketing** in our previous discussion of the elements of the promotion mix and noted the overlap between promotion mix elements:

• The definition of advertising includes web pages which broadcast to large numbers of people but are not interactive.

- Personal selling is increasingly relying on online communication to support the efforts of sales personnel.

- Public Relations professionals have understood the potential impacts of social networking websites on a company's reputation and have developed web-based tools of their own.

- Online media have become an integral element of direct marketing by opening up a channel through which a company can enter an interactive dialogue with its customers.

Communication using online media has gone through a number of stages of development. At the most basic level, a company's website can simply give additional information about its goods and services, for example many hotels have websites which give information about their location and the facilities available. At this stage of development, the Internet is being used simply as an online form of the traditional printed brochure. Although a static, one-to-all website may now seem quite unadventurous, we should nevertheless recognise the advantages that a web page has over traditional printed brochures:

- They are much less expensive to produce.

- They can be updated very rapidly (e.g. in response to a price change) without the need to destroy existing sticks of brochures.

- Information can be provided immediately to prospective customers anywhere in the world, without the need to wait for a postal delivery.

- Comprehensive information can be provided within the site—more than could realistically be provided within the confines of a printed brochure.

- Links can be provided to other related information (for example, a hotel can include a link to local tourist attractions).

The second stage of online development allows some degree of interactive dialogue between a company and visitors to its website. At its simplest, this can allow a visitor to the site to send a message to the company, perhaps to request further information. Interactivity could be added by creating a script which allows the visitor to ask simple questions and for the site to generate answers which are of direct relevance to the customer (for example, the bank's website may include a simple ready reckoner to allow the user to calculate the monthly repayments on a mortgage). More complex interactivity can be developed by linking the customer's request to a database of information. This is used by railway operators (e.g. www.nationalrail.co.uk) to provide precise information on possible rail journeys in response to a customer's request for information on train times between two specified points at a specified time. Many online service providers use targeted e-mail services to encourage customers to visit their sites. The travel and leisure company lastminute.com, for example, claims to send more than 2 million e-mails to customers every week. The content of the e-mail is tailored to fit the recipient's age, lifestyle and other factors (Kirchgaessner, 2003).

The third stage of online development is to allow immediate fulfilment of a request, such as confirmation of a hotel booking or reservation of a plane ticket. By linking a customer's online request to a real-time database of availability, the company is able immediately to communicate a specific price/product offer. Many airline and hotel companies have used the principles of yield management to continually change their price and product offer to reflect the changing balance between supply and demand, so the message that it sends to a site visitor may be quite different to one that it sent even just half an hour ago.

More recently, many companies have started to use Web 2.0 technologies, such as blogs and video clips, to increase the level of engagement with buyers. As an example, when Nissan launched its Qashqai car in the UK in 2007, it offered a game website where visitors could try to shoot the car and it broadcast video clips of the car, which could be linked to blogs and social networking sites. A plethora of social networking sites, such as Facebook and Bebo, plus many specialized niche sites, have emerged through which companies have sought engagement as part of a community.

In the longer term, it is likely that the distinction between Internet and television advertising will become increasingly blurred, as traditional television channels transmit their programmes online, and niche Internet sites develop broadcast digital television channels (e.g. the magazine *Nuts* has developed from a printed magazine to a website and more recently to a broadcast television channel).

In most western countries, the majority of the population now has access to the Internet, either at home, work, or their place of study. Online communication is particularly attractive for services, such as travel and financial services where the costs of delivering tangible elements is not a major constraint. It has been predicted that by 2010, the majority of package holidays will be bought through the Internet and High Street travel agencies will serve only a small niche market (Forrester Research, 2006).

Choice of online channels

As use of the Internet as a communication medium has increased, it has become increasingly cluttered. This effect has been seen during the development of all media, and companies using the Internet have faced increasing challenges in drawing people to their website. Getting a high ranking in search engines has become a critical skill and specialist companies are often employed to raise a client's rankings. From being a very cheap source of messages, companies are having to spend increasing amounts of money promoting their web presence, both online and offline.

There are several methods that online service providers use to charge for advertising. 'Pay per click' involves a company paying a fee every time their advert on another site is clicked on. Google, Yahoo, and other companies offer these facilities, but they are susceptible to abuse—companies can click on a competitor's banner adverts to drive up its costs, possibly getting them removed from the search results page if they reach their maximum ad budget. Other methods of buying advertising include paying per visitor to a website; paying per thousand people exposed to a message; and paying commission only if an actual transaction takes place.

Search marketing has been growing rapidly, and in the UK in 2007 it was estimated by the Internet Advertising Bureau to account for £1.2 billion of advertising expenditure, or twice as much as radio advertising. Search marketing typically involves an advertiser paying to sponsor individual key words on Internet search engines such as Google or Yahoo. When a visitor to the search engine enters the key words, the advertiser's entry is listed as a sponsored link. This puts the advertiser at the top of a long list—possibly thousands or even millions—of websites which match the search criteria. The visitor can then click on this link to arrive at the advertiser's website. Very often, the advertiser will have prepared slightly different pages, to reflect the keyword which was originally searched for. Search marketing is becoming increasingly sophisticated, and now offers targeting which is geographically specific. Until recently, geographical targeting was based on very crude national boundaries, for example a user based in the UK entering 'mobile phone deals' would see UK-based mobile phone companies, while the visitor based in the USA would see American-based companies. As the Internet becomes more widely available through mobile phones and PDAs linked to a global positioning system, a search can be made geographically very specific.

While the level of sophistication in search marketing has been going up, the cost of entry has also been rising. It is no longer realistic to plan the launch of a major brand from a small home office with a budget of just a few hundred pounds—as many entrepreneurs in the early stages of Internet development managed to do. Pricing of keywords has risen steadily as more advertisers have been drawn into the market. Companies in highly competitive markets are likely to bid up the prices paid for key terms such as 'cheap car insurance' or 'mobile phone deals'.

Integrating online with other media

For most companies, online cannot really be considered in isolation from other elements of the promotion mix. Online adverts are increasingly used to support printed and broadcast media, and such ads now routinely include a website address where a reader or viewer can find more information. The Internet should be used to provide a form of communication which is not possible using other media, for example a bank's press advertising may give general information about personal loans, but its website can incorporate a personalized loan repayment calculator. A picture of a car in a glossy Sunday magazine can be supplemented on the manufacturer's website with video clips and information about how the car can be personalized to suit their preferences.

The Internet Advertising Bureau (www.iabuk.net) has made a number of recommendations for companies planning to engage in online marketing, and these emphasize integration with the offline environment. It has noted, for example, the importance of including words used in offline campaigns in their paid-for search advertising.

Although some companies, such as Amazon rely on online channels for almost all of their promotion, most companies recognize that the medium is not suitable for all products or all target customers. Although the majority of the population in most western countries now has access to the Internet, there are still large groups, especially of elderly people, who do not routinely have access and must be targeted through alternative media. Some products are more suitable than others for online promotion. In the case of high-involvement purchases, which require a sense of touch, smell, or feel fully to evaluate the product, promotion through the medium of the Internet may be a limitation. Doubt has been expressed whether it is possible to build a strong brand using Internet media alone.

MARKETING in ACTION

Can you trust word of mouse?

There has been considerable recent excitement about the possibility of online 'peer to peer' websites becoming a primary source of information about a company and its products, while the importance of traditional advertising declines. This trend appeared to be confirmed in 2006 when the UK commercial television operator ITV reported a fall in advertising revenue, while the media conglomerate News Corp acquired the relatively new peer-to-peer site MySpace (www.myspace.com) for $580 million. Would buyers of the future instinctively look first to what their peers were saying in chat rooms and blogs, rather than turning to traditional advertising?

There is a great deal of research indicating that for high-involvement products, consumers turn initially to their friends for recommendations; but how can you trust friends in a global community comprising millions of users who contribute to peer-to-peer sites? Inevitably, when an Internet forum provides free access to all, it will include material posted by cranks, criminals, and smart companies who have learned how to anonymously provide a good recommendation about their own organization, and to criticize their competitors. Peer review sites for restaurants and hotels have become difficult to manage, with many allegations that hotels have simply submitted a glowing recommendation for their establishment, passed off as the comments of a very satisfied customer. Inevitably, some sites have become more trusted than others, on account of their greater diligence in spotting false postings. It seems that there will always be a role for impartial communication by companies and intermediaries that can be trusted. Despite the availability of a plethora of free hotel review sites, paid for hotel guides such as Frommer's travel guides, continue to prosper, based on the trust as a communication source that they have developed.

So, is the idea of a global word-of-mouth recommendation network a powerful new source of consumer information? Or is it a myth, driven by technology, which naively assumes that technology can replicate on a large scale what humans have always done on a small scale?

◼ Chapter summary and links to other chapters

Very few products can be sold in competitive markets without any form of promotion. This chapter has shown how the features of a product need to be communicated to potential buyers as benefits that will satisfy a need. We saw in Chapter 4 that needs can be complex, and can change over time for an individual. Promotion can help to take people through a number of stages of the buying process, from merely being aware of a product through to committing themselves to a purchase. Messages are communicated through channels to reach a target audience. The existence of 'noise' means that the message that was encoded and sent is not the same as the one that is received and decoded. This chapter has reviewed the elements of the promotion mix. Although each element of the mix has a different role to play, they are very much interdependent. The headings this chapter used to define the elements of the promotion mix are to some extent arbitrary, and we have seen, for example, how advertising is often an important part of sales promotion and direct marketing activity.

This chapter has stressed that promotion planning is an integral part of the marketing and business planning process. The promotional message must be consistent with the positioning of a product (Chapters 6 and 7), its price position (Chapter 9), and its availability (Chapter 10). Promotion becomes more complex where overseas markets are involved (Chapter 13).

▢ KEY PRINCIPLES OF MARKETING

- Promotional messages should translate product features into benefits for buyers.
- Objectives set for individual elements of the promotion mix must be consistent with overall marketing objectives.
- The audience for a promotional message should correspond to the target market for the product being promoted.
- There can be multiple targets involved in promoting a product, including all members of a decision-making unit and the intermediaries that handle the product.
- Communication is a process that aims to take a target through stages from awareness to action.
- The promotional objectives for a product must be related to the stage of the product's life cycle.
- Definitions of the elements of the promotion mix are not watertight and all elements overlap with each other.
- The effects of any promotional medium will be greater if its message is integrated with other media.
- All elements of the promotion mix involve a process of analysis, objective-setting, development of strategies, implementation, and evaluation.

CASE STUDY

Online advertising goes mobile

In life generally, it is widely recognized that there can be a time and a place to communicate a message. Your friend may not appreciate an invitation to spend a night on the town just before their pay day when they are broke, but a couple of days later, the message may be more keenly taken up. In the world of advertising media, the past 100 years has seen a dramatic improvement in the ability of media to target messages on the basis of time and place. Years ago, the main medium for advertising was the printed press, which had only a very crude ability to segment by time, but nevertheless it did happen; for example, Friday editions of newspapers have tended to carry more advertising than other days, ahead of weekend shopping trips. Segmentation by place was technically very difficult for national newspapers, and it has only been quite recently that regional editions of national newspapers have become widespread, supplementing local titles for a share of local advertising expenditure. Television improved segmentation by time—for example, the typical audience profile for daytime television can be quite different to the audience for evening peak-hour programmes.

The Internet has opened up tremendous new possibilities for segmentation by time and place. The time aspect has been well developed by many companies' Internet-based communication. The live nature of the Internet means that a company can change its message throughout the day or week to cater for visitors' fluctuating motivations. As an example, some insurance companies have been reported to charge different premiums depending upon the time of an inquiry. The rationale could be that an inquirer for car insurance at 9 a.m. on a Monday morning might have been desperate to renew their insurance because it had just expired, therefore will be less likely to shop around for the best deal, and will more readily accept a higher premium. On the otherhand, an inquirer at 5 p.m. may be casually surfing a few sites before they go home from work, and may be more price-sensitive than the morning shopper.

A problem for Internet advertising so far has been its inability to fully exploit segmentation by place. An advertiser generally has little idea about the geographical location of the visitors to its site. Online advertisers would normally expect statistics showing the domain where a visitor came from, and the country with which that domain is associated. However, it has been technically very difficult to show even which region, let alone in which town or part of the town the visitor is based. There is also a problem that the buyer may be using an office computer with a different location to their home address.

Is mobile marketing about to exploit the opportunities for time- and place-specific advertising? As with any new technology-based advertising medium that comes along, there were initial doubts about the true potential of the medium. In 2007, estimates of the market for mobile advertising varied widely. The consultancy Informa predicted that the worldwide market for mobile advertising would grow from about $1 billion in 2007 to $8.4 billion in 2012. However, analysts at Jupiter Research were more pessimistic, predicting that the European market would grow from a mere €58 million in 2007 to €1.3 billion in 2012, accounting for just 1% of total advertising expenditure.

For search-based advertising companies such as Yahoo and Google, which dominate Internet advertising, the mobile market offers a new, much larger market of more than 3 billion consumers worldwide, compared to about 1 billion on the fixed-line Internet. Media buyers have been enthusiastic about the mobile phone's ability to tailor advertising to specific audiences, particularly teenagers. Moreover, messages could be targeted precisely at the time and a place when the receiver is most likely to be receptive to a message. They were encouraged by early reports of high response rates for mobile campaigns. Vodafone claimed in 2007 that it was obtaining a 2% click-through rate on banner ads on its mobile Internet pages, more than ten times the response rate to ads on the fixed-line Internet. Rival UK operator 3 UK claimed an 8–10% click-through in ads on its mobile portal. However, sceptics urged caution over these apparently good early results, and pointed out that high response rates could be attributed to the novelty of the medium. A decade earlier, when the Internet was still a novelty, click-through rates were similarly high, but have since declined.

Key to the success of mobile marketing is the creation of a user-friendly experience. Many critics have pointed out that navigating the Internet on a tiny screen can be extremely difficult, so mobile advertisers and network operators have been keen to simplify this process, and to link mobile advertising with offline advertising. To this end, mobile operators have been carrying out experiments to try and judge the likely take-up of mobile advertising. As on previous occasions when new mobile technologies have emerged, they have looked to the affluent, technologically savvy countries of the Far East to try and assess the likely take-up in western markets.

In 2007, Singapore operator M1 launched a location-based marketing service. Having opted-in, a user walking along Orchard Road, Singapore's main shopping street, would receive messages offering discounts in stores or restaurants as they approached them. Shopkeepers, who typically cut 10% off their prices, were able to address customers who might otherwise have passed them by. Restaurants could offer discounts to attract early and late diners, filling capacity during their quieter hours. The operator also undertook a trial to link the world of mobile advertising with the real physical world. It had acknowledged that navigating the Internet on a mobile phone was slow and difficult, so sought to simplify the process by linking outdoor billboards to websites. A number of billboards appeared with bar codes, which could be read by mobile phone cameras. As soon as the bar code was read, the mobile phone would be linked to the advertiser's website, giving more information about the product.

Providing a link between the mobile world and the real physical world may be the key to overcoming the problem of navigating the Internet on a small screen. Many have seen hope in the idea of widespread use of barcodes printed on physical objects, such as magazines or product packaging, at which a mobile phone user could point their camera phone and find out more about the product directly from the advertiser's website. This vision led to the creation of the Mobile Codes Consortium, an initiative launched in 2008 by Hewlett-Packard, Publicis, and NeoMedia to push for greater technology standardization in the emerging field of '2D barcodes'.

There were many more problems to overcome before mobile advertising could become mainstream. Many people bought mobile phones which were capable of accessing the Internet, but simply did not use this facility. In 2007, the mobile phone manufacturer Motorola claimed that typically only 10–20% of owners of smart phones had used the browser on their mobile to connect to the Internet. Many may have been deterred by the mobile phone companies' practice of charging on the basis of cost per minute or per byte downloaded. This issue was addressed when operators such as Vodafone moved to a flat-rate charging method.

A further challenge was data protection legislation which required customers to opt in before they received unsolicited messages. Targeting hungry diners as they passed a restaurant with spare capacity may seem attractive in principle, but the legislation of most countries requires permission from the receiver before they can be sent unsolicited messages. There was clearly a great need for the mobile sector to put its house in order if users were not to be deterred from giving permission by stories of relentless spam mail.

Measuring the effectiveness of mobile ads has been a big problem. Click-through rates on banners and messages can be counted, but there is little agreement on how to calculate the reach of a display or video ad, for example. A study by Jupiter Research in 2006 indicated that 47% of executives responsible for mobile advertising said they had problems with measurement and reporting of mobile campaigns. To make matters worse, mobile phone operators have historically been secretive with their key customer data, and nearly half of advertising buyers polled in the Jupiter survey identified measurement difficulties as an important obstacle in mobile advertising. In 2008, the principal UK mobile phone operators agreed, under the auspices of the GSM Association—the global trade association for the handset industry—to pool information on customer numbers and usage patterns. The aim was to develop a common set of metrics for measuring the reach of mobile advertising.

A final problem that mobile advertisers had to face up to was a proliferation of mobile technologies. The 3G phone was just one medium through which to target buyers on the move. It had to compete for attention with WiFi networks, and the prospect of national rollouts of such networks and longer range WiMax networks, which did not directly involve 3G technology. Podcasts which could be downloaded on to a person's home computer and listened to on their MP3 player may have been a more attractive alternative for many people seeking content over which they have control.

CASE STUDY QUESTIONS

1. Critically assess the likely opportunities and problems of mobile advertising for a national chain of restaurants.

2. Discuss methods that could be used to assess the effectiveness of mobile advertising.

3. Discuss the relationship between mobile advertising and other elements of the promotion in campaign planning.

◻ CHAPTER REVIEW QUESTIONS

1. What is the relationship between selling and marketing?

2. Critically evaluate the steps that companies can take to ensure that their direct mail does not become 'junk' mail.

3. What do you understand by the term 'promotional campaign', and how can a firm assess whether its campaign has been successful?

◻ ACTIVITIES

1. Collect publicity material and media reports for a selection of major football clubs (e.g. Manchester United) or leading theatrical companies (e.g. Royal Shakespeare Company). Identify which commercial organizations sponsor them, either as primary or secondary sponsors. Evaluate how well you think the sponsorship works for all parties.

2. Undertake a critical assessment of the last time you purchased a reasonably high-involvement product such as a holiday or university course. Identify the main sources of communication that influenced your eventual choice, noting the effects of messages derived from within and beyond the service provider. Now repeat the exercise on friends to see if a consistent pattern emerges.

3. Go through a glossy magazine and select a sample of adverts for durable consumer goods. Critically assess the messages contained in the adverts and in the context of a buyer response model, try and understand what the intended response of the message may be.

◻ REFERENCES

Cardwell, A. (2002), 'Subliminal Advertising'. *Ziff Davis Smart Business*, 15(3): 51–2.

Chung-kue, H. and McDonald, D. (2002), 'An Examination on Multiple Celebrity Endorsers in Advertising'. *Journal of Product & Brand Management*, 11(1): 19–29.

Cummings, P. (2007), 'The Power of Celebrity Endorsement: do celebrities add value to a brand campaign? How to get the best and what to expect in return'. *Journal of Sponsorship*, 1(1): 67–71.

Direct Marketing Association (2007), *Census of the UK Direct Marketing Industry*. London: Direct Marketing Association.

Drucker, P. (1973), *Management: tasks, responsibilities and practices*. New York: Harper & Row.

Ferguson, R. (2008), 'Word of Mouth and Viral Marketing: taking the temperature of the hottest trends in marketing'. *Journal of Consumer Marketing*, 25(3): 179–82.

Fill, C. (2006), *Marketing Communications: engagement, strategies and practice*. London: FT Prentice Hall.

Forrester Research (2006), *Information Fabric, Enterprise Data Virtualization*. Cambridge, MA: Forrester Research.

Godin, S. (2007), *Permission Marketing: turning strangers into friends and friends into customers*. New York: Pocket Books.

Henderson B. S. (2000), 'Are So-called Successful Advertising Campaigns Really Successful?'. *Journal of Advertising Research*, 40(6): 25–31.

Jones, K. (2008), *Search Engine Optimization: your visual blueprint for effective internet marketing.* Chichester: John Wiley.

Kirchgaessner, S. (2003), 'Need Inflatable Sheep, Fast? Lastminute.com: speed and reliability are essential ingredients for online success'. *Financial Times*, 5 February, p. 4.

Kotler, P., Rackham, N., and Krishnaswamy, S. (2006), 'Ending the War between Sales and Marketing'. *Harvard Business Review* (July).

Lauf, E. (2001), 'The Vanishing Young Reader'. *European Journal of Communication*, 16(2): 233–44.

Lynch, D. (2001), 'The Magic of *Harry Potter*'. *Advertising Age*, 72(50): 26.

Ratner, B. (2001), 'Finding the Best Variables for Direct Marketing Models'. *Journal of Targeting, Measurement & Analysis for Marketing*, 9(3): 270–96.

Richardson, G. W. (2001), 'Looking for Meaning in All the Wrong Places: why negative advertising is a suspect category'. *Journal of Communication*, 51: 775–90.

Rogers, E. M. (2003), *Diffusion of Innovation*. New York: Free Press.

Smith, P. and Taylor, J. (2004), *Marketing Communications: an integrated approach*. London: Kogan Page.

Steward, K. (1993), *Marketing Led, Sales Driven: professional selling in a marketing environment.* Oxford: Butterworth-Heinemann.

Susskind, A. M. (2002), 'I Told You So! Restaurant customers' word-of-mouth communication patterns'. *Cornell Hotel & Restaurant Administration Quarterly*, 43, (2): 75–85.

The Times (2002), 'Media Age Poses Threat to Reputations', 1 May, Business, p. 29.

Walker, L. J.-H. (2001), 'The Measurement of Word-of-Mouth Communication and an Investigation of Service Quality and Customer Commitment as Potential Antecedents'. *Journal of Service Research*, 4(1): 60–75.

SUGGESTED FURTHER READING

For a general overview of communication methods and campaign planning, the following are useful:

Fill, C. (2006), *Marketing Communications: engagement, strategies and practice*. London: FT Prentice Hall.

Smith, P. and Taylor, J. (2004), *Marketing Communications: an integrated approach*. London: Kogan Page.

Advertising is explored in more detail in the following:

Ogilvy, D. (2007), *Ogilvy on Advertising*. London: Prion Books.

Burtenshaw, K., Mahon, N., and Barfoot, C. (2006), *The Fundamentals of Creative Advertising*. Lausanne: AVA Publishing.

Public relations is explored in more detail in the following:

Tench, R. and Yeomans, L. (2006), *Exploring Public Relations*. London: FT Prentice Hall.

L'Etang, J. (2007), *Public Relations: concepts, practice and critique*. London: Sage.

For an overview of direct marketing and online media, the following are useful:

Scoble, R. and Israel, S. (2006), *Naked Conversations: how blogs are changing the way businesses talk with customers*. New York: Hungry Minds Inc.

Tapp, A. (2004), *Principles of Direct and Database Marketing*, 3rd edn. London: FT Prentice Hall.

Chaffey, D., Ellis-Chadwick, F., Johnston, K., and Mayer, R. (2006), *Internet Marketing*, 3rd edn. London: FT Prentice Hall.

The challenges of integrating media channels are discussed in the following:

Clow, K. E. and Baack, D. E. (2008), *Integrated Advertising, Promotion, and Marketing Communications*. Harlow: Pearson.

Pickton, D. and Broderick, A. (2004), *Integrated Marketing Communications*, 2nd edn. London: FT Prentice Hall.

Duffy, D. L. (2004), 'Multi-channel Marketing in the Retail Environment'. *Journal of Consumer Marketing*, 21(5): 356–9.

▢ USEFUL WEB LINKS

Visit the Online Resource Centre for resources that are relevant to this chapter, including web links, multiple choice questions, and additional case studies:

www.oxfordtextbooks.co.uk/orc/palmer2e/

▢ KEY TERMS

- **Advertising**
- **Buyer readiness state**
- **Channel of communication**
- **Communication models**
- **Communication process**
- **Database marketing**
- **Decoding**
- **Direct mail**
- **Direct marketing**
- **Encoding**
- **Hierarchy of effects model**
- **Key account management**
- **Lobbying**
- **Mailing lists**
- **Noise**
- **Online marketing**
- **Personal selling**
- **Press conference**
- **Press release**
- **Profiling**
- **Promotion mix**

- Prospecting
- Public relations
- Sales promotion
- Search marketing
- Selling
- Social network sites
- Sponsorship
- Target audience
- Telemarketing
- Viral marketing
- Voluntary codes
- Word of mouth

PART 4

Bringing it together

12

Managing the marketing effort

CHAPTER OBJECTIVES

This chapter brings together the theory of the previous chapters in a framework that can be implemented by marketing managers. Too many marketing plans fail to be implemented effectively, and this chapter explores the bases for effective marketing management. Marketing management involves a never-ending process of analysis, planning, implementation, and control. Timely and relevant information, acted upon by appropriately structured and motivated management, is crucial to success.

Introduction

A frequently heard comment about some aspects of marketing is that it is 'fine in theory, but doesn't work in practice'. This book has presented much of the theory that underlies marketing management decisions, but theory and good ideas alone will not create long-term profitability. Nor is it good enough just to have the right product at the right time. Good management is crucial to bringing about *sustainable* success.

Most people will have had experience of companies that do not appear to have the management capabilities necessary for success. At the operational level, inadequate investment in staff training and a distribution system that results in the wrong products being delivered late to the wrong place can be signs of bad management. At a strategic level, poor management can be seen by a preoccupation with declining products at the expense of new opportunities and a lack of information about current market conditions.

There is an ongoing debate about whether management is an art or a science. Those who advocate a scientific approach set great value in structured procedures, for example in the way information is routinely collected and analysed. Rationality and reassurance underlie the scientific approach. Most of the top 100 UK companies have systematic procedures for management that make them a relatively safe bet for investors, even if they lack the occasional sparkle of smaller and more volatile companies.

Advocates of a creative, artistic approach would argue that the business environment is changing rapidly and therefore a scientific framework, which works on the basis of previous models, may no longer be valid in the future. Furthermore, under the scientific approach it may take a long time to reach a decision, putting a firm at a competitive disadvantage in a fast-moving market. By taking a scientific approach, managers often end up breaking a large problem down into component sub-problems, and fail to take a holistic overview. If all other firms are following a similar scientific approach, using similar business models, they may all end up with 'me too' strategies. A more creative approach is likely to encourage unique solutions which may either succeed spectacularly or fail miserably. Later in this chapter we will explore how different management structures and processes can either help or hinder the process of developing a sustainable competitive advantage.

Information is a key element of the marketing management process. We saw in Chapter 5 how, in large organizations, information is a medium for keeping in touch with customers, employees, suppliers, and intermediaries. Getting the right information to the right people at the right time is crucial if the management of a company is to be able to develop and implement a strategy. Without appropriate information, strategy formulation can become guesswork and the implementation of that strategy may be half-hearted. Inadequate monitoring may not warn of problems until it is too late to do anything about them.

The marketing management process

Marketing management can be seen as a continual process. This section identifies the key elements of the process, although just who should be responsible for each element is a subject to which we will return later when we explore how marketing management is organized.

There are five key stages in the marketing management process (Figure 12.1).

1. **Where are we now? Analysis of the organization's current market position.** A vital starting point for marketing planning is an analysis of a company's current marketing environment, often undertaken by means of a SWOT analysis or a marketing audit. A **marketing audit** has been defined as:

   a systematical, critical and unbiased review and appraisal of the environment and of the company's operations. A marketing audit is part of the larger management audit and is concerned with the marketing environment and marketing operations. (McDonald, 2002)

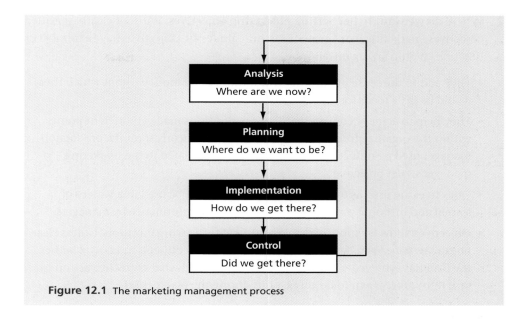

Figure 12.1 The marketing management process

A marketing audit typically includes analysis of the organization's current market share, the size and nature of its customer base, customer perceptions of the organization's output, and the internal strengths and weaknesses of the organization in terms of production, personnel, and financial resources. A marketing audit addresses these issues using both quantitative and qualitative methods where appropriate. But what information should be collected? A company's **mission statement** can provide its employees with guidance about what is relevant and irrelevant in analysing its current position.

How much analysis of the current situation should a company undertake? While it is nearly always true that a sound analysis of the current situation is an essential prerequisite to developing a marketing plan for the future, excessive preoccupation with the current situation can have its costs. Analysis on its own will not provide the management decisions that are necessary for defining the future marketing plan. A 'paralysis by analysis' can occur in organizations that avoid making hard decisions about the future because they are continually seeking more information about the present. A plateau is usually reached at which little additional information is any longer available that will improve the quality of marketing plan decisions. Worse still, in markets that are fast changing, excessive analysis of the current position can put a company at a competitive disadvantage to firms that are more willing to take a risk and exploit a market opportunity ahead of its competitors.

2. **Where do we want to be? Setting marketing objectives.** Without clearly specified objectives, marketing management can drift aimlessly. Objectives have a number of functions within an organization:

- They add to the sense of purpose within the organization, without which there would be little focus for managers' efforts.

- They help to achieve consistency between decisions made at different points within the organization; for example, it would be inconsistent if a production manager used a production objective that was unrelated to the marketing manager's sales objective.

- Objectives are used as motivational devices and can be used in a variety of formal and informal ways to stimulate increased performance by managers.

- Objectives allow for more effective control within an organization. Unless clear objectives have been defined at the outset, it is very difficult to know whether the firm has achieved what it set out to achieve, and what corrective action to take if its efforts seem to be going adrift during the plan period.

To be effective, objectives must be capable of realistic achievement and must be accepted as such by the people responsible for acting on them. If objectives are set unattainably high, the whole process of planning can be brought into disrepute by the company's employees. Wherever possible, objectives should be quantified and should clearly specify the time period to which they relate. Inconsistency between objectives should be avoided. This sometimes occurs, for example, where sales objectives can be achieved only by reducing selling prices, thereby making it impossible to achieve a profitability objective.

3. **How can we get there? Developing a marketing strategy.** There are usually many ways in which marketing objectives can be achieved. For example, a financial return objective could be satisfied equally well by a high sales volume/low-price strategy or a low-volume/high-price strategy. Identifying the strategic alternatives open to an organization relies on interpreting data and evaluating a number of possible future scenarios. Within this evaluation, factors such as the likelihood of success, the level of downside risk, and the amount of resources required to implement a strategy need to be taken into consideration. What may be an appropriate strategy for one company may be quite inappropriate for another, on account of differences in financial resources, past history, and personnel strengths, among other things.

It often happens that the objectives set for the planning period are greater than what could be achieved if growth occurred at the historic trend rate. Where such a **planning gap** exists, the aim of the planning process is to develop a strategy that will close this gap. This can be done either by reducing the original objective downward to a level that is more realistic, given the historical pattern, or by accelerating

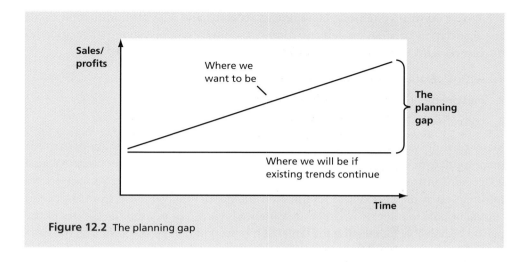

Figure 12.2 The planning gap

the trend rate from its historical pattern to a higher level by means of marketing strategy. In practice, the planning gap is reduced by a combination of revising objectives and amending marketing strategies (Figure 12.2).

There have been many prescriptions for developing marketing strategies, some of which were discussed in Chapter 7 in the context of the development of a sustainable competitive advantage.

4. **How will we implement the strategy?** Having chosen a strategy, the next step is to implement it. This is usually done through a 12-month **marketing plan**, although the length of the plan period can depend on the amount of turbulence in a company's marketing environment. The marketing plan sets out programmes for, among other things, the timing and costing of promotional programmes, pricing plans, and the recruitment and payment of distributors. The plan should clearly show who is responsible for implementing each aspect of the plan. The detailed marketing plan should flow directly from the marketing strategy, which itself starts from marketing objectives. The plan may go through a series of iterative stages of consultation before it is finally accepted. Too many companies develop a strategy that sounds fine, but they fail to think through fully the detail of implementation.

5. **Did we get there? Monitoring and controlling the marketing programme.** Marketing plans are of little value if they are to be implemented only half-heartedly. An ongoing part of the marketing management process is therefore to monitor the implementation of the plan and to seek an explanation of any deviation from it.

Effective **control systems** demand timely, accurate, and relevant information about an organization's operations and environment. Control systems require three underlying components to be in place:

1. setting of targets or standards of expected performance;
2. measurement and evaluation of actual performance;
3. corrective action to be taken where necessary.

Many control systems fail because employees within an organization have been given inappropriate or unrealistic targets. Even where targets are set and appropriate data are collected, control systems may fail because of a failure by management to act on the information available. Control information should identify variances from target and should be able to indicate whether the variance is within or beyond the control of the person responsible for meeting the target. If it is beyond that person's control, the issue should become one of revising the target so that it once more becomes achievable. If the variance is the result of factors that are subject to a manager's control, a number of measures can be taken to try to revise their behaviour, including incentive schemes, training, and disciplinary action.

◖ Strategic, tactical, and contingency planning

From the above description, marketing *planning* is best viewed as a continuous *process*. However, it is necessary to produce periodic statements of a *plan* which all individuals in an organization can work towards. Three types of periodic plan can be identified.

1. The **strategic** element of a marketing plan focuses on the overriding direction that an organization's efforts will take in order to meet its objectives.
2. The **tactical** element is more concerned with plans for implementing the detail of the strategic plan.

    The division between the strategic and tactical elements of a marketing plan can sometimes be difficult to define. Typically, a strategic marketing plan is concerned with mapping out direction over a five-year planning period, whereas a tactical marketing plan is concerned with implementation during the next 12 months. Many business sectors view their strategic planning periods very differently, and in the case of large-scale infrastructure projects such as airports or railways, the strategic planning period may be very long indeed. On the other hand, many small-scale, low-technology businesses may find little need for a strategic plan beyond the immediate operational period.

3. A **contingency plan** seeks to identify scenarios where the assumptions of the position analysis on which strategic decisions were based turn out to be false. For example, a food manufacturer might have assumed that there would be no significant

change in consumers' attitudes towards a particular category of food. However, the possibility of a food scare, such as those associated with salmonella in chickens and BSE in beef, could seriously affect the implementation of a marketing plan. A contingency plan would allow a firm to react quickly to such a scenario, for example by increasing its promotional expenditure and cutting back on production capacity.

The dynamic marketing environment

In developing a marketing plan, it can be very easy to assume a stable market. In Chapter 7 we saw that, in reality, most markets are dynamic and a marketing plan needs to take account of not just competitors' current strategies, but also their likely future strategies. If a market appears attractive to one organization, then it probably appears equally attractive to others as well. These other organizations may possess equal competitive advantage in addressing the market. If all such firms decide to enter the market, over-supply results, profit margins become squeezed, and the market becomes relatively unattractive. This could be observed in the semi-conductor market, which in the mid-1990s looked highly attractive, with a rapid growth in demand and a shortage of supply. This was the signal for many companies to enter the market, with the result that by 2000 oversupply had resulted, the price of semi-conductors had fallen from over £4 to less than 50p, and many manufacturing operations had become unprofitable.

Marketing planning and corporate planning

Marketing management is just one of the specialist management functions that can be identified within most commercial organizations. What is the relationship between marketing management and corporate management? At one extreme, the two can be seen as synonymous. If an organization stands or falls primarily on its ability to satisfy customer needs, then it can be argued that marketing planning is so central to the organization's activities that it becomes **corporate planning**. The alternative view is that marketing is just one of the functions of an organization that affects its performance. Marketing takes its goals from corporate plans just as the personnel or production functions of the organization do. In business sectors where customers have relatively little choice and production capacity is limited, the significance of the marketing plan to the corporate plan will be less than for a company facing fierce competition. Many public-sector service organizations operating in relatively uncompetitive markets claim to go through the marketing planning process, when in fact, although the term 'marketing planning' may be referred to by name, it is given much less significance than the development of production plans or personnel plans to serve a stable market.

The relationship between the processes of marketing and corporate planning can be two-way, again reflecting the importance of marketing to the total planning process.

Marketing information is fed into the corporate planning process for analysis and formulation of the corporate plan in a process sometimes referred to as 'bottom-up planning'. In a 'top-down' process, the corporate plan is developed and functional objectives are specified for marketing.

Planning as an inter-functional integrator

The marketing planning process helps to integrate the efforts of a diverse range of people throughout an organization. The plan allows everybody to 'sing from the same hymn sheet'. Without the plan, individuals may end up doing things that are in direct conflict with their colleagues.

Corporate and marketing planning processes act as integrators in horizontal and vertical dimensions (see Figure 12.3).

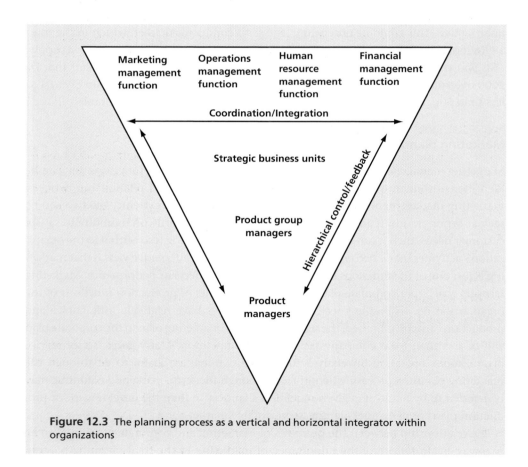

Figure 12.3 The planning process as a vertical and horizontal integrator within organizations

- **In the horizontal dimension**, the planning process brings together the plans of the specialized functions that are necessary to make the organization work. Marketing is just one function of an organization which generates its own planning process. Other functional plans found in most organizations are financial plans, personnel plans, and production plans. The components of these functional plans must recognize their interdependencies if they are to be effective. For example, a car manufacturer's marketing strategic plan which anticipates a 20% growth in sales of its cars over a five-year planning period should be reflected in a strategic production plan that allows for output to increase by a similar amount, as well as a financial plan that identifies strategies for raising the required level of finance for new investment and work in progress and a personnel plan for recruiting additional staff. Within the marketing department, a plan helps to ensure that the activities of advertising personnel are mutually supportive of the activities of sales and market research staff, for example.

- **In the vertical dimension**, the planning process provides a framework for decisions to be made at different levels of the corporate hierarchy. Objectives can be specified in progressively more detail, from the global objectives of the corporate plan, to the information required to operationalize these objectives at the level of individual operational units (or **strategic business units**) and—in turn—for individual products.

The mission statement

A corporate mission statement provides a focal point for the marketing planning process. It can be likened to a hidden hand which guides all employees in an organization in developing and implementing marketing plans. Drucker (1973) identified a number of basic questions that management needs to ask in drawing up a mission statement:

- What is our business?
- Who is the customer?
- What is value to the customer?
- What will our business be?
- What should our business be?

By forcing management to focus on the essential nature of the business it is in and the nature of customer needs it seeks to satisfy, the problem of 'marketing myopia' identified by Levitt (1960) can be avoided. Levitt argued that, in order to avoid a narrow, shortsighted view of their business, managers should define their business in terms of the needs that they fulfil rather than the products they produce. In the classic example, railway operators lost their way because they defined their output in terms of the *technology* of tracked vehicles, rather than in terms of the core benefit of *movement* that they

'To give ordinary folk the chance to buy the same things as rich people'

—Wal Mart

'To organize the world's information and make it universally accessible and useful'

—Google

'To make people happy'

—Walt Disney

'To provide our customers with safe, good value, point-to-point air services. To effect and to offer a consistent and reliable product and fares appealing to leisure and business markets on a range of European routes. To achieve this we will develop our people and establish lasting relationships with our suppliers'

—easyJet

'To be the consumer's frst choice for food, delivering products of outstanding quality and great service at a competitive cost through working faster, simpler and together'

—Sainsbury's

Figure 12.4 Some examples of corporate mission statements

provided. They lost out to the development of cars and buses, which provided similar benefits using different technologies.

The nature of an organization's mission statement is a reflection of a number of factors, including the organization's ownership (e.g. public-sector v. private-sector statements); the previous history of the organization; the resources available; and major opportunities and threats faced by the organization.

In services organizations where the interface between consumers and production personnel is often critical, communication of the values contained within the mission statement can be very important. The statement is frequently repeated by organizations in staff newsletters and in notices at the place of work. An example of a mission statement that is widely communicated to the workforce—as well as to customers—is shown in Figure 12.4.

Organizing the marketing management function

It was noted earlier that the principles of marketing might be fine in theory, but they are difficult in practice. The same can be said for the process of marketing planning. The process may look fine in theory, but it needs the right people to implement the process and make it a success. There have been too many cases of marketing planners developing a plan for which the operational implications have not been fully thought through and which therefore fails to deliver value to customers and profits to the company.

A frequent problem occurs where the marketing planning function becomes cut off from other functional departments. The whole issue of organizing a company so that it has a company-wide focus on marketing is considered in a later section. Here we look inwardly at the marketing department and ask how it can best be organized in order to meet marketing objectives.

Responsibilities given to the marketing department vary from one organization to another, reflecting the competitive nature of a company and also its traditions and organizational inertia. Within marketing departments, four basic approaches to allocating these responsibilities are identified here (shown in Figure 12.5 using the example of an airline)—although, in practice, most marketing departments show more than one approach. The four approaches allocate marketing responsibilities by: functions performed, geographical area covered, products or groups of products managed, and market segments managed.

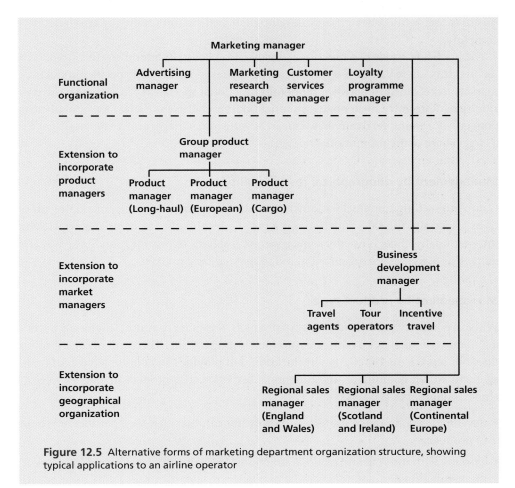

Figure 12.5 Alternative forms of marketing department organization structure, showing typical applications to an airline operator

The great diversity of organizational structures highlights the fact that there is no one unique structure that is appropriate to all firms, even within the same business sector. Overall, the organization of a marketing department must allow for a flexible and adaptable response to customers' needs within a changing environment, while aiming to reduce the level of confusion, ambiguity, and cost inherent in some structures.

Management by functional responsibility

A common basis for organizing a marketing department is to divide responsibilities into identifiable marketing functions. Typically, these functions may be advertising, sales, research and development, marketing research, and customer services. The precise division of the functional responsibilities will depend upon the nature of the organization. Buying and merchandising are likely to be important features in a retailing organization, while research and development will be important for an electronics company.

The main advantage of a functional organization lies in its administrative simplicity. Against this, there can be a tendency for policy responsibility on specific products or markets to become lost between numerous functional specialists. There is also the possibility of destructive rivalry between functional specialists for their share of marketing budgets—for example, rivalry between an advertising manager and a sales manager for a larger share of the promotional budget.

Management by geographical responsibility

Companies selling a product nationwide usually organize some of their marketing functions, especially the sales function, on a geographical basis. For companies operating internationally, there is usually some geographical basis to organization in the way the marketing activities are organized in individual national markets.

Management by product type

Where a company produces a variety of products, it is quite common to appoint a product manager to manage a particular product or product line. This form of organization does not replace the functional organization, but provides an additional layer of management which coordinates the functional activities. The product manager's role includes a number of key tasks:

- developing a long-range strategy and short-term annual plan for a product or group of products;
- working with internal and external functional specialists to develop and implement marketing programmes, for example in relation to advertising and sales promotion;

- monitoring the performance of the product and noting changes in the marketing environment that may pose opportunities or threats.

In theory, a product manager can react more quickly to changes in the product's marketing environment than would be possible if no one had specific responsibility for the product. Although product management structures can allow for a focused strategy to be developed in respect of individual products, there are nevertheless some shortcomings. The most serious one arises when a product manager is given a lot of responsibility for ensuring that objectives for the product are met, but relatively little control over the resource inputs he has at his disposal. Product managers typically must rely on persuasion for the cooperation of advertising, sales, and other functional specialist departments. Confusion can arise in the minds of staff within an organization as to whom they are accountable to for their day-to-day actions—the product manager, or a functional specialist such as a sales manager? Product management structures can lead to larger numbers of people being employed, resulting in a higher cost structure, which may put the organization at a competitive disadvantage in price-sensitive markets.

Management by market segment

Many companies sell basically similar products to different types of customer who vary significantly in their needs. For example, an airline provides services targeted at leisure travellers, business travellers, tour operators, and freight forwarders, among others; each of these groups has differing requirements in terms of speed, reliability, price, etc., and a market segment manager can become expert in understanding these needs and developing an appropriate product offer for each group. Instead of being given financial targets for a specific product, market managers are usually given growth or market share targets.

The main advantage of this form of organization is that it allows marketing activity to be focused on meeting the needs of distinct and identified groups of customers—something that should be at the heart of any truly marketing-oriented organization. Also, new products are more likely to emerge within this structure than where an organization's response is confined to traditional product management boundaries. Market management structures are also arguably more conducive to the important task of developing relationships with customers, especially in business-to-business markets. Where an organization has a number of very important customers, it is common to find the appointment of key account managers to handle relationships with those clients in order to exploit marketing opportunities that are of mutual benefit to both).

Many of the disadvantages of the product management organization are also shared by market-based structures. There can again be a conflict between responsibility and authority, and this form of structure can also become expensive to operate.

MARKETING in ACTION

Marketing the unmanageable?

In any organization, the aspirations of marketing managers can be quite different from those of the employees who have to deliver the promises that marketers make. It can be naive to imagine that marketers simply concentrate on identifying customers' needs, then operations people develop products which will satisfy those needs. In reality, frontline employees may have cherished ways of working which they may feel are threatened by new ideas of the marketing department. This is especially true in services, and a problem can be acute where the frontline employees have considerable knowledge and power. An analysis of marketing management in the National Health Service (NHS) illustrates some of the challenges that marketing managers may face. The NHS has seen an increase in the number of managers who have no clinical background. Increasingly, marketing managers are being appointed by health service trusts, mindful of the fact that in an increasingly market-driven health sector, understanding and responding to patients' needs becomes increasingly important. Indeed, the language of some hospital managers now talks about 'customers' rather than 'patients'. Although the chief executive of a NHS Trust in principle has ultimate authority over all employees, many people would recognize that it is the medical consultants who have the real power in a hospital. If they do not like a change that is proposed by the chief executive, they can point to their professional codes of conduct and years of training that have given them knowledge-based power. Consultants may argue that they have patients' long-term interests at heart, because they have invested heavily in their specialized training and will be around for many years to deal with the consequences of their actions. By contrast, a marketing manager may be perceived as having relatively simple training, and will soon move on to another job with no professional responsibility to see through the consequences of his/her actions. Marketing managers with a non-clinical background may become too focused on relatively superficial quality-of-service issues such as car parking and food, while consultants could argue that only they can judge the true quality of the core service of a hospital, namely the outcome of medical and surgical procedures. They point out that a typical patient is incapable of assessing clinical performance, owing to their limited knowledge, and the fact that the outcome of many clinical procedures will not fully present themselves for many months or even years into the future. In short, only consultants, with their professional training and codes of conduct, can manage the nature of interaction between the hospital and its patients.

For a marketing manager, the professional, knowledge-based power of consultants may be seen as a source of frustration. As an example, it has been claimed that many NHS hospitals' operating theatres are under-utilized on Friday afternoons. For a marketing manager, one method of increasing the number of patient admissions would be to use these very expensive facilities on Friday afternoons, rather than to leave them idle. Consultants would argue that it is bad professional practice to commence operations just before the weekend, when there is only limited cover available in a hospital to rectify any clinical complications. Cynics may claim that consultants are using professional arguments as a smokescreen for giving themselves a long weekend, and a chance to get away early to play golf. Some have pointed out that consultants may nevertheless use Friday afternoons to undertake profitable private surgery elsewhere. How can a chief executive or marketing manager with a non-clinical background argue with the knowledge and professional responsibilities of a consultant? What does marketing management mean in the context of highly skilled professionals? Many would argue that management is not about command and control, but more about facilitating others to achieve their goals. Which model of management is right? Who decides whether consultants are right in their goals of keeping Friday afternoons free for professional reasons, or whether they are doing it because they know a good personal opportunity when they see one?

Integrating marketing management with other management functions

Should an organization actually have a marketing department? The idea is becoming increasingly popular that the existence of a separate marketing department may in fact hinder the development of a true customer-centred marketing orientation. By placing all marketing activity in a marketing department, non-marketing staff may consider that responsibility for getting new or repeat business is nothing to do with them, but should be left to the marketing department. While it is becoming fashionable to talk about everybody becoming a 'part-time marketer' (see Gummesson, 2008), a marketing department is usually required in order to coordinate and implement those functions that cannot sensibly be delegated to operational personnel. Advertising, sales management, and pricing decisions, for example, usually need some central coordination by a marketing department. The importance that a marketing department assumes within any organization is a reflection on the nature of its operating environment. An organization operating in a fiercely competitive environment would typically attach great

MARKETING in ACTION

Should companies build Chinese walls?

The idea of an integrated internal work environment may be fine in theory, and may reassure customers that 'the left hand really does know what the right hand is doing'; but in practice, there are many instances where professional codes of conduct require that staff within an organization do *not* talk to each other. This often happens in financial services institutions where one group of employees may have 'inside information' about the shares, activities, or financial condition of a company, which, if made public, would be likely to have an effect on the price of that company's shares. As an example: information about a proposed takeover bid for a company may be price-sensitive in relation to other companies in the same sector. This leads many institutions to create 'Chinese walls', which are barriers to the passing of information. They are designed to manage confidential information and prevent inadvertent spread and misuse of information. Many banks have set up global Chinese walls policies. Those areas that routinely have access to inside information (e.g. corporate finance), and which are considered 'inside areas', must be physically separated from those areas that deal in or advise on financial instruments (e.g. bonds and shares), which are considered 'public areas'. The problem has become particularly acute in the accounting sector, where a firm of accountants may sell both auditing services and management consultancy services to a company. There have been many allegations that accountants have been too ready to accept compromises in their auditing function in order to pick up lucrative management consultancy business. The investigation of the accountant Arthur Andersen's (now known as Accenture) involvement with the failed energy company Enron in 2002 revealed evidence of unethical practice in the way that the firm had mixed accountancy and consultancy activities, and led to renewed debate about the ethics of 'one-stop' accountancy/consultancy businesses.

Chinese walls are also used by solicitors in cases where they are dealing with clients who may be in dispute with each other. Other service industries can be identified where similar ethical problems can be lessened by the adoption of a product management structure. How do large diversified services firms convince their customers that information given in confidence to one section of the organization will not be used against them in another section?

importance to its marketing department as a means of producing a focused marketing mix strategy by which it could gain competitive advantage over its competitors. On the other hand, a company operating in a relatively stable environment would be more likely to allow strategic decisions to be taken by personnel who were not marketing strategists—for example, pricing decisions may be taken by accountants with less need to understand the marketing implications of price decisions.

In a marketing-oriented organization, customers are at the centre of all of the organization's activities. Customers are the concern not simply of the marketing department, but of all the production and administrative personnel whose actions may directly or indirectly impinge upon the customers' service. In the words of Drucker (1973),

Marketing is so basic that it cannot be considered to be a separate function. It is the whole business seen from the point of view of its final result, that is, from the customer's point of view.

The activities of a number of functional departments can impinge on customers' perceptions of the value they get from a company.

- Personnel plans can have a crucial bearing on marketing plans. The selection, training, motivation, and control of staff cannot be considered in isolation from marketing objectives and strategies. Possible conflict between personnel and marketing functions may arise where, for example, marketing demands highly trained and motivated staff, but the personnel function pursues a policy that emphasizes cost reduction and uniform pay structures.

- Marketing managers may try to respond as closely as possible to customers' needs but encounter opposition from production managers, who argue that a product of the required standard cannot be achieved. A marketing manager may want large numbers of product variants in order to satisfy market niches, whereas a production manager may seek large production runs of standardized products.

- Ultimately, finance managers assume responsibility for the allocation of the funds that are needed to implement a marketing plan. At a more operational level, finance managers' actions in respect of the level of credit offered to customers, or towards stockholdings, can also significantly affect the quality of service and the volume of customers that the organization is able to serve.

The problem of how to bring people together in an organization to act collectively while also being able to place responsibility on an individual is one which continues to generate considerable discussion. Organizations which produce many different products for many different markets may experience difficulties if they adopt a purely product or market-based structure. If a product management structure is adopted, product managers would require detailed knowledge of very diverse markets. Likewise, in a market management structure, market managers would require detailed knowledge of possibly very diverse product ranges. To avoid the problem of functional managers acting and thinking with a 'silo' mentality, there has been a tendency for organizations to develop clusters of individuals who focus on creating value for targeted groups of consumers and profits for their company. Within such a cluster, product managers can concentrate on excellence in production, while market managers focus on meeting consumer needs without any preference for a particular product. An example of a 'matrix structure' as these are sometimes known can be found in many airlines where market managers can be appointed to identify and formulate a market strategy in respect of the distinct needs of private leisure customers, corporate clients, travel agents, etc. Market managers work alongside product managers who can develop and manage specific products and processes, such as business and first-class cabin service (Figure 12.6).

The most important advantages of such clusters are that they can—in principle—allow organizations to respond rapidly to environmental change. Short-term project teams can be assembled and disbanded at short notice to meet changed needs. Project teams can bring together a wide variety of disciplines and can be used to evaluate new products before full-scale development is undertaken. A bank exploring the possibility of developing a mobile phone-based payment system might establish a team drawn from staff involved in marketing to personal customers and staff responsible for technology-based research and development. The former may include market researchers and the latter software developers.

The flexibility of such structures can be increased by bringing temporary workers into the structure on a contract basis as and when needed. During the past two decades there has been a trend for many services organizations to lay off significant numbers of workers—including management—and to buy these back when needed. As well as

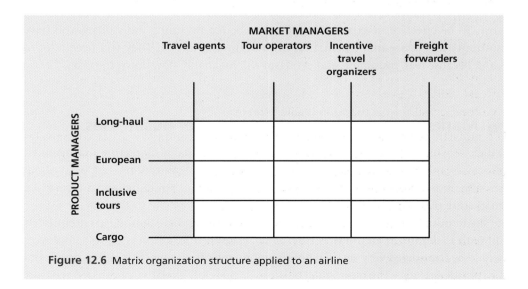

Figure 12.6 Matrix organization structure applied to an airline

cutting fixed costs, such organizations have the potential to respond very rapidly to environmental change.

Where inter-functional clusters exist, great motivation can be present in effectively managed teams. Against this, matrix-type structures can have their problems. Most serious is the confused lines of authority that may result. Staff may not be clear about which superior he or she is responsible to for a particular aspect of their duties, resulting in possible stress and demotivation. Where a matrix-type structure is introduced into an organization with a history and culture of functional specialization, it can be very difficult to implement effectively. Staff may be reluctant to act outside a role which they have traditionally defined narrowly and guarded jealously. Finally, such structures invariably result in more managers being employed within an organization. At best this can result in a costly addition to the salary bill. At worst, the existence of additional managers can also slow down decision-making processes where the managers show a reluctance to act outside a narrow functional role.

Having multi-functional clusters of individuals may represent a desirable structure for an organization, but getting there can be a slow and painful process. Most management change within organizations occurs incrementally. The result of this is often a compromised organization structure which is unduly influenced by historic factors and vested interests which are of no continuing relevance. Some organizations have been more radical and started with a clean sheet of paper and asked 'How would we design our structures and processes if we were starting out today? The underlying principle of *business process re-engineering* is to design an organization around key value adding activities. Essentially, re-engineering is about **radically** redesigning the **processes** by which an organization does business in order that it can achieve major savings in cost, or improvements in service levels, or both. Seen as a model, the organization which is most effective is the one which adds most value (as defined by customers) for the least cost. To be effective, re-engineering needs to be led by strong individuals who have authority to oversee implementation from beginning to end. They will need a lot of clout because fear, resistance, and cynicism will inevitably slow down the task.

● Marketing management and smaller businesses

Much of what has been written so far in this chapter about marketing management processes and structures might sound fine for larger organizations, but what about smaller businesses where the very idea of a 'management structure' and a formalized marketing planning system may seem quite alien?

The term **small business** (or **SME**, standing for small and medium-sized enterprise) is difficult to define. In an industry such as car manufacture, a firm with 100 employees would be considered very small, whereas among solicitors, a practice of that size would be considered large. The term 'small business' is therefore a relative one, based typically on some measure of numbers of employees or capital employed. A large category of 'micro' or 'size class zero' businesses exist which do not have any employees. In these companies, production, finance, and marketing are all vested in the same person.

The importance of small businesses should not be under-estimated. In the UK, the Department for Business, Enterprise and Regulatory Reform's SME statistics for 2006 highlight the importance and diversity of the small business sector: 99.3% of all business enterprises had fewer than 50 employees; 73% had no employees (these are often referred to as micro businesses); small enterprises with fewer than 50 employees accounted for 47.1% of UK employment and 37.2% of turnover; only 0.1% of the 4.5 million business enterprises in the UK employed more than 250 people (DBERR, 2006).

In terms of marketing management, SMEs have a number of important characteristics.

1. They generally offer much greater adaptability than larger firms. With less bureaucracy and fewer channels of communications, decisions can be taken rapidly. A larger organization may be burdened with constraints which tend to slow the decision-making process, such as the need to negotiate new working practices with trade union representatives, or the need to obtain the board of directors' approval for major decisions. As organizations grow, there is an inherent tendency for them to become more risk-averse by building in systems of control that can make them slower to adapt to changes in their business environment.

2. Small businesses tend to be good innovators. This comes about through their greater adaptability, especially where large amounts of capital are not required. Small firms can also be good innovators where they operate in markets dominated by a small number of larger companies and the only way in which they can gain entry to the market is by developing innovatory products aimed at a small niche. The soap-powder market in Britain is dominated by a small number of large producers, yet it was a relatively small company that identified a niche for environmentally friendly powders and introduced innovatory products to the market.

It is not only small entrepreneurs who have been creating new small businesses. Many larger organizations have also recognized their value and have tried to replicate them at a distance from their own structure. Many large manufacturing organizations operating in mature markets have created autonomous new small-business units to serve rapidly developing or specialist niche markets, free of the bureaucratic culture of the parent organization. In the education sector, many universities have established small research companies at arm's length from the universities' organizational structures.

While small businesses have certainly seen a resurgence in recent years, it should also be recognized that they have a very high failure rate. Conclusive evidence of the failure rate of small businesses is difficult to obtain, especially in view of the problem of identifying new businesses that do not need to register in the first place. However, one indication of failure rates comes from an analysis of VAT (value added tax) registrations,

MARKETING in ACTION

Are entrepreneurs born or bred?

Is there such a thing as an 'entrepreneurship gene'? Further developments in the science of genetics may one day add some evidence to the debate about whether entrepreneurs are born or bred. But what about students leaving university today? Evidence abounds of students who are anecdotally attributed with an 'entrepreneurship gene'. As an example, the smoothie manufacturer Innocent was set up in 1999 by three entrepreneurial Cambridge University graduates—Adam Balon, Richard Reed, and Jon Wright—to produce fresh fruit smoothies. The budding entrepreneurs initially tested their dream by buying £500 of fresh fruit and selling their smoothies at a stall during a weekend jazz festival in London. By December 2007 Innocent Drinks appeared at number 40 in the *Sunday Times* Fast Track 100, a list of the fastest growing private companies in the UK. It was the only company to have appeared in this list for the last four years consecutively. In each of the previous four years, Innocent had more than doubled its revenues.

Of course, for every entrepreneurial success story there are scores of failures, and it is commonly estimated that at least a third of new entrants to self-employment leave within three years—even more in periods of economic recession. Very often, an entrepreneur can be good at creating a business, but much weaker at handling the procedures that are necessary to keep a larger organization on track. Typical of this tendency is Michelle Mone, inventor of the cleavage enhancing Ultimo bra. She launched her business, MJM International, in 1996 and enjoyed an annual turnover of more than £1 million within just a few years. Her products went on to achieve global fame when Julia Roberts wore an Ultimo bra for her role in the Oscar-winning film *Erin Brockovich*. In 2001 turnover reached £3 million, and Mone announced plans to float her company. But when the planned float failed to take off, her fortunes seemed to unwind. The bank called in the company's overdraft, she began experiencing problems with designers, and a department store cancelled its order, leaving her business with 15,000 unsold bras. It seemed that designing stylish bras for the rich and famous was one thing, but handling relationships with large retail buyers was quite another. Mone pulled her products out of department stores in 2001 to sell direct to the public via an Internet site, but sales remained static.

So what are the characteristics of an entrepreneur? Most experts tend to agree that a willingness to take risks is crucial—it really does seem to be necessary to speculate in order to accumulate. Of course, taking risks implies that while some entrepreneurs will succeed beyond their wildest dreams, many will fail. Good entrepreneurs are able to pick themselves up quickly following a failure. Being optimistic and spotting opportunities is important, as is the ability to work long hours, and to have a belief in yourself and your ideas (Northouse, 2006).

It would seem that many would-be entrepreneurs do not set out on the road to entrepreneurship, because they have a fear of failure. Some cultures condemn individuals who have failed, but in other countries, such as the United States, there is an environment in which failure is recognized as a sign of a well-intentioned individual who hit a bit of bad luck, and success is about more than having a bit of undeserved good luck. Can this difference in cultural values explain why some countries seem to have a larger number of entrepreneurial companies?

which show that during the 1990s only about one-third of businesses set up ten years previously were still registered. Further evidence of the high failure rate is provided by Barclays Bank which, in 2003, estimated that, on the basis of its business customer records, over half of all new firms fail in the first three years (Barclays, 2004).

Internal marketplaces

Every organization can be considered to be a marketplace consisting of a diverse group of employees engaging in exchanges between one another—the accounting department processing invoices for the sales department; the catering department providing a lunch for a training session run by the HRM department, and so on. Increasingly, organizations are asking internal service departments, such as information technology, human resources, accounting, and media services, to be more accountable and to put in bids to provide goods and services, in competition with external providers. This has resulted in employees effectively trading services with other employees within their organization. In a growing number of instances, organizations have outsourced the services traditionally provided by such internal departments, resulting in extended 'network' or 'virtual' organizations.

One conceptual framework for considering such exchanges is sometimes referred to as 'Next operation as a customer' (NOAC) (Denton, 1990). NOAC is based on the idea that each group within an organization should treat the recipients of its output as an internal customer and strive to provide high-quality outputs for them. Through this internal approach, quality and value will be built into the product delivered to the final external customer. This concept of an internal market of buyers and suppliers is closely related to the concept of the value chain (Porter, 1980). A modified value chain in terms of internal suppliers is shown in Figure 12.7.

There are, however, problems in drawing analogies between internal and external markets for goods and services. External customers can usually take their business elsewhere if they are not satisfied with the value provided, while internal customers may be required to use a designated service unit within their organization. Consequently, the internal customer is frequently a captive customer. Many companies have introduced 'marketing testing' procedures in which the performance of internal service units is assessed against what could be achieved by outsourcing the service provision to an external provider. Such market testing may focus the minds of internal management, who become ever mindful that if they do not sharpen their act, their job will go to a manager of an external contractor. However, the process of market testing may demotivate staff and create a feeling of insecurity and possibly a lack of loyalty to the organization. Many organizations set internal transfer prices on the basis of periodic reviews of prevailing external prices, and then set profit objectives for internal service managers, based on these transfer prices. This itself can be a difficult task, especially where there are complex interdependent cost structures which a service manager has little control over.

🖿 Leadership

Many of the most successful market-led companies, such as Virgin Group, J. D. Weatherspoon, and Dell Computers, attribute their success in part to the quality of **leadership** within their organizations. The results of poor leadership are evident in many failing

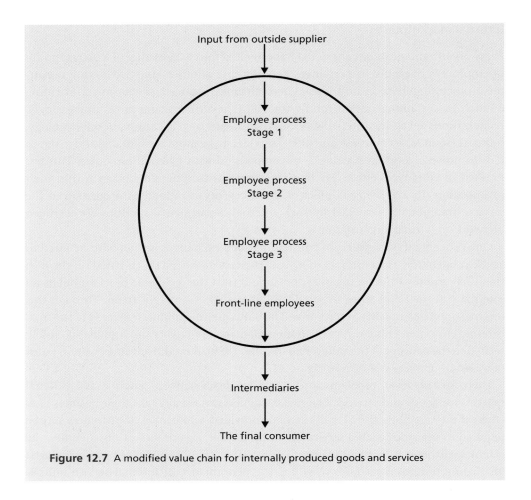

Figure 12.7 A modified value chain for internally produced goods and services

service organizations. Many commentators attributed the decline in the fortunes of Marks & Spencer and Sainsbury's during the late 1990s to poor leadership, which in both cases was reversed with changed leadership styles bought in by new chief executives during the early 2000s.

What is good leadership for one organization need not necessarily be so for another. Organizations operating in relatively stable environments may be best suited with a leadership style that places a lot of power in a hierarchical chain of command. In the UK, many banks until recently had leadership styles that were drawn from models developed in the armed forces, as evidenced by some managers having titles such as 'superintendent' and 'inspector'. Such rigid, hierarchical patterns of leadership may be less effective where the marketing environment is changing rapidly and a flexible response is called for (as has happened in the banking sector).

What makes a good leader of a marketing-oriented company? And are leaders born, or can individuals acquire the skills of leadership? On the latter point there is little doubt that development is possible, and successful companies have invested heavily in leadership development programmes. As for what makes a successful leader of people, there have been many suggestions (Northouse, 2006) of desirable traits, including:

- setting clear expectations of staff;
- recognizing excellence appropriately and facilitating staff in overcoming their weaknesses;
- leading by example;
- being able to empathize with employees;
- showing adaptability to changing circumstances.

In too many companies, bad leadership is characterized by:

- 'management by confusion', in which expectations of staff are ambiguously stated and management actions are guided by a secretive 'hidden agenda';
- reward systems that are not based on performance and are perceived as being unfair;
- the deliberate or inadvertent creation of an 'us and them' attitude;
- failure to understand the aspirations of employees;
- failure to take the initiative where environmental change calls for adaptation.

Managing information

We saw in Chapter 5 how information represents a bridge between an organization and its environment. It is the means by which a picture of the changing environment is built up within the organization. Marketing management is responsible for turning information into specific marketing plans. The marketing management function of any organization requires a constant flow of information for two principal purposes:

1. to provide information as an input to the planning of marketing activities;
2. to monitor the implementation of marketing programmes and allow corrective action to be taken if performance diverges from target.

A timely supply of appropriate information provides feedback on an organization's performance, allowing actual performance to be compared with target performance. On the basis of this information, control measures can be applied which seek—where

MARKETING in ACTION

Managing by example

Beginning with a small shop in Dundalk in 1960, the Irish grocery retailer SuperQuinn has grown to a successful chain of 12 shops and seven shopping centres. In 2008, it employed over 4,000 people throughout Ireland. A large part of this success has been attributed to the leadership style of the company's founder, Feargal Quinn, and the emphasis on linking employees' activities to excellence in service quality. But what makes such leadership style distinctive?

An important principle is that managers should lead by example and should never lose contact with the most important person in the organization—the customer. It is the task of a leader to set the tone for customer-focused excellence. To prevent managers losing sight of customers' needs, Quinn has used every opportunity to move them closer to customers, including locating their offices not in a comfortable room upstairs, but in the middle of the sales floor. Managers regularly take part in customer panels where customers talk about their expectations and perceptions of SuperQuinn. Subcontracting this task entirely to a market research agency is seen as alien to the leadership culture of the company. The company requires its managers to spend periods doing routine front-line jobs (such as packing customers' bags), a practice that has become commonplace in many successful services organizations. This keeps managers close to the company and improves their ability to empathize with junior employees.

Does this leadership style work? Given the company's level of growth, profits, and rate of repeat business, it must be doing something right, contradicting much of the scientific management theories that management is a specialist task which can be separated from routine dealings with customers and employees.

necessary—to put the organization back on its original targets. Organizations also learn from the past in order to understand the future better. For making longer-term planning decisions, historical information is supplemented by a variety of continuous and *ad hoc* studies, all designed to allow better-informed decisions to be made.

Marketing information cannot in itself produce decisions: it merely provides data which must be interpreted by marketing managers. As an inter-functional integrator, marketing information draws data from all functional areas of an organization, which in turn use data to focus on meeting customers' needs more effectively.

You will recall from Chapter 5 that, to be useful to management, information should be collected from a variety of sources in a systematic manner and turned into knowledge that can be shared throughout the organization and acted upon. An important task of marketing management is to plan the collection, analysis, and dissemination of information in a way that balances the costs of collecting the information against the costs of a poor decision based on inadequate information. A number of factors will determine the efficiency and effectiveness of these activities.

- **The accuracy with which the information requirements have been defined:** It can be very difficult to identify what information should be of relevance in a company's information gathering activities and to separate relevance from irrelevance. This is a particular problem for large multi-output firms expanding into new markets/products. The mission statement of an organization may give some indication of the boundaries for its information search.

- **The extensiveness of the search for information:** A balance has to be struck between the need for information and the cost of collecting it. The most critical elements of the marketing environment must be identified and the cost of collecting relevant information weighed against the cost that would result from a poorly informed management decision.

- **The appropriateness of the sources of information:** Information for decision-making can usually be obtained from numerous sources; for example, customers' attitudes towards a product can be measured using a variety of quantitative and qualitative techniques. Companies often rely on the former when more qualitative techniques are really called for. Successful companies use a variety of sources of information.

- **The speed of communication:** A marketing manager must facilitate rapid communication of information to the people capable of acting on it. Deciding what information to withhold from an individual and the concise reporting of relevant information can be as important as deciding what information to include if information overload is to be avoided.

Of course, information itself will not produce decisions, and it was noted earlier that a preoccupation with data collection and analysis can lead to a 'paralysis by analysis'. A crucial skill of management is to interpret information, and a variety of quantitative and qualitative techniques are used to support management decisions. We have seen in previous chapters how rules-based systems have been used to help decisions in relation to such issues as retail location and the allocation of advertisements between different media. Rules-based techniques often need to be supplemented with the intuition and experience of the marketing manager. Rules-based systems for decision support may be fine in stable and predictable environments, where historically collected data may be a good guide to the future. They can be of much less value where the environment is changing and the old 'rules' are no longer appropriate. Many successful entrepreneurs have spotted such changes and, using a combination of intuition, experience, and analysis, have exploited new opportunities.

Using information for control

So far, we have looked at information primarily as a means of improving planning for the future. But it must not be forgotten that marketing managers have a control function as well as a planning function. Indeed, many people have criticized the marketing profession for being good on planning, sometimes lacking in implementation skills, but much worse at monitoring and evaluating their efforts. Control is an important and often overlooked function of marketing, and the key to effective control is to give the right information to the right people at the right time. Providing too much information can be costly in terms of the effort required to assemble and disseminate it and can also reduce effective control where the valuable information is hidden among information of secondary importance. A control system will show variances between budgeted performance and actual performance, and will highlight those differences that are beyond a specified zone of tolerance. An analysis of variance from target should also indicate whether the variance is within or beyond the control of the person responsible for meeting the target. If it is beyond her control, the issue should become one of revising the target so that it becomes once more achievable. If the variance is the result of factors that are subject to an individual's control, a number of measures can be taken to try to revise behaviour.

The following are some of the things about which most organizations will need information if they are to monitor adequately the implementation of their marketing plan:

- Financial targets—sales turnover/contribution/profit margin, disaggregated by product/business unit.
- Market analysis, e.g. market share.
- Effectiveness of communication—productivity of sales personnel, effectiveness of advertising, effectiveness of sales promotion.
- Pricing—level of discounts given, price position.
- Personnel—level of skills achieved by employees, survey of customer comments on staff performance.
- Quality levels achieved—e.g. reliability, complaint level.

Where performance is below target, the reasons may not be immediately obvious. A comprehensive marketing information system can allow an organization to analyse variance. A uniform fall in sales performance across the organization, combined with intelligence gained about the state of the market, would suggest that remedial action aimed at improving the performance of individual sales personnel may not be as effective as a reassessment of targets or strategies in the light of the changed sales environment.

Successful control mechanisms require three underlying components to be in place:

1. The setting of targets or standards of expected performance.
2. The measurement and evaluation of actual performance.
3. The means to take corrective action where necessary.

There is a great deal of evidence of marketers' unwillingness or inability to measure marketing performance (O'Sullivan and Abela, 2007; Seggie, Cavusgil, and Phelan, 2007). Some specific reasons were identified by Ambler (2000):

- The board is not marketing or customer oriented, and has no senior marketing representation on it. Little board agenda time is made available to discuss marketing issues.

- Determination and effort may be considered more important than objectivity. To use an analogy, the First World War would never have been won if the soldiers had known the score—it was won by sheer determination.

- Some company boards believe that accountants should be solely responsible for accounting for all that matters. Internal measures may be interpreted as navel gazing, and are no substitute for measuring sales and market share.

- Marketers may argue against having their effectiveness measured too closely by pointing out that marketing is the business of the whole company, and so they cannot be held specifically accountable.

- Marketers are often too busy fighting the next battle and feel that this should take priority over worrying about the last one.

- Marketing effectiveness may be perceived as something essentially unmeasurable, which should be assessed by more subjective 'feel good' or 'good news' aspects.

- The environment changes too fast, so results need to be judged by the new realities, not those in place or forecast when the plan was drawn up.

- Creating new measurement systems takes too long—the current marketing team will have moved on by the time the report comes out.

It is important to note that measuring overall marketing performance is not the same as measuring marketing expenditure effectiveness (e.g. measuring the recall rate of specific advertisements, or the sales volumes of individual sales personnel). More importantly, the effectiveness of the marketing expenditure budget cannot be assessed without measuring the change in the asset of brand equity. Brand equity is fundamental to assessment of this broader measure of marketing effectiveness, and the results of marketers' actions should live on after the current financial period. You will recall from Chapter 7 that this corresponds to the premium that buyers are prepared to pay for a specified brand rather than a generic product. There is plenty of evidence of organizations whose marketing is ineffective and who have seen their brand equity diminish. Banks who were once trusted institutions have caused anger among many of their customers through perceptions of overcharging, incorrect debits, and poor communication. One result has been that many customers have shifted their bank accounts and credit cards to supermarkets and other competitors, which have achieved high levels of brand equity. Many of these misgivings about banks can be attributed to operational functions, but this only serves to emphasize the point that marketing should be a company-wide integrator. Customers may not care who in the bank is the source of their grievance, but the result is the same: the value they place on a bank's brand is lower than it was before.

Improving organizational effectiveness for marketing

What makes some organizations more effective at marketing than others? And what practical steps can a company take to become one of the best at marketing? One long-standing and widely used framework for analysis—the McKinsey 7S framework developed by Peters and Waterman (1982)—identified seven essential elements for a

---

MARKETING in ACTION

How do patients measure up?

The UK's NHS has increasingly been driven to meet higher 'customer service' standards, in addition to the standards of clinical efficacy that have traditionally been expected from health care professionals. Starting with the publication of a 'Patients' Charter' in the mid-1990s, governments have steadily increased the targets placed on health care administrators, often linking funding to the achievement of targets. But, like many performance targets, their value in the NHS has been questioned by many.

The idea of introducing targets that relate mainly to customer handling rather than to clinical issues has been dismissed by many as mere window dressing. But even the meaning of these non-clinical statistics is open to doubt, as hospitals find ways of making their performance look good on paper, if not in practice. For example, Accident and Emergency (A and E) departments use triage nurses to assess new patients upon arrival, thereby keeping within their Patients' Charter target for the time taken to see a new patient initially. However, A and E departments may be slower in providing actual treatment. Another example, in 2003, some ambulance services were reprimanded for trying to make their response times appear better than they actually were by measuring the response time from when an ambulance set out, rather than when a call for help was received. Good managers would get to understand the system of targets and find ways of appearing to meet the important targets, even if this resulted in dysfunctional consequences elsewhere.

Even the whole value of publishing performance indicators for hospitals has been questioned by many. What does it mean if a consultant or a department has a long waiting time for appointments? Rather than being an indicator of inefficiency, could it be that a long waiting list is an indicator of a consultant who is very popular with patients? And doesn't the very fact that performance indicators are published push up users' expectations of service delivery, so that in the end they may become more dissatisfied even though actual performance has improved? Do health care professionals spend too much time recording data, when really they would create more value for patients by doing what they are good at—diagnosing cancerous cells, replacing hips, and removing appendices? But then how would these professionals be held to account?

successful business, based on a study of the most successful American companies. The elements are broken down into the hardware (strategy, structure, and systems) and the software (skills, staff, styles, and shared values). Formalized strategies, structures, and systems on their own were not considered to be sufficient to bring about success—these could be operationalized only with appropriate intangible 'software'. In other words, the quality of management, in terms of leadership and working with people to achieve stated goals, is critical.

At a strategic level, companies have used a number of methods to try to develop a pervasive marketing orientation throughout their organization:

- In-house educational programmes can aim to train non-marketing employees to empathize with customers' expectations. Some organizations have tried 'job swaps', in which backroom production people spend time at the sharp end of their business, in front of customers and learning about their needs.

- By appointing senior managers who have experience of marketing, marketing values may permeate throughout an organization in a top-down manner.

- The introduction of outside consultants is sometimes used as an external change agent. Consultants can impartially apply their previous experience of introducing a marketing culture to an organization.

- Getting top management to empathize with customers, to understand what they value in a brand, is generally not a problem for small businesses, but formal or informal processes, such as 'Management by Walking About', can help managers in larger organizations to gain the necessary understanding.

- A commonly used method of making management think in marketing terms is to introduce a formal market-oriented planning system. When proposing any initiative, managers must work through a list of market-related headings, such as an analysis of the competitive environment and an identification of market opportunities when developing their annual plans. This prevents a myopic focus on the product alone.

- It was noted above that building brand equity is a primary function of marketing management and is likely to be developed by using brand equity as a basis for rewarding managers.

The overall result of these activities should be to develop a customer-focused marketing culture within an organization. As an organization develops, it is essential that the dominant culture adapts. While a small business may quite successfully embrace a centralized power culture, continued growth may cause this culture to become a liability. There are many cases of businesses, such as the electronics company Amstrad, that have reportedly had difficulty making the cultural transition from small entrepreneur to large corporate entity. Similarly, the privatization of many public utilities called for a transformation from a bureaucratic role culture to a task-oriented culture (see Handy, 1994).

◐ Chapter summary and key linkages to other chapters

This chapter has provided a brief overview of marketing management. There are now many books about how marketing management can be improved, and this chapter has only been able to provide a summary of the main issues involved. Planning and control is central to marketing management. However, marketing plans do not develop by accident, so it is essential that an organization has a structure that facilitates the development of a strategy and its implementation. Marketing management cannot be separated from other business functions, especially finance, production management, and human resource management. Numerous approaches to improving the effectiveness of an organization's marketing implementation have been discussed, and the importance has been stressed of focusing around key processes that create customer value.

There are close links between this chapter and Chapter 7, where we looked at how companies can develop a sustainable advantage through the management of the marketing mix (Chapters 8–11). Information is crucial to management (Chapter 5) in order that it can build a better picture of its operating environment (Chapter 2). It is the task of a marketing manager to ensure sustainable competitive advantage through such means as new product development (Chapter 8) and the development of appropriate distribution channels (Chapter 10).

CASE STUDY

Viva España! Marketing Spain as a tourism destination

It used to be said that the toughest training ground for a budding marketer was to work at one of the fast-moving consumer goods companies such as Procter & Gamble—in such a fiercely competitive market, you would need to use all of your skills and expertise to keep your brand in a strong market position. But more recently, it can be argued that an even more challenging environment for a marketer to cut their teeth in is the increasingly important field of destination marketing. Look through any Sunday newspaper supplement, and it is quite likely that you will see plenty of advertisements enticing you to take a holiday in exotic-sounding places. Destination marketing is now a big and a competitive business. A visit to the annual World Travel Market in London will find hundreds of local, regional, and national destination marketers jostling with each other to persuade tour operators to include their destination in tourists' itineraries, rather than other destinations.

Although the marketing of tourism destinations as brands has received a lot of attention in recent years, the very idea of an all-embracing destination brand can be very difficult to achieve. The main problem is that the destination brand manager has very little control of the 'product' which the consumer receives. The experience of staying in one of the destination's hotels, drinking at its bars and coffee shops or visiting its shops is dependent upon the activities of organizations over whom the destination brand manager has vey little, if any, direct control. There is also a problem that a destination brand manager has to address the interests of different stakeholders who would like the brand positioned in very different ways. Very often, those promoting tourism would like the brand image to emphasize quaint and 'olde worlde' characteristics, while those seeking to promote inward investment want an image based on modernness and the latest technology. Ireland is just one of many countries that has faced this dilemma—should its brand image reflect the traditional image of a simple, rural country with slightly quirky ways, or a high-tech country with an increasingly ethnically diverse population? A further group of stakeholders are the inhabitants themselves—how do they want to be portrayed? Many attempts at creating brand identities for tourist destinations have met with ridicule from local people who do not recognize the brand representations.

Many experts in destination marketing agree that Spain has overseen the most successful implementation of a destination marketing programme. Key to this success was a tourism marketing campaign launched in 1982 on the occasion of the football World Cup held in Spain. The campaign used Joan Miro's sun design to symbolize the modernization of Spain. This logo has since become Spain's tourism logo.

Overseeing the brand is the Instituto de Turismo de España (TURESPAÑA), an administrative unit of the Spanish central government. Its main responsibilities are the planning, development, and execution of activities aimed at promoting Spain as a tourism destination in international markets, and support of the marketing of Spanish tourism services abroad in cooperation with regional and local authorities and the private sector. The organization operates with a staff of 505 working through a network of offices located in Spain and abroad. Its budget in 2007 totalled €148 million, of which 76.8 were used for direct investment in campaigns and activities for tourism promotion abroad.

Key to TURESPAÑA's strategy has been the development of a brand communication strategy which highlights the unique and differentiating elements which a visit to Spain would provide, compared with other competing destinations. The brand values of Spain have particularly focused on: the way of living and the general lifestyle existing in Spain; the cultural traditions of Spain; and the size and diversity of the country.

TURESPAÑA is particularly keen to broaden the brand appeal beyond its association with sun and sea vacations. Like many tourist destinations, Spain experiences seasonality, and over-concentration of tourism in a few key areas. A key part of its marketing strategy has therefore been to encourage visitors to come out of the peak summer season, and to explore the diversity of tourism attractions beyond the coastal resorts.

With a country as big and diverse as Spain, TURESPAÑA recognizes that it must leverage as much as possible out of its budget by working with others. It has therefore worked with regional and local authorities on a variety of regional brand destination campaigns, including the Pyrenees, Green Spain, the Silver Route, the Jacobean Way to Santiago de Compostela, and the World Heritage Sites.

Many commentators agree that Spain has developed and executed one of the most successful examples of national tourism destination branding. The advertising guru Wally Olins noted how until just a few decades ago, Spain was seen as an isolated, backward, poor country on the fringes of Europe. The reality of Spain has changed, and today it is a modern, vibrant, prosperous, and democratic country. The branding campaign has reflected the reality of Spain's new position in Europe. But it can be difficult to tell which was cause and which was effect. Much of the change in perception of Spain has occurred beyond the domain of tourism management—for example the Barcelona Olympics of 1992 and the Seville International Exhibition put the country on the map in many people's minds. The growth, privatization, and globalization of Spanish companies such as Repsol, Telefonica, and Union Fenosa have made many people aware that Spain is now an economic powerhouse. The restoration of Spain's major cities, including Barcelona, Valencia, and Bilbao soon inspired confidence among visitors that this was no longer a backward country.

But brand management for Spain still faces problems. Within Europe, changing perceptions of Spain have matched the changing reality. However, in the United States, the brand image of Spain tends to be confused with that of Latin American countries, where Spain has a historical influence. In Asia and Africa, it is claimed that Spain is largely unknown, and indistinguishable from other European countries.

The marketing of Spain as a tourism destination has succeeded where many other countries have failed. Other countries have tried to promote an image which does not reflect reality, or identified particularly indistinctive aspects of a brand. Many new countries have emerged during the past two decades in central and eastern Europe, but the brand development in many of these has made little impact because of the lack of truly distinctive positioning which has value in the minds of potential tourists. Many attempts at destination branding have failed because of the often conflicting de-mands of tourism marketers to position their brand on the basis of a country's history, while those responsible for inward investment want to drop these images as quickly as possible and portray their country as thoroughly modern. A great achievement of the Spanish tourism branding cam-paign has been to incorporate many modern icons, such as the Guggenheim museum in Bilbao, into the brand image, without having to rely exclusively on outdated images of flamenco dancing.

Source: based on Instituto de Turismo de España (TURESPAÑA) website (www.tourspain.es/TourSpain/Home?Language=en); Wally Olins, 'Trading identities, why countries and companies are taking on each other's roles', 1999.

Case study review questions

1. Contrast the objectives of public and private-sector organizations that are involved in tourism marketing.

2. Summarize the benefits of collaboration between public and private-sector organizations in the tourism sector.

3. Identify the main problems of collective marketing of a tourism destination, compared with the marketing of an individual hotel.

CHAPTER REVIEW QUESTIONS

1. What is the difference between marketing planning and corporate planning? Should they be considered synonymous?

2. Do you agree with the notion that a marketing department can actually be a barrier to the successful development of a marketing orientation? Give examples.

3. What is the value of contingency planning? Identify one sector where the production of contingency plans is likely to have significant marketing benefits, and the factors that need to be taken into account.

ACTIVITIES

1. 'Mission statements are the result of senior managers' undertaking management development courses. They may have the language, but mission statements are invariably misunderstood or ignored by the very people who they are aimed at.' Go to the corporate websites of a selection of organizations with which you are familiar, and examine the extent to which you think this is a fair statement.

2. If you are studying at a university or college, reflect on market objectives that might be specified for your institution. Try setting some specific marketing objectives for the year ahead, and for five years ahead. What problems do you encounter in trying to specify meaningful objectives? Describe how you would monitor achievement of these objectives, and what you might do if performance was below target.

3. Go to the 'corporate information' pages of websites for: a large, established public limited company; a small, rapidly expanding, ethically driven business; a cooperative society; and a charitable organization. Critically examine their stated objectives and identify how these are reflected in their business practices.

REFERENCES

Ambler, T. (2000), 'Marketing Metrics'. *Business Strategy Review*, 11(2).

Barclays (2004), Start-ups and Closures. Barclays Bank SME Market Research Team.

Department for Business, Enterprise and Regulatory Reform (2006), 'Small and Medium-sized Enterprise (SME) Statistics for the UK 2006'. London: DBERR.

Denton, D. K. (1990), 'Customer Focused Management'. *HR Magazine*, 62–7 (August).

Drucker, P. (1973), *Management: tasks, responsibilities and practices*. New York: Harper & Row.

Gummesson, E. (2008), *Total Relationship Marketing: marketing management, relationship strategy and CRM approaches for the network economy*. Oxford: Butterworth-Heinemann.

Handy, C. (1994), *Understanding Organizations*, 4th edn. Harmondsworth: Penguin.

Levitt, T. (1960), 'Marketing Myopia'. *Harvard Business Review*, 38(4): 45–56.

McDonald, M. (2002), Marketing Plans: how to prepare them; how to use them, 5th edn. Oxford: Butterworth-Heinemann.

Northouse, P. G. (2006), *Leadership: Theory and Practice*. London: Sage.

O'Sullivan, D. and Abela, A. V. (2007), 'Marketing Performance Measurement Ability and Firm Performance'. *Journal of Marketing*, 71(2): 79–93.

Peters, T. J. and Waterman, R. H. (1982), *In Search of Excellence: lessons from America's best run companies*. New York: Harper & Row.

Porter, M. (1980), *Competitive Strategy: Technique for analyzing industries and competitors*. New York: Free Press.

Seggie, S.H., Cavusgil, E., and Phelan, S. E. (2007), 'Measurement of Return on Marketing Investment: a conceptual framework and the future of marketing metrics'. *Industrial Marketing Management*, 36(6): 834–41.

⬚ SUGGESTED FURTHER READING

There are many texts on the subject of marketing management which focus on how an organization can implement measures to respond to a changing external environment. The following are useful:

Baker, M. J. (2007), *Marketing Strategy and Management*, 4th edn. Basingstoke: Palgrave Macmillan.

Doyle, P. and Stern, P. (2006), *Marketing Management and Strategy*, 4th edn. London: FT Prentice Hall.

Kotler, P. and Keller, K. L. (2008), *Marketing Management: analysis, planning, implementation and control*, 13th edn. Englewood Cliffs, NJ: Prentice-Hall.

Sargeant, A. (2008), Marketing Management for Nonprofit Organizations. Oxford: Oxford University Press.

⬚ USEFUL WEB LINKS

Visit the Online Resource Centre for resources that are relevant to this chapter, including web links, multiple choice questions, and additional case studies:

www.oxfordtextbooks.co.uk/orc/palmer2e/

⬚ KEY TERMS

- ■ **Contingency planning**
- ■ **Control systems**
- ■ **Corporate planning**
- ■ **Leadership**
- ■ **Marketing audit**
- ■ **Marketing plan**
- ■ **Matrix structures**
- ■ **Mission statement**
- ■ **Planning gap**
- ■ **SMEs**
- ■ **Strategic business units**

13

Global marketing

CHAPTER OBJECTIVES

Markets are becoming increasingly global, and the aim of this chapter is to understand the main challenges facing a company setting out to develop foreign markets. The chapter begins by discussing in general terms the reasons why international trade takes place. For a company that has decided to expand overseas, careful market analysis is necessary to avoid failure. A product may need to be adapted to suit the needs of a local market. Distribution is crucial, and this chapter discusses alternative approaches to gaining access to customers in foreign markets.

Introduction

Few firms can afford to think of marketing purely in terms of their domestic market. To survive and prosper, they must increasingly look to the world as their market. Foreign countries pose opportunities as well as threats. The opportunities for a firm come from its being able to sell its products in a market where it may have a competitive advantage over existing domestic producers. The problems arise where those foreign producers possess competitive advantages that challenge a firm in its own domestic market.

The global marketing environment is changing rapidly, and understanding that environment calls for a great amount of research. The impact of improving international communications and cultural convergence are just two dynamic factors at work in shaping the global marketing environment. The failure of a company to understand these dynamic forces has often resulted in lack of success in seeking to exploit foreign markets, as the following examples illustrate.

- British Airways (BA) failed in its attempts to enter the North American market through its investment in the ailing airline USAir. BA had difficulties in overcoming trade union objections to changes in working practices, among other things, which led the company eventually to pull out of its involvement with USAir.

- The mobile phone company MM02 (now O$_2$) invested over £1.5 billion in the Dutch mobile phone operator Telfort but failed to achieve higher than fifth ranking in the Dutch market. In April 2003 the company admitted defeat and sold the entire Dutch operation for just £16 million.

- Even the fast food retailer McDonald's initially failed to make profits when it entered the UK market in the 1970s and had to adjust its format rapidly in order to achieve profitability.

For firms that persevere, the benefits of developing international markets can be a quite significant contribution to a company's overall profitability. Consider the following cases.

- Although McDonald's may have had difficulties in the early stages of developing many of its foreign markets, these markets now account for the bulk of the company's sales turnover and profits. Had it confined itself to its domestic American market, saturation and increased levels of competition within that market would have severely limited its future profit growth.

- The German yogurt brand Müller was little known in the UK a decade ago, but by successfully exploiting a market niche and rapidly developing its product portfolio, it has now become the leading yoghurt brand in Britain.

- The retailer Tesco has steadily developed markets in eastern Europe and the Far East, and although profits were slow to begin with, overseas expansion has lessened the company's dependence on the increasingly saturated UK market.

Fundamentally, the task of marketing management in foreign markets is similar to the task in domestic markets. Customers' needs remain the driving force of marketing efforts and a company promotes the benefits to customers of buying its products, which are produced as efficiently as possible, distributed through the most appropriate channels, and priced according to local market conditions. The major challenge to **exporting** companies lies in sensitively adapting marketing strategies that have worked at home to the needs of foreign markets whose environments may be totally different from anything previously experienced. 'Global strength and local adaptability' (sometimes inelegantly referred to as 'glocalization') form the basis of many firms' mission statements in relation to foreign markets.

This chapter begins by exploring the reasons why firms should seek to develop foreign markets in the first place. Once a firm has decided to operate at an international rather than a local level, it must go about assessing possible markets, and the bases for such assessments are discussed. If it decides to enter a market, a firm must consider how its product offer might need to be adapted to meet local sensitivities. Most firms enter international markets with the help of partners of some kind, and this chapter concludes with a discussion of market entry strategies.

🔵 Why export?

There is clear evidence that the volume and value of international trade have been rising in recent years faster than domestic growth. Taking the UK as an example, while the value of GDP increased by 49.8% between 1998 and 2006, the value of exports increased by 59.4% (WTO, 2007). This growth can be understood from two perspectives: from the perspective of national economies, and from that of individual trading organizations.

National reasons for trade occurring

From the perspective of national economies, there are many reasons for the increasing importance of international trade.

- Goods and services are traded between economies in order to exploit comparative cost advantages. This means that an economy will export those goods and services that it is particularly well suited to producing, and will import those for which another country has an advantage. A simple example can illustrate this point. Imagine two countries, country A which has ideal conditions for the mining of minerals but a climate that is inhospitable to agriculture, and country B, which is ideally suited for agriculture, but has mineral resources that are expensive to exploit. It would make little economic sense for country A to try to develop its agricultural sector when its output would be much more expensive than for it to buy from country B. Likewise, it may be uneconomic for country B to develop its mining industry. In both cases, it would almost certainly be better for each country to concentrate on what it is good at producing, and to export the surplus in exchange for goods and services that other countries can produce more efficiently.

- Although the theory of comparative cost advantage sounds fine in principle, many countries try to protect their own industries, however inefficient they are, against foreign competition with tariff barriers. The removal of many restrictions on international trade (such as the creation of the Single European Market) has allowed countries to exploit their comparative cost advantages. Nevertheless, many distortions to international trade remain, especially affecting agricultural products and services.

- Rising disposable incomes have resulted in greater consumption of many types of goods and services that can only be provided by foreign suppliers—for example, overseas tourism and the consumption of exotic fruit and vegetables. (On the other hand, many developing economies that previously imported specialist goods and services can now produce these items domestically.)

- Homogenization of international market segments has resulted from cultural convergence, which itself has been encouraged by improved communications and increasing levels of overseas travel. Combined with the decline in trade barriers, apparent convergence of cultural attitudes towards many products has allowed many companies to regard parts of their foreign markets as though they are part of their domestic market.

Firms' reasons for developing foreign trade

For an individual company, the development of foreign markets can be attractive for a number of reasons. These can be analysed in terms of 'pull' factors, based on the attractiveness of a potential foreign market, and 'push' factors, which make an organization's domestic market appear less attractive.

- Foreign markets represent new market segments which a firm may be able to serve with its existing range of products. In this way, a company can stick to making products that it is good at.

- By expanding overseas, a company that has developed a strong brand can stretch the coverage of that brand. By developing in a foreign market, the company will start with the advantage that some visitors from its domestic market will already understand what the brand stands for. Similarly, for residents of the new market, many may have already become familiar with the brand during visits to the manufacturer's home market. In short, there are economies of scale in promoting a brand in multiple markets simultaneously.

- Saturation of its domestic market can force a company to seek foreign markets. Saturation can come about where a product reaches the maturity stage of its lifestyle in the domestic market, while being at a much earlier stage of the cycle in less developed foreign markets. As an example of this, the market for fast-food restaurants is approaching saturation in a number of western markets—especially the USA—but fast food represents relatively new opportunities in many eastern European countries that are in earlier stages of economic development.

- Spreading risk is an important motivation for foreign expansion, and can allow a company to reduce its dependence on one geographical market.

- The nature of a product may require an organization to become active in a foreign market. In the case of scheduled international air services, an airline flying an overseas route will inevitably become involved in marketing at the foreign end of its routes.

- Some companies supply goods and services to business buyers who themselves operate internationally. Such large customers may demand that one single supplier meets their needs in all of the international markets in which they operate. This means that a supplying company has to become involved in international trade. As an example, many multinational businesses seek to engage an advertising agency that can organize a global campaign to launch in all of their international markets.

- There are also many cases where private consumers demand that goods and services be internationally available. An example is the car hire business, where customers often need to be able to book a hire car in one country for collection and use in another. To succeed in attracting these customers, car hire companies need to operate internationally.

- Some products are highly specialized, and the domestic market is too small to allow economies of scale to be exploited. Foreign markets must be exploited in order to achieve a critical mass which allows a competitive market positioning. Aircraft engine maintenance and oil exploration services fall into this category.

- A company may have developed a product that is not suited to its domestic market, so that exporting is the only option for exploiting the product. For example, domestic legislation may make the market for drugs, alcohol, or tobacco-related products less attractive than foreign markets where more liberal legislation exists.

A note on 'exporting' of services

Export of manufactured goods can be represented by stocks of goods moving in one direction, and payment (in cash or in goods) moving in the other. However, the intangible nature of most services gives a different meaning to the export of services. Any analysis of international trade in services is complicated by the diverse nature of producer–supplier interaction, stemming from the inseparability of service production/consumption processes.

International trade statistics for services hide the fact that trade can take a number of forms. Sometimes credits (or 'exports') are earned by customers from overseas travelling to an organization's domestic market in order to consume a service (e.g. a foreign patient visiting a doctor in the UK). On other occasions credits are earned by domestic producers taking their production processes to customers in foreign markets (e.g. a builder travelling to do a job in a foreign country). Sometimes, production and consumption of services can be separated, as in the case of electronic information services, avoiding the need for buyer and seller to meet for international trade to occur.

Analysing foreign marketing opportunities

Foreign markets can present very different opportunities and threats compared with those a company has been used to in its domestic market. Before a detailed market analysis is undertaken, a company should consider in general terms whether the envisaged environment of a market is likely to be attractive. By considering in general terms such matters as political stability or cultural attitudes, the company may screen out

MARKETING in ACTION

Saturated burgers for less saturated markets

A saturated domestic market is often the spur for companies to seek new foreign markets. But is there a moral case against companies seeking to promote a western style of consumption in countries with well-established and sustainable lifestyles?

Cigarette companies have attracted criticism by trying to make up for falling cigarette sales in the west by developing the emerging markets of Asia. Fast-food companies have stepped up their efforts to develop new foreign markets as western markets for fast food have become saturated. Is it responsible to promote burgers that are high in saturated fats to people whose diets are inherently healthier? Is it right that fast-food companies should develop low-fat burgers for the American market, partly out of fear of litigation, while selling higher-fat burgers to less-developed countries, where legislation and consumers' awareness of health issues are more lax? Defenders of fast-food companies point to the fact that they are providing hygienic food prepared in conditions that may be far superior to the norm in many developing countries. They have offered jobs to individuals which can be the envy of their peer groups. Should the solution be greater education of consumers in healthy eating, rather than more regulation? Is greater education a realistic prospect in a culture where fast food has become a cultural icon?

potential markets for which it considers further analysis cannot be justified by the likelihood of success.

The PEST framework is useful for analysing foreign marketing opportunities. This is a starting point for analysis, but it should be recognized that international expansion can take place for a variety of idiosyncratic reasons. (For example, the owner of a business may have enjoyed holidays in a country and chosen that country to set up a foreign venture.)

Political factors

Government and quasi-government organizations influence the legislative and economic frameworks within which organizations trade.

At a national level, individual governments can influence marketing opportunities and threats in a number of ways.

- **Unstable political systems** are often very unattractive to companies considering foreign expansion. For example, the instability of some African governments has posed unacceptable risks for firms considering committing resources to a market.

- **Regulations governing product standards** may require an exporter to reconfigure its products expensively for a foreign market.

- **Legislation** may be used by governments to try to protect domestic producers against foreign competition.

- Sometimes governments impose **import controls** or simply make the task of getting clearance for imports very difficult.

- Where a company is planning to set up a production facility overseas, legislation on **health and safety standards** as well as minimum wages and welfare provision may add to a firm's costs.

- **Restrictions on currency movements** may make it difficult to repatriate profits earned from a foreign operation.

- **Legislation protecting trademarks** varies between companies—in some countries, such as Thailand, a trademark owner may find it very hard to protect itself legally from imitators.

- In a broader context of politics, powerful **pressure groups** in a country may put pressure on legislators to take actions which are harmful to an incoming foreign company.

Exporters also need to consider the political significance of regional trading blocs. The European Union (EU) is an example of a trading bloc that seeks to create favourable trading conditions for companies located within the bloc, regardless of the national borders within the bloc. For companies seeking to develop within one of those countries, the existence of trading blocs creates problems and opportunities. The problems occasionally arise where tariffs or other restrictions are placed on goods and services imported from outside the bloc. The biggest opportunity is that, once an exporter is inside one member country, the process of expansion to other bloc member countries can be made very much easier through the harmonization of standards and dismantling of internal borders. Within the EU, monetary union has also reduced obstacles to international trade posed by the volatility in exchange rates. Fluctuating exchange rates can make it difficult for sellers to predict the value of their future foreign sales in terms of their own domestic currency.

The development of the EU has been paralleled by the development of a number of other regional trading blocs, most notably the ASEAN group of south-east Asian countries and the NAFTA grouping of the USA, Canada, and Mexico.

There have been many attempts to liberalize world trade. Members of the World Trade Organization (WTO) seek greater international economic prosperity by exploiting fully the comparative cost advantages of nations by reducing the barriers that inhibit international trade. Members agree not to increase tariffs or quotas on imports, except in permitted circumstances. However, many critics of the WTO have accused it of pursuing a western capitalist agenda for trade liberalization which less developed economies have little realistic prospect of exploiting. As an example, the Indian Post Office may in theory be able to benefit from the liberalization of trade in services by being able to set up an operation in the United States; but in practice, it is much more likely that Federal Express will challenge the Indian Post Office in its domestic market.

Economic factors

All other things being equal, an exporter would prefer to target prosperous foreign markets. A generally accepted measure of the economic attractiveness of a foreign market is the level of GDP per capita. The demand for most goods and services increases as this figure increases (Figure 13.1). However, intending exporters should also consider the distribution of income within a country, which may identify valuable niche markets. As an example, Indonesia has a relatively low GDP per head, but this still allows for a small but wealthy segment of society which has the desire and ability to pay for luxury western goods.

An exporter should consider economic prosperity not only as it is today, but also as it is likely to develop in the future. While the market for some goods and services in the west may be saturated, less developed economies may be at the start of a growth phase. The level of competitive pressure within the economy must also be considered—again, not just as it is now, but how it is likely to be in the future.

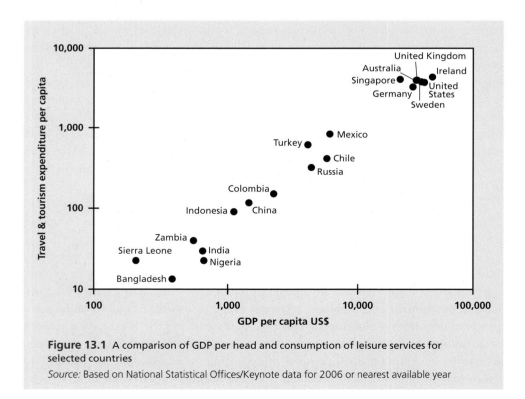

Figure 13.1 A comparison of GDP per head and consumption of leisure services for selected countries

Source: Based on National Statistical Offices/Keynote data for 2006 or nearest available year

Social factors

An understanding of a society's cultural values is crucial for an exporter. Individuals from different cultures not only buy different products, but also may respond in different ways to the same product. Examples of differing cultural attitudes and their effects on international trade include the following.

- Some goods and services may be rendered obsolete by different types of social structure. As an example, extended family structures common in some countries have the ability to produce a wide range of services within the family unit, including caring for children and elderly members.

- A product that is taken for granted in the domestic market might be seen as socially unacceptable in a foreign market. (Loans charging interest may be regarded as unacceptable in Muslim communities.)

- Buying processes vary between different cultures—for example, the role of women in shopping for certain types of product may differ in foreign markets compared with the domestic market.

It has often been claimed that a major driver of international trade is cultural convergence, implying that individuals are becoming more alike in the way that they think and behave. Improved communications and increasing levels of overseas travel have undoubtedly led to homogenization of international market segments. Combined with the decline in trade barriers, convergence of cultural attitudes allows many organizations to regard parts of their overseas markets as though they are part of their domestic market. A 25-year-old upwardly mobile professional female living in Hamburg may have more in common with a 25-year-old upwardly mobile professional living in Manchester, than with fellow Germans in general. Advocates of the concept of cultural convergence remind us that needs are universal and therefore there should be no reason why satisfaction of those needs should not also be universal. If a Big Mac satisfies a New Yorker's need for hygienic, fast and convenient food, why should it not satisfy those similar needs for someone in Cairo? Against this, many observers have noted individuals' growing need for *identity* in a world which is becoming increasingly homogenized. Support for regional breakaway governments (e.g. by the Kurdish and Basque people) may provide some evidence of this. During the build-up to the Iraq War in 2003, many consumers in Arab countries used purchases of Muslim products such as Mecca Cola to identify themselves with an anti-American cause. Many western service brands have become despised by some groups as symbols of an alien identity. Banks in many Muslim countries have reported increased interest in Sharia-based banking services that do not charge interest based on the traditional western banking model.

It is also important to consider the demographic structure of a foreign market. Within the EU countries, the total population in recent times has increased at a natural rate of about 1.0 per 1,000 population (that is, for every 1,000 deaths, there are 1,001 births).

However, this hides a range of rates of increase, with, at each extreme, Ireland having a particularly high birth rate and Germany a particularly low one. This has major implications for future age structures and consumption patterns. By 2030, people over 65 in Germany will account for almost half the country's adult population, compared with one-fifth in 2000; and unless the country's birth rate recovers from its present low of 1.3 per woman, over the same period its population of under-35s will shrink about twice as fast as the older population will grow. The net result will be that the total population, now 82 million, will decline to 70–3 million, and the number of people of working age will fall by a quarter, from 40 million today to 30 million. In Japan, the population is expected to have peaked in 2005, at around 125 million and by around 2030, the share of the over-65s in the adult population will have grown to about half. By 2050, according to the more pessimistic government forecasts, the population will have shrunk to around 95 million. Long before that, around 2030, the share of the over-65s in the adult population will have grown to about half (*The Economist,* 2001).

Much faster population growth has occurred outside the developed countries. Between 1960 and 1994, the population of Africa rose by 150% and Latin America by 100%, compared to just 17% in EU countries. More importantly, these trends seem set to continue.

Marketers are concerned with the rise in immigration to western developed countries, and the resulting ethnic diversity in these countries has presented challenges and opportunities. For an exporter, identifying significant ethnic groups within a country may be an important part of the evaluation of potential export markets (e.g. some Polish drinks exporters have specifically targeted the large number of Polish migrants living in the UK).

Technological factors

An analysis of the technological environment of potential foreign markets is important for companies that require the use of a well-developed technical infrastructure. Communications are an important element of the technological infrastructure. Poorly developed telephone and postal communications may inhibit attempts to respond rapidly to customers' requests. Ireland has attracted many high-technology companies on the strength of the country's commitment to broadband Internet access and its emphasis on training in IT. Where there is only a low level of skills among the population, the ability to produce goods and services in the local market, or to offer back-up support, may be limited.

But, should you instinctively go for a country such as Hong Kong, which has a high level of GDP and a relatively open, incorruptible system of government? At first sight, Hong Kong may appear much more attractive than Tanzania or Zambia, where it may be necessary to bribe your way into the country, only to find a very poor population. The problem with this simplistic analysis is that a country that is attractive to you will

Country	Per Capita GDP $ (2004 estimate)	Index of Freedom (1997)	Ranking of Economic Freedom (1999)	Ranking of Corruption (1998)
Tanzania	700	10	90	81
Zambia	900	9	75	52
Nigeria	1000	13	95	81
Zimbabwe	1900	10	124	43
Pakistan	2200	9	97	71
India	3100	6	120	66
Philippines	5000	5	48	55
China	5600	14	124	52
United Kingdom	29,600	3	7	11
Canada	31,500	2	14	6
Ireland	31,900	2	25	14
Switzerland	33,800	2	5	10
Hong Kong	34,200	9	1	16
Norway	40,000	2	27	8

Figure 13.2 If you were planning to expand your restaurant chain to an overseas market, which of the countries listed above would appeal to you most? The table reports data for a selection of countries linking annual GDP per capita with an index of political freedom within the country (for example, the extent of universal voting rights); a ranking of economic freedom (for example, the ease with which new entrants can enter a market); and ranking of corruption. A casual glance at this table will reveal that many of the poorest countries of the world are associated with lower levels of political freedom and a high level of corruption. Notes: The measure of political freedom comprises a composite of two separate indicators, political rights and civil liberties. The combined score is between 2 and 14, 2 being the freest and 14 being the most unfree. The organization Freedom House considers countries with scores of between 2 and 5 'free'; those scoring between 6 and 10 as 'partly free'; those scoring between 11 and 14 as 'unfree'. The ranking of Economic Freedom consist of one index in which the freest economy (Hong Kong) is ranked 1 and the least free economy (North Korea) ranks 170. Ranking of corruption is based on data provided by Transparency International (1998), with the least corrupt country being ranked 1.

Source: based on United Nations, *Human Development Report 1998*; World Bank, *World Development Report 1996*; Freedom House, *Freedom in the World 1997/8*; Bryan Johnson *et al.*, *Index of Economic Freedom 1999*; Transparency International, 'Corruption Perceptions Index 1998'; World Factbook 2005 (www.cia.gov)

also be attractive to your competitors. So, the competitive pressure for a restaurant is likely to be much greater in Hong Kong than Zambia. If you invest time and effort into Zambia, you may have the market to yourself, reasonably secure in the knowledge that a new overseas competitor would first have to go through the pain barrier that allowed

MARKETING in ACTION

A hotel for lunatics?

Hilton International, owner of many of the world's most prestigious hotels, has joined the race to build the first hotel on the moon. It has developed a project called the Lunar Hilton, which would comprise a complex with 5,000 rooms. Powered by two huge solar panels, the resort would have its own beach and sea as well as a working farm. Experts disagree on the practicalities of life on the moon, but barriers seem to be diminishing as new discoveries are made.

Space tourism received a boost in April 2001, when the determined multi-millionaire Dennis Tito paid $20 million for a round-trip ticket to the International Space Station. Such is the interest in exploiting the moon for tourism that there is now a Space Tourism Association, and a lot of national pride is at stake. Russians launched the first spaceship and now the first tourist in space. In Japan, the Kinki Nippon Tourist (KNT) Company, the country's second largest wholesale tour operator, set up a space travel club in 2002. Back in 1998 KNT helped a Japanese Pepsi franchisee launch a sweepstakes for a suborbital flight. The company received 650,000 applications for five tickets, each going for $98,000. The company is convinced that excursion-class spaceships will become a driving force for the travel industry in the twenty-first century. This is further backed up by Sir Richard Branson's Virgin Gallactica project, which hopes to take tourists into space from 2009.

Three Japanese companies have between them already spent £25 million on development work for their own moon projects. Compared with this, Hilton's expenditure to date of £100,000 looks quite modest. Is the company mad in believing that people will want to visit the moon? Or is this just the kind of long-term strategic thinking that so many businesses lack? With the world becoming smaller and increasingly saturated with goods and services, does the moon offer a unique opportunity for expansion?

you to enter the market. Also, the figures for GDP per person can be quite misleading, because what really matters is the number of people in the population who have disposable income above the level at which they start eating out in restaurants. In many less-developed countries, a low GDP may mask big differences in income distribution. A small but expanding middle class may be a very attractive proposition for a new entrant to the market.

A more detailed analysis of potential markets

A rough environmental analysis along the lines discussed above would have reduced the number of possible foreign markets. At this stage the method of analysis is very qualitative, and is often based on the 'gut feeling' of a company's senior management. Very often, the list of potential markets is reduced through idiosyncratic factors, such as personal links between senior managers and their friends and family in a country. Senior management has been known to target a market for apparently personal reasons, such as the opportunity to get away to enjoy good golf courses. Where the business potential of prospective markets is otherwise fairly indistinguishable, such personal factors may sway the final choice. However, if they are a starting point for a decision, with no underlying business assessment, a foreign venture could be doomed.

Once a company has developed a shortlist of foreign markets, it can set about the task of collecting more detailed information about each of them. The methods used to research a potential foreign market are in principle similar to those used to research the domestic market. Research would normally begin by using secondary data about the potential foreign market, which are available at home. Sources that are readily available include information for exporters published by the Department for Business, Enterprise and Regulatory Reform, reports of international agencies such as the Organization for Economic Co-operation and Development (OECD), chambers of commerce, and private sources of information such as that provided by banks. Details of some specific sources are shown in Figure 13.3.

Secondary research at home will often be followed up with further desk research of materials available locally within the short listed markets. This is most likely to be carried out by appointing a local research agency. Its brief may include a review of reports published by the target market's own government and by specialist locally based market research agencies.

Secondary data have their limitations in assessing the attractiveness of a foreign market. Problems are compounded by the greater difficulty in gaining access to data, possible language differences, and problems of definition.

Primary research would be undertaken in a foreign market when a company has become happy about the general potential of a market, but is unsure about a number of issues that would be critical for success. These might include whether intermediaries would be willing and able to handle their product, or whether traditional cultural attitudes would prevent widespread adoption of it. Prior to commissioning its own specific research (or instead of doing its own research), a company may go for the lower-cost option of undertaking research through an omnibus survey. These are surveys regularly undertaken among a panel of consumers in foreign markets (e.g. the Gallup European Omnibus) which carry out questioning on behalf of a number of sponsors.

A local agency would better understand attitudes towards privacy and the level of literacy that might affect response rates for different forms of research. Language barriers would be reduced but not eliminated, as the problem of comparability between markets remains. For example, when an American respondent claims to 'really like' a product, the meaning may be comparable to a German consumer who claims to 'quite like' the product. It would be wrong to assume on the basis of this research that the product is better liked by American than German consumers.

Government agencies
> Department of Trade and Industry market reports
> Foreign governments—e.g. USA
>> Department of Commerce
> Foreign national and local development agencies

International agencies
> European Union (Eurostat, etc.)
> Organization for Economic Co-operation and
>> Development (OECD)
> World Trade Organization
> United Nations
> World Bank
> International Monetary Fund
> World Health Organization

Research organizations
> Economist Intelligence Unit
> Dun and Bradstreet International
> Market research firms

Publications
> *Financial Times country surveys*
> *Business International*
> *International Trade Reporter*
> Banks' export reviews

Trade associations
> Chambers of trade and commerce
> Industry-specific associations

Online resources
> Eurostat
> Mintel online
> FT online, etc.

Figure 13.3 Sources of secondary information on foreign markets

Adapting the product offer to foreign markets

'Global strength and local adaptability' are the stated aims of many successful companies that operate in international markets. But how can such local adaptability be achieved? And how can a company ensure that the benefits of economies of scale that derive from global size are not undermined by the cost of adapting to each individual market? Too many companies have failed overseas because they did not fully take into

MARKETING in ACTION

Is the glass half full or half empty?

The chairman of Bata, the shoe manufacturer, is famously quoted for his analysis of a foreign market for his firm's shoes. Two employees were dispatched to a potential market in Africa and noticed that very few people were wearing shoes. 'No hope here—the people don't wear shoes' was the response of one. But the other saw it quite differently 'What an opportunity—just think what this market will be worth when these people start wearing shoes!' Facts alone will not make a market entry decision: the facts must be interpreted, and this interpretation can lead to quite diverse conclusions.

account local sensitivities to their products. For example, attitudes towards promotional programmes differ between cultures. The choice of colours in advertising or sales outlets needs to be made with care because of symbolic associations. (For example, the colour associated with mourning/bereavement varies across cultures.) Also, what is considered to be an acceptable method of procuring a sale varies between cultures. In Middle Eastern markets, for example, a bribe to a public official may be considered essential, whereas in most western countries this is unacceptable.

A crucial task of overseas marketing management is the design of a marketing programme that is sensitive to local needs. The following sections examine the extent to which adaptation of the marketing mix to local needs is either desirable or possible. In particular, should a company seek to develop one globally uniform product offer, or make it different in each of the foreign markets which it serves? Sometimes a company may simply change the promotion of its product, while keeping the product itself the same in all markets. Five types of strategy can be identified, based on the extent to which product and promotion decisions vary from the global norm.

1. **Maintain a uniform product and promotion worldwide:** This approach develops a **global marketing** strategy as though the world were a single market. The benefits of this approach are numerous. Customers travelling from one market to another can immediately recognize a brand and the values it stands for. If, instead, the product were different in a foreign market, a traveller purchasing it overseas might come away confused about the qualities of the brand. If Coca Cola tasted too different in foreign countries, could this detract from individuals' perceived value of the brand when they got back home?

   Product standardization can also yield benefits of economies of scale. As well as lowering the unit costs of production, economies can extend to the collection of market research, the design of buildings and uniforms, etc. The use of a common brand name in foreign markets also benefits from economies of scale. Travellers to

MARKETING in ACTION

Miniaturized hotels for miniaturized people?

How does a large American hotel chain adapt its service offer to the Japanese market? Hotels operated by Hilton International in the USA have bedrooms that, to many visitors from overseas, are surprisingly large. But what would an American think of a typical Japanese hotel? Land prices in America are generally fairly low outside the main metropolitan areas, hence the relatively spacious facilities offered. But in Japan space is at a premium, and this has given rise to all sorts of miniaturized hotel formats, aimed at keeping prices at an affordable level. How could Hilton International remain affordable yet retain its generic brand values? Following extensive research, the company developed a hotel format that was appropriate to the Japanese market. To avoid the problem of visitors from America being shocked by the relatively cramped spaces, Hilton International developed a separate brand format, 'Wa No Kutsurogi' ('Providing Comfort and Service the Japanese Way').

foreign markets will already be familiar with the brand's values as a result of promotion in the domestic market. However, care must be taken in selecting a brand name that will have no unfortunate connotations in foreign markets. There are many legendary cases of brand names that have not worked in foreign markets; for example, many English-speaking people are left wondering about the likely taste of 'Bum' crisps or 'Pschitt' soft drinks. There can also be problems where legislation prevents an international slogan being used. In Quebec, for example, companies have been fined for using standard anglicized advertising material without changing it to French as required by the province's legislation.

2. **Retain a uniform product formulation, but adapt promotion:** This strategy produces an essentially uniform global product, but adapts the promotional programme to local markets. The manner in which brand values are communicated in advertisements is a reflection of the cultural values of a society. For this reason, a snack food manufacturer may use a straightforward, brash, hard-sell approach in its American market, a humorous approach in its British market, and a seductive approach in its French market, even though the product offer is essentially the same in each market. Some images and symbols used to promote a product in the domestic market might fail in a foreign market. Animals, which are often used to promote a range of home-based goods and services, present a caring and comfortable image in Britain, but in markets such as Japan animals are seen as unclean, disgusting objects.

3. **Adapt the product offer only:** This may be done in order to meet specific local needs or legislation, while retaining the benefits of a global image. For example, flavourings and colourings used in confectionery may be illegal in some foreign markets, requiring reformulation of the product. Exporters must continue to track changes in consumers' tastes as they become more used to a product. For example,

Figure 13.4 With a name like 'Pschitt', would you buy this product? As the markets for many products become increasingly global, companies are going to greater lengths to ensure that the name chosen for a new product will work in all of the markets in which the company is likely to operate. Pschitt is now owned by Perrier and has, not surprisingly, decided against exporting this product to its English-speaking markets. Had it been developing the product today, it would almost certainly have chosen a different brand name. Creative agencies that develop brand identities for clients are themselves having to work at a global level in order to satisfy the needs of their global clients.

in 2002 the Dutch brewer Heineken changed its UK product offer to a more alcoholic brew after market research suggested the standard lager market was losing its appeal. The company phased out its Cold Filtered and Export products and replaced them with Heineken premium lager (Batt, 2002).

4. **Adapt both product and promotion:** In practice, most companies undertake a combination of product and promotion modification in order to meet local market needs, while still trying to stay true to their global brand values and worldwide economies of scale.

5. **Develop new products:** Sometimes markets emerge for which a company has no product offering that can be easily adapted. In order to gain access to a foreign market, it may be necessary to develop new products. Western financial services companies entering Muslim countries have developed new forms of loans which do not charge interest but pay back a higher amount in capital. The firms may have had no similar product in their domestic market, but development of a new product has been necessary to gain acceptance from significant segments in Muslim markets. This option compounds the risk of a new market with the risk of a new product.

MARKETING in ACTION

What's your Ireland?

How do you promote the image of a tourist destination in foreign markets? The destination itself cannot be adapted to suit the needs of individual markets. Physically, the Tower of London will always be the same for tourists, whether they are from Manchester, Madras, or Melbourne. But the promotional message can be fine-tuned to stress the aspects on which different markets place high value.

Take the case of the Brand Ireland campaign, a joint effort by the Northern Ireland Tourist Board and Bord Failte to increase the number of visitors to Ireland, north and south. Several hours of footage was filmed featuring tourist attractions around Ireland. This was reduced to a series of 15 and 30-second television commercials, but a different cut was made for each of the major markets targeted by the campaign. The German cut stressed the wild, rugged nature of the country, the Italian cut stressed the romance of the island, the American cut stressed Ireland's history, and the English cut stressed that Ireland is so close, but so different. The strap line 'Live a different life' worked well in most markets, but had to be changed in the USA after focus groups identified unfortunate associations with cross-dressing.

Pricing in foreign markets

The issue of whether to globalize or adapt to local conditions arises again in respect of pricing decisions. On the one hand, it might be appealing to customers if a company charged a standard price for a product regardless of where in the world it was purchased. Customers would then always have an idea of how much the product would cost, and this would help to develop a long-term relationship between the company and its customers. However, the reality is that a variety of factors cause global companies to charge different prices in the different markets in which they operate:

• A brand that is highly valued at home may be unheard of in a foreign market, and therefore unable to command its accustomed price premium.

• Competitive pressure varies between markets, reflecting the stage of market development that a product has reached and the impact of regulations against anti-competitive practices.

• Where it is difficult to make a product at home and export it to the foreign market, a company will face cost levels that may be significantly different from those applying to the domestic market. For services that use people-intensive production methods, which cannot be 'exported' from a company's domestic base, variations in wage levels between countries will have a significant effect on total costs, and hence will influence pricing. Personnel costs may also be affected by differences in the welfare provisions that employers are required to pay for. Other significant cost elements that often vary between markets include the level of property prices or rental costs.

- Taxes vary between different markets—for example, the rate of value added tax (or its equivalent sales tax) can be as high as 38% in Italy compared with 17.5% in the UK. There are also differences between markets in the manner in which sales taxes are expressed. In many markets taxes are fully incorporated into price schedules, although in others (such as in the USA) it is more usual to price a service exclusive of taxes, with the amount of tax added in small print on the line below.

- Local customs influence customers' expectations of the way in which a product is priced. While customers in the domestic market might expect to pay for bundles of products, in a foreign market consumers might expect to pay a separate price for each component of the bundle, or vice versa. It has been noted, for example, that UK mobile phone buyers tend to purchase their handset as part of an airtime contract, but in other markets, the practice is to buy the handset and airtime contract separately.

- Formal price lists for a product may be expected in some markets, but in others individual bartering may be the norm. Having a published price list which it sticks to may put a firm at a competitive disadvantage.

- Government regulations can limit price freedom in foreign markets. In addition to controls over prices charged by public utilities, many governments require that 'fair' prices be charged for a wide range of goods and services—e.g. tourism-related services—and that the prices charged be clearly publicized. Retailers that use 'Buy one, get one free' offers in the UK have found this type of price promotion illegal in Germany.

The development of the single European market has tended to reduce price differences between member states, although significant differences remain for many products (refer back to Chapter 9). If wide differences in the pre-tax price of goods emerge between countries, it is open to entrepreneurs to buy goods in the lower priced market and sell them in the higher priced market. The 'grey' market in perfume imported from the Far East to western Europe is evidence of this. Because of their inseparability, it is much more difficult, and often impossible, to transfer a service from a low-priced market to a high-priced one.

Distributing goods and services in foreign markets

Getting distribution strategy right is crucial to success in foreign markets (as indeed it is in the domestic market). The cost of making goods and services readily available to consumers can be quite daunting, and for this reason many exporters choose to go into partnership with companies that are already established in a market. The whole issue of market entry strategy is considered in more detail later in this chapter. Many exporters have failed because they had not fully thought through the costs and barriers of getting their products to the final consumer.

Although the principles of distribution planning in foreign markets are similar to those for the domestic market, the following potential differences should be noted and accommodated:

- Consumer behaviour may differ significantly in foreign markets. What is a widely accepted outlet in one country may be regarded with suspicion in another. For example, buying cosmetics in a supermarket is now accepted as normal in the UK, but may meet resistance in some other countries.

- Consumers vary in the extent to which they are prepared to travel to obtain a product. In less-developed economies where transport and refrigeration equipment are less readily available, consumers may seek very local access to intermediaries to replenish their stocks of perishable products. In car-based economies such as the USA, intermediaries may be selected by consumers on the basis of their range of choice and easy access by car.

- Differences in the social, economic, and technical environments of a market can result in the existence of different patterns of intermediaries. As an example, the interrelatedness of wholesalers and retailers in Japan can make it much more difficult for a foreign retailer to get into that market than into some other foreign markets. In some markets there may be no direct equivalent of a type of intermediary found in the domestic market. (For example, estate agents on the UK model are often not available in many foreign markets.)

- The law of a country can restrict the use of intermediaries which would otherwise be commonplace in the domestic market. Governments of many countries restrict the sale of alcohol, financial services, and gambling services—among others—to a much narrower set of possible intermediaries than may be the case in the domestic market.

People decisions

Should a company employ local or expatriate staff? The latter may be preferable where a company is providing a highly specialized product and may be useful in adding to the global uniformity of the product offer. In some service industries, the presence of front-line expatriate serving staff can add to the appeal of a service; for example, a chain of traditional Irish pubs established in mainland Europe may add to their appeal by employing authentic Irish staff.

For relatively straightforward goods and services, however, a large proportion of staff is likely to be recruited locally, leaving just senior management posts to be filled by expatriates. Sometimes an extensive staff development programme may be required to ensure that locally recruited staff perform in a manner that is consistent with the company's global image. This can often be quite a difficult task. A company moving into a previously centrally planned economy may have difficulty developing values of customer focus among staff members who have been accustomed to taking instructions from above.

Market entry strategies

Although new foreign markets provide a company with opportunities, they can also present high levels of risk. A company's market entry strategy should aim to balance the opportunities with the risks involved.

The main issues here are:

- How rapidly should a company commit itself to a foreign market?
- Who, if anybody, should the company work with in developing a foreign market?

Timescale for foreign market development

Should a company move as quickly as possible to develop a foreign market when the opportunity arises? This approach may have some merit, as being first can give long-term advantages. The market leader's product could become the benchmark by which consumers subsequently judge all products within its class. An early developer could also tie up key distribution outlets, making it difficult for a subsequent competitor to move into the market.

While there may be long-term benefits from being the first company to develop a new category of product in a foreign market, there are also risks. If development is hurried and a product is launched before quality can be guaranteed to live up to an organization's international standards, the company's long-term image can be damaged, both in the new foreign market and in its wider world market. In the turbulent marketing environment of eastern Europe in the late 1980s, two of the world's principal fast-food retailers—McDonald's and Burger King—pursued quite different strategies. McDonald's waited until political, economic, social, and technological conditions allowed it to launch a restaurant that could meet its global standards. Burger King, however, in its desire to be first in the market, got in quickly but was able to offer only a sub-standard service, giving it an image from which it has subsequently struggled to recover.

Risk can be minimized by gradually committing more resources to a market, based on experience to date. Temporary facilities can be established that have low start-up and close-down costs and where the principal physical and human assets can be transferred to another location. Rather than setting up its own distribution system, a company can buy in distribution services from another company, with relatively low close-down costs should the venture fail.

A good example of risk reduction through the use of temporary facilities was found in the pattern of retail development throughout eastern Germany following reunification. Foreign companies were initially reluctant to commit themselves to building stores in specific locations in a part of the country that was still economically unstable and where patterns of land use were rapidly changing. The solution adopted by many companies was to set up branches in temporary marquees or mobile vehicles. These could move in response to the changing pattern of demand. While the location of retail outlets remained risky, this did not prevent retailers from establishing their networks of distribution warehouses, which could respond more flexibly to the changing pattern of retail location.

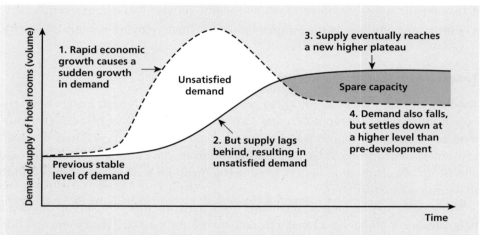

Figure 13.5 In emerging markets, timing can be crucial for success. In the past two decades, major opportunities for hotel operators have emerged as the economies of China, India, eastern Europe, and Latin America have grown rapidly. When these economies emerged as centres for economic growth, one of their first requirements had been for hotels to accommodate the army of architects, engineers, and business people who headed out to these countries to create new infrastructure and trading links. The result was that in the early stages of rapid growth, hotels were very scarce and operators could charge premium prices. As an example, China and eastern Europe are associated with low costs of labour and many manufacturers and service businesses have moved operations there to exploit these low costs. However, their capital cities often had some of the highest hotel prices in the world, reflecting their scarcity at a time of rapid economic growth. This has been a signal for more hotel chains to move into the market, but eventually the steam would go out of the economic boom, probably just at the time when the additional hotel capacity is becoming available. The result is greater pressure on prices, and a less attractive overseas investment opportunity for newly arrived companies, compared with that achieved by earlier arrivals. Of course, it is easy with hindsight to spot the right time to invest, but much more difficult to predict which economies are going to grow, when, and by how much.

Who should be involved in foreign market development?

An assessment of risk is required in deciding whether an organization should enter a foreign market on its own, or in association with another organization. Going in alone increases the strategic and operational control that the organization has over its foreign operations. However, it exposes it to the greatest risk where the foreign market is relatively poorly understood. A range of market entry possibilities are considered below.

Exporting directly to customers overseas

This involves producing goods at a firm's domestic production facilities and shipping them to the foreign market. Choosing to sell directly to customers can be an extremely expensive task where the product in question is low in value and high in volume. Direct exporting is therefore limited to companies who sell specialized, high-value products. In the case of intangible services, it is possible to sell directly to consumers in foreign markets, but a company may find its task made much easier by using some form of information intermediary (see below).

Exporting through an export/import agent

Because of the difficulty in obtaining access to foreign customers, many first-time exporters choose to use an **import or export agent**. In return for a fee or commission, the agent uses its contacts to exploit distribution opportunities in a foreign market. Agency agreements vary in their timescale and responsibilities. At one extreme, an agent can be casually recruited to sell a batch of items on a no-sale, no-fee basis. At the other extreme, an agent may agree to develop a market and be given sole rights to sell the company's product in that market for a number of years.

Direct investment in a foreign subsidiary

Very often it is difficult for an exporter to serve a market from its home base. The cost of transporting goods to foreign markets may put it at a competitive disadvantage. It may even face tariff barriers levied on imported goods. The use of an import or export agent can leave an exporter with very little control over its foreign market.

Direct investment in a foreign subsidiary gives a company maximum control over its foreign operations, but can expose it to a high level of risk where it has only a poor understanding of the foreign market. A company can either set up its own foreign subsidiary from scratch (as many UK hotel companies have done to develop hotels in foreign markets), or it can acquire control of a company that is already trading. When Heineken sought to gain a larger market share in the Islamic market, it acquired the Egyptian brewer Ahram's, whose popular Fayrouz line of non-alcoholic flavoured beers had acquired respectability by being certified by Al Azhar, a prestigious Sunni Islam body, as *halal*, and permitted for consumption by Muslims (Allam, 2003).

Where the nature of the product offer differs very little between national markets, or where it appeals to an international market (e.g. hotels), the risks from creating a new subsidiary are reduced. Where there are barriers to entry and the product is aimed at a distinctly different local market with its own preferences, the acquisition of an established subsidiary may be preferred. Even the latter course of action is not risk-free, as was illustrated by the problems encountered by the UK bus operator Stagecoach, which acquired the American group Coach USA in 1999, but was forced to dispose of most of its operations a few years later after losing over 70% of its initial investment of $1.88 billion.

Direct investment in a foreign subsidiary may also be made difficult by legislation restricting ownership of certain services by foreigners. Many developing countries have complex requirements which allow a foreign investor to acquire only a minority stake in a company.

Licensing/franchising

Rather than setting up its own operations in a foreign market, a company can license a local company to provide a product. A licence allows the local licensee to manufacture and sell the product as if it were made by the licensor itself. The licensee pays an agreed amount to the licensor for the right to sell its products (usually on the basis of turnover or volume of sales) and agrees to maintain specified quality standards. Licensing is widely used for low-value, high-volume products such as soft drinks. The Coca Cola company licenses local bottlers around the world to produce and sell its drinks.

In the case of services, it is necessary for a licensor to retain greater control over the processes of production, and not just the tangible outcome. Licensing or franchising in a foreign market can take a number of forms. Sometimes the franchisor enters into a direct franchising relationship with each individual franchisee. The difficulty in this approach lies in monitoring and controlling a possibly large number of franchisees in a country far from home. To overcome some of these problems, the franchisor normally establishes its own subsidiary in the foreign territory which negotiates and monitors franchisees locally. Alternatively, it could grant a master franchise for an area to a franchisee where the latter effectively would become the franchisor in the foreign country.

Franchising can allow an organization to expand rapidly overseas with relatively low capital requirements. However, it is subject to the same issues of control that affect domestic franchise agreements. (These were discussed in Chapter 10.)

Joint ventures

International **joint ventures** involve two or more firms sharing their competencies to develop a market. Usually one of the partners will be a local company in the target market with detailed knowledge of that market, while another will be a company 'back home' with technical and/or financial competencies but little knowledge of the market. Joint ventures can balance a company's desire for control with risk minimization, and can be attractive in many situations.

- A joint venture with an organization already based in the proposed foreign market makes the task of collecting information about the market, and responding sensitively to it, relatively easy.

- A joint venture can spread risk where the initial capital requirement threshold is high.

- Where foreign governments restrict the rights of foreign companies to set up business on their account, a partnership with a local company—possibly involving a minority shareholding—may be the only means of entering the market.

- There may be significant barriers to entry which a company already based in the foreign market could help to overcome. A common barrier to entry is access to a comprehensive network of intermediaries.

- There may be a reluctance on the part of consumers to deal with what appears to be a foreign company. A joint venture can allow the operation to be fronted by a domestic producer with which customers can be familiar, while allowing the foreign partner to provide capital and management expertise.

- Taxation of company profits may favour a joint venture rather than outright purchase of a foreign subsidiary.

Joint ventures are an important feature of many business sectors where the benefits listed above can be achieved. They have assumed particular importance in the car manufacturing, airline, and financial services sectors. Some recent examples of joint ventures are shown in Figure 13.6.

Venture partners	% holding	Purpose of joint venture
GfK, Germany	40	Creation of ORG-GfK Marketing Services, based in Bangalore, India, to monitor monthly retail sales in retail outlets for consumer technology markets
ORG-Marg, India	60	
Nanjing Automobile Corporation, China	50	Cooperation in commercial-vehicle making and passenger car parts production for Chinese market. This venture ended in 2007, apparently because Fiat was unhappy with the low level of commitment given by Nanjing Automobile Corp. and low sales level and market share
Fiat, Italy	50	
Skype, Luxembourg	49	Agreement in 2005 to bring together Skype's Internet communications expertise and TOM Online's mobile networks to further develop advanced communication features for mobile Internet platforms in China
TOM Online, China	51	

Figure 13.6 Examples of international joint ventures

Strategic alliances

Strategic alliances have become an important form of joint venture in international business. They comprise agreements between two or more organizations where each partner seeks to add to its competencies by combining its resources with those of a partner. A strategic alliance generally involves cooperation between partners rather than joint ownership of a subsidiary set up for a specific purpose, although it may include agreement for collaborators to purchase shares in the businesses of other members of the alliance.

Strategic alliances allow individual companies to build upon the relationship that they have developed with their clients by allowing them to sell on services which they do not produce themselves, but instead are produced by another member of the alliance. This arrangement is reciprocated between members of the alliance. Strategic alliances have become important within the airline industry, where operators share their route networks through 'code-sharing', thereby increasing the range of origin–destination opportunities that can be provided with a through ticket. Some strategic alliances of airlines, such as the 'oneworld' alliance which includes British Airways, Qantas, Cathay Pacific, American Airlines, and Canadian Airlines, allow an extensive range of 'seamless' travel possibilities, to the mutual advantage of all members of the alliance.

Global e-commerce

The development of the Internet has offered new opportunities for organizations to enter foreign markets, especially services companies whose transactions are essentially intangible. At the business-to-business level, a lot of backroom service processing, such as invoicing, data entry, and software development, can now be carried out in parts of the world where there is a plentiful supply of low-cost, skilled workers, and the results sent back to the customer by a data link. At the consumer level, many service providers now promote themselves to global audiences through the Internet. A consumer in the UK, for example, could in principle find a hotel in Australia and book a room online without the hotel needing to use an intermediary. The costs to service providers of reaching global audiences in this way can be low.

Travel-related services and financial services have seen major developments in **global e-commerce**. However, the limitations of the Internet in gaining access to foreign markets should be recognized. For many private consumers, purchasing through the Internet is perceived as being very risky, and this riskiness is likely to increase when the supplier is based overseas. In the case of Internet banking services offered in the UK from overseas, customers may find themselves not protected by legislation that protects customers of UK-based banks. Some service providers are careful about how they make their services available globally through the Internet in order to preserve

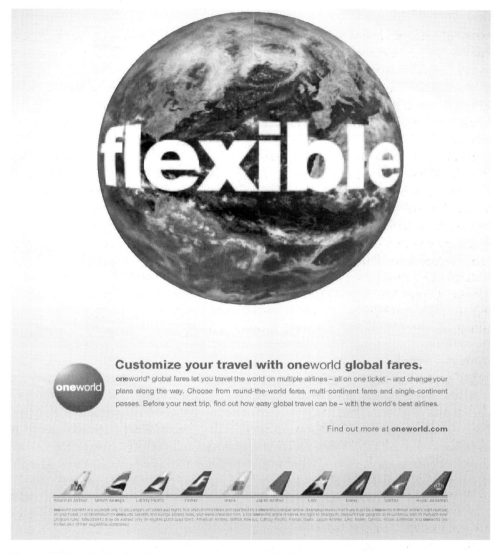

Figure 13.7 With the globalization of markets, strategic alliances are becoming increasingly crucial to facilitate overseas growth. In the airline sector, an alliance such as oneworld allows an airline's services to be marketed by all other alliance members. To its customers, British Airways is able to offer 'seamless' travel around the globe on services of fellow alliance members including Qantas, Cathay Pacific, American Airlines, and Japan Airlines. For the company, there are opportunities to rationalize operations in foreign countries. Strategic alliances allow individual companies to build upon the relationship that they have developed with their clients by allowing them to sell on services which they do not produce themselves, but instead are produced by another member of the alliance. This arrangement is reciprocated between members of the alliance. Strategic alliances have become important within the airline industry, where operators share their route networks through 'code-sharing'. (Reproduced with permission of the oneworld Alliance)

price discrimination between national markets. For this reason, airlines often restrict sales of tickets through the Internet to local national markets, to prevent customers buying in the cheapest global market.

The Internet is becoming increasingly cluttered with websites and it is not sufficient for a global trader to simply have a website. One of the biggest challenges is to get a potential customer to a company's site. For many consumer goods and services suppliers, the only sensible solution may be to pay one of the many information intermediaries such as Expedia.com and ebookers.com that act as a cyber exchange between often geographically separated buyers and sellers. For many service companies entering a foreign market, it may be safer and more cost-effective to work through these, rather than acting alone. Buyers are still likely to be cautious about dealing with a foreign company that they have not heard of. If it is difficult enough for a foreign supplier of television sets to establish itself in the UK market when it has real products available for inspection in local shops, how much harder is it going to be for a foreign-based Internet company? Can the buyer trust an unknown brand to perform as promised? What will happen about after-sales service? Who can the buyer complain to if things go wrong. There is also the question of actually distributing the product which is promoted globally through Internet channels. This has been overcome with some services (for example, music downloads), but for bulky goods, the sometimes difficult reality of global physical distribution has to be balanced against the simplicity of global promotion through a website.

The Internet is undoubtedly offering new opportunities for firms to enter foreign markets. However, basic rules of foreign market entry still apply, and many of the successful uses of global e-commerce have involved more traditional approaches based on joint ventures and strategic alliances. A number of global Internet intermediaries such as amazon.com and Yahoo! have emerged as internationally respected brands. For many suppliers entering a foreign market, it may be safer and more cost-effective to work through these, rather than acting alone.

Future trends in global marketing

Finally, we must never forget that marketing is more concerned with understanding the future than simply recording the past, so what does the future hold in store for globalized marketing? This chapter has discussed a number of trends, some of them mutually contradictory. We saw early in this chapter how cultural convergence has led some companies to see global markets as simply an extension of their domestic market. We saw how the falling cost of transport and communications has assisted this. The Internet and international media now allow consumers in Bangalore to compare their consumption preferences with their contemporaries in Birmingham, so by the logic of cultural convergence, standardized products will emerge to satisfy a similar underlying need.

Against this, many commentators have pointed to the increasing importance of cultural identity, and instead of seeing themselves as similar, consumers in Bangalore and Birmingham may seek to assert their distinct cultural identity, and may achieve this through the types of goods that they buy. We saw how ethnically based goods and services have apparently been increasing in sales, running counter to arguments of global products for global marketplaces.

A further challenge to the assumption of unrestrained globalization of markets has come from the prospects of rising costs of transport. Some have argued that threats of terrorism have deterred some international passenger journeys. From 2008, sharp increases in the price of oil led some companies, for example Procter & Gamble, to reassess their global strategy, and it is reported that the company has moved a greater proportion of its production to be close to the markets served (*Financial Times*, 2008).

What will the pattern of globalized markets look like in ten years' time? An increasingly homogenous market in which goods and services flow freely between countries, facilitated by falling transport costs and greater political cooperation? Or a more localized world, in which the assertion of cultural identity is reinforced by increasing political divisions between countries, and movement between countries is made more difficult by threats of terrorism, and rising transport costs, based on an unsustainable use of fossil fuels for transport? Come back to read the revised tenth edition of this book to find out what happened!

Chapter summary and key linkages to other chapters

Few firms can afford to define their marketing environment only at the national level. Markets are becoming increasingly global in nature, presenting opportunities for expansion overseas, but also the threat of new entrants from overseas in the domestic market. Many foreign ventures undertaken by firms fail, suggesting the need for a rigorous appraisal of potential new markets. Many of the principles of researching markets that were discussed in Chapter 5 apply equally to research in foreign markets. Companies must make a careful study of how buyer behaviour may differ in a foreign market (Chapter 4). If a decision is made to enter a foreign market, care must be taken to be sensitive to local needs by carefully adapting the marketing mix (Chapters 8–11). A balance has to be made between local sensitivity and maintaining the strength and economies of scale of a global brand. Entering a new market involves a high level of risk, and firms often seek to minimize this by sharing risk with other companies, although this can result in a loss of control.

MARKETING in ACTION

How do you find a needle in an international haystack?

In the early days of the Internet, many people assumed, perhaps naively, that international markets could be opened up through the Internet at very little cost. An entrepreneur with a bright idea and a good product proposition would no longer need to distribute expensively printed brochures around the world or employ a network of agents. With direct communication through the Internet, a buyer seeking supplies of fasteners or needles could trawl the Internet for the best source of supplier. The supplier just had to have a website, and buyers would come. Of course, life is not so simple, and one of the biggest challenges is to simply get a potential customer to your site. In the case of many consumer goods and services, the only sensible solution may be to pay one of the many information intermediaries who act as a cyber exchange between often geographically separated buyers and sellers.

But what about the case of specialized business-to-business sales where intermediaries may be few and far between? Here, the importance of getting a high ranking in search engines becomes even more important. It is claimed that there are over 20,000 search engines available to Internet users, but the reality is that the top ten search engines account for over 90% of all searches. Being close to the top of these search engines has become an important part of marketing strategy. Consider the case of a company that specializes in buying redundant manufacturing machinery from factories that have closed down, and reselling it to buyers looking for second-hand equipment. Addressing global markets is often key to success here. After all, if a shoe factory that has just closed down in Leicester is selling off its injection moulding equipment, it is unlikely that there will be many potential buyers for the equipment in Leicester, or indeed the UK—if one company in the UK could not profitably use the equipment, then it is likely that no UK companies will be able to. But the equipment may be just what an entrepreneur in Romania is looking for.

How can a UK-based trader in second-hand equipment get its site to the top of the list that the Romanian is looking at? Relying on searches for 'machinery' or even 'second-hand machinery' is unlikely to be very fruitful—after all, there are likely to be thousands of sites in this category across the world. But including market-specific terms such as 'injection moulding' and 'shoes' in the web page text and meta-tags will help to put a company's site higher in a specialized search category. Having several pages with different titles, text, and meta-tags provides more opportunities to target specific international market segments. And there's another trick that many companies use to get overseas buyers to their site. It costs relatively little to produce a foreign-language version of the main pages of a company's site. If a Romanian entrepreneur entered 'ЄГКНУЗГ ПУРbЯ' in a search engine instead of 'injection moulding' or 'shoes', the seller's site would probably come very close to the top of the search results.

◻ KEY PRINCIPLES OF MARKETING

- The basic principles of marketing apply whether a firm is dealing with its domestic market or a foreign market.
- The competing demands of global standardization and local adaptation must be reconciled.
- Understanding the effects of cultural differences on buyer behaviour is crucial to successful overseas marketing.

CASE STUDY

Can Interbrew sell more beer to the heavy drinking Czechs?

Why would western brewers want to enter the beer market in the Czech Republic, a country that was awash with famous local brands of legendary quality, with intense loyalty to regional brands, and among the lowest beer prices in Europe? True, the Czechs also had one of the highest rates of consumption in the world, which in 1997 stood at an average of 165 litres per person per year, beaten only by Bavaria. But even this high consumption was falling, as traditional hard-drinking working men cut back on their consumption. In fact, consumption fell steadily to 158 litres in 2006 (Euromonitor, 2007). To lovers of real ale, the Czech Republic may have been heaven, but why should western brewers have been so keen to move into an apparently saturated market with low prices and falling consumption? To the UK-based Bass Breweries (as it was then known), the Czech market represented an opportunity waiting to be developed. However, a study of its venture into the Czech Republic illustrates that understanding the environment of an emerging market can involve many risks, and in Bass's case, it ultimately failed to achieve all its ambitions.

In the communist era, Czech breweries operated within a system of production allocations determined by central state planners, with each brewery allocated a geographical area of distribution. This provided for very little competition within a given region, and capital investment into the modernization of production facilities was low. However, the quality of Czech beers was preserved on account of the professional honour of the brewer. The Czech Republic has a long tradition of brewing, with some of the world's oldest and most respected beers, including the Staropramen, Ostravar, and Vratislav brands. One of the reasons for the high consumption of beer has been its high quality and low price. The price of a litre of beer in 1997 was typically less than a quarter of what a comparable litre would have cost in the UK, the low price reflecting low taxes and low margins for producers.

With the collapse of the communist government in 1989, central planning and state ownership gave way to a private, market-driven economy. In this reorientation, Czech breweries found themselves in a new business environment. With government financing severed, breweries were forced to privatize. Profitability, competition, and marketing became paramount, as regional brewers' hold over local customers was weakened.

Czech beer drinkers had become used to a mentality of taking what was available, rather than seeking the best product to suit their needs and preferences. Bass saw that the fragmented market was ripe for consolidation. In 1997, the three largest breweries held only 55% of the market, with another 25% being made up of small regional brewers, none of whom had a national market share of over 3%. Even Budwar, possibly the best-known Czech beer, accounted for just 3% of the domestic market. Many of the Czech Republic's near neighbours had similar structural problems and opportunities in their beer sector and, like other western investors, Bass saw the country as a platform for expansion into the rest of eastern Europe.

In addition to exploiting the Czech market, Bass also saw an opportunity to develop global markets for the high-quality beers that were currently confined to the domestic Czech market. Bass could use its global distribution network to exploit the brands in a way that would have been impossible to domestic companies.

Bass first invested in the Czech Republic in 1994, with a 34% stake in Prague Breweries, later increasing this to 46%. This brought Bass three Prague-based breweries that would have seemed quite small and unsophisticated by UK standards. In 1995 it bought 78% of Vratislavice nad Nisou (with two breweries in North Boherrda) and 51% of Ostravar, a brewery in North Moravia. In 1996 Bass acquired a controlling interest in Prague Breweries when it increased its stake to 51%. In 1997, the three companies in which it had invested were merged under the name Prague Breweries, in which Bass has a 55% stake. This made Prague Breweries the second biggest brewer in the Czech Republic, but it still had only a 14% market share. The market leader, Prazdroj, had 27%. Bass had started the process of consolidation in the industry, but it still had a long way to go if it was to match progress in western Europe.

A further approach to making the Czech market profitable was the development of strong brands that could be sold at higher margins. Importantly, the 'typical' Czech beer drinker appeared to be changing, as the heavy-drinking male gave way to a rising number of young, relatively affluent professionals.

Bass's first new product development in the country was a premium lager called Velvet, developed and brewed in the Czech Republic, but with the help of Bass in the UK. From the beginning, Bass sought to position Velvet as something quite different to commodity beers. It had a distinctive smooth, creamy head and Bass commissioned special glasses for it to be served in. To add to its differentiation, Bass provided training for bar staff on how to pour and serve it. Velvet was aimed at high-income consumers and promoted through bars and restaurants with targeted tastings. Promotional support was provided by advertising in *Elle, Harper's Bazaar*, and *Esquire*, and by a dedicated sales team. Despite the conservatism of Czech drinkers, Bass had successfully found a niche market—the emerging middle classes in stylish bars. Bass's strategy was to invest heavily in brands for the long term. In developing a brand, the company started with a research programme among consumers to learn more about their preferences, followed with research on respondents' perceptions of competing brands. It then undertook lifestyle segmentation, something previously unheard of in the Czech Republic.

Another strength of Bass in its UK home market was distribution and this represented another opportunity in the Czech market. It introduced a new sales, marketing, and distribution structure, making it possible to distribute national brands efficiently and effectively. The structure included national marketing, key account and business development teams, along with a unified sales force and distribution network. In three years, one result of this reorganization had been to increase distribution of the company's products from 50 to 80% of all retail outlets in the country.

Overcoming the cultural barriers of the Czech people proved to be one of the biggest challenges for Bass. It seemed that many people found change to a market-based system difficult to cope with after 40 years of centralized planning. The whole idea of customer focus seemed to lack credibility among employees who had been used to customers having no choice. While Bass might have been expert at brewing, branding, and distribution issues, it under-estimated how much time it would have to spend on change management issues and instilling western values into staff. Problems were encountered in getting people to make decisions, motivating them to act on their decisions, and then having to check that agreed actions were actually being undertaken. Recruitment, appraisal, and reward increasingly stressed a number of key attitudes of mind: being customer-focused, results-driven and innovative, behaving with integrity, treating people with respect, and showing respect for the community. As an example of the problems that had to be overcome, salespeople had a pride that prevented them from listening to retailers, fostered by years of production orientation.

Bass never managed to achieve profitability in the Czech market. Despite being an early mover in the consolidation of the Czech beer market, it was increasingly threatened by other international brewers that had gone through the same process of evaluating overseas markets and decided to enter the Czech market. Most significant was the advance of the world's second largest brewer, SAB Miller, which by 2003 had about 50% of the domestic market, and employed 2,700 people in three breweries (Plzen, Nosovice, and Velke Popovice) and 13 distribution centres.

Back home, all the major UK breweries were undertaking reviews of what business they should be in, and Bass decided that its future should lie in the growing leisure sector (where it owned restaurants, hotels, and fitness centres), rather than brewing. It came to an agreement for the Belgian brewer Interbrew SA to acquire all of Bass's brewing operations. Although the takeover of Bass's UK operations was blocked by the Department of Trade and Industry on competition grounds, Interbrew's acquisition of Bass's non-UK businesses was cleared by the European Commission. Bass was subsequently renamed Six Continents and in 2003 split its pub operations into a new company, Mitchells and Butler.

Interbrew already had a significant part of its business in central and eastern Europe, with operations in Russia, Ukraine, Hungary, Croatia, Romania, Bulgaria, Montenegro, and the Czech Republic. It had a long-term vision for Bass's brands and, following the acquisition of Bass's Czech assets, earmarked 3 billion Czech koruna for development of Prazske Pivovary. Could it succeed where Bass had not been able to make a profit?

Meanwhile, third position in the Czech beer market was taken by Budejovicky Budvar which, despite a wave of privatization and consolidation in the Czech beer industry since the end of communism in 1989, remained in state hands.

The presence of two major international brewers in the Czech market helped to focus attention on exports at a time when domestic consumption of beer was steadily falling. Domestic consumption was stagnating as beer faced increasing competition from other types of drink, particularly wine. Increasingly strict drink-driving laws also helped to hold back beer consumption.

The accession of the Czech Republic and nine other countries into the EU in May 2004 helped to integrate the country's brewing industry into the wider European marketing environment. Accession meant the easing of export administration, long border queues, and prohibitive import duties in some countries. Countries such as Hungary, Poland, and the Baltics previously had restrictively high customs duties, so accession opened up new markets for brewers with an interest in the Czech Republic. The retail price of beer was claimed to be two to three times higher in most EU countries, so exporting appeared to be more profitable than domestic sales. SAB Miller set out to make the Prazdroj's brand Pilsner Urquell its flagship label worldwide. In 2006 over one-third of the 1.5 million hectolitres brewed was sold abroad. It saw that, as the Czech market had reached maximum consumption, the only room for growth was through exports.

Meanwhile, cultural and economic convergence between the Czech Republic and the rest of the EU continued to present new opportunities for imported beers. Interbrew claimed that a growing number of retailers were coming to appreciate that stocking niche brands such as its Staropramen brand could create a clear point of difference in a crowded market, and encouraged consumers to trade up. Belgium's Stella Artois was introduced to the Czech Republic, targeting upwardly mobile, educated, and well-travelled young people. Some claimed that it was sacrilege, but others saw it as normal market development when Czech brewers diversified even further into alcoholic fruit drinks and alco-pops.

Source: based on C. Johnstone (2005), 'Major breweries invest in controversial beer concept for Czech drinks market', *Prague Post*, 7 July; 'Interbrew to invest £1m in Staropramen as sales soar', The Publican.com, 30 June 2005; 'Czech brewers see the world as their oyster', www.eubusiness.com, 26 March 2005; J. Hamm, (2002), 'Foreign beer enters local market', *Prague Post*, 18 December; Euromonitor (2007), Alcoholic Drinks in the Czech Republic, London, Euromonitor International.

Case study review questions

1. Review the alternative market entry strategies that were open to Bass in 1994 and assess each for its level of risk.

2. Identify the principal barriers Bass faced in developing a marketing culture in its Czech operations. How could it overcome these barriers?

3. Critically assess the problems and opportunities for Interbrew's investment in the Czech Republic arising from further integration of the country into the European Union.

▢ CHAPTER REVIEW QUESTIONS

1.   Discuss how a UK designer clothing label might go about researching market potential for its products in Germany?

2.   In what circumstances is a global, rather than a localized, marketing strategy likely to be successful?

3.   What is meant by a strategic alliance, and why are they of increasing importance? Give examples of strategic alliances.

☐ ACTIVITIES

1. Choose two or three international service providers from the following sectors: hotels, airlines, fast food, car rental, accountancy services. Go to their websites and click through to a selection of their national sites in countries with a different socio-economic profile to your own. Analyse what is common between the service offer and the promotional messages between the different countries in which the company operates. Then try and identify ways in which the service offer has been adapted to meet local conditions.

2. Go to the website of an international hotel chain such as Hilton or Holiday Inn. Check out the price of a standard room on a particular date, for a selection of the company's hotels in different capital cities. What dispersion of prices for a basically similar room do you observe between cities? What factors may explain the differences in prices that you observed? Do you think such price differences are likely to persist?

3. Refer to Figure 13.2 which gives information about GDP per person and the level of corruption and economic freedom in a selection of countries. If you were a European hotel operator seeking international expansion for its budget hotel format, how would this information influence your choice of target country to expand into? What specific additional information would you need to further guide your choice between those countries listed?

☐ REFERENCES

Allam, A. (2003), 'Making Near Beer Acceptable in Near East'. *New York Times*, 4 January, p. C3.

Batt, C. (2002), 'Heineken Pumps Up the Volume'. *Daily Telegraph,* 17 August, p. 29.

Euromonitor (2007), 'Alcoholic Drinks in the Czech Republic'. London: Euromonitor International.

The Economist (2001), 'The New Demographics', 11 March, Special Section, pp. 5–8.

Financial Times (2008), 'Oil costs force P&G to rethink its supply network', 27 June, p. 22.

World Trade Organization (2007), *International Trade Statistics Yearbook*. Geneva: WTO.

☐ SUGGESTED FURTHER READING

The following references offer a general review of the factors that influence firms' foreign expansion decisions:

Keegan, W. J. and Green, M. C. (2007), *Global Marketing*, 5th edn. Upper Saddle Rivers, NJ: Prentice Hall.

Cateora , P. R. and Graham, J. (2006), *International Marketing*, 13th edn. New York: McGraw-Hill.

Czinkota, M. R. and Ronkainen, I. A. (2007), *International Marketing*. London: Thomson Learning.

For a general overview of trends in international business, consult the following:

Economic Trends: a monthly publication of the UK Office for National Statistics which includes statistics relating to international trade performance.

Overseas Trade: a DTI–FCO magazine for exporters published ten times per year by Brass Tacks Publishing Co., London.

World Trade Organization Annual Report, published annually.

World Trade Organization *Trade Policy Review* (serial).

Overseas Direct Investment: detailed breakdown of UK overseas direct investment activity, outward and inward, by component, country, and industry (Office for National Statistics).

USEFUL WEB LINKS

Visit the Online Resource Centre for resources that are relevant to this chapter, including web links, multiple choice questions, and additional case studies:

www.oxfordtextbooks.co.uk/orc/palmer2e/

KEY TERMS

- **Export/import agents**
- **Exporting**
- **Global e-commerce**
- **Global marketing**
- **Joint ventures**
- **Strategic alliances**

Glossary of marketing terms

- **Above-the-line** Expenditure on paid-for advertising
- **ACORN** ('A Classification of Residential Neighbourhood') A widely used geodemographic database of residential locality types
- **Adoption process** Rate at which individuals start buying a product
- **Advertising** The process by which an advertiser communicates with target audiences through paid-for messages
- **Advertising agency** An organization which specializes in communication on behalf of clients
- **Advertising campaign** A coherent and planned approach to communication over a specified period of time
- **Advertising media** Communication channels such as radio, television, and newspapers
- **Agent** An individual or company acting in a capacity on behalf of a principal (e.g. a sales agent). An agent does not generally take ownership of goods
- **AIDA model** ('Attention, Interest, Desire, Action') A mnemonic used to describe the process of communicating a series of messages
- **Augmented product** The core product offer with the addition of differentiating benefits, e.g. additional services
- **Awareness** The proportion of a target audience who have heard of a particular product of service (either 'prompted' or 'unprompted')
- **Banner advertisements** Paid-for advertisements on other companies' websites
- **Barriers to entry** Obstacles facing a company when it wishes to enter a market
- **Below-the-line** Expenditure on promotional activities that involves non-commission paying media
- **Benchmarking** Setting performance goals for an organization based on those achieved by its competitors
- **Brand equity** The capitalized value of price premiums that customers are prepared to pay for a brand, compared with a similar generic product
- **Branding** The process of creating a distinctive identity for a product that differentiates it from its competitors
- **Budget** The amount of money scheduled to be spent or received in future periods
- **Business cycle** Fluctuations in the level of activity in an economy, commonly measured by employment levels and aggregate demand
- **Business-to-business marketing** Targeting goods and services at businesses who use the products to add value in their own production processes, as distinct from consumers who are the final consumers of the product
- **Buying behaviour** The way in which customers act, and the processes involved in making a purchase decision
- **Cannibalization** Occurs where one product within a company's range reduces sales of other products in its range

- **Cartel** An association of suppliers that seeks to restrict costly competition between its members
- **Cognitive dissonance** Mental discomfort that occurs following a purchase decision which the buyer may subsequently believe to have been a poor decision
- **Communication mix** The various media and messages that are used to communicate with a target audience
- **Competitive advantage** A firm has a marketing mix that the target market sees as meeting its needs better than the mix of competing firms
- **Consumer** The final user of a good or a service
- **Consumer goods** Goods or services which are targeted at private individuals, rather than at organizations
- **Consumer panel** Research involving a group of consumers who report on their purchases over a period of time
- **Contingency plan** An alternative plan which can be rapidly implemented if the assumptions underlying the original plan turn out to be false
- **Cookies** A small program embedded in a computer which collects information that can be forwarded and interrogated by a remote computer
- **Core product** The essential benefit provided by a good or service
- **Corporate planning** Planning which involves all functions within an organization
- **Cost per thousand** Used in advertising as a measure of cost per thousand people viewing or reading an advertisement
- **Cost plus pricing** A pricing method in which a percentage 'mark-up' is added to the costs of producing a product
- **Coverage** The percentage of a targeted audience that have an opportunity to see a particular advertisement
- **Culture** The whole set of beliefs, attitudes, and ways of behaving shared by a group of people
- **Customer** People who buy a firm's products (although customers may not be the actual consumers of the product)
- **Customer Relationship Management (CRM)** A process of intergrating the multiple contacts which a customer may have with an organization to create a shared knowledge base about the customer's history, preferences, and likely future needs
- **DAGMAR model** ('Defining Advertising Goals for Measured Advertising Results') An acronym for a model of the communication process
- **Database marketing (DBM)** The use of a list of customers (potential and actual) which drives communication between an organization and its customers
- **Decision-making unit (DMU)** The group of individuals who are involved in making a purchase decision
- **Decision support system** Models which are used to inform management decisions on the bases of available data
- **Demand** The willingness and ability of buyers to buy a particular product at a particular time at a given price
- **Demography** The study of population characteristics, e.g. relating to broad population statistics, such as age, sex, household composition
- **Desk research** Research which uses existing (secondary) sources of information
- **Differentiation** Creating a product which is different in some way from its main competitors, in the eyes of the target market

- **Diffusion** The rate at which new products are adopted by different customer adoption categories
- **Direct mail** A form of below-the-line promotion, which uses personalized communication, sent directly from the advertiser to potential and actual customers
- **Direct marketing** Direct communication between a seller and individual customers using a promotion method other than face-to-face selling. Direct mail is one communication channel used by direct marketing
- **Discriminatory pricing** Selling a product at two or more prices, where the difference in prices is not based on differences in costs
- **Distributor** A person or organization who assists in the task of making goods and services available to end-users. Distributors of goods generally take ownership of goods from suppliers and are responsible for collecting payments
- **Diversification** Broadening the spread of markets served and/or products supplied by a business
- **E-business** The ability to integrate local and wide area networks through the use of Internet protocols to effectively remove the barriers between businesses, their customers, and their suppliers in global markets
- **E-commerce** Transactions of goods or services for which payment occurs over the Internet or other wide area networks
- **Economies of scale** Costs per unit fall as total output increases
- **Elasticity of demand** Responsiveness of customer demand to changes in price or some other variable
- **Entrepreneur** An individual who takes risks with a view to profitably exploiting business opportunities
- **Environment** Everything that exists outside the boundaries of a system
- **Environmental set** The elements within an organization's environment that are currently of major concern to it
- **Ethics** Statements of what is right and wrong
- **Ethnographic research** Interpretative research which seeks a greater understanding from the perspectives of the value systems of those being researched
- **Exchange rate** The price of one currency expressed in terms of another currency
- **Experimental research** A research approach which evaluates alternatives within a controlled framework
- **Exploratory research** Initial marketing research used to review a problem in general before committing larger expenditure to a study
- **Fast-moving consumer goods (FMCGs)** Frequently purchased products, usually of low value
- **Field research** Primary research, not using existing published sources
- **Fixed costs** Costs that do not increase as total output increases
- **Focus group** A qualitative research technique in which groups of consumers are brought together to discuss their views and attitudes to a specific topic
- **Franchising** An agreement where a franchisor develops a product format and marketing strategy and sells the right for other individuals or organizations ('franchisees') to use that format
- **Gatekeepers** Members of a decision-making unit who control access to information about available choices
- **Geodemographic analysis** The analysis of markets using a combination of geographic and demographic information
- **Global brands** Goods and services which can have universal appeal and are marketed in numerous countries with little modification to product or image

- **Guerrilla marketing** The use of unconventional promotion tactics which are unexpected by the target audience
- **Hierarchy of needs** A model of consumer motivation proposed by Maslow
- **Horizontal integration** Merging of firms' activities at a similar point in a value chain
- **Image** The perceptions of a product, brand, or company
- **Imperfect market** A market in which the assumptions of perfect competition are violated
- **Income elasticity of demand** A measure of the responsiveness of demand for a product to changes in household incomes
- **Industrial goods** Goods which are bought by industrial organizations. Often also referred to as business-to-business goods
- **Industrialization of services** The process of standardizing and mass-producing services
- **Inseparability** The inability to separate consumption of a service from its production
- **Intangibility** The inability to assess to service using any tangible evidence
- **Intermediaries** Individuals or organizations who are involved in transferring goods and services from the producer to the final consumer
- **Internal marketing** The application of the principles and practices of marketing to an organization's dealings with its employees
- **Internet marketing** Use of the World Wide Web to communicate with customers and potential customers with a view to making a sale
- **Intranet** A restricted access, local Internet communication channel
- **Joint venture** An agreement between two or more firms to exploit a business opportunity, in which capital funding, profits, risk, and core competencies are shared
- **Just-in-time production** Reliably producing goods and getting them to customers just before customers need them
- **Key client** A customer who is particularly important to an organization
- **Ladder of loyalty** A representation of the stages through which a buyer goes in the process of becoming a committed and loyal customer of a supplier
- **Learning organization** An organization-wide sharing of knowledge which leads to better decisions being made by the organization
- **Lifecycle** A phenomenon that exhibits cyclical patterns (e.g. in respect of products, markets, and buyer–seller relationships)
- **Loyalty** Non-random repeat purchasing from a seller, with behavioural and attitudinal dimensions
- **Macro-environment** The general external business environment in which a firm operates
- **Marginal cost** The addition to total cost resulting from the production of one additional unit of output
- **Market** A group of potential customers with similar needs who are willing to exchange something of value with sellers offering products that satisfy their needs. Economists define a market more widely by including sellers who interact with buyers, either in a tangible market (e.g. Covent Garden vegetable market), or a conceptual market (e.g. the UK market for vegetables)
- **Market development** A strategy used by an organization to increase sales by offering its existing products in new markets
- **Market leader** The organization which has the greatest share of sales in a given market
- **Market penetration** A strategy used by an organization to increase sales by trying to sell more of its current range of products to its current target customers

- **Market research** Activity to acquire knowledge of external factors relating to an organization's marketplace
- **Market research agencies** Organizations employed by client companies to collect information about the client company's marketplace (although market research agencies do not strictly act in an 'agency' capacity)
- **Marketing research** Distinguished from market research because marketing research is concerned with research into all of a company's marketing functions (e.g. research into pricing and distribution effectiveness)
- **Market segmentation** A process of identifying groups of customers within a broad product market who share similar needs and respond similarly to a given marketing mix formulation
- **Market share** One company's sales value (or volume) as a proportion of the total sales (or volume) for that market
- **Marketing** The management process which identifies, anticipates, and supplies customer requirements efficiently and profitably (Chartered Institute of Marketing definition)
- **Marketing audit** A systematic review of a company's marketing activities and of its marketing environment
- **Marketing environment** The social, economical, legal, political, cultural, and technological factors, external to the marketing function of an organization, that affect its actions
- **Marketing information system** A systematic way of collecting, analysing, and disseminating information which is relevant to a company's marketing
- **Marketing intelligence** Relatively unstructured information about trends and events in a company's marketing environment
- **Marketing mix** A series of convenient headings for decisions to be made by marketing managers in eliciting a profitable consumer response
- **Marketing planning** A systematic process of analysing a company's environment, then developing objectives, strategies, and action appropriate to the company's resources
- **Matrix organization structure** An organization structure which relies on coordination of management through cross-functional group leaders
- **Media** Channels of communication, e.g. television, radio, newspapers, etc.
- **Mission statement** A means of reminding everyone within an organization of the essential purpose of the organization
- **Model of buyer behaviour** A simplified representation of the processes that buyers go through in making a purchase decision
- **Monopoly** A market in which there is only one supplier. Rarely achieved in practice, as most products have some form of substitute
- **Mystery shoppers** An observational form of marketing research
- **Needs** The underlying forces that drive an individual to make a purchase which will remove a feeling of deprivation
- **New product development** The process of identifying, developing, and evaluating new product offers
- **Niche** A small sub-segment of a market which can be targeted with a distinct marketing strategy
- **Noise** Factors that distort the flow of communication between sender and receiver
- **Non-price competition** Non-price benefits such as warranties or additional features, or merchandising which can give a company's product a competitive advantage
- **Objective** A target towards which to work

- **Observational research** Research which studies customers' reactions and behaviour without any direct interaction
- **Oligopoly** A market dominated by a few interdependent suppliers
- **Omnibus survey** A regular questionnaire undertaken on behalf of multiple clients, usually involving very large samples
- **Organic growth** A 'natural' form of growth in which a company's growth rate is influenced by its previous success rate
- **Perfect competition** An ideal-type market in which there are no barriers to entry, no one firm can dominate the market, there is full information available to all buyers and sellers, and all sellers sell an undifferentiated product
- **Perishability** Services perish instantly, as the service offer cannot be stored for sale at a future time
- **Permission marketing** Communication by a company with customers and potential customers that is based on consent to receive communications
- **Personal selling** A face-to-face communication between an organization and its customers, with a view to achieving a sale
- **PEST analysis** (or 'STEP' analysis) Elements of the macro-marketing environment, comprising political/legal, economic, social/cultural, and technological environments
- **Physical distribution management** The process of ensuring that the right goods get to the right place at the right time, cost effectively
- **Place** The point where a product is to be made available to consumers
- **Point-of-sale (or point of purchase)** In retail, the area where customers make their final decision to buy
- **Positioning** Decisions about how the marketing mix for a company's product should be developed in comparison to the marketing mix of competing products
- **Press release** News story written for, and distributed to, the news media with a view to inclusion in media editorial
- **Pressure group** A group which is formed to promote a particular cause
- **Price elasticity of demand** A measure of the responsiveness of demand for a product to change in the price of the product
- **Primary data** New, original data obtained from field research
- **Product life cycle** The different stages through which a product develops over time, reflecting different needs, sales levels, and profitability
- **Product line** A number of related products offered by a supplier that often cover a broadly similar type of need
- **Product mix** The total range of goods and services offered by an organization
- **Production orientation** Where the focus of an organization is on production capability rather than consumers' needs
- **Productivity** The efficiency with which inputs are turned into outputs
- **Profiling** A description of the characteristics of actual or target customers, based on data analysis
- **Profit** The excess of revenue over costs (although it can be difficult to calculate costs for particular products, and therefore their profitability)
- **Promotion mix** The combination of media and messages which a company uses to communicate with actual and potential customers

- **Prospecting** Techniques to identify potential new customers
- **Psychographics** A basis for segmentation derived from attitudinal and behavioural variables
- **Public Relations** A deliberate and planned effort to create mutual understanding between an organization and its various publics
- **Pull strategy** A marketing strategy in which the manufacturer promotes directly to the final customers, who then demand products from intermediaries, who in turn 'pull' goods from the manufacturer
- **Push strategy** A marketing strategy in which the manufacturer promotes primarily to intermediaries, relying on them to promote to their customers
- **Qualitative research** Research which produces essentially attitudinal, non-numerical data
- **Quality** The standard of delivery of goods or services, often expressed in terms of the extent to which they meet customers' expectations
- **Quantitative research** Research based on large samples, but which may be lacking in interpretation. Sometimes called 'hard data'
- **Questionnarie** A set of questions used to obtain information from a respondent
- **Quota sample** A sampling method where those questioned are numerically in proportion to pre-defined characteristics, e.g. sex, age, occupation
- **Random sample** A sampling method where everyone in the population has an equal chance of being included in the sample
- **Relationship marketing** A means by which an organization seeks to maintain an ongoing relationship between itself and its customers, based on continuous patterns of service delivery, rather than isolated and discrete transactions
- **Repositioning** The development of a new marketing mix relative to that of competitors, to replace the existing mix
- **Sales orientation** The focus of an organization is on selling its products more aggressively, while probably not fully understanding the needs of customers and the types of product they would prefer to buy
- **Sales promotion** Techniques and incentives used to increase short-term sales
- **Scientific approach** Using the rules of scientific procedure in order to develop objectivity and repeatability
- **Sealed bid pricing** Submission of a price quotation for supplying goods or services, in which the identity or price of competing bids is not known
- **Secondary research** Using previously conducted research data
- **Segment** A grouping of customers who have similar needs and respond in a similar way to a given marketing stimulus
- **Segmentation** The process of identifying groups of customers who have similar needs and respond in a similar way to a given marketing stimulus
- **Services** products which are essentially intangible and cannot be owned
- **Social responsibility** Accepting corporate responsibilities to customers and non-customers that go beyond legal or contractual requirements
- **Societal marketing** Marketing which attempts to improve social benefits
- **Socio-economic groups** A grouping of the population based on occupation
- **Spam** unsolicited e-mail
- **Speciality goods** Consumer goods for which buyers are prepared to make an effort to acquire
- **Sponsorship** Payment by a company to be associated with a particular event or activity

- **Stakeholder** Any person with an interest in the activities of an organization (e.g. customers, employees, government agencies, and local communities)
- **Strategic alliances** Agreements between organizations that are based on a long-term recognition that they could each benefit by cooperating on some aspect of their marketing
- **Strategy** The overall, long-term direction or approach which a company aims to follow, in order to achieve its objectives
- **SWOT analysis** An acronym for strengths and weaknesses, opportunities, and threats and used to assess the internal strengths and weaknesses of an organization against its external threats and opportunities
- **Tactics** Operational activities that put into effect a company's marketing strategy
- **Target market** The segment of a market at which a marketing mix is aimed
- **Telemarketing** Sales activity which focuses on the use of the telephone to enter into a two-way dialogue with present and potential customers
- **Test marketing** A trial launch of a product into a limited area to test its marketing mix prior to a full national launch
- **Unique Selling Proposition (USP)** A selling claim based on a differentiated product feature or unique element of the marketing mix
- **Value chain** The sequence of activities and organizations involved in transforming a product from one which is of low value to one that is of high value
- **Vertical integration** The extension of a firm's activities to previous or subsequent points in a value chain
- **Vertical Marketing Systems (VMSs)** The integration of intermediaries at different levels of a distribution chain to improve efficiency and effectiveness of the chain as a whole
- **Viral marketing** Encouraging recommendation of a company or its products through word of mouth
- **Wholesaler** An intermediary who buys products in bulk and resells them in smaller quantities to retailers
- **Word-of-mouth promotion** The act of recommendation by existing customers to their friends
- **Yield management** Using variable pricing to maximize the earnings from fixed resources, e.g. hotel rooms, airline seats

Subject index

24/7 society 95, 386, 439
3G mobile phones 457

Accelerator effect 53, 54
ACORN classifications 176, 199, 216
Advertising 99, 424–32
Advertising agencies 416, 417
Ageing population 59, 188–90
Anti-competitive practices 97–8
ASEAN trading bloc 56
Attitudes 196–8
Auctions 338, 339
Awareness set 122

Banking code 91
Bartering 338, 339
Benchmarking 152, 373
Bio diesel 85
Birth rate 59
Blogs 126
Brand
    characteristics 231–3
    co-brands 243
    equity 491
    extension 242, 243
    families 242
    features 237, 238
    global brands 245, 246
    history 229, 230
    name 235–8
    personality 238
    positioning 249–53
    strategy 239–45
Brandscape 247
Budgets
    promotional 417–19
Business cycles 53–5
Business-to-business marketing 133, 134, 203, 263, 265, 358
Buyer behaviour
    buying process 113–16
    decision-making unit (DMU) 128
    evaluation processes 122–4
    models 130–4
    overseas markets 518

Campaign planning 415, 416
Cannibalization 340
Carbon footprint 28
Carbon trading 104
Cartels 99, 319
Celebrity endorsement 117, 399

Census of population 186, 188
Change
    environmental 66, 67
Channels of communication 410–11
Channels of distribution
    defined 350
    design 356–60
    electronic 451, 452
    foreign markets 517, 518
    integrated 364
    global 366
    power 361, 362
Charities 15
Chat rooms 126
Children 93
Choice set 123
Close circuit television 90, 159
Closed systems 30
Cluster analysis 164
CO_2 emissions 81, 85, 103, 104
Co-branding 243
Codes of conduct 87, 91, 100
Codes of practice 320
Cognitive dissonance 125–7
Collusion 96, 97
Commodity products 269
Communication process 397, 398
Communication, responsibilities 97–100
Community forums 126
Competition Act 1998 320
Competitor analysis 43, 224–9
Competitor based pricing 332, 333
Competitor orientation 7
Conjoint analysis 164
Consideration set 122
Consumer adoption process 325–6, 408
Consumer behaviour
    buying processes 113–16
    decision-making unit (DMU) 128
    evaluation 122–4
    models of behaviour 130–4
    overseas markets 518
Consumer confidence 51
Consumer Credit Act 1974 100, 320
Consumer goods 262
Consumer Protection Act 1987 320
Consumer services 265
Contingency planning 470, 471
Control 490–2
Convenience goods 262
Convenience stores 355
Cookies 90

Corporate planning 471, 472
Corporate responsibility 80
Correlation analysis 163
Costs 329–33
Counterfeit goods 244
Credit crunch 204
Culture
    cultural convergence 501
    diversity 57
    effects on buying behaviour 118
    organizational 64, 65
Customers
    complaints 126
    defined 15, 16
    lifetime pricing 329
    loyalty 139
    privacy 89–92
    satisfaction 139, 150, 151
    vulnerable customers 77, 92
Customer charters 270
Customer orientation 7
Customer Relationship Management (CRM) 135–41
Customer service 126, 371, 372

Data Protection Act 1998 446
Data sources 156–60, 175–7
Databases 419, 444, 445
Decision-maker 129, 130
Decision-making unit (DMU) 124, 127–30, 408
Decoding 401–3
Deletion of products 292–6
Demand
    defined 306–9
    demand curve 306–7
    forecasting 172–5
Demography 59, 60, 187–92, 508
Design 270, 271
Desk research 156
Differentiation 312–14
Diffusion model 408
Direct mail 448, 449
Direct marketing 443–9
Discretionary income 195
Discrimination 193, 335, 336
Disintermediation 13
Disposable income 195
Diversification 292
Dot.com mania 13

Early adopters 274
Ecological environment
    impacts: transport and distribution 386, 387
    issues in the business environment 61–3
    responsibility 82–4
E–commerce 524, 525, 526
Economic order quantity 375
Economies of scale 322
Effectiveness
    marketing 492, 493
Elasticity of demand 314–17

Electronic point of sale (EPOS) 66, 149
Emissions trading scheme 104
E–mail marketing 50, 206, 450
Empty nesters 118
Encoding 401–3
Enterprise Act 2002 320
Environmental change 66, 67
Environmental scanning 152
Environmental set 49
Environmental Threat and Opportunity Profile (ETOP) 68, 69
Espionage 156
Ethical responsibility 85–9
Ethnic diversity 57, 192, 508
Ethnographic research 143, 144
European Union (EU) 56, 91, 104, 505
Evaluation
    buying process 122–4
    promotion 419, 420
Exchange 19, 20
Exhibitions 440
Expectations 158, 384
Experimental research 30
Export agents 521
Exporting 501, 503, 521

Family life cycle 119, 189, 190
Family roles 118, 194
Fast moving consumer goods (FMCGs) 10, 14, 262
Field research 156
Financial Services Act 245
Five forces model 225, 226
Fixed costs 332
Flexible manufacturing systems 184, 185
Flexible organization 65, 66
Focus groups 161, 166, 167
Foreign direct investment 521
Franchising 364, 365, 522
Freudian analysis 117
Functional quality 269, 270

Gatekeepers 128
Gender effects 191, 192
Geodemographic analysis 198–201
Global positioning systems (GPS) 381, 421
Global warming 81, 103, 104, 389
Globalization
    causes 499–500
    channels of distribution 366
    global brands 245, 246
    global e-commerce 524–6
    market development 526, 527
Government policy 45
Green consumers 84, 85
Green products 272
Greenhouse gas emissions 81, 103, 104
Gross Domestic Product (GDP) 51
Growth
    planning 290–2
Guerrilla marketing 90

Hierarchy of needs model 116, 412, 413
Household structure 59, 192

Ideas 281–3
Imperfect competition 304
Impulsive shoppers 114, 115
Industrialization 231
Influencers 127, 128
Information management 170, 171, 487–92
Information processing
  consumers 378–80
Innovation 276–87
Innovators 273
Inseparability 264
Intangibility 264
Integrated marketing channel 364
Integrated marketing communications 395
Inter-functional co-ordination 7
Intermediaries
  foreign markets 517, 518
  functions 352–4
  role in business environment 43, 44
  types 354–9
Internal environment 63–5
Internet
  advertising 441, 442, 443
  banking 91
  channels of distribution 366–8, 386
  marketing 449–57
  mobile 206
  research 155, 159
Inventory management 375–7
Involvement 113, 261

Joint ventures 522, 523
Junk food 29
Junk mail 89
Just in time systems 15, 376–8

Knowledge management 169–72

Ladder of loyalty 138
Leadership 485–7
Legislation 91
Life cycle
  family 119, 189, 190
  products 272–9, 324, 325
  customer lifetime pricing 329
Lifestyles 196, 197
Lobbying 440
Location based services 297
Location decisions 381, 382
Logistics
  defined 369–70
Logos 239
London congestion charge 342
Loyalty programmes 137, 139–41, 198

Macro environment
  defined 41
Magazines 426, 427

Mailing lists 445, 446
Mailing Preference Service 445
Management
  by walking about 171
  information 487–92
  structures and processes 25–7, 63–5, 475–7
Marginal cost pricing 331, 332
Market
  defined 20
  entry strategies 290, 291
  overseas 519–24
  research agencies 168
  structure 302–6
  testing 285, 286
Marketing
  audit 251, 468, 469
  definition 5
  department 63–5, 475–7
  environment
    defined 41
  intelligence 169
  management 25–7, 468–70
  mix 21–5, 253, 254
  objectives 468
  orientation 6
  plan 27
  planning 475
  research 152–6, 148–75
  responsibility 93–7
  services 264, 265, 503
  strategy 468, 469
Mass marketing 208, 209
Matrix organization 481
Micro environment
  defined 41
Minimum wage legislation 95
Mission statement 473, 474
Mobile phones
  3G technology 296–8
  charges 320
  Internet 206, 455, 456
  SMS text messaging 50
Models
  buyer behaviour 130–4
  diffusion of innovation 408
  five forces 225, 226
  hierarchy of effects 412, 413
  hierarchy of needs 116
  pricing 341, 344
  stimulus response 117
Monopoly 318, 319
MOSAIC analysis 199–201
Motivation 116, 117, 132
Multiplier effect 53
Mystery shoppers 159

NAFTA trading bloc 56
Needs 16, 17, 114–16, 133, 150
New product development 276–87
New technology 61
Newspapers 425, 426

Niche marketing 209, 210
Noise 401–3
Not–for–profit organizations 14, 341–3

Objectives
    marketing 468
    physical distribution management 370, 371
    pricing 321–4
    promotional 395–7
Observational research 158, 159
Oligopoly 317, 318
Online marketing 161, 355, 428, 451, 452, 449–57
Open systems 30
Organic produce 12
Organizational effectiveness 492, 493
Outdoor advertising 428
Outlet malls 356

Packaging 271
Patents 271
Payment protection insurance 101
Peer groups 118
Penetration pricing strategy 327–8
Perception 120–2, 403–5
Perishability 264
Personal selling 432–4
Pester power 50, 129
Physical distribution management 369–85
Physical distribution objectives 371
Political environment 55, 56
Political parties 15
Position map 213
Positioning 212–14, 249–53, 261
Positivism 29
Post purchase evaluation 125–7
Postcodes 216
Power
    in distribution channels 50, 361, 362
Press conferences 440
Press releases 440
Pressure groups 46, 47, 505
Pricing
    bundling 340, 341
    competition based 332, 333
    determination 311–12
    discrimination 333, 334
    elasticity of demand 314–17
    fixing 96
    foreign markets 516, 517
    methods 329–39
    models 341, 344
    objectives 321–4
    product range 339–42
    public services 341–3
    regulatory influences 319, 320
    skimming strategy 325, 326
    strategy 324–9
Primary research 154–61
Privacy 89–92
Product
    deletion 292–6

design 270, 271
development 276–87
foreign markets 512, 513
launch 286
life cycle 272–9, 324, 325
mix 267–8
offer 266–71
product range pricing 339–42
strategy 288–90
testing 285
Production orientation 11, 12
Profiling 446–8
Profit maximization 321, 322
Profitability analysis 204, 205
Promotion
    agencies 416, 417
    budgets 417–19
    campaign 415, 416
    mix 420–4
    monitoring and evaluation 419, 420
    objectives 395–7
    planning process 414, 415
Prospecting 433
Psychographic segmentation 196–8
Psychological influences 114, 115
Public Relations 437–42
Public services 341–3

Qualitative research 166, 167
Quality 268–71
Quantitative research 162–6
Questionnaires 159–61

Radio advertising 428, 429
Radio frequency identity (RFId) 159
Reference groups 118, 128, 403
Regression analysis 163
Relationship marketing 135–41
Religious groups 15
Repositioning 252, 253
Research
    primary 154–6
    secondary 154–6
Responsible communication 97–100
Responsible marketing 93–7
Retail power 50
Retailers 354–6
Return on investment (ROI) 382
Risk 113, 233

Sales promotion 434–7
Sampling 157, 158, 165
Search based advertising 456, 457
Secondary research sources 154–6, 156, 157, 512
Security 89–92
Segmentation
    bases 187–204
    business-to-business markets 203
    communication 407
    comprehensive approaches 202
    criteria 183–6

defined 182
demographic 187–92
distribution requirements 372–3
geodemographic 198–201
Internet 453
pricing 333–6
psychographic bases 196, 197, 198
socio-economic bases 194, 195
Selling 432–4
Selling orientation 12, 13, 14
Services
defined 264, 265
Services–exporting 503
SERVQUAL 162, 168
Shareholders 45
Shopping goods 262
Small businesses 482, 483
Smartphones 9
SMEs 482, 483
Smoking 94
SMS text messaging 50
Social class 118
Social network sites 421
Social responsibility 28, 29, 78, 79
Socio-economic groups 194, 195
Sociological influences 118
Spam e-mail 89, 206
Speciality goods 262
Sponsorship 442, 443
Stakeholders 78, 404
Stimulus response models 117
Stockholding 375–7
Strategic alliances 523, 524
Strategic planning 470, 471
Strategy
market entry 519–24
marketing 468, 469
pricing 324–9
product development 288–90
Supermarkets 355
Suppliers 44, 45

Supply and demand 305–7
Supply chains 369–72
Supply curve 309
Surveys 159–60
Sustainable marketing 82–4
SWOT analysis 67, 68, 251, 252
Systems 30

Tactical planning 470, 471
Target audience 405–7
Targeting 206–14, 434, 446–8
Technical quality 269, 270
Technology 61
Television 427, 428
Terrorism 527
Tobacco marketing 87
Trade Descriptions Act 1968 100
Trade shows 440
Trademarks 244
Trading blocs 505
Treaty of Rome 319, 320
Tribal marketing 247
Trigger points 189
Trust 139, 140
'Two for one' offers 99

Value 17, 18, 19
Value chain 47, 48, 351–2, 485
Values 198
Virtual organizations 385
Visual identity 238, 239
Voice Over Internet Protocol (VOIP) 298
Voluntary codes of conduct 100
Vulnerable customer 77, 92

Warehouses 380, 381
Web 2.0 13, 439, 451
Wifi 457
Word of mouse 126, 453
Word-of-mouth recommendation 120, 126, 423

Index of authors cited in text

Adner, R., 278
Ahmad, R., 353
Ambler, T., 491
Ansoff, I.H., 298
Auty, S., 132

Barbaro-Forleo, G., 63, 83
Basu, K., 141
Bateson, J.E.G., 93
Batt, C., 515
Bell, D.R., 312
Bergeron, J., 63, 83
Berthon, P., 234
Besson, M., 350
Boissy, S., 317
Bolton, L.E., 283
Borden, N.H., 22
Brien, C., 196
Brown, A., 288
Brown, G., 196
Brown, S., 30, 169
Bullard, W., 136
Butcher, K., 118
Buttle, F., 353

Cardwell, A., 423
Carson, D., 169
Chomka, S., 12
Chung-kue, H., 399
Cova, B., 133
Cronin, J., 136
Crosby, P.B., 268
Cummings, P., 399
Cyert, R.M., 322

Dahan, E., 288
De Chernatony, L., 229, 233
Dexter, A., 162
Diamantopoulos, A., 245
Dick, A.S., 141
Dipasquale, C.B. 285
Dixon N.M., 169
Doughty, S., 58
Drucker, P. F., 14, 27, 170, 382, 432
Dwyer, F. R., 31

Enright, M., 288

Fagan, M., 286
Ferguson, R., 423
Fill, C., 417

Forlani, D., 283
Friedman, M., 79
Fugate, D.L., 161

García-Rodríguez, N., 288
Gardner, B., 233
Gilmore, A., 169
Grime, I., 245
Gronroos, C., 269
Gross, M.J., 196
Gubar, G., 118
Gummesson, E., 479

Harris, C., 317
Harris, L. C., 26
Hauser, J.R., 288
Hitt, M.A., 385
Holbrook, M.B., 235
Holcomb, T.R., 385
Howard, J.A., 131
Howley, M., 288
Huang, X., 288
Hulbert, J.M., 235
Hult, G.T.M., 7
Humby, C., 177
Hunt, S.D., 140
Hunt, T., 177

Iyer, G., 312

Jai-Ok, K., 116
Jeffery, P.B., 317
Jones, K., 428
Juran, J.M., 268

Keers, H., 369
Kim, J., 288
Kotler, P., 14, 432
Kramer, M.R., 87
Krishnaswamy, S., 14, 432

Lafferty, B.A., 7
Laroche, M., 63, 83
Lauf, E., 426
Levinson, J. C., 90
Levitt, T., 124, 473
Levy, S., 233
Lin, C.F., 196
Löning, H., 350
Lusch, R.F., 265, 267, 371
Lynch, D., 400

March, J.G., 322
Maskell, P., 381
Maslow, A., 116
Mazzarol, T., 120
Mc Donald, M., 234
McDonald, D., 399
McWilliam, G., 234
Morgan, N.A., 26
Morgan, R.M., 140
Mullins, J.W., 283
Munson, J.M., 234

Nairn, G., 370
Narver, J.C., 7,8
Nonaka, I., 170
Northouse, P.G., 487

O'Callaghan, F., 118
O'Neill, H., 161
Odekerken-Schröder, G., 247
Oh, S., 31
Ouwersloot, H., 247

Padmanabhan, V., 312
Palmer, A., 317
Perry, C., 169
Peters, T.J., 124, 492
Phillips, T., 177
Porter, M.E., 87, 125, 126, 352
Posselt, T., 384
Pugh, K., 169

Rackham, N., 14, 432
Ratner, B., 448
Rayport, J.F., 48
Reichheld, F.F., 134

Richardson, G.W., 401
Rogers, E.M., 407

Salle, R., 133
Sasser, W.E., 134
Savage, M., 168
Schurr, P. H., 31
Shemwell, D., 136
Sheth, J. N., 131
Shugan, S.M., 328
Slater, S.F., 7,8
Smith, D., 162
Smith, G., 245
Song, M., 288
Soutar, G.N., 120
Soutar, G.N., 288
Sparks, B., 118
Spivey, W.A., 234
Susskind, A.M., 423
Sviokla, J.J., 48
Sweeney, J.C., 120
Swink, M., 288

Tuckel, P., 161

Vargo, S.L., 265, 267, 371

Walker, O.C. Jr., 283
Waterman, R.H., 124, 492
Wells, W.D., 118
Wilemon, D., 288
Williams, L., 245
Wong, V., 286

Yrjölä, H., 367

Index of companies and brands

20th Century Fox 227
3 297
3M 282

Advertising Association 100
Advertising Standards Authority (ASA) 100
Aldi 139
Amazon.com 13, 526
American Airlines 524
American Express 336
American Marketing Association 5
Amstrad 207
Andrex 237
Argos 355
Asda 50, 171, 228

B&Q 81, 382
Bass 230
Bebo 13, 247, 451
Bennetton 364
Black Tower 151
BMW 205
Boots 80, 137, 140
BP 243
British Airways 97, 141, 525
British Franchise Association 364
British Industrial Society 95
British Retail Federation 98
British Road Federation 47
British Telecom 133

Cadburys 65, 239, 438
Calvin Klein 357
Campaign for Real Ale (CAMRA) 217
Canadian Airlines 524
Carlsberg 247
Carphone Warehouse 173, 174, 207
Cathay Pacific 524
Chartered Institute of Marketing 5, 29
Chartered Institute of Purchasing and Supply 384
Cheltenham & Gloucester 443
Clarks Shoes 119
Classic FM 442
Coca-Cola 58, 243
Colgate Palmolive 242
Competition Commission 228, 362
Construction News 431
Co-op 228, 342, 356
Cosmopolitan magazine 406
Costa Coffee 235
Countryside Alliance 46

Debenhams 51, 354
Dell 126, 354, 485
Deutsche Post 380
DHL 380
Direct Line 155
Direct Marketing Association 89, 444
Domino's Pizza 365
Dr Martens 143
Durex 237

easyJet 62, 207, 315, 368, 404, 474
eBay 339
Ecos organic paints 185
Egg 287
Emma's diary 190
Enron 479
Epson 340
eSure 50
Expedia.com 13, 50
Experian 199

Facebook 13, 421, 424, 451
Fairtrade 28, 88, 97
Fairy Liquid 254–6
Federal Express 506
FHM magazine 406, 448
Fiat 523
Financial Services Authority 101
First Direct 155
Ford 210
Forrester Research 157
Freeview 173
Friends of the Earth 47, 84, 104
FriendsGreetings.com 90
Fujitsu 203
Future Foundation 58, 95, 172

Gala Bingo 94
Gartner Research 157
Gillette 226
GlaxoSmithKline 143
Google 451, 456, 474

Health and Safety Executive 45
Hilton Hotels 514
HMV 355
Hob Nobs 328
HSBC 423
Huntingdon Life Sciences 46
Hutchinson Whampoa 297

IBM 239
Iceland 228
Innocent Smoothies 97, 441, 484
Institute of Direct Marketing 444
Institute of Practitioners in Advertising 100
Institute of Public Relations 437
Institute of Sales Promotion 434
Internet Advertising Bureau 452, 453

J. D. Weatherspoon 485
John Lewis 140

Kit Kat 402
Kodak 239

L'Oréal 35, 36
Labour Party 15
Lastminute.com 332, 450
Laura Ashley 224
Law Society 100
Lidl 139
Loaded magazine 406

Marks & Spencer 63, 71, 80, 252, 486
Maxim magazine 406
McDonald's 44, 58 , 61, 245, 293
Mecca Cola 507
Mercedes-Benz 207
Mintel 70, 157, 195
Mobile Codes Consortium 456
Moneysavingexpert.com 43
Moneysupermarket.com 13
Morrisons 50, 228
Mothercare 369
Motorola 457

Nanjing Automobile Corporation 523
National Consumer Council 87
National Express 85, 98
National Health Service 16, 344, 345, 478, 492
National Market Traders Federation 18
NatWest 364
Nescafé 239
Nestlé 35
Next 224, 355, 369
Northern Foods 71, 358

O₂ 93, 173, 500
Oakley 357
Ofcom 100, 320
Office of Fair Trading (OFT) 89, 96, 99
Ofgem 93, 320
Ofwat 320
OneWorld alliance 524, 525
Orange 298

Parker Pen 226
PC World 366
Pepsi Cola 238

PG Tips 279
Portman Group 98
Post It Notes 280
Primark 371, 384
Procter & Gamble 143, 255, 256, 318
Prudential Assurance 245
Pschitt 515
Punch taverns 215

Qantas 524

Radio Advertising Bureau 429
Radio Times 426
Railtrack 98
Royal Mail 236
Ryanair 83, 100, 103, 104, 324

Sainsbury's 50, 63, 228, 474, 486
Sky 318
Skype 523
Sony 197, 227, 268
Spar 355, 356
Stagecoach 522
Starbucks 48, 88, 97, 235
Staropramen 529
Somerfield 228
Swiftcall 334

Taylor Nelson Sofres 168
Tesco 50, 175, 176, 228, 270, 357, 383, 388–91
TGI Friday 238
The Body Shop 33–6, 44, 97, 364
Thorntons 139
Timpsons 64
Tobacco Advisory Council 47
Toblerone 238
Top Shop 242
Toyota 377
Toys R Us 355
Transparency International 509

Unilever 279, 318
U-Switch 121

Verdict Research 157
Viagra 280
Virgin 80, 85, 97, 141, 318, 485

Wal-Mart 126, 474
Walkers Crisps 270
Walt Disney 227, 474
What Car? magazine 426
WHSmith 366
World Trade Organization 56, 505

Yahoo! 451, 456, 526
YouTube 247, 421

Zara 384